Private Equity

Private Equity

The German Experience

Paul Jowett and Francoise Jowett

First published 2011 by
PALGRAVE MACMILLAN

Palgrave Macmillan in the UK is an imprint of Macmillan Publishers Limited, registered in England, company number 785998, of Houndmills, Basingstoke, Hampshire RG21 6XS.

Palgrave Macmillan in the US is a division of St Martin's Press LLC, 175 Fifth Avenue, New York, NY 10010.

Palgrave Macmillan is the global academic imprint of the above companies and has companies and representatives throughout the world.

Palgrave® and Macmillan® are registered trademarks in the United States, the United Kingdom, Europe and other countries

ISBN 978-0-230-53776-7   hardback

This book is printed on paper suitable for recycling and made from fully managed and sustained forest sources. Logging, pulping and manufacturing processes are expected to conform to the environmental regulations of the country of origin.

A catalogue record for this book is available from the British Library.

A catalogue record for this book is available from the Library of Congress.

10   9   8   7   6   5   4   3   2   1
20   19   18   17   16   15   14   13   12   11

Printed and bound in Great Britain by
CPI Antony Rowe, Chippenham and Eastbourne

Contents

List of Figures

List of Tables

Preface

A journalist writing from the standpoint of April 2010, when we submitted our manuscript to Palgrave Macmillan, might well have been tempted to entitle this book: "The rise and fall of private equity in Germany". There would have been a certain symmetry to the story that followed; perhaps too long on the rise and too short on the fall. But while such a title would make good copy for a newspaper, for a book it would risk being an ill-judged epitaph. The aptness of the journalist's title surely fades over time. As writers of a book, we hope for a longer period of circulation. Even at its nadir, during the doldrums of 2009, the small cap segment of private equity was alive and kicking. Only in large cap and mid cap were the private equity markets temporarily choked off by the widespread collapse in credit.

Private equity's fall from grace after the Lehman Brothers bankruptcy was perhaps in large part both inevitable and predictable. Any industry which enjoys a period of run-away success is bound to hit a speed-bump at some point or another.

Has our story been influenced unduly by being written during the period of melt-down? We think not. A few members of the industry suggested that the industry's fall-out would mark a fitting end to our book. But we cannot believe that the crisis of 2009 marks the beginning of the end for private equity. Far more likely, private equity will regain its poise, and chart once more a course of growth and development. The industry has been written off many times before, and no doubt will be written off many times again in the future.

A more accurate title for our book might have been: "The cyclical development of private equity in Germany during the period 1984–2009". That would hardly have made for catchy copy, although it would have given a better flavour for the real picture. While writing up our verdict on private equity's first phase from 1984–1991, we pondered how the industry managed to survive to the second. Much went wrong during those early years, and large sums of money were lost. Investors could have been forgiven for shunning the sector thereafter. Similarly, the bursting of the dotcom bubble in 2001, which undermined venture capital in such spectacular fashion, could have bequeathed a similar fate to private equity. That it didn't was more by luck than design. For in the minds of many, confusion between the two remained deep rooted.

From the outset, the industry's story has been one of ebbs and flows, with the tide level rising to reach further-flung corners of the economy. No doubt it will ebb and flow again in the future, navigating business cycles, minting good vintages and bad. Some PE houses will fall by the wayside, and new players will take their place. The novelty of working in private equity will lose its shine, and other careers will steal the limelight. But our best bet is that for many generations to come private equity will endure. We haven't come close to reaching the last page in its history, in Germany or elsewhere.

Acknowledgements

This book would not have been possible without the support of many senior members of the German private equity industry. Over a hundred professionals agreed to be interviewed and devoted time to checking transcripts and sections of our book covering their activities. We are very grateful for their willingness to go on the record in the many quotations we have taken from these interviews included within this book. A list of those who helped us in this is provided overleaf. Over fifty additional members of the industry and their portfolio companies helped us with corrections and supporting material, a list of whom can be found after the note on sources. We would like to thank Friedrich von der Groeben, Tim Jenkinson, Josh Lerner, Max Römer, Alex Tcherepnine, for reading a draft of our book and for their helpful comments and suggestions. The views expressed herein are those of the authors and their interview partners and do not necessarily reflect the views of Roland Berger Strategy Consultants, L.E.K. Consulting (including affiliates and partners) or any of the private equity houses for which our interview partners have worked (be that in the past or present).

We would also like to thank Lisa von Fircks and Renée Takken of Palgrave Macmillan for their support of our project, and for providing advice, and suggestions. Shirley Tan of Expo Holdings was invaluable in her help with the copyediting of our manuscript. Any mistakes which remain are of course our own, and we would be grateful if readers who detect such errors, inevitable in a project of such scope based on primary sources, could bring them to our attention.

Paul Jowett
Francoise Jowett
Grünwald, November 2010

The Interview Partners

Hans Albrecht (IMM/Triumph-Adler, Carlyle, Nordwind), Erol Ali Dervis (BC Partners), Philipp Amereller (FBG, Electra/Cognetas, Silver), Ron Ayles (3i, Advent), Clemens Beickler (Bain, Codex), Wolfgang Bensel (Pallas, FBG, Electra Fleming, Arcadia), Wolfgang Biedermann (Schroders, Thomas CJ Matzen, HIG Capital), Martin Block (Mercury/HgCapital), Michael Boltz (3i, Heller, Equita, Electra/Congetas), Burkhard Bonsels (Quadriga), Michael Bork (Barclays), Marcus Brennecke (SMB, EQT), Christiane Brock (Bain), Peter Brock (Bain, CBR/EquiVest), Marco Brockhaus (3i, Brockhaus), Anthony Bunker (Atco, NatWest/Bridgepoint, Avida), Max Burger-Calderon (Apax), Richard Burton (PwC), Thomas Bühler (IMM/Triumph-Adler, Afinum), Matthias Calice (Apax, TPG), Edward Capel-Cure (Granville Baird), Peter Cullom (3i, ECM), Markus Conrad (Bain, MBO manager Libri), Jane Crawford (3i, Chamonix), Eberhard Crain (Thurn & Taxis, Bessemer-Metzler, Vector/LBO France, CBR/EquiVest), Paul de Ridder (Halder), Rolf Dienst (Matuschka, Wellington), Werner Dreesbach (Cipio), Detlef Dinsel (Bain, Industri Kapital), Ray Eitel-Porter (L.E.K.), Mark Elborn (Candover, LGV, Electra/Cognetas, Silver), Olav Ermgassen (EGIT, Ermgassen), Claus Felder (Doughty Hanson), Andreas Fendel (Genes, CVC, CWB, Quadriga), Brian Fenwick-Smith (TBG, Robannic), Manfred Ferber (Matuschka, Barings, Ferber), Nick Fergusson (Schroders/Permira, SVG), Ekkehard Franzke (Deutsche Handelsbank, Bain, Ingenium, L.E.K.), Peter Gangsted (Allianz, Cinven), Tobias Gondorf (CD&R, Carrycastle), Hans Gottwald (Robannic, IMM, Orlando), Henry Gregson (Phildrew, RBS, Pamplona), Martin Halusa (Apax), Peter Hammermann (Deutsche Handelsbank, Hammermann & Stelzer, Odewald, Barclays), Christof Hemmerle (SocGen, Halder, Finatem), Axel Herberg (MBO manager Gerresheimer, Blackstone), Albrecht Hertz-Eichenrode (HANNOVER Finanz), Michael Hinderer (Apax, Altium), Klaus Hofmann (MBO manager Minimax), Heinz Holsten (JP Morgan, CCMP), Axel Holtrup (Investcorp, Silver Lake), Vincent Hübner (Matuschka, Hübner Schlösser), Johannes Huth (Investcorp, KKR), Jan Janshen (3i, Advent), Simon Kenyon (E&Y), Sebastian Kern (3i, PPM/Silverfleet), Hellmut Kirchner (Matuschka, TVM, VCM), Hayo Knoch (3i), Raimund König (Bain, IMM/Triumph-Adler, Grünwald), Andreas Kogler (BBK/capiton), Steve Koltes (CVC), Kai Köppen (IMM/Triumph-Adler, Riverside), Thomas Krenz (Schroders/Permira), Stephan Krümmer (Bain, Rothschild, Ingenium, 3i), Matthias Kues (Nord

Holding), Thorsten Langheim (Blackstone, Deutsche Telekom), Jim Lawrence (L.E.K.), Reiner Löslein (Allianz), André Mangin (DBAG), David Martin (3i, Granville Baird), Jochen Martin (IMM/Triumph-Adler, EQT, MCH), Albrecht Matuschka (TRV, TVM, Matuschka), Thomas Matzen (Schroders, Thomas CJ Matzen), Guido May (3i, PPM/Silverfleet), Aman Miran Khan (3i, FBG, BPE), Walter Moldan (3i, Heller, UBS Capital, Henderson), Nick Money-Kyrle (3i, BHF/Steadfast), Hans Moock (Bain, L.E.K., Treuhand, Carlyle, EQT, Equita), Jon Moulton (CVC, Apax, Alchemy, Better), Dieter Münch (MBO manager Ludwig Beck), Christof Namenyi (ABN Amro, DDN, Axa), Chris Neizert (Advent, Warburg Pincus), Andreas Odefey (DIC/FBG, BPE), Jens Odewald (Odewald), Robert Osterrieth (Rho, Schroders), Chris Peisch (Morgan Stanley, H&P/ECM), Rolf Petzold (Matuschka, Heller), Michael Phillips (Apax), Wolgang Pietzsch (ABN Amro, Axa), Reinhard Pöllath (Pöllath), Thomas Pütter (Matuschka, GS, Allianz), Jens Reidel (MTH, Barings/BC Partners), Andrew Richards (3i, DBAG), Mike Robbins (3i), Max Römer (CVC, CWB, Quadriga), Thilo Sauter (Investcorp), Ervin Schellenberg (Duke Street, EquiGate), Thomas Schlytter-Henrichsen (3i, Alpha), Daniel Schmitz (GS, CVC), Andreas Schober (HANNOVER Finanz), Fritz Seikowsky (Bain, DB Capital, Rothgordt), Norbert Stelzer (Hammermann & Stelzer, Odewald, Ingenium), Georg Stratenwerth (Chase/JPMorgan, Advent), Martin Stringfellow (Kleinwort Benson, Indigo), Marc Strobel (Doughty Hanson, CVC), Klaus Sulzbach (Arthur Andersen/E&Y), Dirk Tetzlaf (Industri Kapital, Equitrust), Jens Tonn (Deutsch Handelsbank, Candover, Vestas), Peter Tornquist (Bain, Lehman, CVC), Friedrich von der Groeben (3i, Bessemer-Metzler, Schroders/Permira), Max von Drechsel (HSBC/Montagu, SMB), August von Joest (Treuhand, PwC, Odewald), Hans-Dieter von Meibom (Pallas/Palladion/OEP), Caspar von Meibom (GS, Industri Kapital, Axa), Herman Wendelstadt (BC Partners), Wolf Wolfsteiner (ABN Amro, 3i, Lehman, Trilantic), Stefan Zuschke (Equimark, Barings/BC Partners)

1
Introduction

This is the story of a group of post-war Germans who built from scratch an industry new to their country. None of them had any explicit ambition to do so. Private equity was at the time unheard of in Germany, and if any of this group had any inkling of the industry they were to help found, it was venture capital they were familiar with, a concept closely tied with American technology, innovation, and transformational change. But on the whole, even those who had heard of venture capital doubted it bore relevance to their lives or their country.

These unsuspecting founders of German private equity belonged to a generation that was enjoying the fruits of reconstruction. Few of them were old enough to experience any of the immediate post-war deprivations. Instead, they were overwhelmingly sons and daughters of prosperous families, raised in comfortable homes, attending good schools, and enjoying a life rich with opportunities.

They were growing up in a society where deference was coming to be challenged. A young person of the period doing a summer job in a German corporation during the 1980s was still likely to see advancement as depending upon age and experience. To be taken seriously, "grey hair" was paramount. A man needed to be quite mature, or at least look it, to get promoted. Women, whether young or older, were trapped under a low-hanging glass ceiling. Such were the prospects at large German corporations. But this straitjacket was donned willingly by hordes of male business graduates because it gave them a sense of security. The confidence within German corporations during the 1980s was at its post-war peak: firms like Siemens, Thyssen, Mannesmann and Daimler were large, global and infallible. Siemens alone, with its 350,000 employees, was like a small country. To be president of a Siemens foreign subsidiary was to command the same status as a German ambassador abroad; membership of the main board ranked equivalent to a government position in Bonn. Such was the status of large German corporations that many West Germans gladly jumped aboard. They might have been be in for a slow ride up a steep escalator, but theirs was a reliable and safe journey. Progress along its path brought prestige and privilege, each milestone marked by a more generous salary, desk, and company car.

This was not the most fertile environment for developing a generation of new entrepreneurs. Ralf Becker and Thomas Hellmann in their paper *"The Genesis of Venture Capital – The Lessons from the German Experience"* comment:

> In the fifties and early sixties a generation of entrepreneurs had built the German after-war economy. By the later sixties, however, the next generation faced a very different set of incentives for entrepreneurship. Young Germans sought to join large companies and banks, which typically provide lifetime employment at high wages and excellent benefits combined with high social status. Given such life-time employment, an employee that left a corporation – say to start her own business – could not expect to be rehired by that company and would have faced considerable obstacles to later take a comparable job with another corporation.[1]

But by the 1980s, not everyone was as easily drawn to this straight, slow, and narrow path. Those not tempted by corporate Germany, and not lucky enough to be the son or daughter of a family company, were increasingly seduced by the allure of fast-track careers in accounting and management consulting. The former had already become "mainstream", a profession, like law, to train for, and to be used as a launch-pad for senior management positions. Management consulting, on the other hand, was more exotic, symbolising many of the virtues that West Germans of the period strove for. Americanism, modernity, change, wealth, and fame were fast becoming an overriding obsession. Strategy consulting firms spoon fed these in concentrated form, with McKinsey, Boston Consulting Group, and Roland Berger leading the pack in Germany. The strategy consulting groups were growing rapidly and offering an elite status that broke through the predominant ageist paradigm. Where else could one be promoted every year on merit, or have direct contact with top management before the age of 30? While the Darwinian up or out process produced its rejects, even those who didn't make the next rung gained the prestige of having worked for

McKinsey or one of its competitors, coupled with the contacts made on assignment that guaranteed a successful direct leap into middle management.

America had a formative influence on the lives of many West Germans coming to maturity in the 1970s and 1980s. The post-war generation had been left in something of a cultural vacuum, the sense of nationality and identity weak if not wholly absent. This vacuum was filled predominantly by American culture and role models. West Germany during the 1970s and 1980s was experiencing the heyday of American influence, transmitted through music, films, television, literature, technology, and education. American forces stationed in Hessen, Baden-Wurttemberg, and Bavaria, brought with them AFN (American Forces Network) with its staple diet of rock-and-roll and American popular music. The upper middle class generation born in the late 1950s and early 1960s learnt to speak English at school, and mastered it listening to popular music. Small wonder that when many young Germans reached their twenties it was to America they turned for finishing school or the first step of their career. America might not have streets paved with gold, but its reputation towered above all others: it was at the absolute forefront, where everything was cutting edge.

A secondary and far less significant influence for young Germans was the United Kingdom, viewed by many as both related and allied to America in Europe. British troops stationed in Northern Germany, brought with them BFBS radio with its similar fare of pop music and light culture. British television and films had their influence too, with the humour of Monty Python appreciated as much in Germany as in England. But the United Kingdom was too close to Germany to command the mystique of America, and the British economy was viewed by many in Germany as moribund. British corporations were failing on the global stage, with names such as British Leyland and ICL looked upon with scorn relative to their German equivalents.

The pioneers of private equity in Germany had very similar backgrounds. They were born predominantly to successful, well-educated, and industrious middle class parents. They were educated in the rigorous Gymnasium state schools, many pursuing sport (whether football, hockey, or tennis), music, and the theatre. Parental influence was pragmatic: the pressure was upon choosing a career early, and taking the appropriate training. A bout of foreign study was also common, typically in the form of a year in the United States. The most frequent careers chosen were in banking, accounting, and consulting. All of the founders, as could be expected, stumbled early across the concept of corporate finance. The finance they encountered during these early years was either in the form of loans from banks, or in the form of equity put up by investors. Almost without exception, the impressions they formed of corporate finance during the 1970s and 1980s were different from those that dominate perceptions today.

An important concept which was practically absent was shareholder value. Indeed the whole concept of equity returns was hazy in the minds of many. While the process by which entrepreneurs accumulated capital was reasonably well understood, how they transferred its ownership to others was almost a mystery. Entrepreneurs started companies, often with minimal fixed assets, and used a proportion of their profits to invest in the plant and equipment to make them more efficient and profitable. The owner's wealth was built up in the company, and tied up in his or her business. The challenge of ownership change could be most easily overcome by simply passing the business on to the family's next generation. This transfer of ownership required no trading of capital, and the only real issue concerned how the transaction should be taxed. Problems arose when there was no new generation to inherit the business. Some successful entrepreneurs generated far more cash than their original companies needed for reinvestment, and were able to become providers of capital for other businesses that lacked it. "Fremdkapital", or foreign capital as it directly translates into English, is the German term used to describe money that comes from outside the company, whereas "Eigenkapital", or own money, is the term denoting capital belonging to the owners. These concepts of "Eigenkapital" (equity), and "Fremdkapital" (debt), have caused confusion in Germany over the "insider" versus "outsider" sources of the capital employed. An assumption developed that "Eigenkapital" belonged to the owner-manager, who in turn owned the company. The identity of the owner-manager was clear for all to see, as most companies were anyway named after their patrons. The concept of "Eigenkapital" being supplied by other people who had no operational connection with the business was much less well understood. This confusion over the definition of the sources of capital, reinforced by the German terms "own" and "foreign" persisted for many years, and had a significant impact upon the story of how finance and private equity developed in Germany. From the start, "own" capital was viewed positively, as something friendly, and in some respects "free" (because such money did not require a fixed rate of return), while "foreign" finance attracted negative connotations, and was to be avoided, because it saddled the company with unavoidable interest payments. We shall hereafter use the English terms equity and debt to refer to these sources of capital, but the German roots of the two terms should be constantly kept in mind.

The financing of German Mittelstand by the beginning of the 1980s was comparatively simple, and unsophisticated. Despite this, it had proven extremely effective during the post-war period. The success of the German approach to finance had embedded itself into a tradition of practice that was both deep rooted and resistant to change. Fundamental to the simplicity of the German approach was the pricing of risk. The distinction between debt and equity, as described above, was very clear. Debt had fixed rates of return, and thus from a management standpoint was viewed as risky (the interest had to be paid in good times and in bad), while the equity returns were variable, and ill-defined, which was considered positive. Owner managers had little conception of what would make an ideal capital structure, but the prejudice was strongly in favour of equity. Debt was something to be taken on in times of necessity, and for the short-term only, in order to help fund the purchase of land and buildings, or plant and equipment. In all such cases, the expectation was that debts taken on would be repaid as quickly as possible. Indeed such was the complicit contract between bank and owner-manager, that if the banker thought there was any risk of the company not being in a position to repay the loan, it would under no circumstances be granted.

Such perceptions mirrored what was practiced: successful Mittelstand companies paid down their debts, and bought land, buildings, equipment and all manner of other assets. This low level of indebtedness meant that Mittelstand companies could weather recessions with comparative ease. If times were tough, a piece of land would be sold or mortgaged to provide the necessary liquidity. In good times, provisions were salted away, which could be released in times of need. The concept of smoothing results was deeply embedded, and viewed as prudent. Smoothing promoted stability, and helped protect a company from the ill-effects of an unpredictable marketplace. Despite this deep commitment to equity finance, German medium-sized companies came increasingly to rely upon house-bank finance to fund their growth, particularly during the post-war economic miracle, such that by the mid-1960s, their overall level indebtedness was in fact very high.

Many concepts prevalent today were not part of the collective consciousness. German owner-managers did not maximise the returns on their equity, or seek to increase shareholder value. It was enough that owner managers made a good living, and built up healthy companies.

Pride came not from the wealth built up in a bank account, but in the size and scope of their business.

It should come as little surprise therefore that managers, bankers, and trade unions across the water in the UK observed the German way of doing things with a mixture of bemusement and envy. The German owner-manager's concern for stability aligned comfortably with the concerns of the employees. The workers' council, and the worker representation on the Board of Directors, enshrined in Germany's Mitbestimmung legislation, resulted in a consensual pact between shareholders, management and workforce. A strike was viewed by employees in such companies as suicidal: completely against the interests of every stakeholder.

Such was the prevailing wisdom throughout German society at the beginning of the 1980s: that debt was bad and equity good. The pricing of risk was turned upon its head, and tolerated because the bulk of owner managers were not extracting their equity returns, but rather ploughing them back into their businesses. Any leverage introduced onto a company's balance sheet for whatever reason was temporary, dispensed with as soon as possible. An indebted company was an unsuccessful and unhealthy one; a company rich with equity was king.

This was hardly fertile ground for the entry of the "merchants of debt", as some were later to describe the practitioners of private equity. On the contrary, the proponents of leveraged buyouts were met with cold and stiff indifference. What they had to offer was fundamentally immoral, short-sighted, and built upon greed. To pile debt onto a company was to weaken it, and put at risk the interests of other stakeholders. Private equity companies were a misnomer, for they were not considered to be real providers of equity. If it had been only equity they were offering they would have been viewed quite differently. In truth, they were wolves in sheep's clothing: what they offered was lots and lots of debt, hidden under a thin cloak of equity.

Such was the mainstream thinking on capital allocation in Germany at the outset of the 1980s. The argument propounded by Henry Kravis that debt made a company tighter and fitter, assumed from a German perspective that it was unfit and unhealthy in the first place.[2] Indeed, corporate Germany's scorecard at the time was a strong one. Whilst British companies had stagnated or underperformed, to be later bought up by foreign companies, their German counterparts had become global leaders in their field.

Given this backdrop, it is hardly surprising that any large-scale change in the financing of companies in Germany had to wait until the companies in question became less healthy. When private equity companies entered the scene, they were told that there were no sick companies to sell. The idea that anyone would part with a healthy company was viewed as preposterous. It can be no coincidence that a number of the early investments made by the pioneers of private equity in Germany were indeed hopeless cases. In some instances, the financial plight of the company was hidden by a fraudulent owner-manager, or it was simply not recognised by the inexperienced investors. It would take reunification, and a deep recession during the 1990s to convince owner-managers and other shareholders that some change in corporate finance was necessary.

It is for these reasons that private equity took hold quicker in the UK than in Germany. The UK had numerous unhealthy companies, many dissatisfied owner-managers, and many unhappy shareholders. The UK also lacked the built-in prejudice against debt found in Germany, where the German language as we have mentioned defined such loans as "foreign". Against this backdrop, private equity received a warmer welcome in the UK. It was viewed as a cure for a particular and pressing problem. A rebalancing of debt equity ratios could indeed make a company fitter.

When private equity jumped the Channel and reached Germany, it typically made the crossing aboard an Anglo-Saxon institution, rather than springing from a home-grown fund. It is little wonder that the "foreign" nature of these funds should therefore persist in the German consciousness. Not only were these people pushing debt masquerading as equity, they were genuinely bringing in foreign money too.

Today it may seem obvious that debt is just another form of corporate finance, and that it can be permanent, and indeed efficient. But we now live in an age where the division between owners and managers has become more prevalent. It is easy for us to assume that equity should make regular and superior returns to debt. It has become clear that equity should be more expensive, and that in constructing a company's balance sheet, it serves equity holders well to have a significant proportion of leverage. Today it is also clearer that the levels of risk vary from industry to industry. We understand that cyclical businesses will need more equity, and that non-cyclical businesses can support higher levels of debt. Indeed the sophistication of financial instruments has produced a profusion of differently priced risk instruments. The financing of a company can be built up like a multi-layered cake, with a strict order of subordination between the layers determining which has the first and last recourse to funds when the going gets rough. While we may have made little if any progress in reducing the market-related risks companies face, we have made it much clearer who bears the risks and who gets the rewards of their financing.

It should be remembered that these views on debt and equity are the result of the trickle down of many ideas that were developed and propounded in the US during the 1970s. Bruce Henderson, the founder of BCG, developer of the growth share matrix and the experience curve, not only insisted that debt was and should always be a permanent part of any company's balance sheet, but that it was an integral component of a company's competitiveness.[3] Henderson held that low-cost competitors would be forced to have a high level of debt on their balance sheet, in order to maximise their cost competitiveness. The first wave of LBOs during the 1970s in the US was driven by investors who recognised that companies with too much equity delivered poor financial returns, measured on an appropriate risk-return basis. An LBO offered existing shareholders an easy way out of their investment, and gave them a substantial proportion of the profit from improving the debt-equity ratio. In other words, the LBO market played a critical role in the US in helping educate investors and managers in their thinking on the appropriate level of leverage to be placed on balance sheets.

Before leveraged buyouts made their first tentative steps onto the German scene during the mid-1980s, the main experiences with private equity had come in three forms. The first was in minority investments, primarily aimed at supplying growth capital. The second was in venture capital, mainly for funding start-ups, or businesses in their high-burn early phase. The third was in funding leveraged buyouts in the US. Other than these three forms, the capital structure could be split into its more traditional forms: the public capital markets organised around stock-listed companies, the owner-managers whose private capital dominated the Mittelstand, and a smaller category of "family offices" making private investments for rich families typically in an array of stocks, bonds, and direct participations in small- and medium-sized companies.

Debt finance, in the form of leverage, existed purely on a house-bank basis. House banks granted loans to companies to help them finance capacity expansions, increases in working capital, even acquisitions. But before the mid-1980s, debt was not used in combination with structured third party equity to execute majority take-overs of companies.

Of these predecessors to LBO-based private equity, those which came closest in structure and approach to what was to follow were venture capital, minority ownership-based growth capital, and family offices.

The major German banks and the government were behind the development of minority-based growth capital, starting with the Deutschen

Beteiligungsgesellschaft (DBG), founded in 1965 to provide equity for companies not publicly listed, which was later in 1984 converted to the Deutschen Beteiligungs AG Unternehmensbeteiligungsgesellschaft (DBAG). The DBG and DBAG fell under the stewardship of Deutsche Bank and Karl Schmidt Bank. A range of similar equity participation departments were set up within other banks, including BdW (attached to Dresdner) and Nord KB (at Norddeutsche Landesbank).

Under government pressure in 1975 an early experiment in venture capital was started, financed by 29 German banks under the Deutsche Wagnisfinanzierungsgesellschaft. This was singularly unsuccessful, and a halt to investments made under the first fund was called in 1984.

A number of family offices emerged during the course of the postwar years. The two family offices which were to have the biggest influence on the emergence of LBOs were the Thyssen-Bornemisza Group (TBG) family office based in Monaco, and the Reemtsma family office (Rho) based in New York.

Finally, venture capital, originally raised in Germany for investment in American high tech start-ups, was later raised to fund local German technology companies. The most prominent, and arguably earliest of these funds was Techno Venture Management (TVM) established by Count Matuschka, along with a string of major German corporate backers (Siemens, Mannessmann, Bayer etc.), although there were some other less famous but similar venture capital funds raised, such as Genes Venture Services GmbH by Professor Dr Klaus Nathusius in Cologne, which also had an influence on the rise of LBO-based private equity.

2
Minority Participations: 1965–1975

It was the "economic miracle" that created the demand for minority-based participations. Mid-cap companies in Germany required injections of growth capital as they expanded. German GDP between 1950 and 1973 increased almost four-fold, and tripled on a per capita basis.[1] The challenge for medium-sized companies was to find the capital to finance this growth. The house bank could not always be relied upon to meet all of a company's needs, especially when increases in debt were not matched by further injections of equity. H.E. Büschgen, in his chapter "Die Deutsche Bank von 1957 bis zur Gegenwart" (published in *Die Deutsche Bank von 1870 bis 1995*) summarised the challenge:

> In the mid 1960s, many medium-sized companies, with no direct access to capital markets, found that they were only able to finance rapid growth using their own resources to a limited extent. It was against this background that the banks began founding Kapital-beteiligungsgesellschaften (capital participation companies), in order to provide small and medium-sized companies with additional equity.[2]

As was true in the UK, with the creation of 3i and its predecessors (in particular ICFC), it was obvious that the banks should orchestrate the creation of these companies tasked to provide growth capital. Unlike the UK, however, one bank was expected to provide leadership to the rest of the banking community: Deutsche Bank. Günter Leopold, one of the pioneers of minority participations within the Deutsche Beteiligungs AG and its predecessors, explains the situation in his book *40 Jahre Investitionen im Deutschen Mittelstand 1965–2005*:

> As in all other cases, the providers of capital were above all concerned to see what the Deutsche Bank would do, as it typically played the

lead in the development of new opinions and then took a market leadership position in any new financial service created. Even within the Deutsche Bank, the first act was to do what any businessman or entrepreneur would do: to conduct some market research. The Deutsche Bank's massive branch network, with its vast number of medium-sized customers in the Mittelstand, clearly provided a good basis to collect information on market requirements. In 1965, a piece of fieldwork was undertaken in a sample of main branches, which clearly supported in its findings the potential for the formation of companies tasked with providing minority participations.[3]

It was the Hamburg branch of the Deutsche Bank that was given the leading role in this initiative, and under its direction, a discussion group was established which quickly latched upon the phrase "Kapital-beteiligungsgesellschaft" (capital participations company) as its draft name for the institutions it sought to establish. This phrase quickly took the lead over other competing expressions such as "Investment-Trust" or "Partner-Investmentgeselleschaft". For as Günter Leopold comments:

The concepts of "private equity" and "venture capital" which had already been developed in the anglo-american vocabulary were completely unheard of at this time in Germany, and were only to be adopted at a later stage in the development of the industry, as were numerous other technical expressions used in this working environment.[4]

The recommendations of this working group were discussed at a meeting of the Board of Deutsche Bank on the 6th September 1965, and the decision was taken to establish a capital participations company, which would largely be owned by the Bank itself. Shortly thereafter, on 23rd September 1965, the Deutsche Kapitalbeteiligungsgesellschaft mbH was formed with its head office in Frankfurt. Deutsche Bank was joined by six other private German banks (Brinckmann, Wirtz & Co, (Warburg) Hamburg, Handels-und Gewerbebank Heilbronn, B. Metzler Seel. Sohn & Co, Münchmeyer & Co., Sal. Oppenheim Jr. & Cie, and Karl Schmidt Bankgeschäft). Incentive AB, a subsidiary of the Wallenberg Group, which was already active in the participations business in Sweden, was also added to provide the know-how for the new venture. Incentive AB had only been established a few years earlier and its focus was on majority investments which meant that its influence on the new German vehicle was less than expected. The initial capital earmarked for the venture was DM 20 million, but there was no ceiling placed on the venture's investments, and the resources available were defined in a framework agreement rather than in a structured "fund". With the addition of these other banks, Deutsche Bank was able to reduce its stake in the company to 40%. Despite this development, the new venture was widely viewed in the market to be a direct subsidiary of Deutsche Bank.

The first practical steps were to rent an office in Frankfurt, and to select two managing directors and a couple of secretaries to run the business. Wolfgang Büsselberg and Günter Seidel were seconded from the office of the Deutsche Bank's CEO to be the first post-holders in the new company. They made their first three investments during 1966, for sums in the range of half a million to two-and-a-half million Deutschmarks. The three companies involved were: Röscherwerke GmbH in Osnabrück, a milk packaging producer; Morawek in Krefeld, active in textile fibres; and Eberle-Werke in Nuremberg, a manufacturer of electrical switchgear. Günter Leopold describes the selection criteria employed in choosing these first three companies:

> In all three cases, the focus was upon growth capital ... The invest-ments were made in established growing medium-sized companies, and in two out of the three investments, this growth was expected to come through innovation. Other than these criteria, however, the choice of investments was purely opportunistic: there was nothing to connect these companies, and in particular, there was no focus upon any specific industries.[5]

From the very first three investments, it was clear that the business of minority participations would concentrate on long-term partner-ship with medium-sized companies, and indeed there were no explicit expectations of how and when an exit from these investments would be made.

Over the period 1967–1970, the DBG made a further 16 investments, for a total value of DM 31 million, with an average investment per company of around DM 2 million.[6] Financially, the experience was a positive one. On the whole, the companies performed well, making profits which, in the absence of exits, helped make the DBG venture worthwhile. The real surprise was the slow rate of investments, run-ning at only around four a year, and the high rate at which investment proposals were being rejected: 95% of applications for growth capital were turned down.

An advisory board had been set up to give the managing directors of the DBG feedback on their activities. During this period, the biggest area of disagreement concerned the appropriate level of return the DBG should be requiring from its investments. Günter Leopold explains:

> From the ranks of the bankers on the advisory board came the suggestion that something like an annual 6% return was acceptable, whereas on the side of the DBG managing directors the strong feeling was that on the contrary the returns should be at least double this figure.[7]

Part of the explanation for why the rejection quota was so high was that many of the projects did not pass the higher return hurdles the DBG managing directors were setting themselves. This gave rise to a prejudice on the side of many entrepreneurs, and also many bankers, that the DBG was too expensive. In later years, even members of the banks that had helped create the DBG accused the company of requiring "usury rates of interest", which was highly derogatory, given that the word "usury" meant an interest rate that was extortionate, and certainly above lawful limits. As Günter Leopold observes, this dispute was eventually resolved by revising the approach to the problem:

> On this issue, the members of the advisory board finally reached a consensus over the fact that equity, from an economic standpoint, had absolutely no costs whatsoever, because the profit participation of the investors depended only upon the profit after costs, and therefore their returns should in no way be associated with costs.[8]

The DBG's successful operation during the 1970s gave rise to suggestions that it should also make investments in companies that were operating in markets acknowledged to be risky, such as in retailing, textiles, and plastics. As a consequence, the DBG made investments in these areas, but unfortunately, the risks associated turned out to be even higher than expected, causing it to suffer its first serious losses in 1972. Some of the investors were appalled at this outcome, and a small revolution in the DBG's investor base was triggered, with some banks deciding that they had no further interest in investing in a vehicle that could lose money. Only the Deutsche Bank, Schmidt Bank, and the more experienced Swedish Incentive AB recognised that making occasional losses was an intrinsic part of doing such business. These three considered the solution to be improved due diligence, particularly in bringing in the opinions of external experts. Given the unrest among the other banks, Deutsche Bank bought them out, and three years later in 1975, also bought out Incentive AB, which had problems with its stake due to Swedish foreign exchange regulations. By the end of the period, therefore, Deutsche held 92.5% and Schmidt Bank 7.5% in DBG.

The experience with minority participations had fairly minimal impact on the rise of private equity in its modern sense within Germany, whether it be venture capital or leveraged buyouts. The DBG had many applications from innovators seeking "early-stage" finance, but refused to grant any such growth capital to this group because of the difficulties in evaluating the market chances for their products and services. The DBG's stakes were non-leveraged, and small, with its equity participations typically accounting for between 5–15% of the total equity. The fact that the DBG and it competitors played no role in raising their own funds, and also had no structured approach to exits, greatly limited the extent to which they influenced the development of venture capital and leveraged buyouts in Germany. The idea that exits should be planned for, and should contribute the lion's share of the returns, at the time would have been viewed as immoral.[9]

Nevertheless, the DBG and its competitors did help raise the profile of equity finance in Germany, and by the mid-1970s, the DBG had taken the lead in setting up an informal working party of German capital participation companies ("Arbeitskreis deutscher Kapitalbeteiligungsgesellschaften").[10] This group produced the first statistics on the industry in December 1975, revealing that the portfolio investments of all capital participation companies at that time amounted to DM 418.6 million, of which DM 47 million related to investments of the Berliner Industriebank AG, which were granted for special reasons due to the political situation of Berlin. Of the remaining DM 371.6 million, 47.5% was held by institutions formed by private banks, and a further 40.4% by state banks. Three private banks dominated, with the DBG (Deutsche Bank) holding DM 74 million, the BdW (Dresdner Bank) DM 38 million, and the AKU (Bethmann Bank) DM 22 million. Within the state banks, the West-KB (a subsidiary of Westdeutsche Landesbank) held the leading position, and Nord KB became a significant player after its entry in 1969.[11]

3
The Failed Venture Capital Experiment: 1976–1991

By the mid-1970s the state, whose focus for some years had been upon providing support for companies too small to be served by the likes of the DBG and its competitors, turned its attention to "young" and "technological" companies. No history of private equity in Germany can avoid mention of the ill-fated government-bank initiated Deutsche Wagnisfinanzierungsgesellschaft which was the result of this initiative. Ralf Becker and Thomas Hellmann in their paper *The Genesis of Venture Capital – Lessons from the German Experience* do an excellent job of analysing why this experiment failed. Becker and Hellmann explain the background to this unusual initiative:

> Throughout the sixties, there was a growing concern about an equity gap in Germany. While in the mid-sixties a typical German company still had 35% equity, this percentage had fallen to 25% by the early 1970s. Small and medium sized companies had even less equity, about 20%. After the first oil shock, the problem became even more pressing as higher interest rates burdened the balance sheets of companies.[1]

The Federal Government and the major banks locked themselves into a debate over how this equity deficit could be compensated. The banks had little interest in holding equity in small- and medium-sized companies beyond those held by companies such as DBG and its competitors. Their interest in "young" and "innovative" companies was even lower. Equity was still viewed by the banks as "charity" because it commanded no fixed returns, and was exposed to substantial risk. Becker and Hellmann explain:

> (The banks) viewed their loan business as their core activity, and were reluctant to take on the additional risk exposure. The Herstatt

scandal in 1974, the biggest banking failure in the history of Germany, reinforced the risk-aversion of banks.[2]

But it was not just an equity gap that was apparent in Germany. Despite being a world leader in science and engineering, there was a growing perception that Germany was falling behind the US in the pace of technological innovation, and particularly in the commercialisation of new ideas and inventions. Becker and Hellmann continue:

> While German universities and research institutions were producing large amounts of high quality scientific output, the transmission of knowledge was seriously lacking. Employment stability in the research sector and the high social status of university professors and research fellows provided little incentive for scientists to commercialise their discoveries. Those researchers who tried to implement their ideas as entrepreneurs often showed a total lack of interest, and skill, as managers.[3]

This perception that America was gaining an advantage in technology was widespread in Europe during the 1970s, as was the concern that this development was somehow linked to the rise of venture capital. The French were among the first to take the threat seriously, as Peter Brooke, who at that time was head of TA Associates, one of the leading venture capital providers explains:

> In 1972, when the Ministry of Industry in France wanted to investigate the forces that created venture capital around Route 128, they hired Arthur D. Little Inc to do a study of what made these burgeoning technology-based companies successful. Part of the study was to look at the role venture capital played. They asked me if I would write an appendix in that report describing the venture capital experience and the role that it had in capitalizing these new ventures. In the course of writing the report I met the Deputy Minister of Industry, Christian Marbach. I convinced him that venture capital had been vital to the success of these companies and it could do the same in France.[4]

The Germans were aware not only that technology was on the rise in the United States, but also that the UK and France were taking steps to reproduce this process in their own countries. Clearly, Germany could not be left out of this process, and it was the government that put pressure on the German financial community to respond to the challenge. The issues of the technology gap, how it should be filled, and the how the growing equity deficit could be bridged, became entwined in a government-bank debate on the need for a domestic venture capital industry.

The creation of the WFG came in response to the public debates about the equity and technology-market gaps. In the German financial system, only banks were credible financiers that could promote venture capital. However reluctant the banks may have been, the government had no other choice but to lean on them to develop venture capital.[5]

Thus from the start it was clear that the political influence on the creation of WFG was to dominate any economic considerations. Hellmut Kirchner, who later set up a private sector venture capital fund, sums it up this way:

> The government basically told the banks that they had to do something for the good of their country. It was all political.[6]

The construct that the government and banks arrived at was a compromise entailing a number of potential conflicts of interest. Both government and banks had had trouble squaring their divergent interests:

> The government was most concerned about the technology-market gap. It preferred the WFG to invest in young, high technology companies, and considered it an instrument of public policy. The banks, however, did not want to take on too much risk and were anxious to not appear to be wielding too much power over small firms – a reluctance that led one interviewee to say that the banks had to be virtually bullied into backing the WFG.[7]

The WFG was provided with DM 10 million in capital at its inception, later raised to DM 30 million, then to DM 50 million, before the experiment was called to a halt. Twenty-nine banks and savings and loan institutions contributed this capital.

The criteria developed for the WFG to select portfolio companies were to have a major influence over the life of the fund:

1. The product or process of the entrepreneur had to be sufficiently innovative from a technological point of view.
2. There had to be an identified target market, and the company had to have a good chance of becoming profitable.

3. The entrepreneur or entrepreneurial team had to be of a sufficiently high quality and have sufficient business experience to be able to lead the company to success.
4. The WFG would only finance companies that could not obtain financing from other sources.

The last criterion was the most bizarre of the four, and did the most to undermine the success of the WFG as a commercial enterprise. The WFG had been defined as an investor of last resort. If any competition arose, WFG was expected to back down. With respect to the other three criteria, the government laid most emphasis upon the first. Karl-Heinz Fanselow, who later became the head of the WFG, recalls:

> (The government representatives) were breathing down my neck, they were controlling my papers, and they kept telling me: Do this! Do that![8]

The WFG had many features that undermined its economic effectiveness. Hellmut Kirchner explains:

> The WFG was laudable, but it was established with a significant birth defect in favour of the targets: if the target performed well, then it had the right to buy back its shares from the WFG. In other words, the WFG was left with the lemons, while the oranges went away.[9]

Even the WFG's own employees were obsessed with the public policy aspect of their work, as Fanselow later commented:

> They were unwilling to pay attention to market aspects. They literally refused to inspect firms on location. They were only interested in the technological side of a project, in ideas.[10]

The record of the WFG was abysmal. Becker and Hellmann summarised their verdict:

> The WFG was an outright failure. It recorded a loss every year during the first nine years and small profits thereafter. The cumulative losses over its lifetime amounted to DM 38.4 million. Through a downside risk guarantee the government bore DM 37.7 million of these losses, leaving the banks with less than a million DM of actual losses. There

were no revenues in the first three years, and the revenues from the government subsidy exceeded the revenue from investments for every year up to 1984 when the government and the WFG parted ways. The internal rate of return for the investment of the WFG was −25.07%. This is the value for the overall portfolio, excluding the government subsidy. If we count the subsidy as revenues for the WFG, the internal rate of return was −11.41%. Note also that these are nominal rates of return ignoring inflation. The real rates of return are thus even lower.[11]

Most of the companies in which WFG invested went bankrupt. It was even joked at the time that the WFG's approach to exit was to file a company for insolvency. Becker and Hellmann continue their catalogue of misery:

> More than two thirds of the WFG's companies resulted in partial or total losses, and less than 20% of the portfolio companies ever generated any returns. By comparison, Sahlman (1990) estimates that in a typical US venture capital portfolio about one third of all investments result in a partial or total loss, and two-thirds of the companies generate a positive return.[12]

The failure of the WFG, which was recorded in its annual reports, was obvious to all, and various measures were taken to redress its poor performance:

> Over the first three years, four new CEOs were hired in the hope of addressing the instantly visible shortcomings, and of turning around the WFG. In November 1978, Karl-Heinz Fanselow (the latest new co-CEO) realised that, as he says, the WFG was essentially bankrupt. The board of directors put him alone at the helm of the WFG soon thereafter, a position he retained until the demise of the operation. Under his leadership the WFG underwent a fundamental transformation. In 1984, the WFG ended its relationship with the government and decided not to make any further investments. At this time, five of the largest banks created a new venture capital fund, called WFGneu (new WFG), which would continue to invest, and also oversaw the liquidation of the existing portfolio of the old WFG.[13]

Undoubtedly, this first experiment with venture capital was a learning experience for all involved, and as with all learning experiences, provided some opportunities for improvement. On some dimensions, practices at the WFG were changed, to good effect. But a number of challenges persisted throughout the experiment, and spilled over into the post-1984 period that we cover under our heading, *Private Equity – The German Experience*.

The most common challenge for any investment made in Germany in the 1970s or 1980s was one of control, or what would be termed today "corporate governance". Up until 1984, equity investments made by third parties in Germany were made almost exclusively on a minority basis with a "passive" or "silent" participation. De facto, the investor exercised no influence over the management of the company in which he or she invested. This hands-off approach spilled over into the WFG experiment, causing Fanselow and his colleagues to be almost powerless to either influence or change management. This lack of control was fundamental to the problems of early venture capital and private equity in Germany. Becker and Hellmann explain that:

> An important aspect of US venture capital is the hands-on support provided by venture capitalists. The WFG soon realised the need for such hands-on support. All of its first portfolio companies struggled to develop their products and did not succeed in the market. Since many of the entrepreneurs had more of a technological background, the WFG focussed on providing complementary legal and tax advice. The notion of monitoring, however, was limited to hiring controllers that helped the portfolio companies to develop and maintain their accounting systems. While the entrepreneurs welcomed such technical help, strategic advice was neither desired nor accepted.[14]

Fanselow quickly saw this as a weakness, and sought to bring pressure on the managers of his portfolio companies to accept more shareholder influence. But, as he later noted:

> Entrepreneurs were not very open to a hands-on venture capital approach. I found them arrogant. They did not see that an idea alone does not imply success – they considered themselves as inventors and disliked and disrespected business aspects.[15]

It could be argued that the WFG's own staff were not appropriate to play such a hands on role, as Hellmut Kirchner later commented:

> They were all bankers running around, and the so called hands-on active role was not played. It was a finance organisation, and not what I

would call the "Dreiklang", i.e. money, advice, and execution. Added to this was that there was a poor connection between the bankers and the young companies. WFG people were difficult to talk to, they were so high up in the sky. While some venture capitalists today would discuss whether it would be appropriate to go to a meeting wearing a tie, WFG people could be counted upon not to arrive at a meeting without a chauffeur.[16]

Without majority holdings, the WFG found itself a hostage to the managements who held the remainder of the equity. The solution therefore was for the WFG to take majorities. But this also turned out to be no solution, for as Fanselow explains:

> Nobody would have accepted to give up a majority stake to the venture capitalist. People called that exploitation.[17]

The only people to be exploited in this environment were the venture capitalists, or, in end-effect, the government. WFG was powerless in dealing with companies that in many cases were managed by inexperienced entrepreneurs. Fanselow summed up the situation:

> That is why the failure rate was so high. We could not replace an incompetent management team.[18]

In Becker and Hellmann's final assessment, they found it hard to believe that WFG had ever offered such unfavourable contracts, let alone made investments with so little investor protection.

> Where did these contracting notions come from? One could conjecture that people simply did not understand venture capital and the consequences of these contracting practices. But this is not true. Just prior to the launch of the WFG, a Professor Gerke (1975) wrote an article in a prominent German economic journal that explained with almost prophetic vision why the approach of the WFG was doomed to fail.[19]

Fanselow drew the most important lessons from the WFG, and used that experience to progressively push the institutions he led towards a majority-based private equity model typical of today. Becker and Hellmann tracked his early steps towards reform:

> Soon after taking charge, Fanselow challenged the investment approach of the WFG. It was his objective to turn the WFG around into a

financially viable and purely market-oriented venture capital firm. After a confrontational board meeting and strong resistance especially from the government-appointed board members, the WFG dropped the fourth criterion. Furthermore, Fanselow received the freedom to apply the first criterion less rigorously: it became possible to justify investments based on market opportunities instead of technological innovation.[20]

These changes came against strong resistance. Fanselow recalls:

> I told the banks that we wanted to make money. Most banks didn't like the idea, and they didn't want me to do that.[21]

Fanselow drew the conclusion that the early-stage market was "a catastrophe". The reasons for the poor performance of the early-stage market were however far less well understood at the time. It was to take a further ten years for a number of Anglo-Saxon originating players to come up with a similar verdict. Possibly the biggest explanation for the poor performance of early-stage in Germany was that the conditions that made this segment successful in the United States were not present in Europe. Peter Brooke explains the US side of the equation in the run-up to the 1970s:

> At that time the federal government was contracting with small under-capitalised companies. They were front-end loading the contracts, providing the progress payments. For instance, a professor could leave with his prized doctoral student and begin an instrumentation company with a modest amount of his own capital – say $10,000 – and manage a $250,000 contract for the federal government because the government would virtually prepay that contract. The first instalment came before the work was even started. With very little capital, these companies were able to get into business. And there was essentially no risk because the contracting officer would accept almost any proposal as long as it pushed the science forward. So even though the lending appeared very risky it wasn't risky at all.[22]

In contrast with this practice, common in the US, German companies were simply being offered venture capital which, on its own, was never likely to be as conducive to the success witnessed across the Atlantic. But even in the US, conditions for early-stage investments were to change over time, as the market for technology inevitably became more competitive. Kevin Landry, a colleague of Peter Brooke who later took over management of TA Associates explains:

> In the late 1980s, we looked at all our data and said, start-ups don't pay off for us. We make more money investing in profitable companies. And, we asked ourselves, where are we spending our time? We are in the free consulting business, that's the business we're in. We're in the business of helping the weak and the lame survive.[23]

Hence even in the United States, the birthplace of venture capital, many were to conclude that better returns were to be made in management buyouts of established companies. It was to take a further decade for professionals in Germany to reach the same conclusion.

4

The Early Shoots: Genes Ventures, Matuschka/TVM, & HANNOVER Finanz

The first early shoots of a more entrepreneurial approach to growth and venture capital emerged in the period 1978–1984. This was a time of much unrest in Germany, coming shortly after the "German Autumn" of 1977, when Red Army Faction terrorism began. It was a period when many West German citizens had grown tired of the Cold War, with its legacy of "mutually assured destruction". Yet despite a growing scepticism of the US's role in the world, many Germans were captivated by the technological miracle of Silicon Valley, and questioned whether such innovation could be stimulated in Germany. The prospects looked poor. Germany's corporations had become conservative and bureaucratic, so heavily divided into functional specialisms that no manager had oversight of the whole. If Germany was to keep up with the Americans, it would undoubtedly require a new generation of entrepreneurs. But where were they to be found, and how could they be empowered to break new ground?

The stimulus for change came from outside of the mainstream establishment. It had already been proven that the banks and the government both through the Kapitalbeteiligungsgesellschaften and the Deutsche Wagnisfinanzierungsgesellschaft had failed. Instead, a university professor, a charismatic Count, and a former strategy consultant were the people who rose to this challenge.

Genes Venture Services GmbH

One of the earliest players in Germany was Genes Venture Services GmbH founded by Dr. Klaus Nathusius in 1978. Nathusius, who had

24

started life as an officer in the air force, became a research assistant at the University of Cologne working with Professor Norbert Szyperski on the topic of corporate ventures in the USA. Nathusius was a keen theoretician and practitioner, who sought to translate academic ideas, mainly derived from his analysis of US experience, into practice in the German Mittelstand. He set up Genes as a consultancy, to advise start-ups and fast-growing companies, usually referred to in the US as ventures. Remaining close to his academic roots, he recruited students to help support his efforts in experimenting with entrepreneurism. One such student was Andreas Fendel, enrolled on the PhD programme at the University. Fendel later recalled that:

> Klaus had family money, and was fascinated early on by the venture business with which he had gained experience by investing in American funds during the 1970s. By the beginning of the 1980s, he had a real vision for what venture capital might achieve. I made a deal to work almost full time with him for two years while continuing to work on my PhD thesis. That was between 1982 and 1984. It was under his guidance that I learnt about venture capital. I had not really heard of it before, other than stories about stars like Apple or Compaq when they were still green grass investments.[1]

In 1981, Nathusius established a joint venture between Genes and Churchill International, a US venture capital firm based in San Francisco and Boston. Genes's role was to help Churchill's portfolio companies enter Germany. One of Churchill's technology funds included investments from BMW, hence their interest in Germany. This partnership was to last until 1985, after which Nathusius concentrated on his own fund.

Nathusius's decision in 1983 to raise his own fund, International Venture Capital Partners (IVCP) with DM 40 million in commitments, was made because he saw opportunities to finance venture capital in German companies having no links to the US. With the exceptions of Metzler Bank and Heraeus, the funds were raised from abroad including Johnson & Johnson, Prudential, and IMB in the US, NatWest Ventures, 3i, Imperio Reinsurance, Nortrust, and Sofigen Mann from the UK, three investors in France, and one investor each from Denmark, Belgium, Switzerland, and Canada. Genes also was one of the first founders of the Bundesverband Kapitalgeber (BVK), and provided Thomas Kühr as its first president.

Nathusius decided later to shift his focus from ventures to more mature businesses, and from minorities to majority-based buyouts. The first fruits of this strategy were seen in 1988, when Genes, together with Pallas,

Figure 4.1 Klaus Nathusius

Candover and Metzler, supported the management buyout of Heide-mann, an automotive components supplier based in Einbeck that boasted a 1986 turnover of DM 155 million. The problem was that it was also losing DM 7.2 million on that revenue. Heidemann fulfilled the typical characteristics of what many Germans considered to be an appropriate private equity investment: it was loss-making, and in need of a com-plete turnaround. At a time when no other bank was willing to lend it a Pfennig, Genes invested DM 2.7 million in the company along-side Pallas, Metzler and Candover. Later, in 1997, Heidemann was sold to Adwest Group plc, a UK-based automotive components company, real-ising DM 15 million on the original Genes investment, or an IRR of 20.4%.

In 1985 Genes joined the EUROVENTURES network of venture capital companies. EUROVENTURES (EV) had been initiated by the European Roundtable of Industrialists (a club of CEOs of the largest European companies), and went on to establish country funds in all of the major European countries. Genes managed the DM 60 million fund "Euroventures Germany N.V." and later made a number of invest-ments in East Germany, including IFA Maschinenbau GmbH, Polystal Composites GmbH, and POLTE Armaturen GmbH.

While certainly a pioneer, Nathusius's enterprise was small-scale and had little influence on the emerging German private equity industry. Hellmut Kirchner, a contemporary of Nathusius in the market commented:

> Nathusius was definitely a peer. We tried to understand what Nathusius did. But I was never completely sure.[2]

Nevertheless, Genes can lay claim to having trained one of the first private equity professionals. After finishing his PhD, Andreas Fendel joined CVC, and benefitted from having worked with this early pioneer. But few others were marked in the same way by the firm, and its activities drew little publicity. Instead, the more important influence on the home-grown industry was to come from Munich, inspired by one of Germany's leading independent wealth management advisors, Count Albrecht Matuschka.

Matuschka/TVM

Albrecht Matuschka lays a strong claim to being one of the first people to establish a German-based approach to buyouts, and to having kick-started the careers of many individuals who were later to make their names in private equity. Born 1944 in East Germany the son of a career officer turned pastor and brought up in Dortmund within the British occupied region of the Ruhr, Matuschka narrowly survived death from polio, caught at the age of three. His mother, herself a medical doctor, refused to take the advice of other professionals that gave her child no expectations of survival. Instead she sought out a benefactor in the form of Erich Warburg, a rich banker, who made it possible for the young boy to be whisked away to a clinic in Switzerland, where he was eventually put back on his feet. Matuschka never forgot the benevolence of this Jewish banker who was willing to help a child he had never seen. Indeed his debt of gratitude was such that he took his first job with M.M. Warburg in Hamburg.

Growing up the son of a protestant preacher, at a time when Germany was struggling to rebuild itself, Matuschka witnessed many aspects of daily life that gave him insights into people's concerns. Matuschka recollected:

> If you grow up in the household of a pastor, you see all the joys and sorrows very close up. The cancer patient at 10.00, the marriage at 11.00, the burial at 12.00, the beggar at 13.00, you see the whole

cycle of life very close up. My father never had any money; all I saw was what was put into the slot at church. We were poor refugees from the east, having to watch every pfennig.[3]

While at secondary school, Matuschka had the opportunity to spend a year as an exchange student in the United States visiting a high school in Jackson, Michigan, the birthplace of the Republican Party. Partly as a consequence of this experience, he chose to focus his studies on economics and finance, and dedicate his life to finance as a tool for betterment of the world. Influenced by his benefactor, he took his apprenticeship with M.M. Warburg, Hamburg, and retained his links to the Warburg family by becoming an advisor to the cousin's firm, S.G. Warburg in London.

> I was for a long time Sigmund Warburg's court jester, in the sense that I was allowed to say anything without being beheaded for it. If you are very stupid you only learn from others, so I was advisor to S.G. Warburg for ten to twelve years. I always had the luck of having much older friends, so that what I know I learned from myself and from others.[4]

During this time, Matuschka commuted back and forth between London and Munich. Munich was chosen because it was fashionable in the post-war years to "go south", just as it once had been attractive to "go west" in America.

Matuschka met Rolf Dienst on an outing while at university, and found him to be a kindred spirit. Dienst was born 1946 in Wuppertal, the son of a family which was into its sixth generation working in the textile industry. He gained his first entrepreneurial spurs as a teenager, trading steel scrap, before going to Hamburg ostensibly to study law. Dienst later recalled:

> I decided to study law, as it allowed me to postpone making a final job decision. I knew I wanted to build something, but it wasn't clear what. I had an entrepreneurial mind. I attended three semesters in Hamburg, I don't remember whether I really saw the university much, but I had very interesting jobs, mostly selling products, the most obscure things. I learned the art of knocking on doors, which unfortunately no one teaches you today.[5]

Dienst moved to Munich during the summer of 1967, having decided to register at the Ludwig Maximilian University. Matuschka left

S.G. Warburg, but continued to serve as an advisor to his old employer, and the pair began selling mutual investment funds in summer 1968. Matuschka recalls:

> We decided to start something together. At the outset we were one-and-a-half, as Rolf was still studying at the time. We moved from one set of premises to the next as we grew, but we always stayed on the modest side.[6]

Dienst recalls of Matuschka that:

> He was only two years older, but ten years more mature than me at the time. But I had the energy and was more practical. We had a very nice twenty-two year relationship, even if the last three were very difficult. Matuschka was a visionary. Although I didn't have a formal financial training we built quite a nice business together.[7]

Matuschka and Dienst progressively developed their business into a wealth management boutique and focussed their energies upon selling two open-ended investment funds, one which was an international selection, and the other centred on Japan, which in 1968 was very much a novelty. They were well rewarded, as Dienst recalled:

> We made lots of money, and used the money to build the firm, which was originally called TRV, and which eventually became Matuschka. TRV stood for Treuhand Vermögensver-waltung.[8]

Dienst realised however, that he would have to finish his studies, and so completed a law degree in parallel to doing their business.

Through a mutual interest in art, Matuschka later met Werner Doettinger, who was another early member of the team. Matuschka remembers the early days of his team:

> Between 1970 and 1975 we slowly built our asset-advisory finance-boutique. We understood families and took care of their interests. At that time banks were following a very top down approach, not a bottom up one. We took a structured approach to managing the private balance sheet of the client, looking at Anglo-Saxon experience, because for historic reasons we had lots of friends in that community. It was very much a transfer of the best prac-

tices you have in England and America, into the German domestic environment.[9]

Matuschka took the title of Chairman, Dienst became President, while Doettinger took charge of money management. There can be no doubting the fact that Matuschka, Dienst, and Doettinger were innovators in their field. They brought sophistication to wealth management, and yet managed to keep the communication of their work to a level that their clients could understand. Matuschka's charisma was such that he only needed to talk to potential clients for them to be captured by his spell. He had a clear talent for marketing financial service products, and he was merciless in his criticism of the sleepy and inefficient approaches of the banks. This was to bring him both friends and enemies. Clients were convinced that Matuschka's team were cleverer and more sophisticated then the people working at banks like Deutsche. But competitors were appalled by both his arrogance and impudence. It was unheard of, especially in a German environment, for competitors to draw each other's reputations into question, and Matuschka regularly engaged in such banter. Undoubtedly Matuschka's approach was well-suited to his group's position: they were the clear underdogs who needed the publicity. They had everything to gain and little to lose from playing rough with the competition. Reinhard Pöllath later recalled:

> Matuschka pitched himself as selling an independent advisory ticket, which was anti-bank. "We're here to tell you how banks are taking advantage of you, and we're on your side" was his message, and the banks felt that they were being confronted by crazy young people. Matuschka and his colleagues were in their thirties, growing aggressively, and not shy. It was the Matuschka posture that provoked the banks' antagonism. Matuschka was unimportant as such, but he was viewed by the banks as a nuisance.[10]

In the late 1970s, Matuschka and Dienst tried their hands at buyouts in the United States. Dienst recalls:

> We did these buyout deals in the US. There were five in total. We're talking single, low double-digit million dollars. Matuschka/TRV's mistake was to make single deals with single investors. We should have done it in a fund. Some went extremely well, and some not so

Figure 4.2   Cover story of *Der Spiegel*: World Power – Deutsche Bank

well and the latter made the water smell bad, so we considered it a mistake.[11]

Matuschka's brand of wealth management[12] could already be styled as a multi-client family office. What he offered was considered by his clients to be different from that which was generally available elsewhere, and the Count was an excellent salesman. He later recollected:

> The times were good. We were much better than the others. At that time, wealth management was not at all well structured. What we did first was the wealth audit. You need your private balance sheet, you need your entrepreneur balance sheet, and you need your consolidated balance sheet. You must recognize where your assets are, how they are structured, what returns they give you. We were like general practitioners. You can treat 99 % of all diseases with 25 prescriptions, or in other words, if you just do the simple things, you have most of the answers.[13]

Dienst branched out to develop a real estate department which was quite successful in investing in Europe and the US. It was not long before the paths of Count Matuschka, and Peter Brooke of TA Associates, were to cross, in October 1978.

Peter Brooke left the army in 1956 to join the First National Bank of Boston as a trainee. He gradually worked his way up to a position in the credit department where he began making loans to the technology businesses that were bursting out of MIT and Harvard as a response to the Sputnik challenge. Peter Brooke explains:

> I was lending small amounts of money to small companies, helping them attract equity capital, and helping them make management decisions. I was very much involved with some of these small start-ups, not simply as a lender, but also as an advisor. This was in 1958, 1959 and 1960. In effect, I was a venture capitalist using the bank's capital, and that was how I got my start.[14]

From an early stage, Peter Brooke began to assemble equity capital from wealthy families to support the debt he was providing from the bank. Brooke explains:

> I got very close to those who were providing equity capital at that time: American Research and Development and the wealthy families in New York such as the Rockefellers, the Phippses, and the Whitneys. I would lend money to a company, and if I thought it was particularly attractive and making good progress, and the loans were exceeding reasonable limits, I would take those companies to

one of the family venture capital providers in New York to see if they'd like to invest.

There was a good deal of altruism in what the Phippses, the Rocke-fellers, and the Whitneys did initially. They wanted to prove that advancing technology and making money were not mutually exclus-ive. So they started to make investments in the 1950s, without knowing whether they would work or not, or what the exit would be. It wasn't until the over-the-counter market became some-what more active in the late 1950s and the early 1960s that the investments were able to be taken public.[15]

Through this contact, Peter Brooke joined Bessemer Securities, the holding company of the Phipps family, in 1961, to reorganise and run their venture capital operation in New York. This he did until January 1963, when because of a desire to stay in Boston rather than move to New York, Brooke quit to form his own venture capital outfit together with a Boston-based investment banking firm Tucker Anthony and RL Day. The company he formed, Tucker Anthony & Co Inc, was jointly owned by the partners of Tucker Anthony and RL Day and himself. The IRS were to persuade Brooke that his company was accu-mulating too much capital, which should be distributed in dividends, and so Tucker Anthony & Co was dissolved in 1967, to be replaced by a $6 million partnership, Advent I, to be managed by TA Associates.

The success of Advent I paved the way for Advent II, a $10 million partnership in 1972, and to Advent III, a $15 million partnership in 1978. It was during this period that Brooke became interested in Europe, first in 1972, after being interviewed by the French Ministry of Industry, and then the following year when he became a founding director of Sofinnova, a venture capital company in France. Brooke describes the process:

> We put a young man in Paris to be the advisor to the company. I travelled to Paris five times a year, and spent a week of each visit with the companies Sofinnova had invested in, helping them to develop their business. Sofinnova, along with a few corporate clients, gave me the opportunity to travel throughout Europe to see if people would be interested in venture capital.[16]

The interest in Europe also extended to seeking investors to support the TA Associates funds. For as the 1970s progressed, it became a challenge to raise all of the money needed purely in the US, as Kevin Landry, also of TA Associates, recalls:

> In 1975 $50 million was raised in the whole industry. It wasn't even clear at that point that we had an industry. No one believed in us in terms of giving us capital. At that point, Peter took the initiative and started going to Europe and developing European sources of capital. It was a big effort, but we developed some European sources of capital.[17]

Peter Brooke describes how his path crossed with Dienst and Matuschka's:

> In 1976, I was introduced to Count Albrecht Matuschka, the co-founder, with Rolf Dienst, of the Matuschka Group, by International Nickel Company ... which was interested in using our network to identify investment opportunities in Europe.[18]

It was Brooke who suggested that Matuschka invest in American venture capital. The response he got was not initially positive, as he later described:

> When I explained my interest in seeing if venture capital could work in Germany, the Count was very polite but let me know he had no interest in exposing his clients to anything as risky as venture capital. Only a couple of years later, however, it was becoming apparent that venture capital in the United States was producing interesting returns, and that a forward-looking firm had to at least have an opinion on this asset class. At my suggestion, Matuschka's partner, Rolf Dienst, came to Boston for a meeting in 1978. Dienst's job was to sort out and make sense of Matuschka's many enthusiasms, some of which were good and some bad. Rolf himself, meanwhile, had all the verve of a true pioneer. He was flamboyant, a great schmoozer, a man who truly loved life, whether he was conducting a band at the Oktoberfest or discoursing enthusiastically about opera (about which he actually knew nothing). In any case, Rolf became sold on the idea of investing in venture capital in the United States.[19]

Given the overlapping nature of their mutual interests, Rolf Dienst and Peter Brooke could hardly have been better suited to one another. Dienst recalls:

> I hit if off very well with him. From then on we had a very good relationship. We developed the first venture capital fund with Brooke,

piggybacking on his funds. This was in 1978 to 1979. Fifteen million dollars were raised, which sounds tiny, but the TA fund was only $80 million in total, so our contribution was 20%. For them that was a nice addition.[20]

Brooke quickly formed a positive impression of the Count, as he later describes:

> He was clearly driven by an ambition to succeed and to prove something to the world. Since starting his firm in 1968, he had developed a simple but very effective strategy. His goal was to perform just a little bit better than the Deutsche Bank, and to give his wealthy clients excellent service. Matuschka picked the best of breed managers in the various asset classes long before this strategy became popular.[21]

The Matuschka money flowed into Advent III, the partnership of 1978, and Advent IV, a $65 million partnership established in 1980. Peter Brooke's influence upon the group in Munich can hardly be overestimated. He introduced Dienst and the Count to the options for investments in the US venture capital scene. Matuschka recalled:

> We co-invested with venture capitalists in the US, the same thing we did on the real estate side. We were sending German money to the US, and learning about venture capital in the process. We felt at the time that the German market was not mature enough for venture capital.[22]

Matuschka and Dienst needed support with setting up a vehicle for investing money in TA Associates. They chose Hellmut Kirchner.

Hellmut Kirchner, born in 1947 the youngest son of five brothers, grew up on the grounds of an ammunition factory. After studying law, he made a trip to India, Thailand and Malaysia, and came up with the idea of importing Chinese umbrellas to Germany. It was this that attracted Rolf Dienst's attention to him, as Hellmut Kirchner later explained:

> We knew each other from legal studies because we shared a private tutor. Rolf already had his cabrio, and had made his first money. I also knew him from local events: we knew each other's girls. But the key moment was when I came up with my Chinese umbrellas. I

bought them for one Singapore dollar, and imported them, so that fully taxed they cost two Deutschmarks. Then I sold the first couple of hundred for 30 DM each, making a tidy margin. This worked so well that others wanted to sell them for me, so I sold them to other people for 20 DM as long as they took at least ten. Then Rolf came back from Thailand with papier maché pigs which you could sit on. It was the time of the hippy movement. The shops were full of Asian articles. My umbrellas fitted well into such collections, until people realised they had a strong smell, and exchanged them with Rolf's pigs which also turned out to have a strange smell. That was how Rolf and I came to get closer. We were like two little boys with their toys.[23]

Kirchner was impressed with Matuschka, and being bored with his job at Münchener Re, he decided to join him in 1978 to help set up the venture capital fund. The first steps were small, as Kirchner later explained:

We started back in 1979 the first legal entity that could be called a fund. It wasn't called a fund officially at the time, but was set up as "Gesellschaft des bürgerlichen Recht zur Verwaltung von US Wert-papiere",[24] not exactly a catchy phrase. We basically structured it so that it would fall under private rather than corporate taxation.[25]

The new fund raised $15 million to invest in TA Associates. But from the start, Kirchner decided that the investors should be heavily involved in the decision-making process, which nearly led to a deal-breaker. There were some within TA Associates who were not keen on the opportunities Kirchner was requesting for his active investors to "second guess" their investment decisions. Fortunately for Kirchner, Peter Brooke agreed to allow him ten days prior to any closing to facilitate this process. Kirchner recalls:

I wanted to involve my entrepreneurial investors in the process. Among Matuschka's thirty investors, there were about five who were active world class entrepreneurs running large family-owned enter-prises. The rest were passive investors and rich kids. I decided that if I was going to build bridges between the US and Germany, I would have to get the attention of these active investors in some way. I wouldn't get their attention by publishing quarterly reports of what had already been done. Besides, they would probably be critical of what we had invested in. Instead I decided to send them information on what we intended to do. I spent every weekend compiling pages sent over to me from America via fax, and then sent my summaries out to our active investors, also via fax, telling them what we were about to close on. This worked very well.[26]

Out of thirty investment proposals, Kirchner hesitated on only one, as he explains:

> It was an Indian company called Tandon. I found out some information which made me nervous about this case. They had a production plant in Bombay for producing floppy disk drives, which was one of the few mechanical elements still left over in computers. At the time, I thought I knew Bombay and wasn't sure this was such a good place to have a factory. And then I discovered that the company was run by two Indian brothers, one who lived in Bombay and the other in the US, the latter allegedly being famous for driving his pink Rolls Royce up and down Silicon Valley. So I said to TA, "Wait a minute, I happen to be in Bombay can I see the operation?" TA hadn't seen the operation themselves, and were surprised at my request. But they quickly organised a meeting. I was picked up by an impressive looking Sikh in a wonderful car, and driven to an area of Bombay that I did not know. It was surrounded by barbed wire and a concrete wall, with automatic sliding doors at the entrance. Behind these gates there was a different James Bond sort of world, with excellent buildings and manicured lawns.

> I looked into the operations of Tandon and realised they were like nothing I had ever seen before. At that time, I had quite an eye for how things should look, and after an hour, I asked if could make a phone call. I rang up TA and told them that everything was fine, and asked if I could double up. I didn't get double, but I did get one and a half. Seventeen months later that company went public for about 15 times our investment. So of course this was luck. Indeed it was good that this worked, because some of our other investments didn't fly at all. In the end, we more than doubled our money in the fund, which caused us to become quite famous by the end of 1982. We clearly experienced a successful start.[27]

Siemens heard of Matuschka's venture capital activities and expressed interest in them. Matuschka was advising the finance department of Siemens at the time on currency trading. Siemens offered to invest in a new fund which was to amount with other investors to $90 million.

Kirchner was sent out to find someone who could provide legal and technical advice on how to set up a much more official fund structure, one which could be exposed to public scrutiny. He found Reinhard Pöllath, who later recollected:

> Hellmut Kirchner came to see me. He was in charge of venture capital at Matuschka, and he had already talked to various law firms about the Foreign Investment Funds Act, and was surprised to find we had worked on it in practice. Matuschka had started investing in TA Associates and were looking around for someone in Germany who had done venture capital and knew how it should be structured from a tax and legal point of view. They came to me, and were surprised that I already had an idea and experience on how such funds would be treated.[28]

Dienst recalled the early contact with Pöllath:

> He was miles ahead of anyone. You had an evening discussion with Pöllath, like from 8 to 10 p.m. and the next morning you had a 20 page summary. He worked 24/7, he was unbelievable.[29]

The challenge for structuring German investments in venture capital was that the government had passed legislation to protect investors from placing their money with foreign funds. This legislation had been passed after the demise of IOS, a foreign fund of funds vehicle, which caused major losses for German investors. Pöllath recalled later:

> The Foreign Funds Act was an anti-IOS piece of legislation. IOS was the name Bernie Cornfeld gave to his fund. It was a very spectacular case. He had set up a fund-of-funds structure, for investing in foreign entities. The whole thing collapsed in the end, and a lot of small investors lost their money. Many countries started enacting anti-IOS legislation, targeted at fund-of-funds. The German banking lobby benefitted from the act to outlaw all foreign investment funds. It was penalty legislation, but no-one really knew much about the act, neither investors, nor advisors, nor tax agents. So, before you advised investors they acted in good faith, because before they hadn't heard of it, and once you had briefed them on it, they were in bad faith trying to get around the law.[30]

Figure 4.3   Reinhard Pöllath

IOS, Investors Overseas Services Inc., had been established in Panama with an office in Geneva, with operations run from across the border in France. Cornfeld's pitch to investors had been "Do you sincerely want to be rich?"

Pöllath provided step by step assistance to the Matuschka Group as it raised the funds for investment in TA. Pöllath recalls:

> Kirchner, together with Thomas Schwartz, was collecting money in Germany to put into TA. Doettinger and Achim Hartz were also collecting money, sometimes in amounts down to DM 50,000. People were cautious of allocating anything to venture capital back then. We set them up a structure for how to put this money into TA which was very much along the lines of what Andreas Rodin and I had done for family offices before.[31]

Inevitably, the experience of investing in venture capital in the US gave people the idea of trying it out in Germany. Peter Brooke had after all been active in venture capital in France since 1972, and consequently Germany was already at least ten years behind the game. Brooke's interest in Europe was increasing at the time, partially provoked by the victory of Margaret Thatcher in the UK, and partly by the impression he gained that the influence of socialism was on the wane. Brooke later wrote:

> When the Thatcher revolution occurred, we were in a position to replicate the TA Associates model in various places in Europe, starting in the United Kingdom in 1981. That was our first foreign affiliate.

> The affiliate was a management company owned one-third by TA Associates, one-third by David Cooksey, who was one of my partners, and one-third by another individual, Mike Moran, who was a partner of David's.[32]

Brooke's increased presence in Europe caused him to play an important role in setting up a venture capital initiative in Germany, as he later explains:

> I asked Matuschka why venture capital should not at least be tried in Germany. His answer was, "No, my clients would not understand this diversion from our strategy". This was his attitude until, during a lunch in Munich in 1983, he suddenly changed his mind. One of those attending that lunch – and sitting next to me, in fact – was Jochen Mackenrodt, a senior officer of Siemens who was in charge of mergers and acquisitions and relationships with Siemens subsidiaries worldwide. Mackenrodt, who was a very capable, well-regarded, and entrepreneurial person, had studied the venture capital industry in the United States and was curious as to why TA Associates had succeeded. "We've never been able to invest successfully in the United States the way you have," he said. "Obviously you've been doing it the wrong way," I replied. "Could be – tell me more," Mackenrodt responded. So we started talking about venture capital in America. Then I turned the tables on him and said, "You know, you really ought to think about doing this in Germany. Siemens would be the perfect investor to try to kick this thing off." Matuschka – who was sitting nearby and had heard this – was horrified that I had made these comments to someone from Siemens. After all, the purpose of this lunch was to attract venture capital investment to the United States, not to divert it to Germany. But Mackenrodt turned to Matu-

schka and said, "You know, it would be wonderful to do something like this." Matuschka, always the opportunist, replied, "Of course!" We had found our champion – Jochen Mackenrodt of Siemens – and another suddenly willing partner, Count Matuschka, in Germany.[33]

Matuschka recalls the purpose of the lunch differently:

> Rolf Dienst, Hellmut Kirchner and myself built a relationship with Siemens, and created the vision for TVM. We co-opted Peter Brooke to give us guidance on how to build such a venture capital franchise in Germany. We also introduced him to Mackenrodt of Siemens at a lunch with the intention that Peter would help us to bring Siemens on board.[34]

The energy and enthusiasm the Count subsequently put behind the venture, and the significant facilitation role he played, inevitably persuaded many people in Germany that it was his idea, and certainly that he was responsible for making it happen as Kirchner, for example, explains:

> Matuschka was the inspiration behind TVM, and he had every right to be proud of its achievements. It was an idea seeded in his courtyard, starting with the first $15 million fund, then the $50 million fund, and finally the DM 150 million TVM fund. The genealogy of TVM can easily be checked, and Matuschka identified as the principal sponsor. He made it happen, promoted it, and was instrumental in bringing in Siemens, which was vital. But without Peter Brooke in the Chair, Siemens would not have participated.[35]

Dienst later recalled:

> Albrecht and Peter Brooke met Jochen Mackenrodt, Vice President of Siemens and convinced him that we should set up a German venture capital organisation. That was the vision, I executed it. Mackenrodt and Brooke got on well together, which led to a good relationship between Siemens, TA, and Matuschka.[36]

Key figures at Siemens were co-opted onto the initiative by Matuschka and Dienst. Pöllath recalls:

> Mackenrodt at Siemens played an important role, as did the late Peter Kaleschke beneath him. Rolf Dienst pushed the idea and pro-

moted the Siemens connection. Siemens liked the idea of alternative investments. At that time, people used to call Siemens a bank with an electronics company attached.[37]

For a moment, there appeared a chance that Matuschka might be cut out of the venture, as Brooke himself recalls:

> Mackenrodt and his driver picked up my wife and me one evening and took us out to his house for drinks. On the way out in the car, he turned around from the front seat and asked me, "Why do we need Matuschka and Dienst in this thing?" "They're my partners," I said, "and I don't abandon a partner. What their contribution will be, I don't know, but if I'm in this, they're in this." I'm sure Mackenrodt was testing me, and I made it clear that I wasn't going to throw away a relationship for the sake of financial advantage.[38]

Once Siemens was on board, they brought in other large corporations including Bayer, Daimler, MBB, Mannesmannn, Zahnradfabrik Friedrichshafen, and even the Austrian state company ÖIAG. The next challenge was to develop a fund structure that could put the vision into practice. This time it was obvious that Reinhard Pöllath would provide the legal framework. Pöllath recalls:

> Then, perhaps two years after my first contact with Kirchner, came TVM. It was 1982, and they had to set up this fund for investing in German ventures. We had to invent it, because you couldn't copy eighty-page US documents. You had to write a German GmbH & Co KG agreement, and it had to look familiar to the in-house legal departments of all the blue chip companies, and it had to be state-of-the-VC-art and to fit its non-German side-by-side vehicle, TVI.[39]

Dienst toured Germany with Siemens fund raising and the targeted funds were quickly assembled. Once it was clear that TVM was ready for launch, an increasingly irritated Deutsche Bank felt obliged to jump on board. Pöllath recalls:

> Deutsche, as had several others, initially declined to be involved in the fund, probably thinking it was a silly idea. But when Siemens, Daimler, Mannesmannn and the others joined Matuschka, and made it fly, Deutsche joined at the last minute and they were taken

on board as a natural participant in a blue-chip environment and held out as a co-leader of the effort.[40]

Brooke was clearly surprised how hard the campaign *vis-à-vis* the banks was, even with Siemens on board, as he explains:

> Even with the name Siemens behind him, Mackenrodt needed all his powers of persuasion to recruit a roster of investors for TVM... The German banks were the hardest to convince, because they had so little comprehension of venture capital that they couldn't understand how it was any different from the kinds of financing they were already providing. The large industrial concerns, for their part, were convinced that no small company could hope to match their own innovative capabilities.[41]

The Count was not persuaded that Deutsche was hostile to his venture.

> Deutsche Bank accepted that they needed a counterpart in Germany, who was independent, and who knew how to do such things. They didn't look at us negatively, but quite the opposite. I always had the backing of Herrhausen.[42]

Peter Brooke became chairman of TVM, and Kirchner and Kaleschke became joint managing directors. But not everything was perfect with the new fund, as Kirchner explains:

> We had to accept two inherent roadblocks of TVM. The first was the supervisory board, and the second was the advisory board. The latter contained representatives of all the investors which in theory were main board directors of some of Germany's largest companies. But of course in practice, the representatives would be Directors, or people one level below the main board, which was what I had originally hoped for. But it turned out that these people were so important that they didn't have time, so it became the assistant to the Director, and then it became the assistant to the assistant to the Director. The problem was that they were all so overworked, and at that time it was difficult to get hold of any of them. So that was one part of the problem. The next was that in principle they were always negative. It was always a grace not to get a "no", or a "don't know". It was very time consuming. They added no real substance, even if technology-wise they had better knowledge.[43]

The challenge of having so many "experts" on the Board, mostly with a technological bent, meant that there were frequent obstacles to deals which were considered to have insufficient technological content. Kirchner explains:

> We were stopped from doing an investment in a street advertising company, because there was not enough technology content. I suggested that we install sensors to measure how many people went into the bus shelter where the advertising was installed, but this still wasn't considered enough technology. But it would have been a good deal nevertheless.[44]

The difficulties of getting investor approval even extended on occasion to deals which did have technology, and did have the full support of the TVM executive team, as Kirchner explains:

> We were blocked to do Diagen, but this time I began to fight. I started out on a trip to visit all the assistants of the assistants, and convince them that we had to do this deal.[45]

It was lucky that the TVM team fought on Diagen (later Qiagen), because this was to be their best investment. Brooke recalls the experience:

> In 1985, TVM invested in Qiagen, a provider of innovative sample and assay technologies and products for the life sciences. TVM's CFO, Peter Kaleschke, guided Qiagen through a long gestation period and remained on the board through the company's IPO.[46]

The rest of the German investments, by comparison, were dire. Hellmut Kirchner recalls:

> The German part of the portfolio during the first five years was close to a disaster, and drove us to the conclusion that we had to do something. After three years, we decided to take the remaining half of the money and invest it instead in the US. We had to run this past our investors. We used the argument that in Germany we could see no exits, largely due to the lack of a stock exchange. We explained that we would have to grow our German companies faster in the United States. So what could be more logical than to look for similar companies in the US to those we had already bought in Germany, buy them, and merge them, so that we could then take them public in the US?[47]

The TVM fund was not a spectacular success: its survival was largely owing to the opening of the Boston office and the switch to US investments. Part of the challenge, in Peter Brooke's opinion, was recruiting the right people to run the company or the ventures in which it invested, as he later explained:

> We were unable to locate anyone in Germany with venture capital experience, let alone the ability to manage a venture capital organisation. Moreover, it was difficult to find talented people who were interested in working for a small company like TVM. In Germany in those days, most talented German university graduates wanted to work for Siemens, Bayer, Daimler-Benz, or one of the other prestigious German companies. If you wanted to join a small entrepreneurial company, people thought there was something wrong with you.

Needless to say, this aspect of German culture also made it difficult to recruit talent for portfolio companies. A second challenge TVM faced in finding young, entrepreneurial companies in Germany and managers capable of running them was the managerial culture of Germany's large corporations. German companies ... had many brilliant researchers in their R&D organisations. Yet their researchers were isolated within their silos, with no chance to develop any understanding of marketing, manufacturing, or other functions crucial to the development of successful new products. The same held true for managers in these other functions. Such managers were very literate within their own functional areas but quite illiterate outside them. This was a major structural difference between German companies and American ones.[48]

The later success of Diagen, floated as Qiagen on the stock market was the fund's only significant German success story, as Brooke recollects:

> When Qiagen became the first German company to go public on NASDAQ, in 1996, TVM realised the current equivalent of €89.4 million on what had been an investment of €1.8 million... The Qiagen deal made up for ... TVM's 1985 investment, alongside Advent Ltd., in European Silicon Structures. ES2, as it was called, was an ambitious ... stab at creating the first European-based designer and developer of integrated circuits at a time when a worldwide glut of silicon chips was wreaking havoc with the industry. ES2's new

chip design and much-touted rapid production process did not bring success in the marketplace, and the company was sold at a fraction of what its investors had paid for it.[49]

The fund earned an IRR of around 10% over its extended life-time, a miraculous performance by comparison with the WFG, and it was both the publicity surrounding this fund, plus its lack of failure, which helped pave the way for private equity, and investments in mature businesses via leveraged buyouts.

HANNOVER Finanz

Very much in parallel to the activities of Matuschka and Genes, HAN-NOVER Finanz was developing from a traditional "participations" department of the HDI[50] to a fully-fledged private equity house. The story of HANNOVER Finanz belongs largely to that of its founder, Albrecht Hertz-Eichenrode.

Albrecht Hertz-Eichenrode was born in 1944 on his parents' large estate in the east of Germany. While still a baby, the family fled in advance of the Russian front line to the Rhineland, to the perceived safety of the British occupied sector. The Hertz-Eichenrodes were able to rent a farm near Dusseldorf, and the young Albrecht grew up in the country. At the age of 18, Albrecht's goal was to become an officer in the army, but a car accident was to deliver him an injury that eliminated this possibility. The choice of an army position had been a pragmatic one: it would have paid for his higher education. Nevertheless, means were found for him to go to Bonn University to study economics and business administration. Hertz-Eichenrode recalls:

> While at Bonn, I was politically active, and worked in the student parliament. It was here that I came into contact with the Flick Group, and discovered that they were providing a scholarship to send one student a year to the University of Iowa in the US. The arrangement had come about because one of the Flick Group board members had been awarded an honorary degree by Iowa. I applied for, and won the scholarship. So I went to the US for a year in 1965–66. That was a time when there weren't many German students in America, especially given the exchange rate of $1/DM 4.20.[51]

Hertz-Eichenrode finished his studies in Geneva, where he studied politics, before taking his first job at the Flick Group as an assistant to the chairman of the board. It was here that he came into contact with McKinsey. Hertz-Eichenrode recalls:

> At that time, in 1969, I thought strategy consulting looked a challenging job. McKinsey had about 20 people in Germany, and were looking for new staff, but they had signed an agreement with Flick not to hire any of their employees, which basically ruled me out. So I applied to AT Kearney, which had also only just started, and numbered about 15 at an office in Dusseldorf.[52]

Hertz-Eichenrode worked for six years at AT Kearney, focussing mainly on Mittelstand assignments. But towards the end of his time with the consultancy he was assigned to a project at Ruhrkohle, a substantially larger company. They too were looking for people, particularly for work abroad, and Hertz-Eichenrode's command of English and French prompted them to offer him a job based in Liberia, as commercial

Figure 4.4　Albrecht Hertz-Eichenrode

director of an iron-ore plant which belonged mainly to the German steel industry. Together with his young family, Hertz-Eichenrode spent four years, from 1974–79 working in Liberia, and it was here that he came into contact with HDI, the Hannover-based insurance company. Hertz-Eichenrode recalls:

> Each year, one of the HDI board directors came down to Liberia to visit us to assess our risk. In 1979, they were looking for a CFO for one of their operations in Germany. I already had an offer from Thyssen, but wasn't convinced about the future of the steel industry. So I met the Head of HDI. He told me of another project he had in mind. HDI was mainly insuring mid-size companies, and in many cases were asked to take equity participations in their policy-holders. The CEO wanted to do something in the participations area, but on a fully professional basis. He needed someone who knew about running industrial companies, and he offered me the job. I decided that developing participations in industry would be a challenge, and so accepted. That was the beginning of what was to become HANNOVER Finanz.[53]

Hertz-Eichenrode learnt some important lessons from his early days:

> The first investment was a bad one made in 1979 in a company focussed on the storage of data on magnetic tapes. We sold this participation a year later at a lower price. The owner bought it back thinking he had done a good deal. In reality, we were very lucky to sell it as the business went into troubled waters. That was a big learning experience.[54]

In 1983, Hertz-Eichenrode felt it was time to improve his education in the field of buyouts, so he went to Boston to visit TA Associates. He later recalled:

> I talked to them, and looked into what they were doing, hoping to learn about their business. Unfortunately, TA worked already with Matuschka at that time, therefore I had to cut off all further contacts with them.[55]

Armed with his freshly acquired knowledge from visiting TA Associates, Hertz-Eichenrode embarked upon his first majority buyout in 1984. Prior to this date, the only investments had been in minorities. The

Table 4.1 Private Equity Transactions in 1980–83

1980–1983

Year	Company	Buyer	Seller	Exit year	Sold to
1980	Rossmann KG	Hannover Finanz	Family	2002	Hutchinson Whampoa
1981	AWECO Appliance Systems	Hannover Finanz	Family	Not yet divested	Not yet divested
1981	HANNOVER Leasing KG	Hannover Finanz	Startup	1997	Helaba
1982	Fielmann AG	Hannover Finanz	Family	1992	Family

Source: Authors' compilation

investment in Völkner, a mail-order company, was significant, because it marked a change in strategy. Hertz-Eichenrode explains:

> We had a lot of discussions with HDI about taking this majority, because the original fund design was to take minorities, but at the end they agreed, and we were permitted to buy it. Nobody talked about management buyouts at that time, although Völkner really was a management buyout. Mr Völkner was 68 or so and wanted to retire. So we took over 75% of the company. A small proportion of the remainder went to two managers working in the company. They took over the management and we gave them a small incentive, not really a big share at that time.[56]

Much of the due diligence work was done in-house, for the view at the time was that this was the core competence of participation management, as Hertz-Eichenrode recalls:

> When we started, we said that we would do the due diligence our-selves. We had to take the risk for the investment, so we needed to be convinced that the risk was acceptable. We hired investment managers who had experience in industry, and recruited lawyers to work up the contracts.[57]

Völkner was sold four years later to Jens Odewald at Kaufhof.

Common characteristics of the early shoots

The first three players influencing the origins of buyouts in Germany all had significant Anglo-Saxon influence. Both Genes and TVM were greatly influenced by US venture capitalists, while HANNOVER Finanz gained some insights from this quarter, but to a much lesser degree. Genes and TVM consequently were more focussed on venture capital, while HANNOVER Finanz remained committed to minority participations. Passing judgement over which of these three was most successful depends heavily upon the criteria chosen for assessing their impact. TVM came closest to the existing German establishment, with its many connections to large corporations such as Siemens and Bayer. But its most successful commercial exploits were in Boston, not Munich. Nevertheless, the experiment was influential, and many Germans learned from the experience. Genes had the closest relationship with Anglo-Saxon venture capitalism, linked as it was to Churchill in the US, and

3i in the UK. But some were later to criticise its approach for being too theoretical, influenced by its university origins. HANNOVER Finanz's importance stems from the fact that a large tree was to grow from its roots. HANNOVER Finanz was commercially successful within Germany, and demonstrated the impact growth capital could have on companies active in the old economy.

5

The First Phase: From Venture Capital to LBOs

The creation of Genes, TVM, and HANNOVER Finanz helped with the process of importing more sophisticated approaches to equity and debt into Germany. It is significant that both Genes and TVM were authentic transplants of US venture capitalism. Those connected with their development would find it an easy step forward into leveraged buyouts, and many of them made this move within a very short space of time.

Roughly four to five years elapsed before the initiative to bring leveraged buyouts to Germany started. Ironically, it was not from the ranks of those at Genes and TVM that the first pioneers came, but from a very similar stable. The first move was taken by a German family office based in New York. It was the Reemtsma fortune that provided the initial capital behind the opening of Schroder Ventures in Germany.

The origins of Schroder Ventures Germany

Jan Philipp Reemtsma inherited the family tobacco empire from his father at a very young age and, following a period of trusteeship, gained full control of his assets at the age of 26. He had shown no particular interest in owning or running his share of the tobacco giant, and opted instead to sell his majority stake, and create a family office to invest the proceeds. He entrusted the establishment of Rho (his family office) to Diethelm (Didi) Höner, an investment banker at Morgan Stanley, who was later joined among others by Robert Osterrieth, the man who masterminded the creation of the first leveraged buyout fund in Germany.

Robert Osterrieth was born in 1950 in Kronburg near Frankfurt. His father ran a steel trading business which had been handed down over three generations. Osterrieth recalls:

> In 1968, when I finished Gymnasium at the age of 18, I had no idea of what I should study, or whether I should become an artist, a lawyer, or a businessman. I had no clue whatsoever. So I decided that doing a banking apprenticeship would give me a window on the real world. During the apprenticeship, there were things that I hated, and things that I liked. I quickly found that interesting areas were things like capital markets, foreign exchange, equity markets, bond markets and investments. The apprenticeship lasted two years, and by the end of that period, it was clear to me that I would focus my studies on capital markets and investments.[1]

Osterrieth began his studies in 1970 at the Ludwig Maximillian University in Munich, but still remained active in business:

> While a student in Munich I had a job on the side. Studying in Germany is far from a full-time activity. I worked as a research assistant with a firm called Portfolio Management. I believe they were Germany's first bank-independent money and equity manager. Peter Hellerich founded it, and he was quite well known at the time. He was sort of one generation prior to Matuschka. Hellerich was an equity portfolio manager, who bought mainly shares. I worked three hours a day for him as a research assistant. My job was to read newspapers, and pick up from them what would be interesting to portfolio managers. It was great, exactly what I loved to do, and they even paid me for it. I didn't have to write briefs. All I had to do was to mark interesting articles and an old pensioner would cut them out and circulate them. Sometimes when I thought I had an interesting idea, I would just go talk to one of the portfolio managers.[2]

After three semesters of study in Munich, and having gained his Zwischenprüfung in 1972, Osterrieth transfered to St Gallen, a leading business school in Switzerland.

> At St Gallen, unlike the typical German university, studying meant real work. I was kept quite busy there. I started in the fifth semester, whereas most people had studied there from the start. I felt I knew nothing and had to work hard to catch up. When I left St Gallen, it

Table 5.1 Private Equity Transactions in 1984

1984

Company	Buyer	Seller	Exit year	Sold to
Elogica	CVC	Family	1986	Insolvency
Interpane AG	Hannover Finanz	Family	1989	Lewag AG
VEMAG Verdener Maschinen- und Apparatebau GmbH	Robannic (Brian Fenwick-Smith)	Reemtsma	1990	Hannover Finanz
Völkner	Hannover Finanz	Family	1988	Kaufhof

Source: Authors' compilation

Figure 5.1   Robert Osterrieth

was clear I wanted to work in stock market investments, or maybe in corporate finance.[3]

A career in corporate finance during the mid-1970s clearly meant for most people moving to New York, therefore:

> In the spring of 1975, I went to New York: It was my first time in America and I knew nothing. I stayed in the apartment of some friends of my parents, and naïve as I was I thought that ten days would be long enough to find a job. That would leave me time afterwards to travel around. I knew that back in Germany I had a fallback position in the form of job offers in corporate finance from Deutsche Bank and BHF Bank, although these weren't the sorts of jobs I really wanted. I had an interview with Goldman Sachs. Their securities sales people were interested in me, but the corporate finance person who interviewed me wasn't at all. "Where did you say you studied?" he asked with a smirk on his face.

With hindsight 1975 was probably one of the worst years on Wall Street since the Second World War. The markets had crashed, and the banks were laying people off. So it wasn't an ideal time to be looking for a job, particularly if you came from somewhere nobody had heard of. I managed to get an offer from Morgan Guaranty, today's JP Morgan, through someone I knew. They had a very well established M&A department, which at the time had a significant market share in international M&A. I liked that. The problem with the offer was that they wanted me to start in Frankfurt. But they promised to move me to New York within six to twelve months.[4]

All went to plan, and within 12 months, Osterrieth was back in New York undergoing the six-month training programme, after which he moved into the M&A department. About six months later his bosses wanted him to return to Germany to help build up the M&A business there. After about one year working in the bank's Frankfurt office, it became clear to Osterrieth that he first had to learn the business from a larger group of experienced professionals before applying it himself in a relatively new market. That meant going back to New York and working at one of the major US investment banks who all had set up M&A departments to focus on this growing business. Through his connection to Didi Höner, who he had met during his first stay in New York, Osterrieth managed to interview with Morgan Stanley, and received a job offer.

Morgan Stanley was his first choice, and, highly motivated, he began working 14 hour days. The M&A department at Morgan Stanley was made up of about 25 professionals, and it was a perfect place for him to learn the business. Then, because of his German background, the firm began involving him in the development of business in Germany. Perhaps one of Morgan Stanley's most important assignments in the region involved advising Jan Philipp Reemtsma, heir to the largest German tobacco empire. Osterrieth later recalled:

One of the projects we got at Morgan Stanley at the time was for the Reemtsma family. Should they sell their cigarette company? What could they get for it? The background was that Jan Philipp Reemtsma had lost his father at a very young age. His father had been a marketing genius, making the Reemtsma family cigarette business the market leader. After the father died his son inherited the bulk of the cigarette company's shares, but control over the assets was exercised by two trustees until he reached the age of twenty-six, which he did on 26th November 1978. Jan Philipp hired Didi Höner, who used to work at Morgan Stanley. It was through Didi that Morgan Stanley got the mandate to sell the company.[5]

At the beginning of the 1980s, it wasn't common to sell a large family business. Morgan approached various potential buyers in a low profile fashion. The challenge, however, was that the cigarette market in Germany was already very concentrated, and there were very few potential parties interested. Osterrieth later recalled:

> We talked to Philips Morris, RJ Reynolds, and some others, and we kind of had Philips Morris and RJ Reynolds competing against each other. Nevertheless, there were a lot of antitrust problems because Reemtsma had almost 50% market share in Germany, and was therefore the dominant player. Marlboro was the single biggest competitor with about 14% market share. Reemtsma had lower market share per brand but when you added up all the brands, it was the biggest player in the market. We hired Joachim Sedemund of Deringer, now Freshfields Bruckhaus Deringer, a lawyer in Cologne, to advise us on the antitrust issues. We were having long and difficult negotiations. But then, out of the woodworks came Tchibo, another Hamburg company, who made an offer and promptly bought the controlling stake.[6]

Jan Philipp Reemtsma received about DM 400 million[7] for his 53% share (including a 2% share held by his mother). This money needed investing, and six months later Didi Höner approached Robert Osterrieth with an offer to join him in building up a Reemtsma family office (later to be named Rho). Osterrieth was intrigued with part of the role that Rho was being asked to play:

> It was something quite different that they wanted us to do, which was to buy meaningful stakes in companies but not take control. Mr. Reemtsma is not a businessman, he studied literature. He didn't want to get coverage in the financial press. He didn't want to run things. He didn't want control. The last thing he wanted was a bank calling him up, asking him to put fresh equity into a troubled company. Reemtsma wanted a passive and diversified investment activity.

> The first question was, what were we going to do with all that money? Invest in real estate, oil and gas like everyone else? It was a

lot of the genius of Höner, that he developed the theory that Paul Volcker, the chairman of the Fed, was a tough guy who would succeed in bringing down inflation (which stood at 13.5% in 1981, and was brought down to 3.2% by 1983). Volker jacked up interest rates to unheard of levels, and really induced a severe liquidity squeeze that killed the financial markets. Our thesis was that in the next phase, once this policy worked, inflation would come down, and along with that, interest rates, and PE multiples would expand making the stock market the place to be. That was our road map.

The Dow started moving, interest rates went down, bonds were flying, it was great. It started in the US, and it was clear to us that Europe would be next. So we started investing into Europe. Bonds, equities, and it was at this time that I started spending time in London.

Finally, with smaller portions of the money, we started investing in venture capital.[8]

The task of setting up a family office tax structure was still a new one. Reinhard Pöllath was pulled in to advise Reemtsma on the tax structure of investing the cash from selling the tobacco stake. Pöllath recalls:

It started out with a general review of how a German family office is organised and should be taxed on its international investments, and then branched out into what are the advantages and disadvantages of one asset class over the other. I remember that was around 1980.

Didi Höner was a very special person. He was very much a lonely wolf. He started off investing in a more classical fashion, achieving great success in stocks and bonds. Then in 1982 he started looking for something else to do. He went into venture capital, taking a 25% share in the first Sevin Rosen fund, and a similar share in Stein Lehman life-science. It was all strictly non-German and turned into a spectacular success.[9]

Didi Höner and Robert Osterrieth gained their initial experience of venture capital by investing small parts of the Reemtsma fortune in US-based venture capital funds. They followed with direct investments into selected companies owned by these funds. Much of the advice they

Table 5.2 Private Equity Transactions in 1985

1985

Company	Buyer	Seller	Exit year	Sold to
A. Friedr. Flender GmbH & Co. KG	Hannover Finanz	Family	1989	Deutsche Babcock AG
Hübner Elektromaschinen GmbH	Hannover Finanz	Family	1998	Berliner Elektro Holding AG
Lewag AG	Hannover Finanz	Family	1991	Lewag Holding AG
Mikron AG	CVC	Private investors	2005	Swiss investors
Progen Biotechnik GmbH	CVC	Private investors	2001	November AG
WIG – West Industrie Gesellschaft	Hannover Finanz	Family	2001	ThyssenKrupp Industrieservice

Source: Authors' compilation

were given was to come in handy when establishing an LBO fund in Germany. As Pöllath recalls:

> Andreas Rodin, myself and others at then Rädler Raupach had to look at the Placement Memoranda and the Limited Partnership (LP) agreements and work out how they would be viewed in Germany. We gave advice on what the tax authorities would request from German LPs and succeeded in liaising everything with the tax authorities. This was terra incognita at the time, at least in continental Europe.[10]

A critical event which had a formative impact upon Robert Osterrieth's interest in moving into leveraged buyouts in Germany was the disposal of one of Jan Philipp Reemtsma's other stray pieces of business. Along with the stake in the cigarette company, Reemtsma had inherited a company manufacturing machines for producing sausages, VEMAG Verdener Maschinen- und Apparatebau GmbH in Bremen. Like the tobacco company, the young Reemtsma had no interest in owning this company. Osterrieth later explained:

> Since Mr Reemtsma did not want to own control of anything, he insisted on selling VEMAG. As junior partner I had to do the job. I started contacting potential buyers. In those days, we spoke to some of the larger machine manufacturers like Thyssen and MAN, but they weren't particularly interested. The only group that listened to us was a very acquisitive conglomerate, based in Monaco, Thyssen-Bornemisza. They ran the family office of Hans Heinrich Thyssen-Bornemisza, the man with the phenomenal art collection. He was the big fish of the Thyssen family. He had at the time an American led management team in Monaco with a pot of money, which they were using to buy companies.[11]

To Osterrieth's surprise, Thyssen-Bornemisza Group (TBG) decided not to go ahead with the transaction, but the Englishman who had been leading the transaction for them decided to do it on his own.

> Brian Fenwick-Smith was his name. He said that if Thyssen-Bornemisza wouldn't do it, he would buy the company himself, using his own money.[12]

Brian Fenwick-Smith, a British born accountant from Hull, educated at St. John's College, Cambridge, had a German wife. He was at the time

CFO of TBG, but until 1982 he had been based in Amsterdam where he was Chief Executive of the European operations of TBG. TBG was already invested in agricultural machinery, and had been identified as a potential bidder for VEMAG. Disappointed that TBG was uninterested in buying the company, Fenwick-Smith sought to gain financing for his own acquisition of the company. He turned to ABN Amro, with whom he had been doing business for TBG. ABN Amro's response was not wholly positive, as the bank was concerned with the low level of equity. Fenwick-Smith recalls:

> The purchase price for VEMAG was DM 22 million, and I was prepared to put up DM 5.5 million myself, which was 25% of the purchase price. I pointed out to ABN-Amro that the equity of VEMAG was DM 17.5 million and that therefore my investment should be enough. Their answer was that the goodwill of VEMAG at a price of DM 22.5 million was DM 5.5 million, and that as they always deducted the goodwill from equity, they considered me to have zero equity, and therefore couldn't lend me a penny.[13]

Fenwick-Smith finally turned to Reemtsma for support in buying his business, asking him to lend DM 10 million to help finance the acquisition. Reemtsma indicated that he was willing to do this, and the two men shook hands on the deal. But with this new vendor loan in place, Fenwick-Smith's deal excited the envy of Höner. Fenwick-Smith later recalled:

> Didi Höner went back to Reemtsma and said that he could give him a better price than I had offered. He offered DM 26 million. I had offered DM 22 million, and only had a handshake agreement with Reemtsma. But at this point, Mr Reemtsma said to Höner that he couldn't very well deal with him on this basis. He either had to make up his mind whether he was his advisor on the deal, or whether he wanted to be a bidder making an offer for VEMAG. Reemtsma told him to please decide on which side he wanted to stand. If he wanted to make his bid, then he should go away and give him his written resignation as his advisor. At that moment in time, Didi Höner was being extremely well remunerated, and he decided that he would be better off continuing to work for Reemtsma. So Höner didn't interfere any more with the deal which was just as well for him. For when I later signed the contract with Reemtsma, he told me this story himself,

and added that as he had shaken hands on the deal with me, even if Höner had resigned, he wouldn't have sold him the company![14]

Höner and Osterrieth had already gone to great lengths to make VEMAG an attractive deal. They had unearthed a tax credit so attractive, that Brian Fenwick-Smith only needed a bridging loan, because within a few months time, he could expect a substantial tax refund. By distributing the retained earnings from VEMAG to his holding company, he could write down the value of the company once acquired and reclaim taxes that had previously been paid on those retained earnings. In the case of VEMAG, this was a large sum of money. Indeed Osterrieth recalls:

> It was a huge number in this deal. All Brian needed was a bridging loan from the bank until the money was refunded by the tax office. I worked it all out with the tax adviser. It was unproven, but we were confident it would work. The only problem Brian had was that the banks refused to believe the scheme would work. It seemed too fanciful to hope that the tax office would pay out such an enormous sum.

> In the end through his connections, Brian got a loan from a Dutch bank. He bought the company, and six months later received the money back from the tax office, exactly as planned, as well as enjoying a level of profitability in VEMAG never foreseen by the sellers. It was a very successful transaction for him![15]

The procedure with the tax refund became an often-used German method in many leveraged acquisitions, and management buyouts, as Reinhard Pöllath explains:

> It benefitted from the German corporation tax credit introduced in 1977 (modelled after the French avoir fiscal), combined with a traditional US IRC feature, the post-acquisition asset-basis step-up. This combination gave a tax boost to German buyouts throughout the 1980s and into the 1990s, when it was curtailed and then abolished by legislation. We spent thousands of man-hours finetuning this and it became state of the art and generally accepted.[16]

After closing the VEMAG deal, Osterrieth thought that from an investment point of view, it was more attractive to be a buyer than a seller in such a transaction. He realised VEMAG wasn't the only company that could be bought.

> I thought, wait a moment, there are hundreds of such companies in Germany. There were lots of medium size companies. It was then 1984, just before I moved to London, and this was a crucial germinating period for me. Moving to London triggered me into action. I was too close to Germany for this idea of investing in Mittelstand companies to leave me in peace.[17]

Once established in London, Osterrieth set out in search of strategies to buy companies like VEMAG that could be bought on behalf of Reemtsma. Höner, however, wasn't convinced by the idea, because he feared that if the Reemtsma name became associated with a company, and things went wrong, Reemtsma would be the first to get calls from people begging him to inject fresh equity. So from the outset, it was clear that Osterrieth needed to get a co-investment partner that would put his name on the activity, as nothing more than minority participations could be expected from Rho.

Bit by bit, Osterrieth developed a passion for setting up a leveraged buyout business for Germany:

> In those days, I was thinking "why am I interested?" As a young man you have role models: mine were people like Ted Forstmann and Henry Kravis. Back in the early days of buyouts, it was very much a people business, driven by just a few early pioneers. I met Henry Kravis while I was living in New York. His second wife, Carolyne is a very old friend. She was previously married to a German, and lived in Darmstadt for a while, which is where I met her. Then she decided that she couldn't take living in Germany anymore, and moved to New York. She lived in a little one bedroom apartment on 3rd Avenue and I spent quite a bit of time with her back in those days. She married Henry in 1985, and so I got to meet him. I tried to interest Kravis in the idea of taking buyouts to Germany, but at that time he wasn't willing. He said "we have so much to do here in the States", which I suppose at the time was right.
>
> Ted Forstmann I knew because we had common friends, and I played tennis with him a few times in the Hamptons.[18]

Osterrieth had also crossed paths with Bain & Company while in New York, and given Kravis's lack of interest, his next thought was to contact

Mitt Romney who led Bain's investment business at the time. Romney, the son of a Massachusetts senator, later to become a senator himself and contest the Republican candidacy for the presidency, was more sympathetic to the idea than Kravis, but said that while he knew a lot about leveraged buyouts, he knew next to nothing about Germany. So he suggested doing a feasibility study.

Romney discussed the matter with his colleagues in Germany, as Peter Tornquist, the head of the Munich office of Bain & Company at the time recalls:

> I had been doing worldwide recruiting with Mitt Romney for three years, and got close to him over that period. Romney proposed a study be done, and the decision on doing it was taken by Romney at Bain Capital, and the representatives of Bain Holdings, which included George Denny, the partners of Bain & Company, including myself, and also Bruno Tiphine. We agreed to look into the German buyout market as it was both interesting for Bain Capital and for Bain & Company as a potential consulting business. The study was done from the Munich office under my leadership by among others Stephan Krümmer and René Mueller, with Tiphine acting as the manager on the project.[19]

In the cold early months of 1985, Stephan Krümmer and Robert Osterrieth worked on the analysis, interviewing bankers, corporates, and M&A boutiques, to gauge their interest in buyouts. Osterrieth recalls:

> I remember vividly sitting in the Bain office at Amiraplatz in Munich. I had an office there, it was where we had all our meetings. I was staying at the Hotel Vier Jahreszeiten. It was freezing cold when walking over to the Bain office. I stayed four weeks, it was January. We went to see people who we felt would have good judgment on this. We met with every senior banker we had a relationship with.

> For example, we met with Metzler bank in Frankfurt. We started by explaining what we would want to do. We even showed them a simple LBO financial model. The fact that one would then own such companies was considered outrageous.[20] The Metzler bankers said "Do you want to become the Boone Pickens[21] of Germany?"[22]

The banking community was outraged at the idea of people buying companies with so little of their own money.

The study revealed that the German market was singularly ignorant of private equity at this point: none of the corporates were interested in the concept, and suspicion among family-owners was equally high. Stephan Krümmer recalls:

> Our conclusion was that for the time being it was not possible to do private equity in Germany. There were three main reasons for this. First of all, bank financing was not available in the way we see it today, and the banks were pretty reluctant to lend a lot of money to private equity houses. Private equity was very young also in the US at this point. Secondly, people were reluctant to sell companies to private equity houses because they really didn't understand what they were doing. Thirdly, the potential for exits was very limited because the stock market back then was almost non-existent. You had the DAX companies, but that was basically it. There was a regulated market but its population and turnover were very low.[23]

The most promising leads were from US corporates dissatisfied with companies they had bought in Germany, or family companies that

Figure 5.2   Robert Osterrieth's Memo to Nick Ferguson Proposing a German LBO Fund

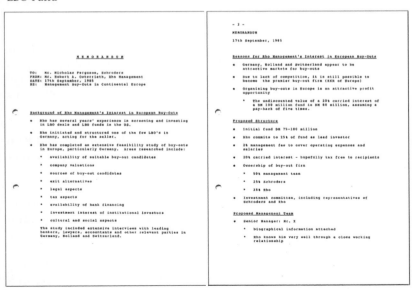

Source: Robert Osterrrieth

were close to bankruptcy. Gerresheimer Glass was one such American owned candidate. Owens Illinois had bought 97% of the share capital of Gerresheimer, only to find that it gave them little control of the German company, whose management continued to act as if they were wholly independent. Bain & Company was brought in to try to influence Gerresheimer management, but Bain's idea was to propose a management buyout. In the end, the suggestion never gained traction, because Bain felt that they would be open to allegations of conflict of interest, especially if the purchasing vehicle had been Mitt Romney's Bain Capital, which until 1986 was still a part of the consulting group. Peter Tornquist recalls:

> Gerresheimer was a very large consulting client to Bain, and we were working to turn the company around, because it was bleeding cash at the time. This reduced Gerresheimer's potential as a true buyout candidate. It was only some years later, once the problems had been fixed, that its candidacy as a buyout target was to arise again.[24]

While the results of this analysis were not particularly positive, there was nothing to suggest that buyouts in Germany wouldn't work. Indeed, the most startling finding was how little one needed to do to make money on a buyout. Peter Tornquist, the head of Bain Munich at the time, recalls:

> The tax impact was in there. I do remember René Mueller saying in his presentation, "you don't need to do a damn thing with the business; just by working with a different capital structure you could make a fortune. Forget about increasing revenues and profits, just keep cash flow steady."[25]

A summary of Bain's findings was passed on to Mitt Romney, but Bain decided to follow their own independent path rather than enter a joint venture with Osterrieth, and instead it was Schroder Ventures which snapped up Osterrieth's proposal.

At the end of 1985, Nick Ferguson visited Robert Osterrieth to try and interest him in investing Reemtsma money in a Schroder Ventures buyout fund dedicated to the UK. Ferguson recalls:

> Robert was a friend of my old room-mate at Harvard. He had a brand new office, all flashy lights somewhere. I went over to see him

while I was raising our new fund. He said he was quite interested, but he was more keen on doing something like this in Germany.[26]

Osterrieth suggested instead creating another fund in which Reemtsma would invest to do buyouts in Germany. Ferguson who had already been considering such a venture with his colleague Jon Moulton, quickly accepted the offer.

> I said this is a great idea. There were literally no buyout funds in Germany, and having seen what we could achieve in the UK, I thought we could make a go of it.[27]

Rho committed DM 25 million from Reemtsma as an anchor investor to the new German fund. With the help of Schroder's placement team, the fund closed at DM 140 million, with Prudential of the US as another investor, matching the Reemtsma commitment. This was a lot of money at the time, and over the target that Osterrieth and Ferguson had set themselves. The institutional investors were drawn from all across the globe, and very few were based in Germany. It took some five to six months to raise the money. Ownership of the management company was split 40% for Rho, and 60% for Schroders.[28] That way Reemtsma remained a minority investor all along the line.

By the summer of 1985, Osterrieth, Ferguson and Moulton went about hiring someone to run the management company in Germany. Ferguson remembers his tour of Germany well:

> I got on the road to find someone to run the management company. Before I went, I typed up some specifications of what we were looking for and showed them Robert. He said I might as well write in "superman". So I went trailing around Germany, visiting lawyers and other intermediaries. I finally met a lawyer in Cologne who put me in touch with Thomas Matzen.[29]

It was a tough task to hire someone for their team, as no-one within Germany could claim to have experience working in leveraged buy-outs. They conducted the search without professional support, and found Matzen through Joachim Sedemund, the anti-trust lawyer in Cologne who had helped Morgan Stanley with the sale of the cigarette enterprise. Sedemund had a connection with Thomas Matzen, the youngest senior manager at EFFEM, the pet-food subsidiary of Mars in Germany, who he had come across when Matzen tried to buy a supplier of Mars, much to the consternation of his employer. Sedemund guessed correctly that this would be precisely the sort of person that Osterrieth would be looking for.

Thomas Matzen was born in 1949 in Hamburg, the son of a long line of lawyers and hanseatic merchants. Matzen was only 15 years old when his father died, an event which was to shape his future life. He felt that he had to work through all of his holidays to help support himself and family. He studied a combination of law and business administration, and was offered a job by Arthur Andersen who at the time were eagerly building up a presence in Germany. While working for Andersen, Matzen audited the books of EFFEM, the Canadian branch of Mars Inc. He was subsequently hired by EFFEM to help with the management of their pet-food business. It was while he was working with EFFEM that he got his first buyout opportunity. Matzen explains:

> I had always wanted to do something on my own, and while I was at EFFEM the opportunity arose to buy Baden Hop, one of our suppliers. So I phoned up John Mars and asked for an urgent private discussion. He said OK, so I got on the Concorde and flew over to Washington. I went to his private house and had dinner with his family. Then we went into the library, and before I could say anything, he said, OK you want to leave and you want to buy one of our suppliers. I was shocked to hear that he knew everything already. I said that yes he was right, but he had just destroyed my path of argumentation, so I asked him to please give me a few minutes to explain. I told him that I didn't have the good fortune of being born heir to one of the Mars companies. Instead, I had a number of years available, during which time I could establish my own wealth. He said that he could offer me the possibility of two jobs, one in France and one in Los Angeles. But I refused, and he accepted my decision and wished me success.
>
> The next morning I went to see Forrest, John's older brother. I was more worried about this meeting. But in the end he stood up behind his desk, and shook my hand and said: "Thomas I wish you every success and I am sure you'll make it one." After that I went back to Germany feeling very pleased. But when I got back to Germany events changed such that the deal never happened. From that very moment I knew I would be leaving.
>
> We had an anti-trust problem at Mars at the time and we had a lawyer, Joachim Sedemund, involved. We became close friends and I told him

I wanted to do something new. He put me together with Schroders. They had been interviewing hundreds of people over the previous two years, but not found what they were looking for. I met Nick Ferguson and Robert Osterrieth in February 1986 at the Four Season's in Hamburg for the very first time, and by the evening we had a handshake agreement. I started on 1st May 1986. The offer they made me sounded interesting, but to be honest, I didn't have a clue.

I had assumed the money for their fund had already been collected. When I joined, I was very surprised to find that they had nothing. I had to pre-pay everything. There was no legal environment for our operation, nothing at all. Then I learnt that I would have to conduct interviews with potential investors. I had to do my own tour of the world! I found out that the fund was a goal not a reality! Now of course in hindsight I realize I was too naïve. It is normal that an investor would never invest blindly into a fund without having talked to the person who is to be in charge.[30]

Osterrieth commented later:

When we met Matzen we could see he was good on the numbers side, which was important. He was young, my age, maybe six months older, with a relevant professional and operating background, which we liked. He understood the LBO concept immediately. His job was to beat the bushes and find companies. He then hired Dirk Brandis and an associate called Matthias Gräper.[31]

Matzen insisted on setting up the office in Hamburg, which while not Schroders' first choice, met with little resistance. Osterrieth recalls:

When Matzen said he wanted to stay in Hamburg, he kind of ran into open doors. Schroders originally came from Hamburg. George Mallinckrodt, who ran Schroders thought it was great: we could get to do something in Germany and it would be called Schroders. Indeed he was so pleased with the idea that in 1987 he organised an exhibition of the Schroders' family silver in Hamburg.[32]

Matzen opened a small office, which could seat six to seven people, plus a conference room, on Glockengießerwall, an old office overlooking the Alster Lake. From there, after being joined by Dirk Brandis and Matthias Gräper, he began looking for companies. Pursuant to a model adapted from

Figure 5.3   Thomas Matzen

the US (with the IRC "Ten Commandments" rewritten into German "Do's and Don'ts") Matzen could only be an advisor to Schroders, a restriction he hated (as did many others after him). But Reinhard Pöllath and Andreas Rodin explained to him, on Schroders' behalf, that this was the law.[33]

The pickings were small as Nick Ferguson recalls:

> We knew that what we were doing was pioneering. It was a tough job to get into places. The leads came through private banks, accountants or lawyers.[34]

Schroder's first deal was Jofrika, a company in Cologne with DM 14 million in turnover. Osterrieth recalls:

> Jofrika was the leading manufacturer of cosmetics for carnival, and to a lesser extent for theater, but mainly carnival. It came to us through a buy-in manager who had read about our new activity. There were no M&A firms in Germany in those days, but there were business brokers like Interfinanz. Matzen and his team wrote the preliminary investment review. Ferguson, Moulton and I in London talked it through.

We had the Hamburg people on the phone, and we asked many questions, much like people do today on investment committees. We bought the company in November 1986.[35]

Jofrika can lay claim to being one of the first buyouts ever exited in Germany, and fortunately, it was a successful one. Matzen found the process fascinating:

> When I really tried out the idea of a buyout in Germany, with Jofrika, there really was nothing upon which to base our experience. Some senior partners of Arthur Andersen stayed on in our meetings to be polite, because I was a former colleague. But I could read their faces. They clearly thought "now Matzen has really lost his mind". To them all that we were trying to do was pure speculation.[36]

The company was acquired by the Schroders led investor group for DM 1.8 million of equity, at a valuation of DM 9 million, and later sold in 1988 for DM 18 million of equity, and a valuation of DM 24 million. It had been proven that a buyout could create money for investors, something which was crucial for helping the new private equity industry get off the ground.

Jon Moulton recalls:

> The tax position on deals in those days was wonderful; a lot of the deals were heavily tax driven. By the time we had been running for about four years, we had already got a net cash return in the lower 30s on our investments, it was fabulous fun. It did not get much better thereafter.[37]

Robannic

Meanwhile, Brian Fenwick-Smith was reaping the profits from the VEMAG deal. As he later recalled:

> I recuperated three quarters of my investment in VEMAG inside eighteen months, so it was a very nice deal. I did the same again, with a second deal in early January 1987, when I bought another company using exactly the same construction. Laetus, which means delighted in Latin, was an extremely good buy. It was based in Ansbach near Darmstadt. At the time I bought that company it was doing about DM 7 million in sales, earning DM 1 million in

pre-tax profit. I paid a lot of money for the company, but of course I got a big chunk back again from the tax authorities. I eventually sold the group in 2001.[38]

Shortly after he had completed the Laetus deal, Fenwick-Smith decided to set up a team to run what was fast developing into a nascent private equity group, to which he had given the name Robannic. Unlike the Schroder's vehicle, however, it was built on Fenwick-Smith's own fast developing wealth, and was therefore more a family-office than a true private equity house in the modern sense of the term. Hans Gottwald was the first to be hired.

Gottwald was born in Dusseldorf in 1958, and after an apprenticeship at Bayer, followed by military service, went to study mechanical engineering at Aachen University. Alongside his studies, Gottwald worked for an institute of the university dedicated to rationalisation, which was more akin to a consulting business. Attracted by the business side of his work Gottwald got a job at BCG. There he stayed for two and a half years until 1987, when by chance he came across Fenwick-Smith, who offered him a job. Gottwald recollects:

I quite spontaneously decided I liked that environment so went to join him, down in Monaco. My first assignment was an acquisition of Louda, a machinery company that made credit card manufacturing machines, which was done in Munich from October to December 1987. I learnt about niche markets, tax and legal structuring from scratch, because I didn't have experience of such things or of doing buyouts. But my experience helped me get considerably involved in the operational side of our acquisitions, with some reorganisation, and even taking some day-to-day decisions in a role as full-time Geschäftsführer of the company.[39]

Gottwald was quickly joined by Christian Hollenberg. Gottwald recalls:

I was joined by Christian Hollenberg about a year after I moved to Robannic. The two of us had met before at BCG. After finishing his MBA at Harvard, Hollenberg talked to many people in the M&A scene, and decided to come into private equity. At the beginning of

1989 we both moved to Munich, and became heads of the German operations of Robannic which included some responsibilities within companies as well as working in the market buying firms in special areas.[40]

But Robannic as a German-based institution was to be short-lived, for soon after their move to Munich, Gottwald and Hollenberg left to join Raimund König's newly created IMM Group, with the intention of creating their own sub-holding.

HANNOVER Finanz

In 1986, two years after Hertz-Eichenrode's first majority buyout at Völkner, HANNOVER Finanz closed its first LBO. Hertz-Eichenrode recalls:

> We acquired WIG as the junior partner in a co-investment with a Swiss private equity house. It was the first time we had injected leverage. Even then, however, it wasn't on a grand scale. Interfinanz handled the sale.[41]

A further two years later, in 1988, HANNOVER Finanz closed its first majority leveraged buyout, as senior investor, of Willy Vogel. The deal was not part of an auction, the contact being made through a lawyer known to both parties. The original owner died in the 1950s, but his wife, an opera singer, had managed to take over the business and run it quite successfully. Now that Mrs Vogel was in her 90s, she felt it was time to pass on the business. The deal coincided with Andreas Schober joining the HANNOVER Finanz team from the Mars strategy consulting company in Paris.

Schober was born 1954 in Washington DC, the son of an Austrian diplomat. After living during his youth in Copenhagen, Brussels, and Stockholm, Schober returned to Washington DC in 1977, when his father succeeded Martin Halusa's father as Austrian Ambassador to the US. Andreas Schober attended the Catholic University of Washington, rather than Georgetown like both his brother and Martin Halusa, because he wanted to study engineering, and Georgetown had no engineering faculty. After completing a masters degree at Stanford, Schober joined Hewlett Packard, and worked for five years near Stuttgart in the medical engineering area, picking up two patents on the way. The move to strategy consulting was prompted by a disillusion that his work at HP was becoming more adminis-tra-tive and routine. Meanwhile, his younger brother was working for Matuschka, having first joined TVM, and then joined Hellmut Kirchner in moving to Boston to set up TVI. Partially through this influence, Andreas Schober also decided to apply for venture cap-ital, and his second interview was with WBB, the Berlin-based ven-ture capital operation of HANNOVER Finanz. Schober recalls the experience:

> Joachim Simmroß, who at the time was number two at HANNOVER Finanz, interviewed me, and offered me a job. In the event, it was to Hannover and private equity I went, rather than to Berlin for venture capital. I took over the position of Dr Naber, who died tragically in the February 1988 crash of the NFD flight from Hannover to Dusseldorf.[42]

The Willy Vogel deal gave Schober his first experience of private equity, as he later explained:

> Simmroß was responsible for the deal, which was a buyout, and we had to learn by doing during the project. We were practically inventing everything, developing the Newco, dealing with the legal issues, none of which had been done before at the time. We had heard of leveraged deals, but it was a big difference having to do one. We had to explain everything to the banks, Commerzbank and Berliner Commerzbank, who didn't like cash-flow based finance. We had to create incentive schemes for the manage-ment, decide how much sweet equity to give them, and produce our own integrated cash-flow models, all of which had to be devel-oped along the way. We had two in-house lawyers supporting us, and a team from Deloitte. Part of the challenge was that we were far away from the Frankfurt and Munich scene, and lacked their net-works of experience in this area. Once we had completed the Willy Vogel deal, this was used as the reference for all of our future buyout projects.[43]

Fortunately for the HANNOVER Finanz team, Willy Vogel had been run by the employee-managers for many years, and they already behaved like entrepreneurs, seeing the buyout as their big opportunity to take over the company.

Lessons from the first phase

Some of the most concrete early steps towards the introduction of leveraged buyouts in Germany were taken by people linked to family offices. Robert Osterrieth of Reemtsma collided with Brian Fenwick-Smith of Thyssen-Bornemisza to create the first buyout at VEMAG. Fenwick-Smith's subsequent "Robannic" investment vehicle was in reality also a family office, rather than a private equity house. But Osterrieth's link up with Nick Fergusson resulted in the first fund aimed specifically at buyouts in Germany. Meanwhile Albrecht Hertz-Eichenrode charted HANNOVER Finanz on a course that was to lead to its first buyout with Willy Vogel.

Both Fenwick-Smith at Robannic and Osterrieth at Schroders recognised early on the tax advantages buyouts could benefit from in Germany. Indeed tax refunds played a major role in financing the paydown of leverage on their early deals. By contrast, HANNOVER Finanz was less influenced by these tax benefits, migrating more organically from an earlier focus upon unleveraged minority participations.

The first buyouts in Germany were to attract new players into the market. Nevertheless buyouts were far from the only focus of those that set up shop over the period 1986–1988: venture capital, growth capital, and minority participations, were to play at least as big a role in the next phase of private equity.

6

The Second Phase: 3i, CVC, Bain, and Matuschka

No sooner had Schroders begun its activities than others began to follow. Indeed the timing of the early office openings is so close that their exact sequence is difficult to pinpoint (quite a few will claim to have been the first-movers). Otto van der Wyck hired Wolfgang Schaaf and Max Römer to open up CVC for him in Frankfurt, Friedrich von der Groeben paired up with Andrew Richards to initiate 3i Germany, and frenetic activity was stirred up within the Munich Office of Bain & Company, which led to a cross-roads decision on whether to stay committed to consulting or switch paths to private equity.

3i

In November 1985, Andrew Richards, who was working in the ICFC London South region, received a phone-call from David Marlow asking him whether he would be prepared to help 3i open up an office in Frankfurt. Jon Foulds, the CEO of 3i, had early in the 1980s decided that the firm should expand onto the Continent, and chose Paris for the starting point. Michel Biegala had been hired to open the 3i Paris office in 1983, and Nick Green, from 3i's Reading office, was sent over to provide support and advice. The Paris office performed well, and Foulds decided that Germany should be the next step. Marlow told Richards that they were looking for a German managing director, but needed someone to go over from the UK to Frankfurt to provide the same support that Nick Green had given to Paris. Andrew Richards later recalled:

> Marlow said they had already found a German managing director, and they wanted me to start immediately. It turned out, however, that the guy they signed didn't show up, and so they had to make a

dramatic search for a replacement. Somehow, through a headhunter contact, they came across Friedrich von der Groeben, who was available, and suddenly everything was on again. I met Friedrich in February 1986 when he visited London, and we immediately hit it off.[1]

Friedrich von der Groeben was born in East Prussia in 1943, and like Count Matuschka, grew up as a refugee immediately after the war. His father was entrepreneurial, trying several business ventures, before settling down with a Coca-Cola bottling franchise. After six years in a Schleswig Holstein boarding school, von der Groeben did a one-year apprenticeship in a bank, and then moved on to study economics in Göttingen and Bonn. He knew from the start that he was destined for a life in business. Like many of the founding fathers of private equity, von der Groeben then got some work experience in North America:

> After university I went to McKinsey in Canada. I wanted to go to an American business school and gathered it might be useful to have some work experience beforehand, so I got a traineeship position at McKinsey in Toronto. I only got to hear of McKinsey through a friend who was the CEO of Massey Fergusson. His son was also working at McKinsey. There were about 20 professionals in McKinsey Toronto then, and indeed the whole company had I think only three hundred people. It was a very interesting experience.[2]

After studying for an MBA at Harvard, graduating in 1972, von der Groeben was recruited back to McKinsey, but this time to the Dusseldorf office, opened in the late 1960s, and consisting of around 30 professionals. He spent eight years in consulting, before joining his father's Coca-Cola franchise, which was at that time one of many. Realising the sector was ripe for consolidation, von der Groeben toured the Rhine-Main area, buying up other franchise operations, until there were no more companies available to buy. Then, in 1985, he and his father sold their business to Coca-Cola, leaving von der Groeben at the age of 42 wondering what to do.

> It was clear that I did not want to join a corporation. What were my capabilities? I had analytical tools from McKinsey, and some entrepreneurial experience through running my father's business. What could I do with that?

At the time, investment banks had started to get known in Europe so I took a few interviews with them. But then I found an advertisement for 3i in the newspaper. It didn't actually mention the name 3i. It only said "Beteiligungsberatung"[3] or something of the sort. I thought, this could be something for me. It was only after I joined that I found out what 3i actually did.

I was interviewed by David Marlow and Jon Foulds. They had had some tough luck, having offered the job to a consultant guy, who had agreed to join, and then not shown up. They were under some pressure. They offered me the job within two weeks, and I was their first recruit in Germany.

I started on the 1st January 1986, and spent half a year in England getting to know the people and the business. Only then did we open an office in Frankfurt. They put Andrew Richards alongside me, he had been at 3i for four or five years, and had an accounting background. He didn't speak much German, but he was someone who was willing to go to Germany.

In order to improve his language, I got Andrew a job for four weeks on a Coca-Cola truck. I told him, you will never learn German in Frankfurt, because everybody speaks English here. So I put him into an environment where nobody spoke English. He took it with great humour. He learnt German, and it was much cheaper than with Berlitz.[4]

Andrew Richards recalls his first visit to Germany, ostensibly to improve his German, in March 1986:

I was going to go on a language course in London, but Friedrich said that this was far too expensive. I only had an O level in German, which was pretty rusty. Friedrich said he would get me a job with his father's old company. So I turned up in Mainz, and they hadn't a clue what I was supposed to be doing there. I ended up filling supermarket shelves with Coca Cola and Fanta bottles, shipped around in crates from the back of a lorry. I thought to myself, is this how I'm supposed to learn German?

Michel Biegala was given the role of supervising the establishment of the German office, which was to cause a number of tensions. Biegala wanted the German office to open in Wiesbaden, but von der Groeben insisted that it should be in Frankfurt. Richards recalls:

> Friedrich was uncomfortable with Biegala's role. Friedrich wanted to report directly to London, not to someone in a parallel position, as all decisions were made in London anyway.[5]

Under Friedrich von der Groeben's guidance, an office was found in Frankfurt, and two secretaries hired, as Richards explains:

> We formally opened the office in September 1986. The first recruits started on 1st January 1987. By the year-end March 1987, we had no deals on our books, but nobody in London was worried.[6]

The brief from London was a cautious one. The team in Frankfurt could only invest in minorities, and the amounts to be invested were to be limited. Von der Groeben recalled:

> David told us "Take your time. There's no pressure. The first deals you'll be doing will be wrong anyway, so keep them small".[7]

This advice was taken, and the Frankfurt team made no investments during their first two years. But it was not all due to caution: as von der Groeben recalls:

> At the time nobody had heard about private equity. Everybody I spoke to thought it was an absolutely silly idea. Why would anyone take foreign capital? It would have to be a bankrupt company. For otherwise, why would any sensible entrepreneur give up his company? So it really took a lot of time to convince people.[8]

Within months Friedrich von der Groeben and Andrew Richards had hired an office manager, Janicka von Engelhardt, and a secretary. Their first professional hire was Thomas Schlytter-Henrichsen, who was born in India, and spent the first two decades of his life living in former English colonies, and travelling on a Norwegian passport. Schlytter-Henrichsen joined 3i in January 1987, having spent five years with Preussag. He moved to Frankfurt after a brief spell with 3i in the UK. Schlytter-Henrichsen later recalled:

> The atmosphere in Frankfurt got pretty depressed. They had been going for a few months, and had had many meetings. Friedrich had been calling up all his McKinsey contacts. Of course being polite they would meet him, even if they didn't have anything for him. We were running around to as many intermediaries as possible. Then we decided to cut up the territory into bits. I became responsible for Southern Germany, still doing the round of intermediaries. I would phone people, and they would say, sorry we do not have any poorly performing companies. I would say, but we also invest in excellent companies. But they would say, sorry we're not interested and bang the phone down. Occasionally, someone would ask "does 3i have anything to do with Bernie Cornfield?"[9]

Even before joining 3i, Schlytter-Henrichsen's former boss at Preussag had sent him a copy of the magazine *Wirtschaftswoche* featuring the story, "Barclays Kapital gleich Pleitekapital" (Barclays Capital equals bankruptcy finance"). Like most of his colleagues, Schlytter-Henrichsen knew very little about private equity:

> My exposure had been limited to buying companies in the mining industry. I knew about discounted cash flows, due diligence, how to do contracts. I knew the whole technical side of M&A. But the first time I heard of the concept of an LBO was sitting down with Friedrich and him explaining it to me. It was completely new to me.[10]

Friedrich von der Groeben quickly saw that the future in Germany was not with growth capital, which was the traditional 3i business in the UK, but leveraged buyouts, and the years that followed were a constant battle with London over what they could be allowed to do in their region. The first deal that he and Andrew came across was Vossloh, as Richards recalls:

> Vossloh Werke had been going through a lengthy process of restructuring, and the deal we were looking at was a rescue. The family was having difficulties finding anyone to lend them any more money.

So we discussed with them injecting some equity. We looked at their accounts, visited their subsidiaries, and in November 1987 we put in a proposal to the investment committee in London to provide Vossloh with some additional equity. The reaction which came back was that while it was all very interesting, it was far too risky for us to be doing this as our first deal. We came back again, not giving up, and insisted that it really was interesting. The investment committee then said, look you said that one of your competitors is DBG, which is run by Deutsche Bank. Go to them, and if you can get them to co-invest, then you can do the deal.

So we went off to meet Fanselow at DBG. He sent his people in, and we came to an agreement. So we wrote to Vossloh saying that we would be able to proceed with the deal, and Deutsche immediately agreed to provide them with bridge finance to tide them over until we made our investment. But by March 1988, the results coming out of Vossloh were so good, that Deutsche wrote us a letter saying that our equity wasn't necessary any longer, and that we weren't needed. We were all completely disappointed.[11]

The challenge for the 3i team was that London was not keen on them making such large investments, and the local banks clearly wanted to keep them out of the market. Schlytter-Henrichsen, recalls his impressions at the time:

The concept of a buyout was very much in its early days even at 3i in London. They were doing some buyouts, but the main product was actually development capital. Friedrich had the right idea, which was to go for investments of 5 to 15 million DM, and 3i was looking to do investments of DM 300.000 to one million Deutschmarks. There was a constant dispute with London. They disapproved of Friedrich running off trying to do 5 to 15 million Deutschmark business deals. They were constantly trying to "calm him down". Michel Biegala, who had set up the French office, also got involved. They were all trying to calm Friedrich down. But he was right. He found exactly the spot where Thomas Matzen was successful. We competed with Matzen, but the problem was that we were only allowed to do minorities. We went into transactions with one hand tied behind our backs. It was difficult for us to compete on an even playing field.[12]

Faced with so many problems, the easiest thing for the team to do initially was to follow London's advice, as Richards explains:

> I remember Friedrich opening a bottle of wine in March 1988, the year-end, and he was at his wits end. So he said, OK, let's do what they want us to do. So we did two or three deals, all of which were junk, to get some deals on the books. By September 1988 we had done three deals with an average size of half a million Deutschmarks, all of which went bust.[13]

The first deal the 3i team closed was TTW Industrie & Messtechnik, based in Waldkirch near Freiburg. 3i committed DM 500,000 in two tranches, first DM 300,000, and then DM 200,000 a short while later. The company, which made welding machines, blood pressure machines and electrical testers, had 2 million DM in sales. Schlytter-Henrichsen commented:

> It might seem crazy but the components were very similar. It was quite funny. One week before we signed, the guy bought himself a new 7 series BMW because he was scared we would not let him drive a fancy company car afterwards. You see that a lot in Germany. That was the first investment. Unfortunately it went bust.[14]

The TTW investment was followed by an investment in Orga Karten-systeme, which was later sold to Preussag and the Bundesdruckerei in 1993 after an extremely difficult period of ownership. But London were sufficiently satisfied that the Frankfurt team was focussing on the right amounts of money.

> London were more relieved that it was only DM 300,000 going in, than knowing whether it was a good business or not. It was an indication that we were starting to toe the line. They were glad that we were doing what they wanted. Andrew and Friedrich were, nevertheless, still trying to do something different.[15]

Nevertheless, the German team had no faith in the small investments they were making, and were determined to develop a business which would make more sense. The decision was taken to pursue a direct marketing campaign, addressing the managers of non-German-owned subsidiaries in Germany. Richards explains:

> We hired PPA Direct, a company from the UK, who identified 500 managing directors of the subsidiaries of non-German com-

panies in Germany. They were asked what their views were on buyouts. This process took about four and a half months, and what we were looking for was an interview, or a visit to some companies. In the end, we were able make about thirty visits to managers who thought that their owners might sell. We had one or two enquiries from that, and basically we came to the conclusion that our future was in these small buyout deals.[16]

It had been Friedrich von der Groeben's decision to limit the search to the subsidiaries of non-German owned companies because of the lower mental barriers to a potential sale. The experience with German-owned companies had thrown up a common pattern, as Richards recalls:

Every time we come across a good German-owned company, all that happened was that the owners went to their bank afterwards and told them that 3i was prepared to give them a capital injection. Then the banks told them that there was no need for this injection, extended their credit lines, and kept us out. It was rapidly becoming clear that there was no hope for development or growth capital in established German companies.[17]

The other problem with German-owned companies was that 3i's restriction to minorities meant that many interesting deals went to the competition, as Schlytter-Henirichsen recalls:

I remember the instance with Kleindienst, a company doing washing equipment for cars. Friedrich had an excellent relationship with the management. We had everything going for us, and Matzen just went in there, and before we could say one two three it was done. Friedrich was in shock. We would have had to find a co-investor. The restriction to minorities within 3i meant that the odds were stacked against us in buyouts.[18]

The next solution the Frankfurt team arrived at was to line-up co-investment partners. Von der Groeben, Richards, and Schlytter-Henrichsen sought out other private equity houses that would be willing to co-invest, finding Candover and Metzler as suitable partners to team up with. The need to find co-investors meant that, despite 3i's lack of majority financing capability, its influence on the buyout community in Germany became pronounced. 3i built up arguably the best network within the German M&A and investment community.

Candover

Candover had possibly the most continuous intermittent relationship with Germany of any Anglo-Saxon private equity house. Roger Brooke established Candover Investments in 1980 in London, and raised a small fund of a few hundred thousand pounds. As a consequence of careful investing, this small fund of money was grown into millions. From the early days, Brooke was interested in Germany, as Jens Tonn explains:

> Roger had spent some time in Germany after the war, and was well connected on the political front and in military circles. He was keen to get back to Germany after starting his business in the UK. He opened up in Germany around 1986, and hired a few German bankers. The team was headed up by Johannes Drerup, an ex corporate finance director of DG Bank.[19]

The German team found the local market to be very different from the UK, however, and faced problems with deal-flow and exits. The main solution to deal-flow was to team up with players restricted to minorities, such as 3i, to do joint deals. Exits, however, remained a much deeper problem. Both challenges were to cause frustrations in London, as Tonn explains:

> They did a few deals, but they were very small. There wasn't really an M&A market in Germany at the time. This meant that it was difficult to exit a deal, even if you had done one. So what was the point of buying an interesting Mittelstand company with DM 20 million in revenues, to develop it into a DM 24 million business? That development might be terrific for the individual owner, but had no real impact on the fund. So Candover found itself stuck with a few investments.[20]

The best deal of the period was the co-investment with Metzler, Pallas, and Genes, in Heidemann, closed in 1988. Brooke took a position on the board of Heidemann alongside Klaus Nathusius of Genes. Tonn recalls:

> Candover made about 4–5 times their money on Heidemann, albeit after an extensive holding period.[21]

The co-investing approach continued in 1990, when Jadog was acquired, together with Metzler and 3i. Nevertheless, co-investments in small companies were not enough, and disappointed with the performance of its German effort, Brooke's team decided to close the office in 1995. Mark Elborn, who joined Deutsche Candover in 1995, recalls his impressions of the old Frankfurt team:

> Drerup at that time must have been in his fifties, and had recruited Christian Schlessiger and Boris Rick. They sat in offices on the 17th floor of the old brown tower block on Platz der Republik in Frankfurt. They had been making minority investments, mostly with 3i, in deals worth DM 20–30 million. Around 10–12 of them went bust. Christian hired me in 1995, after Drerup and Rick had left. Shortly after I was hired, but before I started, Candover decided to save money and time by teaming up with Legal & General, who were considering entering Germany.[22]

Bain & Company

Bain & Company was a relative newcomer to both Europe and Germany even in its core area of strategy consulting. In 1977 the company had won a first project with Siemens, only to see its work wither away without a follow-up. As a consequence, when a similar large project resulted in a team being sent to London in 1978, there was a fear that this too would remain a one-time assignment. But this time, the small team led by John Theroux was successful. A couple of years later, one of the Bain partners in London, Jim Lawrence, left London to set up a second small office in Munich. His reasons for doing so were political rather than operational, and for a short period he reported directly to Bill Bain in Boston. His independence was short-lived, and in 1983 his reporting line was switched to London. Unhappy with this arrangement, he returned to London to suggest to Iain Evans, another of the London-based Bain partners that they leave to set up their own firm. Evans's response was favourable, and with the addition of a third Bain partner, Richard Koch, a new consulting company was born, L.E.K. (Lawrence, Evans & Koch).

The defection of three out of Europe's five Bain partners was a serious blow, and all other members of the European team were offered fifty thousand pounds to stay. Jim Lawrence's second in command in Munich, Peter Tornquist, chose to remain, along with Gary Crittenden, and took responsibility for building Bain's operations in Germany. Peter Tornquist recalls the challenge:

> Gary Crittenden was a key guy for consulting, strong in analytics, enormously committed to Bain and myself. He stayed with us for

three to four years, and was a very strong guy, helping me train a young and inexperienced German team. Crittenden later went on to become CFO of Monsanto and American Express.[23]

Tornquist proceeded to build up a team, hiring Fritz Seikowsky, Raimund König, and Stephan Krümmer. Fritz Seikowsky recalls:

I joined shortly after the L.E.K. people marched out with Jim Lawrence. They changed the locks. The place was in turmoil, and indeed the first years were a big struggle.[24]

Many of the new Bain consultants had been hired with the idea of creating value for clients, and for themselves. Mitt Romney, who went on to head up Bain Capital, played a significant role in recruiting for Bain & Company during the early 1980s. Fritz Seikowsky was one of those captivated by his message.

I really had the feeling I wasn't just joining a consulting firm. Mitt told us that there were three phases of consulting: phase one, selling hours of advice for money; phase two, selling profits at a discount; and phase three, buying profits at a bargain. We were told that Bain didn't do projects, we did companies. I found the value proposition completely unbeatable. This was the alternative to going through the hierarchical career steps of a major German corporation.[25]

Figure 6.1   Mitt Romney and Bill Bain

When Mitt Romney asked the Bain Munich team two years later to investigate the options for leveraged buyouts in Germany, there was plenty of interest within the office. Stephan Krümmer was assigned to the project, and was joined in the work by Robert Osterrieth himself. Peter Tornquist, the head of the office, recalls:

> We all got very intrigued by the findings of the study done for Mitt and Robert. We thought: 'this is interesting'. The office was so small that everyone knew about the work. We started looking for opportunities.[26]

An opportunity for Bain to pursue a buyout in Germany came entirely unexpectedly. Markus Conrad, one of the consultants within Bain's Munich office at the time recalls:

> Rolf Mathies approached us with the news that a family he was close to in Hamburg was discussing whether or not to sell their business. The son of the family was working closely with Count Matuschka to look for a new owner.[27]

Peter Tornquist, Rolf Mathies and Markus Conrad, established contact with the owner of a Hamburg-based book wholesaler. Manfred Ferber at the Matuschka M&A department was indeed trying to line up Libri with Hachette. But Mathies and Conrad seized upon the idea of turning the transaction into a buyout. Fritz Seikowsky later recalled:

> We were all looking for defining opportunities. There was this one consultant, Rolf Mathies, who was the friend of the son of Georg Lingenbrink. He saw an opportunity to get us an exclusive buyout deal.[28]

Conrad and Mathies conducted an initial outside-in analysis on the company to establish whether it would make a good investment. The results were positive, as Conrad later explained:

> I produced one chart which was more-or-less correct, and that was critical. It showed that there were thousands of publishers in Germany, selling through thousands of retailers, who were served by four wholesalers. Libri had never lost money, and the market structure suggested that there was a clear economic need for the service it was supplying.[29]

Peter Tornquist recollects:

> The father basically said: "my son isn't going to run this business so I need a solution". I remember going up to Hamburg and spending time with both the son and the father. I spent most of my time with the father, to firm up the opportunity, with the help of Marcus Conrad. Mathies spent time with the son. We established a trust with them, and we really liked their business. I negotiated a final deal with the father's lawyer. Then we called up Mitt and said we've found a business.[30]

They appointed Reinhard Pöllath to structure the deal for them, and George Denny of Bain Holdings supported the process from Boston. Markus Conrad took responsibility for running the day-to-day handling of the deal, and remembers the final run up to closing:

> On the day of the closing, in February 1989, I remember picking up George Denny at Frankfurt airport, and driving him at break-neck speed in an Audi Quattro up to Hamburg. We got there just in time for the meeting with the notary public.[31]

Mitt Romney backed the acquisition financially, and the deal was done for around DM 150 million – a big deal for its era – the entire execution of the buyout was performed by the Bain Munich consulting team. Tornquist recalls:

> All of a sudden Bain Capital in Boston was owner of Libri, and they never once came to Germany![32]

The Bain Munich team was given a significant finder's fee by Bain Capital, and given co-investment rights. Fritz Seikwosky recalls:

> We bought Libri for DM 150 million, investing DM 15 million of equity, and we later sold it on again for DM 150 million, but this time with no debt. We succeeded in managing the debt down really rapidly. We were all allowed to co-invest on the deal. I invested DM 100,000, and once it sold in 1989 I netted my first million Deutschmarks.[33]

Hypobank, which had begun providing debt for buyouts two years previously, provided 90% of the cash to do the deal, which was bought on a ten times multiple. Peter Tornquist was particularly pleased with the deal as he explains:

> The Hypo financing was wonderful. We got 10% equity to debt, with roughly a 40% mortgage loan tied to a warehouse in Hamburg at some 1.5% margin, and the rest in largely non-amortising five or seven year facilities at a 1.75% spread. They had read somewhere that warrants were "in" and got a 1% kicker. We negotiated directly with the Vorstand at the Hypo, and it was mutually very constructive.[34]

Markus Conrad was given the job of finding a new manager to run the company, which he quickly realised was a major challenge, as he explains.

> We hired Egon Zehnder to look for a manager to take the business on. We were now in possession of a traditional German company, with DM 240 million in revenues, profitable, but heavily loaded with finance. We wanted someone who was fluent in English, who understood private equity, who understood the book retailing industry, and who was competent to run a family company. But it was impossible to find any manager in Germany who met all of these criteria.

> The former owner was 75 at the time, and once I started spending more of my time with the company, he approached me, and asked me whether I would take on the job. He liked the fact that I was from Hamburg. I hadn't made my mind up when six months later in October he died, just a month after I made partner at Bain. I realised then that my heart was not in consulting and that at the age of 29, this was my opportunity to become an entrepreneur. I realised I didn't even like private equity. I'm a holder, not a flipper.[35]

George Denny and Mitt Romney readily agreed to Conrad taking on the management role, and negotiated terms for him to buy shares on the original terms as a buy-in manager. He took up his new role in January 1990, to be confronted by a strike during his first month at the company. Conrad recalls his first day in the new role:

> The old management introduced themselves, and said that they had heard that Bain was a good consulting company. What they

couldn't understand, was why we had bought their company? They saw themselves as working in a declining industry.[36]

Despite the reservations of the old management, the opening of East Germany created the opportunity to expand the business, and Conrad transformed the company, as he later remembers:

> There was a tremendous amount of work to do in the first three-to-four years. We changed the management team, introduced cost savings, professionalised the processes, and made a sale-leaseback on the assets. Within that period, we paid back a substantial amount of our debt.[37]

With a successful buyout behind them,[38] there were tensions within the Bain team in Munich over the office's future strategic direction, as Peter Tornquist explains:

> It was an interesting experience as there were some tensions in the team in terms of where we were going as a firm. There was the big question of whether we should do deals for a living. Some wanted our focus to be only on large corporate clients, while some others wanted also to do work in the private equity arena, including due diligence work and investment evaluations. My task, as head of the business, was to keep the team together, even after I had seen Conrad go. We had only one person, who had joined us recently from McKinsey, who was extreme in his wish that we do only corporate work. For the rest of the team, it was degrees of difference, and more concern about how we would fill the hole left by Conrad's departure. As I had been driving the Libri work, I was sympathetic to private equity work.
>
> There were also a number of big decisions, such as how the finder's fee was to be divided. Some had worked hard on the deal, while others had been keeping up the consulting activity.[39]

But ultimately perhaps the biggest factor which prevented the Munich office of Bain going down the private equity road was the financial crisis within Bain itself.

Bill Bain sold his consulting business to the 60-strong partner group in 1989, in what was itself a very highly leveraged buyout. Only months later, the global economy veered into recession, and the Bain & Company

Table 6.1 Private Equity Transactions in 1986

1986

Company	Buyer	Seller	Exit year	Sold to
Jofrica	Schroder Ventures	Family	1988	Private individual
Loher AG	Hannover Finanz	Family	1991	Flender AG (Hannover portfolio company)
Signalbau Huber AG	Hannover Finanz/Berliner Elektro	Reinhard Müller	1990	IPO

Source: Authors' compilation

business began to crater, leaving the consultants at Bain in Munich, and elsewhere, with internal issues to resolve. As a consequence at the end of the 1980s there was no bandwidth left for thoughts of an aggressive entry into German private equity.

Matuschka Capital

Matuschka's route to leveraged buyouts was not in the event to come directly through its venture capital arm. TVM was only modestly successful, and ran at arms-length to the other Matuschka activities. Rather it was the M&A advisory business Matuschka formed in the early 1980s which was to lead a short and rapid path to buyouts. The value proposition was tax management, following similar approaches to the one developed by Robert Osterrieth for the VEMAG deal at the Reemtsma family office. A group of Matuschka executives, including Manfred Ferber, Michael Hinderer, Adam de Courcy Ling, and Vincent Hübner, showed that using step-up and depreciation techniques, corporate clients could reclaim millions of Deutschmarks in previously paid taxes. At the time M&A had barely begun, as Manfred Ferber, who already had experience of working at both the Bayerische Landesbank and the World Bank at this stage recalls:

> Except for Interfinanz the M&A market was non-existent. Interfinanz was a pure broker, and everyone else was coming and going, with M&A departments appearing and then disappearing. The M&A market was in its infancy. Matuschka Group had an excellent network, and we were the anti-pole from the banks.[40]

When Ferber was hired to develop further the M&A department, he had been impressed with Matuschka's achievements in the area, particularly on the Kühne & Nagel[41] transaction in 1981. Ferber recalls:

> At the start of the 1980s, Kühne & Nagel had had several bad years, and Deutsche Bank promptly found a buyer to take them over. All of a sudden Klaus-Michael Kühne realised that he was about to lose his company. Then Matuschka came in and fixed his problem. It corresponded with Matuschka's mission to be always the anti-pole to the banks. Matuschka brought in Lonrho Plc run by Tiny Rowland to buy 50% of the company, with Kühne keeping the other half. Despite the banks being so overwhelmingly powerful, Matuschka managed to solve Kühne's problem.[42]

The Count was later to comment:

> We helped Mr Kühne in the decisive moments of his life, and that is
> why he is a very old friend. Jens Odewald was an executive at Kühne
> & Nagel at the time, and so I met with him in this context.[43]

Deutsche Bank saw what Matuschka was doing with his M&A team,
and a year later in 1985 set up its own team under Hans Dieter Koch,
using the name DB Consult, to do the same.

Matuschka's M&A experience was to prove very useful later, even if
that experience was to flow, through its alumni to many other firms
in the financial services community. The innovations were manifold:
Matuschka had observed that a second-hand car dealer wouldn't sell
a car with a full tank of gas, and the M&A group started ensuring
that companies sold for its clients were first emptied of cash (to the
substantial gain of their clients, as it did not yet impact the valuation).
Similarly, the Matuschka Group introduced to Germany the concept
of valuing acquisition targets on a debt-free basis, again to the benefit
of their clients.

The Matuschka Corporate Finance Department was very successful, and
indeed the whole Group was very profitable. On the asset management
side, Matuschka was the first institution to invest in Japanese convertible
bonds in Germany. Japan at that time had become a miracle story.
The innovativeness of Matuschka, coupled with the success story in
Japan, helped draw in fresh capital. The Count moved the Group from
Ismaninger Strasse to a big building next to the America House on Karo-
linenplatz. No expense was spared on the redecoration. Seeing the entry
of Schroders into the leveraged buyout market, both Matuschka and Dienst
felt that this was territory they should be in. Their successes to date were
such that they had little doubt that they would be successful also in private equity. Such was the confidence, that it was assumed from the outset
that Matuschka Capital (as it was called, or MatCap for short) should
be the biggest fund so far. The feeling was that if Matuschka was to play
this game, then it had to be much bigger than Schroders, and take the
clear number one spot. The fund had to be multiples of the Schroders
DM 140 million fund.

Armed with a proven track-record of supporting its corporate clients,
Matuschka formulated his goal to raise a fund to make the same sort
of money for his own partners, and their wealth management clients.
Matuschka's ambition for such a fund was years ahead of its time: his
objective was to raise a fund of one billion Deutschmarks. The scale of

Figure 6.2   Overview of the Matuschka Group

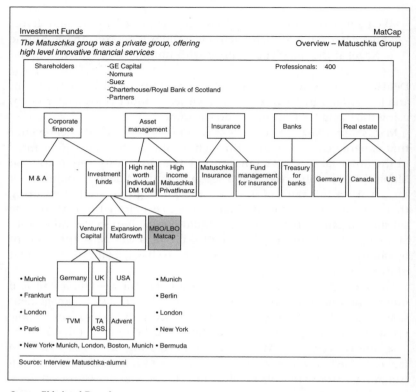

Source: Ekkehard Franzke

this ambition was heavily influenced by the success of the group, and the feeling that everything Matuschka touched turned to gold.

The Count took on board some lessons from his experience with TVM. The first concerned the role of the management company's owners in the investments. He later recalled:

> Matuschka never invested in target companies ourselves. That was important. We always owned part of the management company. We did not co-invest in the portfolio companies ourselves for the simple reason that we were a private partnership, and at that time simply did not have the funds. We were very small. We may have put up 1% of the capital, so if other people put up a hundred million, we put up one million. But we were not George Soros.[44]

The raising of the fund was to prove a long and arduous task. Rolf Dienst later recalled:

> The funds raised for MatCap were a big disappointment to me. It took two years. I said let's do a buyout fund for Germany. Albrecht said that's a wonderful idea, fantastic. I said I'm thinking of raising DM 150 million. Albrecht said, "No! We need a one billion Deutchmarks fund." I said sorry, but we have no idea what to do with it. I said I wouldn't even know where to get a billion. But we agreed on a billion, and then it took two years to raise, with 200 days a year on the road, finding the money. Lehman Brothers did the fundraising in the US, Botts and Company helped us in Europe, Bahrain International Bank helped us in the Middle East.[45]

If there was disappointment in the fund-raising process, it was only shared by Dienst. For as the Matuschka saw it:

> We were extremely happy with the sum we raised. It was a shared vision, and we co-opted the right partners.[46]

The October 1987 crash undoubtedly hindered the raising of such a large fund, and the delays were to put the MatCap team under acute pressure, as Hellmut Kirchner explains:

> We had had quite an easy and fast closing with the Gulf people, but it took longer with the others, and the people from the Gulf became impatient. They wanted to see their money put to work.[47]

Once the fund had finally been raised, it was organised into five separate legal entities, each designed to protect the interests of the specific sources of funds. Norbert Stelzer, who was hired to assist with the controlling of the funds recalls:

> At that time we didn't know how to structure private equity because there weren't any models. Pöllath came up with the structure by which you have an advisor in Germany, and the fund itself is based off-shore. We adopted this for the Matuschka funds. The problem was that we had so many funds: it was an administrative nightmare. They were drawn from the US, the Middle East, Germany, all over the place, and each had different jurisdictions and legislation. We held the first board meeting in Bermuda, because the funds were based there.

I prepared the meeting which was held at the Royal Bermuda Yacht Club. We set up structures, decided how to make investment proposals, how to screen deals, how to make decisions, and all this basic sort of stuff. We even decided how we would calculate IRRs.[48]

The MatCap team had the youthful talent to come up with solutions for many of the internal procedural and organisational problems, but the biggest challenges were external.

The first challenge was the MatCap fund's 2% management fee. The first of the five funds to be restructured contained monies raised from the Arab World, and representatives of these investors soon started calling Munich to ask for news about how their money was being invested. Indeed, such was the pressure from the Arab investors to see their money invested, that they hired someone to sit permanently in the Matuschka Capital office to track the progress of the capital investment, as Kirchner explains:

> They sent Gary de Meester over to look at what we were doing to invest the money. The pressure immediately started building up. You cannot sit on Gulf money for twelve months and do nothing with it and at the same time charge them 2% a year to manage it.[49]

The second challenge was that there were barely enough deals on the market to feed Matuschka Capital alone, which implicitly meant that MatCap needed to achieve a 100% market share for success. But by this time, Schroder Ventures was a credible and active player, participating in every process that Matuschka was looking at, and there were others such as Barings Capital and CVC also bidding. The consequences were obvious: valuations began to inflate at an alarming rate, as Matuschka found itself having to outbid competitors on every deal.

The third challenge was that the quality of the deals available was still very patchy, and the experience evaluating these deals was even thinner. The professionals active at Matuschka lacked the experience of knowing what differences there might be in evaluating say a chain of retirement homes relative to a manufacturer of plant equipment, as Count Matuschka explains:

> No one knew, no one had the experience. We were trying to put our best together, and with the good advice of the Pöllaths and the Arthur Andersens, and all those guys, we were doing the screening

and the valuations. It was just a difficult market environment, and for many reasons during that time you also made mistakes.[50]

A four-headed Geschätsführer team was hired, the experience of which while broad, bore little direct relevance to the running of a private equity fund. This lack of experience was to be expected given the early nature of the market in Germany. The idea behind the appointment of the four managing directors of MatCap was that they would have complementary areas of expertise, and background. Vincent Hübner, the 31 year-old, who had been working for the Corporate Finance department, was chosen for his deal-making expertise. He had just been offered a position by Thomas Matzen at Schroders, and so his appointment was also made to keep him within the Matuschka Group. Industrial expertise was provided by Ulrich Duden, a tall impressive person, who exuded authority simply by entering a room. He was a descendant of the dictionary family, and had established himself as a turn-around manager. He was about 45 years old at the time he was hired. For analytical expertise, Dienst hired a 42 year-old Roland Berger partner, Rolf Petzold. Lastly, private equity experience, something which was in short supply in Germany, came in the form of Gerd Schläger, the CEO of Deutsche Beteiligungsgesellschaft, who was around 55 years old at that time.

As Norbert Stelzer recalls:

> The team was very good on paper, but the problem was that these characters were so different.[51]

The immediate challenge of putting this heterogeneous team together was that they had little in common. From the start, it became clear that there would be little cooperation or co-ordination. Each went off in his own direction, typically influenced by background and experience.

Another challenge was to get out to the market the message of what MatCap was trying to do. Norbert Stelzer explains:

> We started making marketing presentations, travelling around Germany. We visited eight cities, and invited our customers from other departments to attend, plus other people who could act as multipliers. We showed them case studies of how we would buy a company, and tried to spread the word that it was acceptable to sell a company to a financial investor. There was a prevalent view that it was kind of

cheating to do so. We presented to around two hundred to three hundred people at each meeting. We did the first session at the Bayerische Hof in Munich where 200 people showed up thinking they were going to see Henry Kravis, but actually it was his son who appeared.[52]

Within the M&A community, the message that Matuschka was now in the market to buy companies got around quickly, as Hans Moock, who was fronting L.E.K.'s entry into Germany at the time, recalls:

> As it was clear that Matuschka was buying companies, we set up a meeting between Matuschka, myself, and Iain Evans, the Chairman of L.E.K. We had lunch in early 1988, just before we opened our own office, and the Count hit it off with Iain. We left the meeting with a clear view that Matuschka would be a very significant force.[53]

The biggest challenge was the lack of deal flow. Sellers still didn't know or understand private equity. The companies Matuschka and his colleagues approached felt no need to divest. Hübner later commented:

> They were pompous, they were completely conceited and they looked at us as being inconsequential, of no substance, as sort of borderline type people who would just buy companies because we had some capital and then smash them, kill them, do bad things to them. So even if they sold companies, they would sell them privately and usually not in a competitive manner, and certainly not to us.[54]

Given the obstacles, the early investments tended to be very small. Gerd Schläger led the way in this area, having chosen to focus a large proportion of his time on mezzanine and minority participations. Norbert Stelzer explains:

> Dr Schläger was on the whole concentrating on smaller investments. He had the idea of building up a holding company, which would exploit tax advantages, and hold mezzanine and minority positions in a lot of small companies. This vehicle he would then float on the stock exchange. But in the event, the business in minorities and mezzanine performed poorly.[55]

From the outset, it was clear to the MatCap team members that they were running into numerous difficulties. Opinions on the sources of these problems differed. Some were convinced that the group had been too ambitious, raising so much money at a time when the idea of private equity was difficult to bring over to potential partners in the Mittelstand.

Schläger was the first to respond to the pressure from Matuschka and Dienst to close bigger deals. Bahner, a nursing home in Berlin, was among the first of the companies he acquired.

Hübner also began buying companies, beginning with a laundry, which had allegedly just been built, and wouldn't require any capex for the next 20 years. Hübner accepted the story that given the business didn't need capex, it would produce lots of cashflow, but as soon as the purchase agreement had been signed, the capex requirements popped up immediately. Contrary to expectations, the future cashflows were drained away on buying additional equipment.

The second company Hübner acquired was Brause, which produced stationery and folders, a similar business to Pelikan. The owner approached Matuschka with an offer to sell, and Hübner's initial reaction was to consider the company too small, and too poorly positioned to acquire. But six months later, when the deal-flow remained scarce, the owner was contacted again, and the company bought simply to put some of the Matuschka capital to work.

Next on Hübner's list was Startomat, a company based near Frankfurt which produced machines for manufacturing the winding wires of electric motors. Once Startomat was acquired it then became clear that there were only two competitors in the world for this product, one based in Turin called Pavesi, and the other in Japan serving primarily Asian markets. So Hübner came up with the idea of establishing a near monopoly by buying Pavesi. It was of equal size, but manufactured in a lower cost fashion. The company was already heavily indebted, and the valuation at the time of the transaction was very high. Hübner was uneasy, contemplating the post-acquisition integration of the two companies. It looked difficult to combine an Italian with a German company, due to the differences in language and culture.

The decision to buy Pavesi was pre-empted when Hübner sat next to Rolf Dienst on a flight to New York:

So Dienst says to me, "how is this Pavesi deal going?" I said that I was having second thoughts about it. I told him I didn't think we

Table 6.2 Private Equity Transactions in 1987

1987

Company	Buyer	Seller	Exit year	Sold to
Brequet	Investcorp	Previous investors	1999	Swatch Group
Ex-Cell-O	Schroder Ventures	Textron Inc	1989	IPO
Gerhard Schuh	Schroder Ventures	Family	1987	Hein Gericke
Heidelberger Inkasso	CVC	Family	1994	Family holding
Hein Gericke (Eurobike)	Schroder Ventures	Owner	1996	IPO
Helene Strasser	IMM/DBG	Family	1993	Peter Frey/MBO
Laetus	Robannic (Brian Fenwick-Smith)	Family	2001	Robbins & Myers Inc.
Louda	Robannic (Brian Fenwick-Smith)	Family		
Lutz & Farrenkopf	IMM	Insolvency	1992	Alco
Ofner	Luetz & Pfarenkopf/IMM	IMM	1992	Alco
Ofner	Raimund Koenig	Family	1987	Luetz & Pfarenkopf
Polo GmbH	Schroder Ventures	Family	1987	Hein Gericke
Puren	CVC	Family	1991	Family holding
Weiss Tex	Matuschka Capital	Owner	1997	MBI

Source: Authors' compilation

could really handle it. Dienst slapped me on my knee and said: "When are you going to become an entrepreneur, Vincent?" So when I reached New York, I called Munich and advised our people to move ahead.[56]

The acquisition of Pavesi was to be executed fairly smoothly. Ulrich Duden was made Chairman of the Board. The Instituto Bancario San Paolo provided the senior debt, there being no lack of banks willing to finance the company, with no time limits or covenants. Pavesi was acquired for around DM 25 million, with DM 20 million of debt. AT Kearney was hired to help with the process of merging the two companies. Hübner recalled that:

> Duden had no responsibility for the Pavesi deal itself. He was trying to arrange things from a board seat function, sitting in Italy. When Pavesi went bust, the bank pursued Duden, attempting to hold him responsible, which was ridiculous because he had nothing to do with making the investment.[57]

More successful was Hübner's first owner buyout at Rational Grossküchen, which was later to prove the pearl of the entire portfolio.

Despite this spate of deals set in motion, the equity proportions were small relative to the size of the fund that needed to be invested. The pressure to put more money to work was relentless. It fell to Gerd Schläger to alleviate the problem by investing bigger sums of money.

CVC

Citigroup Venture Capital (CVC), which was run in London by John Botts and Otto van der Wyck, was in many ways one of the first venture capital players to become active in the German market, closing its first transaction with Elogica in 1984, followed by Mikron, which was the most successful of the deals, and Progen Biotechnik in 1985. Jon Moulton, who was also working with them at the time, commented:

> It was very early, the pioneering days of development capital deals. I worked on these at CVC from 1982 to 1984. We did I guess a

dozen deals in that period, some successes, some abject failures. It was really pioneering stuff.[58]

CVC opened its first office in Germany in 1984, and focussed initially on venture capital. Wolfgang Schaaf was recruited to run the business. Andreas Fendel remembers:

> CVC invested in venture-capital type companies between 1984 and 1986. The group was run by Wolfgang Schaaf.[59]

Jon Moulton found hiring staff for a private equity house in Germany a challenge. A key hire was Max Römer, who was to succeed Wolfgang Schaaf as head of the office. Max Römer recalled his first day at CVC, dealing with Elogica, the company which Schaaf had just purchased:

> When I joined in June 1984, the first thing I did was to file the first deal that had been done I think in February of that year for bankruptcy. So I went to the Court of Königstein. The company was completely bankrupt. It was a software company, trying to improve the software of telemachines, to make them quicker. Telemachines were only just entering the market at that time. It was a little start-up company.[60]

Max Römer was born in 1951 in Gelsenkirchen (the home of FC Schalke 04), the son of a State University Professor of agriculture. Römer studied business administration in Würzburg, during which time he did several internships inter alia in West Africa where he wrote his thesis about a public transport programme financed by the German government. He started his career in 1977 in the international participations division of the Westdeutsche Landesbank. Römer recalls:

> How did I get into participations? I was fluent in French and English, and had international experience with my African internships which was somehow exotic.[61]

After three years with the WestLB, Max Römer joined the German Development Bank, DEG, initially in their Asian division, and was later given an additional responsibility as Deputy General Secretary of the Bank. The biggest lesson he learnt on the job was that patience was one of the biggest requirements for doing business, particularly in developing countries.

Although they had not worked together, Max Römer and Wolfgang Schaaf had crossed paths and got to know each other, such that when it came time for Schaaf to build up his team for CVC in Frankfurt, it was to Max that he turned for help. Römer recalls:

> I joined CVC on 1st June 1984. At that time, Otto van der Wyck was running the whole thing from London. On our Board were Jon Moulton, Mike Smith, and Otto. Otto was very experienced and later built Baring Capital Europe. Mike Smith was a cool and calculated analyst with a judgement to the point. Jon Moulton was the toughest and for him a deal seemed to be like the composition of chemical elements which initiated inevitably some explosive chain reactions.

> My decision to join CVC was a very clear one. I had been working for seven years abroad and now wanted to join Citibank in my home country, because I knew that there, I would get the quickest and toughest feedback on whether I was really any good or not. That is something you learn very quickly with an American Bank. They are rather unpolitical, being much more cash flow driven. You came into the bank in the morning, and you knew that the coffee had to be earned first before you could pour it into your mug. That was the sort of atmosphere I liked.[62]

After a challenging first two years, with CVC focussed on small growth capital ventures under Schaaf's leadership, the decision was made in London to change both strategy and leader in Germany. Max Römer became the new office head in 1988, and was joined by Andreas Fendel, who had already learnt the ropes working with Klaus Nathusius at Genes. Fendel recalled:

> It was a fresh start in 1988. Max Römer, Wolfgang Engler, Christof Weise and I, we had all gained some experience. Max at CVC, Christof at WestLB, and myself at Genes. We had learned already that you can make significant mistakes in this industry. Therefore it was a restart.[63]

After an analysis of the strengths of Citigroup, and the demands of the German market, the new CVC team quickly came to the decision that it made sense to reposition themselves as a leveraged buyout group. They also decided to have a "German desk" in New York, to help transfer private equity experience from the US to Germany, which turned out to be a very wise decision. Wolfgang Engler was chosen to go to New York. This had a major impact upon the transfer of financial engineering skills to the German team, and upon building credible buyout models.

Shortly after the reorganisation, the first buyout opportunity, Sachtler, a camera-tripod manufacturer with approximately DM 30 million in revenues came CVC's way. As Max Römer recalls:

> Hauck[64] had invited me to deliver a speech about private equity, what a crazy opportunity it was and so on. I delivered my speech in the Colonial Room of the Union Club, here in Frankfurt. After the speech, the M&A head at Hauck approached me and said he had a case for me. It was 1986 at the time. He put me in contact with the management of Sachtler. It was a family situation. They had the idea of floating the company. We convinced the owner and management of our programme. It was very difficult at the time, because it was a small AG generating a modest turnover, with a high profit.[65]

Once Römer thrashed out the details of the deal, he discovered that it was almost impossible to finance:

> The banks complained that the price was three times turnover. None of the German banks would finance our deal. It was absolutely amazing. Even Sachtler's house bank was not in a position to put up the finance. I went to Bankers' Trust, where there was a very bright young guy there, Christoph Neizert, together with Elfie Garthe, in the same department headed by Werner Pfaffenberger, who was later the M&A Head at JP Morgan. They said they would finance the deal, but that they would need an equity kicker.[66]

Chris Neizert later also recalls:

> I was part of the corporate finance division, in the group led by Werner Pfaffenberger, responsible for corporate finance work of all sorts, including a financing function for buyouts. We did a number of debt financings and began at the time to take equity

kickers into this financing. The first transaction of this type was Sachtler.[67]

The deal which finally closed in 1987, revealed how emotional such buyouts could be for the vendor. In Sachtler's case, the owner had inherited the business after the death of his father. Once the time came to sign, he experienced considerable anguish at what he was about to do. Neizert recalls:

> I remember we all went by private plane from Frankfurt to Munich to sign the deal. When we arrived there, the owner was still very concerned about selling the company founded by his father. Max went in there and convinced him to sell it, together with the CEO.[68]

CVC was still hamstrung by US regulations (Glass Steagall Act) preventing them from taking a majority in an acquisition, and so the Dresdner participations business BdW was brought in as a co-investor. CVC fought hard with Schroders in the auction.

The CVC team continued to encounter wide-spread ignorance among management about what they were doing in Germany. Perhaps the most common problem was a mis-understanding of the term management buyout. Römer recalls:

> Most of the managers and owners in Germany were mixing it all up and saying it was "Management Payout". We had managers calling and saying "would you structure me a management payout?" It was really funny.[69]

Not all ran smoothly within CVC during the early years. The fact that the team was embedded in a massive bank clearly had its pros and cons. As Jon Moulton later commented:

> The first three years of CVC, we were so entirely disconnected from the group our accounts were held in dollars, generated in Delaware, and sent to me by federal express. I could not make head or tail of them. They had translation differences, I could not relate anything to anything, and nor could anybody else! But nobody seemed to mind! Anyway, we showed a consistent profit, which was rather odd as we were a venture capital and buyout shop. But it turned out that this was only because we hadn't been allocated any cost of capital.[70]

HANNOVER Finanz

1990 saw HANNOVER Finanz complete its second buyout with the acquisition of Technotrans, a company producing peripheral equipment for printing machines. As with Willy Vogel, Hannover were fortunate with the management involved. Schober explains:

> The management were very much in charge, and knew what they wanted. They were extremely entrepreneurial.[71]

The main competitor to HANNOVER Finanz on the deal was West KB, the participation business of the Westdeutsche Landesbank. Once the news of the competition leaked out, however, a deal between the two institutions was quickly made, as Hertz-Eicherode recalls:

> We found out about West KB competing with us, and so we decided to do it together with them.[72]

In something of a footnote to the end of this period, HANNOVER Finanz can claim to have made the first secondary buyout.

One of the weaknesses of the German private equity market had been from the outset the perceived lack of routes to exit. So it was highly significant that Brian Fenwick-Smith's first acquisition, VEMAG, bought from Reemtsma in 1984, should be sold to HANNOVER Finanz as Germany's first secondary buyout. A sign of the times in this transaction was that HANNOVER Finanz found itself in competition. This too was significant because for many years there was a prejudice among private equity players against buying companies from other financial sponsors, on the basis that all of the low-hanging fruit had already been harvested. Indeed, when VEMAG was acquired, it wasn't perceived by everyone at HANNOVER Finanz as a secondary. For Hertz-Eichenrode it was:

> In 1990, we did one of the first secondaries, acquiring VEMAG from Brian Fenwick-Smith, which was being held via a Dutch holding company for some reason.[73]

Whereas, for Andreas Schober, it wasn't so clear that this wasn't a normal succession issue:

> I didn't think of VEMAG as a secondary. I saw Brian Fenwick-Smith as a hands-on manager and the acquisition logic more one of a

succession issue. Secondaries were never popular with us, although VEMAG worked out fine.[74]

Despite a commitment to executing deals using in-house resources, Hertz-Eichenrode decided to call on external support on VEMAG, as he later explained:

> On VEMAG we brought in Pöllath to advise us, because we had a fairly high leverage on this deal. Pöllath was the pope of such deals.[75]

Lessons from the second phase

There are some common elements to the experiences of 3i, Bain, Matuschka, and CVC during the years 1986–1989, and other aspects which are clearly unique to each of the four new players.

Both 3i and CVC wrestled with the shift from venture and growth capital in start-ups to buyouts in established mid-cap businesses. Both were hamstrung by being restricted to minority investments, and both drew much of their know-how from abroad (in the case of 3i from London, and in the case of CVC from New York). The need to find partners for investments meant that both were forced to develop contacts with other investors and private equity houses. In this respect, 3i and CVC stood at a disadvantage to Schroders, which was equipped from day one to make majority investments and move more quickly than either of its Anglo-Saxon competitors.

The consultants at Bain & Company, through their intimate connections to Mitt Romney, and common dreams of setting up Bain Capital in Germany, were quick to conclude a buyout in their own right. They too, benefitted from importing the required expertise from the US. But what was unique to Bain was its commitment to a pre-existing consulting business. Those less committed to consulting, like Raimund König, ended up leaving, and reducing the pressure from within to transform the office into a branch of Bain Capital. By 1993, when Bain sold its stake in Libri, its position in the buyout market had evaporated.

Matuschka was hardly operative as a private equity house during the period, but the desire of its leader to dominate a market that it had not yet entered, triggered a race to raise a fund dwarfing all others in the market. That the fund was sourced almost entirely from abroad helped draw international attention to the German buyout experiment. The fact that so much was raised meant that the stakes in the next phase were far higher.

7
The Third Phase: Trial and Error with LBOs

With so little experience, it was inevitable that mistakes should be made in the early LBO deals: buyouts were as likely to generate complete losses as the early venture capital investments. Two approaches to portfolio building emerged during the 1989–1991 period.

The dominant approach, pioneered by Schroders and IMM,[1] was to consolidate chosen industries through a series of bolt-on acquisitions (also known as buy-and-build). With IMM, this approach was to develop into the establishment of industrial holdings, which did not necessarily rely on high levels of synergies between the companies acquired within each industry. Whereas at Schroders, once a "platform" company had been acquired, this was used as the first building block for a series of competing companies, from which a high level of integration was expected, yielding significant synergies.

The rival approach, pursued by firms such as 3i, Matuschka, and CWB, was to buy companies with no specific industrial focus: each company acquired purely on its stand-alone merits, with little or no attempt made to force companies together to extract common synergies.

Neither approach demonstrated itself to be superior: the pros and cons of each balanced each other out. Despite the successes at 3i and CWB, the fact that Schroders and IMM were both such high profile and successful players meant that in the periods that followed, the buy-and-build strategy was to prove most popular.

The factors which were to influence the success or failure of these early private equity houses were to be far more varied, but as the case of MatCap demonstrates, deficiencies in due diligence, approach to valuation, and management incentive/participation schemes, were most likely to precede extremely poor performance.

IMM

Of the Bain & Company team, several left in the second half of the 1980s to go into buyouts. First among these was Raimund König, one of the first Germans to have been hired into the office. Born in Munich in 1956, König had studied law to Doctoral level at the University of Munich and after his bar exams had done an MBA at INSEAD before joining Bain in 1984. Being one of the first fluent German speakers among the Bain Munich team, he progressed quickly to play leading roles on projects at Hertie and Gerresheimer Glass. When in 1985 Robert Osterrieth came into the Bain office to work with a local team on an evaluation of the German buyout market, König was curious about the project. But the work that Osterrieth and Krümmer were doing was kept under close wraps, as Stephan Krümmer recalls:

> Raimund was always interested in private equity. We had to make sure he didn't see our results first.[2]

By 1986, König had already made up his mind that he wanted to go into buyouts, being quite certain that he didn't want to be a leading manager at a large corporate, nor wish to stay within a consultancy. He wanted to set up his own company and get himself into a position where he could decide and implement changes. Fritz Seikowsky commented that:

> Raimund König treated Bain like a starting point. He smelt what was going on within Bain in the mid-1980s, and sensed very early on that Bain Capital would be a long way off as far as Germany was concerned. He certainly would have had a big career at Bain, and in his decision to do his own thing he was the smartest of us all.[3]

Together with his friend Wolfgang Stoiber at Hoffman LaRoche, König initially planned to open a generics pharmaceutical company. At the time, Hexal and Ratiopharm were starting their operations. Ultimately, the risks of the generics venture appeared too great, but once König heard of leveraged buyouts at a conference on the subject in London, he teamed up with Arthur Haug, a chartered accountant, to look for "defining opportunities". He soon found one. Another friend asked König whether he would like to buy Ofner, a photocopier dealer. König

Figure 7.1   Raimund König

jumped at the chance, and closed his first deal while still working at Bain. König recalls:

> The privilege of working for Bain is that you have no time to spend your money, so I had savings![4]

The whole payment for Ofner had to be made in cash, and carried to the notary public in a suitcase, because the vendor was so concerned about taking the payment by cheque.

> I went to Kaufhof, and bought a cheap-looking plastic suitcase. I withdrew the money from the Bayerische Landesbank which was opposite the notary public. Then I crossed the street with the money.[5]

In the event, the seller was alarmed to see so much money in cash. König asked him if he wanted to count it, but the seller was more worried by the idea of having to walk into the street carrying so much money, especially as the banks had just closed.

This first deal was done without any formal equity fund. Instead, König sought out some High Net Worth Individuals to help provide the money. Deutsche Bank supported the transaction with senior debt. The credit application König submitted for this debt was unlike anything Deutsche had seen before.
In the middle of 1987 König announced he was leaving Bain. He was asked by London whether he wouldn't rather stay a consultant, and failing that be part of the set up of Bain Capital in Germany. König however was motivated by a keen desire for independence, and stuck to his plans to set up his own buyout firm, which together with Arthur Haug, he initially called IMG (Industrie Management Gesellschaft), but subsequently changed to IMM (Industrie Management München) when a sporting goods company claimed they already had registered the IMG acronym. In the autumn of 1987, Lutz & Farrenkopf, a German copy machine dealer went into insolvency, and König was contacted about whether he would like to buy this company too. After finding some more private investors, König and Haug bought the company, and then sold Ofner to it, making a handsome profit on the deal.
In January 1988 René Mueller, a colleague at Bain, joined them and they established a provisional office at some carved out space within Lutz & Farrenkopf. Their first employee was Angela Lauer, who remained König's assistant for over 20 years. In April 1988 they moved to suitable premises. Peter Frey of Loden Frey then approached König for help with the acquisition of Helene Strasser, a country clothing business. König agreed, but quickly realised that it was difficult to do a string of acquisitions on a deal-by-deal basis. In the spring of 1988, he bought Helene Strasser by means of leverage provided by Deutsche Bank. Deutsche Bank saw that König needed more equity, and so put him in touch with Karl-Heinz Fanselow, head of DBG. Fanselow was very interested and decided to finance the deal.
IMM lacked a fee income arrangement with its portfolio companies, and was running on a shoestring in the early days, financed by König's savings. König saw that there was a viable strategy in consolidating industries, and building platforms on the basis of bolt-on acquisitions. IMM had two platforms by the end of 1988, one in copying machines, and the other in country-fashion textiles. Peter Frey took over the operating management of the country fashion companies, and Dietmar Scheiter, another ex-Bain colleague, who replaced René Mueller, took operational responsibility for the copier companies. It was a paradise time, because the purchasers could fully deduct a part of the purchase price (the so-called goodwill, i.e. the profit that the seller of a business had made in

Figure 7.2   Dietmar Scheiter

the transaction) from tax, whereas the sellers paid half or even no tax on their realised profit. With 25% equity, it was possible to repay the debt within six years. By mid-1988, Markus Trauttmansdorff, another ex-Bainee, and Petra Wibbe, a lawyer, had joined the team.

Once the decision had been made to raise a fund vehicle, König hit the fund-raising road, as he later explained:

> Between the middle of 1988 and April 1989, I gave 170 presentations, touring accountants, lawyers, or representatives of investors. I had one advantage that DBG had already agreed to be the lead investor.[6]

Fanselow was highly impressed with König's approach, and was keen to invest far more than the 25% maximum that König wanted from any single investor:

> Fanselow didn't really want an investment limit. But I didn't want DBG to hold more than 25% of the fund. Fanselow was very clever, and managed to get a compromise whereby DBG would take a 10% direct stake in every industry holding we established, which meant that in reality he would have a 35% stake. I was happy that this

increased my investment volume, but we didn't collect management fees on those 10%, so it was very advantageous to DBG.[7]

By the end of his fund raising, in addition to the DBG, König convinced two other major institutional investors, Bankers Trust, and BHW, along with a number of private investors to join, and raised a fund of DM 100 million. Chris Neizert, who was working at Banker's Trust at the time, later recalled:

> From the beginning, we were very impressed by the drive of Raimund König and his team, as well as their investment strategy. It took quite a bit of convincing to get Bankers Trust management to approve an anchor investment in IMM, not only because IMM was little more than a start-up, but also because Bankers Trust had not been investing in equity capital in Germany before. Investing alongside DBG which at the time was still seen as part of Deutsche Bank made us feel comfortable, and it turned out to become a very profitable investment for the bank.[8]

König wasted no time in starting to spend the money:

> We called up the first DM 25 million, and then basically lined up two to three more copier machine deals, which we had been screening, to do immediately.[9]

Hans Albrecht had overlapped at INSEAD with Raimund König while studying for his MBA. Albrecht, who had studied medicine and law, having done an LLM at Harvard, before moving on to work for BCG in Munich, recalls König's approach to him in late 1988:

> König asked me if I wanted to join him. He was a very convincing guy, but it was a very difficult decision. I felt that as a consultant, you were young and giving all this advice, but I always felt that at some point one of these older more experienced guys would say, young man, if you are so smart, how come you aren't rich?

> So I had already been toying with the idea of leaving BCG, when König called me up. But it still wasn't an easy decision. You did not have to explain to anybody why you worked at BCG. I thought about it, and then had dinner with Raimund and said that I wasn't going to do it, because I had just been promoted at BCG, my wife

and I were just having our second child, and we were building a house. He said that this was not an acceptable decision. So I said, OK, what the heck.[10]

Albrecht joined the team in 1989 after the fund had been established. IMM then went on to purchase a further 14 copier machine dealerships until 1991, the success drivers being service costs (where regional scale was what counted), and being the biggest German purchaser of Cannon and Ricoh etc (procurement leverage). A further significant driver in the development of the business was the fall of the Berlin wall in November 1989. Hans Albrecht immediately took on responsibility for developing a copier dealership business in East Germany. Albrecht saw this as being his chance to carve out a business, and later recalled:

> When the wall came down we said Gee, we have to look into this copier business in the east, because there were no copiers there. At that time, you needed a securities service licence to even own or operate a photocopier. So they had virtually no copiers, and the ones they had were lousy.[11]

Albrecht's first action was to sign up Herr Sparfeld on 15th January 1990, an ex-Robotron managing director and former weight-lifting champion, to set up a dealership in Berlin. Sparfeld was already a significant entrepreneur, running his own discos, and owning a Porsche even before the Wall came down. The company Sparfeld and Albrecht created, Kopier Berlin GmbH, was only the second Western majority-owned company to be registered in East Germany. Once it was clear that the copiers were selling like hot cakes, the decision was made to roll the concept out quickly, as Hans Albrecht explains:

> We said OK, we're going to plaster all of East Germany with these copier dealers. We went in February 1990 to the Leipzig Trade Fair and set up a small stand. It was organised last minute and we couldn't get anything big. All we had were three pictures of nice companies on the wall, and a slogan saying that we were looking for entrepreneurs. Under the pictures we had written in big letters: "this could be your company". I think we had the most crowded stand at the fair. I had ten people interviewing candidates, and I immediately created fifteen companies. We were offering some coaching and stuff for those we chose. We also hired sales trainers, and within

a short space of time we became the largest independent distributor for copy machines in the whole of East Germany.[12]

The ramp up of the East German dealership business was very rapid, with dealerships such as Kopier Leipzig, and Kopier Dresden incorporated shortly after the trade fair. Albrecht continues:

> It was profitable from the start. Within less than a year I paid my equity back. There were of course many challenges. For one thing, you could not wire money to Munich. Instead, I had to collect cash in plastic carrier bags, and bring it down in my car. I went to the bank and said I wanted to put DM 2 million in cash into my bank account, and the banker said, are you crazy, we aren't insured to take sums in cash like this. It was lots of fun, and went really well. We made these East Germans into partners in local companies, and the ones that didn't work, we simply closed down. But we got some really good people, and it is still my proudest achievement that we created seven hundred jobs in East Germany without a single government subsidy.[13]

While the copier business was the core of IMM, the fashion business, MHM Mode Holding München GmbH had to be set up separately because Bankers Trust didn't want to invest in it. Markus Trauttmansdorff took charge and with the support of Thomas Robl and later Cornelia Sailer acquired ARA in 1990 and Basler in 1992, both being very large acquisitions for that period.

During 1989, many others joined the IMM team, including Thomas Robl and Thomas Bühler from Bain. Bühler had joined Bain's London office in 1987 and worked there for two years before moving to Munich to join IMM. Bühler's choice was pragmatic, as he later explained:

> I realised that being a consultant could not possibly be a long term thing for me. I learnt an awful lot at Bain. It was great fun indeed, and my impression of both Bain and the consulting industry in general was positive. But I knew I wanted to do a doctorate, and to do that in parallel to consulting would have been impossible. Raymond König gave me the flexibility to work part time at his private equity boutique, which was perfect because IMM could not really afford to hire me full-time anyway. So for

Figure 7.3   Dr. Markus Trauttmansdorff

about one year, I did both the doctorate and the work at IMM in parallel.[14]

Very few hires had any knowledge or experience of private equity. The only exceptions were Hans Gottwald and Christian Hollenberg, who were hired in 1990 from Robannic. Gottwald recalls:

Chris Hollenberg and I had just done a transaction for Robannic and we felt that we had understood the business, indeed had learnt enough of the lessons necessary to start out on our own. That was in 1989. Then Hans Albrecht, who knew me from BCG days, approached me about joining IMM. So at the end of 1989, beginning of 1990, Hollenberg and I created a sub-group within IMM, focussed on construction services. It was our creation. We did the first acquisition for this vehicle in 1990, and each year thereafter we acquired another one or two companies for the division.[15]

IMM's approach to managing the portfolio companies was hands-on, being actively involved in each company's key strategic and operational issues, as König explains:

> We had a very operational approach. We were never only financially driven. Instead, our people were managing companies. I was doing the yearly negotiation with Canon to buy copiers. When there was a chance an insurance company would buy two hundred copiers, I would go along to visit them. I would never miss the chance to see a customer, and the whole IMM organisation was like that.[16]

By 1993 the IMM team had grown to 28 professionals. They had successfully completed 35 acquisitions in seven buy-and-build areas and had started more than 15 copy machinery dealerships in former East Germany.

Barings Capital

Meanwhile Otto van der Wyck, formerly of CVC, had set up Barings Capital, and after establishing his UK fund, quickly turned to raising one for Germany. Barings had a long relationship with Berenberg in Hamburg, and so van der Wyck contacted Andreas Odefey to ask for his help in setting up the new fund. Odefey recollects:

> I got to know Otto at Barings. Barings had a very close relationship with Berenberg: the two banks had cooperated for over two hundred years. I met the Barings people while they were fundraising at a time when they had not yet opened their office in Germany. Otto sat in his office in the City at Barings wondering where to get DM 100 million from, and thought why don't we ask our friends at Berenberg to help. Otto flew over to ask us for our support.

> We asked him what he expected us to do? But I think it probably took Otto about an hour-and-a-half to talk us round, and I ended up saying that we would use the Berenberg network, and travel up and down Germany looking for investors, which is what we did. We got two insurance companies and one of the best families as an investor, and raised about DM 10 million in total. This established a very nice relationship.[17]

Figure 7.4   Otto van der Wyck

Armed with his new fund, Otto van der Wyck hired Manfred Ferber from Matuschka M&A to set up an office in Munich, and Jens Thomas Lück, who had previously worked for BMW's corporate finance department, was hired six months later. The partners at Barings Capital were impatient to do a deal in Germany, and as time passed, gave increasing attention to their German team. Ferber recalls:

> After 12 months, the French and the English were getting impatient, and I didn't like that sort of pressure. So I decided to set up my own business. Since the Barings people felt they had to do a deal in Germany, they promptly did one 4–5 months later.[18]

The first big deal, Lignotock, was an automotive component supplier, with major accounts at a major American-owned car manufacturer. The owner, and managing director, wanted to sell, and an auction had been initiated. Manfred Ferber saw the start of this process before he left Barings, but was singularly unimpressed with the target:

> The Lignotock financial manager sent me his plans and forecasts for me to take a look at. I saw that the interest payments didn't at all match the debt structure, and two or three other things were

extremely odd. When I told him this, he said no problem, "I'll fix it". Then a couple of days later the statements came back, but there were still many more issues. That was the way things were developing from the start.[19]

Barings closed the deal with a senior debt package from SocGen, and a mezzanine loan from 3i. The deal was valued highly, on the basis of a good growth trajectory, underpinned by a number of likely contracts to be awarded by the American-owned car manufacturer.

Given Ferber's departure, much of the work for this new deal was done from the Barings office in Paris. Paul de Ridder explains:

> Jens Lück was in charge of the Munich office, and actually found himself on the front page of the FT in 1989 for handling Germany's biggest buyout of the year with the Lignotock deal. But it wasn't really all his work. The deal was handled mostly out of Paris, but it was unfortunate for Lück that he got this attention when things went wrong.[20]

No sooner had the agreement been signed, and the cash transferred to the seller's account, than the Barings team discovered that the American car manufacturer's contract had already been lost, and that Lignotock faced an unbridgeable drop in revenues. 3i had syndicated half of its mezzanine package to a large number of others including Kleinwort Benson and First Britannia (later Mezzanine Management), which multiplied the ripple effects the collapse of the deal was to have upon the financial community. One of the syndicatees recalls:

> I phoned up 3i about Lignotock and said that as the deal had been completed two months ago, I thought we were due the first set of management accounts. Their response was "Ah yes! Bit of an issue there". It had already become obvious that there was a huge problem. I sensed that it was going to be something interesting, and we started to rally the other members of the syndicate, banging tables and saying "what's going on here?"[21]

Within 3i, the Lignotock investment was to leave lasting memories, as the organisation in London struggled to come to terms with what had been done, as David Martin recalls:

> I do remember doors being banged angrily. The place was in uproar, and all because of this German adventure which had

gone completely wrong. They brought in a new guy who was able to speak German, and moved in alongside the existing team. It emerged that the warranty claims wouldn't work. It was chaos.[22]

As the truth of Lignotock's situation dawned, attention quickly turned to Arthur Andersen's due diligence. This simply stated that owner manager had assured them that new orders from the American-owned car manufacturer were likely, but there had been no external validation to test this. Arthur Andersen stressed that they had merely documented what the owner manager had told them. Nevertheless, a legal action was started against them on the basis that their due diligence had been negligent, a case which dragged on for many years. Each of the financing parties scrambled to rescue what they could of their money. One of the participants who helped co-ordinate the mezzanine syndicate's onslaught on 3i remembers:

> We wheeled in the Head of our banking division to shout at Ewen Macpherson who was at that point the CEO of 3i. It was a big set piece meeting with huge numbers of people around the table along with all the other syndicate members. It was Autumn 1989. By that stage it was evident that Lignotock was not what it had been cracked up to be, and so the syndicate members, apart from 3i, were having frequent meetings to decide what they were going to do. It had, after all, gone wrong within weeks, not even months, after syndication.

> We just had to recover as much money as we could because it looked very much like the thing was going down the tubes. It transpired that the biggest problem centered on the company's relationship with the American-owned car manufacturer, which represented 30% of the turnover, where the client was simply running off the business.[23]

The collapse of Lignotock was to have serious ramifications for the financial community, and the standing of Germany as a location for leveraged buyouts. Barings' outright loss could be absorbed as part of the risks of doing business, but the substantial write-off of SocGen's senior debt package, not to mention the mezzanine loans syndicated by 3i, were a different matter, and caused shock-waves in

Paris and London. Christoph Hemmerle recalls the challenges within SocGen:

> This was a big deal, with about DM 150 million of acquisition financing, and all the consequences that went with a big failure. All the financial models failed, nearly half of cash-flow was missing.
>
> There were a lot of lessons learnt from the experience. The first is never to rely on the words of only one guy, particularly if he is the founder or owner of the company. The second is to get suspicious if he always uses the same auditor, and it isn't one of the big firms. The third is that in Germany there isn't the same wall between owners and managers that you would expect in an Anglo-Saxon setting. Instead, you have a mix of private fortunes and management issues. You will find people who head the company using money from the firm for private matters. This is something you would go to jail for in France or England, but for a long time in Germany, this wasn't something shocking. Finally, in Germany people had a very different understanding of cash flow. So looking back, the experience had a very big impact on SocGen. Simply from one day to the next there was no more equity, no more mezzanine, and no more senior debt. We had to introduce a very critical approach to risk management, and corporate finance was reduced to bonds and M&A.[24]

3i

1989–1991 was a period of struggle and constant challenges for the 3i team in Frankfurt, balancing the requirements of the London-based investment committee against the requirements and opportunities within the German market place. This translated into a contest between doing small growth capital investments, and larger buyout deals. Following on from the three growth capital deals of 1988, 1989 began with a similar development, as Andrew Richards recalls:

> We ended up in 1989 doing a doing a much better growth capital deal at Ultrafilter, a company in Dusseldorf. This was followed by another deal which Friedrich and I worked on with AS Creation, a wallpaper company with which we negotiated for a year, before finally buying it in January 1990.[25]

Fortunately for the 3i team, a change in the local tax regulations provided them with an unexpected boost in early 1990, as Richards explains:

> We did four buyouts in the first three months of 1990, built off the back of a bunch of tax changes that were being introduced in Germany. Basically, they were going to tax owners when they sold their companies, and so some owners decided that they had better sell out quickly, before the deadline, so that they would have almost no tax to pay. So our market took off for a few months. Indeed, this was to result in the start of an almost exclusive focus on buyouts in Germany, with enterprise values of around 4–5 million Deutschmarks going up to 30 million Deutschmarks. We had about eight deals on our books by the end of 1990.[26]

For von der Groeben, however, the process was becoming too tortuous, and he decided to leave 3i in 1990 to set up his own buyout fund. His departure signalled a leadership change at 3i, which resulted in a bipolar structure arising around Andrew Richards and Thomas Schlytter-Henrichsen. Schlytter-Henrichsen later recalled:

> We got a call from the UK informing us that Friedrich had departed, and David Marlow came across and said to me "Thomas, I am going to make you MD of Germany and because you are too young, 33, we are going to make Andrew joint MD." Andrew and I suddenly found ourselves running the show. We basically just carried on what the three of us, I mean us two and Friedrich, had believed in all along, i.e. that buyouts were where we wanted to be. We were not that keen on development capital, because these were difficult investments to exit.[27]

At the same time, a new generation of professionals was brought in. Brian Veitch, who had joined 3i Cardiff in 1988, transferred to Frankfurt literally in the same month that the changing of the guard took place. He later recalled:

> I started in April 1991, just after Friedrich left. The office was headed up by Andrew Richards and Thomas Schlytter-Henrichsen. There was a new bunch that joined around the same time as me, including Ulrich Eilers and Andreas Kochhäuser. Walter Moldan had been there a little longer. There must have been about ten of us altogether.[28]

The limitation of only being permitted to invest with minority stakes reduced 3i's ability to make an impact on the developing buyout scene.

The only solution continued to be to team up with other investors, as Brian Veitch explains:

> There was one company we acquired which was the closest thing we did to a buyout, which was a corporate spin-off, which was quite innovative at the time. But it ended up with considerable controversy over whether the numbers we were given had been manipulated.[29]

A series of problematic deals tainted the view many UK private equity firms and investors had of Germany. Veitch explains:

> When I joined the Frankfurt team all the talk was about Lignotock in which 3i and other UK based firms had invested. It was a Barings led deal and the fact that no German investors or banks wanted to be involved should have been a warning signal. It was one of those situations of people flying in on jets from outside, doing stuff without getting any local people involved. Lignotock was a really big deal within 3i. It left the perception that German managers weren't as good as managers in the UK. Our own buyout only confirmed this view.[30]

As a consequence, the German 3i team were encouraged to keep their deals small, almost as if this was the only reliable way of containing the problem. Veitch recalls:

> The deals that were done were really quite small. I did the MBO of QVF, a company making specialist glassware for the chemical and pharmaceutical industries, from Corning Glass. That was great fun and exciting, going to New York, to meet in Corning's "Masters of the Universe" conference room at their office in Manhattan. For a lot of us, it was a bit like the "wild-west", doing small investments, and getting lots of experience. Our competition was perceived to be DBG, BdW, and HANNOVER Finanz, because a lot of the stuff we were doing was growth capital. Indeed this perception of 3i's position was so strong; it was a real challenge when I decided to leave. There was a perception, people couldn't possibly come from 3i and go into mid-cap buyouts. One would never be able to make the transition.[31]

The small-investments which 3i made from 1991 turned out, however to be very successful, as Peter Cullom recalls:

The small buyouts, we did from 1991, for which 3i had a good track record, were our bread and butter business for must of us during this period and the dominant business of 3i in Germany until the 1999–2000 boom.[32]

Pallas/Palladion

Hans-Dieter von Meibom had his first experience of a buyout while working for WestLB in the 1970s (he was a contemporary of Max Römer). The company was a producer of frozen meals for small offices, and its founder had sold the company in a very bad deal to a US company). The former owner approached Meibom saying: "I did everything wrong when I sold my company, now I want to get it back and I want to do everything right".[33] Von Meibom helped him to buy his company back, supported by a generous helping of mezzanine finance by WestLB. Later at Metzlers, Meibom teamed up with Roger Brooke of Candover, and Klaus Nathusius of Genes, to do the buyout of Heidemann.

Von Meibom met considerable opposition on the Heidemann deal. The owning family had lost more or less all of the equity, because of the poor performance of its bicycle division, despite the fact that the rest of the business was a successful automobile supplier. The banks took over and wanted to sell the company to Piaggio. Piaggio ultimately agreed with the banks to buy it as the latter were even willing to forgive part of their loans with the company.

The deal von Meibom put together did not require the banks to forgive any of their loans, and proposed leaving the family with a small percentage of the equity, both due to tax benefits and also so that they could help develop the business. At the time, Heidemann was receiving all sorts of support from the state of Lower Saxony. Von Meibom made a presentation to a Finance Ministry official, but the Candover/Metzler offer was considered to be much too speculative. Curiously, the Finance Ministry viewed the Piaggio offer to be the entrepreneurial solution. By entrepreneurial, they meant "industrial". Such was the opposition to the type of buyout deal being offered that Deutsche Bank and Norddeutsche Landesbank fought hard to prevent it happening, and ultimately it was only due to the local Sparkasse that the Candover/Metzler transaction was made possible.

Before the deal closed in early 1988, Meibom had left Metzler late 1987 to set up the German business of Pallas. Pallas was a French fund started by Pierre Moussa. Meibom had come into contact with Moussa because both men had a close relationship with Barings. Meibom had worked with Barings, and Moussa had bought 50% of Rock, Barings' European Venture Capital business. The German business combined an M&A advisory boutique with a private equity activity. The process of raising the fund was a challenge, as von Meibom later recalled:

> I think it was a pretty hard way we took, starting our own fund without institutional backing. Doing that only on the base of some track record was very difficult. Nevertheless, the DM 150 million we raised was nice for those days.[34]

Meibom's first recruit in early 1989 was Wolgang Bensel, who had just returned to Germany after doing an MBA at Chicago and working at Strategic Planning Associates in Washington. Pallas went on to do its first major deal in 1991, the acquisition of VCH Verlagsgesellschaft, a scientific and technical publisher, which they were lucky enough to pick up on an exclusive basis without an auction. Bensel recalls:

> By today's standards we were not as professional when we bought VCH. We did some due diligence, both financial and tax, that was sort of OK. You know, at that time we were all learning how to do deals. But it was a beautiful business. It had the best known periodicals in the world.[35]

The second deal, IMO Industriemontagen Merseburg, an East German company, closed in February 1991, went less well, however (and the company was eventually sold directly to the management in 1999). IMO was Pallas's only deal in East Germany, and was a challenging one, as Hans-Dieter von Meibom recalls:

> It was the monopolist for piping in the chemical industry, with more than 2000 employees. When we acquired the company we had hoped that they would remain monopolists, but the big conglomerates in the East German chemical industry sold off their repair units to western competitors of IMO. So that was the end of IMO in East Germany. They started competing with their Western counterparts in West Germany, but it wasn't easy to persuade people to use IMO, as they didn't have a reputation. The fear was that if something went wrong later with the piping, they would have no-one to fall back on. So they preferred to have Babcock or somebody like this. Fortunately, we had some tough East German managers who managed to keep the company afloat.[36]

Further deals included Boeder and Comtech, both of which were later to fall into insolvency, Mauser, and Edscha, the latter of which was done with NatWest.

The challenge for Pallas, as for all private equity houses in the early 1990s, was the lack of deals. Bensel explains:

> We did not lose deals due to lack of trust during those days. It was simply a problem of finding new deals. There were very few deals to be found.[37]

Equimark

Equimark was set up in 1989 as a 50:50 joint venture between Metzler Bank of Frankfurt and Flemings of London. It was led by four well connected partners. Bertram Plettenberg, who had formerly been working at First Boston, was the prime mover in setting up the group. He was joined by Rolf Gardey, an aerospace engineer by training, who had made his fortune in US venture capital and who now owned a stake in Amoena, a business that made breast replacement underwear and clothing. Heinrich Hoyos, a graduate from INSEAD in 1981 and former McKinsey consultant, who already had an established track record of investing, joined later together with Georg Reutter, a former Bain consultant. Eberhard Crain who knew the team (Hoyos and Reutter were both cousins of his wife) later commented:

> It was quite courageous that they should start doing private equity at that time. They had a consulting background, although Heinrich and Georg were both very entrepreneurial, and tried out several things in their lives.[38]

Hoyos and Reutter together had successfully started, and grown both by internal and bolt-on acquisition means a computer retail store chain which they had sold in 1988. All four of the partners were entrepreneurs, heavily involved in their own existing businesses.

Heinrich Hoyos and Georg Reutter continued to undertake investments together, outside the new Equimark fund. In parallel to setting up Equimark in 1989, the two were using part of the returns from their computer chain venture to invest in a chain of Benneton stores in Munich. The deal had been brought to them by Raimund König at IMM. Christiane Brock, who became heavily involved with this investment, recalls:

König, who was already head of IMM at the time, had been offered a chain of nine Benetton stores. He had negotiated the purchase price, but as the business did not fit into his own concept of an industry fund focussing on office equipment, he decided to find investors, financing and management instead for a finder's fee, thus strengthening his own cash flow in the early stages of IMM.[39]

At the L.E.K. Munich office opening party in early 1989, Christiane Brock, who was still working as a Bain consultant, indicated her interest to König in leaving consulting and moving into the entrepreneurial field. Her major expertise was retail. The following weekend she joined the negotiating team on the Benneton deal. As the potential general manager of the business, she considered her options, which were to buy a majority stake together with her husband Peter Brock, another Bain consultant, or to accept a minority position. Christiane Brock explains:

> Negotiations took place with a group of financial investors consisting of a former Gerresheimer Glas manager, known to König from a Bain project, a lawyer and a tax adviser from Bünde/Westfalen. These negotiations were already quite far advanced when Hoyos and Reutter indicated their interest to invest at the end of March 1989.[40]

Financing was arranged with Deutsche Bank with equity at 25%, the contracts were written by IMM's lawyer Petra Wibbe. On the 17th of April 1989 the contracts were signed with Hoyos and Reutter taking a majority stake as financial investors and Christiane Brock the remaining minority with responsibility for management of the group. Hoyos and Reutter were to remain invested in the Benneton chain until 1994, when Peter and Christiane Brock bought out their majority stake.

It was alongside these activities in 1989 that Hoyos and Reutter, joined by Gardey and von Plettenberg in Equimark began by acquiring Vits Maschinenbau. Once the transaction was completed, the Equimark partners decided to expand their team in order to be better equipped to handle the oversight and direction of their investments. Their first move was to hire Stefan Zuschke, who had just finished his studies in Reutlingen. Zuschke later recalled:

> They were all very successful guys, who spent a significant part of their time doing their own businesses. They did the deal sourcing and networking, while I supported them on ground-work and

research. I was with them in most of the meetings. I learnt a lot. We did three investments in total.[41]

The second move was to approach the newly opened L.E.K. office in Munich, which was run by another ex-Bain consultant, Hans Moock, with the request for consulting support. Hans Moock recalls:

> I knew Georg Reutter from Bain. He had been working as a consultant on Gerresheimer. He was before me at INSEAD, and left Bain in the mid-1980s to set up a chain of shops selling PCs. Georg contacted me after he had moved to Equimark, and asked me if there was someone at L.E.K. we could send over on secondment to support him.[42]

Moock sent in one of his team to assess the areas where support might be of benefit. It quickly became clear that the market for the products Vits was supplying had gone into recession.

The Equimark partners were keen to look at new targets. L.E.K. was commissioned to provide due diligence support, this time to examine a low-price jewellery company. This deal did not however reach fruition. Instead, more time was required to tackle the deteriorating market prospects for Vits. Zuschke recalls:

> Vits was suffering substantially, as were many other machine manu-facturers in the early 1990s, and getting into severe problems. We had to do a huge restructuring job, and Rolf Gardey had to take over the interim CEO position at the end of the investment period. I spent a lot of time up there, and prepared the data room for the sale. It was sold to Deutsche Babcock in 1992.[43]

Heidemann, a bicycle manufacturer, and Sound und Technik, a chain of consumer electronics stores were also acquired in 1990. Heidemann was acquired from the company of the same name manufacturing automotive components, owned by Metzler, Candover, and Genes. It had been the bicycle division that had caused the Heidemann Group problems, prior to the family requiring support from a new investor, as Hans-Dieter von Meibom recalls:

> The family had lost a lot because of the bicycle division in which they had put so much money. They were otherwise an automobile supplier. The banks had taken over. We decided to sell-off the bicycle business as a consequence.[44]

Figure 7.5   Stefan Zuschke

Zuschke co-ordinated the due diligences. He later recalled:

> I did most of the due diligence on Sound and Technik myself. I walked through the stores, made some drawings to give the team an idea of how big they were, and what sorts of products they were selling. We tried to do some price benchmarking. All of the work was done in house where we concentrated on commercial assessments. To my recollection, there was only limited due diligence done externally at that time.[45]

For decision-making at Equimark, Metzler and Flemings contributed one banker each to sit on the investment committee, joining the four partners in approving the investments.

With problems at Vits and Heidemann, the latter of which suffered severe margin pressure through imports of low cost bicycles produced in China, it was clear that the fund would have to stop making further investments, although Sound und Technik, another early example of a buy-and-build strategy, was relatively successful. The Equimark team were left to wind down their activity, and Stefan Zuschke later left to join Jens Reidel at the relaunched Baring Capital Investors.

Bessemer-Metzler

Despite his involvement in Equimark, Christof von Metzler was keen to do more, and contacted Friedrich von der Groeben in 1990 to discuss an additional private equity grouping. Metzler wanted to get involved in private equity as a general partner with an interesting share of fees and carry. Von der Groeben, who was ripe for a change having grown tired of being constrained to minorities at 3i, later summarised the position he was in when Metzler called him:

> It was a great experience at 3i and I learnt a lot, particularly from Andrew Richards. By 1990, I think things were building up and going very well. I told 3i to adjust my compensation to market terms either through a carry/profit share or a fixed compensation. They didn't react, so I left and took another initiative. It was very sad.[46]

Von der Groeben's colleagues had witnessed his tensions with London. Thomas Schlytter-Henrichsen later recalled:

> Various tax changes were being discussed impacting the ability to write-off the goodwill in a so-called step-up model, and increases in capital gains taxes for private vendors of companies were also under consideration. These discussions led to a big rise in activity before 1990, but thereafter it fell into a hole. At the time Friedrich got completely restless, and we had a lot of discussions with London. Friedrich had very good ideas, a very good vision, he knew from his experience at McKinsey where the sweet spots in the market were, and the guys in London just did not understand his style because he was much too entrepreneurial. They had a problem with that and as a result the relationship with London got progressively worse. In the end they parted company.[47]

Von der Groeben recalls his time with Bessemer-Metzler:

> I then had a brief period with Metzler bank. They had a project of raising a fund together with Bessemer, but this never really got off the ground because of the outbreak of the Gulf War in early 1991. Suddenly, nobody was thinking of putting money into anything, certainly not into a new team.[48]

Friedrich von der Groeben turned to Eberhard Crain, who had spent many years advising the family office of Thurn & Taxis on their investment portfolio before leaving under a cloud of press scandal, and asked him if he would like to help him set up the venture. Crain recollects:

> Pöllath played a big role in advising us. Friedrich and I were sitting in New York somewhere, and Pöllath advised us on how to position ourselves *vis-à-vis* the Bessemers and the Metzlers, and to get a fair GP arrangement. But the Americans rewrote our entire memorandum five times, so that we didn't recognise it any longer.
>
> The fund-raising in the US with Bessemer in the autumn of 1990 was very interesting, but it just didn't work out. We mainly visited banks and insurance companies. But it was too early, and they all wanted to see a track record in Germany. They assumed that Germany was a mature private equity market, when we were only just at the beginning. Friedrich had done no exits while at 3i, because there wasn't a route for exits. They didn't understand that the banks were only focussed on minority participations in Germany, or that no-one had a track record in buyouts.[49]

While attempting to raise their fund, Von der Groeben and Crain began work on their first deal, Computer Data Institute, a package school system. Crain recalls the condition he and von der Groeben were in:

> We didn't have the money because we had no fund yet, and then Metzler got a family group from Kansas to put the money down, so that we could buy the company. Friedrich's father had to put some money in too.[50]

At the outset, the investment in Computer Data Institute went well, as von der Groben recalls:

> Once we closed the deal, the company performed very well, repaying most of its acquisition debt within two years. It subsequently got into difficulties because of over-expansion in East Germany and the reductions in government funding of retraining the unemployed.[51]

Crain watched as the East German expansion went wrong:

> We had opened up lots of schools in East Germany, and then politicians started getting involved, and suddenly there was no clear system anymore. The politicians took money from the state and set

up schools in competition with us which had no quality whatsoever. So the whole idea collapsed. We sold the company quickly back to the management. I think Friedrich's father got out with plus/minus zero, and Mr Stevens must have got his money back too.[52]

Once it became clear that Bessemer was unable to raise a fund for Germany, Friedrich von der Groeben mentioned his concerns to Reinhard Pöllath, who put him into contact with Nick Ferguson at Schroders. Eberhard Crain left a little earlier to join LBO France.

CVC to CWB Frankfurt

The CVC team in Frankfurt under Max Römer concluded in 1990 its largest deal to date with the acquisition of UHU, the glue company. UHU was a subsidiary of Beechams, the British company which had recently been merged with SmithKline of the US to produce Smith-Kline Beecham. The newly merged entity reviewed its portfolio and decided that UHU was clearly non-core, hence a priority for divestment. Max Römer recalls:

UHU was sold in an auction managed directly by SmithKline Beecham out of London. They did it themselves; it has to be said very professionally. The M&A department invited a long list of 24 bidders. We were sort of invited, because we had positioned ourselves beforehand, having gone to Beechams a year or so beforehand saying "If this company should ever come on the market please consider us." That is the only reason we made it to the list. They quickly narrowed the shortlist down to eight, and it contained just about everyone in glue, such as 3M, Borden, Loctite, and Henkel. It was a tough situation for us. Citicorp were the only financial sponsor in the auction. So to improve our chances, we formed a consortium with the management of Faber Castell, and Bolton Group, which is still a strong evergreen investor into industrial and consumer brands.[53]

It was a major surprise to the market when CVC won the contest for UHU in 1990, and it firmly established the Frankfurt team as capable of doing larger, and more competitive deals.

But hardly had the ink dried on the transaction, than it became clear that some of the continental teams within CVC would spin off. The negotiations within Citigroup over the schemes for co-investment, and carried interest was one of the issues at stake. The German team felt that they had already put together a solution, as Max Römer later explained:

> Citibank, at the time, still had a problem buying majority stakes, a problem which only got worse from 1989 after the collapse of Drexel Burnham Lambert. Citibank still being a commercial bank at the time very strictly told us that we could only buy minorities.
>
> We saw in Germany that this would be a problem for the future. I went to the board and said: "We are preparing a concept for Europe and for Germany. We are all in on this, and it will be something workable. If it goes through, then everything will be fine and we will stay within Citigroup. But if it doesn't go through, then we will probably have to leave and form our own group."
>
> The discussions were friendly enough. We designed our concept in Germany, which proposed that we keep the name CVC, and still have CVC as an investor in our fund, either as a parallel investor or as the main sponsor. But we were keen to make sure that CVC never had more than an economic share of 40% or a voting share higher than 19.9% to comply with the US commercial banking regulations. I shared this concept with the Citigroup guys in Frankfurt, and they said: "This is it!"
>
> Then I flew to London and presented it to the Citigroup team there. They viewed it as a European concept. Finally, I presented it in New York, where they said that while it would technically solve all of our problems, Citigroup was not about to start franchising out its name.
>
> So we had a showdown on the issue when we met on the Algarve in Portugal. Every Citibanker of the time will tell you about this event. After that meeting, the managing director responsible for the investment banking business told us that the answer was no, and he insisted that we toe the line. So the French left, and then the Italians left, and finally we Germans left. There were no bad feelings however. When I announced that we were leaving, the managing director said that he would organise me a farewell party. I was really surprised at this reaction. If this were ever to happen in a German Bank, someone suggesting they were going to walk out and set up their own company, leaving behind a portfolio without a manager,

I don't think that person could expect a farewell party. Instead, this guy said Citigroup were known for creating entrepreneurs, and that they were proud of the fact. He wished us all the best. It was a very good experience.

So we handed over the portfolio. Steve Koltes, who was fluent in German, came over from London to set up a new CVC team. We still advised Citibank for another year, for which we were paid a consulting fee, and we handed over every mandate, and introduced each of the management teams through a very smooth process.

It would have been a pity to break up such a nice relationship. It has to do with style, and respect. We in Frankfurt had all learnt a lot at Citibank, and remained indebted to our former employer.[54]

Matuschka

When Gerd Schläger signed the agreement in 1988 to acquire Leifeld for DM 120 million, many of the other buyout teams active in Germany were puzzled. CVC, fresh from their experience of buying Sachtler, couldn't understand what formula they had got wrong in their valuation model. The maximum they had been prepared to pay for it was DM 65 million. How could CVC have bid so much lower than the Count and his team? Max Römer later recalled:

We saw Matuschka in many auctions. We saw that they were over-bidding dramatically. On Leifeld, we were just beginning to position ourselves, when Matuschka came in and paid almost double what we were offering.[55]

The Matuschka Group was under pressure to get the money invested as quickly as possible and this pressure was felt by everyone within MatCap and its advisors. Many practices were still at an early stage of development, as Norbert Stelzer explains:

Due diligence was done differently then. You relied a lot on contacts and on management. I remember one instance when Vincent came in, once the problems were obvious, and asked the management to explain the numbers. They had in their possession a completely different set of numbers from those we had been given by the former owner.[56]

Even among the Matuschka team there were doubts about the Leifeld investment from the start. Hellmut Kirchner, who by this point was sitting in the Boston office of TVM, was still responsible for signing off on Matuschka investments. He was far from happy with what he saw:

> I saw the Leifeld proposition and it was not convincing. The numbers in the paper weren't well done. You can mock up papers so that they are consistent, and this paper wasn't even consistent. I said to the MatCap team that I wanted additional information, but they said no, I couldn't delay closing. Still I listed eight questions, and five of them were very much to the point.[57]

Reinhard Pöllath later explained:

> It was said later that at the time the seller of Leifeld had more or less disclosed the facts, and Arthur Andersen had also drawn attention to the issues the company faced. Some in the Matuschka team wanted to do the deal, and decided not to go into these questions. But they later came back to haunt them. I remember well Vincent Hübner was very cautious in making investments, and investors started to push Matuschka.[58]

The deal was closed in 1988 for DM 104 million. The senior debt was put up to competition between Hypobank and Westfalen Bank. Ironically, the Westfalen Bank was a subsidiary of Hypobank, but no-one realised that at the time, and indeed the mother and daughter competed away the margins on the debt package, producing a heavily leveraged DM 80 million structure, that the winner, Westfalen Bank, later found impossible to syndicate.

At the time of the Leifeld closing, the Matuschka Group was riding high, managing DM 4.2 billion of high net worth money on an American family office model. The Count and his men had always been the pioneers in their business. It generated an average annual cash flow equivalent to about 1.8%, because they charged 1% management fee, and 10% profit share, working out on average at about 1.8%, or around DM 80 million per year. This was a huge amount of money for such a small boutique. The success of the business certainly made the Count feel that he and his team could walk on water, and he personally went on record many times to say in public that the big banks were unimaginative. Many at Matuschka were convinced that serious resentment had built up within certain quarters of the banking community, particularly among its middle echelons.

Table 7.1 Private Equity Transactions in 1988

1988

Company	Buyer	Seller	Exit year	Sold to
Arbo Medizintechnik	CVC	Family	2003	Kendall/Tyco Healthcare
Brandt ECCO	Schroder Ventures	Owner	1992	Financial buyer
Brause	Matuschka Capital	Family	1992	Exacompta-Clairefontaine
Ex-Cell-O	IPO	Schroder Ventures	Not yet divested	Not yet divested
Haico	Schroder Ventures	Family	1988	Brandt ECCO
Heckler AG	CVC	Family	1995	Family Holding
Heidemann	Candover/Metzler/Genes	Bankruptcy	1990	Equimark
Höhner & Ortmann	IMM (Office)	Family	1992	Alco
Hörnlein/Chocal	Matuschka Capital	Family	1993	Management
Joffrica	Private individual	Schroder Ventures	Not yet divested	Not yet divested
KVS Gruppe	IMM (Office)	Family	1992	Alco
Lutz Tuetloff	Schroder Ventures	Family	1988	Brandt ECCO
MSP/Statomat	Matuschka Capital	Family	1995	Creditor banks
Orga Kartensysteme GmbH	3i	Private investors	1993	Preussag/Bundesdruckerei
Resi Hammerer	IMM	Family	1993	Peter Frey/MBO
Sachtler	CVC/BdW	Family	1995	Vinten
Scandia	Schroder Ventures	Family	1988	Brandt ECCO
Thermoboy	Schroder Ventures	Family	1988	Hein Gericke
TTW Industrie & Messtechnik	3i	Family	1992	Insolvency
Van Tres	Schroder Ventures	Family	1988	Hein Gericke
Völkner	Kaufhof	Hannover Finanz	Not yet divested	Not yet divested
Willy Vogel AG	Hannover Finanz	Family	2004	SKF-Gruppe
WOFI Leuchten	Hannover Finanz	Family	Not yet divested	Not yet divested

Source: Authors' compilation

There were people who warned the Count that he should tread carefully, and curb his criticism, for he might need the help of a bank like Deutsche one day. But he did not accept that Deutsche was hostile, particularly at the senior level:

> Obviously we were competitors with Deutsche on a day-to-day basis. But this was only on a restricted basis. I always had the backing of the Deutsche Bank. What has been said about a feud between Matuschka and Deutsche is without real foundation. I was very close with Herrhausen, and Herrhausen respected us. When Hans Dieter Koch decided to leave Deutsche's M&A department to join ours, he went to Herrhausen and explained what he was going to do. Herrhausen told him that Matuschka was the only firm he should go to. Do you know how I met my old friend, Jack Welch at GE? It was at a dinner organised by one of the Board members of Deutsche, and he introduced me to him. It was because we were so friendly with the banks, Deutsche, S.G. Warburg, Nomura, Charterhouse, etc. that we had no intention of becoming a bank. I don't believe people who tell me the banks were fighting us![59]

Consequently, Matuschka could not be muzzled, and indeed drew confidence from the many lunches and dinners he attended where those who heard him talk voiced the opinion that he was a genius. For the bankers, however, in some quarters, even if not at the level of Herrhausen, resentment burnt, and the feeling grew that this was another case of the emperor's new clothes.

Matuschka liked to talk in public about how he "collected people", and in the late 1980s, his latest collectibles were a group of ex-Citibank executives. Matuschka empowered them to try to build up a business for high income earners equivalent to what Matuschka had established for the high net worth. It was an idea ahead of its time, but one that a small boutique could ill-afford to develop: it ended up costing the Group between DM 15 and DM 20 million a year, through the build-up of the necessary infrastructure. The ex-Citibank team were seasoned, but extremely expensive people. The retail operation they established took on 50 young people all over Germany, setting up offices in many of the largest companies, with the goal of offering money management services to their senior managers. The costs associated with this large group, with high salaries and company cars, burnt a large hole in the Matuschka cash flow, and saddled Matuschka's balance sheet with massive start-up costs.

In addition to the high income earner business, the Count was persuaded to enter the institutional asset management business. This was a business the newly recruited executives had been pursuing while at Citicorp. The challenge again was that this was a business which required an extraordinarily elaborate and expensive infrastructure: it had to be geared up to the task of managing American pension fund money. The ex-Citibank team hired senior members of the Dresdner Bank Institutional Money Management Group, who brought with them their entire New York team, and moved into plush new offices in Greenwich, Connecticut. The group was used to a certain style of living, and quickly accumulated a lot of expenses. It was not long before this group's enormous start up losses were also making their weight felt.

The Matuschka Group began haemorrhaging cash under the weight of the losses of its two new businesses. Ironically, despite the problems associated with its deals, MatCap at that time placed no such strains on Matuschka's finances. The MatCap investments were completely off balance sheet, and on the contrary the management fee earned on the DM 500 million fund was generating an income of DM 10 million per year. MatCap was more than paying its way. The Corporate Finance Department, now under the leadership of Hans Dieter Koch who had moved over from Deutsche Bank, was also successful, and contributing positively to cash flow.

Neither the Count nor Rolf Dienst realised that from an overall perspective, cash was flowing away. Matuschka was still initiating new ventures, such as the bid for the D2 mobile phone licence, which he had asked Hellmut Kirchner to lead. Kirchner recalls:

Matuschka asked me if I would like to do the D2 thing, and I said no way. We were too late. Others had already started, and we would need a lot of money. He said: "how much money do you need?" I said DM 10 million. He said that he would get me the DM 10 million from outside sources. We ended up having 30 people working day and night, but finally achieved a miracle. We chose the best name, Deutsche Mobilfunk AG, pulled together one hundred Mittelstand partners, and secured all of the roofs necessary for transmission masts from Munich to Stuttgart. We also had every important management position filled. It was an amazing achievement.[60]

From the standpoint of 1988, none of the forthcoming problems could have been predicted. Indeed, the Count and his partners were interested in getting some new cash into the company to finance global growth and the new businesses (high net income, and institutional asset management).

It was against this backdrop in 1988 that Rolf Dienst hired Thomas Pütter to "structure" the company, or in other words, to pave the way for creating a single Matuschka Group out of the myriad of companies which had been established over the years. The Count wanted to offer stakes into the restructured group to new shareholders. He viewed Pütter's role as being to facilitate that process as he later explained:

> Pütter was hired as CFO to get an overview of the company, and he did a very good job. At the time, we were a very strong company, I would argue there was nobody stronger. After having consciously decided that we needed more big guns behind us, Pütter's exercise was designed to make that possible. In doing that, neither he nor we made any false promises to new investors.[61]

Pütter recollects:

> When Rolf approached me, he had been told I was German born, English bred, City trained, and that he should hire me. I did my due diligence. Matuschka got rave reviews from clients. In those days the group was known for its private wealth management, one of his clients knew my father very well. I thought it could be fun becoming more of a principal instead of an agent. Although in fairness, the job that I took over was a very odd position. Matuschka wanted to restructure. He had a notion that restructuring meant taking on board outside shareholders. He wanted to sell 25% of the business, enough to validate the valuation of the business. The four founding partners wanted to cash out a little bit, while at the same time getting a capital increase for growth. They wanted to grow regionally. These institutions were hand picked and all had to have some kind of business logic. The technical restructuring was to take the shape of an internal buyout.

> I then discovered that the Matuschka Group was not actually a group at all. It was a bunch of individually owned businesses around the world, which other partners were being allowed to buy into as well. But there were no legal connections between them. So the challenge

was to build a legal entity out of this. They said to me: "You know, we need somebody to run this as a very complicated M&A, corporate finance, legal project. It will take you six months and when you are done you can build the international M&A business."[62]

Pütter flew around the globe with Ann McOwen, a manager at Arthur Andersen, to try to pull together a preliminary due diligence on all things Matuschka. On completion of his work, he announced to Dienst and the Count that he had good news and bad news: the good news being that they were roughly correct in their estimates of how many people they were employing; the bad news was that on all other matters they were flying blind. The Matuschka empire was a mess, with intercompany loans resembling "spaghetti junction".[63] There was no tax planning, no treasury, and what passed for financial accounts they "could smoke in a pipe". His message, in short, was that the Matuschka partners were in deep trouble.

Matuschka and Dienst were hardly thrilled with the news, and asked how long it would take to put right. Pütter estimated two years. Matuschka and Dienst said they hadn't got two years. Pütter said he would do what he could, but when the time came for him to brief the new share-holders on the Group's financial status, his opening speech infuriated the Count. Pütter later recalled the words he used on the day:

> Gentlemen, thank you very much for coming, I am pleased to show you the results of our internal due diligence. You will see consolidated numbers for the group. You will see statistics about the businesses, margins, growth rates, profitability, and so forth. I would like you to not believe a word I am telling you.
>
> I am telling you, as CFO, that you cannot rely on these numbers and I want to see you all write this down. I will not continue my present-ation until I see you physically writing down these comments: you may not rely on these numbers.[64]

After a stunned silence, the representatives of the parties interested in becoming new shareholders in the Group, duly signed the Pütter state-ment. Pütter made it clear that the new investors were buying goodwill in a series of projects to be run by the Matuschka partnership, but all other financials were "conjecture" even if done in good faith.

Pütter completed the restructuring process, producing the basis for an internal leveraged buyout in six countries in parallel, culminating in a

Figure 7.6   Thomas Pütter

Bermudan limited partnership. The new shareholders acquired a minority stake in the business. The Count recalled that:

> We co-opted into our company some major players. So I sold Rolf and others some shares, and we got on board the biggest finance house in the world, the biggest water company in France, a major UK investment bank, and one of the largest US conglomerates. At that time no-one had better names.[65]

Hübner recalled that:

> They sold the Group on the basis of a quarter billion DM valuation, something of that nature, so each of the institutional shareholders paid a fifth of that. It helped us recapitalize the Group, and in parallel Rolf Dienst and Matuschka set up a partnership for the top 30 individuals within the firm, each of them getting different stakes depending on their importance.
>
> Rolf Dienst approached me and suggested I buy 0.3% or something for what I thought was a huge amount (I believe it was something in the magnitude of DM 350,000). I had never seen

any financials for the Group, and had no idea of its value. Initially I was just expected to give them the money. But it was not my style to do something without looking at the numbers. So I was shown planning projections. They were enormous. I just felt the Group was completely overvalued and flatly refused to participate.

In the end, I was talked into it and the Group simply raised my bonus by an amount sufficient to pay for almost all of my partnership interests. This all happened very shortly before the Leifeld situation came out.[66]

Flush with the success of bringing in additional strategic partners to the group, and unaware of the problems emerging at Leifeld, Matuschka decided it was time to raise a second buyout fund, this time even larger than the first one. Norbert Stelzer remembers:

At the time, Matuschka had the idea of setting up a new mid cap fund, larger than the first fund, and he was touring the US drumming up the commitments. The people he was visiting naturally asked him how the first fund was performing, and he said that it was doing perfect. Then they saw in the press what was happening with Leifeld, and all the problems we were having. That was when the trouble started.[67]

The Count was taken by surprise by the Leifeld affair.

I had myself never seen the name Leifeld before. The operational management of MatCap was solely responsible for Leifeld, and this created a terrific problem for me, for the whole franchise. Of course, at the time, I never made a statement delegating responsibility to third parties. On the contrary, my biggest problem was that I had to carry the blame.[68]

Given its high profile growth, it was hardly surprising that the competition, who were on the look out for any signs of weakness in Matuschka's armour, jumped on the Leifeld story. The Matuschka Group had been growing so rapidly, that many outsiders harboured the feeling that the enterprise could not be stable.

The MatCap business was always likely to provide Matuschka's opponents with the easiest target at which to throw stones, despite the fact that it was not a source of the Group's financial problems. It was felt by many in the M&A community that it was run in a primitive fashion, lacked experience in due diligence, and employed a valuation methodology unfathomable to anyone. There can be little doubt, however, that without the motivation among some in the banking community's ranks to expose the emperor's new clothes, little would have come of this confusion.

It was the press that fired the first broadside, timed as many at the time believed, to collide with the applications for the D2 mobile phone licence, for which the Count had entered into competition against Mannesmann, BMW and others. To many within the Matuschka Group it could be considered no coincidence therefore, that in the weeks during which the D2 bids were judged, *Wirtschaftswoche* produced a string of stories written by a young journalist proclaiming that Count Matuschka was fiddling the books at Leifeld, and supporting Colonel Gaddafi in the supply of components for missiles.

The articles in the *Wirtschaftswoche* were written in an extremely aggressive investigative journalist style which freely mixed insinuations of corruption with allegations of incompetence. Such articles were not only guaranteed to leave many egos at Matuschka bruised, but also to provoke mayhem among banks, government officials, and investors.

The three most damaging articles were published on 18th May, 22nd June, and 29th June 1990. The first focussed upon Matuschka's "flop" at Leifeld, and upon the financial incompetence behind the acquisition and its aftermath. *Wirtschaftswoche* began its tirade against Matuschka with a reference to Leifeld's former owner:

> Over the Matuschka Group, Theodor Leifeld would rather not talk. "There I have only negative things to say," commented the 68 year-old former owner.
>
> The finance house had acquired his Westfalian machinery factory in Ahlen, and then demolished it. From credits came debts, out of profits came losses, out of a convivial provincial working environment came rudeness and aggression. "It hurts to watch such a downfall," Leifeld complains.
>
> Today the managers and workers of the previously family-owned business are fighting for their jobs, and the banks are worried about their credits. The Matuschka customers, whose money is invested in various vehicles, have little to expect from Ahlen. Bad luck for the

money providers. Embarrassment for the Count. His biggest buyout threatens to be his biggest flop.

The once independent Leifeld company became part of Matuschka's holding. The purchase price, as is common in such cases, was booked as a debt on the holding company's balance sheet. The previously debt-free company is suddenly highly indebted. "A flourishing Mittelstand company" complained an ex-manager of Leifeld, "has become a pauper in the poor house."

Servicing the interest and repayment schedules threatens to sink the company. Alone in the previous year, according to the interest and repayment plan, Leifeld was obliged to pay DM 17.5 million. The claims of the Westfalenbank for special repayments of DM 2 million come on top of this. This was too much. "On the basis of inadequate liquidity" according to an ex-managing director, "the requirements of the Matuschka loan could not be serviced in time."

For the Munich-based finance investor, the situation is deadly. The high returns promised to customers can only be achieved if superprofits are achieved. A positive result of DM 15 million per annum before tax would be necessary to service the requirements of banks and investors for the coming years. "With our DM 70 million revenues," comments Helmut Wenzel, a Leifeld manager, "this just cannot be achieved."[69]

The *Wirtschaftswoche* article went on to describe accounting entries that gave the impression the picture at Leifeld was better than in reality. *Wirtschaftswoche* also insinuated that the Matuschka managers were fully aware of this:

The little changes have made the numbers look better: revenues and profits both shot up. The holding reported around DM 13 million earnings before taxes. Ulrich Duden a "trouble-shooter" at Matuschka who has been sent to Ahlen was forced to admit that "the financial year 1989 was not as good as it appears." His colleagues confirm that the books have been dressed up to appear at least DM 6 million better.[70]

Wirtschaftswoche traced all the problems back to MatCap's excessive purchase price.

Figure 7.7   Count Albrecht Matuschka

The purchase price was clearly too high. Vincent Hübner, a managing director of Matuschka Capital admits "I would see it that way too".[71]

The alleged unattractiveness of the purchase price meant that the management of Leifeld refused to participate in the buyout (making it an LBO, rather than an MBO). *Wirtschaftswoche* commented:

> The Leifeld managers turned down Matuschka's offer for participation in the company, to make it a management buyout. All attempts to convince them of the benefits were fruitless.

> One of the widely distributed Matuschka brochures refuses to accept these facts: "The participation of management in the Leifeld Group,"

the brochure states, "has markedly increased their identification with the Group." Absolute rubbish, say the men from Ahlen. From Matuschka they want only one thing – to be left in peace.[72]

The first *Wirtschaftwoche* article was already bad news for Matuschka, as Hellmut Kirchner recalls:

> The *Wirtschaftswoche* article was very nasty and had a big impact.[73]

Unfortunately for Matuschka, *Wirtschaftswoche*'s broadside against Leifeld was not to stop at financial criticism. In his next article, published on 22nd June 1990, entitled "Visit to Baghdad: the Matuschka Group's foray into the arms trade", Matuschka was alleged to be deeply involved in equipping Iraq with equipment and components for the manufacture of missiles:

> The entry into the defence business was organised by the former Deutsche Bank manager Gerd Schläger, hired by Rolf Dienst, who until a few weeks ago was the head of one of Matuschka's subsidiaries.[74]

The long, seemingly well researched article, implicating the Matuschka Group intimately with Leifeld in an apparently incontrovertible set of dealings with Iraq's military and intelligence services, caused uproar in the Matuschka offices. The Count himself refuted all these allegations and later recalled:

> Just look at the papers. Total lies! With my background, they put my full picture next to the rockets of Mr Saddam, and said we had some company that supposedly supported the defence industry, and that company was associated with Mr Matuschka. The conclusion was that Mr Matuschka was supportive of Saddam! Everybody knows why today. These were the days when we were trying to get the D2 licence.[75]

Hübner was the first to feel the impact:

> The article was bad for the reputation of the Group. All of a sudden, people who were already suspicious got concerned. There were two journalists who called us up from *Der Spiegel* and wanted an inter-

view after the first article had appeared. They said "we want to talk about the problems at Leifeld". Interestingly, Matuschka and Dienst got a PR adviser to advise them on the matter. I was supposed to participate in the interview, together with Rolf Dienst. The directive was not to admit anything, which in my view was ridiculous because it was so blatantly apparent that we had deep problems with Leifeld. We could not establish even the slightest personal rapport with these guys. We would just block off any questions, and then later they wrote another article in *Der Spiegel*, which just killed us. They accused us of making false statements, of totally unprofessional behaviour, and so on.[76]

The *Spiegel* article, which appeared on the 9th July 1990, described the activities of Leifeld (also known as Leico) in supporting the Iraqi rocket building business:

Leico received on 5th October 1989 a visit from the emissary of the Iraqi state firm NASSR, the enterprise responsible for mechanical industries. In their briefcases they carried designs for the construction of high-performance rocket motor casings. German technicians have for many years been successfully engaged with the first Iraqi rocket project, Al Hussein (with a range of 670 kilometers) and the successor model Condor (with a range of 900 kilometers). Now Leico is in a position to really get the Iraqi rockets airborne. Already days before the visit from Baghdad, the Leico managers had distributed the designs to the R&D department. The technicians started work on an extremely rugged high performance engine pipe. The company belongs to the Munich-based Matuschka Group.[77]

The news reports, which were later shown to be unfounded (a couple of other German companies were indeed found by the government to have been supplying parts to Libya, but Leifeld was not one of them), may have served their role in swinging the D2 licence to Mannesmann. But tragically for Matuschka, it also drew more attention to a deal which was rapidly running into trouble. The hostile press articles were used mercilessly by Matuschka's enemies to attack its customer base. Thomas Pütter recalls:

Leifeld was the chink in our armour that allowed some banks to start a smear campaign. What they did was they colour-photocopied the *Wirtschaftswoche* article and gave it to their private clients, for them to hand to customers of Matuschka. This was their way to bring Matuschka down, to persuade Matuschka clients to withdraw their accounts. And that is what happened.[78]

The Leifeld EBITDA was in the DM 2–4 million range, completely inadequate to service the interest on the 80 million DM debt package. As the situation at Leifeld, and a string of other investments grew grave, Hübner was advised that he should talk to a certain person who was somehow linked to the secret services. The intimation was that this might lead to a rescue of the group. A meeting was set up, and Hübner went to a private flat in central Munich. On entering the building, he saw the shades being pulled down. Hübner met with someone who refused to give his name. Hübner quickly backed out of the meeting, saying that he wanted nothing to do with the business. He returned to his office, called up the Westfalenbank, and told them that "they could basically forget their DM 80 million". Hübner, who was by now the only member of the original four managing directors on board, later recalled that:

> We informed the bank that we could not service the debt. We would default on the interest payments. Despite the acute situation, we had the right to prevent them taking our shares, unless we filed for insolvency, and if we did that, all the contracts would be cancelled by the customers and there would be a reputation issue here for the whole company which we felt would further depreciate the value of the shares from the perspective of the banks. They had to have an interest in preventing this from happening.

> Now in truth we had lost our shirt on the deal. It was a complete zero. This company was so far away from being worth the DM 80 million the bank had lent us that we felt we had some negotiating leverage. I was negotiating with the Hypovereinsbank, who were by now aware that the Westfalenbank loan belonged to them. The bank was represented by a legal team that was pretty outspoken. They could not believe that I would refuse to give them the shares unless we got some money back or were given some sort of deal. Somehow I felt even more confirmed in my view that I wasn't going to give in to pressure. I had the interests of my investors to defend. In the end we agreed that they would get the shares but we would be given a "Besserungsschein" which entitled us to an earn-out if things improved.[79]

The Economist in its 25th August 1990 edition, gave its assessment of the situation Matuschka found itself in after Leifeld:

> The buyout turned to fiasco. First Matuschka Capital paid too much for Leifeld, other suitors such as Deutsche Bank dropped out of the bidding when the price went above DM 65 million. As a result Leifeld has been struggling under a pile of debt.

Then in July 1989 the new Matuschka appointed management at Leifeld decided to buy an American firm, Autospin, for DM 10 million. Since Leifeld has a healthy export business, taking the firm into the lucrative American market may have seemed like a good idea. But Count Matuschka now says this was "the wrong investment at the wrong time". The acquisition simply added to Leifeld's financial difficulties.

This led to the replacement of Leifeld's chief executive in March by Mr Ulrich Duden, a turnaround specialist. Mr Gerd Schläger, the manager at Matuschka Capital responsible for the Leifeld deal, left the group two months later. Then on June 26 1990, Matuschka Capital unexpectedly sold the stake it managed in Leifeld to Westfalenbank, at a loss of DM 28 million.

Count Matuschka maintains that the "operational" problems the group had with Leifeld did not mean that a sale was inevitable. He said other factors forced Matuschka Capital's hand. One was the public criticism by Mr Theodor Leifeld, the company's former boss, of Matuschka's executives. By accusing them of paying too much for the company, Mr Leifeld damaged its credit standing. Then a series of articles mentioning Leifeld appeared in May and June in *Wirtschaftswoche*, a West German business weekly. In these, the Matuschka Group was accused of massaging Leifeld's balance sheet, and of making unrealistic sales forecasts for the company. Matuschka's reply is that the first involved a conservative accounting practice, and the second was a forecast by Leifeld, not Matuschka.

However the article that really made Count Matuschka's blue blood boil was in the *Wirtschaftswoche* issue of June 22nd. Under the head "Visit to Baghdad: the Matuschka Group's foray into the arms trade," the article implied that the Matuschka Group intended to sell equipment with military applications to Iraq.

Although the Leifeld saga is not the crisis that some uncharitable souls were hoping for, it has had a sobering effect on the Matuschka Group's business – and on Count Matuschka himself. To put it simply, the company and its mentor have been too ambitious. The group has taken on more than it can handle. It offers a host of services, including corporate finance, portfolio management and financial planning, with a staff of only 420. That is probably the size of Deutsche Bank's postroom.[80]

There can be no question that the default on the Leifeld debt accelerated the downfall of the Matuschka Group as a whole. The Hypovereinsbank was a powerful enemy. Hübner found that many of the investors in the Matuschka funds were refusing to pay any more money into the fund, despite their legal obligation to do so. It was not long before the representative of the IBM pension fund, Mr. Petersen, became increasingly concerned. Matuschka himself was deeply bitter, when later it was revealed that Leifeld had no involvement with illegal exports to Libya:

> What brought the Group into difficulty? It was Leifeld. This was the result of a systematic smear campaign. After the event, it was proven that Leifeld had nothing to do with exporting rocket parts to Libya. But this didn't help me. The effect of this slander hurt me a lot. It was not an issue of us making a right or wrong investment: those things can be solved, and we did solve the Leifeld issue. If laws would permit such a thing, the press attack on Matuschka would still be grounds for a libel suit.[81]

The investors began to take a much closer interest in the performance of the MatCap portfolio, and requested meetings at which they could be given more detailed information. Norbert Stelzer recalls one of the most critical conferences once the Leifeld news had sunk in:

> I remember one investor meeting, where we had been going through all the problems and issues with the portfolio, and Matuschka didn't show up until lunch. When he finally appeared, he gave a speech about saving the rain forest and what we should do to protect the Amazon. He also gave an update on his ambitions to make a new fund. Once he had finished, he said that he would have to leave now as he had some important business meetings in the afternoon.

> Once he had gone, the atmosphere with the investors was colder than ice. They were so hostile; it was unbelievable, especially given

the contrast with how understanding and reasonable they had been during the morning.[82]

The Count found himself in a difficult position. His name was on top of his shop, and therefore people looked to him to take responsibility. In reality, however, he had never been operationally involved in running MatCap, and was in no position to be cross-examined on its activities. The Count later explained:

> I was Chairman of the Group, but someone else was operationally responsible for MatCap. MatCap created a problem for me, it was called Leifeld. There was operational responsibility of certain people to deal with this. I wasn't privy to all the information, because the operational people were responsible for that. My role as Chairman was to keep the thing together, and not to make statements about Leifeld.

> I took all the blame, with my background, my picture being put beside the rockets of Mr Saddam. But I never knew anything about it. Everyone knew my position *vis-à-vis* Israel, the Warburgs, and so on. Putting Albrecht Matuschka into Saddam's camp is like blaming a Muslim

Figure 7.8 The Crash of the Leifeld Investment

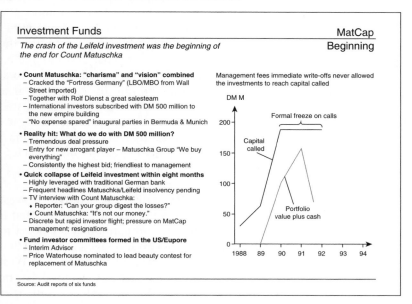

Source: Ekkehard Franzke

for eating pork. In all I have ever done, I have been dead set against anything to do with weapons.[83]

The MatCap team was suffering heavily under the stress. Even with Leifeld, they were not investing enough capital to justify their management fee. The presence of Schroders German Buyouts, another new fund in the market posing as a benchmark for outsiders to see, was a problem as Hübner recalled:

> Matzen played a role in our stress in the sense that he was focussed, he was very good. He was doing it by himself with three people, while we were embedded in this Group. We had meetings with all sorts of people, obsessed with the idea of cross-selling, of synergies. In my view it was exactly the opposite: we were just distracted with meetings, particularly in the corporate finance field. We were a team of something like nineteen in MatCap, compared to three or four at Schroders. We were distracted by all those meetings.[84]

During the course of 1990–91, the Matuschka Group ran into liquidity problems. Although few accurate numbers were available within the group, what had originally been believed to be a profit per annum of DM 20 million became a loss of DM 15 million a year. In reality, the Group was probably never making anything like the DM 20 million. The lack of any process at the beginning for consolidating the various entities was responsible for the confusion. By simply adding up the sum of the parts, the Count had the impression that the Group had DM 120 million in annual revenues, when in reality, as Pütter estimated, the true total was likely no more than DM 75 million, and the cost of the two new businesses was causing a haemorrhaging of cash. As the Group crossed into 1990, the partners were repeatedly called upon for fresh capital to keep the Group afloat. The events at Matuschka continued to draw intense press attention, even outside Germany. As the *The Economist*, somewhat gleefully reported on 25th August 1990:

> Can it be that Count Albrecht Matuschka, the scourge of West Germany's staid banking system, has got his come-uppance? That is the view of some bankers in Frankfurt and London. They point to the problems that have dogged the biggest leveraged buyout (LBO) engineered by the count's upstart financial-services outfit. And West German financiers talk with thinly veiled glee of low morale at the group's Munich headquarters. In reply, Mr Matuschka admits that

Table 7.2 Private Equity Transactions in 1989

1989

Company	Buyer	Seller	Exit year	Sold to
Bäumler	GFT Turin/CVC	Family	1995	Family Holding
Benneton Bavaria Stores	Equimark	Family	1991	Peter Brock
Bethge & Strutz	IMM (Office)	Family	1992	Alco
BMC/Stuba (Bahner)	Matuschka Capital	Family	1996	State of Berlin
Eltec GmbH	Hannover Finanz	Founders	1991	Founders
EWK – Eisenwerke Kaiserslauten	CVC	Family	1994	Management
Friedr. Flender AG	Deutsche Babcock AG	Hannover Finanz	2000	Citigroup Venture Capital
Gebr. Nehl Holzindustrie GmbH & Co. KG	CVC	Family	1991	Management
Goetz und Helimann	IMM (Office)	Family	1992	Alco
Hartmut Ibing GmbH	Schroder Ventures	Family	1993	Private individual
Hugo Ibing GmbH	Schroder Ventures	Family	1990	Merged into OSORNO
Interpane AG	Lewag AG	Hannover Finanz	Not yet divested	Not yet divested
KBHV	Matuschka Capital	Family	1994	Management
Leico Holding (Leifeld)	Matuschka Capital	Family	1990	HypoVereinsbank
Libri	Bain Capital	Family	1993	Tchibo/Hertz Family
Lignotock	Barings Capital	Family	1992	Sommer-Allibert
Müller Mäntel	Schroder Ventures	Family	1988	Brandt ECCO
Nehl	CVC	Family	1992	Family Holding
Rational Grossküchen	Matuschka Capital	Family	1994	Management
Richard Schöps AG	Schroder Ventures	Family (Böhm)	1992	Cinven/Thomas JC Matzen
Rohe GmbH	Schroder Ventures	Family	1990	Merged into OSORNO
UHU Adhesives	CVC	SmithKlein Beechams	1995	Bolton Group
Ursula Neuhäuser Textil-Design	Schroder Ventures	Private individuals	1989	Brandt ECCO
Vits-Gruppe	Equimark	Babcock	1992	Babcock-BSH AG
Wallace & Tiernan	DBAG/Harvest Management	Pennwalt Corporation	1991	North West Water Group Plc

Source: Authors' compilation

morale has indeed been poor, but says that the group's troubles are exaggerated.[85]

In a later article on 18th January 1992, *The Economist* summarised the situation it felt had been witnessed at Matuschka:

> After Matuschka's DM 104 million leveraged buyout in 1988 of a German metal-bashing company, Leifeld, resulted in a DM 28 million loss, its clients began to question its ambitious strategy. To reassure them, in 1989 Matuschka sold 25% of its Bermuda-based holding company to several investors for an estimated DM 45 million. They included Japan's Normura Securities, France's Suez investment-banking group, General Electric Capital of America, and an arm of Charterhouse, a British merchant bank.
>
> The investors thought they were buying into a top-flight German firm. Instead they discovered a group beset by in-fighting and losing staff. In what one shareholder describes as a "face-saving exercise", Nomura doubled its stake in Matuschka to 10% in January 1991 and insisted that it put its house in order. At the same time, Count Matuschka raised his stake in the group from 28% to 51% (and later to 66%) by buying out other executives.[86]

The first move of the investors was to put a stop to further MatCap investments. Norbert Stelzer explains:

> Once we had lost all the confidence of the investors, they told us to just manage the portfolio, but not to buy anything, or sell anything.[87]

Meanwhile, within the Matuschka Group it was becoming clear that restructuring measures were urgently required. The first effort was to sell off the High Net Worth Individuals business. Hübner recalls:

> We tried to sell the retail activity to American Express at that time. American Express was very interested. There were negotiations. There was even one large meeting with Matuschka where the CEO of American Express in New York was personally there, but then American Express decided against it, and all at once there were no buyers for that cash draining entity.[88]

Figure 7.9   Rolf Dienst

The five institutional investors began to get worried about what was going on in Matuschka. Paul de Ridder, who at the time was at Continental Bank, which was not only an investor in Matuschka, but also providing a bridging loan instrument to the buyout fund, later commented:

> I remember one investors meeting where they started to ask very difficult questions due to the performance of the portfolio. It was a very long period between the abrupt decision to block further investments, and getting Bain to take over the portfolio. I was representing one of the smallest investors, but was perhaps one of the only ones on the ground in Germany. Many of the Matuschka people stopped by to argue their case, because some individuals at Matuschka could see that things were going wrong. There were some different settings where various Matuschka professionals were thinking of picking up the responsibility, to try and keep some part of Matuschka going. So I spoke to many of them, and when it came to the point where a decision needed to be made on who was going to handle the fund in future, much of the initial leg work fell to me.[89]

Members of the Matuschka team began teaming up to volunteer to take over the task of managing the MatCap portfolio. Norbert Stelzer explains:

> We had the backing of some of the European investors to manage the portfolio, but the Americans wouldn't let us take on this responsibility.[90]

The investors instead sent in Price Waterhouse to analyse the portfolio, and produce a cash-flow assessment of where money was coming in and going out. They were increasingly concerned with how the portfolio companies were performing.

Divisions quickly arose within the founding partners of the Matuschka Group on what to do. Rolf Dienst and the Count fell out over strategy. Dienst wanted to retrench, restructure, and liquidate parts of the Group. The Count wanted to grow the Group out of its problems. Such were the differences that Dienst asked the Count to buy him out, which he did, taking out a loan from M.M. Warburg to do so. The Count himself recalls:

> I was being asked by investors to take the legal responsibility. I paid a lot of consultants out of my own pocket to clean this up. It was all on my shoulders to sort the mess out.[91]

Various people became involved operationally in grappling with the Matuschka Group's financial plight. Thomas Pütter was one of the key internal figures at the start, but a series of external people were also brought in, tasked with cleaning up the mess. The first of these was Manfred Meier-Preshany who arrived in June 1991. Pütter later recalled:

> When M.M. Warburg brought in Meier-Preshany, they had a big credit exposure. They were worried about it, rightly so. Meier-Preshany was a former board member of Dresdner Bank, and they asked him to solve the problem. I then had to work with him, until I resigned. I agreed that I would carry on helping with the restructuring as an advisor. I was not going to go bankrupt, and I wasn't convinced that Meier-Preshany was the man for the job. He lasted six months, and by then it was 1991.
>
> Once Meier-Preshany had gone, the institutions came back to me and said, Thomas, we know you have this liquidation plan in your drawer. Do you think you can pull it off? I said I don't know. You've left it really late. There was no substance left at all in the group. But I said

Table 7.3 Private Equity Transactions in 1990

1990

Company	Buyer	Seller	Exit year	Sold to
Aixtron	Hannover Finanz	Founders	2002	IPO
ARA	IMM (MHM Mode Holding)	Family	1994	IPO
AS Création	3i	Pickhardt und Siebert	1998	IPO
Bautra Gruppe	Schroder Ventures	Owner	1996	Financial buyer
Bühler + Oberneder	IMM (Construction Services)	Family	2003	MBO
CAM Galaxy Gruppe	Schroders Ventures	Diverse owner	1995	Financial buyer
Cargo Van	Morgan Stanley	Private investors	1992	Deutsche Handelsbank
Computer Data Institute	Bessemer-Metzler	Management	1990	Managment
Copia	IMM (Office)	Family	1992	Alco
Cotec	IMM (Office)	Family	1993	Alco
Denios AG	Hannover Finanz	Family	2005	Family
Erlbeck	IMM (Office)	Family	1992	Alco
Fahrrad Heidemann	Equimark	Heidemann	1997	Adwest Group plc
Jadog	3i/Candover/Metzler	Family	1994	Insolvency
Kleindienst	Schroders Ventures	Family	1990	Merged into OSORNO
Kopierpartner Bonn	IMM (Office)	Family	1992	Alco
Leico Holding (Leifeld)	HypoVereinsbank	Matuschka	2007	Gruppe Georg Kofler
MKT	IMM (Office)	Family	1992	Alco
NGI Norma Goerz GmbH	Global Equity Partners/UIAG	Insolvency	1994	Trade sale
Parexel	SBC Private Equity (Capvis)	Capital increase	1995	IPO
Phonak	SBC Private Equity (Capvis)	Capital increase	1994	IPO
Schneider Verlag	Hannover Finanz	Family	2005	Barclays
Signalbau Huber AG	IPO	Hannover Finanz/Berliner Elektro	1992	Robert Bosch
Sound und Technik	Equimark	Family	1994	Management
Technotrans AG	Hannover Finanz	Family	2004	Management
VEMAG	Hannover Finanz	Robannic (Brian Fenwick-Smith)	2001	Robert Reiser & Co., Inc
Wilken	IMM (Office)	Family	1992	Alco
Willgerodt	IMM (Office)	Family	1992	Alco
Wolford AG	Global Equity Partners/UIAG	Family	1995	IPO

Source: Authors' compilation

that I would give it a go, and undertook to finish the job one way or another, still as an advisor. I told them that Werner Doettinger, one of the founding partners who was still working as an MD, would have to sign everything I told him to sign. I sold off portions, closed down portions, I spun off portions, I satisfied creditors with assets. I fought off claims from people.[92]

The Economist, for the record, described the way that Count Matuschka was out-manoevered during this period:

Count Matuschka had hoped to influence this restructuring himself. With the support of the institutional shareholders, however, Mr Meier-Preschany enjoyed complete freedom. He overhauled Matuschka's finances, cut its costs and narrowed it down to two main businesses, asset management and corporate finance.[93]

The Count remained at the helm until the bitter end, investing the bulk of his own personal wealth in the process of making an orderly downsizing of his group. Reviewing the business he sold during these final days, the Count later commented:

Many of the units we spun off are now leaders in their field. We sold the private banking business to Commerzbank, and we sold the systems business to DG bank.[94]

Lessons from the Barings and Matuschka crises

There can be no doubt that the spectacular failures of Lignotock and Leifeld drew attention to private equity in Germany. These experiences also schooled a generation of German private equity professionals. If the practice of deal-making in Germany had been found wanting, those guilty of inexperience or unprofessionalism were clearly resolved not to repeat their hard-earned mistakes again. "Burnt children" is the phrase Germans use to describe those who have made a mistake, which they are unlikely to make again. Trusting sellers blindly with insufficient due diligence was definitely one mistake. Using valuation techniques that produced numbers twice those of the competition was clearly another.

8
The Schroders' Story of the 1980s

Without doubt, the success story of the 1980s was Schroder Ventures. From the small beginnings of the Jofrica deal, Schroders stunned much of the German establishment with the purchase, and then rapid IPO, of Ex-Cell-O. Thomas Matzen found himself featured in *manager magazin* under the title "The King-maker" for having made the CEO of Ex-Cell-O a rich man.

The Ex-Cell-O deal came to Schroders via an investment banker, in an auction process which within a German context was clearly ahead of its time. The American parent, Textron Inc, had decided to sell its German machine-tool manufacturing plant, and expected a process similar to one run in the US. But the competition was limited, and this undoubtedly helped Schroders to clinch a good deal. Matuschka Capital had only just been established, and Vincent Hübner felt at the time that Schroders' offer was too high. Pöllath recalls:

> Hübner said it was crazy to pay something like that for such a company. He called it absurd. But as it turned out, he erred on the conservative side.[1]

The Ex-Cell-O auction saw fierce competition and at one point Thomas Matzen was given to believe that Schroders had lost the deal, as he later explained:

> We had made an offer for Ex-Cell-O, and in the end it got turned down because they said it wasn't attractive enough. We tried to negotiate several times, but it simply didn't work. Then in June 1987 I went on holiday to Florida and after a few days I thought it might be an idea to give the guys in Boston a call. So I called the vendor and

explained that I was in the US for a few days, so why not meet for a chat. They were very open and said they would be happy to receive a visit. So the next morning I got up very early and flew to Boston.

I had a 14-hour meeting, as a result of which I was offered exclusivity for about 7–8 working days to consummate the whole transaction. My first reaction was to say that this was impossible. After talking amongst themselves, they agreed that what I was trying to pull off would be pioneering.

The upshot was I spent ages on the phone trying to organize lots of little things. The problem in those days was that it was difficult to buy a company with just one holding entity. We also had to make use of the tax situation, and look around for a company with tax losses. This meant negotiating to buy an old German tooling company that had been acquired by a Korean group company that was more or less bankrupt. Arthur Andersen helped us to find it.

Before we made our first offer, I had a discussion with the management. What was interesting is that in those days the management were not at all excited about the idea of a management buyout. They thought it was pure speculation. They said that their industry was not a good fit for our sort of financial restructuring. I had to explain to them what we were about. We spent a couple of hours over dinner, and in the end they said OK, they would support the idea. But I could see they were still sceptical.

I went back to Germany early from holiday and we set up our team room at Ex-Cell-O in Eislingen. The team had already had their first day of work on the premises. I opened the door and I immediately smelt that there was something fundamentally wrong. I saw the faces of the two managers, and I saw my guys. Dirk Brandis was taking the lead, supported by a partner from Arthur Andersen. Then the two managers asked for a break and asked if they could talk to me in private. Once we were alone, they told me that they didn't think what we were doing here was at all serious. They felt we didn't have the experience. They felt it was impossible for us to expect to analyse the structure of their business and come up with a decent financing plan within a week. So the discussion went on for about an hour. Eventually I offered them a compromise. I said I would take the lead now, and at the end of today we would have another meeting. If by then they were still not satisfied, we would stop. I gave them this guarantee. We did not stop. But we also did not make it within the seven days.[2]

As time was running out, Matzen had to press Textron for extra time, knowing that Deutsche was also preparing an IPO process:

> In the end I phoned my contact at Textron. It was quiet on the other end of the line, and then the guy said, Thomas you have tried really hard. I give you three more days.[3]

The conclusion of the process was hair-raising, as the management continuously got cold feet.

> One day before we made the transaction the management phoned me to say that it was all too stressful for them. They wanted to step out. They preferred the offer from Deutsche Bank to make an IPO. So Dr Dietrich and I flew over to Stuttgart, met the management at the Möwenpick, and explained to them that, from theory there is a certain speed at which you have to reach to fly an aircraft, and once you exceed that speed you have to take off or you'll crash. I said I felt we had exceeded the speed to take off on this deal, and we would do it with or without them. We argued all night. At five o'clock in the morning they accepted.[4]

The secret behind Matzen's high valuation of Ex-Cell-O was cash management. None of the other bidders had seen the potential, and considered the Schroders' eight times multiple valuation far too high. Matzen later explained:

> The only thing that was of interest to me was cash management, and I understood a lot about cash management because of my experience at Mars. I looked at the shipping department. There were a huge number of machines that hadn't yet been delivered. Then I looked into the P&L and it was really easy to anticipate that the forthcoming period was a real cash collecting period. That is how we did it. We were able to repay our share of the acquisition debt pretty soon with all the cash that came in from payments.[5]

Once Jofrica and Ex-Cell-O had been completed, Matzen gained an addition to his three-man team in the form of Thomas Krenz, who joined from the Bankers Trust office in Los Angeles.

Krenz was born in July 1959 in Mannheim, but moved to Braun-schweig at the age of three when his father took a senior position at Schmalbach-Lubeca. While Krenz performed well at school, his passion was for field hockey, which he played competitively in the Bundesliga. Turning 18 in 1977, Krenz's life was jolted by the early death of his father, who at the time was only 53. This caused him to settle down, moving to Hamburg University to study business the following year. Graduating in 1980, Krenz briefly began working for Arthur Andersen in Hamburg, but hardly had he started there than he gained a place on the Indiana University MBA program, fully financed from the DAAD (German Academic Exchange Programme). It was at Indiana that Krenz first heard of KKR and its acquisitions. After completing his MBA in 1982, Krenz had no desire to return to Germany, but hoped instead to get a job on Wall Street. He later recalled:

I applied to all the big investment banks in New York. The only people who came to campus in Indiana were the trading outfits from Chicago, and I wasn't interested in trading. I was set on working in M&A. I didn't really know what M&A was, but it sounded exciting. So I sent all these letter to the investment banks. They all invited me, but the phrasing of their invitations was quite funny. They ran along the lines of "if you happen to be in New York, please stop by". Basically, the message was, you aren't good enough for us to pay for your travel expenses, but if you come at your own cost, we'll give you an interview.

We had some nice conversations, but I figured out pretty quickly that none of them had any inclination to keep me in New York. They were basically attracted by my German passport, and were only inter-ested in sending me back to Germany. Some of them had already applied for licences to open branch offices in Frankfurt, as part of a strategy to develop a European presence. Obviously after London the next logical place was Frankfurt, and they thought the hype around M&A in the early 1980s would continue.

I was pretty disappointed. Nevertheless, at Morgan Stanley I met a guy who told me "you know what, you are not going to get a job here on Wall Street. Forget it. There are so many American talents coming out of Wharton, Harvard, Stanford, they are not going to give a job to a graduate from Germany with an MBA from Indiana. If you want to come to New York, you have to do it the other way round. Go back to Frankfurt, sign up with an American investment bank, and then make sure they give you something international to do". By the time I had completed my round of interviews in New York, I realised he was right. I didn't get a single offer.[6]

Krenz took the advice of the Morgan Stanley banker, and joined the corporate finance department of another American bank in Frankfurt. After only six months in Frankfurt, Krenz succeeded in getting a deal whereby he would spend three months in London, followed by a further three months in the US as part of his general training. The work in London was uninspiring, filling in to support German components on UK-based deals, but with the move to the US, his banking experience shifted into overdrive.

> When I went to Los Angeles, it was a very different story. They set me up really nicely. Nice flat, rental car. I got into the office on my first day, and they said, "you're working at our leveraged lending business, here is your first deal, this is the deal team, and this is your boss". There was no messing about. I was put on one of the major buyouts. My first project didn't materialise, it was some jewellery business in New York. But from day one, I was an integral part of the deal team, not really knowing what I was doing, but having great fun.[7]

The experience of working on the leverage for major deals in the US was formative, particularly in his role on a battery deal.

> I was crunching away on those numbers day and night. I looked at them, and it seemed like a huge hockey stick to me. How could we possibly finance this? But the team made all sorts of calculations, just to make the numbers work. Eventually I left before the deal was done, but it was a huge success for the private equity house.[8]

Krenz had first heard of buyout activity in Germany in 1986.

> I read in the paper that there was to be a Schroder Ventures fund. I was just about to set off for London, but I was still clearing out my flat in Frankfurt. I called the guys up, said it sounds interesting, and told them that I was working in the same sort of field. It was a bit of a lie. But anyway, I met Matzen at the Dorchester in London. He made a very good impression on me. Thomas has a very convincing

personality. Obviously he lives off aggressiveness but has a very nice character. He can be very charming and very entrepreneurial. It was while I was still in London that I heard about the Matuschka fund. I thought I might as well speak to them too. So I flew over to Munich and interviewed with Hübner.

Then Matzen started calling me at obscene hours in the morning. I was about ready to fly off to LA but Matzen arranged for me to meet Jon Moulton, again in London.[9]

Matzen warned Krenz in advance that the meeting with Moulton would be unusual.

I had my starter plate in front of me, and Moulton came in, after reading my CV on the staircase. We had a light lunch, and a chat. I thought, O.K. fine. If this guy has any say I might as well not waste my time, I'll go to the US and get on with my life, which I did.

But then Matzen started calling me, and sending me contracts.[10]

Moulton had in fact decided in favour of Krenz after his first meeting, despite appearances to the contrary. Shortly thereafter, Krenz received an offer from Matuschka too, and found himself in the unusual position of having to choose between the two leading private equity houses active in Germany. Krenz's assessment of them is revealing:

Matuschka were at the time still in the midst of fundraising. They ended up raising much too much money. Frankly I did not have the impression that the Matuschka crowd knew what they were doing. They didn't know how to do a deal, and they didn't come across as entrepreneurial. I didn't get the feeling that they would know how to run a company. Instead it was basically a bunch of guys trying to do what they had seen other people doing elsewhere. There is no question that the Matuschka Group was still highly regarded. Indeed, there was a mystique about it. The rich people went there and gave them their money, which was put to work. Nobody knew much about their business, apart from the fact that it was held in high respect by rich people and Matuschka had the reputation for making their money work.

Basically the decision for me was, where would I get to have the most fun and action. I did a bit of due diligence, talked to a few people, because my plan had been to stay in the US. But I felt it was interesting. At the time, I didn't appreciate the risk I was taking, starting work in a brand new industry with people who really weren't sure they knew what they were doing. But then again, I was still fairly young so the risk was probably worth taking. At some point I told Matzen: "fine, I'll join", but that I wasn't yet signing his contract. The contract in itself was fine. But I explained that I wanted to stay in Los Angeles, for perhaps another six months, to pick up the experience I needed. Matzen accepted my terms. At the back of my mind, I thought that I would probably finish the deal I was working on and then join Matzen. That was the plan. Well the plan lasted exactly two days.

I was called into the office by the head of the LA office. I found out later what had happened.[11]

Back in London, Moulton had lunch with a staffer of the American bank in question, having understood from Nick Ferguson that Krenz had signed his contract. Moulton later commented:

I had absolutely no idea Krenz was anything other than a done deal![12]

The fact that the American bank had found out that Krenz was talking to Schroders led to a rapid response, as Krenz later explained:

Of course the news passed on immediately to the bank's office in LA. So I got called into the office by my head of department. I was still very young and was pretty scared. He got straight to the point: "I hear you've signed a contract with Schroder Ventures". I correctly said no, because actually, I had not yet signed a contract. Then of course they started to grill me. I admitted that I had been approached, that an offer had been made, that I was considering it, but that I had not signed anything yet. Then they turned the whole thing around saying "we give you 24 hours to make up your mind and by the way here is an offer for you to stay in LA. We would like you to stay."

I went back to my office and did some serious thinking and the next day I went back to my boss's office and said "I appreciate the offer, thanks, but no thanks, I am going back". Then they tried to do exactly what Americans do, saying "please clear your desk, hand us the keys to your apartment and rental car". They also wanted my return ticket back to Frankfurt.

I said "I am sorry but I have a German contract and in Germany there are such things as employment protection laws. I have some rights. What you are suggesting here won't happen". I sent a fax to Germany to officially quit the job, with all the termination periods. That was OK. I spoke on the phone to Frankfurt and asked them to explain to these people how it works under a German contract. This went on for a couple of hours. At the end of it I got to keep my rental car for another three to four days, and the return ticket was fine.[13]

Krenz started at the Schroders Hamburg office on 8th August 1988, joining Matzen, Brandis, and Gräper. On his first day, he found flowers on his desk.

There was a pile of files on my table. Matzen says "you are off on the road tomorrow morning. There's this little company I want you to visit". I asked him what time we were leaving. He says "not we, you". I asked him what I was supposed to do. Matzen answers: "due diligence". I said OK, but could I have a list of things to ask. He said "no, you have a couple of hours on the train tomorrow which will give you plenty of time to put together your own list of questions. Just come back and tell me whether I should buy the company".[14]

So already on his second day at work, Krenz was sent off to Lutz Teutloff, a global fashion company. Krenz continues:

We had already signed a contract for a company called Brandt, which turned out to be a whopping success, and the idea, which later on got copied by a couple of other people, was to build up a group around a number of Mittelstand companies in the fashion industry. Some of these companies, in those days, still had manufacturing in Germany, although others had already started sourcing from abroad, probably not yet in Asia, but certainly in Eastern Europe, Portugal and Italy etc. So Teutloff was supposed to be the second acquisition for that group. I did not know much because it was my second day, and I didn't know anything about the Brandt deal either. I am not even sure whether we had signed or were about to sign, but the Brandt deal was well advanced. Off I went. I drew up my list on the train, and wrote a really nice report to Matzen telling him what I felt was the right price and why we should buy the business. I also told him what I felt we should be checking further. That was how we operated. We ended up buying the company for something between DM 6.5 million to DM 8.5 million, and it became the second piece in the Brandt jigsaw.

We only did one true capital increase for the group, maybe two maximum. All the other acquisitions, there were six or seven in total, ended up being financed through the Group's cash flows. We convinced the bankers that the cash-flow was strong enough to fund each new acquisition. It was a whopping leverage at the time. Actually I spent more than half my time in the first three years just on this exercise, looking at companies and building up the Brandt Ecco group.

It was funny, while we were doing this, Schroder Ventures in England, were trying to teach us about market standards, what free cash flow was, how to assess the risk, and how to work up the numbers from the banking side, and decide how much equity to put into the deals to make the returns work. But we did exactly the reverse. We worked out a fair price for the business, then went to the bank and said we needed a certain amount of money, which was usually more than a UK bank would have been willing to give for a similar transaction. Whatever finance was missing was the equity plug. There were no covenants. We ended up doing almost all our deals with the DG Bank and the old Hypo bank.[15]

Ex-Cell-O turned out to be one of the most spectacularly successful deals of the period and helped to raise the profile of Schroders, and convince many that Thomas Matzen and his team were the real thing. Schroders achieved its exit after just two years by means of an IPO in Frankfurt. *Manager magazin* gave extensive coverage to the event in an article written by Hayo Koch entitled "The King Maker" published on 1st September 1989. The article commented:

Thomas Matzen is a specialist: he changes employees into dynamic entrepreneurs. With a new variant of buyouts, medium-sized companies are transformed into proud corporations, while investors and managers earn millions in the process.

On 7th July 1989, in the factory halls of the machine-tool manufacturer Ex-Cell-O in Eislingen, the Champagne corks were popping. The nine hundred strong group of managers and employees at the special-machinery factory (with DM 189 million in revenues) were celebrating the IPO of the Ex-Cell-O shares. Over two hundred of the employees had very concrete reasons for being happy. Together with management, in May 1987 they had bought the company out from the American company Textron, and made themselves DM 17 million richer by means of an IPO.

The initiators of the buyout, the old-timer managers Dr. Jürgen Jenrich (aged 53) and Hans-Jörg Waldenmaier (aged 54), began their new jobs as executives of a public company as millionaires. Twenty-one other managers earned enough to buy their own home, and a further two hundred employees cashed in over DM 100,000 each, and all tax free.

Management and staff have Thomas Matzen to thank for this bonanza, which increased their investments of DM 2.4 million from management, and up to DM 20.000 per employee seven-fold within two years. The managing director of the Hamburg-based J. Henry Schroder Unternehmensberatung GmbH, a subsidiary of the London investment bank J. Henry Schroder Wagg & Co Ltd, has a war chest of DM 140 million to invest on behalf of an international group of investors, and has been systematically buying up medium-sized companies in Germany. Eighteen companies with a combined turnover of over DM 1 billion have already been acquired by this means.[16]

A clear feature of the Schroders strategy was buy-and-build. Ex-Cell-O was in this respect the exception rather than the rule. Most of the 18 companies acquired by the summer of 1989 had been bolt-on acquisitions. On the basis of an initial acquisition of the men's fashion company E. Brandt GmbH, Schroders had added four companies, including Maico, the companies of Ursula Neuhäuser, and Lutz Tuetloff, and Scandia, to build the Brandt Holding.

Similarly through the acquisition of Hein Gericke, a motorbike accessories retailer, Schroders added four more companies including: Polo GmbH; Gerhard Schuh's company; Thermoboy; and Van Tres. *Manager magazin*, in its coverage of Thomas Matzen's story, reported that he had plans to build up a carwash-machinery company on the basis of a platform investment in Rohe GmbH, a mining technology company upon the shoulders of Hugo Ibing GmbH, and a hospital cleaning company through adding to Hartmut Ibing GmbH (owned by a distant relative of the mining technology company). In this respect, Schroders was treading a very similar path to that pursued by Raimund König at IMM in Munich. Thomas Krenz recalls:

> With all the portfolio companies, the idea was to professionalize the businesses and try to grow them. Otherwise they would not be interesting for anybody else to pick up later on. We did a lot of add on acquisitions for almost all of the portfolio companies. Brandt ended up at the end having about six to seven subsidiaries. Hein Gericke, the other fairly sizeable deal we did which was renamed EuroBike, I think involved about eleven businesses.[17]

The *manager magazin* article was read by Wolfgang Biedermann, who was studying for his MBA at Harvard Business School, having worked for BCG in Dusseldorf.

> I was sitting in the Baker Library at Harvard, and on the front page of *manager magazin* was the Königsmacher article. I read the story about private equity, how it had paved the way to a successful IPO, and how the guys in management had become rich. I wrote Thomas Matzen a letter, and said that I would be in Germany over Christmas. As a result we met, and he made me an offer.

> I started out as an analyst, did some deals in textiles and I was supposed to do some follow-up work on Kleindienst. I was the youngest guy on the team.[18]

By the start of 1990, tensions arose between Matzen and the London team at a time when discussions were already underway about raising a second fund. Matzen's idea to become independent came after his experience with a construction equipment company transaction, as he explains:

> This was a deal that didn't happen for us. We had done all the due diligence. We even went to the US to do interviews with the target's dealers, and were given comments regarding its asphalt spraying system. We passed these comments on to management, and they were quite impressed.

I negotiated the price for the deal down to an absolute bargain. But then the Gulf War started, and Schroders became a bit afraid. After I had finished negotiations with the seller, I got a call from Nick Ferguson telling me that we had to reduce the price by another couple of millions, or he wouldn't give us permission to complete the transaction. I was really annoyed about this, because I had already reduced the price in my negotiations to an incredible extent, and to have reduced it even further would have been to look no longer serious. Nevertheless, I was forced to do so, and the seller didn't accept this. Even though they had a load of debt on their books, and had to dispose of the construction equipment company at almost any price, they still had their limits. So we lost the deal, and I returned very angry to Hamburg and decided that if this was the way we were going to have to work together in future, I wasn't going to put up with it for long.[19]

After much reflection, Matzen decided to set up on his own, dispense with the Schroders brand-name, and make an offer to buy the existing Schroder's German portfolio. Osterrieth recalls:

It was around the end of 1990 that Matzen and Schroders began to drift apart. The first fund was a success, and one of the fathers of that success was Matzen. Anyway, he clearly decided that he didn't need Schroders, and came up with the idea that he could just carry on by himself. Matzen called me in and asked if I wanted to join him on the next fund without Schroders.[20]

Initially, Matzen's proposal was given a constructive reception at Schroders in London. Nick Ferguson wrote in June 1990 to Matzen saying:

Following our earlier discussions, this is to confirm that in the interest of investors, Schroder German Venture Advisors Ltd agreed that it has encouraged, and is prepared to consider proposals for the purchase of investments held in the Schroder German Buyout Fund by a new company if those proposals offer the present investors in the Fund a cash price for their investment, and a right to reinvest in the new company on the same terms as currently applied to their existing investments in the Fund.[21]

Ferguson discussed the matter with John Strangfeld of the Prudential, who was broadly supportive of the proposal. On the basis of this favourable reaction, Matzen set in motion an exercise to value and bid for the portfolio. Thomas Krenz was given the job of valuing the German portfolio, as he explains:

> I ended up working for Matzen on a model to buyout the entire portfolio from the fund. The modelling I worked on got so big that none of our computers could take it any more. In the end, we had to go out and buy what in those days they called a lap-top, which was probably about half the size of my desk. It was one of those Toshibas, and weighed fifty kilos. Trying to buy twenty companies, and set up the leverage was a complete nightmare.[22]

Osterrieth gave Matzen's offer to join him serious consideration. By 1990, it was clear that alternative funding could be raised, and Matzen's team in Hamburg appeared more crucial to Schroders' German operation than two-thirds of its investment committee. But the choice would have meant too many changes to Osterrieth's own life-style. He later explained:

> I gave the suggestion plenty of thought. I knew I didn't want to live in Germany and that I really liked my lifestyle. I lived in London, and had lived in New York. I had already got into the habit of spending the summers in the Hamptons. If I was going to work with Matzen, I would have to move to Germany.

> I remember on one beautiful day in July, I was walking along the beach at the Hamptons, and I realised that if I went to work in Germany, to help with the team, I could do this for three weeks, perhaps, but not three months or a year. So I said no to Matzen.[23]

Undeterred by Osterrieth's refusal to join him, Matzen asked Thomas Krenz to finalise his valuation exercise on the entire German portfolio, so that he would be in a position to make an offer to Nick Ferguson to buy Schroders out. Armed with the figures he proposed the spin-off to his British colleagues.

Behind the scenes in London, however, the attitude towards the Matzen proposal was changing. Osterrieth recalls:

> In the beginning, Ferguson tried to appease Matzen and probably convinced Prudential that they should support his plan. Ferguson was very close to John Strangfeld who ran Prudential in London at the time, and Strangfeld usually bought into what Ferguson

suggested to him. But then other events happened, and I am not sure whether Prudential was still in favour of the plan thereafter. Also, there were many investors in Schroder German Buyouts other than Prudential.[24]

Matzen's view was that Schroders became reluctant to lose their position in Germany:

My guess is Schroders didn't want us to become successful in Germany. They wanted to build the business on their own. But in the original offer I made to them, I said that I would provide the support necessary to set up a Schroders team for a second German Buyout Fund. So there was no intention on my part to stop them doing future business in Germany.[25]

The change of heart on the London side took place over several months. Meanwhile Matzen and Krenz invested considerable time and effort to go into their offer for the portfolio, as Krenz remembers clearly:

We spent months on an internal exercise of value modelling, and then embarked on long discussions with Robert Osterrieth and Schroders to work out how this buyout could be pulled off. It all went on way too long. Only at the end of the whole exercise did we find out that Schroders had gone around the banking community saying that this couldn't possibly be structured from a debt point of view. We were talking of a financing package in excess of a DM 1 billion, which in those days was unheard of. You needed big guys to play in that league, and Schroders tried to influence the banks behind the scenes and basically call the whole thing off on the debt side.[26]

Matzen discovered the Schroders change of heart after a meeting with a bank in Frankfurt. He had been discussing the senior debt the bank would supply him for his bid. But after the meeting, two of the bankers came to visit him, as Matzen explains:

They came over to inform me that after my meeting with the bank, Schroders had rung them up to say that the Matzen buyout deal was not in their interest. So the bank had turned down the loan application.[27]

With the collapse of his buyout offer out in the open, Matzen met Ferguson at a hotel in London to discuss how the separation between Schroders and the Hamburg team should be managed. Matzen recalls the meeting:

> Nick asked me whether I would like to buy the Osorno Group, which was active in carwash equipment. I said yes. He then asked me if, in return I would approve of Dirk Brandis staying on to run the Schroders Fund for at least two more years. I said that if this was his compromise, I could live with it.[28]

The Schroders London team was wrestling with a major challenge. Matzen, who controlled the management company in Hamburg, and Schroders, who managed the fund which owned the portfolio, were clearly about to cut off all ties with one another. Technically, this was quite easy for the London team to do, because the fund had a contract with the management company in Hamburg, which Schroders was able to terminate. It was the operational challenge that kept the London team up awake at night. Krenz recalled the dilemma:

> How can you possibly separate the fund from your team? Matzen thought Schroders couldn't pull this off. They wouldn't be able to make a sensible story for the investors. Matzen was betting on Schroders not getting away with the portfolio. He calculated on being able to keep at least the management and consulting fees with the companies.

> Another factor in the equation, was that Matzen had already started buying companies on his own, so that by the time the separation happened the Hamburg team had acquired another three businesses including a small company in Austria called Respo, manufacturing women's coats, and a software company which later on turned out to be a whopping success. He was using his own money, with some leverage from banks. The whole Hamburg team were also invested, getting into debt, underwritten by Matzen himself. It was more and more clear that the future was going to be separate.[29]

In practice, it was messy. Schroders desperately began trying to gain at least one member of the Hamburg team to join them. The effort to retain Dirk Brandis was ultimately unsuccessful. Only Thomas

Krenz was willing to stay with Schroders. Wolgang Biedermann recollects the atmosphere among the Hamburg team:

> The question confronting all of us was what to do. Krenz decided to stay with Schroders. For sure they made it worth his while to stay. But for my part, I was young, and hadn't made my experience, and Matzen was clearly the successful guy. So my focus was on Matzen.[30]

For Krenz the decision certainly appeared easier. Krenz later recalled:

> It became pretty clear that there was a choice to be made between either leaving Matzen or staying with Matzen, and that with the latter you would never get anywhere close to running the business, because you would always be at best number two to Matzen. In the end the decision was, do you want to get rich quickly with Matzen, which was likely. With a whopping success on the fund you could see that already. But in doing so, you would always be number two. Or do you want to go somewhere else and try to build your own fortune. At the time I had lots of discussions with Robert Osterrieth who sat on our investment committee as well as on some of our portfolio companies' boards. It was clear I was going to be their target to keep hold of from the team to justify to the investors that the business was being monitored and so forth. The whole thing unfolded in the winter of 1991.[31]

Thomas Krenz was 31 at the time Schroders and Matzen parted ways. He moved over to London, where he joined Robert Osterrieth in looking after the portfolio companies. But the move to London was not immediate.

> Matzen kept the non-compete clause which meant I couldn't work for six months. So I went to Kitzbühel. I was working from Robert's dinner table, both in Kitzbühel and in London. We did not have an office. Robert always worked from home anyway. Robert and I were going back and forth between Kitzbühel and London.[32]

Given Krenz's non-compete clause, immediate responsibility for the German portfolio reverted back to the team in London, as Jon Moulton explains:

> When Matzen left, in the interim period the German portfolio was managed from London. Henry Simon and Eric Walters were

considerably engaged from the London office. They had already made notable contributions on the German deals both on the investment committee, and at operating levels throughout the Matzen period.[33]

Reinhard Pöllath, who was advising both Bessemer-Metzler and Schroders at the time, put Friedrich von der Groeben in contact with Nick Ferguson, shortly before the Bessemer-Metzler experiment dissolved. Von der Groeben recalls:

> I first met Nick Ferguson in July 1991, and we agreed to meet again at the end of the holiday season, in early September, which we did.
> I also met Osterrieth, who had taken over the management of the old fund, which basically meant him spending time on the portfolio. It was clear that I was completely separate from this previous activity. So I agreed to join them, and worked to help raise a successor fund. Within three months we had raised DM 200 million. So I started up the new management company, and rented an office in Frankfurt on the Bettinastrasse in February 1992.[34]

Nick Ferguson was relieved to find a solution so quickly:

> We actually found Friedrich fairly soon. We still had the existing portfolio in Germany, and it was now time to launch another fund around Friedrich fast. So we got him onto the road. Rho was by this time out of the picture, and Robert had left Rho anyway.[35]

Thomas Krenz recalled:

> I needed some time to get to know Friedrich. He was managing partner of 3i before he left, and at the time we got together he had been trying to set up a new fund which had never materialized. So he joined the Schroders team.

> Friedrich started the business and opened an office in Frankfurt in 1992. I was still in London at the time and didn't relocate to Frankfurt until the end of the year. There was a big fuss between Robert, Nick, Friedrich and myself about how I would allocate my time, because I had to spend so much of it on the old portfolio. By the end of 1992 and beginning of 1993 I was still spending all of my time on the old portfolio, at a time when we were only two-to-three

people sitting in one office. We knew each other, but we didn't know what each of us was doing.[36]

Friedrich von der Groeben took responsibility for establishing a management team that could run a new fund. He left all concerns over the old portfolio to Osterrieth and Krenz, who acted almost as an independent unit. After procuring an office, Friedrich von der Groeben recalls making his first new hires:

> The first person I recruited was Wolfgang Reuther who had previously been at McKinsey. Then came Ingeborg von Moltke, from Dresdener Bank, followed by Rick Hoskins, a graduate from Harvard Business School, who although a US citizen, had grown up in Germany as the son of a John Deere manager.[37]

Krenz recalls the recruits who followed later:

> Then came Jörn Karsten, also ex-McKinsey, who had two years experience working in a marketing function at Procter and Gamble, and once we added Thomas Jetter, the new team was pretty much in place.[38]

Lessons from the Schroders Experience

Despite the fact that Ex-Cell-O, the biggest of Schroder's success stories in the 1980s, was a stand-alone transaction, the clear impression within the team, and within many external observers, was that it was the buy-and-build strategy that had been the major driver of performance. In practice, experience demonstrated that corporate spin-offs were typically large enough to be fully self-sustaining, and capable of significant organic growth. They also contained sufficient internal improvement potential to generate substantial additional value, whereas with many family-owned companies of small size, the easiest way to gain scale to foster higher efficiency was through a consolidation strategy.

The Schroders experience also demonstrated the risks to Anglo-Saxon firms of recruiting local teams in Germany. The ties between the Hamburg and London teams were never particularly close, and there were few bonds between the two to help generate a common culture. From the Hamburg perspective, the London arm did little more than raise money, something which, with experience, the Germans felt they were perfectly capable of doing on their own. Any hesitation to approve a German deal in London could only hasten the speed with which the two spun apart. The experience also demonstrated that Anglo-Saxon-based funds, on the whole, preferred to exercise a high level of influence over their teams based in Germany. Such cross-channel tensions in Anglo-Saxon houses surfaced time and time again over the decades that followed. At the time, few players appreciated the investment in integration needed between London and German-based teams. As a consequence, for many years to come, the alignment of Anglo-German interests within private equity teams proved fragile, and in many instances, elusive.

9
The 1984–1991 Experience in Retrospect

It is an amusing coincidence that at the turn of the decade, the most important private equity players should make wholesale changes in their management teams. In hindsight it is now clear that this is one of the recurring themes of private equity: it is typical to have a fairly high level of churn among the players, with individuals switching from one house to another, and management teams leading their own buyouts. But at the beginning of the 1990s this was all new. The stimuli behind the changes of management team were of course very different. The move of the Matuschka portfolio to the stewardship of Bain & Company was clearly a symbol and symptom of the failure of the Matuschka Group, and in part, the MatCap subsidiary which had built up its private equity investments. Over at Barings Capital, the collapse of Lignotock gave rise to a change of team, but the fund remained the same. Jens Reidel came in to provide a new start for Barings Capital in Germany, but without the legacy of a portfolio, given that the single investment made by his predecessors had gone to the wall. At CVC, the situation was far less traumatic. Max Römer and his team made the decision to spin-off, and their decision was met with a generous spirit by their colleagues at Citigroup in London. Steve Koltes took over the CVC German portfolio, which was in good order. The situation at Schroder Ventures was more acrimonious, with the German management team replaced after a failed buyout offer. But as with the Citigroup example, the portfolio was in good shape, and a new team was rapidly put in place.

Within this transition lies the first set of insights into the private equity experience in Germany at its inception. The first is that there

Figure 9.1   Overview of Private Equity Office Openings & Team Changes

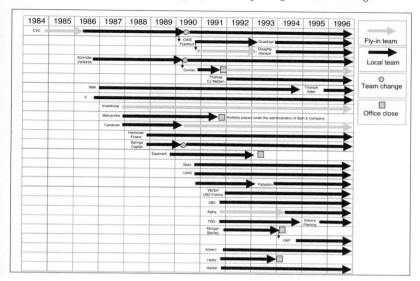

Source: Authors' compilation

was a big difference in the success of the investments made, basically polarising between the good investments made at Schroders and CVC, and the bad at Matuschka and Barings Capital. The second is that there were many reasons why a management team might change, or be changed, not least because of the performance of the investments made.

The year 1991 provides a very fitting cut off between the early and later phases of the private equity industry in Germany. It marks the point when the first assessment of fund performance was in the making. Private equity's first steps in Germany had involved its fair share of stumbles and falls. But what on balance was the outcome at the end of this initial period?

At the turn of the decade, the private equity industry had succeeded in building a beach-head into the German market, even if it had suffered collateral damage along the way. The collapse of Matuschka, the demise of Lignotock, and a number of complete write-offs made on investments concluded by 3i, reflected the initial risks of investing in German companies. Due diligence needed tightening up, and valuation tools had to be more universally applied. Funds raised for German investments also needed to be sized appropriately to the opportunities available in the market. Experience had been gained by 1991, albeit from a low base. Friedrich von der Groeben explains:

> The Matuschka story, which is a sad one, is a typical example of management consultants making poor investors. The same could have happened to me, had I not had Andrew Richards with me. I didn't have the right background. I would have gone down exactly the same route as Matuschka. Management consultants are trained to look for potential. You do not see the risk. Then, if you pay for the potential you typically overpay.[1]

Many members of the financial community in London were already becoming cautious about the German market. As Thomas Krenz recalls:

> I was not on the investment committee during the early years, but what I found out later on was that the investors perceived the German market to be mostly difficult, and massively underperforming. They saw that the money they put to work in Germany in the early years yielded nothing. Matuschka had blown up. We actually had most of our investors come by in 1991 asking us if we would take over the Matuschka fund. There were even some negotiations over whether there

Figure 9.2   Sources of Private Equity Transactions, 1984–1991

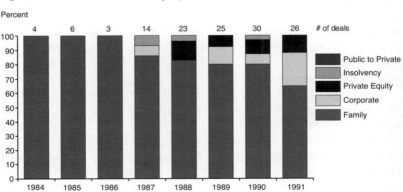

Source: Authors' compilation

could be a structure that would prevent a conflict of interest between the consortium invested in Matuschka and our own investors. The idea was that we would not only get fees but also carry from the old investors. But there were many unresolved issues at that time. The carry was already placed with Matuschka, and how could you possibly fire Matuschka as general partner of the fund? Those debates went on and on during 1991. But the general investor perception was of total underperformance. Germany was difficult to manoeuvre around anyway, because of the tax and legal system. Nobody in Germany seemed to want private equity. All in all, it was considered a subscale and generally underperforming market.[2]

The risk of bad deals being done was definitely enhanced by the unwillingness of Germans to sell anything but an unhealthy, unprofitable, or even downright bankrupt company. Jon Moulton later commented:

A buyout was seen as a failure in the 1980s. It wasn't something to be admired or chased. Another big problem was to recruit good managers into deals. In the early days German managerial mobility was very low.[3]

The view of private equity as something relevant only for failing companies remained deep-rooted throughout the 1980s. Private equity professionals were not viewed favourably by the people they visited. Hans Albrecht recalls:

We called people and said we wanted to buy their company. They made you feel like a cross between a pimp and a second-hand car dealer.[4]

In short, poor performances outweighed positive ones. Nevertheless, there had also been many positive aspects of the market during those early years. Foremost were the tax breaks available. As Jon Moulton later commented:

It was a time of fantastic tax advantages. There was at least one deal in that first Schroder fund where you were going to make 150% of your money, even if the business failed, all based upon the tax breaks. There were huge refunds and mark ups.[5]

Table 9.1 Private Equity Transactions in 1991

1991

Company	Buyer	Seller	Exit year	Sold to
Apcoa	CWB Capital Partners	Apcoa USA	1995	IPO
BAG – Biologische Analysensystem	Hannover Finanz	Family	Not yet divested	Not yet divested
Benneton Bavaria Stores	Peter Brock	Equimark	1996	Benneton
Binder & Co AG	Global Equity Partners/UIAG	Voestalpine-Gruppe	2006	IPO
Büko, Heilbronn	IMM (Office)	Family	1992	Alco
de Maekelboerger	Hannover Finanz	Family	2009	Nord Holding
HTH	3i	Family	1992	Management
Hugo Storz	IMM (Medical Homecare)	Family	1995	Otto Bock/Strategic
IMO – Industriemontagen Merseburg	Pallas	Treuhand	1999	Management
Knürr AG	SBC Equity Partners (Capvis)	Private investors	2000	3i
KTS Kunststofftechnik Schmöllin	Berliner Elektro Holding AG (Ad Capital)		Not yet divested	Not yet divested
		Hannover Finanz	Not yet divested	Not yet divested
Lewag AG	Lewag Holding AG	Family	1994	Family
Nolte GmbH	Hannover Finanz	Family	1997	Corporate Express/Strategic
Ortloff	CVC/NatWest	Everest & Jennings International Ltd	1992	Meyra GmbH
Ortopedia GmbH	IMM (Office)	Family	1992	Alco
Overkott & Keil	IMM (Office)	Family	2003	MBO
Quinting Betondeinstleistung	IMM (Construction Services)	Family	1994	Ericsson
Schrack Telekom AG	Global Equity Partners/UIAG	Family	1995	al bohn ALU elemente GmbH
Tebau	Alpha/3i	Family	1996	John Wiley & Sons
VCH	Pallas	Gesellschaft Deutscher Chemiker		
Vögele Kunststoffenster GmbH	CVC	Family	1995	Management
Vogtländische Musikinstrumentenfabrik – B & S	IMM (Music)	Treuhand	1994	Gerhard Meinl/MBO
Wallace & Tiernan	North West Water Group Plc	DBAG/Harvest/Management	2006	Siemens
Wenzel Meinl GmbH	IMM (Music)	Family	1994	Gerhad Meinl/MBO
Werner Tobler	IMM (Office)	Family	1992	Alco

Source: Authors' compilation

Irrespective of the source of Schroders' routes to value creation, many viewed the success of Schroders' as lying in Thomas Matzen's hands, for as Chris Peisch put it:

> During that time, the only guy generally considered to have a "name" was Thomas Matzen. The Schroders guys were the only ones who seemed to be systematically doing well.[6]

The arrival of Matuschka undoubtedly had a major impact on the market. On the one hand, Matuschka increased awareness and even to some degree the understanding of private equity. But on the other hand, it was a loose cannon on deck. As Jon Moulton later commented:

> Matuschka was a fine competitor: he never took a moderate position when an extreme one was available. Sometimes he was incredibly right, and sometimes he was incredibly wrong. There was the very exotic diversity of the people who seemed to work for him. He was a colourful competitor. The Matuschka Group did train a lot of people, and their activities probably raised the profile of the industry. Matuschka was a pretty important pioneer, no question about that.[7]

Another feature of the 1980s was the lack of competition. The role of intermediaries in running auctions was minimal, and there was plenty of scope for finding proprietary deals. As Jon Moulton pointed out:

> A lot of the Schroder deals in those days were generated on the whole by charging around talking to intermediaries and to individual entrepreneurs. It was pretty easy actually because there was so little competition.[8]

10
The Fourth Phase: Frustrating Times 1992–1994

Given the trials and tribulations of the early phases, it may seem difficult to comprehend that later phases of private equity in Germany were possible. One explanation for the next phase must be that newcomers thought they would never make the same mistakes as the pioneers. Indeed many of the individuals who helped set up new private equity houses at the beginning of the 1990s were well familiar with the problems of Matuschka, 3i, and Barings. A second explanation is that the market was considered too promising to be tarnished by a few bad deals. Succession problems were considered to be rife in Germany, providing opportunities for new funds to prove their worth. A final, perhaps more cynical explanation, is that bankers have been known to have short memories. Money had been lost, but there were still abundant opportunities for future gain.

Heller

One of the first spin-offs from the collapse of the Matuschka empire was formed by Rolf Petzold. He was approached by a head-hunter interested in his background in private equity.

Heller was a Chicago-based factoring company, active around the world, which belonged to Fuji Bank. It resembled GE Finance, and indeed many of its staff came from that stable. Despite its Japanese ownership, Heller was a very American institution, filled with successful and dynamic people. Among its other business lines were aircraft leasing and project finance, the latter of which entailed equity-related risk. In 1991, the Head of Heller decided that he wanted to diversify further into private equity. He turned to Rolf Petzold to support his initiative. Petzold was given the task of opening an office and recruiting a team.

One of Petzold's first hires was Michael Boltz, who had been working for five years at Bank of Boston's debt finance department. Michael Boltz recalls:

> I had to move to Munich. We found a new office in Marsstrasse, hired a secretary, talked with people, and were told we were allowed to invest from two to twenty million DM, with no limitation on participation, so we could do majorities. The reason Petzold hired me was because I had the skill set. He was a very good boss. We did two deals, the first of which was Heyne & Penke Verpackungen GmbH, a small packaging company in Holzminden. They produced printing paper, laminated paper to wrap anything, Golden Toast, Haribo gummibears, lots of export to Arabian countries, for candy companies. The firm had revenues of maybe DM 25–30 million. We bought a 40% stake and the owner kept the rest, but we had the right to determine when the company was sold; it was an interesting structure for the time. I spent four weekends on his sofa, in his private home. The deal only happened because of Petzold's charm. It was purely relation-driven. The owner liked Petzold. It was a lot of work for him. That was 1992. In those days he wrote letters, made cold calls, and that sort of thing.[1]

In 1992, Petzold hired Walter Moldan, the first 3i defector after Friedrich von der Groeben's departure. He was viewed as a man of considerable experience, with three years under his belt working for 3i. The newly enlarged Heller team went on to do a deal with a company producing electronic devices and computer screens for dusty environments. Again this was a minority deal, and the equity provided was used for growth capital. Michael Boltz recalls preparing his first commercial due diligence on the deal:

> I got in touch with L.E.K. for the first time. I had a meeting with Ray Porter about a commercial due diligence in 1992, and engaged them to support us on the deal.[2]

The other two Heller offices in Europe, based in Paris and Milan, also closed two deals respectively during the period, and the companies acquired were making solid if unspectacular progress. It therefore came as a bombshell to the teams, when the signal arrived from the US, that a course change had made their activities no longer relevant. Michael Boltz recalls:

> Then in August 1993, Malcom Lamp from Heller's in-house council came to Munich. He told us that Heller had a new CEO, who had a

new strategy, and that as a consequence the decision had been taken to close our office by December. He was a friendly lawyer. It was not his fault. He told us that we hadn't done anything wrong, nor had Paris or Milan. Private equity was no longer considered core. Instead it had been determined that Heller should concentrate on factoring. Our pay lasted until December, and then I was out of a job.[3]

Heller's entry and exit from Germany was the first instance of such changing moods within a financial service institution, and was to be become a pattern, particularly for banks, later in the 1990s and early 2000s.

Halder

Even before Paul de Ridder had completed the task of deciding what to do with the Matuschka portfolio for Continental Bank, he had decided to enter private equity himself. As a Belgian, born in 1956, raised and educated in Antwerp, he was not necessarily the obvious candidate to set up a private equity house in Germany. He began working for Continental Bank in 1978, spending five years in Belgium and six in Milan, and then some time in Chicago and London, before ending up in 1988 heading up the bank's corporate banking business in Frankfurt. De Ridder recalls:

At that time Continental was one of the leading foreign banks in Italy and Belgium. But on arriving in Germany I discovered that the bank was only a marginal player in this market, with no particular reputation, people, customers, or specific projects. It was my challenge to build something up. So I said let's focus on buyouts.

Continental had a strong reputation in the US for buyouts because Henry Kravis had worked a lot with the bank in the 1970s. Continental and Chase were the two banks in the early days that were most active in financing buyouts. When I moved to Germany there was some buyout activity already in the UK, but nothing in Germany. So I told my new colleagues we should start an MBO business. We began by publishing a book in German on MBOs, and then, every six months, we organised MBO seminars. We asked Matzen, Matuschka, von der Groeben, and Jens Lück to be special guest speakers. The first time we did it, we wondered how it would work. We only wanted to invite entrepreneurs, which was overly ambitious at that time. Our message was that we could do MBOs, we could finance them, and we could bring in private equity sponsors, such as Schroders, 3i, and many others.

It took us about two years to get the business off the ground, by which time we had looked at a lot of Mauschka deals, and set up a blind bridge finance facility for them.

When it came to my time to jump ship to set up Halder in Germany, I was asked if we should take on the Matuschka portfolio. I didn't like the idea. What I was most worried about was the types of contracts they had entered into with the sellers. They didn't leave much flexibility to make decisions and hire and fire.[4]

De Ridder joined Halder in May 1991, and subsequently hired two other team members, Joachim Kramer, and Susanne Quint, a management assistant at Continental who started as office manager and later became investment manager. Karl-Heinz Funke was added shortly afterwards, who joined Halder from Matuschka. Paul de Ridder explains:

Halder wasn't a typical entry of a foreign player into the German market. Entering Germany for Halder meant Germany becoming Halder's largest market, so this required a much stronger commitment than for the Anglo-Saxons, who would come in and out of the market knowing that the bulk of their business was either in the UK or the US. We were typical of a Benelux player in any industry, having the biggest part of our market outside our domestic market.[5]

De Ridder started investing out of Halder's third fund, which was dedicated to the Benelux and Germany. His first deal was closed in 1992, when he acquired Schmidt + Link from Lignotock. Lignotock was owned at this point by Societe Generale, after the Lignotock LBO for which they provided the original senior debt had collapsed. De Ridder describes the process:

It was an auction run by the M&A department of SocGen. It was one of those situations where effectively the management team themselves were looking for a sponsor, and they managed to own slightly over 50% of the Schmidt + Link equity. The remainder was acquired by Halder.

We won the deal because we appeared so eager to do our first deal, and because we convinced management that we were focussed on them, and had many conversations with them. Indeed, they told us afterwards that they felt we had been fighting on their side. We structured all the financing for them and got BHF bank to back the deal.[6]

Christophe Hemmerle was on the other side of the negotiations at the time, working for SocGen, selling a part of Lignotock at a very difficult time, as he later recalled:

I met Paul de Ridder for the first time while we were selling Schmidt + Link. It was a time when the private equity community was nearly dead. Matuschka was no longer in the market. Paul de Ridder and Joachim Kramer had just started Halder, but it was not very well known. The investor community was disappearing. If we talked to French investors about Germany, they just left the room. The discussions went well with Halder, and that's how I ended up joining them in 1994.[7]

Surprisingly, the deal was closed with a very high level of leverage from BHF Bank, the total equity only accounting for around 13% of the purchase price, as de Ridder explains:

Those were the days when you could write off goodwill for tax purposes, so just by doing the deal you had an enormous cash flow improvement, because you essentially didn't have to pay taxes for a couple of years. That's why the equity proportion was initially so low.[8]

Halder looked at some of the Treuhand deals which came onto the market, but decided against them all. Also deals seizing on the East German opportunity after unification appeared difficult to do.

The companies were all too unpredictable. We looked at a company importing television sets from Asia, whose business was booming. But they were a typical example of a short-lived wave of business. Once the East Germans had bought a television they moved onto something else. People had no way of assessing whether a market they were focussing on was sustainable or not. This was particularly the case in construction and building materials, which reached its peak in 1995, and then declined thereafter for ten consecutive years. I've never seen so many window manufacturing deals offered to us as in 1995. The markets back then for East German focussed companies were very difficult to assess.[9]

Halder's second investment came in 1993 with Bernd Steudle, a company making electrical parts for various industries including washing machines and automotive, which was acquired from the founder-entrepreneur. The banking included finance from HSBC, represented by Scott Greenhalgh, which was to be significant once it came to the exit. Greenhalgh moved on to set up the German office of Alchemy and bought Steudle from Halder in 1998. 1994 saw Halder close a small expansion finance deal in a construction company, Schukraft, which was to prove a total write-off (the only one in the German team's history). Chrisophe Hemmerle joined the team in 1994, in time to support the investment in Jaeger and also the sale of Schmidt + Link for a second time, as Halder made their exit. He recalls the experience:

Halder sold the operation at a time when the economic situation wasn't so good, but the IRR realised was a good one. At the time, without doubt, Schmidt + Link was an impressive deal, a classical buyout.[10]

The investment in Erich Jaeger GmbH in the same year was to prove one of the most successful of Halder's third fund. Hemmerle remembers the curiosities of the process:

Jaeger was an impressive medical care company. We brought Krüger in again to take over the company in a management buy-in. They were facing a lot of change in the industry at the time, there was quite some price pressure in the market, and the unions were pretty unco-operative too. This was another of Krüger's restructuring jobs. But Jaeger also grew and became more international under our ownership. We sold it to a US strategic in 1999 for a good capital multiple.[11]

Despite its Benelux roots, Halder had made a good start to doing business in Germany. The strong track record allowed the German team to raise its own Germany dedicated country fund in later years. Unlike Heller, Halder's entry into Germany was not made on a whim, but on the contrary was a major decision that would mark Halder's ambition to become a much bigger private equity player. Halder was the first non-Anglo-Saxon entrant into the market, and set an example for a number of French and Scandinavian houses that were to follow the same strategy in later years.

IMM

As the 1990s progressed, IMM continued to grow in size and scope. Thomas Bühler acquired the first medical homecare supplier, Stortz, in 1991, Kai Binder and Christian Eckart joined as managers of the sub-group; Arthur Haug acquired Zapf in 1992. Given the success of its copier dealerships in East Germany, IMM was also emboldened to set up a musical instruments division, beginning first with the acquisition in 1991 of Wenzel Meinl, co-opting Gerhard Meinl to run the business, and then proceeding to acquire Vogtländische Musikinstrumenten-fabrik – B&S from the Treuhand in 1991. Christoph Tiefenbacher, an ex-BCG consultant, who had stepped in from Siemens started a stationery business in Leipzig, Büro Depot, and after persuasion, acquired Ortloff, a large stationery products distribution company in Cologne. Albrecht recalls:

> Ortloff was really a give-away, and Christoph didn't want to have it. He preferred starting something from scratch. It was a time when consolidation in this sector had only just started, driven by the fact that there were now these fast third-party logistics systems. Beforehand, every town had had its own independent stationery distributor, because there was no third party fast logistics and you could distribute as far as the truck load. With third-party logistics, obviously the economies of scale and purchasing and warehousing came into play.[12]

IMM's concept was rapidly becoming well-honed and comprehensible, as Kai Köppen realised when he applied to join the company in 1992:

> IMM was still a comparatively small company when I joined. I started in the summer of 1992. I understood at the time that they bought companies in fragmented industries, mid-size build ups, and then consolidated them. They were mainly interested in companies in mature phases of the life-cycle, usually suffering declining profit margins. Once these companies had been grown and made more profitable, they would then be sold to strategics.[13]

Walter Moldan had a similar view:

> I remember the mood of IMM when I joined: their key characteristics were: the spirit of hard work; great success in building business concepts; and detailed in-house due diligence. We had the duty of getting hands-on involved in the businesses. I wasn't just managing director of the holding company; I was also co-managing director of every portfolio company. This made you really involved in those companies.
>
> It wasn't just the money at IMM, it was the way they worked: very many hours, lousy equipment, but it was a spirit that we were a family that developed something, everyone had a career opportunity, and everybody at the end of the day could run his own business somewhere.[14]

Not everything went smoothly, however, and the first serious differences within the IMM team emerged at the time of the acquisition of Zapf, as Hans Albrecht explains:

> Arthur Haug brought in his friend Matthias Eckhard, who had possession of the Zapf deal, on the condition that he would get a 10% share in the company. But Raimund didn't want him to get this stake, and Arthur was so angry that he and Eckhard left over the issue.[15]

König had been encouraging managers who took operational control to acquire significant percentage stakes in their industry holdings. Gerhard Meinl had a 20% stake in the music group, Gottwald and Hollenberg had 10% each in the construction services holding and Kai Binder and Christian Eckart owned 10% each in the medical home-care business. IMM effectively had a two-tier structure, as Thomas Bühler explains:

> There was the partner group, then there were senior managers who were under the partners but responsible for a branch, who were officially employed by IMM, and who received their equity-kicker or carry from IMM. Then below them there were the branch managers who didn't belong to the core group, but who were managing directors in a branch and got their shares

that way. Under them were the participations which also had managing directors and minority shareholders.

In my area, for example, I was a senior manager, or effectively a junior partner, with a carry in IMM, but no stake in the branch I was overseeing. Under me were two managers in the health products division, Kai Binder and Christian Eckart, They were the operative managing directors, and had shares in the branch. I was ultimately responsible. That was a typical picture of how it worked.[16]

In the case of the new toy division, however, König decided that Dietmar Scheiter would take operational control of Zapf, and therefore Eckhard was not offered a minority participation in either the division or Zapf. König later explained:

It was clear that Dietmar Scheiter would take responsibility for the toys division, under which we would put Zapf.[17]

Haug and Eckhard left to set up their own participations business, H & E Kapitalbeteiligungen GmbH & Co KG. This successor company to IMM was also focussed on majority buyouts, whereby the partners of the buyout company would play a significant operational role in their acquired companies.

Walter Moldan, whose job at Heller had been brought to a sudden end, also joined IMM in early 1994, and teamed up with Kai Köppen at the toys division. Moldan recalls:

Zapf was my first assignment with Kai, and my job was to review the logistics. Zapf still had a going-direct concept, which implied that you didn't ship whole pallets, but instead took off single boxes from a pallet, and then returned the pallet to the warehouse, which was an absolutely terrible approach. So we had to change all of this before the Christmas season started, otherwise Zapf wouldn't have survived.

I did a lot of analysis of all the shipments and started talking to engineering logistics companies. Once I was experienced enough, I found an excellent engineering company, which helped Zapf develop a completely new logistics system. It was my first time working with Kai, and it was a great experience. Mr Zapf was a fascinating entrepreneur; indeed his whole family were very nice.[18]

Zapf was to become a major success for IMM, as König explains:

> When we bought Zapf, it had sales of DM 80 million, and reasonable profitability. They had just launched Baby Born. Dietmar Scheiter developed the company aggressively. We invested in a huge television advertising campaign, on a scale that no-one had done in the German toy industry before. Baby Born was a tremendous success. We sold more Pampers for Baby Born dolls than all the German hospitals did for real new born babies in their care.[19]

In 1993, Thomas Bühler and Henriette Lorenz acquired CJD Clinic & Job Dress, a mail order house for professional clothing which was to be the core of Mercatura Holding. Mercatura, like the fashion business, was not a sub-group of IMM. Two further acquisitions followed in 1993 and 1994.

IMM was no longer only buying companies. It was also beginning to sell them. Chance encounters demonstrated how exits could be orchestrated quite quickly, as Hans Albrecht discovered with the office division:

> By 1991, we were the largest independent distributor of photocopying equipment in Europe. We were planning to be active in Germany, Austria, the Czech Republic, Russia, and Hungary, and I wanted to see how this business was done in the US. So I went off on a trip to Texas, to visit a dealer there. While on the visit, I found that the dealership in Texas, was owned by a consolidator, and the guy I was meeting so much liked my story of consolidating businesses in Europe, that he put me in touch with his boss at Alco Standard. Alco Standard had been consolidating photocopier dealerships in the US. Alco was immediately interested, and that's how we came to sell them our company.

> Raimund König charged Alco more than twice the sum for half the company than I would have dared to ask for the whole of the company. They only acquired half, because for some reason they didn't want to consolidate it. We made a lot of money when we sold to Alco.[20]

Kai Köppen, who had recently joined IMM, was called in for reading support during notarisation. He remembers the evening of the transition:

> We were standing in the cellar level meeting room of IMM with the notary public, all reading out loud at the same time. We had a tight deadline, and the notary said that there was nothing to prevent us reading in chorus.[21]

The sale of IMM Office Systems to Alco was to lead a further set of management changes at IMM, as König explains:

> Hans Albrecht effectively left us to become the Office Systems business's CEO. Dietmar Scheiter had been overall responsible for Office Systems, but pretty much at the same time we sold this division we acquired Zapf, so after handing over to Hans, Dietmar took over responsibility for toys. He then bought euro-play in June 1993.[22]

Subsequently further businesses were sold: following the acquisition of Otto Kern in 1993 the IMM fashion division was floated on the stock market in 1994. Mercatura Holding was sold to Quelle in 1997.

The size, scope, and growth of IMM, meant that in the early 1990s, it became one of the leading buyout companies in the market. Like Schroders and 3i, this inevitably meant that it would also continue to generate spin-offs, as its professionals decided to leave and do their own thing.

HANNOVER Finanz

At the beginning of the 1990s, HANNOVER Finanz's parent, HDI, ran into financial challenges which required it to look for ways of raising extra equity. HANNOVER Finanz was quickly identified as a non-core business which could be sold. HDI ownership of HANNOVER Finanz had already drawn criticism from some of the HDI board members, as Hertz-Eichenrode explains:

> When we bought Signal Huber from Bosch, one of the HDI supervisory board members said that this was a business unit which competed with one that his business owned. How could they be

making such an investment? Similarly, when we invested in Flender, we got the same reaction from another member of the HDI board: they had a business which was competing in the same area.[23]

Not without a certain amount of relief, therefore, the board engaged Morgan Grenfell to look for potential buyers. Hertz-Eichenrode recalls the initial results of their search:

The only offer they got within Germany was from another major German bank, which offered DM 140 million at the time. We had other investors like Apax interested in buying us, but when our portfolio companies heard about this, they raised their hand in protest. They pointed out that it was a German company, HDI, which had invested in them: they wouldn't accept us being sold to foreigners.[24]

The obvious solution for the HANNOVER Finanz team was to orchestrate their own buyout. Hertz-Eichenrode put this proposal to the board, as he later recalled:

We suggested making a buyout, where HDI kept a 25% stake, management took 25%, and we looked for five other investors which would each take a 10% stake. We suggested that the MBO be priced at the same level as the offer from the major German bank. We also asked HDI to give us a vendor loan of DM 10 million. HDI agreed to our concept, and in the event it was very easy to find the additional investors. We had a good reputation and track record, and we already had partner companies on a number of the other funds we were running, such as the venture capital fund in Berlin.[25]

With the new non-captive status, and the increasing professional-isation of the industry, HANNOVER Finanz came under pressure to start to upgrade its due diligence, as Andreas Schober explains:

Once private equity started to become commonplace towards the middle of the 1990s, we started to spend more time on due diligence. We continued to do most of this in-house, and were convinced that this was an advantage, proven by the fact that we had hardly any failures. Our belief was that you tend to lose your gut feeling if you outsource due diligence.[26]

A constant concern of the team was to keep out a watchful eye for fraud, as inevitably, HANNOVER Finanz suffered its share of unscrupulous former owners and managers, as Schober recalls:

> We had one big flop which was due to criminal activities. We had invested into a company with many subsidiaries, and it was operating a snowball system, such that it was bankrupt long before we got in. They managed to confuse our auditors and everyone else. In such cases, you end up receiving a call from the person responsible saying "I'm a really bad person and can't keep the company from bankruptcy any longer". One of our investments went bankrupt because the former owner, who was still running the company, was incentivising his clients to continue buying his products out of his own pocket, but then pulling the liquidity out of the company. Often the problem is that something has gone wrong, and the manager thinks of doing something to get by, or to cover it up, and then they end up denying reality for a while, and lose their realistic view of things. It is tragic when they then call up twice a day, and try to make the impossible possible, and you end up seeing grown men cry.[27]

Nevertheless, the HANNOVER Finanz experience was generally good, in that the due diligence process gave the team opportunities to get to know management:

> We've had positive experiences most of the time. If you establish a good relationship with the entrepreneur, usually they are grateful to have someone to talk to, and are happy to take advice.[28]

CWB Frankfurt

Once it was clear in 1990 that the Frankfurt team was leaving CVC, the market was abuzz with speculation about what they would do next. The first approach came from the shareholders of the Matuschka portfolio who were rapidly becoming convinced that the time had come to part with their management team. Max Römer recalls:

> Paul de Ridder approached us from Continental Illinois at just the time we were considering leaving CVC, and he asked us if we could help with the Matuschka portfolio. He introduced us to the limited partners group.

We embarked on a valuation of the companies. The nominal investment amount that had been made was about DM 200 million, and the residual value we found was nil! We said let's be positive. If we invest here and there and there and infuse equity, the valuation of the portfolio might be raised to the mid DM 30 millions. We didn't really want to be the bearers of bad news. But the limited partners were pretty insistent. They said: "have it all and fix it". They made us a very attractive offer that would have covered the cost of the whole group. So we ended up sitting down and thinking what would happen if we accepted their offer.

We realised that all the bad news would fall on us if we took it on. The Matuschka portfolio would also block our capacity to build up our own company in the direction we wanted to go. So we left all that money on the table. It shows you that from the outset we were quite independent and not compromised by money. That is very important in our business. You can be offered all the money in the world, but if it is for a bad concept you shouldn't embark upon it.[29]

The second approach came from West LB. Max Römer was more favourably impressed by this one, as he explains:

Hans Peter Peters approached us. He was at the time the managing director of the West LB. Peters said that the West LB was thinking of creating a management buyout fund jointly with Standard Chartered Bank. The two had formed a joint venture at the time called CWB Merchant Bank. Peters said he wanted to embark on buyouts, for the north of Europe, UK, Scandinavia, Germany, and Benelux. They came along to us with the Standard Chartered acquisition finance team, made up of Nigel Doughty and Dick Hanson.

On the one hand, Doughty and Hanson had never done a proprietary acquisition. But on the other hand they had engaged in a huge range of equity kickers, and were very knowledgeable from their experience in the UK, which was so much more developed than the German market.

So we pooled our track records in the placement memorandum. All the equity kickers related to the deals done by Standard Chartered, all the participations to those held by West LB, and all the buyouts to those we had been involved in while at Citibank.[30]

In the end despite all the synergies, it was to be a tough process for Doughty, Hanson, and Römer to raise a new fund. Every possible objection was raised by pension funds and insurance companies in the US and the UK. Max Römer recalls:

> It was difficult. Nigel Doughty and I were travelling the whole world. The investors were saying: "Why should we give you our money? West LB and Standard Chartered both have money, why do you want money from us?"

> Then there was all the bad experience international investors had had with Matuschka.

> And to add another element: the first Gulf war started on February, 22nd 1991. The whole world came to a standstill. Literally, we started fund raising in 1991 not to be in a position to close it until the middle of 1993.[31]

The CWB Capital Partners fund finally closed with 166 million pounds sterling. But the marriage between the London and Frankfurt teams was strained from the outset, with the London team tending towards large deals, and the Germans favouring mid-cap transactions. To make matters worse, the London team did not feel itself constrained to the UK and considered large-cap deals in Germany to be fair game, even though the Frankfurt team sent strong signals that this was their home turf.

The largest of the deals closed by the Frankfurt team was Apcoa, which was acquired in 1991, under the lead of Andreas Fendel. The other deals closed in Frankfurt were smaller, as Römer explains:

> We did a couple of other deals, medium size, no flashy milestone deals. There were a couple of deals in the furniture business, in the construction supply business. Meanwhile the British team first did Bran + Luebbe in 1993, and then Tarkett in 1994.[32]

Such was the divergence between the two CWB teams that their story needs to be told separately, albeit in parallel, up to the point at which they parted company.

CWB London

Despite the agreement with Max Römer and his team, the early 1990s saw Dick Hanson operating in the German market from London, and pulling off some of the largest buyouts of the period. The first of these came in 1993, when Bran + Luebbe came up for sale. Richard Burton, who had recently moved to Hamburg with Price Waterhouse, recalls the events:

> In January 1993 we had a call from Price Waterhouse London saying that they needed help with a big acquisition project on Bran + Luebbe, a pumps manufacturer in Norderstedt, just north of Hamburg. They told me it was a due diligence for an outfit called CWB Capital Partners. The team was basically Dick Hanson and Chris Wallis and the deal took about six months to close. It was a massive acquisition at the time, worth several hundred million Deutschmarks. I think the reason it came from London was that it was such a large transaction and therefore London were in the lead, and probably sourced it, as it was coming out of Alfa Laval. It was a corporate disposal to a private equity house.
>
> The London Price Waterhouse team produced, with our help in Hamburg, an impressive tome telling you everything you could want to know about Bran + Luebbe. The goal of the due diligence seemed to be to understand the business in as much detail as possible, including commercial. The supply chain was described in utmost detail, and a major focus for Dick Hanson was the achievability of the financial projections. The initial work took about six to eight weeks.
>
> It was a whole new world for a young accountant such as myself, with a predominantly forward-looking commercial and cash-flow oriented approach. For some reason the financing dragged on. Completion wasn't until September, and we had to keep updating the report. I imagine our fees were well in excess of one million pounds, a very sizeable fee in those days.[33]

The deal was large enough that Dick Hanson decided from the outset to take on a co-investor, in the form of Goldman Sachs Principal Investment Area. Thomas Pütter, who had only recently joined Goldman, explains:

> I had joined Goldman in September 1992, after retiring from Matuschka in February, and having taken six months off in Asia. I asked to

work in the principal investment area, but they said "no you can't, because it is partners' money and newcomers can't manage partners' money, that would be preposterous". But then Goldman got a call from Doughty Hanson (CWB Capital at the time) asking them whether they wanted to work with them on Bran + Luebbe. Suddenly the Goldman partners realised they knew little about German tax, German law, or German company investments. Fortunately, somebody remembered that they had just hired a former CFO of a German company, and felt sure that he would know all this stuff. And I did know all this stuff. So the rest is history.

Bran + Luebbe was one of the largest industrial buyouts in Germany at that time, with an enterprise value of DM 240 million in 1993. For Goldman, this was a minority investment, with the majority held by Doughty Hanson. A year later, in 1994 they came back and asked us whether we would like do Tarkett, a parquet flooring company, with them as well. We said yes, but only if we could do it on an equal fifty-fifty basis. We no longer wanted them to have the whole say on the deal. So we did Tarkett, and it was the largest industrial buyout in Germany. It was also the largest high yield bond issue ever done in connection with a buyout, DM 660 million. Later, it became the largest IPO out of a German buyout. A lot of firsts.[34]

The involvement of the CWB London team in the German market was to provoke tensions with the CWB team in Frankfurt. Peter Sewing and Peder Prahl were effectively posing as a rival German team in London, focussed on larger buyouts. These tensions between London and Frankfurt could only create faultlines that would eventually push the two teams to a break point.

Schroder Ventures

Once the split with Thomas Matzen and the old Schroders' team was complete, Friedrich von der Groeben and Thomas Krenz began the work of kick-starting a second beginning for Schroder Ventures in Germany.

Armed with the newly raised DM 230 million fund, von der Groeben acted quickly to get the successor management company up to speed. The new and old funds were run in parallel. Osterrieth and Krenz focussed heavily on Kleindienst within the old portfolio, which required a lot of restructuring. Meanwhile, von der Groeben set his sights on closing a new landmark deal, which would re-establish Schroder's position as the leading player in the market. Krenz recalls:

> Friedrich was trying to re-establish the Schroder Ventures brand name in the market, which basically meant closing a big new transaction. It took a year-and-a-half to get there.[35]

The timing of the Schroders relaunch, in early 1992, was unfortunate. The recession in the US and the UK was deepening, the situation in the Middle East was fragile, and the first signs of a recession were showing through in post-reunification Germany. Von der Groeben recalls:

> By August 1992, the German economy had collapsed, and there were no deals. All the people who wanted to sell their companies had valuations in mind that were pre-recession. All the others were too busy rescuing their companies. So for the next two years we did not do any deal.[36]

Nick Ferguson too found he had to be philosophical about the delay in closing new deals:

> We went for another two years without deals. I didn't lose sweat over that. Once we started investing, the second fund ended up being one of the best in our history.[37]

Having made no investments in 1992 and 1993, and just five investments amounting to DM 48 million in 1994, the pressure within the organisation for more money to be put to work in Germany was palpable. Investors were growing anxious over the fund's progress, and there were concerns in other offices that their fund-raising efforts could be undermined or at least made more challenging by an underperforming fund in Germany. Despite these pressures, the Frankfurt team remained committed to only looking for deals which they felt would make money: better to do no deals than bad ones.

The economic difficulties in Germany were eventually to provide some opportunities for Schroders. Starting in 1993, Kässbohrer, a vehicle manufacturer in Ulm producing buses, coaches, vehicle transporters, trailers, and snow groomers, began to fall apart. The division's truck bodies, semitrailers and trailers were sold to the competitor Kögel, and in 1994 Kässbohrer's insolvency administrator was in the process of selling the bus division to Daimler Benz. Daimler had no interest however in the snow groomer vehicles division, and therefore an investment bank was mandated to find a buyer for this entity. This looked an interesting opportunity, and Friedrich von der Groeben decided that it could be the key deal for Schroders. Thomas Krenz recalls:

> When the Kässbohrer auction came along, basically the whole office was put to work on it. This was the big re-launch break. It was a fairly sizeable company, and it was high profile. This put Schroders back on the map. From an outsiders' perspective, we had been out of the market from 1991 through to 1994, doing a lot of things but not buying companies.[38]

Success with Kässbohrer was fundamental to restoring Schroder's credibility in Germany. The following year, in 1995, another opportunity came along, which von der Groeben initially thought of rejecting. Oerlikon had acquired Leybold from Degussa AG in November 1994. Degussa had itself taken over Leybold from Metallgesellschaft AG a few years earlier, but had experienced heavy losses with the company, forcing it to dispose of the asset. Although the price Oerlikon paid for Leybold was not disclosed, it was generally thought to have been low, due to Leybold's losses, and Degussa's desire to part with the company.

Bringing Leybold into the Oerlikon family, which also owned Balzers, meant that approximately ninety percent of CD metallisation equipment production would be concentrated under common ownership. Given the small size of the business in question, this did not contravene German law, but in the US the Federal Trade Commission (FTC) ruled that one of the two businesses should be divested. Leybold's CD metallisation machines were sold under the name of Singulus, and consequently Leybold complied with the FTC's ruling, and put the business up for sale. The origins of the Singulus deal came not with a private equity house but with a small company in America that had been contacted by the anti-trust authorities investigating the Balzers-Leybold merger. Denton Vacuum Inc (DVI), based in New Jersey, manufactured vacuum deposition equipment for precision optics, and had tried unsuccessfully to enter the CD metallization equipment business in the 1980s. Peter Denton was good friends with the Leybold US sales manager, who encouraged him to make a bid for the Singulus business. Denton gave it some thought, but it wasn't until a Harvard Business School reunion, and a chance meeting with a former classmate, Don Nelson, an investment banker, that the idea of bidding for Singulus gained traction.

Nelson told Denton that if it was a good deal, he would he able to get the money. In the event, finding the funds to buy the business proved a challenge, but Nelson encouraged Denton to put in an offer letter to Leybold. Nelson emphasised that they had nothing to lose from simply putting in a bid.

Denton sent in a letter offering $18 million for the business, one third in cash, one third in delayed payments, and one third financed by advanced payments of Singulus metallisers that Leybold would still need during the first few years for its line business. This offer was rejected by Leybold as being too low, and containing too little cash.

Denton's efforts to find a bank to support him in the US continued to prove fruitless. The common reaction of banks was to consider Singulus to be lacking substance, in particular due its absence of assets. The response from US venture capital was no more positive. It was clear that if Denton was to raise money, it would have to be in Europe. Again, it was Nelson's contacts that played a critical role. He put Denton in touch with a colleague at Schroder Ventures, who in turn put him together with Friedrich von der Groeben.

On seeing the proposal, von der Groeben's initial instinct was to reject it immediately. The deal which was on offer, DM 30 million in revenues and DM 8 million in EBIT for a purchase price of DM 30 million, appeared to be good to be true. Consequently, von der Groeben assumed that there had to be something very wrong with the deal, and in some respects he was right.

In essence, Singulus as it was being offered, was little more than a collection of patents, together with a manager who had been running a part of Leybold. The challenge was not winning over customers, as the due diligence quickly established, nor were there any technological threats. The big issue was who would leave Leybold to join the new stand-alone Singulus team and make it function.

In the event, von der Groeben and his team managed to convince many sceptical people, be they managers or bankers, and master their own doubts about the transaction. Their success in ironing out all of the potential problems on what was a significantly challenging deal, firmly established the new Schroders team as a quality outfit, and a worthy successor to that which had served under Matzen.[39]

Apax

The story of Apax's start in Germany originates with Michael Hinderer, born in 1955 in Stuttgart to a family with a thriving textile business

Table 10.1 Private Equity Transactions in 1992

1992

Company	Buyer	Seller	Exit year	Sold to
Aschenbrenner	Heller	Family	1995	Management
Autodorado	DIC/Fleming Berenberg Gosla	Treuhand	1993	Liquidated
Basler	IMM (MHM Mode Holding)	Family	1994	IPO
Beissbarth (part of Kleindienst)	Schroder Ventures	Osorno	1999	International trade buyer
Boysenburger Fliessen	DIC/Fleming Berenberg Gosla	Treuhand	1993	Insolvency
Brandt ECCO	Financial buyer	Schroder Ventures	Not yet divested	Not yet divested
Cargo Van	Deutsche Handelsbank	Morgan Stanley	1999	Group AFU/ABN Amro Capital France/Paul Capital
Dragoco	Harald Quandt (Equita)	Family	2002	EQT
EW Hof Antriebe und Systeme	Berliner Elektro Holding AG	Family	Not yet divested	Not yet divested
Fielmann AG	Management	Hannover Finanz	1995	IPO
Freitag Elektronik	Hannover Finanz	Family	1995	Vivanco
Haushaltsgeräte-Service HGS Holding	EGIT	Treuhand	1993	Treuhand
Hengstenberg Beteiligungs GmbH	Hannover Finanz	Family	Not yet divested	Not yet divested
Heyne & Penke	Heller	Family	1994	Hans-Peter Penke-Wevelhoff
IMM Office Systems	Alco	IMM	1994	Triumph-Adler
Instore Marketing	Hannover Finanz/3i	Family	2000	Management
Kleindienst Aufzugstechnik	Schroder Ventures	Family	1996	Corporate buyer
Kleindienst Datentechnik	Schroder Ventures	Family	1999	IPO
Krings	CWB Capital Partners	Family	1998	Mezzanine
Logo	Apax	Previous investors	1997	Strategic
Malitz	Advent	Treuhand	1994	Boral
Märkische Baustoff-Service GmbH (MBS)	EGIT	Treuhand	1993	Treuhand
Mondi	Investcorp	Family	1999	Management

Table 10.1 Private Equity Transactions in 1992 – *continued*

1992

Company	Buyer	Seller	Exit year	Sold to
P.A.L.M. Microlaser Technologies AG	CWB Capital Partners	Family	2004	Carl Zeiss AG
Peter Butz GmbH & Co	Hannover Finanz	Family	2003	BOS GmbH & Co. KG. (Hannover portfolio co.)
Reha Technik Schneider	IMM (Medical Homecare)	Family	1995	Strategic
Richard Schöps AG	Cinven/Thomas JC Matzen	Schroder Ventures	1996	Thomas CJ Matzen
SEHO	CWB Capital Partners	Family	1998	Management
S.M.I. Strasser Marigaux (Paris)	IMM (Music)	Previous investors	1994	Gerhard Meinl/MBO
Schaltbau AG	Berliner Elektro Holding AG (Ad MAN)	Previous investors	2002	Vossloh AG
Schlott Gruppe	3i	Family	1997	IPO
Schmidt + Link	Halder	Lignotock	1996	Management
Schuch	IMM (Medical Homecare)	Family	1995	Strategic
Suspa Compact	3i/Family	Family	1998	PPM Ventures
Time/System GmbH	Hannover Finanz	Family	1996	Management
TTW Industrie & Messtechnik	Insolvency	3i	Not yet divested	Not yet divested
Vits-Gruppe	Babcock-BSH AG	Equimark	2002	WD Beteiligungs GmbH
Zapf Creation	IMM Industriebeteiligungs GmbH	Family	1999	IPO
Zementol	IMM (Construction Services)	Family	1999	Insolvency/MBO Thorsten Quent

Source: Authors' compilation

in the Black Forest. Hinderer's first instinct was to reject the capitalist path his family had taken, and to go off to a Kibbutz in Israel. But his interests soon took a U-turn, and in the late 1970s he studied business administration at St. Gallen, where he met Max Burger-Calderon. Before Hinderer had finished at St. Gallen, Max moved on to Harvard Business School, and when the two met in Cambridge, Mass. to compare notes, Hinderer became convinced that further studies were necessary, and so enrolled at ETH in Zurich to do a PhD. On completion of his thesis in 1981, the choice was either consulting (BCG or McKinsey) or corporate finance. Michael Hinderer later recalled:

> A former colleague, Claus Löwe at JPMorgan, introduced me to Matu-schka, because he wanted to open up in corporate advisory. So after doing my interview with McKinsey in Munich, I passed by Matuschka late at night, literally on my way back to the airport. I had a fascinat-ing interview with the Count, who called in Rolf Dienst to join him. Before I left for the airport, they had already made me an offer.[40]

After three years working alongside Hellmut Kirchner, Manfred Ferber, and Vincent Hübner, Hinderer had learnt and earnt a lot. Indeed, he was having so much fun that he had no thoughts of leaving. But an ex-Matuschka partner, Georges Huber, planted the idea in his head that he should set up his own shop in corporate finance. The Matu-schka team was constantly being approached by head-hunters during the mid-1980s, and one such approach caused Georges Huber's idea to bloom. Hinderer recalled:

> The first time I was really intrigued by a head-hunter was when one approached me on behalf of Robert Osterrieth in mid 1986. He told me that Robert was trying to set up a buyout fund in Germany. I knew Robert from St Gallen and through other St Gallen friends and so went to see him. He offered me a position as a partner along-side Thomas Matzen for the first Schroders' German buyout fund. I also met Nick Fergusson, and the two of them made an offer in December 1986 valid for three months until March 1987.[41]

Meanwhile, Georges Huber came clean with the fact that he had a concrete opportunity for Hinderer to pursue: Huber had set up a con-sortium of investors in Switzerland prepared to fund a corporate finance boutique which would simultaneously make co-investments. By coincidence, Max Burger-Calderon turned up in town, interested in a job at Matuschka, and Hinderer floated the idea that the two of them should take up Huber's opportunity.

> Max and I made a handshake deal, and then I introduced him to the other guys. We started with SFr 1 million in 1987, with a little office, and some deals in the pipeline. I called Robert, thanked him for the offer, and said that I would have to turn him down. And that is how Corporate Finance Partners (CFP) was born.[42]

The early days of CFP were not easy however. Some small deals were done, but in the October 1987 financial crash, CFP's investors lost a significant proportion of the company's capital, and then refused to participate in subsequent co-investment opportunities. Hinderer recalls:

> So by the end of 1987, Max who was a braver guy than me, went in to see our other shareholders, and had a boardroom fight. He insisted that they sell us their shares. Only Georges Huber was willing to do so. But by January 1988, we had an option in place whereby through a Chinese auction we could establish a price by which the shares would be bought or sold. In the end we bought the other shareholders out. I was leveraged to the hilt. This was in 1988.[43]

Shortly after the dust had settled on the deal, Hinderer attended a conference on Venture Capital organised by the *Handelsblatt*, at which Alan Patricof was a keynote speaker. Patricof was interested in finding a partner to work with in Germany, and Hinderer, along with a number of others, including Hans Albrecht, signalled his interest.

> By coincidence, while I was talking to Alan, I found out that we had a buyout deal in common with his team in Paris. We were representing the management of a company Patricof wanted to buy. The company had a great brand but no assets, sales, or anything, just some managers interested not to be sold again to an industrial buyer. We were representing these guys, who were trying to spin-off from a French pharmaceutical company. We came up with the idea of selling distribution rights to their products, as a way to finance their buy. Alan thought that this was a very good idea, and quickly began talking to his colleagues in London. And that's really how we went into business with Alan.[44]

Hinderer and Burger-Calderon originally renamed their CFP business MMG Patricof operating from a base in Switzerland. Events moved quickly however, and with German reunification in 1990-91, many of Patricof's investors were interested to see a presence established in Germany. Hinderer initially saw his role as simply being to help Patricof find a team:

> So I approached various people, and we discussed whether it would be possible to set up a DM 25 million fund. After writing prospectuses, and conducting the executive search, I approached Martin Halusa whom I knew from boarding school, and who was also going out with the sister of my then girlfriend. Coincidentally, we had also studied under the same PhD supervisor. We met at a restaurant. He was clearly not that happy at Swarovski, and having had a background at BCG, seemed keen on what we had to offer.[45]

Martin Halusa was born in Bangkok in 1955, his father being Austrian ambassador to Thailand. Halusa moved continuously, switching from language to language, from Thailand to India, to Austria, to France. Only at the age of ten was he put into a German boarding school to ensure he didn't lose his German (he had already lost Thai and English). But even this proved short-lived, when he went to the US as an exchange student, only to find while he was there that his father had been made Austrian ambassador to the US. He stayed in the US therefore to study first at Georgetown, and then at Harvard Business School, graduating in 1979 to join BCG, and move to Munich. After six years at BCG, during which he did a PhD at Innsbruck University, he joined Swarovski where he took charge of marketing.

Halusa decided to join Hinderer and Burger-Calderon in Munich in 1991 to start up the new fund, which quickly attracted a total of DM 96.5 million in commitments, all from Anglo-Saxon investors. The new vehicle was named Apax. Max Burger-Calderon agreed to stay in Zurich to run the Swiss operation.

The first two years began inauspiciously, with only two small deals concluded. Halusa recalls:

> Our very first deal was Logo, where I think we barely got our money back. We sold it indirectly to Transoflex, which we were really happy about. The second deal we did was PKG, a cable company, and on this we did extremely well. This closed in 1992. PKG wasn't a buyout, but rather growth financing. We found an entrepreneur through a friend of mine at Barclays, Ralf Haerforth. I liked the guy a lot. We put money behind it, and at the end of the day, we made three and a half times our money. We must have sold it in 1994 or

1995. It was a big winner, and it was really the one that gave us the confidence to continue.[46]

Another key addition to the Apax team was made during 1992. Halusa was looking at a Bavarian waste management company and asked a friend responsible for waste management at McDonalds for advice in identifying the best young waste management manager in Germany. Halusa explains the train of events which followed:

> My friend at McDonalds said there was a young Canadian at Otto, called Michael Phillips, who had studied at INSEAD, that he could certainly recommend. So I phoned Michael up and asked him if he could give me some advice. He said sure, and came down to Munich, and we drove out to this waste management company. We were regaled at a breakfast of Weisswurst and beer at eleven o'clock in the morning. Michael asked a lot of very clever waste oriented questions and I thought it was going pretty well and Michael seemed pretty enthusiastic. But when I got in the car to drive back and asked him what he thought, he told me to trash the deal. I was really impressed that he was able to exude enthusiasm, while at the same time calculating in the back of his head that this was a total no-go. This is a skill you really want from a private equity person. So I decided that Michael was the kind of guy I needed for this business, because I was looking for a partner to work with me.[47]

Michael Phillips was at the time convinced more by waste management than private equity, as he later explained:

> Back in 1989, waste management was hot, in Germany. The Duales System had just been created, and it was actually a pretty sexy industry to get into. I began as the manager of Otto's recycling operations in Germany, having worked for four years in the plastics and specialty chemicals area. Otto was building a business from scratch which didn't exist. It was a nice job. Otto was a classic German business, family owned, just developing professional management structures. You couldn't have had a better preparation for private equity.
>
> A lawyer I knew, Peter Oehl, called and said that there were two guys he knew who had just started a private equity fund in Munich. They were looking for deals, and one of their targets was a Bavarian waste management company which needed a buy-in manager. So

Table 10.2 Private Equity Transactions in 1993

1993

Company	Buyer	Seller	Exit year	Sold to
AHT Austria Haustechnik	CVC/NatWest	Family	1998	IPO
Arbo Medizintechnik	Kendall/Tyco Healthcare	CVC	Not yet divested	Not yet divested
Autodorado	Liquidated	DIC/Fleming Berenberg Gosla	Not yet divested	Not yet divested
Bernd Steudle	Halder	Family	1998	Alchemy
Boysenburger Fliessen	Insolvency	DIC/Fleming Berenberg Gosla	Not yet divested	Not yet divested
Bran + Luebbe	CWB Capital Partners/ Goldman Sachs	Alfa Laval	1998	IPO
CJD Clinic + Job-Dress	IMM (Workwear Clothing)	Family	1997	Quelle
DIFI Dierk Filmer	Halder	Family	2000	German strategic buyer
E Missel GmbH & Co KG	3i/Alpha	Family	1996	Masco Corporation
europlay-Gruppe	IMM (Toys)	Family	1999	Strategic
Finkeldei GmbH	3i	K.A. Niggemann & Partner GmbH	1997	Management
Format Tresorbau	Atco/ABN Amro	Family	1996	Management
Haushaltsgeräte-Service HGS Holding	Treuhand	EGIT	1994	Treuhand
IFCO GmbH	Hannover Finanz	Family	2000	IPO
KabelMedia (PrimaCom)	Advent	Previous investors	1999	IPO
Koelbel Group	Cinven/Thomas JC Matzen	Family	1996	Haleko
Lignotock	Sommer-Allibert	Barings Capital	Not yet divested	Not yet divested
Märkische Baustoff-Service GmbH (MBS)	Treuhand	EGIT	1994	Treuhand
Medima	Harald Quandt (Equita)	Family	2001	Insolvency
Orga Kartensysteme GmbH	Preussag/Bundesdruckerei	3i	2005	Sagem
Otto Kern Gruppe	IMM (MHM Mode Holding)	Family	1994	IPO
Planta-Subtil-Arzneimittel GmbH	Nord Holding	Family	1995	Boehringer Ingelheim AG
PPS Group	Cinven/Thomas JC Matzen	Family	1995	Thomas JC Matzen
QVF Engineering GmbH	3i	Corning	2000	De Dietrich
Remaco	Robannic/BHF	Brian Fenwick-Smith	2000	Robbins & Myers
Respo Mode International	Cinven/Thomas JC Matzen	Family	1995	Thomas JC Matzen
Sicorell	Atco/ABN Amro	Family	1997	IPO
Technische Orthopädie Habermann	IMM (Medical Homecare)	Family	1995	Strategic
Temco	Vector/LBO France	FAG Kügelfischer	1998	3i

Source: Authors' compilation

I met Martin Halusa to discuss it. I ended up spending six months working weekends and nights, travelling up and down from Dusseldorf to Munich, because I was still working at Otto. In the end, we didn't do the deal, but Halusa said "Why don't you join us", which I did in 1992.[48]

Halusa considered the six months to be more a process of convincing Phillips to join, rather than wrestling with a waste management deal that had already been trashed:

> We dumped that deal very quickly. What then took a long time was the recruiting process. It took about six months of flying back and forth, over which period the two of us could see if we would get along. That took about six months until he finally said "fine I take the plunge" and he moved his family down to Munich. I think, from then on, basically until we raised Germany II, there was no deal we didn't work on together.[49]

The new Apax team struggled in the early years. For try as they might, like Schroders, they couldn't find any deals to do. Michael Phillips recalls:

> The first three years were fantastically unsuccessful. We only did one transaction, Logo, a start-up package logistics company competing with Transoflex. We looked at hundreds of companies, but for a host of reasons every single one wasn't worth buying. We had our first fund of DM 100 million waiting to find an investment. Three years later we had drawn down DM 12 million of management fee, and invested DM 4 million in Logo, and that deal wasn't doing particularly well.[50]

When Michael Boltz lost his job through the closure of Heller, and interviewed for a job at Apax, deal-sourcing was the first topic he was asked about. Boltz explains:

> I interviewed with Halusa at Apax. He was very curious, and he asked me "how did you source deals at Heller?" Again and again he asked me "How do you do sourcing?" He was interested to learn how we conducted our business at Heller. After all, the two deals in three years we had closed at Heller wasn't bad for the time. He wanted to know how we found them, and how we convinced those guys.[51]

Michal Phillips didn't feel that investors were overly critical of the lack of deals done, as he later explained:

> The investors were relaxed. It is true that everyone was cautious about Germany. It was a first time fund. They were all American investors, who were actually quite happy that we were being so thoughtful, and that we were really struggling, and not making investments just because we felt we had to. We put ourselves under pressure. After all, it wasn't that we had seen twenty great deals and lost them. We simply hadn't found any good companies to invest in.[52]

However serious the situation, it was clear by 1994, that a new approach to the market was needed, both in Germany and the UK. Max Burger-Calderon recalls:

> Our low point was in 1994. We were trying to do venture capital and growth capital, and nothing really worked. No-one was doing extremely well in Europe. The UK wasn't doing well either. It was all based on hope and self-belief.[53]

Patricof had moulded his business around venture capital, funding start-ups, entrepreneurs, seed-capital, growth capital, almost every type of funding except vanilla buyouts of going concerns. What was clear was that in Germany entrepreneurs were thin on the ground. Michael Phillips recalls:

> So we sat down at the end of 1994 and asked ourselves what was wrong with our business model. We did an analysis. We were doing venture capital because that was what Apax did. Apax was, after all, a venture capital company. We had been trying to do venture capital in Germany for three years and discovered that this was the wrong market to do it in. There were few entrepreneurs, there was a very small venture pool of technology companies, there's no start-up mentality, the red-tape is too expensive, people are too expensive. It was clear from our analysis that this was a buyout market, and consequently we needed to become a buyout house. So we called up our partners and told them that we were going to start doing buyouts. So we called up a bank and got hold of a buyout model and literally reengineered on a computer for 5–6 days how a buyout actually worked. Because at that time it is true we didn't know how it worked.[54]

After initial scepticism, the investors played along with the strategy change. The Apax team in Munich was able to argue that the German market was wide open for a buyout play. Michael Phillips recalls:

> The industry was the Western Merchant Bank (CWB), the precursor to Doughty Hanson. It was Raimund König's IMM, which had just started up. It was a bit of Schroders. Thomas Matzen had just left, and he was the hot shot in Germany in 1991 and 1992. There was HANNOVER Finanz. Those were the big addresses to go to.
>
> Deutsche Beteiligungs Gesellschaft, BdW, 3i, projected a good footprint, but were very minority oriented. They weren't really doing buyouts. The average ticket deal in those days was DM 5–10 million.[55]

The first deal that came along in the buyout space was Infox, a company with a quasi monopoly in the distribution of advertising materials to travel agencies, which while of interest was clearly not without its complications. On the plus side, the management team appeared to be strong, and the business prospects were at least average. Infox had an extremely defensible business, as it collected and collated the brochures of Germany's many tour operators and distributed them to all of the nation's travel agencies. It was a near monopoly service. But on the negative side, the owners' asking price seemed high, and the indications were that one of the sellers in particular was unlikely to accept much of a reduction. The Apax team were very concerned not to overpay for deals: their lack of deals had not made them price insensitive. The other big problem was that the exit route for Apax was not entirely clear, given the limited number of strategic buyers and the immature poorly developed nature of the German IPO market. Last but not least, Halusa and Phillips were not sure how the optimal deal structure should look like, particularly in light of the fact that the banking community appeared to be very reluctant to finance the acquisition of a business with so little in the way of tangible assets.[56]

The deal had been brought to the market by Berenberg Consult, the Corporate Finance subsidiary of Berenberg Bank, and it was being handled by Peter Urbanek and Aman Miran Khan. For the latter it was his first deal in a new job. Miran Khan had just completed three years working for the Treuhand, where he had worked on, and completed, several privatisations. Miran Khan recalls his first meeting with Halusa.

The first deal that I did at Berenberg Consult was the sale of Infox to Apax. It was on this transaction that I met Martin Halusa. It was a very interesting experience, and without knowing it, he gave me a very good view on his business. Halusa is a really impressive guy, very low key. I remember when I picked him up at the airport, I expected something totally different. We had a very nice conversation during the ride from the airport to the company. Once we had arrived, and I was sitting down next to the Infox entrepreneur, I had this nice warm feeling. Martin Halusa had asked me a lot of questions, during the three quarters of an hour ride from the airport, much of which he used during the meeting to try to win over the entrepreneur to his side. It was really impressive. I will never forget that.[57]

The Infox auction was one of the most modern, hard fought battles of the early 1990s. Apax struggled for many months to conclude negotiations with the owner managers, Elmar Brandschwede and Hans-Joachim Krause. The two owners, like many other successful German entrepreneurs who had proven their business concept, were engaged in new endeavours, and had reduced their involvement in the original business.

Figure 10.1   Martin Halusa

It was Brandschwede's idea to sell the business, and with Krause's agreement, he approached Berenberg Bank, an investment bank in their region, with the request for support with the sale. The two entrepreneurs had originally thought that their business might be worth as much as DM 50 million, but the Berenberg bankers suggested that the company might sell for twice that amount. It was the prospect of making DM 50 million each that really fired the imagination of the two entrepreneurs.

During the course of November 1994, Berenberg proceeded to present the deal to various parties, including Apax, 3i, CVC, Nord Holding, and another local bank. After some initial discussions, Apax began due diligence in early February 1995, once most of the bidders had withdrawn, leaving Apax and CVC as the last two serious contenders. Apax's hope had been to buy the business for a value closer to Brandschwede's own initial valuation of the business at DM 50 million, but they perceived CVC to have a reputation for offering high bids with conditions, only later to cut the price while negotiating over details. Consequently, getting a low price at the outset was likely to be very difficult.

An added complication was that one of the sellers discovered during the negotiations that he didn't want to let go of the business. Despite it having been Brandschwede's idea to sell the business, he appeared in the midst of the discussions to have fallen in love afresh with his enterprise. This was true also to a lesser extent for Krause, and the two men began to show signs of being reluctant to let it go. Fortunately for Apax, there were sufficient tensions between the two owners to keep the process alive, giving the two bidders the opportunity to keep the deal in play.

Apax fought through the complexities of the deal and closed Infox in 1995. The price was seven times EBIT, DM 70 million, of which DM 28 million was equity, and DM 42 million in debt. The company was kept for two-and-a-half years, and sold in a secondary transaction to Vector/LBO France with a return of 2.3 times the original investment.

Apax was now on a roll. Success with Infox gave the team in Munich credibility in the market. Michael Phillips recalls:

> From 1994 to 1996, in those two years we invested the entire DM 95 million in our fund.[58]

The second deal was Utimaco, a software house near Frankfurt, specialised on encryption software. Unlike Infox, this wasn't a majority position. Michael Phillips explains:

With Utimaco, there was a kind of capital increase structure and owners buyout. We were a minority player, but it was still a leveraged transaction.[59]

By the mid-1990s, Apax had largely transitioned its focus from venture capital to private equity, putting behind it a number of deeply frustrating years. It found there were few if any venture deals to be done in Germany, whereas buyouts of mature companies held great potential. Many other private equity houses concluded that buyouts were the place to be by the mid-1990s, particularly those focussed on minority participations. One of the few exceptions to this trend was 3i.

3i

The frustration that had clouded the early years of 3i's entry into the German market under Friedrich von der Groeben persisted. But despite all the obstacles, 3i made a success of its business as Schlytter-Henrichsen comments:

According to the BVK statistics of the time we quickly moved up the ladder and became the fourth largest private equity firm in Germany. Despite all the frustration, we made it work, and the first three funds which I was involved in (fund one, fund two, and eurofund one) actually made between 2.5 to just under 3 times their money.[60]

One of the deals closed by the 3i team in 1993 brought to light some of examples of the curiosities of family-run companies. Schlytter-Henrichsen later recalled:

We bought a company from a family shareholder. It was quite an amazing company, highly profitable and well managed. However we later discovered that the owner of the company was at some point having an affair with the wife of one of the Directors, the MD was having an affair with his secretary, and the daughter of the MD was very friendly with the Sales Director. Due diligence nevertheless confirmed that this was an excellent company with a great future. At the time we had a problem regarding the CEO. As in any MBO, 3i required the CEO to put money into the company. The CEO however said "I have built this company for this old guy, and I am certainly not going to put a single Pfennig into it". So in order to make the transaction work, I basically convinced the vendor to give the guy a loyalty bonus on the condition that he put it back in the company. It was well deserved as he was not earning a lot of money anyway. We also had a successful entrepreneur and ex-Arthur Andersen accountant take a 25% stake in the business to help us manage this complex situation. And we brought in a junior partner as we could not take a majority position.[61]

Later in the 1990s many of the 3i team-members came to view their time with the firm as training, and a spate of defections took hold. The attraction of other houses was that they could do majorities, they had a carry, and they gave scope for bigger deals to be closed. As other teams set up shop in Germany, the most likely sources of experienced professionals were either ex-Matuschka, or ex-3i. Sometimes even a combination.

The Missel deal closed in 1993 provided Thomas Schlytter-Henrichsen with his opportunity to leave 3i. He later recalled:

What is quite funny is that we syndicated one of our investments, a company called Missel, with Alpha at the time, in 1993, that was how my relationship with Alpha began. They originally came and met Andrew in 1991, and bought Tebau, a company manufacturing aluminium windows, with him. That was the first deal they made jointly with 3i.[62]

The 3i team was gradually added to, with Nick Money-Kyrle joining from KPMG in 1994, on a controversially high salary, suited to his experience as a senior manager at KPMG and a chartered accountant. Money-Kyrle recalls his early impressions:

3i was split between north and south, Thomas running the south, and Andrew the north. I ended up working for the north, together with Tom Geller, Ulrich Eilers, Stefan Lehman, and Brian Veitch. I was confronted by raised eyebrows over my salary, and something of a culture shock at becoming a trainee project leader. But it was fascinating. 3i was the only business of its sort to offer courses in the UK, which meant for example that you could have several days training in negotiation skills. They had a very structured programme.

We were doing micro cap and small cap deals. A big deal would be DM 100 million, and the normal range was around DM 10–20 million, and we couldn't take majority in stakes, so we had to find a syndication partner. The amounts of money involved were small enough that you could afford to lose a bit of it. After you had been on board for a year, the expectation was that you would do 2–3 deals a year on your own.[63]

Events in London were to have a significant impact on the Frankfurt team. Schlytter-Henrichsen recalls:

> 3i toyed with the idea of opening up offices all over Germany. And these offices would report directly to London. Andrew and I would become local Directors representing one each of these offices. As with many of the ideas coming out of London, in the end it became clear that Germany had to be run from Germany and not from London. I was always a protagonist of a local approach; centralised rules and values but local and independent management.[64]

Money-Kyrle too, had strong impressions of sometimes frantic and frenetic activity between Germany and the UK:

> The story did the rounds that in Friedrich von der Groeben's day, he would actually finance a deal personally until he got approval, sometimes even before the investment proposal had been written. We would typically pitch a deal by telephone, submitting an investment paper in advance. Either you were psyched up, or you would lose. Nonetheless, when it came to approval processes, it may have been easier than at our competitors, certainly we were doing more deals than anyone else.[65]

Thomas Schlytter-Henrichsen left 3i in the beginning of 1996 before the regionalisation strategy could be implemented, opening up an office for Alpha in Frankfurt. But those he left behind were faced with the task of making London's new concept for Germany work. Aman Miran Khan recalls:

> Thomas Schlytter-Henrichsen had just left 3i, so I missed the cultural dilemma he experienced. When I arrived, Andrew Richards was leading the Frankfurt office having five or six more senior guys below him: Andreas Kochhäuser, Tom Geller, Ulrich Eilers, Stefan Helmstedter, Stefan Lehman, and Harald Rönn. They were more or less leading the transactions, as senior investment managers. But

nevertheless my perception was that it was still very dominated from the UK.[66]

Part of the cultural challenge between London and Germany was that the background of the professionals differed significantly. Miran Khan explains:

> People recruited in Germany had some experience, a couple of years let's say, five to ten years of professional experience, compared to very young people recruited by 3i in the UK, that had of course studied shorter, started earlier and they were in their early-to-mid 20s while we were in our late 20s early 30s. But I don't think it was so much a cultural difference, but one of seniority. We were not more senior than them but we had different experiences. I didn't have to go to London very often, perhaps only a couple of times. I was more often in Birmingham because the industrial advisors were there rather than in London.[67]

A further cause of frustration for the German 3i team was that they had to sell an approach to entrepreneurs that appeared extremely foreign and unclear. Miran Khan found the task very difficult:

> It was an incredibly difficult task to convince a second or third generation entrepreneur to sell to a big UK private equity fund with offshore vehicles investing out of Jersey or Guernsey, with titles like Equity Partners number three and four. We visited entrepreneurs together with experienced industrial advisors, but they did not understand or speak German. All that type of stuff was very difficult to explain, and some of the people we talked to simply didn't want to hear us. They just didn't want what we were offering. So that was the first time I got the impression that with simple structural changes it would help a lot to win the entrepreneur over. 3i was of course an absolutely top company, with a very good reputation. But it was very difficult to bring that over to these people, at least to the people we were aiming at. I remember for example we were looking at Paals Packpressen Georgsmarienhütte, a company that was later sold to GMM, or Orlando as they are known today. I was there at Paals Packpressen and it was impossible to explain to the entrepreneur that we would be a good solution for his company. Meanwhile, the guys from GMM came along and told this family that they had a German entrepreneurial approach and so on. 3i clearly needed a

more customised, less institutionalised, less foreign solution. In other words, they needed a German solution.[68]

3i was also increasingly committed to ventures in Germany, as Miran Khan recalls:

> 3i made a significant strategic move in 1997 reducing the focus on the smaller German Mittelstand business. They bought Technologie Holding, and expanded into venture capital. I think for anyone who looks at the German market, and knows the landscape of the companies, it is easy to say from today's perspective that it was a mistake to go that way. But it was definitely a mistake to leave the focus on the succession problems aside.
>
> That was one of the main reasons for me to leave 3i. 3i had a pearl in the German Mittelstand. I don't understand why they didn't exploit it. If anyone in Europe had long-term experience of private equity, then it was 3i. If 3i had been focussed on the German Mittelstand with a more national strategy, today it would have an unbeatable position.[69]

By the turn of the mid-1990s, therefore, 3i was moving in a different direction to most private equity players in the market. Far from having come to the conclusion that buyouts were the most profitable niche in the market, 3i had decided to switch focus from buyouts back towards venture capital. This was a strategy which would yield good results in the short-term, but was later to cost the organisation dearly.

CVC

A Managing Director of CVC London since 1987 and fluent in German, Steve Koltes was the obvious choice for a move to Frankfurt in 1991 to pick up from Max Römer, who together with his team had left as head of CVC Germany to join CWB. Koltes, an American who first moved to Europe in 1983, had learned German as an exchange student in Braunschweig. He married a Swiss German.

Koltes had mixed views about taking over the German operation, as he later explained:

> The positive was that we could get control of CVC's activities in Germany. From London we had been actively working to integrate

Citicorp's European private equity investing activities into one business. Max and his team had always worked somewhat independently, for instance, reporting into Citicorp Germany rather than CVC and having their own local investment committee. The negative was that Max's team had been effective, a rare quality in the German private equity community at the time, so losing them was initially a blow.

We didn't know much about the portfolio at the outset. There were a handful of investments: Sachtler (professional camera tripods), Mikron (microprocessors), Heckler (cold-formed metal parts), Progen (biogenetic pharma products), Baümler (men's clothing) and UHU (consumer adhesives), the latter two having been done shortly before the team left.[70]

One of Koltes's first decisions was to integrate the new CVC Frankfurt into the rest of CVC Europe. This turned out to be relatively simple, as Koltes recalls:

At the time Günther Rexroth was head of Citicorp in Germany, and we had a very friendly relationship. He was a politician turned banker. Joachim Faber, now a member of the Allianz Vorstand and then head of Citicorp's German investment banking activities, was also on the investment committee. Faber understood the basics of buyout investment, but had his focus elsewhere. So we arranged things in a way that allowed German deals to be moved to our European investment committee in London, while I undertook to keep people in Citicorp Germany informed.[71]

Despite a host of apparent challenges, starting with having to rebuild the team from scratch, Koltes succeeded in doing his first German deal quickly, closing Ortopedia, Germany's largest manufacturer of wheelchairs and mobility devices, in September 1991. The company had been sold by its US owner, Invacare.

Koltes settled in quickly, bringing his family to Frankfurt in April 1991. He took stock of the market and was quite surprised by what he saw:

It was a lot different than I expected. The general attitude towards finance and banking was very negative. People were biased toward the "real" economy and were quite sceptical about the role and value of private equity investing and for that matter any form of finance. They did not really understand what we did and assumed it was a turnaround or venture activity. The idea that we would want to buy majority control of a good business and make it better was totally alien. How would we make it better? Where were the synergies? How can you evaluate a business if you are not experts in the sector? So we were put into the "banker" category and left to pick up orphan businesses that attracted little or no interest from trade buyers. Overall M&A activity was limited anyway. It was made up mainly of foreign companies buying and selling their German subsidiaries. German sellers were rare. For Germans then, selling a business was considered an admission of failure.

I don't think the Matuschka implosion in the early 1990s had much of an impact on us because the business they were doing was not on our radar screen. The Lignotock fall-out was much more visible and damaging. Indeed, Lignotock's problems had knock-on effects for Mercedes and BMW, and I think the Lignotock mess helped augment the prevailing antipathy towards financial investors.

Also different was the lack of deal infrastructure. When I was working in London in the 1980s, some law firms operated 24/7, with perky receptionists answering the phones at 4:00 a.m. In Frankfurt there was nothing of the kind. Law firms were traditional and local in approach. Accounting firms had great tax advisers who participated in the passionate sport of minimising company taxes, but their local due diligence teams were often thin and dominated by a bookkeeping mentality that showed little grasp of the underlying businesses. The M&A world was dominated by small boutique brokers. The first class-act investment banker I can recall in Frankfurt was Paul Achleitner, then with Goldman Sachs and subsequently CFO of Allianz. Paul and his small team advised us when we sold Ortopedia in what was Goldman's first ever German-to-German sale. Market consultants were corporate-focussed and due diligence accountants needed to be imported from London.

The quality of managers was generally poor. Most were not very international and had had little exposure to the basic measures of value creation. You tended to find three types of manager. First, there were the "corporate administrators" who managed businesses within conglomerates or large groups. They were usually uninspiring, although you could be positively surprised from time to time. The second group were the "entrepreneurs": managers who either owned their own businesses or flitted from one to another. They could be excellent managers in a family setting, but were too intuitive to work closely with the analytical approach of a private equity investor. Lastly, you had the "internationals", a small group of well-educated and internationally-experienced Germans coming out of the big multinationals like Unilever, Mars and Smithkline Beecham. Often they had acted as autonomous general managers for a country operation – Australia, for example, and gained valuable experience in all aspects of management and in calling the shots without interference. These were good managers to work with.[72]

Only a year after the change of team in Germany, CVC achieved its spin-off from Citigroup. The partners, including Koltes, bought their management company, at a point when CVC had five offices in Europe (UK, France, Germany, Netherlands, and Italy). The process was made easier by the fact that the team had already raised a third party fund, EuropEnterprise, in 1990. Citicorp continued to commit capital to CVC's deals.

Koltes's next major deal, in 1993, was to come from neighbouring Austria. This came to market through an auction run by Dietrich Becker, then at Merrill Lynch. The sellers were the Rothenberger brothers. Koltes liked the CEO:

Austria Haustechnik was run by a very dynamic German woman, Almut Graefe. She showed great stamina in assuming responsibility for a company that was one of the single largest employers in that relatively undeveloped part of the Austrian Steiermark. Singlehandedly, she used this base to revolutionise the European freezer market for food retailers by convincing them to adopt her "plug-in" version instead of the vastly more expensive but traditional centralised system offered by Linde and others. No one thought it was possible, but she took market share from 1% to 20% based solely on her determination and persuasive skills.[73]

Like Schroder Ventures, CVC had succeeded in replacing its management team in Germany, and re-launched itself successfully on the market. The biggest challenge for CVC was that none of the previous German team remained (Schroders effectively had not only Thomas Krenz but also the support of Robert Osterrieth), and Koltes was faced therefore not only with the task of finding new deals for the firm in Germany, but also with managing the existing portfolio.

Barings Capital

The catastrophic Lignotock deal was the worst possible start for Barings in its German market entry strategy. In many ways it is surprising that Barings continued trying after bloodying its nose so badly. Jens Reidel was given the task of relaunching, but with a difficult starting point given the fall-out over the Lignotock affair.

Reidel was born in 1951, and grew up in the Frankfurt-Mannheim area. He spent most of his schooldays in a boarding school, which in Germany was an unusual choice, and spent a year-and-a-half in San Diego, staying as an exchange student, and finishing his high school studies. Reidel's first job back in Germany was with Beiersdorf. He recalls:

> I was probably lucky because everyone else went to marketing and sales, while I joined the organisation division. Before I started, the CFO gave me a call to say that they had just acquired a big company and didn't have anyone around to do the integration. Was I willing to do it? Of course I jumped at the chance, and that's how I spent my first two years, drowning most of the time.[74]

In 1986, Reidel was sent to Kansas in the US to run one of the Beiersdorf companies. It was here that he first became attracted to private equity. He later recalled:

> It was the year of Nabisco. I knew of private equity, it was there, and I had friends who were bankers and consultants, who were always talking about these management buyouts, and made it seem interesting. I got a little virus over there not really knowing what it was all about.[75]

Returning to Germany, Reidel was put in charge of overall Beiersdorf planning, controlling, and business strategy. This brought him into contact with strategy consulting. Reidel explains:

> We called in Boston Consulting for a complete strategic review. This took thirty consultants two years, so you can imagine how big the

job was. The managing director of BCG at that time, Burckhardt Witte, was heavily involved in the exercise. He was my age, he had been thirteen years with BCG, while I had been thirteen years with Beiersdorf, and we spent a lot of time together, talking about all sorts of things.

On one of those occasions, after a couple of bottles of red wine, we detected that we both had the private equity virus. So in 1990, he left BCG, and I left Beiersdorf, and we rented an apartment in Munich, hired a secretary, and bought some furniture, to start our own little private equity fund. We called it MTH, Munich Trust Holding.[76]

Despite a promising start, Reidel and Witte's venture was short-lived.

Our set-up was a bit like IMM, which also had people like Hans Albrecht from Boston Consulting. We were hoping to get our money from several people, but mainly one guy in Switzerland, who then unfortunately died at the age of 49, before he had signed our contract. We managed to get some money from Paribas, and a few Dutch families. During this time we worked on a transaction where we invited Barings Capital as coinvestors, and I got to meet John Burgess.[77]

Detecting that Reidel was not happy with his own set-up, Burgess asked Reidel to join Barings, to re-boot their operation in Germany. Reidel signed an agreement with Barings in October 1991, and joined officially on 1st April 1992. Reidel soon moved the Barings Capital office from Munich to Hamburg, his preferred place to live.

Reidel had crossed paths with Mathias Gräper, who was working with Thomas Matzen at Schroders, and the original idea was that Gräper would join Reidel at Barings immediately. In the event, Gräper didn't join for another year and a half, making Stefan Zuschke the second member of the new team, after he left Equimark.

The first target of the new Barings team was a company focussed on baggage scanning machinery, which was owned at the time by a large German conglomerate. Despite getting close to the seller, it proved impossible to get him comfortable with private equity money. Jens Reidel explains:

In the end he didn't want to sell to us because he kept asking "can you really prove where your money is coming from, can you prove it is not really coming from drug money?"[78]

It took until 1994 for the Barings team to close its first deal, when the team acquired Tierschmidt, an apparel company. By this time patience was already running thin. Reidel was driven to compare notes with other members of the industry. He recalls:

> I spent some time chatting with the Apax guys with Halusa and Hinderer, discussing how on earth we were going to get things going.[79]

The Tierschmidt deal broke the Barings duck, and took the new team through the ropes of how to get an MBO completed. They lacked buyout models, even a computer, and had to bring in Arthur Andersen to redress some of their in-house deficiencies. But at least the new Barings team had got a deal over the finishing line.

Morgan Stanley

One of the early fly-in teams from London to do a deal in Germany was led by Chris Peisch, an American, who married his German wife in 1984. He was responsible for European private equity at Morgan Stanley, and became disillusioned with the UK market in the late 1980s, and was looking for new pastures on the continent. Peisch recalls:

> Partly due to intellectual interest, and partly due to frustration with the deal flow in the UK, I started to spend more time on the Continent in 1989 and 1990. In the winter of 1990, I had a marketing call with Frankfurt Consult, the M&A arm of BHF Bank, and I was shown a company with sales of DM 80–90 million, which produced pre-assembled truck body kits. It was called Cargo Van, and it was based in the Pfalz, an hour and a half south of Frankfurt. It was being sold in an auction, in so far as that existed in those days.

> The sellers were a group of local investors and management, and included a couple of truck body distributors, one of which had a distribution contract for these Cargo Van kits in Italy. It was a fairly eclectic investor group, about twenty percent of the shares were held by the management, who were interested in reinvesting and did. We showed an interest, and I started to work hard on it. My boss in New York said it was OK to pursue, although a few tens of million dollars was a pretty small investment for a $2.5 billion fund. He took the view that it would at least print us a ticket, get us a name, and help us learn about the market. From this perspective, the small

size of that investment probably helped. If it blew up, then it was better that it wasn't $200 million.

I got support from New York with the deal. I think we competed with Steve Koltes at CVC, and von Meibom at Pallas, who had Wolfgang Bensel working on it. Neither 3i nor Schroders were in on the deal. The only other bidder was also based in London, but looking at German deals, the Sutton Group, led by Peter Lampl, with mezzanine support from Martin Stringfellow at Kleinwort Benson.[80]

Peisch closed his first German deal successfully in September 1990. He moved to Germany during the economic recession which hit the UK in the early 1990s. His move had involved a lot of debate.

A big discussion point at Morgan Stanley was whether I could cover Germany from London. There were a lot of successful investment bankers that had done this. Many were staying in London because

Figure 10.2   Chris Peisch

their wives had said no to moving out of London. But the German private equity market in 1992 was in its early stages of development. It was thin, and completely small cap to maybe mid-cap. If you're doing the big cap deals, you can live anywhere in the world, but if you're doing the smaller stuff you're going to be dealing with clients and owners, people for whom there will always be a benefit of functionality in the local language, and demonstrating that you live here.[81]

Peisch looked at DoDuCo, which was being sold by the Thurn & Taxis foundation, but after consideration decided against it. The pickings were thin, as Peisch recalls:

1992 and 1993 were years of looking and doing no deals. The pressure was building up, but then the German market began to slide in 1992–93. The reunification boom died. There had been overbuilding. Then there was the whole cost crisis discussion, particularly about labour costs. It was the first time people began to look at the cracks in the German system. People looked at the way the country was put together economically, at the way companies were run. It was clear that the wage bills were out of whack. There was a period of horrible press on Germany in the international Wall Street Journal and the FT. Every other day there was an article on the German cost crisis. There were hundreds of German companies slipping into losses.

Some of my colleagues, including my boss, were reading the WSJ on the way to work, and saying "Gee, do I want to invest in that part of the world right now?" So the few deals I was generating were getting a pretty cool reception in New York, and another issue emerging was that the market was remaining very low to mid-cap in size.[82]

Chris Peisch left Morgan Stanley in May 1994 to raise his own fund: German Equity Partners.

Investcorp

Investcorp's approach to doing deals in Germany was in many respects very similar to that of CWB/Doughty Hanson. Sitting on a large fund, Investcorp was only interested in large deals. Almost by definition, therefore, this meant that the initial interest in Germany was limited: Germany lacked large deals. The London team had hired Johannes

Huth in 1990, but he was chosen because of his qualifications, not because he was German.

Johannes Huth was born in 1960 in Heidelberg, and went to school in Frankfurt. He spent a year in his late teens studying in Paris in preparation for entry to the Science Po, but changed his mind on finishing and went to study at the L.S.E. instead. He graduated in 1984, and feeling he was neither finished with his studies, nor ready to work, decided to enrol on an MBA course at the University of Chicago. He chose Chicago mainly because it took students without work experience. After finishing his MBA, he was recruited by Salomon Brothers, and went to work in their international department in New York. After little more than a year, Dan Tyrie asked Huth to join him in setting up an M&A department in London.

Despite difficult timing, the pair moved to London just before the October 1987 crash. The Salomon M&A department grew rapidly, and by 1990, Huth was getting headhunter calls, one of which was for a job at Investcorp. Huth was attracted by the idea of becoming a principal, having worked in investment banking for five years.

The London Investcorp team numbered nine, and had done the Gucci deal on the continent, but not taken much interest in Germany. Huth met early on with Robert Osterrieth to discuss a potential acquisition of Hein Gericke, but these talks came to nothing.

Two years after Huth's move to Investcorp, the London team acquired Mondi, a fashion retailer, but without involving their only German team-member. This lack of concern with the nationality of team-members was to continue through-out Investcorp's engagement with Germany. A deal-team was as likely to be led by a Frenchman as a German. As if to confirm this approach, in 1994, Ebel, a Swiss watch company was acquired, again without Huth's involvement.

Investcorp reached the mid-1990s having made a significant name for itself within the German-speaking region, working with a multinational team from London. The early success of this model was to imprint itself on Investcorp's strategy for the late 1990s and 2000s: i.e. to remain based in London, and staff deals with professionals of different nationalities irrespective of the country and language group of the target. Inevitably, this strategy prevented to a degree Investcorp from being viewed as a "German" player. It also made it likely that it would go up the deal-size ladder, as smaller deals typically required more local presence than large ones.

LBO France/Vector

After his short experience with Bessemer-Metzler, Eberhard Crain was determined to continue with a career in private equity. Through Herr Sachse, a lawyer contact, Crain was put in touch with Jean-Daniel Camus of LBO France, who together with Renato Mazzoleni and Gilles Cahen-Salvador were looking for a German angle. Mazzoleni and Cahen-Salvador had set up LBO France in 1985, focussed principally on investments in France and Italy. Camus had joined them later, having graduated from ENA in 1971, and having worked for both the French Ministry of Finance, and the President of the French Republic. Crain remembers his first meeting with Camus:

> I met Camus at the office of Herr Sachse in Frankfurt. He was a very elegant and nice guy. He told me that when they had told their investors they wanted to go to Germany, they had shown no interest. They simply wanted them to stick with France and Italy. But they had convinced them to be allowed to try at least something. I told him that I was keen on being an independent entrepreneur. He said fine, but who would give me money? At the time, I wasn't sure. So he said they could give me a guarantee for two million, on the basis of which I could go to BHF Bank and borrow two million to set up a private equity General Partner-

Figure 10.3   Eberhard Crain

ship in Germany. They had a €600 million fund which I could draw upon, but they weren't prepared to give me any of their 2% management fee.[83]

Crain liked the prospects of having high levels of independence under the arrangement, even if the financial terms were challenging. The Paris team wanted Crain's company to be given the name LBO Germany, but as a demonstration of his independence, Crain chose instead to call it Vector:

> The reason why it is called Vector is because Jean-Daniel was calling me up, together with his lawyer to encourage me to finalising our arrangement. I hadn't chosen a name for my company at that point. The lawyer working for Camus got impatient and asked me where I was standing. I said I was on Avenue Victor Hugo. So the lawyer suggested Vector as a name, simply on the basis of where I had been standing at the time.[84]

Crain needed support, and in the summer of 1991 called Wolfgang Behrens-Ramberg, a close colleague he had worked with at Thurn & Taxis, asking him to join him in his venture. Behrens-Ramberg agreed, and the two proceeded to set up shop in Frankfurt, as Crain recollects:

> I always wanted to have an elegant office, and elegant cars. We found a white villa on the corner of Wilhelm Hasse Strasse.[85]

One of the first deals Crain and Behrens-Ramberg looked at was Cargo Van, which Chris Peisch was selling from Morgan Stanley:

> We liked the company, and would have bought it. We knew about the cyclicality, and saw the main challenge as being to keep the management. My brother in law had been involved in a similar company, and the whole management had walked out and set up in competition. But the fact that Cargo Van had a French subsidiary gave us a French connection which was a slight advantage, particularly when we were visiting the French plant. We lost on price, because we simply didn't offer enough. Plus Hammermann at Deutsche Handelsbank had some former connections with the company which gave him an advantage.[86]

Having failed to secure Cargo Van, the Vector team started looking at Temco, a small machine manufacturer focussed upon synthetic fibres owned by FAG Kugelfischer. The mother company was going through the process of restructuring and needed to sell some subsidiaries to raise cash. Again, personal chemistry was to play a major role in the outcome, as Crain explains:

> We got that deal because the president of the company took snuff, and when we first met, sitting down at a table, he was taking his snuff, and I asked if I could have some too. That was the moment I won. There were not too many competitors at the time: 3i, CVC, and CWB. It was a very tight market.[87]

The process of securing Temco took almost a year and a half, and the deal was finally closed in December 1993.

Vector's next deal came served on a plate, and took very little time to complete. Crain remembers the day Kruse & Meinert, one of Germany's largest kitchen furniture manufacturers, was presented to him:

> Wolfgang Alvano, who at the time was an M&A broker, called me up and said he had a company we could buy on the condition that we paid a 2% commission, double the normal amount. Obviously I asked him why, but he said he couldn't explain, but if I was willing to sign, he would let me know the details. The facts of the matter were that the CWB team in Frankfurt had already signed the deal, and completed all their due diligence, but had been prevented from closing the investment. The reason was that the London team had already acquired an English kitchen furniture manufacturer which had subsequently gone bankrupt. CWB Frankfurt had settled all the financing before their English colleagues said no. That was a critical factor in Max Römer's team splitting off to form Quadriga.
>
> So we agreed to pay the 1% of fees which covered CWB's due diligence and costs, plus the 1% for Alvano.[88]

Vector closed Kruse & Meinert in 1994, giving LBO France its second significant transaction in Germany.

Cinven/Thomas CJ Matzen

Only a few months elapsed before the estranged ex-Schroders team in Hamburg found a source of capital. Thomas Matzen's path crossed with Andrew Marchant's, an investment executive working for Cinven.

Marchant knew Matzen from Schroders. A graduate of Exeter University, Marchant had left Schroders to join Cinven in 1988. Cinven was established in 1977 as the "in-house" private equity manager for the British Coal Pension Funds, and subsequently, took on responsibility for managing the private equity investment allocations of two additional pension funds, the Railways Pension Schemes in 1988, and the Barclays Bank Pension Fund in 1990.[89]

Cinven was looking for partners on the Continent, and Matzen's team seemed an ideal fit. Matzen was able to negotiate a favourable partnership arrangement with Cinven and receiving a 20% by deal carry in return for an exclusive relationship, as he explains:

> The structure was pretty special, because we got a 30% investment stake in the companies acquired, 10% of which we were putting up ourselves. The 30% applied to the voting rights too.[90]

The Cinven team were quite prepared to travel to Germany, to work with Matzen's team which was unusual, as typically it was the Germans flying to London for regular meetings rather than vice-versa at the time.

Armed with the new partnership arrangement, Matzen's team was able to close those initial deals which he had been preparing. One of these was Richard Schöpps in 1992, which Matzen agreed to acquire from Schroders.

> When we acquired Schöpps we invested a lot in the shops, renovating them to keep up with the competition, and took the chain up to 135 stores in Austria.[91]

In the same year, Matzen found the opportunity to buy Respo Mode International AG, a manufacturer of fashion clothing for women.

A year later in 1993, two more acquisitions were made, Koelbel Group, focussed on fitness-training equipment, and PPS Group, a supplier of services to professional photographers. The final investment of the Cinven/Thomas CJ Matzen partnership was made in 1994, with the acquisition of A&S Bäder. But once again, the Hamburg team was confronted by problems with their London partner, as Matzen recalls:

> The end of our relationship with Cinven came at the very moment when the decision was taken that they should buy themselves out from the National Coal Board. They informed me that based on the new situation they couldn't afford our original structure. Their

investors insisted on a change, to comply with the standard terms acceptable to investors. We said we couldn't do that. So they asked us to dispose of the companies that had been acquired together, which I think was pretty sad.[92]

The relationship reached a crossroads in 1995 when Cinven was subject to a privatisation process. The basis of its contractual relationship with its clients moved to a mandate for direct investing in larger buyouts. This prevented them from sustaining coinvestment arrangements in respect of any new investments.

Although some investments offered potential upside, the performance of the portfolio from the Cinven perspective was mixed and coupled with the change of strategic focus, Cinven decided that it would be optimal for the existing portfolio to be realised in an orderly manner.

Cinven's change of strategy led to an orderly disposal of the seven companies over the period from June 1995 to June 1998. Out of the seven investments which were made, five were realised at less than cost. In three of these instances, Cinven sold their interests to Matzen having taken the decision not to participate in the financing round.[93] Matzen did not always agree with Cinven's decision.

I think the best example of this was Köhler & Krenze Fashion AG. I told them it didn't make any sense to dispose of this company, because at that time we would get a very low price. They said that this didn't matter, we had to dispose of it. So we decided to buy the business ourselves. We brought in some external offers, such as from Barings, who made a good offer, but then Cinven said that they couldn't sell to our team because it was against their standards. We discussed this for quite a while, until we found a solution. We allowed the manager to take a 51% stake, and based on that, we got permission to buy 49%. So we really made the manager a rich man, and about a year later we took the company public and made about three-four times our money.[94]

Inevitably, the Matzen team ended up buying most of the other companies from Cinven, including PPS Group, A&S Bäder, and Richard Schöpps AG, the Austrian retailer which had been acquired from Schroders.

The partnership faltered partly because of a change to Cinven's own structure and partly because the financial backing which Cinven afforded to Matzen during this period was not replaced by any other institution.

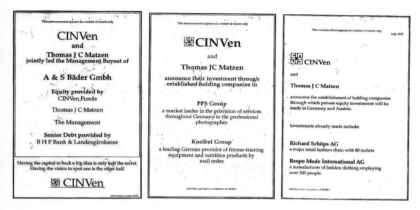

Figure 10.4 Tombstones for Cinven & Thomas CJ Matzen in Germany

Matzen's model with Cinven, was an unusual one. He provided Cinven with a partner in Germany as a substitute to Cinven opening its own office in the region. This was similar to the approach Eberhard Crain adopted with LBO France. The few examples of this model, however, would suggest that for both parties the arrangement tends to be temporary. If the partnership succeeds, the international player prefers to set up its own operation in the region, and if it fails, the international player will either look for an alternative partner, set up its own operation, or exit the region altogether. Cinven opened its own office in Frankfurt in 1999.

DBAG

The team at DBAG, which included the remnants of the old DBG and WFG, under the leadership of Karl-Heinz Fanselow, was still focussed at the beginning of the 1990s on minorities, and was not a player in the majority buyout market. The only buyout DBAG had supported was for Wallace & Tiernan, done jointly with Harvest, the US private equity group in 1989. DBAG's stake had been kept to a minority by virtue of co-investing with Harvest and management. Even in this case, the initiative for the buyout came from Harvest, as André Magnin explains:

An important factor in DBAG coming to consider buyouts and majorities was when the group became the largest investor in the Harvest partners fund in the late 1980s. The investment was made principally so that DBAG could exchange knowhow with the American team. We were allowed to send our guys over there, so that they could pick up the Anglo-Saxon way of doing business.[95]

Given that DBAG was still investing from an evergreen fund, based on a listed company, for tax reasons it was not able to buy majorities at the time. But the stimulus for change came from a growing concern that minorities were no longer the sensible way forward, as André Mangin explains:

> It was around the mid 1990s that DBAG realised that its minorities weren't running smoothly, over which it had no control. They also realised that the deals they were doing were a bit too small, which meant that in many cases the companies were only active in one or two products, which meant that they were very exposed to competition and market fluctuations. This encouraged a rethink on focus.[96]

Jens Tonn, who had recently joined the DBG from the Deutsche Handelsbank, recalls a formal review of the strengths and weaknesses of the business:

> They had a strategic review done by Roland Berger in 1995 which found that DBG/DBAG had made most of its money in majority stakes, and so called leveraged build-ups. This included their investment in IMM at the time. They were also invested in Harvest. It turned out that those people who did majorities and build-ups were bolder and more successful than those doing the core DBG/DBAG minority investments in the German Mittelstand. Indeed the core business was not very profitable, and it was very difficult to do anything with minorities, because the old owner was always influencing decisions. The Roland Berger study recognised that we couldn't exactly exit our core business, because that was what Deutsche expected us to do. Indeed Deutsche didn't really want us to do leveraged buyouts. But the report did recommend that we do bigger deals, in fewer sectors such that expertise could be established, and that we could gain control, like IMM had been doing.[97]

The investment which caused DBAG the biggest problems at the time was Balsam, a company making floor coverings for sport halls. Unfortunately for DBAG, and many other providers of finance, manufacturing floors for sport halls was only a part of what the management of Balsam were really doing. In a spectacular fraud which had been running for many years, management were issuing false invoices on real projects for anything up to 66 times the real value, and sending them to a factoring company, Procedo, which provided them with cash in advance of the project's completion. The Balsam management used the funds raised in this way to speculate on the foreign exchange and stock markets. This behaviour passed unnoticed by everyone in the financial community. It was not until December 2002, when a former Balsam employee put together a folder of documents exposing the fraud and posted it to the public prosecutors office in Bielefeld, the tax authorities, *Der Spiegel, manager magazin*, and the Verein Business Crime Control in Frankfurt, that the fraud was eventually exposed.[98] Indeed, the informant's whistle-blowing actions were initially ignored, and it took many attempts before the information produced any reaction. Karl-Heinz Wallmeier, a member of the criminal police force, on being included in the recipients of the information, gave up his holiday to travel to France to check the validity of the evidence provided. Despite clear evidence of fraud, and additional information being provided by other former Balsam employees, it took the entrepreneurial detective one-and-a-half years to persuade the Bielefeld public prosecutor's office that there was a case for prosecution. The trial of the management, and the exposure of the fraud, pushed Balsam into insolvency, leaving DM 2 billion in liabilities, the bulk of which was borne by the banks and finance providers. Fortunately for the management of DBAG, Raimund König was in the process of selling IMM to Triumph-Adler, which gave them the opportunity to realise their investment to partially compensate for the complete loss on Balsam, as König recalls:

In doing the Triumph-Adler transaction, we lost DBG, who had been co-investing in IMM from the start. They sold their stake in the IMM II fund vehicle and all of their 10% stakes in our industry holdings, and made a lot of money. It was the year when DBG had the big Balsam scandal, and DBG lost a lot. So DBG needed to make up for these losses, and through the tremendous profits they made on IMM, you don't see these losses from Balsam on their balance sheets of the period.[99]

The process of reorientation was to take considerable time at DBAG however. Even its regional structure, which 3i was about to mimic, was of the type that would support small deals, as Jens Tonn recalls:

DBG was a big team at the time, with something like 60-80 professionals, with offices in Berlin, Frankfurt, Hamburg, Munich, and Stuttgart. But it was difficult to switch this infrastructure away from the core business. I remember situations where we got ourselves into some perfect positions with targets, and then Steve Koltes or Michael Phillips would turn up. You could see that the Anglo-Saxons were taking over.[100]

Minority investments continued at DBAG throughout the mid-1990s, and it was not until 1997 that the next buyout was made.

Bain & Company – The Matuschka Portfolio

Having overcome the transition challenges of becoming a true partnership, the consultants at Bain were in a position to carve out a new role in the emerging German private equity landscape. The opportunity to manage the Matuschka portfolio literally came out of the blue. Fritz Seikowsky, who became head of the Munich office of Bain in 1993, later recalled:

A friend of mind from the HypoBank, an investor in MatCap, called me and said that all of the Limiteds were extremely dissatisfied with the performance of Matuschka, and that he was happy to propose Bain as one of the alternatives to the current GP. This was in 1991. We were put into a beauty contest against Goldman, Kleinwort Benson, and Lehman Brothers.[101]

The investment banks and Bain were offering rival approaches, as Detlef Dinsel explains:

Basically there were two parties: on the one hand there were the investment banks offering to do a fire-sale, in which they would kick all the participations out, and on the other there was a consulting company, Bain, offering to do value added services work on the portfolio, and keep in there for two to three years.[102]

Fritz Seikowsky recalls the show down between the two parties:

The pitches were made in London and New York. The banks behind Matuschka had to decide simultaneously, with a 100%

consent, whether to take-over the keys and who to give them to. Romney, Tornquist and I did the pitch. Romney just sat there, and did not say much, but being the highly respected co-founder of Bain Capital his personal endorsement for us was palpable. We probably wouldn't have won the pitch without him.[103]

Peter Tornquist, who led the pitch with Seikowsky, also held similar memories:

I can recall the presentation very vividly, as it was a day-trip from Europe, and we had rehearsed over and over again, and also got input from Mitt. The key European investors, who we had already won over, were also supporting and pushing for Bain.[104]

The Matuschka investor-base was impressive, as Tornquist recalls:

There were actually two investor groups that were separated, and needed different pitches and dialogues, although in the end they coordinated. Both of them had a lot of the "who's who" in investors

Figure 10.5   Finding a New Home for the MatCap Portfolio

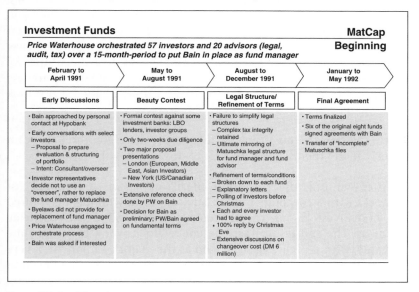

Source: Ekkehard Franzke

at the time. In retrospect, it was amazing to see the quality of the investor group Matuschka assembled to invest in his fund. The North American pool had names like Met Life, IBM Pension Fund, as well as some of the well-known pension savers. The other group was the European and Asian investors, which included investors such as GIC Singapore, Prudential UK, and some Dutch funds.

A key deciding factor for why Bain won was that the investors saw an opportunity to gain a substantial premium over the firesale value the investment banks had pitched. The option value, even though it would take some years longer to achieve, was attractive enough for them to vote for Bain, as it also involved little extra work for them, and the compensation structure for Bain was highly geared to success.[105]

The beauty contest organised by the investors was itself something of a last resort. Many of the private equity houses had already been approached with the offer to manage the Matuschka portfolio. But not a single house was interested, as Thomas Krenz recalls:

> We looked at it, but in the first place, we could not make the model work because of the conflict of interest with Schroder's existing investors. There were uncontrolled minority positions, structures you could not unwind because the vendor still had a say in what you wanted to do. There were businesses that from our point of view had no strategic place to go. So after looking at the whole thing, we realised we would have to be paid a really big amount of money, because from our point of view, this portfolio really did not look attractive.[106]

Having beaten the investment banks to the mandate, the Bain team quickly found themselves with a lot to do, as Seikowsky recalls:

> After winning the "beauty contest" we spent and fought for weeks with a corporate finance advisory firm, who had been hired by the investors, over the right compensation and incentive scheme for us. The end result was a decent retainer over a four-year time frame, with a declining scale, and as the major component, a very handsome success fee for the returns to investors over and beyond the "fire-sale value" of the portfolio with an aggressive increasing scale. Simply put: the more value we created and realised, the more

we got. The important constraints were: no fresh money was available, and no re-investment of realised proceeds was possible.

What followed thereafter was an administrative nightmare in that the entire Matuschka fund structure had to be dissolved and, at the same time, replaced by a new structure of offshore Bain entities, exactly mirroring the original set-up in order not to threaten the tax optimisation structure and system that had been developed by Pöllath and Partner.[107]

For the Bain consultants involved on Matuschka, however, the new assignment was a welcome change from the work they had been doing. Clemens Beickler, who at the time was a consultant on Bain's MatCap team, later recalled:

> When Matuschka came along, it was an exciting change. This was something completely different: an opportunity to put the entrepreneurial spirit of the Bain team into action. Bain put quite a large team on the project. The first phase was taking stock to understand how we could add value to the companies. The next question was how to sell them off. There was never any question of making any extra acquisitions. There were only two ways to get out. One was to wait and try to improve the business, and the second was to sell it off fast.[108]

Bain began its assignment with a two-week assessment of the assets, the task being to establish its own fire-sale value. Next on the agenda was to determine the additional value that could be available, and the cost of achieving it. Seikowsky recalls:

> We basically analysed in more depth than was possible before, what the value enhancement potential in Deutschmark terms for each company was, and what the required effort would be in manpower terms to get there. Having reviewed the portfolio, we then developed our exit strategy, which was to sell the hopeless cases first, and "invest" in the few potential winners for the profitable endgame. For example, Brause was close to bankruptcy, and as we had no money to invest, we handed over the keys to the banks just before we would have had to file for insolvency. On the other side of the spectrum, we were confident that with operational improvements, an improved economic climate, and clever exit tactics, we could achieve nice returns on Weiss, Bahner, and Rational.[109]

Figure 10.6   The MatCap Portfolio of Companies

Investment Funds					MatCap
The investments represented a very diversified lot – **MatCap Portfolio of Companies**					
both in industry direction and geographically					
Overview of Portfolio Companies – 1993 Status					
Company	Business description	Equity held by funds* in %	Sales in DM/ M	EBIT in DM/ M	Employees
Brause	Office supplies distributor	75%	30	2.0	400
BFM/SGHB	A diversified holding company; interests in building, automotive supplier, video, sporting goods, fashion	Redacted	Redacted	Redacted	Redacted
Rational	Manufacture of steam ovens for food preparation at professional kitchens	Redacted	Redacted	Redacted	Redacted
MSP/Statomat	Design and manufacture of equipment for the production of stators for electic motors	Redacted	Redacted	Redacted	Redacted
KBHV	Design and production of high quality cloth consisting of wool and wool mixtures of men's and ladies' wear	Redacted	Redacted	Redacted	Redacted
BMC/STUBA	Ownership and operating of nursing homes and related businesses, including property	Redacted	Redacted	Redacted	Redacted
Weiss Tex	Provision of laundry and washing services for hospitals and large commercial customers; finishing of textiles	Redacted	Redacted	Redacted	Redacted

* Six fund advised by Bain & Comapany (out of eight)
Source: Preliminary 1993 financial statements, company
  estimates, quarterly report December 31, 1993

Source: Ekkehard Franzke

Within a short space of time, Brause was sold off to Clairefontaine, a large French company, for a small consideration.

Bain quickly found the task much more difficult than expected. Many of the companies were still run by managers who had previously owned them, and in some cases, the Matuschka stake was only a minority. Detlef Dinsel recalls his initial experience:

I became one of the two managers working on the portfolio, together with Roman Zeller. We split up the companies between us. I was given Statomat and Weiss among the companies under my supervision.

We started off with a hand-over meeting with Norbert Stelzer. It lasted about two hours, and we were shown a room full of files. He told us a bit about the various managers. Then he got up to go, and said "Goodbye". I couldn't believe he was going already, but he had already left Matuschka, and was doing this meeting on his own time.

It was clear that Matuschka had made a structural mistake, and that they hadn't understood what they were doing, buying companies, with very little equity, in the hope that they could then sell them on again to new investors. These weren't buyouts in the management sense.

What we underestimated from the start were the covenant issues. We missed the fact that these companies were basically over-leveraged, and the banks were so nervous that they gave us little room for manouvere.

The next problem was that the managements were not particularly cooperative. At Weiss Tex, for example, the owner manager held a blocking minority stake in the company, and he was super annoyed about the situation in which he found himself. He had sold his company to Matuschka, and got a nice price. But he wasn't only interested in the money. Within Miltenberg, the small town he lived in, he was an important man, and now that the company he was managing, and which bore his name, was in deep difficulties, with the local bank making these problems very visible locally, he was deeply dissatisfied about what had happened. When I showed up, he didn't differentiate between me, and my Matuschka predecessors. It took some time for him to understand that the mess had not been my responsibility. But then he began to see that there was an opportunity to get his company back. He had no incentive to help us, there was no alignment of interests. We hadn't given him any sort of incentive programme. Instead he was going to sit it out and watch for an opportunity to take back the ownership of his company.

Then on top of that we had the challenge that a recession was starting. Statomat went into crisis because machine tools were hit first.[110]

Beickler recalls his first experiences with the companies:

The former owners were tough and had a "Mittelstands-mentality". It took some time and effort to earn their respect.[111]

Seikowsky recognised that the challenges of running the portfolio required an additional skill-set and outside support, and sought help from a variety of lawyers, tax advisers, and accountants. One of the most influential of the outsiders brought in to help was an American accountant. Clemens Beickler recalls the role played by David Giauque:

He was a highly qualified fund manager, who was instrumental in optimising particularly the administrative handling of the Matuschka portfolio. He was a CPA and had a lot of M&A experience. Bain realised that in the management of a fund, you needed to have a profound knowledge about legal issues, reporting, all the formal ways to administer the different societies and investors, etc. Bain set up an organisation to achieve all this.[112]

The Bain team found that putting together a mix of skills and know-how from their own management consultants and other professional service providers was crucial to the successful handling of the Matuschka portfolio. Nevertheless, while Bain could support the companies in making operational improvements, they were still dependent upon management being willing to follow their advice.

The remainder of the portfolio, after the exit from Brause, was a very mixed bag. Seikowsky recalls:

Bahner was about nursing homes in Berlin. This was really two businesses, a nursing home, and a retirement home. The first was subsidised by the government, the second was subject to the free market. There was even a third element, the real estate. We made a very nice return for the investors on Bahner. Also on the high end was Weiss

Figure 10.7   The Bain & Company Structure for Managing the MatCap Portfolio

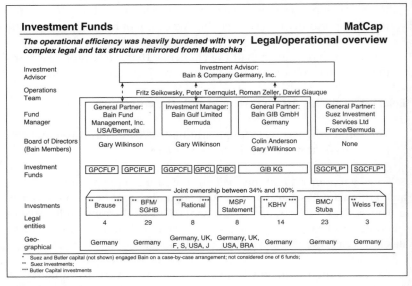

Source: Ekkehard Franzke

Tex, which stonewashed jeans. The big problem with this business was that it had only one client, Levis. But this too we sold for a good price. And last but not least there was the one jewel in the portfolio, Rational Grossküchen, unfortunately a minority position. It took a lot of armtwisting, to get the majority shareholders to agree to a deal.[113]

Bain's challenge in selling off the businesses was not made easier by the onset of the post-reunification recession. This transformed some companies that had been growing profitably during the immediate post-reunification boom into restructuring cases. Consequently, selling off the remaining companies was a difficult job that took until 1997. Detlef Dinsel recalls the key events:

> We ended up selling the laundry to the son of the previous owner and two private investors. Statomat was saved by the banks. But it was Rational which saved the whole fund. Management bought the company out, together with the banks, and took it onto the stock market. It was an incredible success.[114]

Peter Tornquist later took stock of Bain's experience with the Matuschka portfolio:

> In the end, the investors made the right decision, as they received a significant premium over the firesale value, and for Bain also the economics were attractive. Bain learned a lot about the practical aspects of value creation in real life, and it helped with our marketing to be able to say "been there, done that, seen that" which is hard to put a dollar value on, but it's big.[115]

Fritz Seikowsky's take on the experience was similar:

> We increased the return to the investors two-and-a-half fold, compared to the fire-sale approach as proposed by the other bidders for the task. The investors were highly satisfied with the results and gave us plenty of references. MatCap was a very difficult job, but a big success, as measured from the starting point when we took it on. In the internal Bain rankings, it was amongst the most profitable of Bain's assignments world-wide.
>
> The quality of our work on MatCap formed the basis for the creation of Bain's highly successful and profitable private equity consulting and

co-investment business in the nineties, and provided us with a unique positioning in the consulting marketplace.

Also, it gave us, for years to come, a strong story for the recruitment of superb young talent to Bain against our core competitors. MatCap was the "proof of concept" of a differentiated and unique approach to consulting.[116]

In short, Bain's learning experience on managing the Matuschka portfolio was a tough one, but nevertheless the goals set in their initial pitch to investors had been achieved, and skills had been acquired which were to serve the team well later on in the marketplace.

Lessons from experience

By the end of the 1992–1994 period, the German private equity industry had begun to take shape (17 firms are given coverage during this period within these pages alone). The pattern that was to reinforce itself over the years had established itself: the majority of the private equity houses opened offices in Germany, while a minority continued to operate from London. In many respects, the addition of so many new houses caused the supply of private equity to exceed demand.

Among the players, there remained differences of approach. IMM continued its industrial concept strategy, building up divisions devoted to particular industries. Schroders, however, became more interested in larger spin-offs, which lent themselves less readily to the buy-and-build approach. 3i moved more decisively in the direction of buyouts, taking advantage of the increased number of players to co-invest with, while Apax began as a venture capital player, only to conclude by 1994 that buyouts were the only hope for the future.

The tax benefits behind deal making were no longer as favourable as in the 1980s, and the emphasis upon value creation was far more upon financial engineering and operational improvements in the business. Fortunately for the private equity houses, most of the 1992–1994 period saw the fruits of the domestic boom caused by German reunification. Given that in many other countries the early 1990s were a period of recession, the post-reunification boom was an added attraction for Germany. Part of the initial interest, as the next chapter describes, was around the creation of the Treuhand, and the expectation of deals to be done in East Germany. But, on the whole, the deal flow of the period was disappointing, both in volume and quality.

11
East German Adventures

The Treuhand

From the start of the 1990s, the Treuhand and reunification of Germany dominated much of the M&A agenda. But even before the establishment of the Treuhand, Count Matuschka campaigned to encourage a completely different approach to the privatisation of the DDR's assets, as he explains:

> Kohl appointed a number of people to give him advice on how to handle the privatisation process, and I was one of them. I developed the coupon programme, which would have helped to enrich the East German managements and employees of these companies, and given them a stake in the development of their businesses. But in the end, our government did the reverse. In eastern Germany, out of a peasant paradise, we created an unemployment paradise. We left those people without equity, and instead gave a DM 1,200 billion subsidy to West German companies to take them over. I was not alone in speaking out against this. Karl Otto Pohl of the Bundesbank for instance expressed a similar opinion. So there were those who made an open stand against this approach. Instead, huge subsidies were spent helping West German investors put capital intensive businesses into East Germany, which in the case of Bitterfeld meant an investment of DM 14 million for every place of work preserved at the site.[1]

The Treuhand was established on 17th June 1990 by the Volkskammer, the East German parliament, and was given responsibility for privatising 8,500 companies with some four million employees. For a time, it was the world's largest enterprise. But its approach of rapidly preparing companies for sale to Western investors, which included wide-scale lay-offs within its portfolio companies, drew criticism from many quarters.

Detlev Karsten Rohwedder, the first Chairman of the Treuhand, was murdered on 1st April 1991, possibly by the Red Army Faction. This intervention of the domestic terrorist organisation followed a pattern. Alfred Herrhausen, the Chairman of the Deutsche Bank, had been assassinated by means of a roadside bomb on 30th November 1989. The targeting of senior industrialists had begun in the Red Army Faction's "German Autumn" when on 30th July 1977, Jürgen Ponto, the Chairman of the Dresdner Bank had been shot and killed in front of his house. The decline of the Soviet Union in the late 1980s was a blow to left-wing groups, and their new victims included Ernst Zimmerman, the CEO of MTU on 1st February 1985, and Karl-Heinz Beckurts, Head of R&D at Siemens and key man on the Board of TVM on 9th July 1986. Matuschka later lamented:

> I don't have an axe to grind. This is just history. But the point is that in Germany innovation is a very difficult thing. You would never have thought, for example, that my friend Beckurts from Siemens, and all those other people, such as my friends Rohwedder, Ponto, and Herrhausen, all got killed. Why were they targeted? The fact is that those revolutionaries were very smart. They killed people who understood that the system had to change, and who were capable of making it happen. The revolutionaries didn't go after billionaires who had money. No, they went after the smartest people who understood that change was needed. This is typical of Germany. Rohwedder, for instance, was our one chance to change something at the Treuhand. But they killed him before he had the chance.[2]

Despite the inducements, private equity houses sustained little interest in what the Treuhand had to sell. On the whole, the companies available lacked viability without a strategic partner, and indeed it was West German companies that took over most of the Treuhand's assets. A few private equity houses were to venture east, but most of them burnt their fingers. Those that did dabble in buying Treuhand companies did so either because they had specifically set out with this mission, or because they were frustrated by the lack of decent deals available in the West.

The Treuhand played a major role in improving the German business community's understanding of the M&A function within investment banks. This had long been lacking. It also helped Goldman Sachs gain its first significant foothold in Germany, as Daniel Schmitz recalls:

> The breakthrough for Goldman was the mandate Paul Achleitner won from the Treuhand. It was the first real evidence in the public eye of why an M&A adviser might be useful. Up until then, the attitude tended to be: "I have a handshake with the buying CEO, now our lawyers and accountants can figure out the details" This changed after the Treuhand had some considerable success, notably in the privatisation of the East German utility industry. Before Goldman got involved, this was basically a done deal, distributing the utilities among West German incumbents for little or no value. Goldman was awarded the mandate for this work and said "we are doing an auction." This meant that the West German utility companies ended up buying the East German assets on completely different terms, saving the tax payer billions and causing people to rethink their prejudices about what M&A advisers can bring to the party.[3]

Hans-Dieter von Meibom also saw the major change in German M&A as having been brought about by the Treuhand:

> In the 1970s and mid 1980s, it was not just that no German family or corporation would sell something to a private equity house, it was that nobody would sell their business to anyone. To sell anything in Germany was a sign of weakness. It was against the German ethics or culture to sell a company like merchandise.
>
> The big change came in the early 1990s when the Treuhand in Berlin had to sell hundreds of East German companies. All of a sudden the big investment banking institutions sent people to support the Treuhand in selling many of their businesses. This helped the investment banks prove themselves, develop networks, open new branches, and continue on from there. After the dissolution of the Treuhand, all those people had nothing else to do but to find out which West German companies might be prepared to sell some of their businesses. M&A activity in Germany went up tremendously from that point in time.[4]

Fresh from having left Matuschka, Norbert Stelzer gained the support of some investors and Credit Suisse to set up a new private equity fund dedicated to East German investments. But having hired a team, and opened an office, Credit Suisse and Stelzer decided to pull the plug before a single investment was made. Stelzer recalls:

> The fact was that we found out very quickly that the only thing you didn't need in East Germany was money, and the only thing you did need was management, which most private equity funds didn't have.[5]

Advent International

Norbert Stelzer was not the only former associate of the Matuschka Group whose thoughts turned to setting up a new private equity house, and looking at the opportunities in East Germany. Indeed, the collapse of Matuschka unleashed a generation of professionals to take up positions throughout the German M&A scene, which was at the time dominated by the Treuhand. It was the first and largest M&A/private equity alumni imaginable of its time.

Peter Brooke, who had played an important role in internationalising the Matuschka Group's venture capital and leveraged buyouts exposure, decided quickly to pursue his own course in the region. He had also in the meantime decided to split off from TA Associates. Peter Brooke explains how this happened:

> It became obvious in 1983 and 1984 that I had more of an interest in globalizing TA Associates than did my partners. I remember at the end of one year after we had raised a lot of money and the income was high that my partners said, "Well, how much money are you going to take out of our pockets and spend on advancing the company in Europe and Asia?" And I said, "Well, probably $1 million." There was a deathly silence. I knew then and there that if I was going to build a global company, I had to do it outside the profit-and-loss statement of the partnership; it had to be done in a separate company that was self-financing. That's when I arranged for the capitalisation of Advent International and negotiated with my partners the trans-ferral of the international program from TA Associates into Advent International.[6]

Much has been written and spoken of about why TA Associates and Advent International split. One part of the explanation is certainly the different geographical focus of US versus Europe and Asia. But another explanation is over short-term versus longer-term approaches to making money, as Kevin Landry who remained behind to run TA Associates explains:

> Peter had a vision, and it was a long-term vision. It was just something he wanted to do. Peter was less interested in making money than I am. I've always been amazed that people would give me capital to manage. I came from a family that didn't have capital. For someone to trust their capital to me is an incredible compliment and an incredible responsibility, which I've accepted. I just love making people money. I get a kick out of succeeding that way. Peter marched to a different drummer – he had a vision, and he wanted to see it succeed.
>
> My team looked at that in the mid-1980s and said: "We've got a lot of money to manage here. We've got our hands full with lots of responsibilities and opportunities. We don't believe in that dream." We were correct for the next five to ten years. We were correct in the short term. Peter was correct in the long term.[7]

Brooke began with an affiliate approach to developing his global network, supported by an International Network Fund (INF), but by the late 1980s began to feel that this did not give him the quality control he needed. He later recalled:

> What we really needed was US-style due diligence. We were not getting the return on the International Network Fund that I wanted. So in 1990, we established our first office in London to coordinate our affiliates and to build a direct investment organisation. I sent Doug Brown over to run that office. He established and executed a strategy for us, opening offices in Milan and Frankfurt.[8]

Doug Brown, an American with a Harvard MBA, played a leading role in establishing Advent's presence in Germany. Through a head-hunting contract with Spencer Stuart he came across Chris Neizert, who had been working since 1983 at Bankers Trust. After a series of senior departures from the Bankers Trust Frankfurt team, most notably former TVM founder Uwe Burkheiser, Neizert was looking for a new opportunity. Neizert joined Advent in January 1991, and was entrusted with establishing an office. Neizert recalls:

> I had a friend at the time who was running Hauck consultants in Frankfurt. They were trying to enter corporate finance and private

equity at the time. They later bought Jagd und Sport Waffen Suhl, in Thüringen. There were two guys, Johannes Rosendahl und Ulrich Gerlein running the Hauck office, and they had an office on the 5th floor of an old house in Niedernstrasse. They gave me a desk in their office. It didn't cost me anything. A little while later, I got an office at the Westendplatz in Frankfurt and in October 1991 made my first hire in the form of Ralf Huep.[9]

Neizert and Huep began building up a network of intermediaries, industrialists, consultants, accountants and lawyers. Deal-flow was still limited, and their hope was that they could source deals via proprietary routes, as Neizert later recalled:

> In 1992 we did two deals. Our first transaction was TG Chemie, a Bremen based manufacturer of clinical chemicals, which had been going through a succession upheaval. We got it through Angermann in Hamburg.[10]

Seeing the opening up of Eastern Germany by the Treuhand, Neizert and Huep were one of the few teams to look for privatisation opportunities. Neizert explains:

> The first Eastern adventure was a brick factory that we bought in Mecklenburg Vorpommern, near Lauenburg. It was actually a brick factory that had been shut down. Malitz was its name. It was a brick-works with a large clay pit and a business plan that had been prepared by an engineer from Hamburg, an old-timer who had experience and planning. He had identified the opportunity. He wanted an equity partner. We liked the idea of construction, bricks, and buildings. We had to tear down the old factory and build a new plant from scratch, and had quite some trouble making it work. There was always some white stuff on the bricks, they should be truly red, but there was always something.
>
> Everything took longer than expected. At some point we thought the money might be running out. Then the Treuhand discovered that they had sold us something that did not belong to them. It turned out that about half of the claypit, which had reserves for 700 years, didn't belong to us. That hardly made any difference to us, because a hundred years of clay was enough. But the Treuhand

gave us half the purchase price back. That money came in very useful. It meant that we could finish the plant.

By the time it was all up and running, and we had built up a distribution structure, Boral, a large Australian construction materials company came in and wanted to buy it. The business was sold six weeks before the outbreak of the German construction industry crisis. We got out just in time.[11]

Neizert's initial success in East Germany, although it had been a close call selling just before the collapse in the construction market, inspired him to look for more opportunities in the region.

The next acquisition from the Treuhand was Thuringer Behälterglass, a manufacturer of container glass. The process was far from smooth, as Neizert explains:

Buying that business was a big adventure because the local Treuhand manager had met an Indian fellow during his vacation, and they had become friends. Subsequently, the Treuhand manager tried to sell that business to his Indian friend for a few cents. So in the first round we lost against this Indian, although we had offered money, whereas the Indian hadn't, and we had presented a concept, and again the Indian hadn't. So we had some good contacts in the Treuhand and decided it would be worthwhile to complain. Once we had done so, the Treuhand reopened the process, but again we lost, even though we had made a better offer. But we didn't give up. This time we went to the Bundestagsbeauftragte für die Treuhand and complained officially, and they opened the process a third time. In this round we finally won.

By this time, the company had been through years of due diligence and every competitor in the glass container business had taken a look at it. The company had been due diligenced to death. All the customer relationships had been stolen by western companies, who wanted to kill that competitor in Thuringia.[12]

Hardly had they taken the company over than an accident occurred in the plant, in which a big tank collapsed spilling molten glass over the floor and into the basement. Fortunately, no-one was harmed, but this material had to be drilled out before work could begin again. Despite the overwhelming challenges, Advent managed to turn the Thuringer company around, making the investment a successful one.

Neizert's biggest success at Advent was his purchase of Deutsche Wagonbau (DWA), the East German company producing railway rolling stock. Peter Brooke explains the background:

> At DWA, the Treuhand stepped in and undertook a restructuring that shut down three plants and reduced the number of employees from twenty-five thousand to about seven thousand. The dramatically downsized company put up a valiant effort to survive. While the East Germans had no experience running a business in a market economy, they had excellent skilled labour, including well-trained engineers who were used to improvising. They wanted the company to succeed, and managed in just a few years to dramatically change their product portfolio, developing double-decker railcars and smaller cars for regional trains that were innovative and low cost. On the strength of this effort, they landed a few major supply contracts with Deutsche Bahn, the German national railway system.[13]

In 1994, the Advent team had acquired Dowald Werke, a small rail vehicle supplier in Bremen from the former owner of TG Chemie. The company specialised in making door systems for the ICE. Overnight, Advent had established credibility in rail equipment supply. Neizert explains:

> In early 1994 we were approached by Trinkhaus & Burkhardt because they had heard that we knew something about rolling stock. They said they wanted to bring us together with Herr von Rauchitsch at the Treuhand because he had something for sale in that sector, and that was Deutsche Wagonbau.[14]

L.E.K. had been hired to support the Treuhand in selling Deutsche Wagonbau, having originally conducted a buy-side commercial due diligence of the company for an earlier bidder. The Treuhand had been using JP Morgan to assist with the sales process, but decided to substitute them with the strategy consultants who had spent considerable time working on the asset. This was L.E.K.'s first sell-side mandate in Germany, and the team-members sat in on all the meetings with bidders, and evaluated the bids that were made. Brooke recalls what he learnt about the early process:

> It turned out that thirty-nine bidders had already looked at the company and either passed on the opportunity after seeing the due

diligence results or failed to agree on terms with the Treuhand. The asking price was only about 28 percent of the revenue generated the previous year but was also roughly equal to the negative earnings before interest, taxes, depreciation, and amortisation (EBITDA) for that year. The company was haemorrhaging cash – about $100 million annually – and was a disaster. A small group of West German executives had recently joined DWA and were transferring necessary commercial know-how. But when our people looked at the numbers and the considerable uncertainties the company faced, the situation did not look promising.[15]

The final bidders included Begemann, Berliner Elektro, Siemens, and Vossloh. Neizert recalls:

We saw the presentations from L.E.K. At the time we had to put together a business plan, which McKinsey had helped us on. We had not used strategy consultants before and they did a good job, as they knew the sector and had already done some work on Deutsche Wagonbau. We were bidder 39. It was a company which had 25,000 employees in the late 1980s. When we came they still had 7,000, and by the time we sold they were down to 3,500. The company had been mainly providing the Comecon block with rail cars. After the empire crumbled, while the Russians changed their economic system and East Germany became part of a new united Germany, orders for rail cars slowed down to a trickle. As a result Deutsche Wagonbau had to find ways to survive by building products for Deutsche Bahn. The French market was closed. The company was making triple digit losses when we came in.[16]

Brooke describes the process by which Neizert put together the deal:

In a long series of conversations with officials from the Treuhand and with DWA's new CEO, Chris developed the level of confidence necessary for the long process of drawing up a restructuring plan and selling it to the various constituencies involved. Chris brought an initial plan to Doug Brown, who said that although there might be something here worth pursuing, the restructuring plan needed to be more detailed and have better cost figures. So Chris, Doug, and another Advent team member, the resourceful John Walker, spent a tremendous amount of time hammering out a restructuring plan that would reduce DWA's head count from seven thousand to three thousand employees and close two more plants. The only problem was what it was going to cost to do it. Doug finally told Chris; "I'm sorry, but even if the government gave us the company for nothing, we can't put this much money into it." It looked like that was the end of the deal.

Chris Neizert wasn't ready to give up, however. He went back to the Treuhand, showed them the restructuring plan, and convinced them to put up the money it would take to restructure the business. Advent offered to buy the company at less than 10 percent of the original asking price and split the profit from the eventual sale 50/50 with the government. It took a full year to convince the German federal government, regional and local politicians, the unions, and key decision makers in German industry to accept our plan, but in the end they agreed to it.

When Advent acquired DWA in 1995, we were lucky to be able to persuade Otto Wolff von Amerongen, whom Helmut Kohl had asked to become the chairman of the company after reunification, to stay on in that post. Whenever delicate issues arose, Wolff (who made a name for himself in postwar Germany by opening up trade relations between West Germany and the Soviet Union) was able to make a few calls to the right people. Both Wolff and DWA's CEO, Peter Witt, worked well with Chris and the rest of the Advent team.[17]

Advent signed the Deutsche Wagonbau deal in 1995, and finally closed the transaction in 1996. They were judged by the Treuhand to have prepared the best bid, and Begemann was the only other party that remained in the race to the end, Berliner Elektro, Siemens, and Vossloh all having withdrawn their bids.

Some aspects of the way in which the deal was transacted in Frankfurt was still to clash with the approach Peter Brooke was advocating. Brooke himself later explained the approach he wanted the Europeans to emulate:

Our affiliates in Europe were inclined to do business the way merchant banks still do business in that part of the world. When they get a deal, they subcontract the accounting work and the management and marketing studies to outside vendors, gather the data, do some analysis, and then decide whether they're going to do the deal. That's not the way we do our business. Our people dig into all of the data on their own. We spend a tremendous amount of time training our people how to do in-depth due diligence, how to do the appropriate kind of checks with suppliers and customers. We use outside sources but we conduct a lot of market surveys ourselves. We do a tremendous amount of background checking on the management team. This is a method that was not known in Europe when we opened our first office. It's getting better known now.[18]

The acquisition of Deutsche Wagonbau, which was to generate the biggest capital gain for Advent in eight years, concluded Advent's engagement with the Treuhand. Peter Brooke commented proudly on the deal:

The largest investment we've made was in the privatisation of an East German company that manufactured railway cars. We sold that out to Bombardier for fifteen times cost, for cash, earlier this year.[19]

Berenberg and Fleming/Deutschland Investment Corporation

East Germany was also attracting other funds into the region. Robert Fleming, the UK investment bank, teamed up with Berenberg Bank in Hamburg, to establish a fund, Deutschland Investment Corporation (DIC), targeted at buying East German companies. The fund was the brainchild of Roddie (Rodderick) Fleming and Leonard Ingrams of Flemings and Claus Budelmann of Berenberg. Their initial target had been to raise DM 250 million, but once the Kuwait crisis hit, their fund-raising stalled at DM 110 million. Budelmann turned for help in finding a team to run the fund to Andreas Odefey, Berenberg's head of M&A. Odefey later recalled:

These chaps raised the money and then looked around. They had DM 110 million, which was nice, but who was going to manage it? So they came along to me and said, "Andreas you know a lot about wheeling and dealing. Why don't you do the job?" So I told them that there was another guy in Berenberg, Max Drechsel, who had been on a training programme at Fleming. I said why not give him the chance?[20]

Max Drechsel, who had been working at Berenberg since 1986 and just completed a secondment at Flemings in London, agreed in 1991

Table 11.1 Private Equity Transactions in 1994

1994

Company	Buyer	Seller	Exit year	Sold to
A&S Bäder GmbH	Cinven/Thomas JC Matzen	Family	1995	Thomas JC Matzen
Augsburger Aktienbank	Harald Quandt (Equita)	Previous Investors	Not yet divested	Not yet divested
Bragard	IMM (Workwear Clothing)	Family	1997	Quelle
Brahms Diagnostica	Alpha	Family	2000	HBM Partners
Carl Schenck AG	Harald Quandt (Equita)	Family	1999	Dürr AG
Certec (Burton-Werke GmbH)	Schroder Ventures	Burton	1999	SocGen Private Equity
Deutsche Waggonbau AG	Advent	Treuhand	1997	Bombardier
Dowald-Rollen Beteiligungs	Advent	Family	1996	Deutsche Waggonbau AG
Dressel GmbH	Halder	Family	1999	Management
Ebel	Investcorp	Family	1999	LVMH Moet Hennessy Louis Vuitton SA
Erich Jaeger GmbH	Halder	Family	1999	US strategic buyer
Glashütter Uhrenbetrieb GmbH	Aureus Private Equity	Treuhand	2000	Swatch Group AG
Goetz + Müller	Atco/ABN Amro	Family	Not yet divested	Not yet divested
Heyne & Penke	Hans-Peter Penke-Wevelhoff	Heller	Not yet divested	Not yet divested
IMM Office Systems	Triumph-Adler (Office)	Alco	Not yet divested	Not yet divested
IMM portfolio	Triumph-Adler	IMM	Not yet divested	Not yet divested
Jadog	Insolvency	3i/Candover/Metzler	Not yet divested	Not yet divested
JCK Holding GmbH Textil KG	Global Equity Partners/UIAG	Family	Not yet divested	Not yet divested
Kässbohrer Geländefahrzeug	Schroder Ventures	Karl Kässbohrer Fahrzeugwerk	1998	IPO
KMH Industrie Service Holding GmbH	Nord Holding	Capital increase	2007	KMH Partners GmbH
Kruse & Meinert	Vector/LBO France	Family	1997	IPO
Küpper Weisser	Schroder Ventures	Private individuals	2000	Corporate buyer
MJ Media Werbe	Advent	Family	1996	FiWo Plastik GmbH

Table 11.1 Private Equity Transactions in 1994 – *continued*

1994

Company	Buyer	Seller	Exit year	Sold to
MobilCom Holding GmbH	Hannover Finanz/3i	Family	1997	IPO
NGI Norma Goerz GmbH	Trade sale	Global Equity Partners/UIAG	Not yet divested	Not yet divested
Offset Gerhard Kaiser GmbH	Nord Holding	Family	2002	Alpha
Passport Fashion Group	3i/IBG GmbH/BHF	Gunter Speidel (Founder)	2004	BHF Private Equity
Sachtler	Strategic buyer	CVC/BdW	Not yet divested	Not yet divested
Schukraft	Halder	Family	1996	Insolvency
SOTEC/OMT	Schroder Ventures	Family	1997	Merged into Singulus
Sound und Technik	Management	Equimark	2006	Insolvency
Sporting Dress, Gütersloh	IMM (MHM Mode Holding)	Family	1997	IPO
Tarkett	CWB Capital Partners	Stora AB	1995	IPO
Thuringer	Advent	Treuhand	1998	GTH Glastechnik Holding
Tierschmidt Apparel	Barings Capital	Family	1998	Bayerische Landesbank
TA Triumph-Adler AG	IMM (reverse take-over)	Olivetti	Not yet divested	Not yet divested
UTT	IKB	Family	2003	BPE Private Equity
Visolux Elektronik GmbH & Co.	Harald Quandt (Equita)	Family	1998	Pepperl + Fuchs
Walter Schuhversand	IMM (Workwear Clothing)	Family	1997	Quelle

Source: Authors' compilation

to run the joint venture, DIC, while Odefey joined James Nicholson of Robert Fleming on the Investment Committee. The mandate to invest in East Germany quickly turned out to be a poisoned chalice. Odefey later explained:

This was a terrible experience, because we were forced to invest in East Germany, a non capitalist country. We invested in a chain of petrol stations, which was a disaster. We invested in a tile factory that was terrible. On one we lost around 50 percent of our investment, and on the other we lost completely.[21]

Drechsel had the first-hand experience:

These two horrible investments were my post-graduate education. I was deputy chairman of Boizenburger Fliesen, a company which had 1800 employees initially, and which we cut down to 350, and eventually turned around. The second investment, Autodorado, was a complete write off.[22]

In the event, only DM 10 million of the original DM 110 million was invested in East German companies, and Drechsel together with Odefey insisted that the focus of the fund be changed. Odefey explains:

We turned round and said that what we were doing didn't generate returns. There were no entrepreneurs. The market might be nice but most companies simply had to be shut down. So I said let's step out and do West German investments instead. The investors agreed, which was a relief.[23]

Out of the ashes of the Deutschland Investment Corporation, FBG (Fleming Berenberg Gossler) was born. Once the strategy had been changed to a focus on West German investments, Wolgang Bensel joined the team, moving over from Pallas. Wolgang Bensel recalls:

They had raised DM 110 million during the hype of reunification, and had already made two deals in East Germany before I joined them. Fortunately, it wasn't more than two deals. It was Boizenburger Fliesen, a tile manufacturer in Boizenburg, about 50 kilometers from Hamburg, and Autodorado, a chain of gas stations, which was about to go down the pan, but hadn't quite reached that point yet.[24]

Wolgang Bensel started his new job by winding down Autodorado, the chain of gas stations, which DIC had already acquired.

From the remaining DM 100 million, FBG did seven deals, most as lead investor but together with co-investors. The first of these was done with 3i and Alpha. Bensel recalls:

> The first investment was in Brahms Diagnostica in 1994. We never disclosed how much was invested in that.[25]

FBG, and its successor Electra Fleming, lead investments in 1&1 (renamed United Internet), an internet telecom company (jointly with 3i and Halder), Heim & Haus, which made and sold window blinds, SHK, a company in heating and airconditioning which was built by a buy-and-build strategy, Kamps (an Apax deal in which FBG took a small position), and WAP. Only SHK was a failure. Odefey remembers:

> These were small deals in companies with about DM 50–80 million in sales. Normally the debt to equity ratio was two thirds to one third. What was good in those days was that the tax structure allowed you to choose which depreciation method you felt was favourable. Even if you were only able to make the most of tax advantages you got a good deal. If you could keep cash-flows stable, you could easily make 3–4 times your money.[26]

In 1996, Max Drechsel left the team to join HSBC Private Equity in Dusseldorf, and FBG looked for fresh blood, quickly found in the form of Christof Tiefenbacher, an old friend of Odefey. Odefey explains:

> Tiefenbacher and I both grew up in the East of Hamburg. We played hockey and tennis together. Our parents were very close. We knew each other well, and at the time Drechsel left, Tiefenbacher was with IMM in Munich, running a wholesale business for office supplies, which he had created in Leipzig. So I gave him a call, and said, Christof, you've been with BCG, and you've travelled the world, and now you're building this small business in Leipzig. Why don't you become an entrepreneur. He said that he was already an entrepreneur.

So I told him that he should become a famous entrepreneur, by joining FBG. He joined FBG, and it became a wonderful cooperation between Wolgang Bensel, Christof Tiefenbacher, and Mathias Turwitt. Turwitt was the first man to be hired by Drechsel and Bensel.[27]

Shortly after Max Drechsel left, Philipp Amereller put in a stint as an intern at FBG. At his interview he was asked to estimate bread consumption in Germany, an exercise relevant to the Kamps deal, closed by Apax, in which a small piece of the equity went to FBG. His internship was the first step towards Amereller joining, as he later explained:

> After that, I worked for them as a freelancer while I was doing my studies. They were interested in hiring me, but had to wait until they had settled the transition from FBG to Electra Fleming.[28]

The deal concluding FBG's conversion to Electra Fleming closed in 1997, shortly after Fleming bought itself into Electra Kingsway, which was itself a sizable private equity business. Odefey explains:

> The guys from Electra turned up and said they wanted to invest more money in deals. The sorts of sum we had been investing, in the DM 5 million range, didn't make sense for them. We said that we didn't want to become a big player, but wanted to stay in the German Mittelstand. So we asked them to make us an offer for our 50 percent stake in the joint management company, and that's what they did. So Electra bought us out of the joint venture, which was renamed Electra Fleming.[29]

Up until 1997, the team was using the original DIC funds. From 1997 onwards, the money came from Electra. The first deal to use Electra funds was WAP Alto Group, a company making floor cleaning equipment, and the second and last deal was Deutsche Woolworth, which closed in 1998. Bensel remembers that the due diligence process on this last much larger deal, had become more professional:

> We used BCG for the commercial due diligence on Woolworths. But everything was still on a smaller scale than was to come later.[30]

Amereller, who by this point held a permanent position, also recalls the disappointments of the deal:

> Everything the management told us, the opposite happened.[31]

LGV[32] took a minority stake in Woolworths, as Mark Elborn explains:

> We had been bidding for Woolworths, and we came to an agreement that whoever won would give a slice to the other. So LGV took a minority after the deal was closed. It was never the strongest business, and the market moved away from the company. The main logic of the deal was the enormous perceived downside protection offered by the property, which was worth more than the company. We all told ourselves that if things didn't work out, we would always have the property. The reality was that Woolworths continually lost ground, and if it hadn't been for the property, it would have gone bust. They had a lot of prime sites, which were very expensive, but it had the wrong format.[33]

Amereller also remembers the difficult days on the German retailer:

> From the start onwards, none of the budgets were ever achieved. We were lucky in a way that the first year was goodish. We had significant working capital improvements, and we managed to repay the acquisition within 18 months. That was the good news. Afterwards the remaining debt was only mortgages with no covenants to breach and this meant that things got less disciplined. The other problem was the structural changes within Electra which were happening at the time.[34]

The end of the road for the Hamburg team came once Electra in the UK became the object of a hostile take-over bid from 3i. Overnight, the sole focus of Electra management became one of fending off the unsolicited offer, and no-one had any bandwidth to think of doing new deals. Bensel recalls:

> It was at that point that the three of us developed the idea of spinning off and raising our own fund. We had a good track record in fund raising, and thought it would be plain sailing. But by 2000, investors had come to consider internet deals to be more attractive. They were no longer interested in the old economy. We were still fund-raising by

2001, when many investors lost most of their money in the dotcom collapse. It was much more difficult than we had expected.[35]

EGIT – East German Investment Trust

The challenges that Odefey and Drechsel faced with their Deutschland Investment Corporation nevertheless appear relatively minor when compared to the tortuous experience of EGIT, the fund raised by Olav Ermgassen for a similar purpose.

Olav Ermgassen was born in Schleswig Holstein in 1946, the son of a refugee family from Pomerania and Silesia. He attended school in Hanover, and did his 11th grade at an American high school in Michigan. After completing his military service, Ermgassen studied law, and finished his education at INSEAD in 1977. He then moved to the US to pursue a career in investment banking, working for JP Morgan. Ermgassen returned to Europe joining the energy project finance group within JP Morgan's London office, before moving to Morgan Guaranty, then JP Morgan's investment banking arm, and in 1984, put in a stint at their Japanese office. In 1986 he joined Morgan Stanley as head of their German-speaking region corporate finance business. He founded and was the first managing director of Morgan Stanley's Frankfurt office. In 1988 he started his own corporate finance firm which was immediately joined by several professionals from JP Morgan and Morgan Stanley.

A few months later, shortly after the Berlin wall came down, Ermgassen received a call from the West German Ministry of Finance, asking for his advisory support at the Treuhand. After a year-and-a-half advising the privatisation agency, Ermgassen decided to raise a DM 200 million fund (later increased to DM 350 million), sourced from a range of international pension and insurance companies, dedicated to buying companies in East Germany. The fund was christened EGIT, or the East German Investment Trust.

The fund had a competent and very prominent board, chaired by Rudolph Escherich, former CEO of VIAG and VAW and chairman of DSL Bank. Other well known members were the former EU commissioner Sir (now Lord) Christopher Tugendhat and the former Kleinwort Benson chairman and then Scottish Widows chairman Colin Black. Head of the management team was Walter Zinsser, who as Chief Investment Officer of JP Morgan's International Fund Management operation had been probably one of the world's largest and most successful international equity managers.

Ermgassen recalls:

> Walter Zinsser was a prize catch: he was experienced and well res-
> pected in the industry. He also thought this was a once in a lifetime
> opportunity to really make a difference. He said that he had spent
> most of his professional life making rich people even richer. Now
> there was a chance to do something for those who, having been left
> behind the Iron Curtain, had been less lucky than us. It was just
> after 1991, and since he knew the market very well, Zinsser found
> a lot of investments and invested the money reasonably fast. We
> were investing at that time in a portfolio that was very much real
> estate related. It was a good mix of things, including companies in
> the construction industry.[36]

EGIT was instrumental in the set-up of n-tv, Germany's first 24 hour
news service, for which Zinser found Ted Turner's CNN as co-investor.
EGIT funded and became co-investor with Hubert Schrodinger's Lein-
felder Group in the buyout from the Treuhand's largest paper group,
Schwedt Papier und Karton, which it turned into a green investment
by sourcing only from recycled paper. Its largest investment was in
MBS, Märkische Baustoff-Service GmbH, the concrete company which
had been making most of the panels for the Berlin wall, and still had
the forms to prove it. Together with the BKK-Investment fund (a joint
venture between the Berliner Bank and the Kuwait Investment Office),
EGIT also invested in Haushaltsgeräte-Service HGS Holding GmbH, a
seller, installer, and ongoing service provider of household white-goods.
This investment turned into a disaster for the fund. After having become
one of the Treuhand's most important customers, the EGIT and its investment in HGS fell under the spotlight of hostile press attention, and matters
quickly spiralled out of control. Ermgassen recalls:

> This fund turned out to be the biggest mistake of my life. We were
> very good, I think, in selecting and managing the portfolio. It was very
> professional, and we spent a lot of time on it. But then ultimately, we
> got a very bad press because there was an article in *Der Spiegel* mag-
> azine in April 1993 that said we had insider knowledge on HGS and
> that we didn't have enough money to put further liquidity into EGIT's
> investments.[37]

The article in *Der Spiegel*, entitled "Against every rule", claimed that the
Treuhand had begun a legal process against EGIT, the fund having failed

to honour its obligations. The *Spiegel* article also suggested that EGIT had run out of money, and far from being in a position to acquire additional companies, lacked the liquidity to finance those already acquired. *Der Spiegel* alleged that:

> The fund has in the meantime acquired more than 20 companies, among which are the Märkische Baustoff-Service (MBS) and the Haushaltsgeräte-Service HGS Holding GmbH. The Treuhand would have been happy to sell more companies to Ermgassen's trust, but now it would appear that the big investor doesn't even have enough money to administer the empire it has already acquired.[38]

Another criticism made of EGIT was that it was extracting more money for the companies out of the Treuhand to compensate the losses they were making and that EGIT was also raising money from the sale of real estate. *Der Spiegel* commented:

> The Treuhand has already had to provide the DM 25 million that was urgently required by the EGIT-owned company Märkische Baustoff-Service. The privatisation agency, which had placed its blind faith in its biggest client, took over the liability for DM 50 million.

> Ermgassen is attempting to burden the Treuhand with a further DM 25 million, which would be used to clear the debts of MBS, a holding company of five building materials companies, which would otherwise fall insolvent. Some three hundred jobs would be lost in such an instance.

> The Treuhand is not standing idly by while the previously highly valued client pursues extortion tactics. On the 12th March 1993, the Treuhand began a court battle against the EGIT-owned company MBS.

> "All in all, we are concerned not to throw good money after bad", the Treuhand commented in one of its documents.[39]

Ermgassen was accused of having "promised too much". EGIT's board and management simply did not understand what was happening to them. By its statute, EGIT was only a minority investor and therefore did not have full control of its investee companies. Furthermore, the MBS investment had a serious legal defect: the Treuhand had discovered a so-called foundation error, which meant the ownership of the company was still with the Treuhand. It had actually never been privatised. Ermgassen explained what he later discovered to be the real reason behind the frontal attack on his fund:

> It took a long time to discover the motivation behind the article. We fought for those companies, and I really spent a lot of time in our business looking after the portfolio. I'm an honourable person. So we told the privatisation agency that they could have everything back that we had bought from them for the fund. Rudolf Escherich, who was the Chairman of our fund and one of the most competent, nicest and most honourable business leaders in Germany promptly resigned and died. For my part, I also ultimately thought "I'm going to get killed here", and because I now was seen to have a personal vendetta against the privatisation agency, I decided I was probably a handicap to the business. So I too stepped out. I think our business was destroyed deliberately.

> Before Dr. Escherich's and my departure from the fund, EGIT hired Kroll Associates, a company of private detectives, to investigate the Treuhand's allegations against EGIT and in particular all the circumstances surrounding the privatisation sale of HGS.[40]

The Kroll Associates private investigation revealed that another party had a strong interest in acquiring the Treuhand owned company RFT Brandenburg, a Potsdam-based retail chain for brown goods. At the time of the appearance of the *Spiegel* article, this company was about to be sold to EGIT's investee company, HGS, which wanted to convert the retail chain from a brown goods' to a white goods' seller. Ermgassen explains:

> Kroll Associates concluded that the motivation behind the defamation of EGIT was not to destroy EGIT, but simply to prevent the sale of RFT Brandenburg to EGIT's investee company HGS. For, unknown to EGIT, RFT Brandenburg was much more than an electrical retail chain. It was a very valuable asset because it had more than 70,000 cable television connections and held 130,000 connection rights to households in the Postdam region. Whilst we did not know that the company was essentially a cable television company, another party saw the opportunity to buy it at a bargain "retail chain price". The Kroll team summarised its findings and submitted them to the Central

Figure 11.1   The East German Investment Trust Portfolio

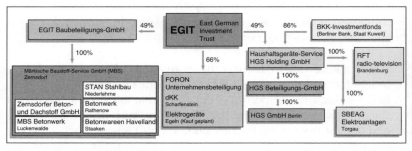

Source: *Der Spiegel*, 17/1993, 26th April 1993

Prosecutor for Crimes relating to Unification in Berlin. This submission was too late to give justice to EGIT.[41]

The publicity around the demise of the EGIT was quite sufficient to terminate any remaining interest that private equity investors might have had for establishing funds dedicated to doing deals with the Treuhand.

HANNOVER Finanz

HANNOVER Finanz was pulled into its East German adventure by an enthusiastic West German entrepreneur who wanted to take over an industrial bread factory in Neubrandenburg. As such, Hertz-Eichenrode and his team did not go looking for East German opportunities, rather an East German opportunity found them. Michael Hedtstück, one of the authors of *Zwischen Rendite und Verantwortung* a book covering the history of HANNOVER Finanz, describes how this happened:

> Only one manager from the West wanted to step into the bread-factory, which was making products that had been predominantly sold in East German state-owned shops. The would-be buy-in manager had management experience in food-retailing, and was keen to prove himself as an entrepreneur.

> Despite its commitment to privatising the Neubrandenburger company, the Treuhand felt that its acquisition by a single manager was too much for one man. The entrepreneur was informed by the representatives of the Treuhand that he could expect their support for

his plan, but only if he could prove that he had a financially strong equity partner behind him. He went out and found that partner in HANNOVER Finanz.

The buy-in manager took a 40 percent stake, and the HANNOVER Finanz was allocated 30 percent. The remaining 30 percent was split between three East German senior managers on the second level. The Treuhand subsidised the acquisition with credits which ran into millions. This included coverage for all losses that had been accumulated by the company at the point of acquisition, and the provision of a healthy opening balance of working capital. This made it financially possible for the company to begin restructuring: its headcount of 370 employees would clearly need to be reduced by at least half.[42]

In the event, HANNOVER Finanz was to have some nasty surprises with the investment, and needed all its patience to see the company through the coming years. Wolfgang Lampel, a restructuring manager from the West, who had experience in the bakery industry, was brought in to help turn the company around. Lampel was confronted with a financial situation at the newly renamed De Mäkelbörger which was very serious. The company was losing money every month, and its equity was bleeding away. It quickly became clear that refinancing was necessary. The only possible source of funds on the scale required was from the public coffers, this time in the form of the local government of Mecklenburg-Vorpommern. Public support was forthcoming, but on the condition that 20% of the sum be provided by private sources. The banks weren't willing to risk any more money in the venture, and HANNOVER Finanz had no alternative but to put up the money itself. It also injected an additional €1 million in equity, to further shore up the balance sheet.

After a difficult start, attention at De Mäkelbörger turned to more strategic and operational concerns. Lampel and the one of the East German managers had very different views on what the next steps should be, as Hedtstück explains:

There was a long debate over many months between the East German manager and her new boss. The former was convinced that the company should go ahead with the investment necessary to modernise the company's production of industrial bread. But Lampel was convinced such a strategy was doomed, predicting that the prospects for the industrial-bread business were poor. He compared the market structure of East Germany with that of West Germany, and predicted that the East would soon come to resemble the West as the two markets converged. The industrial bread market in the West was stagnant, and powerful rivals such as Harry and Wendel were consolidating the market rapidly. Within a few years, there would be no place for a small independent in the industrial bread market. Lampel therefore recommended progressively withdrawing from the industrial bread market, and moving into the hand-made bread segment.[43]

The HANNOVER Finanz team backed Lampel's strategy, and new bakers were hired with experience of baking hand-made bread. The strategy change was difficult. De Mäkelbörger could only attract shops at the outset which no-one else wanted to serve, and which were largely unprofitable. But gradually the company established a reputation. A crucial decision was to enter the market for frozen semi-finished products for sale to hotels and restaurants. This increased not only the accessible market, but also the capacity utilisation of the company's facilities. Nevertheless, it took until 1999 for the company to turn the corner to profitability. By 2002, the company was in a position to forward integrate, by acquiring progressively its own chain of bakery-products retailers. By 2008, the company opened its 125th retail outlet, and was producing 300,000 frozen baked products per day. Its turnover reached €50 million with a satisfactory level of profitability. But it had been a long and difficult path for the private equity sponsor.

Deutsche Handelsbank

One of the most unusual new players on the private equity scene at the close of 1991, was the Deutsche Handelsbank, East Germany's only merchant bank before the wall came down. The bank had funds of DM 1 billion under management. Peter Hammermann, born in 1954 the son of an entrepreneur, took over the job of managing the bank, while the Treuhand was in the process of privatising it. Hammermann had been to school in Hamburg at the same time as Thomas Matzen. He spent a significant proportion of his early career, some four-and-a-half years while working at Bosch, travelling around the world. At the end of this period, he decided he wanted to do something more financial, and joined the corporate finance world of BHF Bank. But the event which had the biggest impact on his career was the falling of the Berlin wall, as Hammermann himself explains:

> The reunification of Germany came, and I was very familiar with the environment in Berlin from my Bosch days. Shortly thereafter, I had the opportunity to join the board of the Deutsche Handelsbank, which at that time, was the owner of some brand new airbuses. So the bank sold the aeroplanes, and the money raised went into our bank. When I joined in 1991, the Deutsche Handelsbank was trying to enter the merchant banking business, but actually got into something more comparable to private equity. Buying companies gained more attention. The idea of buying companies was also something that was in people's minds because of the Treuhand situation. People were flocking to Berlin to get heavily involved in all sorts of trans-actions, advisory services, and the like. We had the idea of trying to develop the Deutsche Handelsbank into a merchant bank. Our approach was to take minority positions in companies, build a port-folio, and then try to trade our assets within this portfolio.[44]

Hammermann recruited Norbert Stelzer, Ekkehard Franzke, and later Jens Tonn to help him invest the bank's money. But the money was destined for West Germany, not East Germany. Franzke recalls:

> They had a Western team, they wanted to build a merchant bank like Warburg or Schroders. They were the largest private equity player in Germany at the time, overall translated in today's money it would be DM 500 million equity. Peter Hammermann started on 1st January 1992, and I joined him on 1st April 1992, the same day as Norbert Stelzer.
>
> Our strategy was clear: equity, participations, minorities, the financing of transactions, and consulting. The Deutsche Handelsbank originally had 86 participations which had been sold down to 16, so that there was an increase in equity value. The shareholder was BFG Bank, who were afraid of the risk in the transaction. It turned out to be one of the best investments they ever made. There was no risk at all in any of the participations. BFG got something like a three-to-four times return on its money.[45]

One of the team's first investments was in Kühne & Nagel, where the owner from the founding family and CEO, Dr Kühne, had decided that the time had come to part with Lohnro, for although the deal Matu-schka's M&A team had organised to save the independence of the logistics company had been both welcome and successful, the time came when Klaus-Michael Kühne was keen to buy back the stake held by Lohnro. The new Deutsche Handelsbank team saw an opportunity to make a name for itself. As Norbert Stelzer explains:

> Knowing that Dr Kühne wanted to buy out Lohnro, we decided to call him up. We went to Zurich, and were about to buy the stake, then VIAG came along and clinched the deal. We ended up with a 10% share as a consolation prize for having got in first. But for us it was an important step towards getting our bank on the map. We got a good return on that investment. The company was later taken public.[46]

The team's first majority buyout was in Cargo Van, a company which Hammermann knew well from an earlier point in his career. Franzke recalls:

> Hammermann knew the transaction because he had sold it to Chris Peisch and two years later he saw it was on the market again. He liked that company a lot so he said we have to get it! It was a departure from the strategy of doing only minorities because it was a 100% takeover. We had been committed to taking only minorities.[47]

Cargo Van had previously been a very successful deal. Chris Peisch, who at the time was working for Morgan Stanley merchant bank, recalls:

> Cargo Van had developed really well, and we sold it in the summer of 1992. We sold it during a time when our US portfolio was under pressure because of the US downturn. This deal had been a real winner, and had greatly benefited from the increased trucking volumes between the former East Germany and the west. It was a very strong market, driven primarily by reunification. But there were also some other factors. My boss said that we had to sell our winners, and this was a winner. We made between two and three times our money, by the time we closed that deal.[48]

But under the Deutsche Handelsbank stewardship, the investment quickly turned into a difficult one, and it took a lot of effort to keep the company alive once the transaction closed.

One of the members of the Deutsche Handelsbank's supervisory board had a high respect for Matuschka, and encouraged Hammermann to involve the Count in the Deutsche Handelsbank's activities. Hammermann recalls:

Matuschka brought in a couple of deals and individuals. We quite often flew to Paris together. Our chairman was also bringing in a number of projects, often involving Americans. Matuschka fronted quite a number of attempts to convince GE of certain deals, which was naturally quite difficult at that time, given the whole fall-out from the Matuschka collapse. On the other hand, the American approach to German private equity at that time was kind of "we're going to show you how this works, and we're going to bring in the big money."[49]

The life of the Deutsche Handelsbank as a private equity vehicle was to be cut short however, once the BFG was acquired in 1994 by Credit Lyonnais. The French bank was not happy with the industrial participations, and insisted that they be divested. Hammermann recalls:

On reflection, there are a number of reasons why things didn't go smoothly. Firstly, this sort of equity business doesn't fit well into a bank's organisation. Secondly, our parents within the bank were having many troubles, and there was a significant change of ownership. Then a third point would be that our team lacked experience. There were various other reasons. Initially we had a partial success story, as a couple of the deals we did went well, and drew a lot of attention. At the outset it had seemed like the management board had the intention to give us the opportunity to co-invest on the equity investments. But to make this become real was very difficult in the banking world. So we didn't get the options to develop our personal investment accounts. We were also frustrated in our ambitions to become more deeply involved in the companies, that is to say to develop a relationship with the portfolio businesses. In fact the opportunity to act like some kind of shareholder did not materialise. These were just some of the aspects why this venture eventually failed.[50]

The end came suddenly, and for some team-members, rather unexpectedly. Franzke recalls:

In August 1994 I came back from a vacation in Brittany and found a letter in my pigeon hole informing me that there was no more private equity basically.[51]

Franzke left the team almost immediately, and after various discussions with other consulting companies, joined Bain & Company in 1995. Hammermann and Stelzer remained on board a few months longer, but it was clear that they were now developing plans to set up a private equity venture of their own.

The mid-1990s recession

The winding down of the Treuhand in the period 1994–1995 coincided with the onset of a major economic recession. The reunification had created a boom for many German companies, as they tapped into the East German market. But this massive growth in demand reached a plateau, before falling sharply backwards off a cliff. Many German companies which had added capacity to meet the growing demand suddenly found themselves with substantial surplus capacity, particularly in consumer products, building materials, and construction.

The M&A community that built up in Germany during the height of the Treuhand's privatisation activities, shifted its focus towards advising German companies on how they could best preserve shareholder value during the recession. Shareholder value was something of a new concept to the German corporate elite, and was met in many quarters with great scepticism. But a few, such as Jürgen Schrempp at Daimler, decided to rally to the cause, and slowly but surely the spotlight was shone upon poorly performing businesses within the large German conglomerates. The recession made it easier to see which units were poor performers, and the M&A advisers pressed for them to be put up for sale. Indeed the "shape up or get out" culture trickled into German board rooms. Schrempp defined a minimum 12% ROCE for the Daimler divisions, and many other German corporates such as Siemens, Degussa, and Mannesmann began to follow suit.

12
The Fifth Phase: Retrenchment & Spin-offs: 1995–1996

By 1995, Germany was turning, approximately, its tenth anniversary of LBO activity. Eleven years had passed since Brian Fenwick-Smith acquired VEMAG from Reemtsma, and it was nine years since Schroders bought Jofrika. In that time, many young Germans and ex-pats had cut their teeth on buyouts in the German Mittelstand. Arguably, the worst years were over, and not only had experience been gathered, but a culture of M&A activity, partially provoked by the Treuhand, had spilt over into a nascent concern for shareholder value. Perhaps more significantly, Germany had witnessed some larger buyouts, particularly the joint CWB Capital/Goldman Sachs acquisition of Bran + Luebbe in 1994.

All of this activity drew attention to Germany. Many investors, who had, up until now, shied away from backing buyout activity in the German-speaking region, began to reappraise the situation. At the same time, many of the people within existing private equity houses based in Germany began to think of branching out on their own, preferably with the support of an international team based either in the UK or the US, but some by direct fund-raising of their own.

In many respects, the mid-1990s were a period of flux, and many inside and outside Germany felt that the economy was being stress-tested on multiple levels. With the mounting costs of supporting East Germany, and the home-made recession influenced by over-investment during the reunification boom, many German companies lost their shine, and some of their profitability. This transition from an over-whelmingly healthy West German economy in the mid-1980s, to a much more fragile and creaking unified German economy in the mid-1990s, did much to increase the potential for private equity. It had always been said a decade previously that owner-managers would only be willing to sell unhealthy companies, and that there were none for sale. By the mid-1990s there were plenty of owner-managed companies, and conglomerate subsidiaries that were in an ailing state of health. That the buyout market didn't explode in volume (as it was to do five years later) was mainly due to the fact that the private equity houses were still very concerned about the poor quality of the deals on offer. The experience in the first half of the 1990s had been both frustrating and troubled. This frustration was driven by a combination of a lack of volume, and a host of troubles with the companies acquired.

The fact that the private equity industry had matured by the mid-1990s, and was reaching the stage where some professionals were ready to spin-off from their parents, only made the conservatism stronger in this time of economic distress.

Thomas Matzen can lay claim to be the father of spin-offs in Germany. The parting of his team from Schroders at the end of 1991 was dramatic, and largely unexpected. The spin-offs of the mid-1990s were, on the whole, less traumatic. Römer's team had already spun-off once from CVC, and was to do so again from CWB and Doughty Hanson. Chris Peisch's spin off from Morgan Stanley to form H&P was a stepping stone to further morph into ECM. The Atco team, which was serving an ABN-Amro and Alpinvest joint venture, jumped ship to NatWest, Nord Holding span out of Norddeutsche Landesbank, and BC Partners emerged from the ashes of Barings.

CWB Frankfurt to Quadriga

By the mid-1990s, the team which had both held together, and arguably gathered the most experience, was that of Max Römer at CVC. Römer's team can also lay claim to having had the highest number of spin-offs and name changes in Germany. For having spun-off from CVC in 1991 to form CWB Capital Partners, Römer's team finally mounted its own unilateral spin-off to become independent at Quadriga.

A number of factors drove the Römer team to jump ship so many times. The initial challenge that had forced the group out of Citigroup was undoubtedly the restriction on majority stakes. The next tension which drove them out of the alliance with Doughty and Hanson was the commitment to small- to medium-sized Mittelstand deals. Last but not least, was a desire to be master of their own destiny.

The Frankfurt team had enjoyed little success in convincing investment committees outside Germany of their strategy. Independence therefore seemed to be the best route forward. Max Römer explains:

> By 1994, we were already done with our original fund that was closed in 1993. We had always invested in parallel, rather than waiting to finish raising a fund before investing. But by this stage, West LB had started to extricate themselves from buyouts, despite the fact that they had taken over the whole Chartered WestLB Merchant bank, which had been renamed West LB Merchantbank.
>
> The marriage between West LB and Standard Chartered had always been an unhappy one. The same was true for the buyout teams. Nigel Doughty told us that the London team were going for the big deals, and that we in Frankfurt should forsake our own management company but rather integrate into one centralised fund dedicated to big buyouts.
>
> We explained that this was not our turf. We preferred to create our own brandname and stay focussed on the mid market. So, in 1995, we started raising our own fund. In parallel, we got a mandate from the European Bank for Reconstruction and Development (EBRD) to set up in Russia, which meant we set up Quadriga Russia and Quadriga Frankfurt at practically the same time.[1]

The tipping point in the split was when Römer's team had finalised all the negotiations necessary to close the Kruse & Meinert deal, and the Doughty Hanson team in London refused to give it their approval. For the London team, Kruse & Meinert was considered to be both a risky deal (they had had bad experiences with kitchens in the UK) and a small one. It didn't match the strategy the London team was developing. This left Römer and his team with the options of either: throwing in their lot with the London approach, or going their own way. The latter seemed the most preferable.

CVC

1995 was busy for Steve Koltes and his team as they closed two deals in what was still a thin market for available opportunities. Work on both deals, Empe and Dixie, had started in 1994. Steve Koltes recalls:

> Empe was being sold in an auction run by Christian Wildmoser at Bankhaus Metzler. Chris is now a Partner at CVC. As I recall, Apax were active counter-bidders.
>
> Empe manufactured components for the automotive OEM markets. Their products fell into three product groups: door panels, headliners (the ceiling panel) and technical surfaces (wood trim). The door panel and headliner businesses were difficult and subject to intense competition, while the wood trim business was not. As a result, I was keen that we exit the two difficult divisions and focus on the wood trim business which, though much smaller than the others, was far more stable and profitable. Wood trim was the original business of Empe and had been neglected by the incumbent management team and used as a cash cow.
>
> As it turned out, the two managers were reluctant to follow a strategy that would reduce the size but increase the quality of the business, and we quickly parted ways. Changing management at the time was controversial in Germany, especially if it was a private equity investor making the change. *manager magazin* ran a piece criticising the way it was handled, at least in the eyes of their unnamed sources.[2]

Koltes brought in three new managers: Gerd Siekmann, then CEO of an Empe competitor, Olivier Roux, an ex Bain consultant based in London, and Werner Daniel, ex Controller of Tarkett Pegulan, to run the company. Within a year they had executed a successful sale of the two divisions and a turnaround of the wood trim business. Empe was then renamed Novem and sold in 2003.

The next deal, Dixi, was the largest provider worldwide of portable toilets used primarily on construction sites but also for special events. The auction was managed by Credit Suisse. Koltes recalls:

> We were bidding against Dixi's biggest competitor, Toi Toi, which was owned and run by Harald Müller, a successful "toilet entrepreneur". Müller was not that familiar with private equity investors and was surprised that an outsider would want to enter his small industry. He was even more surprised when we won the auction.

It was clear from the start that Dixi and Toi Toi belonged together: as the two largest players they could extract easy synergies by optimising overlapping service routes. I quickly opened a dialog with Mr. Müller about merging the two businesses. Meanwhile, the German construction market was in the early stages of a ten year decline, hastening the need to get a deal done. It took nearly two years, but in 1997 we managed to agree and execute the merger. During the long period of negotiation we kept things focussed by selling Dixi's mobile container business to GE Capital.

Following the merger Mr. Müller became group CEO, and the two businesses exceeded their plans in terms of cost savings. They also made a successful and extensive move into the US and Asian markets.[3] Today Dixi Toi Toi is the clear number one worldwide.[4]

From H&P to ECM

When he left Morgan Stanley in May 1994 to establish a private equity firm, Chris Peisch invited Onno Hogerzeil to join him. Peisch explains:

> Onno had worked for me on a project basis during my last few years at Morgan Stanley and he was at that time with a small consulting firm comprised of former Bain Munich people.[5]

It took almost two years to raise German Equity Partners I, which had total commitments of roughly €80 million, in a slowly developing market. Peisch recalls:

> The market was relatively new and most of the capital came from existing relationships with European and German banks. Many prospective non-German investors were deeply sceptical of the market, reflecting limited deal activity and adverse publicity surrounding the Matuschka portfolio. I had a lot of tough meetings.[6]

The fundraising process was supported by a transaction which Chris Peisch had developed during his time at Morgan Stanley and which he negotiated and closed in the summer of 1994. The target company was Vestas, a Danish wind turbine manufacturer. The Dutch bank Mees-Pierson, one of the early sponsors of German Equity Partners I, agreed to provide "bridge" equity to fund the deal with a view to placing it with the fund when it closed. Because of difficulties and delays in fundraising, it instead syndicated portions of its 83% shareholding, primarily with other Dutch private equity firms. Peisch comments:

> The deal showed early indications of success as the company entered a sustained period of outperformance, which was very supportive of the fundraising effort. Some prospective investors showed an interest in the fund with the understanding that they would acquire a piece of the syndicated Vestas equity.[7]

Vestas tripled its sales in the 1994–1998 period and went public on the Copenhagen Stock Exchange in May 1998. The investment produced roughly a 15 times return to the 1994 investors. In addition to his Cargo Van transaction at Morgan Stanley it provided enough of a track record to ensure the ultimate success of the fundraising.

Another deal closed during the fundraising period, with financial support from MeesPierson, was Geyer Werke, a family-owned film post-production services business. Peisch recalls:

> The transaction was sourced and organized by a member of our Advisory Board, Jochen Tschunke, who was a successful Munich-based entrepreneur. It was a classic financially undermanaged German Mittelstand company of that period with an asset-heavy balance sheet which lent itself to significant financial optimization.[8]

Ulrich Gleissner and Onno Hogerzeil worked on the deal with Jochen Tschunke and a significant equity interest was eventually acquired by German Equity Partners I. This transaction also developed well and the company was the subject of an IPO on the Neuer Markt in January 1999. Although the stock price eventually collapsed it was nevertheless a successful investment due to an attractive purchase price and the benefits of various financial engineering measures.

In early 1999 Chris Peisch formed ECM, which acquired most of the assets and personnel of H&P. Peisch explains:

> I did a major restructuring of people and processes and was actively supported by our investors, most of whom made early commitments to German Equity Partners II. That fundraising process took less than a year and resulted in a €125 million fund which closed in November 1999.[9]

As a small outfit, Peisch and his ECM team were always on the lookout for partners and co-investors, particularly if they represented no direct competition. Early on, Georg Stratenwerth, who at this time was based in London at Chase Capital, found in Peisch both a sparing partner, and a potential co-investor:

> In the early days of my marketing for Chase in Germany, I met up with Chris Peisch at ECM, and Thomas Schlytter-Henrichsen, who at that time was still working at 3i but shortly to open up with Alpha. The three of us met every week to discuss large and complex buyouts, and to think about what we could do together. We looked at Kässbohrer when that came out, and got quite close to it. This was a useful and interesting forum, and when we came up with the Casa Reha lead in 1998, I included Chris Peisch in the process, and we eventually co-invested with ECM.[10]

Chris Peisch set an example for professionals, either spinning off from an existing private equity house, or setting up for the first time in Germany, evolving an Anglo-Saxon approach tailored to Germany for leveraged buyouts in the small-cap segment of the market. Many other private equity houses were to follow his example.

Atco

One of the many curious winding stories in the development of private equity in Germany concerns the team that started at Atco, a joint venture between ABN Amro and Alpinvest, and moved over to join NatWest, the forerunner of Bridgepoint. Atco was set up in the Netherlands by ABN Amro and Alpinvest to undertake private equity transactions. In 1993 Atco decided to branch out into Germany. The first two investment were in Format Tresorbau and Sicorell. Nick Money-Kyrle, who was working for KPMG in Dusseldorf at the time, recalls his work on the due diligence:

> At that time, most of the financial due diligence work was being undertaken by foreigners. Our due diligence teams were drawing people from the audit side, and the first one I was involved in for a private equity client was for Frits Vromen at Atco on Format Tresorbau, a safe manufacturer. This gave me my first exposure to private equity, but it was still done at a distance.[11]

Tony Bunker recalls:

> I met Frits Vromen, the founder, and Wolfgang Lenoir, who had opened a PE house for ABN Amro and Alpinvest which they called Atco, in

Table 12.1 Private Equity Transactions in 1995

1995

Company	Buyer	Seller	Exit year	Sold to
1&1 Aktiengesellschaft & Co KGaA	Halder/3i/FBG	Management	1998	IPO
AHC Oberflächentechnik	Alpha	Family	2000	Aalberts Industries
APA Basic Beteiligungsgesellschaft mbH	Advent/KabelMedia	Previous investors	1999	IPO
Aquatec Peter Schmidt	TA Triumph-Adler (Medical)	Family	1997	Warburg Pincus
BFR Beteiligungsgesellschaft mbH	Advent/KabelMedia	Previous investors	1999	IPO
Colortronic	Atco/ABN Amro	K-Tron International Inc	2004	DDN
Disetronic	SBC Private Equity (Capvis)	Original investors	1996	IPO
Dixi (ADCO)	CVC/3i	Family	2007	Amcotec
Eilenburger Fenstertechnik	Schroder Ventures	Owner	2000	Private individual
EMPE/Novem	CVC/GS Capital Partners (Ad)	Family	2004	NIB Capital (Alpinvest)
FRAKO Kondensatoren- und Anlagenbau	Berliner Elektro Holding AG	Family	Not yet divested	Not yet divested
Geyer-Werke	H&P/CineMedia Film AG	Family	1999	IPO
HWS Energy Corporation	Global Equity Partners/UIAG	Electrolyser Corporation	1996	Canadian investor
Infox	Apax	Previous investors	1997	Vector/LBO France
Infratest	Harald Quandt	Previous investors	1998	NOK/Equita
ISIT GmbH	Advent/KabelMedia	Previous investors	1999	IPO
Kabel Plus Gesellschaft fur Kabel und Sat.	Advent/KabelMedia	Previous investors	1999	IPO
Kabelcom GmbH	Advent/KabelMedia	Previous investors	1999	IPO
Klein & Weiden	Atco/ABN Amro	Family	1998	Management
Köhler & Krenze Fashion AG	Cinven/Thomas JC Matzen	Family	1997	Thomas JC Matzen
KSW GmbH & Co KG	Advent/KabelMedia	Previous investors	1999	IPO
Ludwig Beck	Barings Capital	Family	1998	IPO

Table 12.1 Private Equity Transactions in 1995 – *continued*

1995

Company	Buyer	Seller	Exit year	Sold to
Oettinger Bier Brauhaus Oettingen	Hannover Finanz	Family	2000	Family
PKG Holding GmbH	Advent/KabelMedia	Previous investors	1999	IPO
PPS Group	Thomas JC Matzen	Cinven/Thomas JC Matzen	Not yet divested	Not yet divested
Singulus	Schroder Ventures	Leybold AG	1997	IPO
Sodawerk Staßfurt	BVT-Finanz-Gruppe	Lars Christensen A/S	2007	ECM
TAG Heuer	Doughty Hanson	TAG Group	1996	IPO
TBK Telecable Betriebsgesellschaft mbH	Advent/KabelMedia	Previous investors	1999	IPO
Telecable Betriebsgesellschaft Halle mbH	Advent/KabelMedia	Previous investors	1999	IPO
Toi Toi	CVC/3i	Family	2007	Amcotec
Ulrich Alber	TA Triumph-Adler	Family	1997	Warburg Pincus
Utimaco Safeware	Apax	Capital increase	1998	IPO
Wandel & Goltermann Management	Hannover Finanz	Family	2001	Management
Wego System AG	Halder	Family	1997	Scandinavian security firm
Wiedmann-Dettwiler St. Georgen GmbH	Advent/KabelMedia	Previous investors	1999	IPO

Source: Authors' compilation

1993. I worked for them as a consultant from 1994. They had opened up an office in Dusseldorf. This went on for two years, until it became clear that ABN Amro had a completely different strategy from Alpinvest. So eventually Alpinvest and ABN Amro parted ways, and each opened its own office.

Atco acquired quite a few companies, but a number of these deals were driven from the Netherlands. Atco bought Götz Müller, a labelling business, then Klein und Weiden, a window business in Cologne. We bought TTB in 1995, a plastic components company in Fulda, and Sicorell, an electronic circuit board manufacturer in Switzerland, not to mention Format Tresorbau, a safe manufacturer. The average value of these deals was about a maximum of DM 30 million. We were competing with HANNOVER Finanz, BdW, and 3i.

In those days we had a statistic that fifty per cent of our sourcing came from local lawyers or tax advisors, or people who knew people. Today we would say that these leads were proprietary, but in actual fact they were limited auctions. The boutiques would talk to 2–3 people at the same time, without telling you.

Due diligence, by today's standards was low-cost. We would spend a maximum of DM 25,000 for everything, financial, tax, legal etc. Commercial due diligence didn't exist, but we spent a lot of time on tax. We did not have transaction support offices, or teams. Just local tax advisors. There were no specialist lawyers then.[12]

The parting of the ways between ABN Amro and Alpinvest forced the Atco team in Dusseldorf to look for a new home.

NatWest Ventures

The Atco team's search for a new investor didn't take long. As Tony Bunker recalls:

At the time I knew Charles Matthew, a guy in Oxford, who had good contacts with NatWest. We had heard that NatWest wanted to open a German office. They had already hired two consultants, Tony Kirk, who was a South African, and Renee Maeder, a Swiss national. At the time, NatWest Ventures and later NatWest Private Equity wanted to become a pan-European player. They had an office in Berliner Allee, which we moved into after Kirk and Maeder left.[13]

The Atco team quickly agreed to take over where Kirk and Maeder had finished, as Bunker explains:

> The new team was made up of Frits Vromen, Wolfgang Lenoir, Jeroen de Bruijn and me.
>
> When we met NatWest, they were doing about 50 transactions a year, a lot of them were in minorities. What we were doing in Germany was very detached from the UK. We had our own local carry, and people in London were not too concerned about what we were doing. We did Lloyd Werft, which was successful, in 1997. In 1998 the MBI Manager, Mr Kuschetzki did Edscha together with us and PCI Parcom.[14]

The Edscha deal was inspired by Hans-Dieter von Meibom's team at Palladion (the successor name for Pallas, the fund itself was called PCI). Von Meibom recalls the process, and how he came to pull NatWest in on the deal:

> Our biggest deal in the 1990s was with Edscha, which we closed in 1998. Kuschetzki came to see me because a big law firm Baker & McKenzie had suggested he should talk to me. He wanted to buy Edscha from the former owners, and they had given him an option to do so. He had a letter from a bank agreeing to finance the transaction, but he told me that the discussions with the bank had become difficult. He wanted me to help him manage these discussions because we were also offering M&A advisory services at that time. I took a look at that letter and told him "listen, this is most probably a letter from some junior guy. Nobody in a large bank would be willing to give 100% finance to a private individual. This is absolutely impossible. You should look for a private equity investor." I told him that we provided private equity, but it was only fair that I should give him some names, so that he could make up his own mind. The only condition I insisted on was that if he chose us, we would want a majority.
>
> Chris Peisch became our competitor, indeed he was about to buy it, and we thought we were miles behind. Then, on a Monday, we learnt that they were going to notarise their contract on Friday. At the time, we had no bank financing in place, Bayerische Vereinsbank was prepared to provide half of it, but they were some distance away from making a decision. Ultimately we decided it was too large, and that we needed to bring someone else in. We thought we had found a partner in NatWest, but at the last minute we brought in van Fliessing, our

biggest Dutch investor. Once we had signed the deal, NatWest also joined and we pooled it. But we had to tell them that unfortunately we could no longer give them all the equity they had been asking for, because now there was someone else on the deal.

The NatWest team had started not long before in Germany, and they didn't have many contacts. Essentially they had money, but were still building their network.[15]

The NatWest team focussed mainly on co-investments in the early years, before moving on to lead investments, as Bunker later recalled:

We had two legacy companies, AHT (Austria Haustechnik) and Hauser. AHT was owned jointly with CVC, and it wasn't long before I met the CVC guys, Steve Koltes and Charles Schwab, who were managing companies and doing things with them. We got four times our money on AHT when it was later IPO'd. Hauser had been done by Kirk and Mader before we joined. It was an office supplies retailer, and during the IT hype we span off the IT part, called Computer Partner, and sold it in 1999 to Einstein Net, and made quite a bit of money. Other successful deals were Erftcarbon in 1998 and Eurocom Depora. Less successful were Autinform in 1998 and Dutch CompuTrain in 2000. Management 2000, a staffing company which we acquired in 2000 was a reasonable deal, although it encountered some market difficulties. Kaffee Partner in 2002 was successful, and Forstinger in 2004 less so. Swiss Caps was done in 2005. IMO Car Wash bought in 1998 was a German deal, and very successful, but was managed entirely from London with hardly any input from the German team.

In the NatWest days you had to fight for deals. We had a Cases Committee, in London, for which we had to prepare papers in advance. It was seen as a battle. There was one guy who was playing the devil's advocate, who came from the bank. He was a nice guy, a marathon runner, who would evaluate the credit risk. Later decision making changed to become much more of a team effort.

The guys in London were in two minds about Germany. On the one hand, they wanted to move into the market, because it was the largest economy in Europe, and by so doing fulfil their pan-European vision. But on the other hand, they had been hoping to do much more in Germany. Our returns were always higher than the group's overall, but the amounts invested were considered tiny. That was the main criticism from London, and because of that, we weren't taken too seriously. Also, German deals did not have the quality of British, Scandinavian, or even French deals.

Added to this was the fact that we were always behind, in terms of experience, knowledge, and techniques. Mezzanine didn't exist in Germany in those days. When it first came along, our London colleagues were the first to use it, and we had no idea what it was. We were always treated with a smile. I insisted on flying to London every Monday morning, getting there by 9 a.m. for the weekly meeting. Wolfgang and Fritz didn't think it necessary to attend regularly. But I still believe it is absolutely vital for any German office of a British organisation to attend such Monday morning meetings. If you don't, you won't pick up on developments from within the organisation. It is a fundamental part of British business mentality that decisions are taken in the corridor, and you need to be there to take part.

Our industrial focus was driven by the guys in the UK. We had trouble, of course, with getting approval for automotive components deals. England had just gone through the British Leyland experience, and consequently doing the Edscha deal was incredibly difficult. Having eventually succeeded, it was easier later to do the TTB deal, which did not do well, although it had returned two times money for ABN Amro and Alpinvest.[16]

L&G Candover

Having exited the German market in 1994, Roger Brooke continued to take an interest in Germany, while at the same time overseeing the sell-off of the Candover portfolio. The excitement and activity around the Treuhand stimulated this interest, although East German companies were not considered to be particularly attractive. To mitigate the risks of a second entry, however, Brooke decided that Candover should team up with Legal & General Ventures, who were also preparing to enter the region. Jens Tonn recalls the developments:

Candover and Legal & General set up an office in Frankfurt, under the name of L&G Candover GmbH. But as with Candover's first experience, the local team's deals were too small for anyone in London to get excited about. The first significant deal was Tally, acquired from Mannesmannn in 1996.[17]

Legal & General were interested in smaller deals, and Candover in larger ones, but deal flow in both categories was poor and of questionable quality, as Mark Elborn recalls:

> We didn't see very many deals. The 1995 deal-flow Candover brought in probably included twenty deals.[18]

A further challenge for the German office was that the interests of the two houses began to diverge. Although the relationship between the two teams was amicable, and it had been agreed from the outset that neither party was forced to coinvest alongside the other on any deal, Candover became interested in doing bigger deals than L&G.[19] This became an issue for the German team given that most of their deals were small, as Tonn explains:

> When the proposals from Germany came up for the investment committee in London's final approval, the Candover reaction was typically "interesting proposal, but we don't really want to invest". The other issue was that the Frankfurt team was more linked to L&G than to Candover.[20]

Despite the challenges, the Frankfurt team succeeded in getting Tally, a dot-matrix printer company sold out of Mannesmann, through the two London investment committees, but the decision on when to divest the company was more difficult to make, as Elborn recalls:

> We bought Tally for about five times EBIT. No-one really wanted it at the time. CVC had taken a look, and a lot of others stuck their head in before dropping out. The London team at Legal & General asked us what we had, and liked the sound of it. After we bought it, the company trundled on, churning out an EBIT of around DM 20 million a year. Once the Neuer Markt came along, we should have sold it. Everyone was making a lot of money at that time, and we talked to the IPO managers, and they were confident we could too. But the team in London said hold it a while longer, make it bigger, because they thought it was nowhere near IPO-able.[21]

The Frankfurt team also acquired Burkhalter, a Swiss electrical contracting company, again for five times EBIT. This was to be one of the team's most successful investments, as Elborn explains:

> Burkhalter had about SFR 220 million in revenues, and was the biggest company of its type in Switzerland. It was made up of lots of little companies, run by entrepreneurs, and it ran like clockwork. We did an add-on, doubled profits, and ended up selling it for ten times EBIT.[22]

Burkhalter had been turned down at investment committee at Candover because it was considered too small. Once the Chairmanship of Candover passed from Roger Brooke to Stephen Curran, differences over deal size focus led to the decision in 1998 to terminate the joint venture in Germany. Legal & General was left to run the renamed LGV in Frankfurt on its own. As Elborn explains:

> Candover were doing bigger deals, and the German market wasn't generating deals big enough to share with another private equity house. When JPMorgan put Electrocom up for sale on behalf of Daimler, which was one of the biggest deals around at the time, which ultimately went to Siemens, Candover felt that there was no more logic in the joint venture.[23]

Nord Holding

Norddeutsche Landesbank, like many other German banks, had established a unit in 1969 to manage its so-called "silent" or "passive" participations: equity stakes in companies over which it exercised little or no influence. It was to this small team, which was run fairly independently, that a young Mathias Kues was to move.

Mathias Kues was born 1959 in Lingen, a small town in Lower Saxony, close to the Dutch border. After studying economics at the University of Münster, Kues worked for two years as a freelancer to the broadcaster, NDR in Oldenbourg, as much as anything because his girlfriend had a job in the town. It was at this time that his path crossed with the Chairman of the Norddeutsche Landesbank, who asked him bluntly what he intended doing with his life, before suggesting a career in banking. Kues was open to suggestions, and guided into Nord KB's ranks.

In 1989, Nord KB closed its first investment into an MBO. After this initial MBO experience, and many years of developing passive participations, the bank became aware in 1993 of a potential problem with a paragraph governing shareholder loans that had entered into German law. Holding equity in a company which it was lending money to could be risky, as the loans might, in difficult times, be viewed as a substitute for equity, and be given less preference than other liabilities should the company be liquidated. Kues was brought in to help solve the problem. The solution appeared to be to set up a new company, the Nord Holding, in which the Norddeutsche Landesbank would hold no more than a 10% stake. The remaining 90% would be farmed out to other banks and insurance companies, ensuring that none of the other parties held greater than a 10% stake either. Kues consequently found himself in charge of a vehicle tasked with making direct, active investments. He later recalled:

> The first direct investments were for expansion financed minorities, and then in 1995 we made the first buyout when we acquired Planta Subtil, a pharmacy company producing for the OTC market. It was a cream for women of 40–50 years of age, suffering from varicose veins. It was a very successful investment. We had discussions with the insurance companies to find out whether there were other kinds of illness where people were able and willing to pay for themselves.[24]

In the same year, Nord KB achieved its first IPO with IFA AG. Nord KB's experiences were mirrored by many other of the Kapitalbeteiligungs- gesellschaften set up during the mid-1960s and thereafter.

BBK

Prior to 1995, the Berliner Bank Kapitalbeteiligungsgesellschaft resembled many of its other bank competitors. The BBK had been established at the beginning of the 1980s, led by its first director Axel Hartmann. The BBK initially co-invested on a number of HANNOVER Finanz's deals, including ATU and Willy Vogel, or invested together with WestLB in Triumph-Adler. But the majority investments were influenced by Berliner Bank's lending business.

In 1991, Gothaer Insurance Group acquired a 50% stake in BBK, having itself for many years been investing both in funds and directly in German medium-sized companies. Gothaer's investments up to this point had been unleveraged, which was considered to be attractive particularly to

Table 12.2   Private Equity Transactions in 1996

1996

Company	Buyer	Seller	Exit year	Sold to
Blaurock GmbH	Alpha	Family	2000	Management
California Rohé GmbH	Schroder Ventures	Family	2000	Wash Tec
Computer Partner (part of Hauser)	ABN Amro/NatWest	Deutsche Systemhaus AG	1999	Einstein Net
Elexis Elektroholding	Doughty Hanson	AEG	1999	IPO
ESW Extel Systems	Schroder Ventures	Daimler Benz Aerospace	1997	Jenoptik
Hauser Computer GmbH	ABN Amro/NatWest	Deutsche Systemhaus AG	2004	DDN
Heim und Haus	Fleming Berenberg Gosla/Apax	Family	2003	Management/Max von Drechsel
Hoffman-Menü	Schroder Ventures	Grand Metropolitan plc	1999	Pricoa Capital
Huss Group	Schroder Ventures	Private individuals	2000	Pricoa Capital
Idéal-Loisirs-Gruppe/Majorette	TA Triumph-Adler (Toys)	Insolvency	2003	Smoby SA
Info-Sat Elektro- und Kommunikationstechnik GmbH	Advent/KabelMedia	Previous investors	1999	IPO
Kamps	Apax	Borden	1998	IPO
Komax Holding	SBC Equity Partners (Capvis)/HSBC PE	Max Koch	1997	IPO
Leim & Potthoff	TA Triumph-Adler (Construction)	Family	2003	MBO
Mettler Toledo	AEA	Ciba Geigy	1997	IPO
Neumayer Tekfor Gruppe	Equita	Family	2005	Barclays
Niersberger Facility Management	Schroder Ventures	Family	1999	Private individual
OSORNO	Schroder Ventures	Merger of PT companies	2000	Wash Tec
Paals Packpressen GmbH	GMM Active Equity	Family	2001	ECM
Palfinger AG	Global Equity Partners/UIAG	Family	1999	IPO
Quexco	Apax	Metallgesellschaft/Enirisorse	2000	Strategic
Richard Schöps AG	Thomas CJ Matzen	Cinven/Thomas CJ Matzen	2001	Borghetti
SAIA Burgess Electronics	Quadriga/SBC Equity Partners (Capvis)	Williams Holdings	1999	IPO
Schaffner Elekronik	HSBC PE	Elektrowatt	1998	IPO
Tally	L&G Ventures	Mannesmann	2003	Genicom
Techem	BC Partners/Halder	Public to private	2000	IPO
Teles AG	Apax/3i	Previous investors	1998	IPO
TTB	Atco/ABN Amro	Family	1998	Bridgepoint
Wilhelm Weber	Apax	Borden	1998	IPO

Source: Authors' compilation

family-owned companies. Gothaer's first direct investment was made into SG Holding AG in 1979, and five years later in 1984, Gothaer became one BC Partners' founding investors. Reinhard Blei and Stefan Theis were at the time running Gothaer's investment, as Blei later recalled:

> Banks were not the natural private equity players, mainly because they couldn't offer real equity from their balance sheet, whereas insurance companies could do this. As a consequence, it came as little surprise that very few bank-owned and sponsored private equity houses survived as captive entities.[25]

In 1994, Eberhard Witt succeeded Axel Hartmann as managing director of the BBK. Witt had been running DBG's office in Berlin. Following Hartmann's departure, there was a significant churn in the BBK team, with old members deciding to move on to new positions inside and outside the Group, and new joiners coming on board from DBG, the Deutsche Handelsbank, BdW, Christoph Spors from ZLU and Andreas Kogler from Preussag AG.

Andreas Kogler recalls the portfolio the new team inherited:

> We found a portfolio of around forty minority participations, many in media, and many in companies where the bank had made loans. Around a quarter were in Berlin, another quarter in East Germany, and the remainder in West Germany.[26]

Like the other Kapitalbeteiligungsgesellschaften at that time, BBK's owners remained focussed upon minority investments.

Barings Capital to BC Partners

Strictly speaking, Barings Capital barely needed to spin-off from Barings Bank. Its origin was not like that of Barclays, NatWest, or HSBC. Its inception was the result of Otto van der Wyck's decision to set up his own fund outside Citigroup (and therefore Barings was itself a form of spin-off). Van der Wyck wanted an appropriate brand to make his new venture credible. Jens Reidel explains:

> When Barings was founded, we did it the other way around. Otto knew that he had the experience, but he needed a name. So he went to Barings and convinced them that this was an interesting business and that he could set up a fund that would be solid and reputable

enough to bear their name. He struck a deal in which Barings got 25% of the company, in return for the use of the Barings name, plus some infrastructure, and support with fund-raising. So from the start, Barings Capital was independent. One gentleman from Barings Bank was on our board, which met once a year over a very nice dinner.[27]

The mid-1990s saw Barings build rapidly on the success of its first deal with Tierschmidt in 1994. The next break came when Reidel was approached with an offer to support a management buyout at a struggling department store chain in Munich. The DM 100 million deal Barings closed on Ludwig Beck was one of the largest deals of 1995. Dieter Münch, one of the buyout managers of Ludwig Beck explains the background:

The situation was quite simple. Ludwig Beck had invested heavily in a big new store in Cologne, the roll-out costs of which knocked out the company's paper thin finances.

The Cologne store was opened in 1991. It was the boom time of German reunification, and we thought it would go on for years. The Cologne store brought with it a wide range of problems. The rental price was too high, and the revenue too low. Ludwig Beck was undercapitalised, and hopelessly ill-equipped to finance such a start-up store. In the event, we were confronted by a worst case scenario. We had revenues of DM 40 million in Cologne, but the break-even point was DM 50 million.

We took advice from Roland Berger. One option they suggested was that we look for a strategic partner. The second option was to find a financial investor. Ludwig Beck was at the time highly indebted, with a big loan from the Hypovereinsbank. It was clear that Cologne would have to be closed. But nobody was sure how much it would cost to do this.

We were in discussions with other stores, who wanted to come in cheaply, requiring a big haircut from the banks. But then Roland Berger brought Barings Capital into the picture. They had a different concept, and it was all very interesting. For the first time we were confronted with a valuation of the company. Barings ended up taking an absolute majority, and everyone sold out their shares to them. Barings then settled the situation with the banks. The shareholders got a price which wasn't viewed as unfair. It was clear that this wasn't going to be a long term relationship, but more like one lasting five years, after which they would sell the company.[28]

Against the background of the Ludwig Beck deal, Barings was dealing with its own internal crisis provoked by the rogue trader, Nick Leeson, whose activities brought down the bank. Reidel recalled:

> The Barings collapse, because of our independent structure, had prac-
> tically no impact upon us. That's not to say we weren't impacted by
> the consequences of Nick Leeson. First because of the damage to the
> professional reputation of the Barings name. Then we were basically
> forced to buy back our 25%. We had to pay something for this share,
> which was difficult. We had to go to our banks and ask for loans. But
> we succeeded, and then changed the firm's name. We hired an agency
> to look into some options, but the short version of our name had
> always been BC, and as we were a partnership, it seemed a logical
> decision to call ourselves BC Partners.[29]

The breakthrough transaction for the newly rebranded BC Partners came one year later when Reidel's network of bankers and lawyers threw up an opportunity at Techem, a submetering company. The Techem management had originally thought of having an auction between two parties, Doughty Hanson and BC Partners.

Reidel had achieved a complete turn-around for the London-based fund in Germany. It is undoubtedly easier for a larger international private equity house to survive a terrible start in a country. A small domestic fund would almost certainly not have survived the Lignotock collapse. Nevertheless, Reidel and his team proved that a team change could bring with it a dramatic improvement in performance. By the mid-1990s, players and observers in Germany were rapidly coming to associate BC Partners with the premier league of domestically located players that included Permira, Apax, and CVC.

Hammermann & Stelzer

After the demise of the Deutsche Handelsbank, Peter Hammermann and Norbert Stelzer began thinking about their next steps. Stelzer recalls:

> The two of us sat down and decided to do something together. We
> both wanted to stay in private equity, and we thought of pursuing a

kind of IMM model, combined with offering M&A advisory services. That's how we started out, offering advice on M&A deals, while looking for private and institutional investors.[30]

The first change for Hammermann and Stelzer, was to move back to Munich. In parallel to looking for M&A advisory work, they began the process of raising a fund. Hammermann recalls:

> I started my own Munich-based business, together with Stelzer in 1995. The concept of fund raising at that time didn't really exist in Germany. Clearly the country lacked a lot of experience with private equity. So we started with a combination of trying to provide advisory services plus making equity investments. We had some leads into large wealthy German families, by means of what today you would call family offices.
>
> We called the company Hammermann & Stelzer. It was really a bit of a high risk situation. But on the other hand there was confidence in the development opportunities, with the consequence in the end that we got to know Jens Odewald via Hellmut Kirchner.[31]

Rolf Dienst also contacted Norbert Stelzer, as Stelzer himself recalls:

> I got a phone call from Rolf Dienst, asking whether we wanted to team up with Jens Odewald, who had more than ten years of experience working as CEO of Kaufhof. He had also been Chairman of the Board of the Treuhand. Apparently, Odewald had been approached by CD&R with a request to become their door-opener in Germany. This had given him some exposure to private equity in Germany, and now he had set out to raise a fund on his own.[32]

The overlapping interests, and complementary skills, meant that a merger of the two interests, Odewald on the one side, and Hammermann and Stelzer on the other, made eminent sense, and in a pattern that was to be reproduced in many corners of the German private equity industry, the remnants of the Deutsche Handelsbank team morphed via their own vehicle into the new entity Odewald, Hammermann, and Stelzer. Odewald and his fund remained close to CD&R, joining them on a number of co-investments.

IMM to TA Triumph-Adler

On Christmas Eve 1993, IMM and most of its businesses were sold to Triumph-Adler in a reverse take-over, which was finally closed in summer 1994 and another name in private equity was to change forever on the German market. Whilst IMM was fairly typical of a private equity company Triumph-Adler was to act as a "Mittelstandsholding". The transition blurred the distinction between a buyout house, and a typical publicly-held conglomerate. This was to result in many changes, the effects of which were to make the new vehicle less and less like a private equity house. The Triumph-Adler deal originally came through a call from Marija Korsch of Bankers Trust, one of IMM's board members. Hans Albrecht recalls:

> She had called me because I was doing the office systems. I took a look and said that I didn't think Triumph Adler's business was of any interest per se, but the loss carry forward on the company's balance sheet might be of interest for our buyout concept. So I passed this lead on to Raimund and he ultimately did the deal.[33]

Raimund König explains the background to the deal which emerged:

> Olivetti wanted out of Triumph-Adler, which was losing serious amounts of money. But we were the only ones who could see what positives it offered.
>
> First, it had a huge pile of money. When we bought Triumph-Adler, it had assets of DM 400 million, of which only DM 30 million were tied up in the typewriter business. This left DM 370 million in cash or claims against Olivetti. On the liabilities side, it had DM 230 million in pension responsibilities, and DM 170 million in equity. That was a huge pile of money to invest.
>
> Second, we thought once we have invested all that money, we could easily do further capital increases, being a public company, just like Hanson Trust. Thirdly, Triumph-Adler had a huge tax-loss carry forward of some DM 1.4 billion. This meant that all the proceeds from both selling companies, and the operating profits of the divisions, would be tax free.
>
> Finally from our perspective the key difference in Triumph-Adler was management's shareholding which increased from 20% (for IMM) to

50% (for Triumph-Adler). We no longer worked primarily for institutional or financial investors. This was to be "our" company.[34]

Unlike 3i and DBAG, Triumph-Adler had every intention of consolidating acquired companies in order to use its tax credits, there being no obstacles to buying majority stakes, and indeed its tax credits were its principal value added, as Reinhard Pöllath later commented:

> The tax loss carry-forward was Triumph-Adler's main asset, confirmed by a tax ruling obtained for the IMM acquirers. Part of its value was later lost when in 2000, tax legislation exempted inter-corporate capital gains. But its use against taxable operating profits was valuable. Only much later did German legislation further restrict and finally almost eliminate "tax-loss companies".[35]

Hans Gottwald and Christian Hollenberg took the opportunity of the reverse take-over to cash in their stakes. Their departure meant that someone within IMM had to be found to take over construction services. Walter Moldan was given the task, as he later describes:

> I was offered the opportunity to take over IMM construction services between Christmas and New Year's Eve 1994. Hollenberg and Gottwald stayed around for a few days to give me advice, and for one meeting with each of the portfolio companies.

> The portfolio included Bihler + Oberneder for roof and facade construction, Hess hollow-filler blocks for office buildings, and two engineering companies in concrete construction, Zementol and Quinting Betondienstleistung. The latter two were direct competitors. I was surprised to find that the managing directors of these different companies had never met each other before.

> The best advice Hollenberg and Gottwald gave was to be very careful in trying to generate synergies between the portfolio companies. They were absolutely open about this: they said there were none. These companies had been acquired on a purely opportunistic basis.[36]

Raimund König's efforts to restructure the shareholdings between the divisions and the central holding company were not well received by some members of the team. König needed to make the

Triumph-Adler holding own 100% of the divisional shares, so that he could introduce profit-transfer domination agreements between the holding company and its subsidiaries. König explains:

> For tax purposes you needed to consolidate profits upwards, so we basically wanted to have 100% shares, and that is the only reason we bought the shareholdings in the divisions out, and in turn offered people Triumph-Adler shares, or cash.[37]

The newly established corporate structure had further implications which played a significant role in the coming years. Financing, accounting and risk management eventually became more central tasks biting into the perceived independence of the industry sub-groups. Also the focus was no longer on retaining earnings and repaying acquisition debt as quickly as possible but upon generating cash-flows for Triumph-Adler to fund the pension liabilities and to pay dividends. Inevitably the issue of corporate career perspectives began to trickle into the minds of senior team members, as König recalls:

> Seats on the management board (Vorstand) were occupied by Markus, Dietmar and myself for many years to come. Only Thomas Bühler was eventually promoted. We did not fully succeed in maintaining the cosy IMM-structure in the new world.[38]

The issue of when a partner in a division could realise the value of his shares was a continual problem for IMM/Triumph-Adler. Hollenberg and Gottwald had been willing to have their division sold "internally" once, at a time when legally they had the right to realise their capital gains. But once IMM sold to Triumph-Adler, they were not willing to forgive this right a second time.

Kai Binder and Christian Eckart, who had held on to their direct stakes, eventually solved the issue in a surprising way. König recalls:

> Neither Thomas Bühler, who was responsible for the homecare supplies business nor anybody else in our team was aware of the fact, that Kai and Christian had actively negotiated the sale of their entire business (including themselves) to a strategic buyer; so one morning I received within my daily mail a notarised complete and unconditional offer to sell our stake for a super

attractive prize. We only had to say "yes", and that's what we did. And the cheque arrived in time.[39]

Disagreement over both the future strategy and the operational performance of the Office Systems Business caused one of the most high-profile departures, Hans Albrecht:

> It is a pity I had to leave, because IMM at that time was at least in the same position as Carlyle was, relatively speaking, in the US. Plus we had a one-and-a-half billion Deutschmark loss carry forward. We had a huge competitive advantage over everybody. We had a good track record, we had a lot of credibility and we had really good people.[40]

Lessons from experience

Private equity in Germany in the mid-1990s had become a rough and tumble environment, in which a much closer community was establishing itself, and standard codes of practice and behaviour were becoming ingrained. The increasing maturity and experience of the teams was a major motor behind spin-offs, and head-hunters found more people to call upon while looking for people to hire. That said, the number of professionals who had experience of exits was still very limited, largely due to short histories, and the lack of exit opportunities.

Several foreign players were still hesitant in their approach to the market, and it was considered difficult to put large sums of money to work in Germany. This caused a spate of joint ventures (such as Atco, and LGV Candover) in order that foreign players could gain experience without investing too much money. Despite the modest size of deals, co-investments continued, and even became more common. The German market was considered to hold out potential for private equity players, but much of this potential still had to be realised. It was to take until the late 1990s for the level of deal flow to improve substantially: precipitating a veritable Tsunami of new entrants to the market.

13
The Sixth Phase: The Tsunami Begins

In many periods of history there are defining years, whether they be crises, turning points, or moments of high fashion. In our story of the private equity experience in Germany, there can be no question that 1997 marked a sea change, when major corporations awoke to the potential of divesting under-performing businesses. Overnight, the deal-flow increased, and the deals which flowed were larger, more global, and of considerably higher quality. Some of the new sellers were no longer owner-managers of medium-sized firms, but senior executives in publicly traded companies. André Mangin, who at the time was working as an investment banker in Barings and Merrill Lynch, remembers:

> It was around 1997 that private equity really started gaining ground. It was at this time that the large German corporates realised that private equity houses made up an interesting group of buyers. They had never really been considered to be serious before. That's not to say that large German corporates didn't retain their doubts about whether private equity houses could execute large deals. But Merrill, Goldman, and Morgan Stanley were touring around, explaining to the German corporates that they needed to clean up their portfolios, and convincing them that private equity houses were viable partners to help them do this. Banks were still hesitant to provide financing, but even they were beginning to warm to this new kind of asset class.[1]

Another factor triggering the change was the arrival of the American companies. Before 1997, a few US companies such as Citigroup and Morgan Stanley had dabbled in the market, mainly from their London and Frankfurt branch offices. But no bids had been made directly from private equity houses based in New York.

The government's decision to sell its stake in the motorway roadside service network, Tank & Rast, combined with Unilever's decision to sell Nordsee, its chain of fish shops, restaurants, and fish processing factories, and Siemens move to sell Sirona, its dental chair business, attracted private equity interest to Germany like moths to a flame.

The sudden release of so many high profile corporate spin-offs prompted a tidal wave of new private equity houses to enter the market, largely by setting up German offices of mostly Anglo-Saxon firms based in London (PPM, HgCapital, HSBC, etc.). Ron Ayles, who at the time was working in the M&A department of Degussa, recalls:

> In 1997–1998, things really started to kick-off. It was assumed among corporates that private equity houses couldn't outbid strategics. But under the influence of investment banks, private equity houses were getting added to the lists of potential buyers as a fallback position. The dominant mind-set among corporates remained looking at who would be the logical buyer that would be able to develop a business. It was difficult to believe that private equity could fulfil that role. But as capital became available, and pricing became more competitive, things started changing. That's when private equity started to become important.[2]

In parallel, the late 1990s saw the take-off of venture capital, and technology stocks, and the rise of the Neuer Markt. The rise of the Neuer Markt was extremely important for private equity, because it opened up a significant new channel for exits. CVC succeeded in Austria in floating Austria Haustechnik (AHT). 3i experienced a major change of strategy from 1997 onwards as it shifted towards a focus on venture capital, ultimately acquiring the largest German venture capital institution which had emerged, Technologie Holding. The well-publicised rise of venture capital and the Neuer Market helped communicate the benefits of alternative finance, and also the merits of entrepreneurship, and management participation.

The bursting of the dotcom bubble in early 2001, followed by the terrorist attack on the World Trade Center on 11th September of the same year, caused a crisis that was to wreak havoc on the venture capital market, but left the private equity market relatively unscathed. 3i, straddling the two markets, was the worst impacted by the collapse, followed by Apax, which suffered a complete loss on its investment in the

Bundesdruckerei (which had a credit-card chip business that accounted for almost all of the acquisition value). For the rest of the private equity industry, the main influence of the crisis was its immediate aftermath, when the financial community became concerned with the effects of the ensuing recession, and the contraction in the credit markets.

Schroder Ventures

Perhaps the most spectacular example of this change in the German M&A landscape was the decision of Siemens to sell its dental equipment unit. Heinrich von Pierer, the CEO of Siemens, announced the company's intention to sell its dental products business in April 1997. The dental products business was a component business of the Medical Division of Siemens. Siemens as a whole was suffering from increasing global competition by specialised and smaller competitors, and the decision had been taken to refocus its energies on a number of core businesses, while divesting those which did not offer sufficient synergies with the rest of the group. Much of the pressure for these changes came from investors, who through the evolving German capital market were becoming increasingly vocal about their need for DAX listed companies to build shareholder value. The concept of portfolio management was relatively new to German conglomerates, which historically had only rarely sold off businesses, and the decision of Siemens to strategically exit from a group of businesses was viewed as something of a revolution within corporate Germany.

From the moment the Siemens announcement was made, the private equity community moved into high gear. It was clear that this was a different class of deal, one which would require a level of effort and professionalism not yet seen in Germany. At Schroders, Thomas Krenz and Thomas Jetter agreed early on that they had to win the deal. Ekkehard Franzke had recently visited Krenz to market Bain's commercial due diligence product, and so Krenz gave Bain a call. Franzke recalls:

> We had visited Thomas Krenz in June 1997, and I remember him calling me a few weeks later asking "do you know anything about dentists' chairs?" I told him to give me three days and I would have an idea. So we had a hard three days and in the end all he asked me was: "do you think it is a good business or a bad one?" I answered "it depends". He was concerned about regulations. I said regulations were not the problem. He asked us to come over to Frankfurt. When we arrived, Krenz had an admission to make. "I have never worked

Table 13.1 Private Equity Transactions in 1997

1997

Company	Buyer	Seller	Exit year	Sold to
Antennen Lindemann GmbH	Advent/KabelMedia	Previous investors	1999	IPO
Burkhalter	L&G Ventures	Zellweger Luwa	2000	Domenig family/management
Charles Vögele Holding	Schroder Ventures	Family	1999	IPO
Corposan	CVC	Family	2001	Wessanen Nederland
Demedis (part of Sirona)	Schroder Ventures	Siemens	2004	Henry Schein Inc
Domus Homecare/WP Gesundheits	Warburg Pincus	Family/Triumph-Adler	2004	Invacare
Edscha	NatWest/PCI Parcom/Flint Echo	Family	2000	Carlyle
Fahrrad Heidemann	Management	Equimark	Not yet divested	Not yet divested
Geberit	Doughty Hanson	Family	1999	IPO
GMT GmbH	Halder	Family	1997	UK strategic buyer
Haefely Trench	CVC	BBA Group	Not yet divested	Not yet divested
Impress	Doughty Hanson	Merger of Schmalbach-Lubeca + Pechiney	Not yet divested	Not yet divested
Infox	Vector/LBO France	Apax	2000	Trade Sale
Kalle Nalo	CVC	Hoechst	2004	Montagu
Köhler & Krenze Fashion AG	Thomas JC Matzen	Cinven/Thomas JC Matzen	2000	BdW
Libro AG	Global Equity Partners/UIAG	Wlaschek	1999	IPO
Mac Fash	Hannover Finanz	Kaufhof	1999	Karstadt
Memorex-Telex (MSH International Services)	Schroder Ventures	UK receiver	2000	IPO
Niedermeyer AG	Global Equity Partners/UIAG	Family	1999	Interdiscount
Nordsee (Retail)	Apax	Unilever	2005	Kamps/Nomura
Nordsee (Wholesale/Deutsche See)	Apax	Unilever	2002	BPE Private Equity/HSH Kapital GmbH

Table 13.1 Private Equity Transactions in 1997 – *continued*
1997

Company	Buyer	Seller	Exit year	Sold to
NWG	Quadriga/SBC Equity Partners (Capvis)	Family	2000	ISS
Otto Sauer Achsenfabrik	DBAG	Family	2004	Pamplona
Petrick & Wolf Energietechnik	TA Triumph-Adler (Construction)	Family	2003	Insolvency
Roventa-Henex	PPM	Incentive Investment SA	2005	Management
Rungis	CVC	Previous investors	2005	Insolvency
Schoeller & Hoesch Gruppe	DBAG	Schoeller Gruppe	1998	P. H. Glatfelter Company
Schottdorf	Alpha	Family	2004	Management
Schwerin Kabel-, Antennen- und Kommunikationsanlagen	Advent/KabelMedia	Previous investors	1999	IPO
Sebaldus Druck und Verlag	DBAG/Alpha	Previous investors	2000	Schlott AG
SIA Holding (Swiss Industrial Abrasives)	SBC Equity Partners (Capvis)/Quadriga	Family	2003	IPO
Single Temperiertechnik GmbH & Co. KG	Schroder Ventures	Heraeus Holding GmbH	2000	Halder
Sirona Dental Systems Group	Schroder Ventures	Siemens	2004	EQT
Spectro	ECM	Family	2005	Ametek
Süss Microtech AG	Alpha	Family	2001	IPO
TelDaFax	Apax	Family	2000	IPO
Telekommunikation Doebis Antennenservice	Advent/KabelMedia	Previous investors	1999	IPO
Toi Toi (ADCO)	CVC	Family	2007	Amcotek
Tropon	Advent	Bayer	2004	Viatris (Advent portfolio co.)
TTH	Alpinvest/NatWest	Family	Not yet divested	Not yet divested
Winkler & Dünnebier	Doughty Hanson	Owner family	1998	IPO

Source: Authors' compilation

with consultants before, so I do not know what to expect. I do not even know what to ask. But we'll try this." So Bain got its first contract for a commercial due diligence, worth DM 800,000 in fees. The project lasted from June to November.

Damon Buffini at Schroders London was responsible for the distribution side, which is the area I worked on. Jetter was the project manager. It was a complex transaction, and Bain had to beef up the team massively. We could not allow a failure. We knew it would be a landmark project for us. We got in Wulf Weller for purchasing, Roman Zeller for overhead, Jochen Duelli as out healthcare expert, and even Fritz Seikowsky, who was head of the Bain Munich operation, got involved. We ended up saying that there was big potential. We said they could double the EBIT within 3 years. That was our idea. Then Thomas Krenz asked us how he should believe this, that Schroders could double the EBIT in 3 years? We said that Bain would co-invest DM 1.5 million of our own money on the deal, which was almost double what we got in fees. Would that help him believe us? He said "good".[3]

The Schroders team decided to pursue the deal aggressively, putting in a preliminary bid of DM 800 million, which later appeared to have been far higher than any rival's. One private equity house was believed to have dropped out of the process with a final bid below DM 500 million, considering the deal to be fully priced at that level. Thomas Jetter and Richard Winckles believed at the time that no other bidder had offered more than DM 700 million, and their approach was that Schroders should either lead the auction, or bid low and wait for everyone else to drop out because of their problems on the deal. Bidding in the middle ground they considered to be a waste of time, and with Sirona they were confident that the first strategy was the one that made sense.

On the other hand, the Schroders team were fully conscious of the fact that the deal had to earn a sufficient return, should they be successful in acquiring the business. The team's concerns over the valuation were not helped by the time constraints Siemens had set, having decided that it wanted the transaction completed quickly. Perhaps even more challenging, however, were the limits Siemens placed upon bidders' access to management. The Schroders team found itself constantly battling for both time and management access. Siemens rationed both out so tightly that the Schroders team was literally counting the days.[4]

The success of Schroders in closing the Sirona deal dazzled many in the industry, and made some observers feel that, as with Matzen ten years earlier, the Schroders team had again proven that it could walk on water. Over the years that followed, Schroders built up a substantial portfolio, including the Charles Vogele and Memorex-Telex deals in 1997, plus the successful IPO of Singulus of the same year, followed by the addition of Leica Microsystems and California Kleindienst, plus the IPO of Kässbohrer in 1998.

ABN Amro

Having fallen out with Alpinvest in their Atco joint venture in Germany, ABN Amro moved swiftly to set up a captive office in Frankfurt in 1996 under the leadership of Farzin Assayesh, a Persian with a corporate finance background. Farzin, was joined by Richard Gritsch, from Helaba. Wolfgang Pietzsch, formerly of PriceWaterhouse, who joined together with Gerald Oertel from Commerzbank in October 1998 recalls:

> ABN Amro had done a deal with the old Atco team, who went off to join NatWest, and split the portfolio with Alpinvest. The old portfolio included Colortronic, Computer Partner, MultiZoom, and some others. Most of them were MBOs, while the new deals we were embarking upon were expansion capital, or pre-IPO capital as it was called at the time.[5]

Partly as a function of the timing of the office's opening, the team was focussed almost exclusively on growth capital for dotcom and technology companies, with short-term ambitions to be IPO'd on the Neuer Markt. Despite the frenzy of activity, there were discussions over the strategy of the private equity team. The bank wanted to keep a close control over the team's activities, whereas Assayesh preferred a lighter touch, an approach he could not gain acceptance of, and so he left ABN Amro in March 1999.

Wolf Wolfsteiner, who had joined the team in 1999 coming from a managerial role in one of the portfolio companies, recalls his impressions of the period:

> We had a very flexible mandate at the time. The bank's balance sheet was the source of our money, and the beauty was that our investment committee was chaired by Reijkman Groeninck, who was the bank's CFO at the time, and later became its CEO. We had certain degrees of freedom: we certainly wanted to do mid-cap buyouts, but there weren't many of them around.[6]

The churn in the Frankfurt team came at the height of the dotcom bubble, as Pietzsch explains:

> All that had mattered was crazy business plans, put together by all those ex-McKinsey, ex-BCG type of guys. Then the dotcom boom collapsed. That was the time when Richard Gritsch decided to leave ABN Amro Capital to join Marco Brockhaus from 3i in setting up Brockhaus Private Equity.[7]

Alarmed at the staffing challenges Frankfurt was facing, Amsterdam initially expected to have to headhunt a new leader, but after quite some time chose instead to move the head of the German structured finance unit, together with his senior team, over to run the private equity business. The project finance team included Henk Droege, Christof Namenyi and Peter Davidzon. Namenyi recalls the structured finance team's move:

> ABN Amro decided to close the structured finance division in 1999, of which I was a director at this time. The team impacted by this decision were asked by the German CEO of the bank if we would join ABN Amro Capital in early 2000, a group that had been doing pre-IPO investments, but which they intended to switch to typical LBO financing.

> The team they already had in place had done some buyouts, such as Colortronic with Alpinvest and Hauser, but neither of them were leveraged.[8]

Inevitably, the team change provoked further splits in the ranks. In the years that followed, few members of the original ABN Amro team would stay to work with the new group parachuted in from structured finance to help with the refocus upon leveraged buyouts.

HSBC Private Equity

When Max von Drechsel was poached from the Berenberg Fleming team to set up an office for HSBC Private Equity in Germany, he was able to build on HSBC's historic presence in the German market:

> HSBC had a small operation in Munich although the focus was different and had been very much on small deals, investing from the balance sheet of the bank. This was a useful place to start but we wanted to reinvigorate our approach to the German market and I

thought carefully about where to base the business. Ultimately the choice was between Frankfurt or Dusseldorf. I chose Dusseldorf, because I wanted to use the relationship with HSBC Trinkaus, which was very well connected in the region.[9]

Having set up office, von Drechsel made his first investment in 1998, with the acquisition of Evotec Biosystems. This was to prove an excellent investment, as von Drechsel recalls:

Evotec can be described as my one free shot. We took the company public in 1999, only twelve months after the buyout, and made close to seven times our money. It was very good timing too.[10]

After six successful years establishing the business model of acquiring defensive businesses alongside their chief executives in Germany, von Drechsel decided the time was right to explore a more entrepreneurial future and left to join SMB,[11] while Nico Helling and Peter Kroha took over the reins of the HSBC office in Dusseldorf.

BC Partners

The success with Techem firmly established BC Partners' new brand in the German market, indeed many advisers and bankers were to forget quite quickly that the team had ever been known by any other name. The Hamburg team took Ludwig Beck public in 1998 in a process which, while not without its problems, was nevertheless successful. Dieter Münch, a managing director of Ludwig Beck, recalls:

In 1997, BC Partners came up with the idea that we should do an IPO the following year. The initiative came late, it was already November, and we thought that the suggestion was completely impossible. We had the financial year to close. But BC Partners wasn't going to be delayed, or put off.

Fortunately for them, the environment on the stock exchange was good. It was just before the Neuer Markt became so important. If we had waited half a year more, the IPO would have been impossible.

This was the first IPO for BC Partners, and they wanted to make sure that it worked. They took on Morgan Stanley, who were also doing their first IPO in Germany.

Much of the organisation for the process was done from England. While the IPO provided BC Partners with an exit, it didn't bring any fresh capital into Ludwig Beck. This made it difficult to sell to investors. It only worked because Morgan Stanley and BC Partners pushed the thing so well. Another problem later was that the pricing of the share issue was too high. At €17.30 on 18th May 1998, the share price began at a level that was never to be seen again.[12]

The BC Partners team grew over the period, first with the addition of Hanns Ostmeier in 1996, and then Herman Wendelstadt and Ulrich Biffar in 1997.

BC Partners closed a minority participation in KTM shortly before the start of the new millennium, in 1999. Wendelstadt, working on KTM as one of his first deals, recalls the experience:

We had met the management through a motorcycle world champion we knew. We were very impressed by the management team. The firm had grown out of its office space and management had given up their respective offices and decided to manage the business "by walking around", constantly keeping people on their toes. The staff never knew when the management might walk in on them. The two managers had different roles, one as CEO and the other CFO, and there was an incredible compatibility between the two of them. One was visionary, an engineer with high flying but technologically backed ideas, and the other one was stringent, and diligent. They were both very intelligent. It was really impressive.

We thought that it was a smallish deal, and wouldn't pose much of a risk to the firm. The key thing for the management was the growth potential of their business. We used Bain to do our assessment, as I know Rolf Weddigen through my brother who also worked for Bain. There was one big regulatory issue they needed to win, which concerned the import of non-American goods into America. At the time they were having to dismantle their bikes, to reassemble them in the States, in order to comply with American standards. Eventually the ruling went in their favour.

The only challenge was that we had little influence over management. It was difficult to contain them: because they had the majority, we were the ones having to say yes. The real problem came when we wanted to exit. You cannot exit a company without the support of management, and these guys knew this. I was travelling the world to get Harley Davidson and others to express interest, but it was a huge effort to get management to understand that we needed to get out. In three years they tripled their EBITDA, doubling revenues after four years. The management ended up making us an offer themselves, in which we made three times our money. We said fine, let's take it, and leave the relationship intact. The business continued to develop well in the years following our exit, which is important to the buyer and the seller. KTM was one of the better buyouts in Austria.[13]

Another defining deal for BC Partners came in 1999 when Grohe came up for sale. This was a hotly contested auction, in which almost every major buyout firm active in Germany participated. The victory of BC Partners placed them effectively in the position of buyout house of the year in 1999.

Clayton, Dubilier & Rice

The entry of Clayton, Dubilier & Rice into Europe was a direct consequence of Joe Rice's personal interest in Europe. The choice of Germany as the first step was driven by an opportunity: Joe Rice forged a relationship with a high ranking banking figure in 1995, and for three years flew over periodically to be introduced to senior managers and business people in Germany. Rice gained the impression that there was a lot to be done in Germany, certainly in terms of carving out orphaned divisions from large conglomerates and improving some of the local businesses, something that was at the core of CD&R's investment focus and approach. Rice was introduced to Jens Odewald in 1998, and very quickly this led to a deeper relationship. Odewald had already opened his own private equity business by this point together with Hammermann and Stelzer, and became a co-investor in CD&R's first European deal, Schulte Bautechnik.

Schulte was done in June 1998 for $226 million close to the height of the real estate cycle after reunification. Tobias Gondorf recalls:

In hindsight, this was a very challenging time to buy a distributor for sanitary and heating equipment given that the underlying construction market had just entered a prolonged downturn after the reunification bubble, shrinking by double digits over the next seven plus years.[14]

Table 13.2 Private Equity Transactions in 1998

1998

Company	Buyer	Seller	Exit year	Sold to
AHAG Hospitals	Quadriga	Industrial roll-up	Not yet divested	Not yet divested
Anders & Kern Präsentationssysteme	TA Triumph-Adler (Office)	Family	Not yet divested	Not yet divested
Atlantic Zeiser	ABN Amro Capital France	Family	2002	Orell Fuessli Holding
Autinform	NatWest	Family	2005	HAITEC AG
Badenia Bettcomfort GmbH & Co. KG	Halder	Family	2004	Scandinavian strategic
Bernd Steudle	Alchemy	Halder	2002	Finatem/Invest Equity
Bettmer GmbH	Nord Holding	Family	2005	Afinum
Brandl	TA Triumph-Adler (Office)	Family	Not yet divested	Not yet divested
Casa Reha	ECM/Chase Capital	Covenant Care	2005	Advent
Casolute GmbH	Nord Holding	Family	2003	RLE
Coming Home GmbH	Global Equity Partners/UIAG	Family	Not yet divested	Not yet divested
Copytex	TA Triumph-Adler (Office)	Family	Not yet divested	Not yet divested
Deutsche Woolworth	Electra Fleming	Venator	Not yet divested	Not yet divested
Dialog Semiconductor	Apax	Ericsson/Daimler Benz	1999	IPO
Doerries Scharmann Technologie	DBAG	Voith AG	2007	A-Tec Industries
DPS-Engineering	Berliner Elektro Holding AG (Ad Capital)	Family	Not yet divested	Not yet divested
dtms (Deutsche Telefon and Marketing Services AG)	3i	Previous investors	2005	D+S europe
EMAG Machinenfabrik	Hannover Finanz	Family	2005	Family
EMS Engineering Maintenance Services	Nord Holding	Family	2003	R&M Technische Dienstleist
Emtec Magnetics	L&G Ventures	Kohap Group	2003	Imation
Erftcarbon	NatWest	VAW Group	2005	Tokai Carbon

Table 13.2 Private Equity Transactions in 1998 – *continued*

1998

Company	Buyer	Seller	Exit year	Sold to
Erich Jaeger	Berliner Elektro Holding AG (Ad Capital)	Family	Not yet divested	Not yet divested
Essanelle	Halder	Corporate	2001	IPO
Eurocom Depora	NatWest	Microgen Holdings	2001	Finland Post
EurotaxGlasse's Group	Hicks, Muse, Tate & Furst	Family	2006	Candover
Evotec BioSystems GmbH	HSBC Private Equity	Previous investors	1999	IPO
Floristik	Alpha	Raab Karcher	2004	New investor
Frigoblock Grosskopf	Hannover Finanz	Previous investors	Not yet divested	Not yet divested
Frimo	Palladion	Family	2004	Nord Holding
GAH Anlagentechnik	DBAG	Public-to-private	2000	Atel Holding
Henkelhausen GmbH	NIB Capital	Family	2003	Hannover Finanz
Henneveld	TA Triumph-Adler (Office)	Family	Not yet divested	Not yet divested
Highlight Communication	ABN Amro Capital	Previous investors	1999	IPO
Highway One	Apax	Previous investors	2002	Telefonica
Hübner Elektromaschinen GmbH	Berliner Elektro Holding AG (Ad Capital)	Hannover Finanz	2002	Baumer Electric AG
Hüco Electronic GmbH	TA Triumph-Adler (Presentation & Media)	Family	2002	LRP Capital
I-Center Elektrogrosshandel	Industri Kapital	Siemens	2001	Insolvency
Inometa	Gothaer	capital increase	2006	Secondary Gothaer
Jost Werke	Alpha	Previous investors	2005	PPM Ventures
Kirsch & Lütjohann	Hannover Finanz	Family	Not yet divested	Not yet divested
Klein & Weiden	Management	ABN Amro/Alpinvest	Not yet divested	Not yet divested
Landis & Gyr Communications	TPG	Electrowatt	2001	Insolvency
Leica Geosystems	Investcorp	Lancet Investments	2000	IPO
Leica Microsystems	Schroder Ventures	Leica Holding	2005	Danaher Inc
Leobersdorfer Maschinenfabrik (LMF)	Andlinger & Company	Deutsche Babcock	2004	Invest Equity
Lieken/Wendeln	Apax	Family	2001	Kamps AG

Table 13.2 **Private Equity Transactions in 1998** – *continued*

1998

Company	Buyer	Seller	Exit year	Sold to
Lloyd Werft	NatWest	Bremer Vulkan	2003	Management
MAP Medizintechnik für Arzt und Patient	ECM	Family	2001	ResMed Inc
Markenfilm	Hannover Finanz	Family	Not yet divested	Not yet divested
MPA Pharma	Hannover Finanz	Family	Not yet divested	Not yet divested
Neuman & Esser	Hannover Finanz	Family	2008	Other investor
Pickenpack Hussmann & Hahn	Gilde/RaboBank	Previous investors	2003	Orlando
pitti Heimtierprodukte	Hannover Finanz	Family	2004	BHF Private Equity
Pongs & Zahn (mezzanine)	BBK	Mezzanine finance	2002	Repayment
Rhiag Group	CVC	Family	2007	Alpha
Schulte Bautechnik	Clayton Dubilier & Rice/ Odewald	ThyssenKrupp	2004	Management
Soudronic	Doughty Hanson	Family	2001	Capvis/Gilde
Suspa Compart	PPM	3i/Family	2009	Tyrol Equity/ Management
Systematics	Odewald	Management	2001	EDS
Tank & Rast	Allianz Capital/ Apax/LSG	Privatisation	2004	Terra Firma
Tartex Ritter	CVC	Nestle	2001	Wessanen
Temco	3i	Vector/LBO France	2006	Saurer AG
TTB	Bridgepoint	Atco/ABN Amro	2005	Management
UFA-Film Theater OHG	Apax/Pricoa Capital	Family	2003	Insolvency
UNI-DATA AG	Odewald/Nord KB	Family	2001	UPS
Vianova Resins	Morgan Grenfall Dev. Cap/ DB Capital	Hoechst	2000	Solutia Inc.
WAP Alto Group	Electra Fleming	Jungheinrich	1999	Danish competitor

Source: Authors' compilation

Schulte was bought out of Thyssen AG by CD&R together with Jens Odewald's firm as co-investor. It was a corporate orphan with significant improvement potential, and on the face of it, in CD&R's "sweet spot": CD&R had significant, highly successful experience in similar situations in the US, in the general distribution sector and in the markets Schulte served (e.g. WESCO in the US). But besides the underlying market turning against it, a transformation of a business like this presented somewhat different, local challenges relative to the ones CD&R faced in the US. In addition, in order to control and execute change in a business like Schulte, to be effective it was necessary to be able to speak German. Gondorf recalls:

> In order to understand what was happening in the business, you needed to talk to the branch manager, sales people, customers etc., otherwise you just got the message that the top guys wanted to tell you; and you relied on how they translated what you suggested to their team.[15]

The on-going downturn in Schulte's relevant market, and the extent of the decline in sales it precipitated, on top of the significant inefficiencies existing in the business, led to the situation becoming more and more challenging. Irrespective of how hard the CD&R team worked together with the Schulte management, and tried to support the business, the situation at the company grew more serious, as Gondorf explains:

> We invested a lot of resources into Schulte, because we didn't want to just walk away from the problem. We wanted to be good citizens towards the employees, the business, and the banks involved, and not just hand them over the keys. So we spent a lot of time and resources on it more from a reputation point of view than with the expectation of achieving any significant economic gains. We finally sold it to a small private equity house in 2002.[16]

CD&R's challenges were not however confined to Schulte. In 1996, the majority of Dornier, a German aircraft manufacturer, had been acquired from Daimler Benz by Fairchild, led by a group of investors under Carl Albert, to form Fairchild Dornier. But within a short space of time, it became clear that the new US-German concern needed additional equity to see it through the development of a new regional jet.

CD&R teamed up with Allianz Capital Partners to take over as new shareholders, injecting a total of $1.2 billion into the company, of which $400 million was in growth capital from CD&R and ACP, and $800 million was in debt finance mainly from a consortium of German banks, partially guaranteed by the German and Bavarian governments. Gondorf recalls:

> Ultimately, the European Union became involved as well, because it had to approve the German government loan guarantees.[17]

Fairchild Dornier was certainly a challenging investment for a private equity firm, given the capital intensity of its business, specifically the development of a new aircraft. In addition, as witnessed by many if not most examples in the aircraft industry, the development of a new aircraft almost always missed budget with regard to cost, timing, and capital required. Gondorf explains:

> The development of the new aircraft was somewhat out of our total control, hence we planned for significant cushions in our financing.

> CD&R's overriding objective with Fairchild Dornier was to reshape and rebuild a company that, in turn, could successfully build and roll out a new, advanced family of regional jet aircraft (the 70 seat 728Jet and 90 seat 928Jet models) that could capture a significant share of the fast growing regional aviation market, which at the same time was by far the most attractive segment of the aviation industry. While Fairchild Dornier was an existing aircraft manufacturer, this mission required the recruitment of literally hundreds of technical personnel and engineers and the development of a brand new manufacturing facility. And all of this activity was to be undertaken while production of the existing line of aircraft continued in order to finance the company's transformation and its development of new products.

> The premise underpinning the investment was that the infusion of sufficient capital, coupled with the addition of management operating expertise, would allow Fairchild Dornier to transform itself into a cutting-edge aircraft manufacturer.[18]

CD&R was familiar with the regional jet market as a result of its successful investment in Allison Engine in 1993. Like Allison, where CD&R helped to commercialise a new regional jet engine, CD&R knew that the success of the Fairchild Dornier investment depended upon converting a set of designs into an actual product, and carefully managing and executing all of the steps in between. Gondorf recalls the challenge that presented itself:

> Shortly following our initial investment, we launched an all-out programme to give Fairchild Dornier the infrastructure it required to build a new company and to support rapid growth. During the first six months, we instituted a number of significant changes. In support of our investment case, Fairchild Dornier had already received bookings by 2000 for sizable standing orders for its new jets from leading industry players such as Lufthansa, GE, and Delta. At the end of that year, the company's order backlog amounted to 545 aircraft worth a total of $12 billion.[19]

CD&R, with assistance from ACP, kept the momentum moving forward. At mid-year 2001, important progress was being made, as Gondorf recalls:

> Before September 11th, we were pretty active with some major new aircraft procurement campaigns, where Fairchild's new aircraft was a very hot contestant to win its fair share. With the expectation of winning a major new order on top of the launch order we had from Lufthansa, we were offered by our banks the opportunity to place a high yield bond, which would have allowed us to inject significantly more new capital into the business. There were also some other additional financing sources (e.g. for our finished goods inventory of aeroplanes to Hainan Airways). We were at advanced stages in working on further ways of increasing the available liquidity in the business.[20]

Then came 11th September 2001, which swiftly and resoundingly devastated the aircraft manufacturing industry throughout the world. Announced orders for large civil jet aircraft declined from 1,138 in 2000 to 709 in 2001, and then fell further to 551 in 2002. The decline in tourism and business travel pushed many well-known airlines to the brink of, or into, bankruptcy. For Fairchild Dornier, the impact was immediate, as orders for new planes were cancelled or delayed. The net effect was to deprive the company of an essential source of cash, in the form of customer downpayments. Gondorf remembers the critical day well:

> I was just getting off a plane flying with my colleague Michael Babiarz from London to Dusseldorf on the way to another bank meeting for

Schulte. I arrived at Dusseldorf airport, and people were running around talking of what had happened, but we didn't really understand. We couldn't imagine it. I rang my mother, who was watching the events unfold on TV. She said a tower had just collapsed, and we just couldn't believe that. Then we went to our meeting in Dusseldorf, and they had big video screens. Michael tried to call his family in New York, obviously without success as you couldn't get a line.

Within a couple of weeks we realised that airline travel was and would continue to be significantly down for a while, and nobody wanted to commit to anything. All the campaigns we had been working on were put on indefinite hold. Financing couldn't be had, and the financing alternatives we had been working on just dropped dead.[21]

In the aftermath of 11th September, it became clear that Fairchild Dornier would not have enough cash to complete R&D on its 728Jet programme, which was essential to the company's survival. Compounding an already difficult situation, the Chinese government refused to issue licences for 21 328Jets that were already in production for a regional Chinese airline, which meant that yet another important source of cash had evaporated. In October and November 2001, CD&R and its co-investor, ACP, proposed a recapitalisation plan for Fairchild Dornier to provide the liquidity that management considered would put the company onto a sound financial footing. Under the plan discussed and agreed upon, besides additional equity to be invested, the German banks were to provide additional funding with further capital coming from the German government, contingent upon EU approval. By February 2002, circumstances worsened dramatically. Fairchild Dornier management released projections revealing that they would not have enough cash to get through March 2002, the month that the EU was expected to approve the German government loan. Continued delays in customer orders meant that even more cash would have to be raised than the company had previously anticipated.

At CD&R's recommendation, Fairchild Dornier hired Alvarez & Marsal, specialists in financial restructuring, to provide an independent assessment of the company's cash position. In addition, CD&R directed a team of its own personnel to analyse the situation. Based on the Alvarez & Marsal report, management determined that more cash than the original plan estimated would be required for the recapitalisation because of customer delays in orders and purchases.

At this point CD&R determined that a new strategy was required. A strategic buyer for Fairchild Dornier was sought, but CD&R was unable to complete a transaction before the company was mandated to declare insolvency under German law in April 2002. Gondorf remembers the events:

> Early in 2002, we started talking to potential strategic partners, but they weren't open for any real discussions or new investments as at the time they had major problems of their own.[22]

After Schulte and Fairchild Dornier, CD&R had a major success in Germany with the $1.65 billion purchase of VWR from Merck KGaA in April 2004. The transaction was representative of a long line of CD&R acquisitions of corporate orphans in complicated carve-outs. In 2007, after a three year value building process in which VWR's EBITDA grew by over 60%, CD&R sold VWR to Madison Dearborn Partners in a transaction valued at approximately $3.8 billion for a 4.6 times multiple of the investment. Gondorf reflects on this happier experience:

> On a broader basis, the VWR transaction reflected the type of attractive investment opportunity that CD&R was and is positioned to capture as German corporations address the competitive implications of a global market, regulatory reform, cost structure issues, and increased focus on shareholder value. In addition, the close collaboration between CD&R's US-based and European-based professionals proved to be an important competitive advantage in winning and completing the VWR transaction.
>
> VWR played to CD&R's core strengths. First, VWR was a distribution business, a sector the firm knew very well and where it had considerable success, including Alliant, WESCO and Brakes. Second, it was a complex carve-out of an underperforming orphan division from a large global parent, where a critical element of value stemmed from the negotiation of a long-term supply agreement. Third, VWR offered tremendous opportunities for transformation and growth under CD&R's stewardship. The key elements of success that we identified for VWR, purchasing, product breadth and profitability, customer mix, and scale in distribution centers, were not a priority for Merck, since VWR operated primarily as a captive distributor for Merck's chemical products. As a firm, CD&R was very experienced in addressing these issues.
>
> The sourcing of this investment began more than three years before the investment when Joe Rice first started informal discussions with Merck and VWR's senior management.[23]

CD&R hoped that it would be well positioned when Merck finally decided to sell VWR. CD&R's presence in Europe through its London office helped to maintain a strong relationship with the company and ensured that it had the opportunity to participate in the limited, but highly competitive, sale process. Gondorf explains:

> We met with Merck's senior management team to emphasize the importance of selecting a partner with the operating capabilities to grow sales of the Merck-branded products that VWR distributes. The company would retain its exclusive distribution agreement with Merck for laboratory products in certain European countries.[24]

CD&R's successful experience with similar ongoing agreements at Lexmark, WESCO and Alliant, provided Merck with the added level of confidence they needed to select CD&R over the other private equity firms competing for the company. Gondorf adds:

> VWR was a classic CD&R deal. It also reflected the close coordination between CD&R's financial and operating partners in New York and London around sourcing, negotiations, due diligence, structuring, financing and post-close transition.[25]

Clayton Dubilier & Rice learned valuable lessons from its early investments in Germany, which the firm successfully applied with VWR and other successful European investments in the years that followed.

Odewald, Hammermann & Stelzer

Jens Odewald was one of the first successful managers with a track record in German industry to decide to enter private equity with his own investment vehicle. Born in Hannover in 1940, Odewald was the son of a police chief. After harbouring an early ambition to become a diplomat, which faded as soon as he had seen first hand the workings of an embassy, Odewald took up his first job in 1968 working for Esso in Hamburg, where he stayed for six years. He then accepted the offer to become the CFO of Kühne & Nagel's German operations. Three years later he was offered the CFO position at Kaufhof. Here Odewald's financial training enabled him to unlock hidden value:

> I saw lots of equity bound up in expensive locations occupied by the department stores, all built by famous architects. I saw that there

were assets worth billions of Deutschmarks, producing a profit of less than a couple of hundred million Deutschmarks. This could happen because the owner only looked at the results of the retail company, and overlooked the values bound up in the property. It was also clear that we had to diversify if we were to move forward. We had to look for new activities. So I bought two small companies, one with about DM 100 million turnover, and the other with DM 60 million turnover. These were MediaMarkt and Saturn Hansa. In my view it seemed logical that since department stores were being attacked by specialist retailers such as garden centres, IKEA, drugstores, and food discounters, we should get into these businesses ourselves.[26]

Odewald's rapid development of the brown and white goods retailing specialists, quickly ran foul of the Kartelamt which considered him to be building up a dominant position. But Odewald found that the solution was simply to bring in additional investors.

I had a good relationship with some big insurance companies. When I wanted to buy Saturn Hansa, and the antitrust authorities wouldn't permit it, I had the idea, not to buy it alone, but to ask four big insurance companies to buy it with us. These were Allianz,

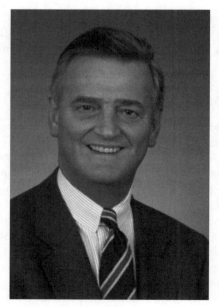

Figure 13.1   Jens Odewald

Axa, Gerling, and Albingia. They got nearly twice the profit they were expecting from co-investing on this with Kaufhof.[27]

When the German government asked Odewald to work part-time as Chairman of the Treuhand, to oversee the privatisation of the East German economy, he couldn't turn down the opportunity, and moved to Berlin to fulfil his new role with zeal. But the deal-making at Kaufhof continued:

> Kaufhof grew significantly during those years. I bought a share of Hapag Lloyd and of Hawesco, at that time a small wine and champagne company, now the European market leader. We also bought Vobis computer, which they sold once I had left, in 1995 after the merger between Metro and Kaufhof. It was at that time that I was asked to leave my job as CEO, which I had held for ten years. I was 55 at this time.[28]

It was in the mid-1990s that Odewald discovered private equity. Rolf Dienst and Hellmut Kirchner suggested that Odewald should turn his hand to the activity. Odewald realised that his relationships with many of the leading insurance companies would make his task of raising a fund relatively simple. His first thoughts were to raise DM 50 million, but his banking advisers recommended him to raise DM 200 million, which he managed very quickly. Rolf Dienst and Hellmut Kirchner also put Odewald in touch with Peter Hammermann and Norbert Stelzer, who had themselves been trying to raise their own fund. Odewald recalls:

> While fund-raising in London, a few bankers came up to me and asked the question "what happens if something happens to you?" It was this comment which made me look for a team.[29]

Stelzer recalls the decisive moment:

> The three of us looked straight into each others eyes and promised, if we manage to raise DM 50 million, then we will go for it! In the end, we reached DM 216 million, and we found that for some time we were running Germany's largest domestic private equity fund.[30]

The first deal, the acquisition of Schulte Bautechnik from Thyssen AG, was done together with Clayton, Dubilier & Rice (CD&R). Schulte was one of the largest building materials wholesalers in Germany,

Figure 13.2   Norbert Stelzer

distributing sanitary and heating equipment and civil engineering materials. CD&R had just developed plans to open an office in London to serve Europe, which was to be headed up by Christopher Mackenzie, and Schulte gave them and Odewald their first deal. Norbert Stelzer recalls:

> Odewald got the deal through his contacts, but it was clearly too large for our fund. Hence he brought in CD&R. Jens was convinced it would be easy to improve. Having CD&R on board, one of the most reputable investors in world, was very promising too. So we did an asset deal. But the recession in the building industry, which came a few years later, was always one step ahead of our improvements. Sales continually went down, and we could never catch up. We were just in the wrong industry at the wrong time.[31]

The Odewald team also closed some smaller deals, where they were a strong minority shareholder, beginning with the acquisition of Systematics in December 1998. This was a DM 350 million turnover IT services company that was being groomed by its owners for the stock exchange. Within two years, the Odewald team executed a buy-and-build strategy, acquiring ten additional companies, and successfully completing the takeover of a competitor of comparable size on the Neuer Markt. Systematics was later sold to EDS with revenues of more than €600 million, almost four times its original size, accompanied by an even larger increase in profits. The company subsequently formed the backbone of EDS Germany.

In the same year, Unidata was also acquired, which was a logistics business, in a segment that Odewald knew well from his Kühne & Nagel days as CFO. Hammerman and Stelzer had acquired and successfully exited a minority stake in Kühne & Nagel on behalf of Deutsche Handelsbank in former times, and so the team liked the industry's dynamics. Unidata was clearly number one in its segment in Germany. Ironically, a portfolio company of Clayton, Dubilier & Rice was number two, but as the managers of the two companies resisted, a conceivable merger was not achieved. Nevertheless, two years and 11 add-on acquisitions later, Unidata was either number one or number two in its segment within 12 European countries, having become the clear European leader. Again, Odewald served as an industry builder, Unidata later forming a large part of UPS Germany.

Hardly had the Odewald team finished these deals, however, than it experienced its first significant change of team. Given that the team's base was in Berlin, it was a logical consequence that the team members would eventually move to Berlin. Hammermann was living in Munich at the time, and decided that he would rather stay put for family reasons, and therefore decided to leave. Almost at the same time, August von Joest, whom Odewald knew privately, jumped in to fill Hammermann's place. Von Joest worked for the Treuhand during 1990–1992, before becoming a partner at PwC, where he supported Doughty Hanson and Charterhouse in the mid-1990s. Von Joest brought a technical dimension to the Odewald team, as he later explained:

> My role was, and remains, to take care of technical aspects. I looked at the nuts and bolts projects in the businesses. One of the charms of the Odewald partnership is that we encompass such a broad range of skills. This contrasts with the Anglo-Saxons, who tend to be staffed by financial people and lawyers.[32]

Barclays

The precise timing of Barclays entry into the German private equity market was strongly influenced by Peter Hammermann's decision to leave Odewald, to find a new opportunity in Munich, as he later explained:

In a way, it would have been logical for me to move to Berlin if I had stayed. Odewald had a very strong dedication to the city, having strong links to politics at that time, and so he was travelling from his own home town of Cologne to Berlin every week. It was effectively a fly-in team. I was flying in from Munich. If you think about how private equity works in Germany, you have to travel, so it isn't really a problem, but I preferred to have a base closer to home.

As the outcome of the fund raising had been very successful, and I was in my early forties, I had to consider whether I really wanted to spend my life in Berlin. Initially I had been happy enough commuting. I worked on one deal at the start, which was a logistics business, which turned out to be very successful, but rather quickly, I came to the decision to leave. One of the big reasons was that with Odewald there was a natural disproportion between him as an industrial heavyweight and me. I wanted to be responsible on my own. I wanted to develop a business.[33]

Via an acquaintance, Hammermann got to know Barclays in London. He met with Graeme White at the Plaza of Barclays Capital on Canary Wharf.

They have two types of meeting rooms. One set has wooden panels with windows, and the other set has the same wooden panels, but without the windows. We were in one of the latter. The meeting with Graeme White lasted over three hours. It was the sort of meeting where you get to know each other. On the one side of the table, you had someone with a great track record of working within 3i, and who had joined Barclays Capital two years before. On the other side of the table was me, who had only the benefit of being German, and having had the courage of raising his own fund, and having done a couple of deals with the Deutsche Handelsbank, and one with Odewald, but it was a limited track record.[34]

What particularly attracted Hammermann to Barclays was its approach towards developing private equity on the Continent. France was already up and running, and set an example of the procedures Barclays was developing. Hammermann explains:

The approach was very unusual, and not a typical UK approach to the Continent. They were setting up local entities, and giving them freedom, showing them patience and understanding. I thought this was an intelligent approach. It made for a good local understanding of the market, and for a good chemistry between the regional teams. Graeme's approach to the market was a great thing, and a precondition for the success of both France and Germany. London provided back burner support that was extremely valuable.

I joined Barclays on 1st July 1998. At that time they had already funded their entire business. What took time in Munich was finding an office, a secretary, and some people.[35]

Peter Hammermann first met Michael Bork privately, at a christening. By coincidence, both had talked to Graeme White at Barclays, as Michael Bork at the time was working for Dresdner Bank sorting out some acquisition finance and corporate lending problems for their Bankhaus Reuschel subsidiary in Munich. Bork later recalled:

I had strong contacts with English private equity houses, through my intensive work with these houses and with Citibank in London. So I took a chance and approached Barclays through Graeme White. It was 1998, and they didn't yet have an office in Germany. I had a meeting with them, and at the week-end I went to a party in Pullach back in Germany, where by then I was living with my family. I met Peter Hammermann who was formerly a board member of Deutsche Handelsbank, and in this function, he had provided some mezzanine finance for transactions I was involved in as well. He had established his own fund with Norbert Stelzer and Jens Odewald. I found out that he lived in Pullach too and that we had both talked to Barclays. Barclays had already hired Peter by this point, and I was quickly interested to join him.[36]

Bork joined Barclays in March 1999, on the same day as Jan Wiechman, previously of DBAG. The Barclays team hit the ground running, doing the first deal only a few months later. Hammermann recollects the course of events:

MTH was a non-integrated business of three separate units and brands owned by Bodycote, and was a spin-off. At the outset, it was a competitive deal out in the market, but after some months a number of our competitors had already put MTH aside. We were approached by a guy from DKW in the UK. We liked the business, and gained a different understanding of it from most of our competitors. The management were not convinced that a buyout could work, but they could build and sell furnaces.

We then ended up in a very complicated negotiation with the vendor. We tried to be very cautious with the tough British lawyers, whose approach was very aggressive. We weren't willing to accept a lot of the things they were pushing onto us. There was a lot of confrontation, but it ended up in a good under-standing. We had lots of late night sessions. People on the other side kept saying "Peter you are always saying no, and I can't stand it". But in the end, we came to exactly the structure we wanted. We got guarantees, and a significant escrow amount. The guaranteed business from Bodycoat was a great contribution, and helped us a lot over the time, giving us some level of security.

During the negotiations, we also had the experience of staying in an advantageous hotel in Manchester, where the walls were covered with pictures of Spitfires and Messerschmitts. We stood there with pints of beer in an interesting atmosphere. We were all of the post-war generation.[37]

Barclays hired a team from Bain & Company under the leadership of Ekkehard Franzke to conduct the commercial due diligence on MTH. But the assignment was a small one, and Franzke and his colleagues moved over to bainlab to ride the dotcom boom, leaving the Barclays team to look for fresh advisers for their next deals.

With Nici, a plush toy company in Altenkunstadt, North Bavaria, Barclays used a consulting group which performed badly, and brought in L.E.K. to redo the work in August 2000. But the biggest break for Barclays was to come with Minimax, negotiations for which also began in 2000. Hammermann describes the process:

Through good connections into Preussag, we were introduced to Minimax. That was in the winter of 2000. We were told that we had to do the deal by December 2000. It was a difficult process, but we were able to demonstrate our strengths to the management. Especially our initial analysis, which was to reduce the number of foreign subsidiaries, was well accepted, because this was their target as well. Helaba was very helpful on the financing side. They were also in an early stage situation in terms of their own development.[38]

A particular attraction for Barclays was that Preussag had already found an MBI manager that they were offering to bring in to help turn around the company. Klaus Hofmann, born 1967 in a town south-west of Munich, had begun his career in Europe's largest meat-packing company, before leaving in 1996 to join Schindler. After four years, he received a call from Preussag to ask if he would join Minimax, a company they were in the process of divesting. After lengthy discussions, Rainer Feuerhake, the Preussag director asked Hoffman whether he would be willing to take on the job if Minimax was bought by a private equity house. Hofmann's remembers his own response well:

> I told Feuerhake that this was the only way in which I would work with Minimax.[39]

Hofmann had already come into contact with private equity, when Robert Osterrieth had been looking for a CEO for California Kleindienst. Hofmann recalls:

> I came across Osterrieth in 1999. He had supported the merger between California and Kleindienst. He told me that he had bought ten companies out of the Schroders fund, and still owned California Kleindienst, which was both loss making and cash burning. I ended up working as an advisor to the company, and also took part in several advisory board meetings, where I met the representative of HypoVereinsbank, who was also involved in Minimax, and hence the connection with Preussag.[40]

Inevitably, Hofmann's association with one of the founding members of the German private equity industry was to be formative. The two men even found they shared a passion for tennis:

> Then we played several games of tennis. Robert was very motivated, and worked hard on developing his skills. He made me an offer in 2000 to become the number two managing director at

the California Kleindienst organisation, with an option to get to number 1.[41]

However, Hofmann was still not convinced that he should leave Schindler, either for Minimax or for California Kleindienst. To help him make up his mind, Feuerhake explained the management participation scheme that was being discussed for Minimax. Hofmann recalls:

> I did not believe what I had heard at first. I told him that the story sounded great, but the company was in a bad situation, so it had a long way to go. In short, it did not sound too interesting. I wasn't too enthusiastic.

> I became enthusiastic about six weeks later when I checked all the information about the company. I began to realise that on the contrary, the wait would not be that long. Minimax had a good basis in the market, especially in Germany. It had good technological expertise and experience. But it also had a lot of subsidiaries and foreign entities which were burning a tremendous amount of money. So it was clear that we could reorganise, and make the business profitable within a reasonable space of time. So I checked the numbers that Preussag gave me again, and just around Christmas, for the first time, I really had the idea to become "a big player in the game".[42]

Once Hofmann accepted the challenge, Preussag brought him into the process, offering him as an MBI candidate to help turn the company around. At the time, Hammermann was working his way through a difficult set of negotiations with Hans Gottwald, the Minimax CEO, as he later recalls:

> I especially remember the negotiations in Hanover, where Bork played the bad guy and I the good guy. It was really a very stressful time, but we enjoyed it.[43]

Walter Moldan, who was running the new UBS Capital operation in Munich, was convinced that he was a front runner in the negotiations:

> The industrial bidders had been kicked out with a valuation of DM 100 million at the time; we had offered DM 160 million. We were the only ones of the three left who had their finan-

cing in place, the other two, Bridgepoint and Barclays hadn't. Bridgepoint committed to doing the whole transaction with equity financing, and Barclays just weren't there yet.[44]

Moldan's hopes were dashed when Goldman stopped the process to give Barclays time to get their financing together:

> I don't even know whether Barclays paid a higher price. I think they had a better relationship with Gottwald, the CEO. They had certainly offered him a much better deal than we had done. We wanted to see real commitment in cash from the management team, something reasonable like two times fixed annual salary.[45]

Ironically, Bridgepoint had been Preussag's preferred bidder, and UBS Capital was bidding far too low, as Hofmann later explained:

> Bridgepoint had offered DM 180 million, and the old management team was driven by bonus agreements from Preussag. So they wanted the bidder with the highest price. If necessary, they could always leave afterwards, and they certainly didn't want to reinvest much money.

> But my aim was totally different. I had no bonus agreement with Preussag. I wanted a lower price, and Barclays was the second of the three. I took my holidays in December and got in touch with the three bidders, including Michael Bork at Barclays, who had offered DM 18 million less, but were offering a reasonable concept and a credible schedule. They offered DM 162 million. I would have preferred DM 120 million, but Barclays would never have got the deal for that, and they needed this, because it would be their first big deal in Germany. The real beauty for us was that whereas the other bidders were talking 8–9% stakes for management, Barclays were giving management 16.8%.[46]

The only challenge was how the Minimax management team should finance their 16.8% stake. Gottwald came up with the solution, as Hofmann explains:

> Gottwald was the interim CEO, who joined in 1999 to see the deal through. He was the one who conducted the negotiations, and solved the financing of the management stake. Two days

before going to the notary public, at a time when Preussag were feeling very lucky to be getting rid of Minimax and for good money, Gottwald went in to Preussag headquarters and told them that private equity was no longer an option, because the management couldn't pull together the million Deutschmarks necessary for their stake. "Let's talk again with Tyco" Gottwald told them. "You're kidding" they said to him. So Preussag gave management half of the money necessary, on the terms that they would not have to repay the money if they themselves didn't make at least this amount when the company was later sold.[47]

Barclays won the Minimax deal, with a management highly incentivised to turn the company around. Hammermann sums up the importance of the deal for Barclays:

Minimax was a breakthrough so to speak. It provided us with the cream on the cake in 2003 when we exited the deal. We had done exits before, such as with Nici, and had paid back investments including high returns, but 2003 was the first time that Germany made the largest contribution to the overall success of the firm. After five years of work, we were fully accepted team members of Barclays Private Equity.[48]

3i

3i was in many respects the market leader in the period 1997–2000. The era began with the hugely successful IPO of Mobilcom, an investment made by 3i in 1994 along with HANNOVER Finanz and others. 3i was the best placed firm to benefit from the growth in the technology and internet markets, putting growth and pre-IPO capital to work for a wide range of young enterprises. 3i quickly transferred some of its resources from minority and majority participations into growth and venture capital investments. Marco Brockhaus, who joined in May 1997, recalls his impressions of the firm at that time:

Harald Rönn hired me, and then left on the day I arrived for Alpha in order to join Thomas Schlytter-Henrichsen, the former 3i managing director in Germany. Someone left the company every now and then for different reasons and we had a huge inflow of new talent too. When I started we were ten investment managers, when I left we were forty! It was the college for private equity. I was able to do many deals during my two-and-a-half years, and invested around DM 50 million. There was no split in the work between the different product lines. I started off reviewing a call option on Gretag, a company making photo imaging machines, and that's when I first me Brian Veitch at Candover, because they had an option too. I then went on to a wide range of investments including ACG, which turned into one of the most successful exits for 3i. In addition, I worked on Nanogate, where we provided seed finance for a small company together with Bayer, and Beldona, a Swiss lingerie business, which turned out to be very difficult to manage.

It was an easy time, people were free to choose the work they wanted to do, and you could gain a lot of experience very quickly. Peter Cullom was my direct boss. Inevitably, I too left in November 1999 to set up my own business.[49]

The regional structure that was springing up around the country gave 3i a clear advantage when dealing with small companies. The growth extended to hiring new staff. Ron Ayles, who had met Peter Cullom for the first time while working for Degussa, and selling the dental division, was impressed with the people and the firm. Ayles recalls:

3i was extremely successful on the Neuer Markt making significant bets on technology companies at the time. Meanwhile, in order to balance the business, Peter was building up the buyout team to invest in more established companies, hiring Wolf Wolfsteiner, Wolfgang Maennel, Ulf von Haacke, André Deloch, and myself. I had always wanted to work for a UK firm and found them fascinating, plus they had a name. Coming from an industrial background I also saw an opportunity to join an established player recognised as a good training ground for the private equity industry.[50]

Despite the feverish focus on new technology and ventures, some of the new recruits were still interested in older economy buyouts. Guido May, who joined 3i in their Stuttgart office at the end of 1998, was one of these, and explains where people of his kind fitted in at the time:

Two months in, I started work on Fuchs Treppenbau, a manufacturer of staircases. We did this as a co-investment with DZ private equity, closing the deal in 1999. This was one of the few old economy deals, because everyone was dreaming of tech deals. This deal was learning by doing. I had not that much of an idea how to organise banking, or management participation schemes. However, I got some support from Andreas, who was head of 3i Stuttgart, but most of the time you were on your own.

Although Co-create, which I worked on next, a buyout from Hewlett Packard, looked like a tech deal, in reality it was large, had real cash flows, and was leveraged. We did this with Triton, because while we were allowed to do majorities, no-one was tough enough to do a deal on their own at this point in time.[51]

3i's growth was not restricted to the organic roll-out of the regional offices. Such was the commitment to venture capital, and the high-tech sector, that 3i opened up negotiations to acquire the largest local venture capital firm, Technologie Holding.

3i finished the millennium extremely well-positioned as a venture capital firm. Its presence in the buyouts market was however much reduced. This imbalance between new economy venture capital, and old economy buyouts, was to cause the firm major challenges once the dotcom bubble burst at the turn of the new millennium.

Granville Baird

David Martin, who was running the Granville Baird office in Leeds, was asked by Mike Proudlock, the head of the firm, if he would support a deal that was being done in Germany on Elmeg, a telecom handsets deal. The lead on the transaction had come through a Hamburg-based M&A boutique, run by Wolfgang Alvano and Rolf Steffens. Martin recalls:

Having tasted a German investment, our UK team wanted more. Mike sprang on me the suggestion that I should help this M&A team become a management company for the firm in Germany. My first thought was how do you achieve that? None of the three guys had any private equity experience, and Dirk Schekerka was very young at the time. I insisted that I should have the chance to meet them, so that then I could decide if I wanted to get involved even though there was already momentum in both countries to raise a German fund.[52]

HSH Landesbank had been brought in by Alvano to co-invest in the deal, and were immediately interested to contribute to the new fund, which closed at €177 million specifically for Germany. After meeting the team, David Martin joined the investment committee sitting in London, and began screening the investment proposals.

My role was as advisor, making recommendations. I wasn't operating in Germany at the outset. Dirk Schekerka learnt quickly, and Rolf Steffens turned out to be very well connected. My concern was to make sure that the first deal was a good one. I flew over regularly, and because we had no portfolio we could spend a lot of time planning our strategy. Often the best ideas came over lunch or dinner. It took me a long time to understand the cultural differences between England and Germany. Everyone was obsessed with revenues, rather than profit or cash. I had always learnt that sales are vanity, profit is sanity, and cash is reality. Everyone seemed to have huge inventories, which I learned was partly because of the hangover from the post-war period when the primary concern was to fully utilise machines, then in short supply, to have long production runs creating a lot of inventory. The British hate machines, and the Germans love them. The other obvious difference was concern for quality. The Germans cared about quality, and spent a fortune on it. To get ahead in the UK, you became an accountant, and looked at how to cut costs, whereas the German counterpart became an engineer and got obsessive about quality and innovation. The differences ran deep: in Britain direct labour was counted as a variable cost, whereas in Germany it was viewed as fixed. Germans viewed high profits as inconveniently incurring high taxes, and therefore it was better to have low profits. In one case, it was even considered better to put the money into the local football club.[53]

Martin's first concern was that the market which Granville was addressing in the UK, didn't seem to be significant in Germany, as he later explained:

One of the first things I noticed was that expansion capital was not something people really wanted, because banks were supporting people with risky loans. The relationship between entrepreneurs and banks was quite good.

Steffens had said there were stacks of deals waiting for money, but when he showed them to me, I said that none of them were of investment grade. The guys got annoyed with me, turning stuff down, but Wolfgang was very patient as he picked up new skills.[54]

Granville Baird was positioned somewhere between small-cap and mid-cap, as Edward Capel-Cure explains:

We saw ourselves as bridging the gap between the Nord Holdings and the Barclays of this world. In the first fund, if we had found a €20 million equity ticket deal, we would have been able to underwrite it, but would then have brought in a co-investor, like we did on Berkenhoff, my first deal, with 3i.[55]

Inevitably, some new talent needed to be recruited, particularly in the areas of financial due diligence and spreadsheet modelling. In came Kane Pirie and Olaf Kensy from KPMG, Jan Hähnel, and Volker Hichert from BCG.

The big break came with mobile.de, brought in by Dirk Schekerka. This was to prove Granville Baird's first successful deal, as Martin recalls:

I met the mobile.de management and liked them. I said we should take a minority stake, although it did mean we had some problems when it came to implementing professional standards. We had to explain what a finance director should be doing, as one of the founders said he could understand how 10% of a finance director's time would be spent, but what about the other 90%? Later we agreed to conduct a management audit and the new CFO said he would take care of it and brought in Booz. They didn't quite do what we intended, presenting 13 new ideas for increasing revenues, rather than the results of a management audit, but the revenues did go up. We eventually sold our stake to eBay for an excellent return.[56]

The M&A background of the Hamburg team proved an advantage when it came to deal sourcing. Alvano found Westfalia, a tow-bar company, and Steffens found Eisenworld, and Nobis came in on the back of mobile.de. In less than two years, the team had closed four transactions providing a solid foundation for the new business.

Investcorp

Over at Investcorp, it took until 1998 for Johannes Huth to get involved in the German-speaking region, when he began discussions with Gerresheimer. Axel Herberg, the COO of Gerresheimer at the time, recalls:

> Private equity got in touch with me at Gerresheimer in 1998. It was around that time that I came into contact with Investcorp for the first time. Thilo Sautter and Johannes Huth visited me; Johannes Huth was still at Investcorp at that point. One of the controllers of VIAG had been in touch with them. We thought a buyout would be a good idea.[57]

Herberg was keen on Gerresheimer being spun out of VIAG, which was going through a number of consolidation attempts in its main business including an attempted merger with Alu Suisse, followed by the fusion with VEBA. But the timing was not yet right. Gerresheimer itself had other priorities, as Thilo Sautter explains:

> When Johannes and I met the Gerresheimer COO, they were considering disposal of the standard glass container business which was focussed on things like bottles for beer, and they weren't ready yet to do a transaction with private equity.[58]

Huth travelled around Germany looking for deals, visiting Gerresheimer, looking closely at Tarkett, and putting in a bid for Geberit. The senior team then moved on to Kappa packaging, while Axel Holtrup, who had joined from Morgan Stanley at the same time as Thilo Sautter, picked up an information memorandum on Leica Geosystems. Holtrup recalls:

> This was one of the first things I looked at. It seemed good enough, although it had some track record issues. I wrote a memo on it, and took it to Johannes. But everyone's focus was on Kappa Packaging. I was persistent, and in the end Yves Alexander agreed to join me in Switzerland for the management presentation. So it was just the two of us, facing 18 people from management and

Credit Suisse. We liked what we saw, in particular the passion of the CEO Hans Hess, and when Kappa died shortly afterwards, Johannes took charge. At that point, Schroders was rumoured to be the front runner.[59]

Once he turned his attention to Leica Geosystems, Huth led a successful bid for the company. Hardly had Huth tucked away his first deal in Switzerland, and completed his first round of talks with companies in Germany, than he got a call from Henry Kravis, asking him to join KKR. He signed a contract in October 1998, and joined them in March 1999. His ambition was to move up into larger deals, having seen that even Leica Geosystems was a large deal for Investcorp.

KKR's gain was Investcorp's loss. It was left to Thilo Sautter and Axel Holtrup to keep the game going. Nevertheless, Investcorp was runner-up in the bid to acquire Wincor Nixdorf, being pipped at the post by Johannes Huth in his new position at KKR. Holtrup recalls:

> We got very close on Wincor. Our due diligence checked out well, we saw the potential in the business. However, we never got the right traction with Siemens. Also during dinner with management, I could sense that Johannes had won them over. Overall, KKR always seemed to be a step ahead.[60]

Thilo Sautter had similar recollections:

> I'm sure that our inability to win on Wincor Nixdorf was partially through the lack of a senior German. Johannes had actually done deals, and we were runner-up on Wincor Nixdorf against him. If Johannes had been on our side, would we have won it? Yes, first because we wouldn't have had the competition, but second, and most important, we would have had slightly more comfort having a senior German guy to do the deal. At the time Axel and I had been at Investcorp for a number of years, and were trusted to pursue deals but not yet to close them.[61]

Fortunately for Investcorp, the Gerresheimer deal was too small for KKR, and here the route was clear for victory. Thilo Sautter explains:

> Subsequently, after the sale of the standard glass container business, Gerresheimer approached private equity through Lehman Bothers. The loss of Johannes definitely put us on the back foot, but the foundations were laid for me being able to pick up the phone to call

Axel Herberg. This was possible because of the meetings we had had before, organised by Johannes. The early contact was absolutely a key success factor.[62]

The Gerresheimer auction was closely fought. Axel Herberg describes the final round:

The close runners at the end were Chase and Investcorp. There were a few trade guys but they were not successful. Saint Gobain looked in during the second round but they were not really serious. It was mainly private equity. Then Chase came up with an Indian company, which I knew, because the world of glass is not very big. We thought it would be unfriendly if they took us over. So they dropped the Indian partner and in the last round joined forces with Investcorp.[63]

Investcorp teamed up with Chase in the final phase, giving Georg Stratenwerth's team a 40% stake in the company, and a seat on the Board.[64] Axel Herberg found the process challenging, as he explains:

At the start, there was a lot of talking on the side. The private equity people wanted to get your personal views. They all wanted to line up something with me. I had to be very careful, given I was the COO of a publicly listed company. It was a difficult process, especially as we had majority shareholders. You got calls from people who were your "best friends", whom you hadn't even seen before. Everybody offered you the same cocktail of sweet equity. If you achieved your buyout business plan, you would get between 10 to 15 times your equity.[65]

Industri Kapital

After leaving Bain in 1993, Detlef Dinsel worked at Hilti, and was responsible for a number of divestments which brought him into contact with the likes of Max Burger-Calderon at Apax, and Thomas Pütter at Goldman Sachs. Looking around for a new more entrepreneurial position, Dinsel found Industri Kapital looking to open up in Germany, as he later explained:

IK had nothing in Germany. Christian Lorenzen, a Dane who had previously worked for Enskilda, was assigned to get the entry into Germany going, and I joined on 1st April 1996, starting off by working for one-and-a-half years in London. This was a good thing, because it meant I got to know all the people, and was integrated into the firm, which helped a lot later on.[66]

Dinsel and Lorenzen went knocking on doors, visiting investment bankers, lawyers, and corporate M&A departments. Their first process experience came through teaming up with Quadriga on Tetra, which was eventually withdrawn from the market because the bids failed to meet the vendor's price expectations. They also put in their own offers on Nordsee, feeling initially that their Scandinavian roots might be helpful differentiation in a business involving fish, but losing confidence in the management's plan as the process developed.

Peter Welge joined the IK team in 1996, in time to begin work on i-Center, a business which Siemens had put on the market. IK quickly emerged as one of the leading bidders. Detlef Dinsel recalls the process:

We got on well with the management, and after their presentation, they called me up while I was travelling back to London. They wanted to talk, so we set up a meeting a week later in Nuremberg. This gave us lots of insights. They clearly recognised that they would need to do deep restructuring, but they had a plan to do so in place. We brought in Booz Allen, because we had used them before on a couple of previous projects, and together with management we identified a cost savings potential of DM 80 million. As the company was losing around DM 25–30 million at the time, off the back of DM 1.7 billion in revenues, this would translate into an EBIT of around DM 50 million a year.

Siemens put up a vendor loan of DM 200 million, and we bought the company in February 1998 for DM 280 million, without senior debt. Already in the first year, Siemens started talking to other wholesalers, and gave them listings, and subsidised these new channels. The loss in share came on top of a major drop in the market. We fundamentally underestimated the cyclicality and depth of the German construction recession. Even after cutting DM 110 million in costs out, the combination of volume and margin drops killed the company.[67]

Ironically, Clayton, Dubilier & Rice, having lost the i-Center deal, went on to look for a substitute, finding it in Schulte, which came to similar grief at the hands of the German construction recession.

The conclusion of the i-Center deal coincided with the opening of the IK office in Hamburg. Fortunately, publicity surrounding the later failure of the deal was kept to a minimum, and IK kept out of the headlines in 2001 at the time of the insolvency, for as Dinsel later commented:

> The insolvency coincided with the start of the Gardena process. It was well managed with respect to the press. Goldman wasn't worried about it, and the management team at Gardena didn't feel affected, and trusted me. If we had made a fuss with Siemens in the press, I don't think the Gardena owners would have handed the keys over to Industri Kapital.[68]

KKR

KKR's first steps into Germany began with a bid for Herberts. In 1997, Hoechst decided to sell off Herberts, a massive DM 2.7 billion company focussed on coatings used mainly in the automotive industry with 7,500 employees. This was a deal-size that none of the existing players based in Germany had contemplated. It was left to Doughty Hanson in London and KKR in New York to come up with offers.

KKR quickly became the preferred buyer, but the Hoechst Board was impatient to release details of the sale to the press before the price or the details had been fully agreed upon. The press release at the time announced that:

> "Hoechst is focusing on the life sciences businesses of health and nutrition because they offer above-average growth and earnings potential. As part of this strategy, we are seeking new options for our industrial chemicals businesses that will enhance their long-term value," said Utz-Hellmuth Felcht, member of the Board of Management of Hoechst AG and Chairman of the Supervisory Board of Herberts. "The acquisition of Herberts by KKR will open up new international expansion possibilities."[69]

But KKR was far from being as advanced in the discussions as the press release suggested. KKR had been concerned that the management team at Hoechst were too keen to get an announcement out early, and these concerns were confirmed when the market collapsed, undermining the basis upon which the deal was to be financed. KKR's refusal to close on the original terms caused the Hoechst management to go public with the news that KKR had reneged on the deal. This experience left a strong feeling within KKR that it was difficult to do deals in Germany.

The biggest impact of the Herberts experience was that within KKR deal-making responsibility for Germany shifted firmly from New York to London. The hiring of Johannes Huth was itself recognition that KKR needed a far more local touch to be successful with German companies. The market by the late 1990s was clearly opening up for deals in KKR's size category, and a quick start off the block might ensure that KKR captured the lion's share of the biggest deals on the German market.

When Siemens decided to put its personal computers business up for sale, KKR recognised that this was a good business they wanted to win, with a management team they particularly liked. Huth worked intensively with Karl-Heinz Midunsky at Siemens, and was at times concerned over whether it would be possible to make a good deal. It was common knowledge that Industri Kapital had lost everything on their investment in i-Center, sold to them by Siemens. KKR faced Schroders and Investcorp in the auction run by Morgan Stanley.

Even for KKR, Nixdorf, or Wincor as the company was promptly rebranded, was a complex transaction, requiring a huge carve out. The service business had to be created from scratch, and there were also a host of functions, like treasury, that needed to be newly established.

A big advantage of the Wincor deal for KKR was that it forged the closest possible relationship with Siemens. This was to put KKR in pole position for future Siemens deals, a factor that was to be extremely important once KKR entered the new millennium.

Cinven

Despite having parted ways with Thomas Matzen, the Cinven team in London remained interested in investments in Germany. Hugh Langmuir led a team to look at the Herberts deal, at the same time KKR was active on the transaction. Feeling the need to have a German angle, he approached Allianz Capital Partners, teaming up with Thomas Pütter. After falling out of the process, the Cinven team became more convinced that it needed a German office, which ultimately kick-started a head-hunting process to recruit a team for Frankfurt.

Carlyle

When a headhunter from the Rose Partnership phoned Hans Albrecht, who had emerged from a brief retirement after leaving Triumph-

Adler to begin deal-making again, her interest was in getting potential names that Carlyle could talk to about setting up an operation in Germany. Albrecht said he would give her the names, on the condition that she arranged him a meeting with David Rubenstein and Chris Finn at the Four Seasons Hotel in Munich. Albrecht wanted to discuss a deal with him. Albrecht recalls:

> She was as good as her word, and I met Rubenstein in early 1997. I wanted to discuss a deal I was working on with him, and perhaps get him interested in a co-investment.[70] Rubenstein has this funny way of not looking at you when he's talking, looking at his shoes instead. I don't know how he talked me into it, but three days later I flew to Washington, met Bill Conway, and the following day began working for Carlyle.

> It kind of intrigued me at the time because their message was, "Hans look we want to do this European fund, which we think we can get, so we would want you to build a private equity firm in Germany. Oh and yes you will probably have to finance it yourself for a year because we don't have the money yet".

> So I financed Carlyle myself for a year. It was actually quite fun to build something in Germany from scratch. We wanted to raise a $300 million fund, and then David said I think we can get a $ billion. I said, how are we going to use a billion? David said if we can get it, we should take it. So I said fine, and I thought then that this should give us a monopoly on big deals. Well obviously six months later, one billion dollars was a comparatively small fund![71]

Albrecht was interested in Daemon at the time, an internet company which owned the largest number of email addresses in the UK. His hope was to buy the company, and roll-out its concept to the rest of Europe, but there was internal opposition within Carlyle.

Albrecht's next target was Honsel, which he hoped to do in parallel to the fundraising, but again there was internal opposition to the deal. But unlike the Daemon deal which was quickly sold to Scottish Telecom, Honsel remained an option that could be pursued with greater leisure, and Albrecht was able to revive the deal, as he later recalled:

> With the help of Bill Conway, we closed the first ever public-to-private transaction in Germany. It was not only the first, but it

remained the fastest ever achieved, after just two months it was entered into the commercial registry. This owed much to the good work of Rieger (today with Millbank, back then with Freshfields).[72]

Hans Moock, who was hired by Albrecht from Bertelsmann, also recalls the Honsel process:

> I had just started on the Carlyle payroll in September 1998, and in my first week we had the management presentation at Honsel. The process dragged on, and then got pulled. But Hans Albrecht managed to get it kick-started again, and we reached an agreement in April 1999. Hans put me in charge of arranging the public-to-private transition, in preparation for the AGM. This meant spending three days a week at Honsel, and working day and night with the lawyers.
>
> We also had a buy-and-build strategy, and in particular we wanted to establish the company in the US. We had identified a number of add-on targets, one of which got done pretty quickly.[73]

Carlyle was now in position to gain momentum in Germany. AGIV, a German conglomerate owned by BHF Bank, was considered too big as an acquisition target by the Carlyle partners in Washington, but once it was split up into separate deals, Albrecht was able to piggy-back on the MBO plan of Wolfgang Leitner, the dynamic CEO of one of its subsidiaries. Albrecht recalls:

> When ING bought BHF Bank, they looked at AGIV and said: "OK we'll sell Andritz from within it". They had to do the deal before the year-end because that was when the tax benefits from the deal would expire. We were the only ones who had done due diligence, and that's how we managed to buy the company.
>
> Andritz was the largest buyout to be done in Austria at that time. We didn't have much to do. It was Leitner who did that deal. He was ex-McKinsey, and had made some money himself before becoming Chairman of Andritz, at a time when it was in a shambles. He restructured it, brought down the break-even point, outsourced lots of stuff, and made it a breathable company that could be profitable. He did it very well. We bought some additional companies with him, and grew it very nicely.[74]

Carlyle finished the millennium with a reputation for being an established large-cap player, already on a par with Apax, BC Partners, and Permira, which considering its brief history in the market, was clearly a considerable success.

Duke Street Capital

As the 1990s drew to a close, the level of fly-in activity from private equity funds based in London, was steadily increasing. But there were risks inherent in private equity houses attempting to do deals from such a distance that they would miss out on local information. Such was the fate of Duke Street Capital, which acquired Steiner Industries, an Austrian plastics company in 1999. The story was reported by the *Daily Telegraph* in May 2001:

> Police have made house-to-house searches after allegations that a British investment group was given false information when it agreed to take over a plastics company that last week became the third-largest bankruptcy in Austrian history, with debts of more than £200m.

> Duke Street Capital claims the previous owner of Steiner Industries manipulated the figures to cover up the dire financial status of the group. Steiner Industries, which is based near Linz and manufactures plastic garden furniture and fruit baskets, filed for bankruptcy last week.

> Duke Street Capital, which acquired a two-thirds majority stake in 1999, has accused company boss Alfred Steiner of falsifying documents in an attempt to cover up exactly how bad the financial picture was.

> Duke Street claims he manipulated the balance sheets in an attempt to fool shareholders and creditors. He is also accused of falsifying end-of-year figures for 1997 and for end-of-year reports thereafter to cover up the company's real financial status.

> A spokesman at the court in Wels, Upper Austria, where the investigation is taking place and which ordered the house-to-house searches, said Mr Steiner is also accused of embezzling £15m – and transferring it to bank accounts in Liechtenstein and the Netherlands.

Mr Steiner, whose family still owns the remaining third of the company, has denied all charges and said bad management by Duke Street was to blame for the bankruptcy.[75]

The fraud was eventually proven in court. Alfred Steiner had indeed falsified much of the description of his business, particularly in the valuation of stocks and receivables, and then tried to cover his tracks after the deal had closed. The company went bankrupt with debts of more than £200 million. Both Alfred Steiner and his father Leopold Steiner later went to jail for their actions. Once again, investors in London were given cause to doubt the honesty of owners in the German-speaking region.

Duke Street learnt three lessons from their experience with Steiner. First, they decided to get tough with the advisers, in particular the accountants who had been responsible for due diligencing the company.

The second response of the Duke Street team was to put in place psychometric testing of the management of all companies it thereafter sought to acquire.

Edmund Truell, chief executive of Duke Street Capital, said: "Ever since we were defrauded in Austria we have put every single management through psychometric testing, however much we love them."[76]

The third response was to make senior hires on the Continent such as Frederic Chauffier in France, and Ervin Schellenberg in Germany, and to form Iberduke Participaciones in a joint venture with a local General Partner in Spain. This was viewed as the best approach to underpin their strategy for Europe.

Schellenberg joined in 2002, to help with fund-raising and spearhead their activities in the region. Looking back on the situation Duke Street had experienced, Schellenberg later commented:

I think this is something that can happen to any investor, particularly if he lacks a proprietary network of relationships in the local business community. Local business men, if they trust you, will often volunteer to help you confidentially to understand what's going on behind the scenes if they know you and trust you. Being part of the regional business community makes a big difference in transactions.[77]

Parallel to the events with Steiner, Schellenberg was making progress with establishing Duke Street in Germany:

We had built an excellent team of investment professionals and senior industrial advisers, a strong pipeline, and had several transactions lined up, e.g. Polymer Latex, which Soros eventually bought, and which was something we clearly could have won. We had a tremendous sales effort, and 300 leads were generated.

However, the recession came, and large exits were delayed. By the end of 2002, Peter Taylor and Eddie Truell decided that they had to consolidate and to focus their limited management resource. Germany was shut down. Iberduke JV was dissolved, and considerable changes were made in the UK team and French teams: there was too little time for us to establish Germany, the German venture was almost still-born.[78]

Allianz Capital Partners

Thomas Pütter had been working for Goldman Sachs for six years when the Allianz insurance company approached him via a headhunter with a request for his support in building up a private equity presence in Germany. The approach from Allianz was far from conventional, as Pütter explains:

> The approach was not done as a hiring. Instead the head-hunter said "Mr Pütter, the Allianz wants to take up discussions with people who know about private equity, because they would like to learn about the market, and they have asked us as a head-hunter who

Figure 13.3 Sources of Private Equity Transactions, 1992–2000

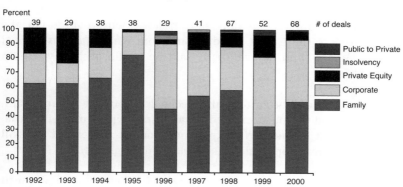

Source: Authors' compilation

knows the scene to set up some of these meetings. Would you be willing to participate?" I said "sure". Goldman was told about the approach at the time, and I asked the powers at be if they were happy for me to do this. As Allianz was one of Goldman's key targets for corporate business in Germany at the time, the local head of the financial institution group gave me his blessing. The discussions took place over a period of around two years.

In one meeting I said "would it help if I wrote all of this down for you? We could then put it through the photocopier and distribute it so that we wouldn't need too many repetitive discussions." They agreed. So I sent them a 28 page business plan. It wasn't just a memo. I gave them the plan and said: "This is what I would do if I were you. This is the opportunity. These are your challenges". It took them a few months to digest and come back to me. Then I was invited back for more senior discussions and at one point was asked whether, if I was given a blank sheet of paper and a corporate GmbH, I could build up a private equity business for them. I agreed to do so in the summer of 1997.[79]

As Pütter headed off to the Allianz, he asked Stefan Sanne, who was a leading equity analyst at Goldman, whether he wanted to join him. Pütter recalls:

Stefan said: "I want to change career. I want to go into private equity. As a friend would you introduce me to private equity houses?" I asked him to let me think about it, but got back to him a week later. This came just after the Goldman pitch for the sales mandate on Tank und Rast, which we lost. On the way back to the airport I told Stefan about what I had just agreed with Allianz, and he eventually said he would be happy to join me.[80]

Another old friend of Pütter's also decided to join the Allianz team. Peter Gangsted was pursuing a corporate career with Unilever in Asia. Pütter felt that his industrial experience would complement the skill sets required in the original business plan. Pütter recollects:

Stefan joined with me on 1st March 1998. Peter joined a month later because of his contract with Unilever. For Allianz it was like

Christmas all over. They suddenly had their three core guys and a secretary, who also came along with us from Goldman. The only condition Allianz made was that we had to set up shop in Munich. But I knew Munich well from my Matuschka days.[81]

Pütter, Gangsted, and Sanne started in a basement within the Allianz head-office, which could hardly be described as an office, as Peter Gangsted recalls:

> We started work in the Allianz archive room. There were no other rooms available in Königinstrasse. The archives contained paternoster filing cabinets, which made a lot of noise when someone came in to find something. People coming in were pretty surprised to see us working down there. I remember thinking; I wonder whether I've done the right thing![82]

Reiner Löslein, who joined later from Deutsche Bank, was also very surprised by the modest conditions:

> The good thing about working in the archive was you got to know a lot of people very quickly. I was sitting there with my computer, without even a real desk. People coming in to the archive looked at me in surprise, and asked me what I was doing there. I said that this was my office. People laughed, and probably thought "this poor guy!"[83]

The time in the basement was, however, to be of limited duration, and may have been simply a test of their entrepreneurial commitment. The new team was quick to get into action, as Gangsted explains:

> On Tank and Rast we paired up with Apax. The target was a privatisation from the government. From an execution point of view, it was a relief to have the Apax organisation just down the road. We were also working with another private equity house which ended up not proceeding. Instead Lufthansa stepped into their place, which had originally been part of a competing oil company consortium. Lufthansa considered it to be a diversification strategy for their LSG catering business unit. We did the full analysis and liked the risk return characteristics. We thought that it was a good idea, and we were successful, closing one of the first big buy outs. It was a DM 1.8 billion deal. For Allianz it was a first, and Apax too had never done such a big investment in Germany at the time.[84]

Allianz hadn't originally intended for its nascent private equity group to be doing such big investments, as Gangsted remembers:

> Allianz didn't want us to do big deals at the beginning. But all the smaller deals tended to be high tech ventures. Instead we continued doing big deals such as Schmalbach-Lubeca, Fairchild Dornier, and Messer Griesheim. In most cases we teamed up with people. We called it the extended workbench. So we did Messer with Goldman, and Dornier with Clayton, Dubilier & Rice.[85]

The status of Allianz, as Germany's largest domestic insurance company, meant that the formation of Allianz Capital Partners not only attracted significant media attention, but also prompted many people inside and outside the industry to assume that Allianz would play a leading role in representing private equity to Germany AG, and the government. Thomas Pütter's election later to head the BVK (Germany's Private Equity Association) confirmed this expectation.

CVC

CVC's acquisition of Kalle from Hoechst in 1997 followed the pattern of corporate spin-offs which was rapidly emerging in the last years of the 1990s. Kalle was the first of numerous subsidiaries that Hoechst spun off in the process of restructuring its portfolio to become a pure-play pharmaceutical company. Steve Koltes recalls:

> Kalle was a market leader in the manufacture of cellulosic and plastic sausage skins. CVC knew the industry well because we had owned a competitor, Devro, based in the UK. Kalle was run at the time and still today by a fabulous manager, Walter Niederstätter. Walter was a classic private equity "find": a competent and hard-driving manager lost in a large and bureaucratic organisation that he longed to be freed from. Once out of Hoechst, Walter flourished, quickly doubling the EBIT and executing one good idea after another.

> The auction was run by Deutsche Bank, and we were up against Apax and Odewald. For the latter, Kalle was one of his first deal attempts in Germany.[86]

With six platform deals, CVC closed the highest number of deals in its history in 1997, acquiring in addition to Kalle, Corposan, Haefely

Trench, Rungis, and Tartex Ritter. This was at a time when the local team was composed solely of Steve Koltes, Jakob Förschner, and Charles Schwab. Koltes hired a headhunter, and Thomas Rubahn was recruited in April 1997 from 3i. Rubahn recalls his first impressions of CVC:

> CVC was totally driven by doing good transactions. I had a good start in September 1997, closing Tartex Ritter, acquired from Nestle, which was selling vegetarian pates to health food shops. Nestle thought it was too Germanic, and didn't like the fact that the factory in Freiburg was only working on one-and-a-half shifts. This was a proprietary deal.
>
> The following year, I had no transactions, and I talked to Donald McKenzie, and said I felt I had had a bad year because I hadn't done any deals. He told me: "that's not a bad year. A bad year is when you do a bad deal".[87]

Rungis was also acquired in 1997, which was a food logistics company, in a deal led by Jakob Förschner, and in 1998 the Frankfurt office led the purchase of Rhiag Spa in Italy, bringing the Empe management team into this leading auto components distributor whose primary suppliers were based in Germany. In 1999 CVC purchased Asbach Uralt and Metaxa, which were sold by Diageo. Nonetheless, Steve Koltes considered that the period 1998 to 2000 was slow for the office. He later felt, however, that these years were some of the worst vintages for private equity, as bubbles in the US technology markets, Russia and Asia were bursting or well on their way to doing so.

Apax

The period 1997–2000 marked a peak for Apax in Germany. The most important part of the track record came from exiting the investments made during the 1992–1995 recession over the boom years of 1997–1999. Halusa recalls:

> I think we won a 36% IRR, on our fund during those years, because basically we sold in the upswing of the 1996–1999 period when the stock market was really going up, assets that we had bought in 1992–95. We were a tiny office at that time, Michael Phillips, Max Burger-Calderon and myself, and we were working together on everything.[88]

Table 13.3 Private Equity Transactions in 1999

1999

Company	Buyer	Seller	Exit year	Sold to
Andritz	Carlyle & Global Equity Partners/UIAG	AGIV	2003	IPO
Argo Personaldienstleistungen AG	Nord Holding	Family	2008	Management
Asbach & Metaxa	CVC	Diago	1999	Bols
Bally	Texas Pacific Group	Oerlikon-Bührle	2008	S-UBG AG/Labelux
Bell-Hermetic GmbH & Co KG	TA Triumph-Adler	Juventas/Berliner Elektro	2001	Legris Industries
Beru AG	Carlyle	Family	2004	BorgWarner Inc.
Bürger AG	Nord Holding	Capital increase	2006	Family
Burton-Werke GmbH	SocGen Private Equity	Schroder Ventures	2006	Nord Holding
Cargo Van	Group AFU/ABN Amro Capital France	Deutsche Handelsbank	Not as yet divested	Not as yet divested
Vantico (Ciba Performance Polymers)	Morgan Grenfall	Ciba Speciality Chemicals	2003	Huntsman
Concord Kinderautositze	TA Triumph-Adler (Child Car Seats)	Juventas/Berliner Elektro	2004	Jane
D + S int.com AG	UBS Capital	CHS	2006	Arrows
DKV	Gothaer	RWE-DEA	2006	Secondary Gothaer
Eschenbach	Hannover Finanz	Family	2007	Barclays
Euro Dental Holding/Müller & Weygandt (M&W)	Schroder Ventures	Family	2004	Henry Schein, Inc
Fiege Merlin	Odewald/Fiege Intl. Bet. GmbH	Granville Baird/ 3i/Prudential	2005	Liquidation
GAB Robins (SGS Insurance Services)	Brera Capital	Societe Generale de Surveillance	Not yet divested	Not yet divested
Geka Brush	Halder	Family holding	2004	Equita
Grohe	BC Partners	Public to private	2004	Texas Pacific/CSFB
Happich Fahrzeug	Halder	Johnson Controls	2003	Ellamp

Table 13.3 Private Equity Transactions in 1999 – *continued*

1999

Company	Buyer	Seller	Exit year	Sold to
Haverkamp Sicherheitstechnik	TA Triumph-Adler (Home Security)	Juventa/Berliner Elektro	2001	MBO Cornelia Sailer
Hoffman-Menü	Pricoa Capital	Schroder Ventures	2005	HgCapital
Homann-Feinkost	Gilde	Unilever	2004	Henderson
Honsel	Carlyle	Public to private	2004	Ripplewood
IBS Brocke	Quadriga	Family	2005	ICE
Komtel	Hannover Finanz	Stadtwerke Flensburg	2000	Versatel
KTM	BC Partners	Public to private	2004	Cross Holdings
Labnet	NatWest	Family	2000	Management
Mapress GmbH	Bessemer Venture	Mannesmann	2003	Geberit
MEKU Metallverarbeitung GmbH	3i/DZ Private Equity	Family	Not yet divested	Not yet divested
Meyer & Burger	BBK	Family	2006	IPO
MIGUA Fugensysteme GmbH & Co. KG	TA Triumph-Adler (Construction)	Juventas/Berliner Elektro	2001	BPE Private Equity
Mobile.de	Granville Baird	Family	2004	ebay
MTH – Metall Technologie Holding	Barclays	Bodycoat	2003	BLB Private Equity/ BdW
Myonic AG – Miniture bearings	Capvis	Schäublin SA	2006	Süd Private Equity/ DZ Equity
Myonic AG – Systems business	Capvis	Schäublin SA	2003	Faulhaber Group
PBSG (Professional Business Solutions Group) AG	Alpinvest	WEKA Group	2006	Addison/HgCapital
Pipetronix (to PII Group)	HgCapital	Preussag	2002	GE Power Systems
Polis Immobilien	Hannover Finanz	Family	Not yet divested	Not yet divested
Porcelain Products Company	Riverside	Frauenthal Keramik AG	2007	Seves Spa

Table 13.3 Private Equity Transactions in 1999 – *continued*

1999

Company	Buyer	Seller	Exit year	Sold to
PPE Presentation Products	TA Triumph-Adler (CAN.media Group)	Family	2004	SELLTEC Communications GmbH
Schoeller Wavin Systems	Chase Capital	Family	2003	Stirling Square Capital Partners
Steiner Industries	Duke Street Capital	Family	2001	Insolvency
Stinnes Reifendienst	L&G Ventures	Stinnes (VEBA)	2003	Euromaster (Michelin)
Telecolumbus	DB Capital	Veba/RWE	2003	BC Partners
Temmler Pharma GmbH	3i	ASTA Medica-Gruppe	Not yet divested	Not yet divested
Tornos-Bechler	Doughty Hanson	Rothenberger	2001	IPO
UTAX GmbH	TA Triumph-Adler (Office)	Family	Not yet divested	Not yet divested
Vestolit	Candover/DGH&A	Degussa	2006	Strategic Value Partners
Visinfo	TA Triumph-Adler (Office)	Family	Not yet divested	Not yet divested
Weru	Triton	Caradon	Not yet divested	Not yet divested
Wincor Nixdorf	KKR/Goldman Sachs Capital Partners	Siemens	2004	IPO
Winterthur Technologie AG	Morgan Grenfall	Rappold Gruppe	2003	Vision Capital
Zapf GmbH	DBAG	Werner Zapf	2006	Les Nouveaux Constructeurs SA/GS/Deutsche

Source: Authors' compilation

The acquisitions Apax made during the period were a mixture of solid transactions that doubled their capital, such as Nordsee (with Chase Capital and Pricoa), and the privatisation of Tank & Rast (with Allianz Capital Partners and Lufthansa Service Gesellschaft), and more spectacular transactions such as Wendlen, a consolidation of the German packaged bread industry (over five times their capital) and Dialogue Semiconductor, a tech buyout from Daimler, where Apax achieved over thirty times their capital. Michael Phillips recalls:

> At Nordsee, under our ownership, one thousand jobs were added, and at Wendeln, we created a leading international bread company. At Tank & Rast, there was a tremendous effort to revamp a previously government-owned entity to dramatically improve service quality and efficiency. In the latter, this was achieved in harmony with unions and tenants. In all, we avoided over-indebtedness in all these companies, and really built them up into strong companies.[89]

The successful exits boosted fund-raising, and prompted a significant expansion in the office size. As Apax entered the new millennium, a pool of talent was flooding into the firm. Apax now belonged to the top tier of private equity houses in Germany, together with Permira, Carlyle, and BC Partners.

Doughty Hanson

After the schism with Quadriga, Doughty Hanson had little trouble establishing a new German team, having been active for many years in the German market. Alexander Hanke and Peter Sewing were active with the second fund, but when Sewing left in 1997, together with Peder Prahl to set up Triton Partners, Hanke hired Christian Fritsch from Merrill Lynch, Andreas Torner from McKinsey, and Claus Felder from KPMG to beef up the remaining German team. Fritsch stayed in London, while Felder joined Hanke in Germany. A year later, Fritsch moved over to join his fellow Germans, and Marc Strobel (ex Lehman) was hired to succeed Andreas Torner, bringing the local contingent up to five. Strobel recalls his start with the firm:

> I wasn't much focussed on Germany at the start. I was based in London, and working mainly on UK deals. It was a very London-centric firm, and even those who were based in Milan and Frankfurt spent a lot of time in London. It was a great set of people, with a good deal-flow.[90]

Table 13.4 Private Equity Transactions in 2000

2000

Company	Buyer	Seller	Exit year	Sold to
A. Friedrich Flender	Citicorp	Babcock-Borsig	2005	Siemens
AMC Pancke	Hannover Finanz	Family	Not yet divested	Not yet divested
Armstrong Insulation Products (Armacell)	CVC/Gilde	Armstrong World Industries	2006	Investcorp
Astyx	Hannover Finanz/Deutsche Venture Capital	Family	Not yet divested	Not yet divested
auratis	Odewald	Family	2006	Radiate Group
austriamicrosystems	Schroder Ventures	Public to private	2004	IPO
Bamberger Kaliko GmbH	BPE Private Equity	Continental AG	2010	Management
BBA (TMD Friction GmbH)	HSBC PE	BBA	2008	Insolvency
BE Semiconductor	AdCapital	Private investors	Not yet divested	Not yet divested
Bi-Log	Odewald	Family	2006	Management
BMF/ADI (BFMH)	Duke Street Capital	Family	2001	Private investors
Brahms Diagnostica	HBM Partners	Alpha	2010	Management
Bundesdruckerei	Apax	Federal Government	2002	Heleba/Federal Govt
Burkhalter	Domenig family/management	L&G Ventures	Not yet divested	Not yet divested
Chemson	BVP Europe/Invest Equity/Leman Capital	mg Technologies	2008	Buy-Out Central Europe/Global/UIAG
CoCreate	3i/Triton	Hewlett Packard	2006	HBK Private Equity
Coperion	West Private Equity	Georg Fischer AG	2007	DBAG
Coventya (Chemetall's Plating Technologies)	Quadriga/Natexis	Chemetall GmbH	2006	Natexis
Dietrich Reimelt GmbH & Co KG	Kero Private Equity	Kero Holding	2007	MBB
DT Cable – Hesse/NRW	Callahan, Klesch & Company	Deutsche Telekom	2003	Insolvency
DVS AG	Nord Holding	Capital increase	Not yet divested	Not yet divested
EDH Euro Dental Holding	Schroder Ventures	Previous investors	2004	Henry Schein Inc
Eisenworld (Apptimum)	Granville Baird	Management	2006	Microsoft
Element 5	3i/Earlybird	Capital increase	2004	Digital River
Essmann	Alpinvest	Skanska	2007	Quadriga

Table 13.4 Private Equity Transactions in 2000 – *continued*

2000

Company	Buyer	Seller	Exit year	Sold to
Fairchild Dornier	Clayton Dubilier & Rice/ Allianz Capital	Capital increase/ Previous investors	2002	Insolvency
Flabeg	Equivest	Pilkington	2008	Industri Kapital
Fläkt Woods Group	Compass Partners	Marconi	2007	Sagard PE/Barclays/ICG
Flender AG	Citigroup Venture Capital	Deutsche Babcock AG	2005	Siemens
Gebrüder Tobler AG	Capvis	Family	2003	Wolseley Group
Gerresheimer Glas	Investcorp/ JP Morgan Partners	Viag/Veba	2004	Blackstone
Identec Solutions	Hannover Finanz/ UBF/UIAG	Gantner Electronic	insolvency	insolvency
Interbrandpro	3i	Previous investors	2005	Equivest
Interhyp	3i	Growth capital	2005	IPO
Kabel Baden Würtemburg	Callahan Associates	Deutsche Telekom	2001	Blackstone/CDPC/ Bank of America
Katz Group	3i	Family	2005	Equivest
Kiekert AG	Schroder Ventures	Previous investors	2006	Deutsche/Morgan Stanley/ Blue Bay/Silver Point Capital
Knürr AG	3i	Capvis/Family	2006	Emerson Electric Inc
Köhler & Krenze Fashion AG	BdW	Thomas CJ Matzen/H & E	Not yet divested	Not yet divested
Linos AG	Nord Holding	Family	2006	IPO
Lonstroff Holding	3i	Private investors	2007	BV Group
M&W Müller & Weygrandt	Schroder Ventures	Previous investors	2004	PPM Ventures
Management 2000	Bridgepoint	Family	2007	Vebego
MAPS – Metzeler Automotive Profile Systems	CVC	Invensys	2007	Cooper-Standard Automotive Inc
Messer Griesheim	Allianz Capital/ Goldman Sachs	Aventis/Rhone Poulenc SA	2004	Air Liquide
Müller Brot	DB Capital Partners	Family	2002	Klaus Ostendorf

Table 13.4 Private Equity Transactions in 2000 – *continued*

2000

Company	Buyer	Seller	Exit year	Sold to
Nici	Barclays	Family	2002	Family
Nobis	Granville Baird	Family	2005	ISS Group
Nybron Flooring	HIAG and Nordic Capital Funds	Family	2006	Vestar Capital Partners
Odlo Sports Group	Partners Group	Previous investors	2006	Towerbrook
Offset Kaiser	3i/Nord Holding	Family	2003	Alpha
Paion	3i	Private investors	2005	IPO
Poggenpohl Küchen	Industri Kapital	Skanska	2004	IPO
Polytec	Capvis	Family	2006	IPO
Refresco	capiton/Residex/ISIS	Spin off	2003	3i
REMP	Capvis	Capital increase	2005	Tecan Gruppe capiton
Reum Automotive	UBS Capital	Family	2003	capiton
Richard Fritz Group	Quadriga	Family	Not yet divested	Not yet divested
RMF	Gothaer	Family	2002	MAN Group plc
SAV Group	Arcadia/E.ON Kraftwerke GmbH	Private investors	2008	Indaver NV/ NIBC Infrastructure
Schmalbach-Lubeca	Allianz Capital	E.ON (Viag/Veba)	2002	Ball Corporation
Single Temperiertechnik GmbH & Co. KG	Halder	Schroder Ventures	2005	Swiss family company
Steinbeis Temming	BdW	Public to private	2008	Steinbeis Holding
Takko Modemarkt	Schroder Ventures	Tengelman Group	2007	Advent
Tenovis Germany GmbH	KKR	Robert Bosch	2004	Avaya
TH Technologie Holding	3i	Private investors	Not yet divested	Not yet divested
Trevira	DB Investor	Multikarsa/Aventis	2004	Reliance Industries
Tropon	Advent International	Bayer	2004	Viatris (Advent portfolio company)
Vinmolit & Vintron	Advent International	Celanese & Wacker-Chemie	Not yet divested	Not yet divested
Westfalia Automotive GmbH & Co KG	Granville Baird	Westfalia Group	2005	Odewald/West LB
Zumtobel	KKR	Family	2006	IPO

Source: Authors' compilation

It was impossible to avoid discussion over the reasons for the break with the previous German team. Claus Felder, who later took over Doughty Hanson's German private equity operations in 2001, recalls the explanations given:

> I only know the Doughty Hanson side of the story and what I was told at the time was that on the basis of differing views on strategy and independence, a rift had developed between the respective English and German teams. Our vision was to be seen as one European private equity team united in approach and corporate culture. That is what Dick and Nigel wanted. We were an English private equity fund, but at the same time we were able to raise a German flag on top of the local office if a transaction in Germany needed such an approach. For instance, if there is an entrepreneur who only speaks German, he would not need to care about our English roots. That's why we are a private equity firm with offices in multiple jurisdictions; we are international but we understand the local culture and can put the local flag out. It appears that the professionals at Quadriga wanted to follow a different approach which did not fit with our view of having country heads but no country turfs.[91]

The new German team began working in the mid-90s on transactions such as Tarkett, Elexis, and Winkler & Dünnebier. Winkler & Dünnebier was IPO'd in 1998, just before the market became dominated by new technology. Indeed the market trend towards high-tech companies posed challenges for the Doughty Hanson team, as Felder recalls:

> Doughty Hanson was pretty conservative during those years and in the aftermath of the dotcom boom. We felt that sellers' price expectations were excessive even in more conservative industries. We didn't know where this would all lead so we looked at a lot but did little in terms of new investments, which I think with hindsight wasn't a bad thing.[92]

As had always been the core strategy, the Doughty Hanson team continued to focus upon family owned, mid-cap, industrial companies. 1998 and 1999 saw the team close two deals in Switzerland, both sold by families: Tornos-Bechler SA, a machine-tool manufacturer, and Soudronic, a manufacturer of metal packaging. As the tech-boom expanded, however, the Doughty Hanson team's search for appropriate deals became more difficult, and it took until 2002 before it completed its next investment in ATU.

Triumph-Adler

The second half of the 1990s saw the Triumph-Adler team addressing further acquisitions and many operational issues.

An anticipated problem was that, in order to keep the tax loss carry forwards, Triumph-Adler had to continue manufacturing typewriters, a business which was in terminal decline. In order to sustain a sizeable operation in Nuremberg the headquarters of the Office Systems Business were moved from Munich to Nuremberg and "genuine Triumph-Adler personnel" assumed the tasks of centrally managing the operations. The remaining production facility in Frankfurt could only be closed down five years later.

The second challenge for Triumph-Adler was that the office business, which had been bought back from Alco in autumn 1994 shortly after the IMM/Triumph-Adler merger, had fallen into poor performance.

The decision to buy back office had largely been driven by its sudden availability, as König later explained:

> Alco had a change of leadership, and the first thing the new CEO decided was to get out of IMM office systems. Also in retrospect I would say that this constituted a super attractive opportunity. I personally think the Americans had misinterpreted the way the business was financed, and were surprised to find out that the bulk of our rented copiers were refinanced with leasing companies, and that a good part of the cash generated went to cover the financing of these leases. I think as soon as they understood this, they realised they had paid a pretty high price for a business which had missed its profitability target for 1993 and 1994. So the new CEO, who had been responsible for buying IMM office systems, decided to write it off in his first year, which is what he did.[93]

Dietmar Scheiter reassumed responsibility for the business once Triumph-Adler had purchased back the stake from Alco.

By 1995, a year after the office division had been bought back from Alco, it became apparent that there was trouble at one of their companies, where the sellers had clearly perpetrated a major fraud. König was particularly disappointed by the revelation:

> We had invested in this company, and there was an earn-out scheme with the managers. It turned out that the numbers they had been giving us were misleading. The profitability in the year we bought the

company came from the fact that the inventories were too high. There had been nothing to indicate that anything was amiss, and according to the numbers, the profitability was just fine. What kept the practice concealed was the fact that several parties were involved, corroborating each other. This policy they continued throughout the earn-out phase, so for three years in a row the company's earnings continued to look good, and were in line with cash-flows. It was a perfect scheme, but inevitably it eventually blew up. That hurt us a lot, and took a long time to resolve.[94]

In the following years the office systems business was fundamentally restructured. A fairly loose assembly of copy machinery dealers with some centralised procurement was to become a strictly managed operation. Up to 1999 another seven larger acquisitions were done and the scope of the business was enlarged to include presentation and media technology. Only in 1998 Triumph-Adler regained exclusive control of its traditional brand name from Olivetti and was therefore in the strong position to replace the previous suppliers' (e.g. Canon, Toshiba, Ricoh) products with its own brand "Triumph-Adler" products. In 1999, UTAX, a lesser known OEM of copy machines was acquired to handle the complex logistics associated with the change of brand strategy. The prospering of the business was also facilitated by the changing industry environment; in the digitalised world a copier machine had become a network printer. By 2000 the sales volume of the office systems business had increased to €383 million and the EBITDA amounted to €39 million, almost twice the level of 1992.

But perhaps the biggest challenge of all, even if not the most expensive, was when Triumph-Adler's toy division acquired in January 1996 a major French player, which it was hoped, once combined with Zapf and europlay, would spearhead the consolidation of the European toy industry, and create a player second only to Lego in the sector. Jochen Martin remembers his first contact with Idéal Loisirs/Majorette/Solido,[95] a distributor of licensed toys and manufacturer of die cast cars which at the time was in financial distress:

I was on a plane from Paris travelling back to Munich with Raimund König. We had just visited Idéal Loisirs in Paris, and Raimund said to me: "Jochen do you think we should buy this company?" We were still concluding the due diligence phase at that point, and my answer was an emphatic "no". I said let them go bankrupt, and then buy the moulds and the brandname. We could then headhunt a few good managers, and do our own thing in Germany. Even though I was only a junior associate at the time, I pressed my point hard: "Raimund, let's not buy this company". Raimund said: "OK, I hear you, but let's think about it. We want to be big. We want to effect a change in toys. Big is beautiful, we can do a turnaround."[96]

König was possibly influenced in his decision to go ahead with the deal by a favourable experience two years earlier when Mercatura Holding, the professional clothing holding business of which Thomas Bühler was the managing director, had acquired Bragard, a French producer of professional clothing. This was a restructuring case which Thomas Bühler turned around, and made into a successful business.[97]

Hardly was the ink dry on the Majorette deal, than things began to go seriously wrong, as Jochen Martin explains:

The first thing that happened was that the company ran into serious financial problems. It was sliding downwards. What made things so challenging was that we didn't have sufficient people competent in French. Cornelia Sailer was the only one who was fluent. I spoke it, but not well enough to restructure a company from top to bottom. Kai Köppen went over to Paris and took over the finance function. I think his French was almost non-existent at that time.[98]

Köppen's challenge would have been great even if he had been a native speaker, as he later explained:

We bought Ideal Loisirs/Majorette on the assumption that it was a break-even business which had been heavily leveraged. The valuation was based on a financial due diligence report recently given to us during the process on behalf of the banks involved. The negotiations were under the care of a French ministry, responsible for insolvent companies.

It was clear right from the beginning that I would have to go to France. That was a bit of a challenge, at the time, as my wife was pregnant. When I found out what it looked like, I said let's see, this will need a three year restructuring plan. It sucked in quite some money. It was a nightmare, and ever since this experience, I won't buy a restructuring deal.[99]

In the event, König was more convinced that his own team's due diligence had been at fault:

With Majorette, in hindsight it is clear we were very unfortunate in how we performed the due diligence. The day we arrived there we found out that whatever we had invested was gone.[100]

Despite the weaknesses of the financial due diligence, the Triumph-Adler team had put together a thorough turn-around plan, as König describes:

The tragedy is that prior to the acquisition we had an operating concept for how to turn the company around, and basically the profitability improvements which we achieved over time were larger than expected. Cornelia Sailer and Richard Mamez, the newly retained operating manager, did a great job there. However upon arrival in 1996, not only were there FFr 100 million missing in cash, we had a different starting point as to profitability. Instead of zero, our starting point was minus FFr 100 million. We had calculated about FFr 100 million in profit improvements over the five years, which suddenly would bring us back only to zero. That was the tragedy.[101]

The challenges at Majorette were more than compensated by the positive development of Zapf. By 1999 the Zapf sales volume stood at almost four times the level of 1992, at a very high level of profitability. The decision was taken to IPO the company independent from the other toys operations and the company was successfully floated in 1999. The share price skyrocketed to unexpected levels – for some time the market capitalisation of Zapf exceeded the market capitalisation of Triumph-Adler. Triumph-Adler sold its last Zapf shares in 2001.

In contrast the development of the construction business was solid if unspectacular, largely as a consequence of the onset of a long down cycle in the construction industry. Only two smaller acquisitions were added, Leim + Potthof in 1996, and Petrick & Wolf Energietechnik in 1997. Walter Moldan, who was in charge of the business up until the end of 1997, noticed that there had been a clear mood shift within the holding company:

Nobody was really interested in construction services, which was doing reasonably well. But it became clear that there wouldn't be any funds available for its further development.[102]

Meanwhile the Triumph-Adler acquisition team had experienced another home run. In 1995 the group had acquired two manufacturers of medical devices for the elderly: Aquatec and Alber both of which were further developed successfully under Thomas Bühler and Tom Harder. Bühler and Harder sold these businesses, with the support of JP Morgan, in 1997 to Warburg Pincus.

In 1998 Hüco was added to the portfolio in a process led by Thomas Bühler and Gernot Eisinger, with the initial intention to set up another sub-group. This however never materialised and the business was sold for a profit in 2002 to LRP Capital.

The public markets however did not appreciate Triumph-Adler's performance. Indeed, a number of disadvantages of being a public company were surfacing, as Thomas Bühler explains:

> By the mid 1990s, it was already becoming normal for private equity houses to raise money by fund-raising using a classical GP/LP structure, and we were outside this typical structure. This was a disadvantage, because the capital markets were becoming a difficult place to raise money. Indeed, the whole public company status of Triumph-Adler was requiring a ridiculous level of public disclosure. For two years we had major dramas at AGMs about things that took place before our times under the Olivetti period. This was covered by the press, and was a burden to us. We also had the problem that a private equity house would typically have its success measured in terms of cash or NPV multiples, but as a stock listed company our success was measured in terms of revenue and profit growth. In a year when we exited more companies than we acquired, Triumph-Adler's revenues and profits both declined. This was viewed negatively in the public perception. This made us extremely uncomfortable, and pushed us to start looking for deals which would look to the outside world as if they fitted.
>
> Then in the period 1997–98, the new economy came along, and suddenly analysts were no longer interested in Triumph-Adler. This was not at all funny for us: everyone being interested only in dotcoms, and considering Mittelstand holdings to be simply uninteresting. We weren't considered modern. We only earned money, which in those days wasn't interesting. Consequently, our share price stagnated. By the end of the 1990s, we were frustrated. Even though we had been running the business well, and paying out good dividends, the public listing had failed to bring us the advantages we had been expecting, but instead it brought a lot of disadvantages.[103]

Despite the high dividend payouts the few analysts that covered the company's developments, came to the conclusion that diversity was a bad thing. But this was a view that had been influenced by the Triumph-Adler partners themselves. In 1999, they decided to make one last major acquisition. The opportunity for which had come up when looking at an investment in Migua, a company held by Juventas AG, an investment vehicle targeting small to mid-cap companies.

Juventas wanted to sell Migua, Raimund König was interested and proactively asked Juventas Manager Marcus Brennecke what other companies were in the portfolio. They showed him what they had, and König then was prepared to buy everything, the main reasoning obviously being to utilise the loss carried forward from Triumph-Adler. Juventas had not made any preparations to sell the entire group, and had not undertaken any assessment of what the full potential might be of each of the various businesses. Juventas was also worried about upsetting the managing directors of their portfolio companies in case they would keep the other businesses; therefore they wanted to keep the discussions highly confidential and clearly refused upfront a meeting between Triumph-Adler and the respective managing directors of the portfolio companies. Despite all these restrictions and limitations, König bought the whole group.[104]

Triumph-Adler's strategy was now to divest all of its divisions with the exception of the office systems business. König later recalls:

> When we bought Juventas, a holding company for other businesses, it was from our perspective the last acquisition we were doing. Then a year later, we publicly announced a change of strategy towards focussing the company. The environment for being a diversified holding company at that point wasn't really that good. So by arguing that we were focussing, we had a good clear reason for eventually selling off all the businesses at a huge profit. Our intention was to reinvest about half the proceeds into the office division and dividend out the rest.

> With the hype surrounding the Neuer Markt, there was no way to use Triumph-Adler for fundraising anymore. Plus there had been a change in the tax laws which meant that in selling off participations the gains were tax-free anyway. That's why we actively decided to get out of Triumph-Adler.[105]

In the wake of the Juventas acquisition Thomas Bühler, who had been responsible for new business development, left to set up Afinum together with Gernot Eisinger.

The idea of exiting the divisions deliberately was a new concept both for Triumph-Adler, and its predecessor IMM. Companies had never been acquired with an explicit strategy to sell them, as König explains:

> You will never find in our investment proposals a page on exit, even from the very beginning. We always worked in the belief that if we developed and grew businesses nicely, sooner or later somebody would come in and want to buy. With a few exceptions, that is exactly what happened.[106]

Slowly but surely, the Triumph-Adler team began an orderly liquidation of Triumph-Adler's private equity activities, shrinking it back to the office system core. Some of the smaller businesses were eventually taken over by team members: Gerhard Meinl bought the majority of the music business, Thorsten Quent bought parts of the Zementol business and Cornelia Sailer bought Haverkamp.

This strategy was also driven by the expectation that the focussing strategy would result in a rising share price. The continuously declining Triumph-Adler share price had been a challenge, as König explains:

> The quoted share price at the outset for less than 0.5% of the outstanding shares had been unrealistic, in fact it was more than twice what we had paid per share. With a gradually growing free float of shares, which we encouraged in principle, the share price "normalized" – nevertheless I did not like the notion from 1994 onwards, that I was the CEO of a company that had a miserable public shareprice-performance of up to minus 40% over five years which continued basically through 1999, and became hyper-critical during the development of the new economy, and the Neuer Markt. Investors looked at König and all his boring industries. No analyst would consider us being an attractive company despite our high dividend pay-outs. In 2000 the share price turned significantly upwards. Suddenly selling the shares became a financially attractive option especially for those Triumph-Adler partners who had not yet used the dividends to pay back their private leverage.[107]

A further consideration was the new and growing threat of insider-trading which made selling via the stock market almost impossible:

There was this newly established BAFIN to regulate insider trading that was just looking desperately to get some insider-trading case. Given the scope of our activities we were in a very narrow market, and it would be evaluated with hindsight that something was relevant or not. In fact we had established the position that we wouldn't sell any shares via the stock market, which we adhered to. Only after retiring could I sell my shares.[108]

In the summer of 2001, when Raimund König stepped down as CEO of Triumph-Adler, the end of the IMM/Triumph-Adler era as private equity company was a mere formality. The crisis following the 11th September 2001 made the divestment strategy more difficult, and it took longer than expected to complete the orderly liquidation of the portfolio. König recalls:

When I retired in 2001 and Dietmar took over, he eventually sold off all the remaining businesses. Unfortunately however the general market conditions and the sudden reluctance of Triumph-Adler's banks to support reinvestment, forced him to pay back the banks and reduce the company's leverage. So the plan to reinvest all this nice money into the core business could not be implemented.[109]

But for those that had invested in IMM and Triumph-Adler, the returns had more than justified the experience.

In 2003 Kyocera of Japan, a leading manufacturer of copiers and printers bought a minority stake in Triumph-Adler to secure its access to Germany's largest distributor in the copier and printer business. Kyocera appreciated the strategic value and by 2009 made a successful public takeover bid – the squeeze out was announced for 2010.

Afinum

The change of strategy at Triumph-Adler left Thomas Bühler and Gernot Eisinger with the option to leave and set up their own business. It was clear from the start that it would be private equity, and that they would be later joined by some of the other members of the Triumph-Adler team. Bühler recalls the events which led to the establishment of Afinum:

For my part, I simply wanted to do something on my own. The opportunities revealed themselves in my eleven years experience at IMM/Triumph-Adler. I clearly wanted to copy the positives and avoid the negatives. I knew that a couple of other people were prepared to leave with me to set-up something new. I started a few weeks before Gernot Eisinger because I was able to gain release from my contract with Triumph-Adler a little quicker than he was. Jochen Klemmer, who had supported us on Hüco and a number of other deals, joined us in 2000.

One of the lessons I learnt from Triumph-Adler, was that industry concepts don't always make sense. I doubt that half of all the industry concepts had synergy benefits big enough to compensate the holding group costs. We learnt that the individual deals must work on a stand-alone basis, and each deal must be strategically relevant. There will be time enough to talk about add ons later, but each deal must make sense on its own, not as part of some concept, where further deals need to be done.

The other lesson learnt was that it is not always sensible to keep the old shareholders locked into the new company for two–three years with a significant minority stake, and in particular, if this involves an earn out, because it is too easy for these people to influence results during such periods. So we have focussed more on buying 100% stakes, hiring new managers as employees, and later giving them minority participations. We are much more insistent upon taking over the company, and implementing the succession process.[110]

The name Afinum was chosen at a ski-resort. Bühler and Eisinger borrowed a pen and paper from a waiter, and wrote out a list of 20 names, all beginning with "A". They had ruled out family names, or abbreviations. Of the 20 names they came up with, only two were not already registered as company names, and Afinum won out in the contest with Agirax.

Fund-raising was straight-forward, and DM 94 million was quickly raised, although many advised Bühler to go into venture capital, rather than private equity. Bühler recalls:

People told me to start in venture capital, because that was much more modern, but I told them that I had no idea of venture capital, and people would say that didn't matter, because the others didn't either. I stayed with the old economy, and we had already found in 2000 sufficient conservative thinking investors that wanted to invest in classical Mittelstand successions. It wasn't so difficult to raise money in 2000. We were a so-called first timer, but we had a track record. It was almost more difficult to find an office in Munich than to raise the fund. There were hundreds of dotcoms and their advisors looking for office space.[111]

Once the fund had been raised, Bühler and Eisinger began building up their team. After Jochen Klemmer joined, they were able to add Berthold Schmidt-Förger from Bain. The new firm was positioned to compete with the likes of Halder, Equivest/CBR, ECM, Arcadia, and Steadfast. The first deal, Kinshofer, came in via Bühler and Eisinger's traditional intermediary contacts, built over eleven years at IMM/Triumph-Adler. The second deal, SIGG, however, came via more proprietary channels. Bühler describes the context:

> SIGG came to us through the personal network. It was a turnaround case, which had been taken over by a small group in Switzerland. I knew the guy leading the turnaround personally, and this enabled us to do our entry deal into Switzerland. It was a relatively uncomplicated acquisition with people we could trust. We only acquired the aluminium bottles business. The turnaround manager had already separated this business from the other cutlery business.[112]

Bühler and his team had resisted the new economy temptations, bucked the trend to stick with old economy buyout transactions, and closed two deals before the technology bubble finally burst.

BBK to Capiton

The BBK team had to wait until 1997 to make their first new investment, which was to prove a small one, a silent participation in the chemicals company, Pongs & Zahn. This did not lead to an unleashing of new investment activity. On the contrary, the team were restricted to just two more investments prior to 2000. The challenges confronting the team were again internal, as Andreas Kogler explains:

> In 1998, the Berliner Bank merged with the Landesbank Berlin (LBB) to form the Bankgesellschaft Berlin. The LBB also had its own participations business, which became known as the Berlin Capital Fund. With the merger, the extended bank preferred the 100% owned Berlin

Capital Fund as its vehicle for alternative investments, and discussions took place with the Gothaer about BBK's ownership being transferred to a single party. The outcome was that Gothaer took over BBK in summer 1999.[113]

The takeover matched Gothaer's existing investment strategy, which was to increase the allocation of their assets within direct medium-sized company investments. Gothaer's in-house team had already made a number of direct investments in companies such as ARI Albert Richter, Classen, Studienkreis, Inometa, and DKV. Gothaer merged its own private equity activities with the BBK team, subsequently renamed capiton. The Gothaer team brought in the management of its portfolio companies as well as its distinctive investment approach: avoiding high risk leverage structures, improvement of operating results, and multiple enhancement via growth strategies like buy-and-build. Stefan Theis was appointed the first managing director of the merged entity, and Reinhard Blei became head of the supervisory board.

Capiton's biggest challenge in the months that followed was the structuring of its commitments along Anglo-Saxon lines into an off balance sheet fund, that would be suited to include new investors: a precondition of capiton's future independence. The new structure also made possible a shift in strategy towards majority buyouts.

Under the new strategy, the first majority deal was closed in 2000 with Meyer & Burger, a Swiss machinery company serving the semiconductor and solar power industries.

Capiton entered the new millennium with plans well advanced to set up a fund sponsored by third parties, and positioned to move quickly towards independence.

Vector/LBO France/PPM Ventures

Eberhard Crain's small team at Vector Beteiligungsberatungs GmbH, working with LBO France, LBO Italia (Fund: Europe Capital Partners/ ECP), made a final acquisition in 1997 by buying Infox from Apax before moving into exit mode during the late 1990s.

The first major exit was achieved when Kruse & Meinert was taken public in April 1997. Crain recalls:

It was a big success. We sold 74% of the company in an IPO. I remember that the day of the IPO was also the first day for the Neuer Markt, and I was disappointed because Herr Seiffert, the then

Head of Deutsche Börse whom I interviewed for McKinsey, didn't join us to celebrate our launch. We made a 48% IRR on Kruse & Meinert.[114]

A year later, Temco was sold to 3i achieving a 30% IRR.[115] During the holding periods, Vector made several add-on acquisitions for both Kruse & Meinert and Infox. But once capital constraints began to set in, Crain and his team were faced in 1998–1999 with the question of what to do once the ECP fund was fully invested.

We were fully invested in the ECP fund in 1999, and we didn't have a new fund yet. We started working with an American investment bank, who said that in order to help LBO France, LBO Italia and us bridge the period between the end of the ECP fund and a new fund raising, we could work for them on a retainer basis. They offered the same package to the French and Italian offices.[116]

Crain was given an early opportunity to look at Sirona, before it went into an auction. But he was unhappy with the response from New York:

First of all, New York was slow, which gave Sirona the time to contact JP Morgan and give them a sell-side mandate. But despite this set-back, we still thought we could get the deal done before it went onto the market. Then the second response from the Americans in New York was to start contacting the JP Morgan people across the street. A group within the American investment bank came to the view that everything could be done out of New York, but it still took them a month to sign a letter of intent. This was no way to cooperate, and it was certainly no way to do business in Germany. So we lost the deal.[117]

Despite the difficulties, through lack of other options, Crain continued trying to work with Americans, bringing them in on a deal to buy the BHF Industrial Holding group AGIV.

I started negotiating with the president of the industry group. I was showing off that we had the American investment bank behind us, but when it came to the most important meeting, the guy didn't show up. So again we lost a beautiful deal. I started getting rather annoyed.[118]

The last straw for the cross-Atlantic relationship came when Vector was at the point of closing on Suspa, a company that was being sold by 3i and family shareholders. Crain recalls:

> We had everything done, including due diligence, and were full-financed twice from the Bayerische Landesbank and BHF. Then the American investment bank held a management meeting in New York, to which we weren't invited. They had sent some guy over to Germany over the weekend to look at the deal, and present it alone to the investment committee. But at the meeting, somebody said they knew someone else who was a very small, dissatisfied customer of Suspa, who had said that it was a bad company. So they turned the deal down. This left me furious again. I thought: what shall I do?[119]

Through old contacts made while at Thurn & Taxis, Crain got in touch with Neil MacDougall and Jean-Lou Rihon of PPM Ventures, who were in Frankfurt looking for people to work with in Germany. Crain moved quickly:

> I jumped onto a plane, and went to explain to them that I had a super deal that was all set to go, if they wanted to step in. The only difficulty was to go to the seller, with whom we had a close personal relationship, and tell him that everything was the same, but we wanted to change investor. I explained the change by saying that I didn't think the Americans would suit him, and that these English would be better. He said he didn't care who the investor was, as long as we stayed on board. So we did the deal, but for PPM, not for Vector, the Americans, or anyone else.[120]

PPM conducted an extensive due diligence on Suspa following on from the work done by Crain's team.[121]

Sebastian Kern, who was at 3i after the Suspa sale, and later joined PPM, recalls the PPM side of the story:

> Neil MacDougall and Jean-Lou Rihon, who was looking after the French office, found that the Suspa deal was well prepared. It later emerged that there were technology issues, quality issues, and production issues. There was a high currency dependency, and the currency went in the wrong direction. We had fallen out with the original banking group. The lesson learned from them doing that deal was that PPM would find it helpful to have their own office on the ground.

Despite having successfully closed the deal with PPM, Crain decided that his days of working with other partner's funds were over, and resolved to become fully independent. Crain and Wolfgang Behrens-Ramberg promptly formed CBR-Management GmbH, and in 1999 went on to raise their own fund under the name of EquiVest, which was closed in 2000.

Candover

Candover, who had hired Jens Tonn from Citicorp in 1997, having exited their joint venture with Legal & General in Germany in the same year, were far more interested in the size of deal that could be easily done from London. Jens Tonn describes the change of heart towards Germany within the Candover team in London:

> After the boring years of 1994–1996 in Germany, suddenly things started to get much more interesting. In 1997–1998 you had people like Siemens announcing they were going to sell DM 25 billion worth of turnover of their subsidiaries. You had Jürgen Dormann at Hoechst saying that he was going to focus on pharma, and get rid of the rest. Then in 1999–2000 you had the *Handelsblatt* reporting on a list of approximately twenty businesses that Degussa wanted to divest. This suddenly got the market going, and raised Candover's interest.[122]

Candover made its first major deal in 1999 with the acquisition of Vestolit from Degussa. The experience brought with it many insights into the differences in mentality of managers in Germany compared with the UK, as Tonn relates:

> We met many managers from the so-called "Deutschland AG"/corporate Germany, and realised that many of them were as far away from being entrepreneurs as you could imagine. The classic example was when we gave management presentations to show them how much wealth they would create if they achieved the business plan, and the key questions which came back from them were: "but will we keep our company car arrangements?"; and "what will happen to our corporate pension entitlements?"
>
> It was a question of attitude. They were used to their company car, their bonus at the end of the year, and their benefits. We were talking about them becoming independent, calling the shots, investing some

of their money, and becoming wealthy. But the lawyers also made things very difficult for us. Lawyers were scaring managers away from what it meant to be an owner, and entering into new responsibilities. This was a classic German situation.[123]

Ironically, the Candover team had fewer problems convincing the workforce at Vestolit of their intentions than some of the key decision makers. The works council listened patiently to the Candover presentation, and showed themselves to be very co-operative:

> We had nothing to hide. If you do things properly, and you believe in your business case, then it is best to share it with others.[124]

Bain & Company

Bain & Company had had little involvement in the provision of consulting services to the emerging private equity industry during the first seven years of the 1990s, other than managing and running down the Matuschka Portfolio. All this changed with Sirona, when Bain was hired to perform the commercial due diligence for Schroder Ventures, and thereafter to execute a substantial piece of post-acquisition restructuring work. This included splitting the business between its equipment business, retaining the name Sirona, and its wholesale business which was sold off under the name of Demedis. Bain opted for a co-investment approach to the business, offering almost all of its initial fees for the initial work plus a similar investment by the Bain & Company partners that amounted to some DM 1.5 million. This approach was pursued on a series of subsequent transactions, and was to be influential in stimulating the creation of bainlab, which was set up to channel the Bain & Company consulting and investment activities into venture capital investments.

Fritz Seikowsky and Peter Tornquist had been overseeing the rundown of the Matuschka portfolio, which took five years from 1992 to the divestment of the final company, Weiss Tex, in 1997. Almost all of the companies were sold to management. The only trade sale was with Brause, which went to Clairefontaine. Ekkehard Franzke recalls:

> I came to Bain at the point when they were asking themselves "how do we exploit our experience?" Bain created investment vehicles, it was a worldwide initiative, but we had, with Matuschka, a unique experience on which we tried to capitalize.[125]

L.E.K.

Despite its early involvement in the commercial due diligences for Charterhouse, Equimark, Heller, and the Treuhand, L.E.K. gained little traction from its early experiences, and it wasn't until an initial flow of projects were sold from L.E.K. London that the office's interest in private equity was kindled. These included projects to support Toby Wyles at Apax in his acquisition of Nordsee, and Guy Hands at Nomura for his unsuccessful bid for Tank & Rast. But ironically, these were not the most influential projects for the office. Instead it was an entry strategy project conducted for Close Brothers that stimulated L.E.K. Munich's interest in serving the German private equity market.

The L.E.K. Munich team analysed many segments of the M&A financial services market in Germany to pinpoint how and where Close Brothers should establish itself in Germany. This included a review of the private equity houses, and the L.E.K. Munich team discovered that their office was just a few houses down the street from the Apax office on Possartstrasse in the suburb of Bogenhausen. Ironically, L.E.K. diversified its private equity client base at precisely the time that the consultants at Bain & Company were moving over to bainlab, effectively reducing their firm's commitment to serving the "old economy" private equity market. By the turn of the new millennium, L.E.K. had jumped from four private equity clients to 20, and by 2001 increased this number to 30.

2000: The tax and legal watershed

The year 2000 marked a watershed in the German tax and legal environment for almost all parties touched by private equity, including their managers (the "GPs"), their investors (the "LPs"), the sellers of target companies, and the target companies themselves, as Reinhard Pöllath explains:

> Fund formation in Germany in the early days tried to mirror Anglo-Saxon limited partnership models (including the "Ten Commandments" from the US Internal Revenue Regulations), using the German tax tools of "advisory versus management activity in Germany" and "investment versus business status of the fund" (including elaborate "do's" and "don'ts" for managing and advising the usually foreign-based funds). These early structures were heavily influenced by the

experience gained with foreign funds, beginning with the advice given to the sophisticated Rho German family office, which invested in funds like Sevin Rosen or Schroder Ventures.[126]

Pöllath himself, and his colleague Rodin, helped shape that experience into an established practice, working closely with the German authorities. Later they felt that formal "tax rulings" were preferable once more and more funds used advisory offices in Germany, and domestic funds like Odewald were born. In a lengthy process, and with some policy support, Pöllath and Rodin started to obtain these tax rulings in states like Bavaria, Berlin, Hamburg, and North Rhine Westphalia. This assurance by rulings was also needed because more and more German investors, private and institutional, invested in mostly foreign funds, and required comfort as to how their German tax offices, initially unknowledgeable without exception, would view their investments, as Pöllath later recalled:

"Non-business" (investment) capital gains were largely tax-free up to 2000, while "business" capital gains were taxed at up to 50%. So, certainty of tax treatment could decide whether or not an investment was made, whether it be by a foreign fund in a German target, or by a German investor in a foreign or German fund. Through this practice, tax rulings became the "gold standard" of fund formation. At the same time, they and private equity publicity in the media attracted tax policy attention. One significant element was the largely tax-free status of "carried interest" earned by fund managers based in Germany. This tax treatment was attacked from about 2000 onwards, resulting in much fighting, lobbying[127] and the threat of a freeze on private equity activity in Germany.

Certainty was reinstalled after much intricate drafting by a Government decree on Private Equity taxation.[128] It established a new regime and protected (grand-fathered) the tax treatment of earlier funds under the prior tax ruling practice. Carried interest taxation was legislated, roughly on a "one-half" capital gains tax basis, effectively similar to Anglo-Saxon tax burdens. This new certainty of tax treatment let private equity in Germany flourish more openly[129] and better organised,[130] just in time for the rise of private equity after 2000. The (then restricted) tax exemption of capital gains of individuals also benefitted fund managers and target company managers. The full exemption was only more recently replaced by a "half" tax burden on these capital gains, and other investment income of individuals.[131]

The rise of private equity affected investors resident in Germany as well as foreign and some German funds active in Germany. Pöllath was heavily involved in developing clearer structures:

> In the early and mid 1980s, Didi Höner, and the Rho family office he managed, was often the only German investing in the funds he chose to invest in, and these funds were in no way adapted to German needs, either tax or otherwise. At this time, it was necessary to make the first tentative steps, beginning with the seemingly incompatible terminology.

> The first Schroder German Ventures fund had only two other German investors, which were big institutions with small stakes. The MatCap funds had at least 90% or more non-German investors. Gradually, German investors were introduced to private equity, sometimes through intermediaries, feeder or side-by-side funds, sponsored by the likes of VCM, Hartz Regehr, Döttinger Straubinger, CAM, Solutio (all with Matuschka backgrounds), von Braun & Schreiber (with an Allianz background), Feri/ Sauerborn, Harald Quandt, and others. For institutional and "retail" investors alike, tax certainty was vital, initially provided by tax rulings without a statutory basis, then on a firmer legislative and administrative basis.[132]

The owners of the target companies were also touched by tax and legal issues, which in turn impacted the opportunities for, and development of, private equity in Germany. The steep rise in the number of transactions at the end of the 1990s prompted many advisory firms to set up shop in Germany to offer their services to foreign funds, as Pöllath himself experienced:

> German funds were rare, after early examples like TVM and MatCap, and even today, German funds such as Odewald are the exception rather than the rule. In the 1980s and in much of the 1990s, the tax exemption of most capital gains of individual sellers and the full tax on capital gains of corporate sellers twisted the sourcing of deals towards family businesses (owner-operated Mittelstand). Tax legislation restricting and finally eliminating the tax exemption threatened to dry up that deal source by the late 1990s. So, the Christmas 2000 announcement of the SPD Government of a full inter-corporate tax exemption[133] was a timely reversal of a seventy-five year old tax policy. Full tax on corporate capital gains had frozen Deutschland AG

structures, and full tax exemption unfroze them, turning corporates into a major source of deals for private equity after 2000.[134]

Parallel developments were taking place regarding the target companies themselves. Up until the mid-1990s, buyouts of German target corporations had benefitted from a double tax advantage: a post-acquisition potential refund to the acquirer of all German corporate tax paid by the target on earnings since 1977, and a post-acquisition asset-basis step-up procedure sheltering subsequent earnings by depreciating the above-book-value premium reflected in the purchase price,[135] plus a full acquisition-interest deduction.[136] Pöllath later commented that:

> These tax benefits were little publicised initially,[137] then became well known,[138] and were essentially abolished from the late 1990s and after 2000.[139] Their rise in the early days helped popularise M&A and financial buyers including private equity funds, since they were willing to reflect these benefits in the purchase price they calculated and offered.[140]

Lessons from experience

The 1997–2000 period saw Germany take a central position on the global private equity stage. No longer merely a backwater, for some firms Germany was becoming the second or third biggest market. After a long period of development, the amount of capital put to work in German buyouts had at last become material.

The only drawback, in hindsight, was that Germany attracted a disproportionately high share of venture capital, and that the Neuer Markt became such a significant driver of investment activity in the region, primarily on the basis of the new economy. Buyouts in mature companies were by the end of the period attracting little interest because of the dotcom hysteria. Very few, at the time, were aware that they were being buoyed up on top of a rapidly expanding bubble.

14

The Seventh Phase: 2001: The Collapse and Its Aftermath

Many times a collapse in one market brings with it unexpected beneficiaries. The bursting of the dotcom bubble in 2001, and the fall from grace of venture capital, had some spill-over into the area of private equity. For a while, the rise of the stock markets helped the development of private equity, particularly in Germany, where for the first time, there was a feeling that the options for exits were growing. But at the peak of the bubble, old economy deals were suffering. Few people were interested in the IPO of a long-standing business with a modest growth rate, even if it was well-positioned and international. Hordes of professionals were upping sticks to move over to ventures, either to set up new companies, service them as principles, or to act for them in an advisory capacity. So while the events of 2001 had negative side-effects for private equity, the impact was not all negative. Indeed, after a brief fall back in the number of buyouts closed in 2001, private equity activity was to enjoy its own boom, reaching undreamed of heights of activity and valuations by the spring of 2007.

The sheer size of the private equity industry in Germany by the start of the new century was staggering compared to its stage of development ten, or even five years earlier. The number of private equity houses active in German leveraged buyouts now ran into triple figures, and the number of professionals employed by them had long since exceeded a thousand. Indeed, the supply of private equity had over-shot demand prior to 2001. There were too many houses chasing too few deals. Auctions were becoming massive: investment banks routinely sent out books to at least 30 private equity houses with requests for indicative offers. A second round could still involve anything up to ten financial sponsors competing with one another. Final round exclusivity was by now a thing of the past.

Inevitably in this changed environment, some of the most established private equity houses found it difficult to adapt, although how long an institution had been present on the market was little guide to its collective experience. Some older houses had substantially grown their teams, and by so doing introduced large numbers of inexperienced professionals into their ranks. While other houses, newly formed, were sourced from seasoned professionals, head-hunted from firms with a deeper pool of experience.

The addition of new private houses, created the curse of the headline deal. As Michael Philips explains:

> The competition increased staggeringly from 2001–2002. You had every company coming to Germany intent upon making a headline deal. On every transaction, there was some guy who wanted to make his mark. There were many moments when we at Apax felt we should let them win a deal so that they could at last get into line. During the period 2002–2004, prices weren't overly aggressive, but nevertheless the competition for the deals had increased dramatically. The simple truth was that during 2002–2004, you didn't have a huge number of deals on the market. Instead, you had lots of new entrants, and lots of inexperienced hires.[1]

The other major challenge of the immediate post dotcom years was the lack of credit, and the unwillingness of many investors to put money into Germany. Christophe Hemmerle, who left Halder in 2000 to set up Finatem his own private equity house, remembers the challenges of the market over the 2002–2003 period:

> Getting finance for deals at this time was difficult and very expensive, because Deutsche Bank, Dresdner Bank, and the Commerzbank had basically quit the Mittelstand. The Anglo-Saxon banks were not there. Only the Scots were trying to set things back up again, led by the Royal Bank of Scotland, and the Bank of Scotland. The mezzanine people were charging 17%–20% rates, and senior debt rates were very high. We sold out our investment in Hügel and Gutbrod too early to Barclays partly because the financing we had committed to in 2002 was so expensive.

> Meanwhile, fundraising in 2003 was a major challenge. Everywhere in the world, the first thing you had to do was to explain why

Germany wouldn't go bankrupt, and how Germany would raise itself out of its disaster. The question on every American's lips was: "why do you believe in the German economy?"[2]

We labelled the years 1992–1994 as "frustrating times". Ironically, a decade later, the same title could be applied again.

Apax

Apax had a very difficult couple of years, in the immediate aftermath of 2001 with two challenges, one revolving around the collapse of its investment in Bundesdruckerei, and the other, the last minute withdrawal of its bid for Mannesmannn Plastic Machinery (MPM). Max Burger-Calderon recalls:

> For a while, we were wobbling, and yes we made mistakes. We were lucky to get into trouble so early. What didn't kill us made us stronger. So while 2001–2003 were absolutely nightmarish years, they paved the way for us performing well later on, when many other firms were doing terribly.[3]

In some respects MPM, while costing Apax nothing other than its broken deal costs, posed more serious external challenges. Michael Phillips recalls the events:

> For various reasons Siemens wanted us to sign the deal on MPM. The numbers at MPM had clearly been going down. Everyone knew that. We were the last man standing, and we told Siemens that we would sign a deal on the condition that if the numbers continued to go down, then we wouldn't proceed to closing.
>
> In the event, the numbers continued to decline in a dramatic fashion and we informed Siemens we would not close the transaction. Clearly they were upset, but this was not a surprise.[4]

Of course, not everyone reading the newspapers knew the full facts of what Apax had or had not signed with Siemens. Many thought Siemens would sue Apax. It was generally believed that it was the senior debt providers who had pulled the plug on the transaction, leaving Apax having to say that it would let its investment vehicle go bankrupt before being forced to finalise the closing.

Internally, however the problems with the Bundesdruckerei, were far more serious. Halusa recalls the experience:

> Because Bundesdruckerei was a co-investment with the Apax UK fund, we had a joint approval committee, so it was big group reviewing the proposal. When the Gemplus data came through we all started worrying: Gemplus was crashing, and yet Bundesdruckerei was going up. We thought: "How can that be?" And then Michael said: "you know what, I'm just going to go up there and meet management." So he went up to Berlin, and two days later came back saying "I think the numbers provided by our own team are misleading."[5]

Michael Phillips bore the brunt of dealing with the crisis, Halusa being on holiday at the time. Phillips explained the situation which confronted him:

> We have a rule within Apax that if you have a problem you tell it on day one. At the time, back in January 2001, it was clear that the chip market was experiencing some very big problems. We were told by our people that at Orga, the chip unit within the Bundesdruckerei, there weren't any problems. But come June 2001, Gemplus had announced that they were having big problems, and still we weren't hearing any bad news from our colleagues responsible for Orga. So I flew to Berlin, and immediately discovered that we had a huge problem, just as everyone had suspected. Within 24 hours we made some team changes.
>
> It must be emphasised that we don't change people for making bad decisions. Decisions are made by everyone. As well, the fall-out in the telecoms market to the degree that it happened was hard to foresee. Many technology companies had severe issues during this period. It's by making bad decisions that you learn from your mistakes.[6]

CVC

CVC entered the new millennium, by its own account, having had a quiet period, and the team was to endure further frustrations during the period 2000–2002. The first deal which was nearly done was on Lenzing, which ultimately didn't get competition approval. Marc Strobel, who joined the team from Doughty Hanson in 2000, recalls those years:

When I moved to CVC, I found that it was a lot more decentralised than Doughty. This meant that I was much more involved in Germany. Some of the work was cross-border, but you still spent most of your time in the German-speaking region. Lenzing was the first thing I worked on, which was signed but didn't close. That was very frustrating.[7]

The Frankfurt team worked extremely hard on Dynamit Nobel (which went to KKR backed Rockwood) and VAW Aluminium (which went to Norsk Hydro), but finally prevailed on Viterra Energy Services (subsequently renamed Ista), as Strobel later explained:

On Ista we didn't have any particular angle, but then no-one else did either. Permira were batting hard to win this one.[8]

The Ista transaction was substantial, and confirmed CVC's position as a leading player for the run-up into the mid-2000s.

Allianz Capital Partners

Through Reiner Löslein's contacts at Deutsche Bank, the Allianz team came up with the idea of buying Schmalbach-Lubeca, a packaging company owned by Viag. Reiner Löslein recalls:

It looked an interesting asset, because the industry was highly consolidated, but there was still scope for further consolidation. Schmalbach-Lubeca on its own wasn't that interesting. But if it was sliced up, its pieces looked more attractive. Viag had hired CSFB to advise them on how to divest the business, but we approached Timotheus Höttges, who was at that time responsible for M&A at Viag, to signal our interest. We told him that we thought an outright sale wouldn't give his group the full amount they needed to earn on the deal. We had come up with a more attractive structure that kept Viag in with a participation.

Höttges said that while Viag needed to divest the business, he wasn't sure that the structure we had suggested would work for them. But during our discussions, Viag was running an auction for Gerresheimer and had just given exclusivity to Investcorp. The trouble for them was that once Investcorp got exclusivity, they started knocking the price down. They couldn't withdraw exclusivity from Investcorp because time was running out. They had told the market that they would have all these issues resolved by June 2000. This put them in a difficult situation, draining their motivation for another auction. That's how they came back to us to accept our suggestion.[9]

Axel Holtrup, who at the time was with Investcorp, remembers the incident at Viag well:

> I was in the negotiations at Viag with Ferdinando Grimaldi. In these sorts of negotiations, there is always some give and take. Not retrading, but both sides trying to optimise the deal.[10]

Allianz was to do extremely well out of the Schmalbach-Lubeca deal, selling the PET business to Amcor, and the beverage can unit to the Ball Corporation. As Reiner Löslein explains:

> Schmalbach-Lubeca made up for everything. With the returns from Schmalbach-Lubeca, we repaid everything, including the money we lost on other deals.[11]

At roughly the same time as Schmalbach-Lubeca, the Allianz team came across another similar transaction with Messer Griesheim which was being led by Goldman Sachs:

> We created a structure which allowed Stefan Messer to do what he wanted, and that gave us a decent return. We cut the business into sizable pieces. Stefan Messer kept the part he wanted, and we sold a major part on to Air Liquide. Again this was a kind of industry consolidation. Air Liquide couldn't have done the deal on their own, because then they would have been forced to buy the whole of Messer, and would have run foul of the cartel authorities. We acted as a kind of facilitator.[12]

The Messer family pursued a similar strategy with one of their other companies. Stefan Messer later confirmed that he, Goldman Sachs and Allianz Capital Partners made a good deal, although the PE houses "a fortune – for my feeling too much within only three years – and that was the reason I had to sell our entire German business",[13] as Reinhard Pöllath explains:

> Messer Griesheim was a particularly happy private equity-plus-family transaction. Likewise, the other Messer company, a

welding machinery and tools business, went to Carlyle, in a joint venture with the family, who finally bought Carlyle out to retain its heritage family business. In the end, this left everyone happy: the sellers, the private equity investors, the managements, and the members of the Messer family.[14]

The successes with Schmalbach and Messer helped Allianz Capital Partners compensate for the total loss made on its investment in Fairchild Dornier. Like Clayton, Dubilier & Rice, the Allianz team experienced many trials and tribulations with the investment, as Löslein recalls:

I guess everyone was shocked on 11th September 2001. When I first saw the pictures, I thought it was one of those disaster movies, because such a thing couldn't possibly happen. Only over time did people realise what had happened. The stock market collapsed, and within 2–3 weeks Fairchild Dorner experienced a withdrawing of orders. All the airlines were very insecure about how air traffic would look in the future.

We were only a minority investor on Dornier. We bought into the concept of Clayton, Dubilier & Rice, that they had an experienced operating partner, who would make sure the business would be a success. What a lot of American investors underestimated, however, is that it's a different country and culture here. What works in one country won't necessarily be successful in another. There were problems at Dornier even before 9/11.

Once we realised there was something wrong, we sent Robert Frost, one of our guys into the company. He did some analysis of the status quo, the outcome of which was that he said that if we wanted to continue with the venture we would need to inject somewhere between $800 million and $1.2 billion of extra cash into the business. That was basically the point when everyone involved said it's just not worth while.[15]

The period 2002–2003 was difficult for Allianz, as it was for many other players in the industry. In 2002, Bartec was acquired, a much smaller deal, and the team focussed mainly on providing mezzanine for other PE transactions.

Industri Kapital

Detlef Dinsel's team at Industri Kapital in Hamburg had also been going through a difficult period. Memories were still fresh over the i-Center failure, which crashed into insolvency after its acquisition from Siemens in 1998. Dirk Tetzlaff, who had joined the team from BCG in September 2000, recalls:

> After the i-Center experience, the German team was in need of a deal, and preferably a good one. One of my first assignments was to work on ContiTech, where we were up against fierce competition. But we got exclusivity for a couple of weeks, and had a meeting set for 12th September 2001. The day before, we had a secretary running around screaming about a plane having crashed into the World Trade Center. We were all stunned, yet trying hard to concentrate on preparing for our meeting. In the evening, we received a call to cancel it. Stefan Kessler, the Continental CEO, had just been replaced by Manfred Wennehmer, the head of ContiTech.[16]

Hardly had the dust settled, than a new deal attracted the Hamburg team's attention. In November 2001, the process began for the sale of Gardena, in which Dinsel took an immediate interest. Again the competition was fierce, with Electrolux viewed by many as the most likely winner in the auction. Tetzlaff recalls:

> Electrolux wanted Gardena so badly, that they offered Werner Kress, the Chairman and one of the two main owners a price that was somewhat higher than our best offer. We owe our success to the management team, which was very much in favour of a buyout. They did a lot of preparation, which greatly assisted the process.[17]

McKinsey had been advising Gardena with a big-ticket consulting project for several years, and was secured by Dinsel's team to undertake the commercial due diligence. Many of the other private equity firms were concerned by the seasonality and weather dependency of the business, but these were of little concern to Industri Kapital, as Tetzlaff explains:

> We focussed on the strong things relating to the underlying business. We had a high regard for Gardena. With such a strong brand, nobody could threaten to take you off the shelves. We saw continuous underlying growth in the main segments and the prices were always a couple

of points higher this year than last, which was a luxury that few other suppliers could aspire to. Later on, Martin Bertinchamp was hired to become the new CEO. As far as we were concerned, everything was in place.[18]

Success with Gardena put Industri Kapital firmly back on the map for private equity in Germany, as Tetzlaff experienced:

> Gardena was an ice-breaker. All of a sudden, IK was in the spotlight. Doing successful deals is the best publicity.[19]

Dinsel too was relieved to have closed a deal so shortly after the i-Center insolvency:

> We were lucky and happy with Gardena. The Gardena process had started in September 2001, and the i-Center insolvency was filed in November 2001. So we were lucky that we had the Gardena process running, although my colleagues in Sweden never threatened me with closure.[20]

Arguably, the Industri Kapial team had bucked the trend twice, closing a disastrous deal in the heady days of 1998, when most were making fortunes, and closing a successful deal in 2002, when many other players were finding it challenging to find anything to do. Nevertheless, the team was to endure a long stretch until its next deal, as Caspar von Meibom recalls:

> After Gardena, we were very successful at winning silver medals, on Apcoa, AHT, and Tetra among others. Racking up full due diligence costs on five projects and not doing a deal for more than three years was not a pleasant experience.[21]

Electra

With the core of the team around Wolfgang Bensel, Christoph Tiefenbacher, and Mathias Turwitt leaving to form their own company at Arcadia, Electra in London was left with the problem of making new hires for Germany. Philipp Amereller and Frank Hermann were the only two members of the former Electra Fleming team left. Through headhunters, Electra London quickly found Brian Veitch and Mark Elborn, the core of the old Legal & General Ventures team. Veitch signed before Christmas

1999, and started work in the first quarter of 2000. He recalls his first actions:

> I had to move up to Hamburg, but only so that I could then relocate the office to Frankfurt within six months. Frank and Philipp both wanted to be part of a European fund, and so they had stayed behind. I had to persuade them of the merits of relocation.
>
> Once we had moved into the new office in Frankfurt at the Haupt-wache, we spent eighteen months marketing, and not getting any deals done. We were sending out offers, but there were not that many deals around in 2000–2001.[22]

It was not until the Electra team dug in on the Gardena deal that they began to realise that some changes of approach were required, as Veitch explains:

> We saw we needed to change the way we did deals. In reality Gardena would have been quite a big deal for us at the time. But we were a bit hesitant, probably because it was so big. It made us realise that we should probably get experience on something smaller.[23]

Through the work on Gardena, the Electra team came across Oase, a company making equipment for garden ponds, which had been a possible bolt-on acquisition for Gardena. Veitch and his colleagues decided to pursue this option instead. Veitch recalls the process:

> We managed to get an exclusive negotiation going, and quickly became persuaded that it was a better business for us to buy. It was smaller, and more compact.[24]

Some of the attractions of Oase, which Electra closed in 2002 and was the new team's first transaction in Germany for the new fund, turned out to be not all that they had seemed, as Philipp Amereller recalls:

> On the positive side, it had a leading market position and an excel-lent brand recognition as well as reputation. But on the negative side, management's business plan proved to be somewhat optimistic and it didn't materialise at all. Then we had the problem that the

company had become too over-sophisticated relative to the market it served. They were too product innovation driven, adding new products at a rate that the channel couldn't keep up with. The end-customers were also getting confused, and didn't know what to buy anymore. Last, but not least, was their appalling delivery ratio. They just couldn't get the product out when it was needed, which annoyed the dealers, and caused costs to increase. So we had to make a lot of changes in strategy.[25]

Close on the heals of the Oase transaction came Scholz & Friends, a deal which was picked up by Michael Boltz, who had joined the Electra team from Equita. Boltz explains the source of his lead:

> I was talking to Kai Kraft from Deloitte, and he mentioned that he had been mandated by the management of Scholz & Friends to find a suitable private equity house to help them buy themselves out from Cordiant, their parent company in the UK. Cordiant was hurtling its way towards insolvency. I mentioned that I had done the Infratest deal at my previous employer, and that a market research company was as close as you could get to an advertising agency. So he introduced us to the management team.[26]

Boltz prepared Electra's pitch for the beauty contest that the Scholz & Friends management were running. Fortunately, help was on hand from London, as Boltz explains:

> I felt it would be wrong and too proud not to pick a UK operating partner. Advertising had after all been historically strong in the UK. I was put into contact with John Spearman, and he said that he knew of Scholz & Friends, thought they were a super company, and had wanted to buy them himself in a former life. We also had another operating partner who was about to join our London team, Chris Jones, who used to be CEO of J Walter Thompson in New York. So in the second phase of the Scholz & Friends pitch, we brought John Spearman over for a dinner with the management, and this was a very lively affair. Then we had a second dinner at which we wheeled in Chris Jones, a completely different person, but equally impressive, and afterwards the Scholz & Friends management said they wanted to go with us.[27]

The Scholz & Friends deal was a complicated deal, being an acquisition from a public company which was close to bankruptcy. Boltz describes the transaction:

> It was so stressful. I couldn't sleep at night, because the value of Cordiant's share price was dropping so fast that the Scholz & Friends valuation was becoming ever more material. If it crossed 20% of Cordiant's market capitalisation, we knew we would need approval for the sale from an AGM. Once this point passed, we had to pray that the banks wouldn't force Cordiant into insolvency before the AGM had approved the sale.[28]

Scholz & Friends closed in 2003. Keeping up the rhythm of a deal a year, Electra moved on to bid for Thyssen Fahrzeugguss in 2004. But this was a deal which died a thousand deaths, as the Frankfurt team were quickly to find. In the middle of the first auction, the process collapsed because one of their OEM clients sent a letter informing management that the OEM would stop sourcing one of their components from them. Boltz recalls the event:

> Automotive suppliers are used to being treated badly, but this was brutal. The client asked in the letter how much it was going to cost them to close the plant which was producing the component in question. We had a meeting with the Thyssen Board and discussed the situation amicably, saying that we really could not close on a deal with such a level of uncertainty, which they perfectly understood.[29]

Four months later, Boltz received a call from Citigroup to inform him that the process had been restarted, and to ask him whether he wanted to be included. Boltz had to clear this with his investment committee, as he explains:

> We had a Monday morning investment committee meeting, and I said that I would like to make a bid for Thyssen Fahrzeugguss, which was for considerably less than what we had bid earlier. I don't think any of them took it that seriously. They thought it would never happen. I kept coming back and pressing for approval until I got it. At the next meeting I told them that we had agreed to buy the company for this lower amount.[30]

In the event, the OEM client discovered that they were more dependent than they had thought upon Thyssen Fahrzeugguss, subsequently renamed KSM Castings, and the business developed far better than any of the Electra team could have hoped for.

ABN Amro

Henk Droege's new team proceeded in 2001 to close its first successful deal with Löwenplay, a chain of amusement arcades, followed by Nau Umwelt, focussed upon solar panels. L.E.K. was hired to do both commercial due diligences. Christof Namenyi, who invested considerable time in the deals recalls:

> Löwenplay was our first LBO, developed under the typical newco structure, and it was followed by another buyout of Nau Umwelt at the end of 2001. We all learnt with the latter that a business driven by government subsidies can be quickly brought to a halt.[31]

Up until the beginning of 2003, further deals were closed including Steco, and a reinvestment in Colortonic, one of the older deals.

Several members of the ABN Amro team left to pursue other activities. The first to leave was Richard Gritsch in 2000, who joined Brockhaus, followed by Wolf Wolfsteiner, who moved to 3i in 2001, Gerald Oertel, who joined Halder in 2002, and Wolfgang Pietzsch, who signed up with Axa in 2003. Pietzsch explains the main reasons for his move:

> ABN Amro was a special environment. It was of course captive. We were talking for years about carry but these talks were leading nowhere. The challenge was that too many countries would have needed a solution. The bank spent a lot of money looking for one global solution for numerous tax systems, and lots of smart managers flicked through them. But at the end of the day, it was a banking driven environment. With hindsight, I realise I left a bit too early. Some months later, it became clear that ABN Amro was going to exit private equity in Germany, and Henk Droege, Peter Davidzon, and Christof Namenyi, the only remaining guys, got a great deal in buying the portfolio from them.[32]

The ABN Amro decision to pull out of private equity in Germany came as little surprise. Namenyi recalls the environment which led up to the decision;

> During 2002, the markets were in a crisis, and throughout this period, ABN Amro was not sure whether it should be supporting ABN Amro

Capital at all, whether it be inside or outside the Netherlands. As a consequence, we never knew whether money was available. The market challenges persisted into 2003, when we didn't do much, and by then people started to leave, and the office shrank. Finally, we ended with just the three seniors, Droege, Davidzon, and me.[33]

There were a number of options discussed, once it was clear to the German team that ABN Amro was going to pull out of the German private equity market. This process was not, however, without its challenges, as Namenyi explains:

> First of all it was clear we would lose our jobs, so we said that we either would be willing to run down the portfolio or come to a reasonable agreement, and make them an offer to buy the portfolio. ABN Amro wanted to avoid creating the impression that they were selling down the overall commitment. None of us in the Frankfurt team had substantial funds available. We had only enough to provide some commitment. Nevertheless, it was agreed by the bank that we could buy the six companies, if we could get the financing in place.[34]

The Bank of Ireland in its first leveraged deal in Germany provided the newly formed DDN Capital with the bulk of the financing, via a holding company, under which all the participations were lodged. A recap of Löwenplay was also used to help fund the acquisition of the portfolio. Namenyi recalled the process of liquidating the ABN Amro portfolio once the deal with the bank was done:

> Löwenplay was the most stable of the deals, which is why we used the recap to help with the refinancing, but on the other hand we had to pay the highest price for it to the bank. The three minorities had lower valuations, partly because they were complicated in terms of shareholder structure and we therefore couldn't expect much from them. In the event, we managed to sell them surprisingly quickly and successfully. Finally we sold down TomTec, Dyconex, Hauser, and Colortronic. Hauser and TomTec were sold back to management, Colortronic to a competitor, and Dyconex was sold in 2008 to a strategic buyer.
>
> The most important investment, Löwenplay, was sold to Waterland in 2006 at a valuation which proved very successful for us, and later very successful for Waterland. The last company to be sold was Steco, which was sold to IFCO at the end of 2008.[35]

BHF Private Equity/Steadfast Capital

In 2000, it was the turn of BHF Bank to decide it wanted a piece of the private equity action. Nick Money-Kyrle, who had left 3i to work for GE Equity, received a headhunter call on behalf of a German bank wanting to enter the PE market, and took the meeting. He later explained the events that unfolded:

> The board of BHF had decided to put €150 million into private equity, and wanted someone to set it up and manage it. I stressed that, in my opinion, private equity only worked with independent structures, and explained that a direct bank subsidiary was a no-win situation. If the team was successful, the carried interest would be more than board members of the bank would earn, and thus be unacceptable, and if it underperformed, in the short term, the team members would inevitably be sacked. They accepted that if I took on the task I wouldn't be an employee, but own the management company, and that the team would take 20% carried interest, with a 2% management fee on the funds committed.[36]

Once established, Money-Kyrle found that the bank already had fund of fund investments, and two direct participations, which he took responsibility for. One of the direct investments was in Remaco, which was 80% owned by Brian Fenwick-Smith. Negotiations over this stake were one of Money-Kyrle's first challenges:

> Remaco was making machines for the pharmaceutical industry, and it was an old investment that had been made by the bank many years earlier, but which had ceased to pay a dividend for many years. The bank had already entered into a process to sell its stake to Brian, who was offering to buy it for a significant discount. My first reaction on learning this was to say no to the deal. Consequently, the initial upshot was a cessation of communication. So I went down to Monaco to meet Brian, and we got on well. In the end, it was decided that we would both sell the business, achieving a con- siderably better result for the bank.[37]

The other direct investment was in Passport, a deal which had been closed with 3i and IBG in 1994. As the 3i fund was coming to an end, there was also a pressure for an exit on this deal, as Money-Kyrle explains:

> It didn't look a good time to sell Passport, so I told 3i that we would either be willing to sell at one price, or to buy their share

with management at a somewhat lower price. 3i and the bank accepted the offer. We had to do a refinancing, but closed a successful secondary buyout, with the new BHF Private Equity funds taking a stake and management reinvesting its proceeds for an increase in equity.[38]

The fund of funds had a broad range of investments in vehicles such as Charterhouse V, Odewald I, and German Equity Partners I. During the process of finalising the arrangements for the private equity activities, the BHF Bank sold off its stakes in AGIV, and decided as a consequence to increase its commitment to private equity to €350 million. Given the sums now involved, the bank hired Bain to give independent advice on the investment strategy. Money-Kyrle recalls the results presented by the consultants:

> Bain put in 2–3 months work, analysing the players in private equity, producing a big wadge of paper in preparation for the key board meeting. Bain had gone for the pure buyout option as being the preferred strategy, but with a generalist investment fund as the second choice. I suggested the latter since I had the strong impression that certain of the board members had made the decision they wanted the generalist strategy before they commissioned the project. The board members were frustrated that the bank was giving good deals away to other parties, and also convinced they needed some exposure to fund-of-funds.

> What came as surprise, however, was that during one of the key board meetings working off the back of the Bain project, I found €45 million of the €350 million had already been committed to another private equity start-up, CMP, a Roland Berger sponsored fund in Berlin. I suggested that my team should manage the €305 million commitment that was left, and we signed the management agreement on 21st September 2001. I and my partner, Clemens Busch, became self-employed and found ourselves an office.[39]

Having secured the necessary commitments, and infrastructure, Money-Kyrle proceeded to hire a team, securing first Marco Bernecker from Arthur Andersen in 2001, followed by Sebastian Ribbentrop, Kay Buschmann, James Homer and Thomas Rubhan by the beginning of 2002. It was then that the problems with the bank began, as Money-Kyrle explains:

One big lesson I've learned in life is not to trust corporates. They tend to change their strategies regularly and if they change their minds, they will pull out. I had this in mind during my contractual negotiations with the BHF Bank. One of the reasons I like doing business in Germany is that Germans tend to stick to the letter of the contracts they sign. In February 2002, literally five months after signing the agreement, I was confronted by an investment freeze. We had at that point made seven fund-of-fund commitments, acquired Elaxy, and made three venture investments, and thus around €60 million was committed or drawn down. The freeze continued for nine months, and then as we moved into 2003, I went to the bank and said that it was crazy to make such a commitment, and pay a fee thereon, whilst preventing the team from investing the money. They needed to decide what they wanted to do. We then spent six months negotiating a new agreement, which would allow us to raise further outside funds, and in June 2003, just as they were due to sign, I was called in to the Bank to be told that the board had decided that private equity was no longer a core business. They wanted to sell the fund, or reduce the 2% management fee to apply only to the €60 million we had already invested.

I pointed out that they could hardly sell a €305 million commitment which was only 20% invested and that, since we had entered into a joint venture, they should read the contract before deciding upon a course of action. The bank's lawyers clearly saw we had a good case, and the bank capitulated, and continued to honour the original agreement. Almost overnight, ING lost patience with BHF, and we suddenly had a new manager from Holland to deal with. The investment freeze was lifted at the beginning of 2004 and we were allowed to invest again, completing three transactions that year in Passport, Pitti, and MPS, the latter being in Holland.[40]

The brief return to normality, however, was shortlived. By the end of 2004, the bank was put up for sale, and it was clear that the private equity group had no future. Money-Kyrle could see the writing on the wall and approached the bank for approval to find alternative investors. In this he was successful.

In December 2005, Money-Kyrle closed off the first fund, and finalised its spin-off of the Fund, which was subsequently renamed Steadfast Capital.

EQT

In August 1999, shortly after completing his work on transitioning Honsel from public-to-private status, Hans Moock received a call from Stephan Krümmer, asking him if he would like to join him in opening a new office for EQT. Krümmer was travelling the following week to Stockholm to finalise his contract, and Moock was welcome to set up a meeting to talk to Conni Jonsson the day after. Moock found the idea appealing and set up the meeting, but, as he later recalled, things didn't exactly go to plan:

> The day before I was scheduled to fly to Stockholm, I got another call from Krümmer saying that Rothschild had made him a vastly improved offer to stop him from leaving, and informing me that he had decided not to take up the EQT offer. So I called up Conni, and asked him if he still wanted me to come. He said of course: there was a new job on the table. So I flew up to Stockholm and got the top job to open up EQT's office in Germany.[41]

Having opened up L.E.K.'s office in Germany in 1988, starting a new organisation from scratch was nothing new for Moock, but nevertheless retained its appeal. The first task was to decide where to locate the office. Conni Jonsson wanted to open up in Hamburg, because that was where their archrival Industri Kapital was based. But Moock had other ideas:

> I said let's do a location analysis. The options were clearly Hamburg, Frankfurt, and Munich. I ensured that the final discussions took place in September 1999, during the Oktoberfest, at the Käfer restaurant in Munich. They had an advisor who was keen on Frankfurt, and they had their original ideas of Hamburg, but in the end they accepted Munich.[42]

Moock's task was to build up a team, and his first call was to a colleague, who had worked as a consultant with Moock at L.E.K., and then joined him at Bertelsmann a few years later.

> My colleague was happy to join. The rest of the team was quite difficult to hire. 1999 had been a great year for investment bankers, and those we approached laughed at us in the face when we told them what our package was. So we ended up mainly with ex-consultants like ourselves.[43]

The first deal closed was Leybold Optics, a deal which was quickly to experience challenges in its main markets, as Hans Moock explains:

> At the start, in summer 2001, we weren't even on the list to get the book for Leybold Optics. I was asked by WestLB whether I was interested in being in the process. We only had two days to get our first bid in before the deadline. My colleague from Bertelsmann and L.E.K. days went to the management presentation, and then hired BCG for support, having found that L.E.K. was already conflicted. We ended up buying the company, but it was a cyclical business, and we caught the nose-dive into a downphase. On the other hand, maybe that's the price you have to pay to get market entry. The first deal is always difficult: you need it to get yourself established. Certainly we were taken more seriously in the market after we had done the deal.[44]

It was EQT's second deal, however, which was to revolutionise the firm's position in the market place. In 2002, Bayer decided to sell off its flavour and fragrances business, Haarmann & Reimer, leading to one of the hottest auctions of the year. Moock had already visited Horst-Otto Gerberding at Dragoco, one of the other German flavour and fragrance players in September 2001, hoping to buy him out. This meeting had been pleasant but not led to a deal, as Moock explains:

> We had a very nice meeting. It was one of those where the chemistry is right. Gerberding said we were welcome to buy the minority stake in Dragoco, which at that point was held by Equita. But he wasn't going to sell out the majority. He wanted to stay in the driver's seat.[45]

Knowing Dragoco's commitment to keeping majority control, EQT began the process without a strategic partner, until it realised that it could no longer justify the price they needed to win the deal without one. The first solution, put together by the Scandinavians, was Christian Hansen, a food additives company in Denmark. The idea was that Christian Hansen would get the flavourings part of the business, while EQT would keep the fragrances. The Danes quickly lost interest, however, leaving the EQT team to find another partner. Moock decided that another visit to Dragoco would make sense, as he recalls:

> By now, it was beginning to look certain that Givaudan would buy Haarmann & Reimer, and this wouldn't necessarily be a good thing for Dragoco. My colleague met with Gerberding again, and convinced

him that putting Dragoco and Haarmann together would create a strong number four in the industry. Even if Gerberding only held a minority in the company, at least it would guarantee the survival of his company. He eventually gave his agreement on the condition that he would run the merged company as CEO.[46]

Once EQT emerged as the front-runner on the deal, together with Dragoco, it became clear that a €500 million equity ticket transaction would benefit from another private equity house as a co-sponsor. Allianz Capital Partners was approached, and discussions proceeded up until the last days of the process, but a deal could not be reached before the deadline. Consequently, EQT underwrote the equity cheque, only to look for parties to syndicate equity to, after the process was over.

The closing of the Haarmann & Reimer deal demonstrated to the market that EQT could scoop a spectacular and complex deal in Germany. Internally, however, it revealed that the Scandinavians intended to keep tight control over an investment so large. Stockholm made the decision to put Björn Hoj Jensen onto the Board of the new company, and to send him to become co-head of the Munich office. This signalled a change of guard in the Munich office, as Moock explains:

> I underestimated the cultural dimension of working for a Swedish firm. In hindsight, I realise I should have joined their Stockholm office, and worked alongside the other Swedish partners for a couple of years. I could have learnt the language, and launched them into Germany gradually, once bonds of trust had been forged.[47]

Moock stayed with EQT until the summer of 2005, before leaving to join Equita.

Advent

Having acquired Vinnolit and Vintron at the turn of the millennium, the Advent team continued to focus on complex large corporate spin-offs. Jan Janshen, who had been working at 3i in Hamburg in the late 1990s, joined the Advent team, convinced that this was the sort of buyout house he was looking for:

> Advent was focussed on buyouts, and put in a long and deep due diligence on targets. Ironically, the first thing that lay on my desk when

I joined was an info memo from Goldman Sachs who were trying to sell off Asta Medica, Degussa's pharmaceutical activities. Ironic, because the business was finally sold in pieces, and it was from them that we bought the remaining Viatris, which I worked on, in 2002.[48]

Ron Ayles, who joined later, from 3i Frankfurt, held a similar view:

> I wanted to invest in a sector I understood, not something I tried to learn about in a few weeks. At Advent there was a significant track record in chemicals, I had full support, and my industry experience was seen as of value.[49]

Advent had dabbled in venture capital during the dotcom boom, but the venture team were quickly spun off. Janshen was confronted with a completely different approach to deal-making, and was working very hard to develop Viatris into a deal:

> Viatris was a complex situation. It was diverse regionally, being in Europe, the US, and Brazil. Functionally, it had a lot of sales and marketing in the various countries in combination with R&D and some production. In the US, Viatris was operating a joint venture with Carter-Wallace. Perhaps even more significantly, however, the pharma market itself is pretty complex: it is highly regulated and a multinational set-up.
>
> If all these complexities weren't enough, we were just coming up in Germany to another health care reform, and we had to develop scenarios on what the outcome of this reform might be.[50]

Hard on the heals of the Viatris deal came Moeller, a distressed deal which had been floating around the market for several years. Hans Albrecht, who had left Carlyle to set up his own vehicle Nordwind, had been trying to buy this company, as he later explained:

> Moeller was one of my absolute favorites. It had been in an auction run by Deutsche Bank, but no one was interested and the auction was called off. I was trying to do this deal while at the same time raising a fund. When I started fundraising in 2001, I thought that it would be easy, that the police would have to organise lines for people queuing up to give me money. But 2001–2002 was a terrible time to be trying to raise a fund, and I just couldn't pull the money

Figure 14.1   Ralf Huep

together quickly enough. Advent took advantage of the fact that we had no money. There were terrific deals in 2001 and 2002, if you were interested in restructuring, where you could make ten times your money. Unfortunately, I didn't have money in time.[51]

Despite being in the process of retiring from Advent, Chris Neizert picked up the initial lead on Moeller, and suggested making it his last major deal before leaving the Frankfurt office. A critical factor for Advent was their operating partner, Uwe Alwardt, an ex-ABB manager, who worked with the Advent team and the Moeller management, pulling together a restructuring plan. Advent backed him, and also brought in Dave

McLemore, another operating partner who had previously worked for GE. The two men joined the Moeller management. Janshen watched as the management pulled off an impressive turnaround:

> They did a fantastic job, turning the company around, growing revenues at twice the rate of the industry, and with good profits. It was surprising when we came to sell that it didn't go straight to Eaton, because they were the obvious candidate. Instead, it was Doughty Hanson that pulled it off, only to sell it on to Eaton two years later for half a billion Euros more than they had paid to us.[52]

While the period 2001–2003 was difficult for some, for those with money and a focus on restructuring these were the heydays of deal-making, as the experience of Advent demonstrated.

BC Partners

After its string of successes with Techem and Grohe, BC Partners was convinced in 2001 that it was about to chalk up another victory with Klöckner Pentaplast. The indications were positive that the management were on Board, and that the BC Partners' offer was in pole position. The deal was their's for the taking. Jens Reidel later described the events that unfolded:

> We had Klöckner Pentaplast served up to us on a silver plate. Our success in getting to pole position on the deal had a lot to do with soft factors: the way we handled the management; the way we always respected people.

> So on the 11th September 2001, we were at the Frankfurt airport club together with the Klöckner Pentaplast management on a conference call with Citi in New York. Suddenly we were told that a plane had crashed into the World Trade Center, and that various parties needed to hang up. Everyone was in shock. We realised that the Pentaplast business was driven by oil prices and the dollar, and so our take-away the next day was that the Pentaplast business plan could no longer be relied upon to happen. We shied away from the deal. We just couldn't be certain of the business plan any longer, and we basically chickened out. On 12th September we withdrew from the process. Cinven, who at that point were the runners up, were more courageous than us.[53]

Erol Ali Dervis, who had also been sitting in the Frankfurt airport club room, considered this moment to have been one of the most memorable in his life:

> We were sitting with the Klöckner Pentaplast management at the Frankfurt airport club. Citigroup was advising us. We wanted to make a conference call at 15:00 German time, 9:00 New York time, linking up with a managing director of Citigroup who was in New York. Two minutes before 15:00 we got this call from Citigroup saying that their team had been forced to evacuate the building as a plane had crashed into one of the towers. We were joking about this, saying "Oh OK, a drunken Cessna pilot. Fine let's go out, in 15 minutes they will be back and we'll be able to do the call". So we went out, and in the airport club they had this big screen switched on to NTV, and right then the second plane flew into a tower. It was a big plane. It wasn't a Cessna. It was immediately clear that something was fundamentally wrong. OK, we were under shock. There was no way we were flying back to Hamburg, and instead we rented a car quickly at Sixt before there was any risk of them closing down Frankfurt airport. Nobody knew what was going on, so we rescheduled the meeting.

As it turned out, Citigroup was in the building directly adjacent to the twin towers. Their building collapsed the day after, because of structural damage. It was a sad memory. The meeting we were supposed to have had was an important one, and in the end we blew the deal.[54]

Cinven

Peter Gangsted left Allianz Capital Partners at the beginning of 2001, in time to join the Cinven deal-team on Klöckner Pentaplast. Cinven had looked for internal resources after ending its relationship with Thomas Matzen, hiring Christian Dosch and Oliver Frey to open an office in Frankfurt in 2000. Karin Himmelreich joined Cinven on the same day as Gangsted, and also worked on Pentaplast. Gangsted recalls the days around the critical day in September 2001:

> We knew it was down to BC Partners, Bain Capital, and ourselves. We had to put in an offer on 12th September. When we saw what was happening on television the day before, we realised that it was serious. But we thought that Pentaplast was in a long-term business, and believed that the events shouldn't impact our bid. We felt deci-

sions needed to be made on the basis of whether it was a good business, or a bad one. I think Bain put in a higher price than us, but WCM felt more comfortable that we would close the deal.

JP Morgan joined us after we closed the deal, as they had been one of the close runners up. That was good for Tom Goeke, one of the three leaders of Pentaplast, and the future CEO, who was based in the US, and felt out on a limb.[55]

The link-up with JP Morgan was to become more typical of PE houses joining forces at the end of a process, once substantial deal costs had been incurred. In part, this was an inevitable part also of the growing auction processes, as Georg Stratenwerth, who was at JP Morgan at the time, explains:

> We had our own bid on Klöckner Pentaplast, and then various bidders started teaming up. That was a process where at least six bidders were forced to go all the way to the finishing line, and have all the financing in place. So we got a 20% stake in the company, which was still a sizable investment.[56]

The Cinven team pushed ahead to do the Springer deal, together with Candover, the following year, having already acquired Kluwer, also with Candover, in the Netherlands. Gangsted recalls:

> Thomas Middelhof announced that he was selling Springer while we were still doing the Kluwer deal. This made us feel more comfortable about our strategy. We had Bain working on Kluwer, and got them to work immediately on a plan to put the two businesses together. This put us into a much better position when CVC, Blackstone, Apax, and the other houses were competing with us for the deal. On this one, we clearly paid the highest price, but the work we had put in made me feel comfortable about winning.[57]

Candover had probably the best angle on the Kluwer deal, as Tonn describes:

> Candover had a very good relationship with management of the scientific publishing division of Wolters Kluwer. The fact that we knew the former chairman of Wolters Kluwer meant that the team was comfortable that we would win the deal. In the very final round,

we were concerned a trade buyer would probably outbid us, and we knew that Cinven were keen on the asset, and that they probably had the same idea as us to buy-and-build. Both of us had relatively modest sized funds at the time, and given that Thomas Middelhof had already announced his intention to sell Springer, we knew it would be a good time to join forces, so that we would have the firepower to do both deals.[58]

Much of the work on both publishing deals was done in London. Neither Candover nor Cinven had a problem with this approach. Tonn comments:

Local presence doesn't matter for large deals such as Springer or Klöckner Pentaplast. These sorts of deals are done at Frankfurt Airport Center, or the Arabella Airport Hotel Dusseldorf.[59]

Gangsted was also completely comfortable with the London role on the Cinven side:

Cinven has a pan-European view. The local offices are advisory, and the decisions are made in London. The local teams help to get the deals going, but the sector teams are the most important part of the matrix. Cinven is more centralised than most others, because of our history, but I don't think people really care. If you talk to the boss of Siemens, he will tell you they love to do deals with KKR. Why should they worry that KKR is based in London? The biggest issue is industry competence, and being able to pay the top price.[60]

KKR

Apax's refusal to close on MPM opened up opportunities for KKR. On its own, MPM would not have been a compelling auction for a private equity house focussed on mega-deals. But once Siemens realised that it no longer had an automatic process for disposing of its portfolio of non-core businesses, an alternative option became possible. Johannes Huth began a series of discussions with Heinz-Joachim Neubürger at Siemens, which was then followed-up by a meeting between Kravis and the Siemens team. Siemens made it clear that they needed a simpler process to get out of a long list of portfolio companies. KKR offered to do a deal to acquire such a portfolio in late 2001.

Once the confidentiality issues had been cleared, the KKR team looked at a portfolio of a dozen companies, and short-listed those that they were keen to acquire. KKR offered a valuation of DM 2 billion, which after negotiations, was accepted by Siemens.

The approach Siemens and KKR were taking did not lend itself to an auction. In effect, the manner in which KKR chose its targets was customised. It was clear that the price KKR was paying to get this access to the portfolio was the commitment to taking over MPM at a fair value. But KKR didn't view this as a problem. Its team did not view MPM as a bad business, but rather one that had been mispriced.

The KKR deal closed in 2002 causing some dismay within the private equity community, as two processes had already started, one for the sale of the Demag and Gottwald crane businesses, and one for the disposal of Stabilus. Many private equity houses had invested effort in attending management presentations, conducting preliminary due diligences, and drafting bids before these two deals were taken off the table, to be sucked up into KKR's package. The scale of KKR's deal also gave the impression that Kravis and his team were playing in a league of their own, far above the rest of the competition in the German market.

KKR weren't always able to get their way on every deal however. In the auction for ATU, a retailer and installer of car accessories (particularly tyres and exhausts), the KKR team felt they had the inside track, but were pipped at the post by Doughty Hanson. But Huth and his team kept in close touch with both ATU and Doughty Hanson, such that when the latter came round to the idea of selling the company two years later, KKR was in pole position to buy the company from them.

KKR kept up a rapacious level of deal-making by acquiring Zumtobel in 2002, an Austria-based lighting business, proving that they could not only clock up high value deals, but also win several deals a year. KKR had previously acquired the UK-based Thorn Lighting, and was later able to merge the two businesses.

KKR's *coup de grace* came in 2003, just a year later, when it acquired MTU aero engines from Daimler. If the Siemens deal had started the process of KKR becoming accepted as a serious player in Germany, closing the MTU deal pushed them over the final finishing line. During the negotiations, the KKR team met with Chancellor Schroder in Berlin, ministers and officials in the ministries of Defence, State, and Economics.

KKR had overnight extended the reach of the private equity industry in Germany, in a way which fundamentally changed its contours. In

Table 14.1 Private Equity Transactions in 2001

2001

Company	Buyer	Seller	Exit year	Sold to
SaSec	Milestone Capital (E.A.C.)	Family	2007	ING Parcom PE
Agrolab GmbH	Hannover Finanz	Family	Not yet divested	Not yet divested
Askys (CWW-GERKO Akustik)	DBAG/Süd Private Equity	Rüttgers	2003	PPM Ventures
Brüder Siegel GmbH & Co. KG	Quest Capital Beteiligungs Ges. m.b.H.	BayBG Bayerische Beteiligungs GmbH	Not yet divested	Not yet divested
Buch + Kunst	Barclays	Family	2008	Thalia
Cognis	Permira	Henkel	2010	BASF
Dorotheum GmbH & Co KG	Global Equity Partners/ UIAG	Family	2004	Management
Elaxy	BHF Private Equity	Heyde AG	2005	GAD eG
Getmobile	IVC Venture Capital AG	Family	2005	Fitzwilliam Capital
Grammer	Permira	Public to private	2005	Public Block Trade
Hettich	capiton	Family	2006	Family
Hügel GmbH & Co KG	Finatem	Family	2002	Gutbrod (Finatem portfolio company)
Illbruck Automotive (Carcoustics)	NIB Capital Private Equity	Illbruck GmbH	Not yet divested	Not yet divested
Kabel Baden Würtemburg	Blackstone/CDPC/ Banc of America	Callahan Associates	2006	Blackstone
Kemmer Technology AG	Hannover Finanz	Family	insolvency	insolvency
Klöckner Pentaplast	Cinven/JP Morgan	Klöckner & Co	2007	Blackstone
Konrad Hornschuch AG	Halder	Decora Industries	2006	DZ Equity Partner/ L-EA Priv. Equity
Maillefer	Argos Soditic	Nextrom/Nokia	2008	Alpha Groupe
MBB Liftsystems	Finatem/Natixis	MBB	2007	Palfinger AG
MCE	Andlinger & Company	VA TECH Hydro	2007	DBAG

Table 14.1 Private Equity Transactions in 2001 – *continued*

2001

Company	Buyer	Seller	Exit year	Sold to
MIGUA Fugensysteme GmbH & Co. KG	BPE Private Equity	TA Triumph-Adler AG	2005	Indus Holding AG
Minimax	Barclays	Preussag	2003	Investcorp
PEPcom	GMT Communications Partners	Management	Not yet divested	Not yet divested
Pfaff Haushaltsnähmaschinen	Industri Kapital	Insolvency Administrator	2006	Kohlberg
Phoenix Xtra Print GmbH	BPE Private Equity	Phoenix GmbH	2005	ContiTech AG
Richard Schöps AG	Borgetti	Thomas CJ Matzen	2006	PHI Private Holdings of Investments
RT Recycling Technologie GmbH	ECM	GMM Active Equity	Not yet divested	Not yet divested
Schollglas	Alpha	Family	2008	Strategic investor
Soudronic – Automotive Division	Capvis/Gilde	Doughty Hanson	2006	VTC
Soudronic – Metal Packaging Division	Capvis/Gilde	Doughty Hanson	2006	Keystone Group/ Leonhardt Holding
Strähle + Hess (Sellner Group)	EquiVest	Family	Not yet divested	Not yet divested
TA Musik GmbH (renamed JA Musik)	Gerhard A. Meinl MBO	Triumph-Adler	Not yet divested	Not yet divested
Telecom Nescom Systemhaus	Hannover Finanz	Family	Not yet divested	Not yet divested
TFL	Permira	Ciba & Degussa Hüls	2003	Odewald/WestKB
titus	ECM	Family	2007	Investor Group
Völker Informatik AG	Norddeutsche PE	Family	Not yet divested	Not yet divested
Wendt	BPE Private Equity	Family	Not yet divested	Not yet divested
Zarges Tubesca	NIB Capital	VAW/Zarges Family	2007	DZ PE/Granville Baird

Source: Authors' compilation

Table 14.2 Private Equity Transactions in 2002

2002

Company	Buyer	Seller	Exit year	Sold to
Accovion GmbH	HeidelbergCapital	Aventis	Not yet divested	Not yet divested
Agrolab	Hannover Finanz/BayBG	Family	2006	Management
AHT Austria Haustechnik	Quadriga	Public to Private	2006	Equita
Alukon	Granville Baird/ECM	Family	2004	Axa
ASCAD Engineering Solutions GmbH	IKB Private Equity	Family	Not yet divested	Not yet divested
ATU	Doughty Hanson	Owner family	2004	KKR
Balzac	Granville Baird	Management	Not yet divested	Not yet divested
Bartec	Allianz Capital Partners	Family	2008	Capvis
Basler GmbH	Alpha	Hucke AG	2006	Triton
Bernd Steudle	Finatem/Invest Equity	Alchemy	2008	L-EA
BHS-Cincinatti Getriebetechnik	EquiVest	Micron Cincinnati	2005	Halder
Breitfeld & Schliekert GmbH	Nord Holding	Family	Not yet divested	Not yet divested
CAN.media Group	TA Triumph-Adler	Previous investors	2004	SELLTEC Communications GmbH
Demag – Mannesman Plastic Machinery	KKR	Siemens	2006	Madison Capital Partners
Demag – Stabilus	KKR	Siemens	2004	Montagu
Demag Crane & Components	KKR	Siemens	2006	IPO
DeTeSat (Plenexis Group)	3i	Deutsche Telekom	2005	Stratos
Deutsche See	BPE Private Equity/ HSH Kapital GmbH	Apax	2006	Management
Dragoco	EQT	Equita	2006	IPO
Ecoroll	Hannover Finanz	Family	Not yet divested	Not yet divested
Etimex	Barclays	BP Specialty Chemicals	2006	Alpha
Fleming Dental	CMP Capital Management-Partners GmbH	Family	Not yet divested	Not yet divested

Table 14.2 Private Equity Transactions in 2002 – *continued*

2002

Company	Buyer	Seller	Exit year	Sold to
Flottweg	Invest Unternehmens-beteiligung AG	Siemens/Kraus Maffei	2006	Management
Forstinger	Orlando	Insolvency	2005	Bridgepoint
FTE Automotive	Hg Capital	Dana	2005	PAI Partners
Gardena	Industri Kapital	Family	2006	Husqvarna
Gealan	Halder	Family	2004	Axa
Gutbrod Holding GmbH	Finatem	Voestalpine AG	2007	Barclays
Haarmann & Reimer	EQT	Bayer	2006	IPO
HDW	One Equity Partners	Deutsche Babcock Borsig	2008	ThyssenKrupp
Heide Park Soltau	Charterhouse/Tussauds	Family	2005	Dubai International Capital
Hengstenberg	Hannover Finanz	Family	Not yet divested	Not yet divested
Herbst Beteiligung	Norddeutsche PE	Family	Not yet divested	Not yet divested
Highway One	Telefonica	Apax	Not yet divested	Not yet divested
Hirslanden	BC Partners	UBS	2007	Medi-Clinic Luxembourg
Hörmannshofer Fassaden	BdW	Family	2006	Equita
HTE – Blast Furnaces	DBAG	RHI AG	2004	Paul Wurth S.A
HTE – Cimprogetti S.p.A.	DBAG	RHI AG	2007	FMW Industrieanlagenbau
HTE – Hochtemperatur Engineering GmbH	DBAG	RHI AG	Not yet divested	Not yet divested
HTE – Kaefer-Raco Engineering GmbH	DBAG	RHI AG	2006	Camfil Group
HTE – Maerz Ofenbau AG	DBAG	RHI AG	2006	Polysius AG/Thyssen Krupp
HTE – RCE Industrieofen Engineering GmbH	DBAG	RHI AG	2006	Polysius AG/Thyssen Krupp
HTE – StrikoWestofen GmbH	DBAG	RHI AG	2007	BPE Private Equity
HTE – Z&J Technologies	DBAG	RHI AG	2006	Equita

Table 14.2 Private Equity Transactions in 2002 – *continued*

2002

Company	Buyer	Seller	Exit year	Sold to
Hüco Electronic GmbH	LRP Capital	TA Triumph-Adler AG	Not yet divested	Not yet divested
Jack Wolfskin	Bain Capital	Johnson Outdoor	2005	Quadriga/Barclays
Kaffee Partner	Bridgepoint	Family	2005	Odewald
Kannengießer	TA Triumph-Adler (Office)	Family	Not yet divested	Not yet divested
Kinshofer Greiftechnik GmbH	Afinum	Family	2005	Paragon Partners
Landis & Gyr	KKR	Siemens	2004	Bayard Capital
Leybold Optics	EQT	Unaxis	Not yet divested	Not yet divested
Machalke Polsterwerkstätten	Afinum	Family	2005	Capvis
Microdyn-Nadir	Global Equity Partners/ UIAG	Previous investors	2005	Sinomem Technology Ltd
NOI	Odwald	VC Fund	2003	Management
Oase Wuebker GmbH	Electra	Family	Not yet divested	Not yet divested
PDS Entwicklungs- und Service GmbH	MUK Kapitalbeteiligungs- gesellschaft mbH	Family	2006	NordHolding
Raith	Hannover Finanz capiton/ACA	Family/Financial Investors capital increase	Not yet divested	Not yet divested
Repower	Cornerstone/Heptagon	SER Systems	2005	IPO
SER Banking Software	Madison Private Equity	Family	Not yet divested	Not yet divested
Similor Group	JP Morgan Partners	Siemens	2007	ROCA
Siteco	AdCapital	GE Capital	2007	Barclays
Softpro GmbH	3i/Star Capital	Swiss Air (Insolvency)	Not yet divested	Not yet divested
SR Technics			2006	Mubadala Development/ Dubai Aerospace Enterprise

Table 14.2 Private Equity Transactions in 2002 – *continued*

2002

Company	Buyer	Seller	Exit year	Sold to
Strohal Rotationsdruck	Invest Equity	OIAG	2006	Let's Print Holding
Tesion Communicationsnetze Südwest GmbH & Co. KG	Arques	Energie Baden-Württemberg	Not yet divested	Not yet divested
Tetra	Triton/Axa	Pfizer	2005	Rayovac Corp
Trespaphan	Bain Capital/ Dor Chemicals	Celanese AG	Not yet divested	Not yet divested
Uster	Capvis/Quadriga	Zellweger	2006	Alpha
Viatris	Advent	Degussa	2005	Meda
Vits-gruppe	WD Beteiligungs GmbH	Insolvency of Babcock	2006	Granville Baird
WAS – Wietmarscher Ambulanz und Sonderfahrzeug GmbH	Norddeutsche PE	Done AG	Not yet divested	Not yet divested
Werner Kammann Maschinenfabrik GmbH	Arcadia/Nord Holding	Family	Not yet divested	Not yet divested

Source: Authors' compilation

addition to the large-cap, mid-cap, and small-cap segments, there was now a giga-deal category, in which for a period it held a 100% share. KKR gained many advantages from this position, as it was able to make offers for huge undertakings such as Kirch Media and DB Capital Partners without having to face much competition, and while at the same time gaining a "conglomerate discount" in return for solving big problems.

Barclays

The 2001–2003 period was to witness feverish activity within the Barclays Munich team. After having closed Minimax in early 2001, Barclays was to seal another deal, Buch + Kunst, a chain of bookstores, only a few months later.

The Buch + Kunst deal was a good example of the Barclays London team leaving Munich considerable independence, and relying upon the judgement of the German locals. Hammermann explains:

> Our UK colleagues didn't like Buch + Kunst, but there was limited downside, and it had good management. A lot of people had looked at it and decided to turn it down, which probably had an influence. We had long meetings, with many ups and downs. It is often said that a deal has to die many times before it gets done. Well this one died at least fifteen times before we closed it. It was very painful. But we succeeded finally.[61]

Buch + Kunst closed in 2001. In 2002, Barclays won a limited auction to acquire Etimex, a carve-out from BP Specialty Chemicals. In the same year, Barclays exited from Nici, the plush toy manufacturer, because the management were clearly unhappy with the amount of information Barclays needed, the request Barclays had made that a highly professional CFO be installed in the company, and the worsening situation on the capital market, since the target had been to IPO the company. This reluctance of the owner to be subjected to tight controls was later to gain significance, when it emerged that the he had fraudulently inflated Nici's revenues and returns, plunging the company into insolvency, with the result that he was arrested, convicted, and jailed.

The exit from Minimax was transformational for the Munich team at Barclays. Hammermann and Bork had proved what the local team could achieve, and were emboldened to push on ambitiously do a string of further deals.

The final acquisition of the 2001–2003 period was Wessel Werk Group which was acquired from Garbe, Lahmeyer & Co.

JPMorgan Partners

The original Chase Capital team, under the leadership of Georg Stratenwerth, made its transition to Munich in 2001. Stratenwerth recalls the early years:

> We built up critical mass, and did some smaller mid-market deals, where local presence made all the difference. The German team now stood at six, and we staggered our moves over from London, Max Liechtenstein moving half a year after me.[62]

The strategy of making co-investments with other houses had been a successful way of entering the German market, with experience on AHC Oberflächentechnik (with Alpha and Alpinvest), Nordsee (with Apax), Gerresheimer (with Investcorp), and Klöckner Pentaplast (with Cinven), and gave the organisation comfort, as Stratenwerth explains:

> In the early days our investment committee felt more comfortable with us working with local partners. It allowed us to make a second check on the investments. The view was that playing the role of meaningful minority investor would bring us extra know-how. We didn't have ten-plus years of experience to draw upon.[63]

The move to lead arranged buyouts proved more challenging, however, as Heinz Holsten explains:

> The transition from co-investor to lead investor was longer and harder than we expected. It was probably not helped in Munich by the fact that we were further removed from where the decisions were being made. Munich didn't have much leverage over the rest of the organisation. Instead, we tended to get roped into a lot of international investments.[64]

The team nevertheless closed its first deal in 2002, with the acquisition of Siteco, which was to turn out to be Stratenwerth's last deal with the firm. He went to Advent, leaving the Munich team to become more tied to London, as Holsten recalls:

I spent about half my time working in London, while Max Liechtenstein and Ralf Jäger spent more time in Munich.[65]

The life of JPMorgan Partners was however soon to change. For the merger between its parent, and the parent of One Equity Partners in 2005, meant that the new combined bank was left with two private equity activities. This was to lead to the JPMorgan Partners team engineering its own spin-off and buyout, resulting in CCMP in Europe and North America, and Unitas in Asia.

Investcorp

Having experienced a number of years without a deal in the German-speaking region, 2003 became a pivotal year for Investcorp, as Thilo Sautter explains:

> We started working on Apcoa July 2003, and we closed Minimax in June 2003. Thomas Middelhof was now running the shop in Europe, and was doing extremely well. We got a lot more calls, and he generated a lot of publicity for us. It was much easier to get meetings with managements.[66]

Klaus Hofmann, the CEO of Minimax, recalls the process by which Investcorp succeeded in winning the auction for his company:

> We had three interested companies in the last round: Investcorp, Compass, and HgCapital. HgCapital gave in the highest bid with €234 million, and they made a very good management participation offer, because by then we knew how to negotiate such things. Trevor Bayley and Stefan Winterling were heading their bid. Investcorp were the second highest with €229.5 million, and they only won because HgCapital's financing broke down. HgCapital had a debt package from WestLB, and on Sunday evening, after a tennis tournament in Turkey, I had just decided to give them exclusivity when Winterling called me up to say their financing had fallen through. He pleaded with me to give him time to find an alternative. I told him he would never get it fast enough, and then called Yves Alexander at Investcorp, who had financing from Dresdner.

> One of the arguments for Investcorp was that they buy from their balance sheet, and then go around private sponsors in the Middle East on a syndication tour. They took me along, and I

could meet people and see what their investments were in fire protection.[67]

By contrast with Minimax, the Investcorp team faced significant challenges on the Apcoa deal, which took 12 months to complete. Thilo Sautter recalls the extensive due diligence process:

> Apcoa needed a lot of attention, and was a difficult due diligence. It was just a portfolio of contracts, we didn't really have any tangible assets.[68]

Holtrup recalls the difficult route the Investcorp team travelled to close on Apcoa:

> We were actually thrown out of the Apcoa auction at one point, but made a comeback thanks to Thomas Middelhoff's relentless efforts. But the problems weren't just with the vendor. There was a good deal of internal resistance to the deal within Investcorp. Thilo really absorbed himself in the operations and plan, while I focussed on the SPA negotiations which became a very drawn out and complex process.[69]

After the acquisition, Sautter was to spend twelve months, working four days a week, effectively as a shadow CFO, as he later recalled:

> Apcoa was a major turnaround, night and day. A complete refurbishment, everything inside changed.[70]

Hofmann at Minimax was also surprised to see how much more hands-on the Investcorp team were after the acquisition:

> Their approach was totally different. They had a four-person post-acquisition team, and held regular advisory board meetings. Mr Hammermann at Barclays was much more informal, although we talked every week, whereas with Investcorp, all the meetings were very formal. It was a much more exhausting time, I have to say, because the low hanging fruits had been picked, and so there was a lot more ground work.[71]

Quadriga

The bursting of the technology bubble vindicated the commitment Max Römer and his team at Quadriga had made to the mid-cap buyout market, as he later explained:

After the hype crash we saw that there was a sudden appetite in the middle market, for solid companies with not too high leverage. Our biggest temptation came in 2000 when we raised Quadriga Capital II. We had written a target of DM 500 million in our book, and within six months had commitments on the table for DM 1.5 billion. So we had to turn a lot of it away. It was quite frightening. What we did was to increase the fund to DM 525 million, and then close it a couple of days later, which in hindsight was one of the best moves we ever made. Entering the large-cap market would not have served our purpose. We wanted to make Quadriga the private equity house for mid sized companies.[72]

Römer and his team were relieved not to have raised more, because the years which followed were quiet ones, during which the team had difficulty finding deals they could close.

3i

After the acquisition of Technologie Holding, 3i found itself with a substantial infrastructure, including nine offices (Hamburg, Berlin, Leipzig, Dusseldorf, Frankfurt, Stuttgart, Munich, Vienna, and Zürich). Once the dotcom crash came, it was clear that many of these offices would have to close.

Andrew Richards began the restructuring process in 2001. In London too, a change of strategy was in progress. Jonathan Russell had assembled a dedicated buyout team, initially in the UK, but quickly this was extended to encompass the whole of Europe. Having raised external funds, 3i was now free to do majority buyouts. All of the professional staff within Germany came under review. It was decided early on that Rudolf Kinsky, an Austrian with an investment banking background who had already been working for 3i in London, would be given the job of running the German buyout team, rather than Peter Cullom, the most senior of the buyout executives in Germany, and this led to Cullom's departure in 2002. Peter Cullom explains the background to this outcome:

Jonathan Russell was key in the transition. Once he became head of buyouts, he quickly came to the view that it can't be that the top two people in Germany should both be Brits.[73]

Andrew Richards, who had become heavily associated with Ventures, was replaced as Head of Germany late in 2002 by Jane Crawford, who came in from Asia where she had been since 1997. Crawford recalls the discussions which led to her move to Frankfurt:

> Brian Larcombe, the 3i Group CEO, called me up to discuss the possibility of me moving over to Germany. He said that Germany was 3i's biggest problem at the time, and the capital invested largely in the cash hungry Venture business was very material to 3i's total business. 3i wanted somebody to go into Germany and tell them whether it would stop going down, and if so, to turn it around. Things were very bad in Germany and 3i wanted someone it trusted to reassure them. It's a natural international organisation tendency to send someone from the 'home' country at such times.[74]

Crawford had two immediate tasks in Germany. First, she had to restructure an operation which, with the collapse of the venture capital business, was now over-sized. This meant implementing cuts across the board. Second, she had to reorient the business back towards majority buyouts. The first of these two tasks was the most difficult and painful. The transition was also a challenge, as she explains:

> When I arrived, it was a tough and pretty unwelcoming environment. Most of my direct reports had disagreed with my appointment. But it was also a hard job because there were so many pieces of the jigsaw that needed to be fixed.[75]

She quickly initiated a process of refocus and retrenchment. Inevitably there were some within the ranks who feared losing their jobs, and resented being managed by a non-German speaker without a local track-record.

Once installed, Kinsky was supported by a fly-in team from London, led by Stewart McMinnies and David Osborne. Under this model, two acquisitions were made in Switzerland, the largest being SR Technics, a spin-off from Swiss Air, and the smaller being MIB AG, a spin-off from Credit Suisse. This was a significant achievement. Indeed the SR Technics investment was the largest buyout 3i had done in the region to date.

PPM Ventures

Sebastian Kern had come into contact with PPM Ventures while at 3i. In 1998, when 3i sold Suspa, via Eberhard Crain, to PPM Ventures, it

Table 14.3 Private Equity Transactions in 2003

2003

Company	Buyer	Seller	Exit year	Sold to
2 D Holding (Süddekor/ Dakorgruppe)	Odewald/Bain Capital	NIB Capital/Family	2007	Quadriga
Aksys (CWW-GERKO Akustik)	PPM	DBAG/Süd Private Equity	2008	Family
Almatis (Alcoa Specialty Chemicals)	Rhone Capital/Teachers	Alcoa	2007	Dubai International Capital
Amann Druckguss GmbH & Co KG	Granville Baird	Family	2007	Endurance
Babcock Borsig Service Division	DBAG/Harvest	Borsig	2005	Bilfinger Berger AG
Bally Wulff	Orlando	Alliance Gaming Corp	Not yet divested	Not yet divested
Bärbel Drexel	Finatem	Family	Not yet divested	Not yet divested
Bertelsmann Springer	Cinven/Candover	Bertelsmann	Not yet divested	Not yet divested
Borsig GmbH	capiton	Insolvency administrator	2008	KNM
BOS GmbH	Hannover Finanz	Family	2004	Strategic player
Breitfeld & Schliekert	Nord Holding	Family	Not yet divested	Not yet divested
Brenntag	Bain Capital	Eon	2006	BC Partners
Büsing & Fasch	Hannover Finanz	Family	Not yet divested	Not yet divested
Cablecom	Apollo/Soros/Goldman	NTL	Not yet divested	Not yet divested
Coveright (Casco Impregnated Paper)	DBAG/Harvest	Akzo Nobel	Not yet divested	Not yet divested
DMS Dynamic Micro Systems	Brockhaus PE	Private investors	2006	Arcadia
DSM	Ströer/Ceberus	28 cities and towns	Not yet divested	Not yet divested
Edscha	Carlyle	Public to Private	2009	Insolvency
Eisfeld Datentechnik	Heptagon Capital/Equinet	Family	Not yet divested	Not yet divested
Enorm Schmidt Beschläge GmbH & Co.	Arques	Ehlebracht AG	Not yet divested	Not yet divested
Epigenomics	3i	Capital increase	2007	Share sell-off

Table 14.3 Private Equity Transactions in 2003 – *continued*

2003

Company	Buyer	Seller	Exit year	Sold to
Etavis (ABB Gebäudetechnik Schweiz)	Capvis	ABB	2007	VINCI Energies Group
Frigoblock Grosskopf GmbH	Hannover Finanz	Family	Not yet divested	Not yet divested
Goebel Schneid- und Wickelsysteme	Nord Holding	Family	Not yet divested	Not yet divested
Guillod Gunther	Léman Capital	Private investors	2007	Providente (Natixis PE)
Hahl-Group	Granville Baird	Family	2007	Lenzing Plastics
Henkelhausen GmbH	Hannover Finanz	NIB Capital	Not yet divested	Not yet divested
hde Solutions GmbH	Nord Holding	Insolvency	2007	Fischer Holding GmbH
Hirschvogel Umformtechnik	Hannover Finanz	Family	Not yet divested	Not yet divested
ICM AG	Alchemy	Private investors	Not yet divested	Not yet divested
IFCO	Apax	Public to Private	Not yet divested	Not yet divested
Infosystems GmbH	Arques	Schaltbau Holding AG	Not yet divested	Not yet divested
Intradent Zahntechnik AG	Hannover Finanz	Family	2006	PPM Capital
Kabel Baden Würtemburg	Blackstone	Blackstone/CDPC/ Bank of America	2006	EQT
Kabel Deutschland	Apax/Goldman Sachs/ Providence	Deutsche Telekom	2006	Providence
Kirch Media/ProSiebenSat1	Saban/Blackstone	Insolvency	2007	KKR/Permira
Lemo Machinenbau	Tequity	Jagenberg/Rheinmetall	2005	Auctus
Mauser GmbH & Co KG	One Equity Partners	PCC Parcom	2007	Dubai International Capital
MBM Grossküchentechnik	EquiVest	Family	Not yet divested	Not yet divested
Melvo	Norddeutsche PE	Salamander AG	2008	Management
MIB AG	3i	Siemens Building Technologies	2007	ETDE
Miles Handelsgesellschaft International	Hannover Finanz	Family	2004	Other investor

Table 14.3 Private Equity Transactions in 2003 – *continued*

2003

Company	Buyer	Seller	Exit year	Sold to
Minmax	Investcorp	Barclays	2006	Industri Kapital
Moeller Holding	Advent	Family	2005	Doughty Hanson
MTH	BLB Private Equity/ Hannover Finanz	Barclays	2006	European Capital
MTU Aero Engines	KKR	Daimler Chrysler	2005	IPO
MultiVision GmbH	Afinum	Family	2003	Management
Offset Kaiser	Alpha	3i/Nord Holding	Not yet divested	Not yet divested
OPS Ingersoll	3i	Ingersoll	2006	IKB Private Equity
Perrin GmbH	Nord Holding	RHI AG	2009	Kitz Corporation
Pharmexx	Süd Private Equity	Private investors	2006	Celesio
Pickenpack Hussmann & Hahn	Orlando	Gilde/RaboBank	2004	FAB GmbH
Polymer Latex	Soros Private Equity	Bayer/Degussa	Not yet divested	Not yet divested
Polytan	ECM	Family	2006	Industri Kapital
Preh	DBAG	Rheinmetall AG	Not yet divested	Not yet divested
Premiere	Permira	Kirch Group	2005	IPO
Profil	Arcadia	Family	Not yet divested	Not yet divested
Rademacher	Arcadia	Family	2007	Nord Holding
Reum Automotive	capiton	UBS Capital	Not yet divested	Not yet divested
Rodenstock	Permira	Family	2006	Bridgepoint
Röhren- und Pumpenwerk Bauer	Invest AG	Willi Kopf	Not yet divested	Not yet divested
SAM Electronics (Euromarine)	EquiVest	STN Atlas	2006	L3 Communications Inc
Schierholz-Translift-Gruppe	Arques	Swisslog Gruppe	2005	Management
Schoeller Wavin Systems	Stirling Square Capital	JP Morgan Partners (Chase)	2008	One Equity Partners
Scholz & Friends	Electra	Cordiant	Not yet divested	Not yet divested
Sirona Dental Systems Group	EQT	Permira	2005	Madison Dearborn

Table 14.3 Private Equity Transactions in 2003 – *continued*

2003

Company	Buyer	Seller	Exit year	Sold to
Suspa Compart	Tyroll Equity/Management	PPM Ventures	Not yet divested	Not yet divested
TDS Informationstechnologie	General Atlantic	Public to Private	2007	Fujitsu
Telecolumbus	BC Partners	DB Capital Partners	2005	Unity Media
TFL	Odewald/WestKB	Permira	Not yet divested	Not yet divested
Tom Tailor AG	Brand Invest	Family	2005	Alpha
Trenkwalder Personaldienste AG	capiton	capital increase	2007	Trenkwalder Foundation
UnityMedia	BC Partners	Deutsche Bank	2010	Liberty Media
Utimaco	Investcorp	Existing shareholders	2005	IPO
UTT	BPE Private Equity	IKB Private Equity	2007	DZ Equity Partner
Visinfo AG	TA Triumph-Adler	Family	Not yet divested	Not yet divested
Viterra Energy Services (Ista)	CVC	Viterra/E.on	2007	Charterhouse
VVA Kommunikations GmbH	Nord Holding	Capital increase	2008	Management
W.E.T. Automotive	HgCapital	Public to Private	Not yet divested	Not yet divested
Wessel Werk Group	Barclays	Garbe Lahmeyer	2006	DZ Equity Partner
Winterthur Technologie AG	Vision Capital	Morgan Grenfall	Not yet divested	Not yet divested
Wohnprofil	Afinum	Family	2005	Paragon Partners

Source: Authors' compilation

had retained a small 5% stake in the business, which Kern was put in charge of. This, as Kern recalls, is what led PPM to hire him:

> I didn't know Neil MacDougall at the time, despite being responsible for looking after the 3i stake. But the PPM guys knew me, and contacted me via a headhunter. When I had my interview, I had already decided to leave 3i after the Technologie Holding acquisition.
>
> My motivation to join PPM came mainly from seeing a chance to return to the buyout business. Also, instead of having to run a large office, with lots of administration work interfacing with a large organisation which included growth and venture capital, I would get the chance to build up a new team. From a very early point on, I talked to Guido May. I met him at a 3i internal event, and told him what I was going to do and it was clear then that we would do it together. Guido was responsible in Stuttgart for the buyout business of 3i. I asked a former colleague, Thessa von Huelsen, to join me as well. The three of us started the office. I had only just hired Thessa at 3i, so she stayed there for six months before she joined our team.[76]

Kern spent his first two months at the London office getting to know the people, before opening up an office in Munich. Kern was quick to recognise that it was not the best time to be starting out afresh, as he later explained:

> It was not an easy time, when I joined in 2001. There was the crisis on the Neuer Markt and a general depression in our industry. It was, to a degree, a recessive period, and it wasn't easy to do buyouts. Indeed for quite a while we didn't do any deals. It took us until 2003 to do the first deal, and that was a co-investment in Aksys.[77]

Fortunately for Kern, PPM was still part of the Prudential group, not formally having a fund of its own, and consequently there was less pressure within the organisation to do deals than there would have been in an independent fund.

> The people in London were also very aware that it took time to build a business, and I never really felt a high degree of pressure on our finally having to do a deal here in Germany.[78]

The closest PPM got to a deal in the early years of 2001–2003 was on Salamander, a portfolio of businesses which the energy utility, EnBW, was attempting to sell. This included a chain of shoe shops by the same name, a facility management company (Gegenbauer), a company producing window profiles (also called Salamander), and Apcoa, a car park management company. Despite much effort, the negotiations ended in failure.

PPM Ventures was renamed PPM Capital, to reflect its focus on buyouts rather than venture capital. But before long it was to go through another name change, as preparations began for the group to spin-off from Prudential.

DBAG

The turn of the millennium saw changes at DBAG on almost every front. In August 2000, Karl-Heinz Fanselow went into retirement, concluding one of the most important careers in professional minority investments in Germany. Wilken Freiherr von Hodenberg joined in July 2000 to fill his predecessor's shoes. Günther Niethammer left in 2001 to join Odewald, and Axel Dorn moved to join one of DBAG's portfolio companies. Von Hodenberg, who had previously been an investment banker with Barings and Merrill, and his new board colleagues, set about raising a classical private equity fund which would enable DBAG to become a player in the majority buyout market rather than keeping its focus on minorities. With Schoeller and Hoesch and GAH, DBAG had already tapped the MBO market successfully in the late 1990s. André Mangin, who joined the team from Merrill Lynch in 2001, recalls the early days of the new strategy:

My job was to improve deal sourcing, because beforehand, DBAG was mostly considered to be a minority investor in small deals. The idea was to reposition DBAG into a truly mid-cap buyout firm. We were able to do that successfully, using hype around private equity, and playing on the roots of the firm. We supported our marketing process by developing our own CRM tool on the IT side. We wanted to rigorously capture our network and develop it.[79]

The first deals under the new regime came already in 2001, as Mangin describes:

DBAG did Aksys first, which was the result of merger of CWW-Gerko from Rüttgers and Pfeist, one of our existing portfolio companies. Then came HTE in 2002, a group of a number of small entities, which DBAG bought from RHI, an Austrian listed company.

I think it was the first time DBAG bought a portfolio to split up and sell off, and we got it at a conglomerate discount: the price was very attractive. Then we bought Coveright in 2003 from Akzo, and finally we acquired Babcock Borsig Service out of the Babcock insolvency, also in 2003. That was DBAG's landmark deal.[80]

By 2003, DBAG's repositioning as a mid-cap buyout fund was complete.

Mercury Private Equity/HgCapital

The entry of HgCapital into the German market closely coincided with preparations for its spin-off from Merrill Lynch, where the team was trading as Mercury Private Equity. Mercury, a UK fund established in 1985 as part of Mercury Asset Management, a company owned by SG Warburg, was acquired along with its parent by Merrill Lynch in 1997. Trevor Bayley, who started his private equity career with Grosvenor Ventures, acquired by Mercury in 1994, was given responsibility for building a German business in 1999. Bayley quickly set about hiring a small team to work for his branch in Frankfurt, taking on Joachim Pieper, a former consultant at Bain & Company in Munich, and Michael Hehn, another former consultant from BCG's Munich Office.

Early on his travels, Bayley met with Martin Block, who had moved over to Germany in 1998 to set up the Royal Bank of Scotland leveraged finance team in Frankfurt. The two hit it off, and Block joined Mercury in 2001. The early years were challenging, and the deals were difficult to come by, as Block recalls:

The early days were quite difficult in Germany. We suffered somewhat from the legacy of being part of a big bank. The initial hires Trevor had made felt more comfortable working for big names in corporate environments, and the plans to spin-off into a small independent team didn't suit them 100%. Once I joined, we had to begin the rebranding process over the period 2001–2002, getting to know people, and recruiting new people who were happier with our set-up. It was a difficult time deal-wise. It wasn't until the end of 2002 that we closed our first transaction, with FTE.[81]

The FTE deal was not entirely straightforward, as it involved some important changes of management, as Block explains:

When we met the FTE team, we could see that it was solid and dependable. The company had a great client list, and we were reassured by the fact that clutches and brakes were indispensable products. The line management was very strong, and you could see that they had a good track record. As the CEO wasn't staying with the company, we put in Franz Scherer, the former CEO of Sirona, who I had met during the Sirona transaction in 2002. I got on well with Franz, and we knew that he would handle the spin-off from FTE from Dana just as well as he had handled Sirona's spin-off from Siemens. We also recruited a new CFO.[82]

Having gained confidence with the acquisition of its first automotive component supplier, HgCapital proceeded in 2003 to close a semi-proprietary investment in W.E.T. Block recalls:

> We had done a trawl through the MDAX and Neuer Markt companies, and one of the potential public to privates was W.E.T. which had been IPO'd in 1998. Bodo Ruthenberg, the main shareholder, had already tried to take it private. He still held 66% of the stock. We liked W.E.T. because it was a world leader, with a global footprint. But we didn't manage to take it private, and were left with a rather illiquid shareholding in the company.[83]

Franz Scherer was installed, this time as chairman of W.E.T. HgCapital's reputation for tackling challenging transactions grew further in 2004, when it closed Hirschmann, a portfolio of very different companies, sold by Goldman Sachs on behalf of Rheinmetall. Unlike FTE and W.E.T., Hirschmann was difficult to assess from the outside in. L.E.K. was brought in to help review Hirschmann's market position in its various non-related segments. The key to HgCapital's success in closing the deal was to ring-fence different parts of the portfolio for financing purposes, as Martin Block explains:

> Inside the Hirschmann bag there were some gems, and some complete unknowns. Nobody knew how to finance the company. So we stripped out the difficult businesses, ring-fenced them, and financed them purely with equity. We split these further into a workout group, and those which were simply unknown. The other good businesses we got leveraged. That was the key, positioning the conglomerate as at least two businesses.[84]

HgCapital formed close relationships with the people involved in the transaction, and Klaus Eberhardt who was representing Rheinmetall in the sales process became chairman of Hirschmann once it was sold. This gave HgCapital another high-profile German executive to guide its team and extend its network in Germany.

HgCapital did have some important near misses during 2004, the most significant of which was on Kalle. This was a secondary transaction, CVC having acquired Kalle from Hoechst in 1997. In the final stage of the process, Montagu and HgCapital were running neck to neck, and Block remembers:

> With Kalle, we were distracted by other transactions, and took our eye off the ball. I think in this instance, our teams were just too stretched.[85]

The proliferation of new private equity houses in Germany

The troubles of many of the established private equity houses in the period 2001–2003 did not deter a record number of new entrants to the German market. Many of the teams had dipped their toes in the market by means of fly-in activities from London, while others had hired local talent through head-hunters, as did EQT when it poached Hans Moock from Carlyle to open their new Munich Office. As Michael Phillips of Apax lamented, the behaviour of the new players was considerably different from those who were established in the market. Indeed the tenure of the private equity players could now be classified into three categories, which included: (i) the "grandfathers" of the industry such as 3i and Permira which had been in the market for decades, possessing substantial track-records and portfolio companies; (ii) the "fathers" of the industry, who had been around for 5–10 years, and had a modest portfolio; and (iii) the "new boys on the block", who had set up shop in the period 1999–2002 and had few if any portfolio companies. The fact that the new boys possessed virtually no portfolio companies meant that they spent almost all of their time hunting for deals, whereas the houses which had been on the market for longer were investing more time working on their portfolio companies. It was little surprise, therefore, that many of the 2002 deals went to the new boys on the block.

The pickings for the "new boys" were thin on the ground, and the year 2002 saw major obstacles in the path of getting deals done. A major factor was the growing anxiety of the banks, who were worried about their potential bad debt exposure. Banks became the pivotal factor in determining the timing of many of the transactions, particularly in instances where they had seen liquidity dry up, and equity fall below debt value. There was a clear case of "negative equity" in many segments of the market. The choice for many banks was whether to crystalise their losses by pushing for an asset sale, or whether to hang on, and inject fresh funds in the business in the hope that the climate would improve, and with it the chances of recovering their capital. Typically banks seeking to recover their money from problematic investments were not willing to help finance those interested in buying them. This meant that on a wide range of transactions, particularly where a consortium of lenders was involved, it was a challenge for many private equity bidders to find finance.

Given that 2002 saw a number of large transactions completed, most notably EQT's acquisition of Haarman & Reimer, in addition to KKR's mega-deal with Siemens, it was clearly the mid-cap segment of the market that was most exposed to the vagaries of the recession. Very few mid-cap transactions were closed, and in a fair number of cases, vendors simply walked away on seeing the prices on offer. There were a number of explanations for this behaviour. Perhaps the most significant was the wide gap that had opened up between vendor and buyer valuations. Vendors persisted in down-playing the recession, and writing a near immediate recovery into their business plans. The second explanation for the malaise affecting the market was that many companies put up for sale were underperforming against plan. At the time, vendors, and many managements, dismissed this as a short-term blip, and insisted that such deficits could be made up within a few quarters. Nevertheless, few buyers believed them. The third explanation was that given the poor state of the market precipitated by the recession, many vendors were reluctant to put attractive companies onto the market. As a consequence, many companies which were for sale were either poor performers that might benefit because their poor performance could be blamed on the recession, or they were companies which possessed significant levels of risk, such that they might as well be sold sooner rather than later.

While the number of deals closed in 2001 collapsed relative to the late 1990s, it was significant that private equity transaction volumes recovered very quickly. The number of LBOs in 2002 was already higher than in 2000. The main reason most of the participants viewed the period 2002–2003 as being difficult was that competition had increased dramatically at the turn of the millennium. New capacity flooded into the German market to execute leveraged buyouts on a grand scale. Justification for this expansion would have required the market to chart a course of unbroken growth. Nevertheless, the much needed upswing was just around the corner. As the year 2003 drew to a close, few in the industry could have imagined how quickly transaction volume would climb to unforeseen heights.

15
The Eighth Phase: The Booming Market: 2004–2007

As the economy climbed out of recession in 2004 the scale of private equity deal making began to explode, with an annual growth in the number of transactions of 20% per annum. New private equity houses entered the market at all levels: large-cap, mid-cap, and small-cap. Even PE houses that had deliberately avoided the German market for some years, such as Charterhouse and Clayton, Dubilier & Rice, changed tack.

The most spectacular development of the period 2004–2007 was the commoditisation of debt. Leverage became easy to obtain for almost any private equity house that required it. Indeed, the ease with which debt could be syndicated after closing caused the structured finance departments of many banks to focus heavily on arrangement fees: what counted was to win the debt package, and then syndicate it on. Due diligence requirements became less demanding, as banks became less concerned with a deal being approved by their credit committee, and more concerned that the debt once won could be effortlessly syndicated to third parties.

It was inevitable in this environment that prices for companies should rise. By the end of 2005, the debt multiples were rapidly reaching EBITDA multiples that companies had been valued on only a couple of years earlier, and over the course of 2006 and 2007 valuation multiples rose in a fashion familiar to that seen in the dotcom boom less than ten years earlier.

As competition for companies between the private equity houses became more brutal, and the valuations rose, it was also inevitable that the business plans of the targets would be forced to become more optimistic on revenue development, and more aggressive on cost cutting. The latter feature was to pitch private equity into the middle of the political spot-light.

Charterhouse

Charterhouse Capital Partners[1] was first established in 1934, making it one of Europe's oldest private equity firms. In 1976 the Firm raised third party capital for the first time, through Charterhouse Development Capital Fund, which focused upon UK private equity investments. The investment activities of Charterhouse Bank, including its participation in Matuschka Group during the late 1980s, were completely separate from those of Charterhouse Capital Partners. At the end of the 1990s, Charterhouse Capital Partners significantly increased its earlier activities in the French market, and with the dawn of the new millennium turned its interest towards other Continental European markets. In 2001, Charterhouse engineered its own management buyout from HSBC, the owners of Charterhouse Bank, to become a partner-owned independent firm with offices in London and Paris.

Christian Fehling, was hired to the firm in 2003, and began tracking Ista International from the time of its acquisition by CVC from E.on. Ista's attraction was that it fitted well with Charterhouse's investment philosophy, which was to back incumbent management teams of well-positioned companies, and support them with their growth plans. Four years later, in 2007, these efforts ensured that Fehling and his colleagues were well placed to become management's preferred bidder when Ista was sold by CVC, which ultimately saw Charterhouse acquire the company. Walter Schmidt, Ista's CEO, said after the deal that he was confident that Charterhouse would make a strong partner with whom his team could work on the next phase of growth. This €2.4 billion secondary transaction represented a major milestone for Charterhouse's expansion into the German-speaking region.

Industri Kapital

For the Industri Kapital team in Hamburg, the period 2004–2007 saw a significant uptick in fortunes. The first change came in 2005 with the acquisition of Dywidag-Systems International (DSI) from Walter Bau. The auction over DSI was hard fought; Barclays and Triton being close runners up, and the DSI management team proceeded to consolidate their business, focussed on supplies of components to mines, tunnels, and bridges, via an aggressive buy-and-build strategy. The IK team's experience with the i-Center insolvency played a helpful role in buying DSI out of administration, as Detlef Dinsel explains:

> I was probably the most experienced guy when it came to dealing with the fasteners industry and a mother company in insolvency.[2]

Part of the attraction of the DSI deal was that being sold by the insolvency administrator of the mother company, the management were highly incentivised buyers, rather than sellers of the business, as Caspar von Meibom explains:

> The management had actually already agreed to do the deal with a UK buyout fund a year earlier, and the fund was convinced that they would be the winners. But it was a complex buyout, with its insolvent mother and a sector – Germany related building materials – that banks hated at the time. It was a great transaction: without additional equity, DSI completed thirteen add-ons over the years that followed and we saw revenues about triple, and EBITDA increase more than six-fold.[3]

The following year, Industri Kapital succeeded in winning the auction for Minimax, and securing its position in the German market. Klaus Hofmann, the Minimax CEO recalls the set of events that led the Dinsel team to victory:

> We had a final handshake on Thursday night in London with a large American conglomerate, who had come late into the process. They were offering big money, €580 million, which was €60–70 million more than anyone else. We had a notary date for Sunday, and on Friday, while I was in my office packing, the Americans in London were asking for some more contracts they wanted to check. I sent my assistant over to London with all the documents they needed in a suit-case. But although my assistant arrived in London, the suit-case didn't. British Airways searched for the suit-case for three to four hours, and the Americans thought we were holding information back from them. They said that if they didn't have the documents by Saturday morning, they would fly back to the States.
>
> The Americans waited up until 1 a.m., but the suitcase still hadn't arrived, and the Head of Corporate Development called Yves Alexander to complain. I had already flown to Frankfurt ready

for the notary meeting scheduled for Sunday. But then Yves called me up, explained what had happened, and told me he had called Dinsel, who was already on an aeroplane over to London. Dinsel signed Saturday evening, and we kept the notary appointment on Sunday morning. The notary was a little bit surprised, as he expected the American conglomerate to be the buyer, so he had to delete all mentions of this company, and insert Industri Kapital in the document. Within 62 hours, everything changed, so I repacked my things and went back to my office on Monday.[4]

This and DSI were the game-changer deals for Dinsel's Hamburg team, both investments being substantial. The good times continued into 2007, when Industri Kapital sold DSI at the peak of the market to CVC, making a very significant return on its investment and being awarded the European Mid-Market Deal of the Year by Real Deals/EVCA.

3i

Despite the success in completing SR Technics and MIB AG, 3i had a high reliance on London professionals to support the execution of German deals. Jane Crawford explains the dilemma:

> The view in London was that there was an interesting German market in which the German team needed the London team's assistance to operate. There was an overhang of mistrust of German companies from Lignotock, one of 3i's biggest disasters involving big losses, which still lingered among the members of the investment committee.[5]

Investment proposals were regularly being thrown out by the investment committee. Crawford later acknowledged that there were problems in the German camp:

> There were only two investments on the WIP list of fifteen which I thought we should be pursuing, and Betapharm was one of them. The investment proposal for Betapharm had already been bounced by the investment committee in London once, and even after I wrote another paper couched in terms that the committee would better understand, it was still bounced again, because it had had a bad start.

The only solution was to work with London on it. Ian Nolan was already over in Germany leading the London originated bid for Lichtwer, which was an investment I had been less keen on up till then. So we basically cooperated on the two deals. Germany needed to get more credibility on Betapharm, and London wanted Germany's support for Lichtwer. Nolan brought in Mike Robbins from London to support me on Betapharm, and also asked his chairman for Lichtwer to become Executive Chair on Betapham.

So it went back to investment committee for a third time, and this time it got through, and in the end we not only made great money on Betapharm, we also made decent money on Lichtwer too.[6]

Working on the Betapharm deal, Mike Robbins gained a critical overview of the way 3i's buyout operation in Germany was functioning. It was clear that the combination of the fly-in model, coupled with the regional structure, was not delivering the impact that could have been expected from such a resource commitment. At the same time, it was increasingly obvious that the German market was becoming more interesting. 3i clearly needed to increase its hit rate to be in a position to capitalise on this potential.

The solution was to move some element of the "fly-in" solution physically to Germany. The motor for change came when Chris Rowlands took over in London. Crawford explains:

Rowlands immediately understood that I needed someone who could write investment proposals, and who was trusted by the UK, to move into the German buyout team. Mike had worked with us in Germany and had liked it.[7]

Mike Robbins was asked to head up the Germany Buyout team, initially for a three-year period. His presence would also help knowledge transfer on buyouts from London to Germany. The first deals to be closed under this new model were sourced from outside the German region. These included Jung Pumpen, which was sold out of Masco, and Wendt, which was spun out of Boart Longyear, a South African/UK quoted company. Crawford felt a huge weight fall from her shoulders:

Mike made an enormous difference, because he was trusted by both Chris Rowlands and Ian Nolan in London, and by me in Frankfurt.

Everything fell into place and the German Buyout team started to be really effective. This just turned the corner really, and so then my involvement in the buyout team could go down dramatically and I could move focus to the Growth and Venture parts of 3i's German business.[8]

In parallel to working on the deals, Robbins began the process of pulling together the buyout team into one location. Frankfurt was the obvious choice, and there were even some advantages to be gained from having so many professionals working away from home, as living in rented apartments during the week, it was easier to build a close knit culture.

Inevitably, the process of downsizing and closing regional offices meant that some of the personal contacts and networks in Germany were weakened or lost during this period.

In 2004, Philip Yea moved from Investcorp to become the new CEO of the 3i Group. Yea believed there should be a German in charge of the German operation, and made finding the right person a personal task. Crawford fully understood Yea's thought process, as she later explained:

> Philip Yea knew that 3i had a very strong culture, and that he would have to take a tight grip to gain control. Even before he started, he personally instructed headhunters to look for a new Finance Director, and new Head of Human Resources, and a new Head of Germany. He realised that private equity was about money, people, and markets. The new Finance Director would give him control over the money, the Head of Human Resources would give him power over the people, and he would be sitting in the UK and have control over that market, so if he added control over the Head of Germany, he would have 80% of 3i's marketplace within his grasp. His was the shortest and quickest route to power, and I've always thought it was a clever tactic.[9]

Stephan Krümmer, the consultant who had worked on the MBO feasibility study for Robert Osterrieth in 1985, had left Bain to join Bertelsmann, before heading up Rothschild's investment banking activities in Germany, where he worked with Yea on an Investcorp transaction. The lure of private equity had eventually caused him to leave Rothschild in 2003 to join Ekkehard Franzke and Norbert Stelzer in trying to set up a new fund, Ingenium Capital. Krümmer recalls:

I had talked with Norbert Stelzer about setting up a new fund. He and Ekkehard were aggressive about building up their team and wanted me to join them. In fact it was not a bad team. What was lacking was a private equity track record. At that point, Systematics was the only deal that Odewald had done which was clearly a good one, and that was the deal which Norbert alone could point to. It quickly became clear to me, after half a year, that Ingenium wasn't going to work. Then Phil Yea hired me to run 3i's German operation in February 2005: it was a very fast decision.[10]

The fruits of the 3i turnaround became obvious in 2005, with the sale of Betapharm to Dr. Reddy's, which yielded an extremely positive return. This, and the progress in making buyouts, reassured opinion in London that the German operation was now on a firmer keel. It was even possible to consider adding talent to the group, with the hiring of Frederick Roth from Permira, and Hayo Knoch from Dresdner Kleinwort Wasserstein.

Hiring Frederick Roth from Permira's Frankfurt office sent a particularly strong signal to the market that 3i was now firmly out of restructuring and into rebuilding, and Roth's appointment had an immediate benefit, in that it brought them the Scandlines lead. Running a ferry service between Germany and Scandinavia, Scandlines operated as a 50:50 German/Danish joint venture. Roth presented the investment case, and brought 3i important industrial and political connections which would help make the deal possible. From the start, 3i was well positioned to be a front runner on the deal. The deal was led by Steffen Thomsen, and Gustav Bard from Copenhagen, and Stephan Krümmer in Frankfurt. Wolf Wolfsteiner, who led the financing for the transaction from London, recalls:

> Through the 3i Danish team in Copenhagen we established some strong angles into the industry. There were various parties who knew Scandlines from past activities that gave us a pretty good understanding of the company and its markets. We were also able to field people from the shipping industry we had contact with in the UK.[11]

The biggest challenge on Scandlines was that while the Danish state shareholder favoured 3i as the highest bidder, the German shareholder, in the shape of Deutsche Bahn, strongly favoured 3i's competitor on the deal: Allianz Capital Partners and their partner Deutsche Seereederei. Wolf Wolfsteiner recalls the final stages of the auction:

In the final stage of the auction, and per our request, bids had to be submitted in sealed envelopes to be opened by a notary public. Jonathan Russell encouraged us not to lose the auction at this stage for some small amount of money. We targeted an offer of around €1.5 billion. But a round number was considered too likely for our competitors also to have come up with. So we agreed to bid an odd number, and when the envelopes were opened, we found that we had won the auction literally with the last €5 million.[12]

The Deutsche Bahn resistance to selling to 3i was deep rooted, and for a while it looked as if the deal would be cancelled altogether. Stephan Krümmer recalls the events:

The deal was basically put to sleep for six months until April 2007, when I had lunch with Horst Rahe, the CEO of Deutsche Seereederei. I made the point that 3i would not give up buying Scandlines and that either we joined forces or nobody would have a deal for quite some time. So over four weeks, we developed a proposal for the sellers that the new buying consortium would be ACP 40%, 3i 40%, and Deutsche Seereederei 20%. The sellers accepted this offer and the deal was signed in the summer of 2007.[13]

By the end of 2007, therefore, 3i had fully re-established its position in the German market, and successfully repositioned itself as a mega-deal player, able to compete with the likes of Allianz Capital Partners.

PPM Capital

2004 was to see the first domestically generated independent buyout for the local PPM team, with the acquisition of Mueller & Weygand. The following year, in 2005, two closed deals followed, with the acquisition of Jost and BST Safety Textiles. The Jost deal was a particularly hard fought auction, as Guido May recalls:

Fortunately, we had already been working on Jost six months before the official process started. We had met management, and lined ourselves up with Alpha, giving them presentations, and getting over the message that we were dedicated to doing this investment. We had a good understanding of the uniqueness of the Jost business model, and were confident that there would be a long time to go before the next downturn. We had L.E.K. support us with commercial due diligence, and we felt we were on top of Jost's market position.[14]

In 2006, in addition to exiting the BST Textiles deal, discussions began internally within PPM Capital about a buyout from Prudential, as Sebastian Kern recalls:

> The buyout from Prudential happened in November 2007, and discussions probably started one and a half years beforehand. A trigger point was the handover of the leadership from Jonathan Morgan to Neil MacDougall. On the one hand, there was pressure at the time from some of the younger directors keen to do more deals. But perhaps more significantly, there was also a hostile take over bid for the Prudential. This alerted us to the question of what would happen if the Prudential were taken over by some other company, such as the Allianz or Axa, both of which had their own private equity groups. Neither would necessarily have been interested in keeping PPM Capital. We were motivated to try to get a higher degree of independence, in order to make sure that whatever happened to the Prudential, the impact upon us would be minimal. In addition, the team wasn't getting the returns from the business that we would have done if we had been independent. We approached the Prudential, held some negotiations, and these lead to the deal which was closed in 2007.[15]

Independence meant having to raise a fund. The new firm, which was six months later renamed Silverfleet Capital, had a difficult time adding to the initial amount committed by the Prudential in 2007 and 2008, but finally achieved a €665 million fund, as Kern explains:

> Fund raising was difficult, and we were doing this both before and after the Lehman bankruptcy. We raised money from Europe, the US and the Arab region. With the change in funding structure, we had to take a lot more care of the limited partners. They were lucky we didn't do a deal in 2008, and managed to exit Jost and TMF before the market fell out of bed.[16]

HgCapital

Barely was the Hirschmann deal closed in 2004, than Stefan Winterling chose to leave. He had joined HgCapital from Apax, and put in much of the leg-work on the Hirschmann transaction. His departure reflected, once again, some of the stresses and strains of relations between Britons and Germans, as Martin Block explains:

> We had two British nationals running the shop in Frankfurt. We didn't think it was right to have two Brits taking the lead, and as Trevor Bayley had been in Germany since 1999, and was happy to return to the UK, I said I would stay to head up the German team. Stefan wanted to run his own show, and was also not so keen on us gravitating towards ever larger deal sizes. He ended up co-running his own fund at Paragon Partners.[17]

Philipp Schwalber, who had been hired in the London office in 2000, helped take up the strain, working on secondment to the Frankfurt office, while Justin von Simson, who had been hired in 2002 for Frankfurt, put in a spell in London. The HgCapital partners were keen to ensure that their private equity house was a single team, as Block explains:

> We had enough people in London to support the German team, and it was important for us to have the flexibility to move people backwards and forwards. We have always been able to flex our teams. Both Philipp and Justin played key roles on Hofmann Menü, and each of us ended up forging a relationship with someone important during the transaction. While we have a local German team, I continue to have one foot in both camps. We act as one seamless team, and have always been one team.[18]

Nevertheless, even with flexing from London, the HgCapital team was stretched the following year, when in 2006 it was simultaneously trying to close Minimax and Schenck Process. On Minimax, the HgCapital team had been convinced they were in a good position to win the transaction, until their financing crisis hit, as Block explains:

> We really liked Minimax and fumbled it at the last moment. We were using WestLB for the debt, and in the eye of the storm they called us up to say that the loan had not been given credit approval. We managed to get replacement finance from Fuji at short notice, but it cost us two weeks. So we were ultra close, but we just didn't win.[19]

HgCapital's luck held out instead during the Schenck Process transaction, which was being handled by Lazard. Martin Block's memories of this deal were happier:

> Schenck was the best run process I can recall. Lazard were ultra professional: slick with their deadlines, and really followed through each phase well. Another private equity house was very close to us on this deal, and they lost Schenck in the same way we lost Minimax, by a whisker. We had a good rapport with Jochen Weyrauch, the CEO, but I don't think he picked us over the other PE house. He was far too professional to do that.[20]

HgCapital's intensive spell of deal-making was to continue a while longer, closing Schleich, a toy-manufacturer in 2006, SLV, a lighting manufacturer, and Mondo, a manufacturer of industrial talc, both in 2007. But despite their flurry of deals, the team at HgCapital could see that all was not right with the market by this point:

> We had a strong view that the market was looking overblown. The debt market felt all wrong. It made no sense at all. Credit terms which included "pay if you can" were ridiculous, and I knew then that the debt market was going to fall over. Our house view was that we should sell our good businesses, and then keep our powder dry. So we sold Hirschmann, Schenck Process, and Hofmann Menü in rapid succession. That gave our investors good returns. They were very relieved that we did more exits than new deals.[21]

By the end of the period, HgCapital had shown that a tightly knit UK-German team could work extremely effectively, with a mix of different skill-sets. HgCapital had established a position as one of the leading mid-cap players alongside local champions such as Quadriga, Equita, Odewald, and Capiton.

Allianz Capital Partners

Even during the boom years, the team at Allianz had its concerns about the developments in the market. Having moved into mezzanine during 2002–2003, one of the first moves in 2004 was to exit this market, as Reiner Löslein explains:

> In 2004 the market changed completely. Towards the end of that year, we decided to get out of mezzanine because there were now

too many players offering highly competitive conditions. In 2005, we saw the valuations of companies rising, and ended up selling Four Seasons, a company we had acquired in the UK, because we were approached by real estate players, with amazing offers. It was clear that there was a huge property bubble.[22]

Allianz continued to benefit from being a local large-cap player, and in 2006 the team acquired MAN Roland from MAN, in a proprietary transaction, taking the market completely by surprise. Löslein recalls:

I really like situations where we don't have an auction. We had screened the companies in the printing machinery industry, and seen that it was dominated by three German players. Our initial idea was to bring Heidelberg and Roland together, but on closer examination, we realised that Roland was much more interesting. It was also a corporate orphan. Achleitner was really helpful in the process which followed, getting a meeting organised with the guys at MAN Roland for us. Again we offered MAN a structure whereby they could remain an investor, to share in the upside.

I was pretty shocked when we went out to look for financing on MAN Roland. We knew this was a cyclical market, but despite this we were getting offers from banks for financing at multiples equivalent to what we were expecting to pay for the business.[23]

It was a troubled team at Allianz in 2007 that watched the market rise to new heights in transaction volumes and values. Instinctively, they knew that there was no way this development could last.

EQT

In 2004, Marcus Brennecke was approached by EQT as envisaged Head of Germany. After the sale of the Juventas AG portfolio to Triumph-Adler, Brennecke had joined Christoph Schoeller and Hieronymus Graf Wolff Metternich in their investment vehicle SMB (Schoeller Metternich Beteiligungen), which had made in the 1990s a very successful investment in Trans-o-flex. With Brennecke's support, SMB then acquired a further three companies, including Helsa Automotive, Chereau, and Kögel. At that time the EQT portfolio consisted of Leybold Optics, Sirona, Symrise, and Carl Zeiss Vision. So far there had been no exit from the German portfolio.[24]

Brennecke started in Stockholm at the beginning of 2005, and worked on portfolio companies and transactions in Scandinavia. During the summer, he also started working on the acquisition of MTU Friedrichshafen, later renamed Tognum, which was signed at the end of the year. Brennecke moved back to Germany eight months later, and succeeded the current Head of Germany, Björn Hoj Jensen who moved back to Denmark.[25]

EQT moved into overdrive in the period 2005–2008, acquiring nine companies in Germany with their three funds, Equity, Expansion Capital, and Opportunity. These included MTU Friedrichshafen/ Tognum, Kabel Baden Württemberg (in a secondary from Blackstone), CBR (in a secondary from Apax and Cinven), and SAG (in a secondary from Advent) – all of which were Equity; Pharmazell, Sausalitos Holding, Cinterion Wireless Modules – all Expansion Capital; and Pfaff Silberblau and Strauss Innovation – both funded by the Opportunity Fund. In 2005, EQT exited Sirona to Madison Dearborn, in 2006 floated Symrise, and a year later in 2007 IPO'd Togum. All three exits were a great success. By the end of this period, EQT had become one of the leading private equity funds in Germany.

Blackstone

Despite its size in the US, Blackstone was a latecomer to Europe. Blackstone's engagement with Germany began from afar, with the acquisition from Callahan Associates of Kabel Baden Württemberg, together with CDPC and Bank of America, a transaction managed out of New York in 2001. Thereafter, David Blitzer moved over from New York to establish the private equity presence of Blackstone in London in 2002. Indeed his first comment in subsequent media interviews concerned his opinion on the timing of his arrival:

> If David Blitzer has a regret about Blackstone's private equity activity in the UK it is that he did not arrive here sooner. As senior managing director for the American giant's European private equity operations, his issue had not been finding the money to spend but identifying enough targets to buy...

> "We came in late to Europe. We started in January 2002. It has taken until the last twelve months to be fully up and running with the profile we should have. If we had come in 1998–1999 we would be in an even better position."[26]

A challenge for Blackstone arriving so late, was that its team started buying companies at precisely the time prices were rising to great heights. Interviewed in *The Observer* in 2005, Blitzer pointed to the challenge his firm faced with leverage:

> Leverage is driving deal prices. In general I love debt and you will catch me on the phone in five minutes yelling at the banks for more. But anybody can get debt now. Competitors can get the same financing as Blackstone. Debt has become a commodity and I don't like commodities by definition. Too many people on deals are taking the leverage they can get, then adding the equity cheque and that is the purchase price. We never do that at Blackstone.
>
> We calculate what it is worth and then we work out how to finance it. People can bid up these prices. It might be worth seven times earnings but somebody will come and pay eight times.[27]

Blackstone's first hire for Germany came almost immediately on entering Europe in 2003: Hanns Ostmeier, a former BCG consultant, was recruited from BC Partners where he had led the firm's engagement on Grohe. Ostmeier chose to locate Blackstone's first office in Hamburg, and began the process of recruiting a team.

The next hire in Germany was Thorsten Langheim, a former JPMorgan banker, whose path crossed Blackstone's when Langheim's client Degussa explored an acquisition of Haarmann & Reimer and teamed up with Blackstone for the project. Ultimately, this initiative was to lead nowhere, but Joseph Baratta, a senior managing director at Blackstone, was impressed with the German banker, and at the end of 2003 approached him with the offer to join the new Hamburg team.

The Hamburg team experienced challenges, largely due to lack of integration into the rest of the Blackstone organisation. Like many other private equity organisations recruiting local teams to open new offices, without having them first spend extensive periods in established offices, Blackstone experienced tensions between its teams in London and Germany. Given that the Hamburg team was small, a large proportion of the work on German deals was executed from London.

Seeing the need to become better integrated within the Blackstone organisation, Langheim went to New York in 2005, where, despite working primarily on US assignments, he retained an interest in Germany, and his return was always on the cards, as he later explained:

When RAG was about to raise its 50% stake in Degussa in 2005, we proposed a leveraged joint venture for Degussa's fine chemicals and construction chemicals divisions, as a way to refinance RAG's acquisition of the remaining Degussa stake. However, RAG and Degussa finally decided to sell the division in an auction. BASF had deeper pockets than us in that process. But this put me back on flights to Germany. The time in the US was very well spent on internal communication, getting to know the people as well as the New York-led investment process, and building credibility, the key requirements if you want to successfully integrate in a private equity firm, especially if you work out of a satellite office.[28]

In 2006, Langheim returned to Europe, while Hanns Ostmeier became a non-executive director. At the time, Langheim joined the team around Larry Guffey that was responsible for the acquisition of a 4.5% stake in Deutsche Telekom from the German Government.

Blackstone proceeded in April 2006 to acquire from the KfW a packet of Deutsche Telekom shares equivalent to a 4.5% stake for almost €2.7 billion. The KfW placed the shares on behalf of the German government, reducing its own stake in the company to 17.3%, the government itself holding a further 15.2%. Stephen Schwarzman said in a press statement:

We are looking for a long-term engagement with the company. We believe that Deutsche Telekom is an excellent company, with a strong management, and attractive numbers and market opportunities.[29]

The investments raised widespread curiosity among the private equity industry in Germany. Opinions on why Blackstone had made the investment varied, but many felt that Blackstone hoped to gain favourable publicity in Germany, and to get close to both government and those in power generally. Thorsten Langheim, however, later argued that the investment was made entirely on its merits, even if the timing was unfortunate (the stock price plunged shortly thereafter, wiping off a significant part of the equity proportion):

We believed at the time that the acquisition had an attractive risk/return profile given Deutsche Telekom's undervaluation compared to its peers, its size and stability of cash flows, the attractive financing structure for the stake purchase, massive cost and asset reallocation opportunities and most importantly the invitation by the German Government to join the supervisory board and help drive change with the Government's support. The jury is still out as Deutsche Telekom is trading at a range between €12 and €14 this year versus a buy-in price of €13.28, but we believe that we have initiated change that mid term should result in a higher Deutsche Telekom share price.[30]

Alongside its minority investment, Blackstone continued to make its more conventional buyouts, having acquired Sulo and subsequently Cleanaway together with Apax in 2003/2006, the public-to-private of Celanese in 2004, exited its investment in Kabel Baden Württemberg to EQT in 2006, and the acquisition of Gerresheimer from Investcorp in 2004. In the latter, the Gerresheimer management were pleased to be acquired by a larger fund, as Axel Herberg explains:

> We were three-and-a-half years into the first buyout, and so it was hard to get fresh equity out of Investcorp when we were so far down the line, I wanted to grow the company but I couldn't get the extra money to do so. Blackstone and a few other houses approached us

Figure 15.1 Thorsten Langheim

speculatively, and helped give our investors the idea of doing more than a recap, which was planned at the time. Once we were acquired by Blackstone, we performed very well. In the first buyout there had been problems because of our US business, but under Blackstone we were always spot on our budget, and had nice acquisition opportunities. We were viewed by Blackstone as the good guys.[31]

The bigger challenge for Blackstone was when in 2007, at the peak of the market, it acquired Klöckner Pentaplast, in a secondary buyout from Cinven. Almost immediately, raw material prices and volume demand developed unfavourably, as Langheim recollects:

Obviously, you have issues in the market place which aren't always foreseeable, such as the current combination of unprecedented raw materials cost inflation and slowdown in volume. However, Lionel Assant who leads this investment is very experienced and successful in investing and monitoring packaging companies and has assembled a strong team. Colin Williams, who became the chairman at Klöckner Pentaplast, was previously the CEO of one of Pentaplast's biggest customers in the US and helped Blackstone on various packaging acquisition opportunities. Another board member is Philippe Meyer who has significant experience in plant rationalisations, cost restructurings and had been a long standing senior advisor to Blackstone.[32]

With the closing of Deutsche Interhotels in 2007, Blackstone had also proven that it was serious about Germany, and a major deal-maker, even if its arrival on the scene had been a little late.

TPG

Texas Pacific Group established its office in London during the mid-1990s, and from the early days took an interest in the German-speaking region. Andrew Dechet had worked in Frankfurt, and Stephen Peel, previously of Goldman Sachs Principal Investment Area, had also plenty of interest and experience in the region. The first major investment came in 1998, when TPG acquired Landis & Gyr Communications from Electrowatt. The focus remained on Switzerland a year later, when in 1999 the target was Bally, acquired from Oerlikon-Bührle. The former Gucci manager Marco Franchini was put in as CEO of Bally. The business was refocussed upon shoes, and returned

Table 15.1 Private Equity Transactions in 2004

2004

Company	Buyer	Seller	Exit year	Sold to
AHT Austria Haustechnik	Equita	Quadriga	2006	Equita
Alukon	Axa	Granville Baird	2007	Halder
AMEOS Hospitals	Quadriga	Industrial roll-up	Not yet divested	Not yet divested
Apcoa	Investcorp	Salamander AG/EnBW	2007	Eurazeo
ATU	KKR	Doughty Hanson	Not yet divested	Not yet divested
AZ Electronic Chemicals	Carlyle/Vestar	Clariant	Not yet divested	Not yet divested
Bakelite	Apollo	RAG	Not yet divested	Not yet divested
BASF Printing Inks (Flint Group)	CVC	BASF	Not yet divested	Not yet divested
Bene AG	Global Equity Partners/ UIAG	Other investors	2006	IPO
betapharm Arzneimittel	3i	Santo Holding (Deutschland) GmbH	2006	Dr Reddys
CBR Holding	Cinven/Apax	Family	2007	EQT
Celanese	Blackstone	Public to private	Not yet divested	Not yet divested
ddp Deutscher Depeschendienst GmbH	Arques	Insolvency	2009	BluO
debitel	Permira	Swisscom	2008	Freenet
Delticom AG	Nord Holding	Family	2009	IPO
DocMorris.com	3i/HgCapital/ Neuhaus Partners	Family	2007	Celesio
DOCUgroup	GMT Communications Partners	Family	Not yet divested	Not yet divested
DSD	KKR	Private investors	Not yet divested	Not yet divested
Dufry Group	Advent	Patrick Laurent	2005	IPO
Dynamit Nobel	Rockwood/KKR	MG technologies	Not yet divested	Not yet divested
Dystar	Platinum Equity	BASF/Bayer/Hoechst/Avenus	Not yet divested	Not yet divested

Table 15.1 Private Equity Transactions in 2004 – *continued*

2004

Company	Buyer	Seller	Exit year	Sold to
E. Missel GmbH & Co KG	Arques	Masco Corporation	2008	Kolektor Group d.o.o.
E.H.R.	capiton	Technip	2007	Bilfinger Berger
Eduard Ubrig & Sohne GmbH	BPE Private Equity	Family	2006	Insolvency
Eismann	ECM	Nestle	2007	Intermediate Capital/ Management
Elisa Kommunikation (Tropolys)	Apax	Elisa	2007	merged with Versatel
Fennel Technologies AG	Carlyle	Family	Not yet divested	Not yet divested
FEP Fahrzeugelektrik Pirna	Barclays Private Equity	Family	2006	Steadfast
Findlay Industries	Capvis	Other investors	2006	IPO (as part of Polytec)
Forstinger	Bridgepoint	Orlando/Value Management Services	2009	Insolvency
Frimo	Nord Holding	Palladion	Not yet divested	Not yet divested
G.E.V. Großkuchen-Ersatzteil-Vertrieb	Equivest		Not yet divested	Not yet divested
Gealan	Axa	Halder	Not yet divested	Not yet divested
Geka Brush	Equita	Halder	2007	Halder
Gerresheimer Glas	Blackstone	Investcorp	2007	IPO
Gries Deco	3i	Management	2006	Management
Grohe	Texas Pacific/CSFB	BC Partners	Not yet divested	Not yet divested
Gutbrod/Hügel	Barclays	Finatem	2007	Voestalpine Motion
Hego Holding GmbH	Hannover Finanz	Family	Not yet divested	Not yet divested
Heidel	Frimo/Nord Holding	Rheinmetall	Not yet divested	Not yet divested
Helsa-automotive	Schoeller Metternich Beteiligungen	Family	2007	Mann & Hummel
Hirschmann Automation and Control GmbH	HgCapital	Rheinmetall	2007	Belden

Table 15.1 Private Equity Transactions in 2004 – *continued*

2004

Company	Buyer	Seller	Exit year	Sold to
Hirschmann Car Communication GmbH	HgCapital	Rheinmetall	2007	Management
Hirschmann Multimedia Electronics GmbH	HgCapital	Rheinmetall	2005	Triax
Holmer	Afinum	Family	2006	Avida
Homann Feinkost	Henderson	Gilde	2007	IFR
Honsel	Ripplewood	Carlyle	Not yet divested	Not yet divested
Ionbond	Stirling Square	Oerlikon Saurer Arbon AG	Not yet divested	Not yet divested
Isola	Texas Pacific	Rütgers AG	Not yet divested	Not yet divested
Jung Pumpen	3i	Masco Corporation	2007	Pentair Inc.
Kalle	Montagu	CVC	2009	Silverfleet Capital
Karl Konzelmann Metallschmelzwerke	BayBG/Nord Holding	Aluminiumschmelzwerk Oetinger GmbH	2009	New investors
Kautex Maschinenbau	Adcuram	Thyssen-Krupp/SIG	2007	Steadfast
Kögel	Schoeller Metternich Beteiligungen	Insolvency	Not yet divested	Not yet divested
Kolbe-Coloco Group	Invest Equity	Family	2008	Equita
Konzelmann Holding GmbH	Nord Holding	Agor AG	2005	Aluminiumschmelzwerk Oetinger GmbH
KTM	Cross Industries	BC Partners	Not yet divested	Not yet divested
Landis & Gyr	Bayard Capital	KKR	Not yet divested	Not yet divested
Leobensdorfer (LMF)	Nord Holding/ Invest Equity	Andlinger & Company	2007	Equita
Lichtwer Pharma	3i	Family	2006	Klosterfrau
Löwenplay	DDN Capital	ABN Amro	2006	Waterland
LR Health & Beauty Systems	Apax	Family	Not yet divested	Not yet divested

Table 15.1 Private Equity Transactions in 2004 – *continued*

2004

Company	Buyer	Seller	Exit year	Sold to
Ludwig-Reiter Schuhmanufaktur	Hannover Finanz	Family	2007	Other investor
M&W Müller & Weygrandt	PPM	Permira	Not yet divested	Not yet divested
Melvo	Hannover Finanz	Salamander AG	2008	DZ Private Equity
Nord Süd Speditions	Argantis	Hella KgaA Hueck & Co	2008	BIP
Novem	NIB Capital (Alpinvest)/3i	CVC/GS Capital Partners	2008	Barclays Private Equity
Oesterle SLR	Equivest	Family	Not yet divested	Not yet divested
OKIN	Equita	Indus Holding AG	2009	New investors
Otto Sauer Achsenfabrik	Pamplona	DBAG	2007	IPO
Palmers	Quadriga/Lead Equities	Family	Not yet divested	Not yet divested
Passport Fashion Group	BHF Private Equity	3i/BHF-BANK AG	Not yet divested	Not yet divested
pitti Heimtierprodukte	BHF Private Equity	Hannover Finanz	2009	New investors
Prüm GmbH	Halder	Hochtief	2007	Looser Holding AG
Rudolf Riester	Afinum	Family	2005	Paragon Partners
Saargummi	Orlando	RAG (Ruhrkohle AG)-Saarberg	2007	Odewald
SF-Chem	Capvis	Syngenta/Clariant	2007	CABB/Axa
SIG Hamba Filltec	Bavaria Industriekapital	SIG	2007	Cystar-Gruppe
SIG Kautex, SIG Blowtec	Adcuram	SIG	2004	Insolvency
SKW Stahl-Metalurgie-Gruppe	Arques	Degussa	2006	IPO
Solvadis	Orlando	GEA/Mg technologies	Not yet divested	Not yet divested
Sportfive	Advent/Goldman Sachs	RTL Group/Canal+	2006	Lagardere
SSB Antriebstechnik	Granville Baird	Private investors	2004	Parcom Deutsche PE
Stabilus	Montagu	KKR	2008	Paine & Partner
Starkstrom Gerätebau	HCP Capital Group GmbH	RWE	2008	BC Partners
Sulo	Blackstone/Apax	Previous investors	2007	Veolia Environment

Table 15.1 Private Equity Transactions in 2004 – *continued*

2004

Company	Buyer	Seller	Exit year	Sold to
SWB – Stahlwerk Bochum	Norddeutsche PE	ThyssenKrupp AG	2006	Management
Tank & Rast	Terra Firma	Allianz Capital/Apax/LSG	2007	REEF Infrastructure
Team BS Zeitarbeit	Granville Baird	Family	2007	Randstad
Teutonia Kinderwagenfabrik	Arques	Insolvency	2007	Newell Rubbermaid
ThyssenKrupp Fahrzeugguss (KSM Castings)	Electra	ThyssenKrupp AG	Not yet divested	Not yet divested
Time Partner Gruppe	Auctus	Family	2006	Investcorp
Transnorm System Holding GmbH	Nord Holding	Swisslog AG	2007	Equita
Tropon	Viatris (Advent portfolio co.)	Advent	2005	Meda
Tuja	Odewald	AHL Services Inc	2007	Barclays
Unterland Flex. Pack.	Capital-Management Partners	Near insolvency	2007	Mondi
VAG Armaturen	Equita	IWKA	2008	Halder
VTG-Lehnkering	Triton	TUI	Not yet divested	Not yet divested
wwd Vereinigte Wirtschaftsdienste	Cornerstone Capital	FAZ/Handelsblatt/Dow Jones	Not yet divested	Not yet divested
VWR	Clayton Dubilier & Rice	Merck KGaA	2007	Madison Dearborn Partners
Werner Kammann	Arcadia/Axa/Nord Holding		Not yet divested	Not yet divested
Zanolli	3i	Growth capital	2005	Insolvency
Zehnacker	Odewald	Family	2008	Sodexo

Source: Authors' compilation

from 2004 to profitability after a long period of losses. The turn-around task at Landis & Gyr Communications was however to end in failure, and the company filed for insolvency in 2001. TPG began the new millennium by switching its attention to Germany, and during 2001–2002 an attempt was made to acquire Bankgesell-schaft Berlin from the Berlin state government. The bank had fallen on hard times, and had to be refinanced by the local govern-ment, which now wished to divest its holding. This process stalled however in 2003, and was only restarted in 2007, by which time TPG declined to participate. The bank was eventually sold to a consortium of local Berlin-based savings banks.

The deal which catapulted TPG to a household name in Germany was its acquisition of Grohe in 2004 from BC Partners in a secondary transaction. The auction was hotly fought, and TPG teamed up in the final round with Credit Suisse. Matthias Calice recalls the process:

> Inevitably the highest bidder wins, but at 8.3 times EBITDA, the price was in a normal range for the period, and with around 35% equity, it was not over-leveraged. We had our own CEO manage-ment team, with whom we had worked up a business plan. It was clear from the start that we needed to restructure the company, and get its cost base down. It had seven plants in Germany, and didn't purchase anything in Asia. I'm not sure anyone in procurement had a passport from the region. Under BC Partners, they had built up some revenues abroad, but it was still very old fashioned.

> The people we brought in were either focussed on the brand or on the costs. For the brand, we brought in a bunch of people with an FMCG background.

> On the cost side, it was totally obvious that one plant would have to be closed. We made investments of around €30 million into the plants, and for the closures, negotiated from June to December 2004 with the unions, the works councils, and the management, and got a unanimous agreement on a social plan with which we were very pleased. In May 2005, two weeks before the election in North Rhine Westphalia, we announced our restructuring plan, with its 950 social-plan layoffs. What we didn't realise was that Grohe's headquarters was in Franz Münterfering's constituency, and when he heard our news, he lumped us in with the locusts. That was a mess, and all of our competitors jumped onto that.[33]

TPG might have feared some negative publicity on announcing the lay-offs, but they could not have reckoned with the political storm that was unleashed by the SPD Chairman, placing them very much at the centre of what he termed as the locust debate.

Texas Pacific rode out the storm, keeping as low profile as possible, while continuing its restructuring work at Grohe. The TPG team's work was not aided by the immediate macroeconomic changes, both during the boom, which caused material prices to sky-rocket, and in the later recession, which particularly hit the building materials industry, as Calice explains:

> In the first year of ownership, what with brass prices going up so dramatically, and the dollar/Euro rate changing so substantially, it was tough on the business. Then the recession came, which was tough for pretty much every business, and Grohe was no exception. Nevertheless in Germany the effect on Grohe was minimal, and they had some of their best years, built on a lot of market share gains.[34]

Fortunately, Grohe's financing structure was never put under strain during the difficult years which followed:

> Grohe had a bond financing structure which goes out to 2014, with no covenants. So while the bond prices could go up and down, this had no direct impact on the company.[35]

Despite a challenging macroeconomic climate, the results of TPG's restructuring programme were to bear fruit some eighteen months after the acquisition. In 2007, for the first time in its history, Grohe recorded revenues of over €1 billion, and increased its consolidated EBIT by 6% to €216 million. Even during the financial crisis, revenues stayed fairly constant, and by careful stewardship, the operative margin increased from 20% to almost 21%. What had been cast by the politicians as a victim of private equity had in fact been a success story under both BC Partners, and the TPG/Credit Suisse consortium. Calice recalls the actions put in place to influence the company's development:

> What we did at Grohe was to introduce a transformation process. We completely modernised the factory in Sauerland, and moved the process from workshop manufacturing to serial production. We also completely reorganised the logistics and the factories. The

throughput of products was reduced from 20 days to 4 days, so that Grohe could react quicker and more flexibly to the demands of the market. The factory in Hemer even won the "Best Factory" prize, against 180 competitors with production facilities in Spain, Germany, France, and Eastern Europe.[36]

In what was a very busy year for the firm, TPG acquired Isola in 2004, a company manufacturing base materials for printed circuit boards, from Rütgers. TPG's goal with Isola, as Calice later explained, was to pursue a consolidation strategy:

> Isola served customers predominantly in Asia and the US, despite its base and origins in Europe. We proceeded to buy one of its competitors, and created a much bigger and stronger business out of the combination of the two.[37]

In May 2005, TPG acquired France Telecom's 27% stake in mobilcom, giving it a minority stake in a public company. France Telecom had acquired its stake in 2000, and used mobilcom as a vehicle to win one of Germany's UTMS licences. Only two years later, however, a major dispute broke out between France Telecom and the former owner which escalated into a potential law suite. At the same time, mobilcom's finances foundered, and the company teetered on the brink of insolvency. Calice explains the rationale behind the investment:

> The reason it was attractive for France Telecom to sell this stake to us was that they had a very large contingent liability on their balance sheet of some €4 billion relating to a potential lawsuit between themselves and mobilcom's founder. When we took over that stake, we solved that contingent liability. As far as the business was concerned, we wanted to merge it with freenet, which we knew would create a boost to its business.[38]

With TPG's support, the merger between mobilcom and freenet was eventually agreed in 2007, after which TPG sold its stake, and made an attractive return on its investment.

TPG's last investment during the boom was its investment in Media Broadcast GmbH from T-Systems, using an innovative financing structure, which brought the company into the TDF-Group. By the close of this period, Germany had become a significant market for the firm, as Calice explains:

Germany had become one of our most important markets. We pursue a country focus, and have a team of five professionals focussed on the German-speaking region. In 2006, we asked Ludolf von Wartenberg to join us as a senior adviser. He was the former head of the German federation of industry, the BDI. He is in regular contact with Angela Merkel and Peer Steinbrück, and an excellent person to guide us through the German domestic scene.[39]

Von Wartenberg's understanding of his role for TPG was similar:

I help them to understand Germany.[40]

manager magazin described von Wartenberg's political and industrial contacts as "legendary".[41] TPG had clearly found its way in Germany.

The locust debate

Nobody within the private equity industry had expected their industry to become an election issue. It was unfortunate for TPG that the announcement of the Grohe redundancy scheme should have both coincided with the election campaign, and been announced in the home town, Hemer, of the Chairman of the SPD, Franz Müntefering. On reading the press coverage of the restructuring plans at Grohe, Müntefering gave an impassioned interview with the *Bild am Sonntag* denouncing the "locusts" that had descended upon innocent German companies, swallowing them up, and squeezing out all of their value, before moving on to their next victims:

Some financial investors waste no thoughts on the people and their jobs which they destroy. They remain anonymous, have no face, and fall like locusts on our companies, gobbling them up and pushing on further. We will fight against this form of capitalism.[42]

Although the press leapt onto this quotation with glee, Münterfering had already singled out private equity for criticism in a speech given in November 2004, and in his original list of locusts, TPG had been given no mention:

We support those companies, who act in the interest of their future and in the interest of their employees against irresponsible locust swarms, who measure success in quarterly intervals, suck off substance and let companies die once they have eaten them away.[43]

Overnight, all private equity houses were in the dock of public opinion and at the centre of the political spotlight.

The locust debate within Germany saw references to private equity in the media increase by 100% per annum, to reach levels where hardly a single edition of any national newspaper or magazine failed to mention private equity somewhere within its columns. One of the first to develop a feature based upon the Münterfering story was *Stern* magazine, which produced an article on 28th April 2005 entitled "The names of the locusts" based on an analysis of an SPD internal memo-

Figure 15.2   Der Spiegel Coverstory: The Greed of the Big Money

randum, which having been produced before the Grohe press release, did not include either Grohe or TPG:

> The SPD-paper names many additional locusts, in particular participations business WCM, which took over Klöckner, and alongside them the private equity companies: Apax, BC Partners, Carlyle, Advent, Permira, Blackstone, CVC, and also Saban Capital, which is still the current owner of Prosieben Sat1. The victims of these acquirers include: Siemens Nixdorf, Tenovis, Rodenstock, Autoteile Unger (ATU), Debitel, Celanese, and Dynamit Nobel. The named individuals included: Michael Phillips of Apax, Jens Reidel of BC Partners, Hanns Ostmeier of Blackstone, Steven Koltes of CVC, Johannes Huth of KKR, and Thomas Krenz of Permira.[44]

For many members of the industry, the locust debate was viewed as a good thing. While the tone of the communication was aggressive, a

Figure 15.3   *Stern* Coverstory: The big feast – why we are all locusts

Source: *Stern* magazine

significant proportion of the press coverage included articles explaining what private equity was doing, and passing judgement on successes and failures. Within the space of a year, almost every manager in Germany had heard of private equity. This unexpectedly positive development was picked up in an article published a year later in the *International Herald Tribune*:

> Müntefering's comments seemed aimed at the time to rally his Social Democratic faithful before the general elections in September 2005, and he drew predictably outraged comments from business leaders. Since the elections, which elevated Angela Merkel to the chancellorship, he has been labor minister, a traditional redoubt of leftist politicians in Germany, and has spoken barely a word in public about private equity.

> The industry, meanwhile, took his comments in its stride and with good humor. In offices around Germany, pictures of locusts quickly started appearing on T-shirts and computer screen savers.

> And by highlighting the activities of an industry that – in contrast to Britain or the United States – was not well-known in Germany, even among some investors, Müntefering may actually have helped rally other politicians to support the business.

> "I think the politicians found themselves in the position where they had to demonstrate that this was a subject that mattered to them," said Patricia Lips, a member of Parliament who represents a district south of the financial capital of Frankfurt.[45]

capiton

capiton's march to independence took a further step in 2002 with fundraising for capiton II. This saw the addition of other insurance companies, the KfW, and a number of family offices to its investor base. The new fund specialised in mid-cap buyouts, a pre-requisite for the move to full independence. In 2004, the team executed its own full MBO, and within three years Gothaer no longer held a minority stake in the management company. Stefan Theis comments on the process:

> It was the typical exit of a private equity company, comparable with spin-offs from other banks or insurance companies. History is littered with such examples. Our move was well timed, because when

we came to raise capiton III two years later in 2006, fundraising sentiment had further improved towards both capiton, and its MBO. If we hadn't done the MBO when we did, and gained third party investors, we would have been in trouble, because a few years later our former sponsor, like many other financial service firms, decided to change its investment strategy.[46]

The capiton team acquired Reum Automotive from UBS in 2003, which at the time was liquidating its private equity investments in Germany, and then provided Trenkwalder Personaldienste AG with significant growth capital. Andreas Kogler recalls the latter to be one of the first private equity investments in temporary staffing:

> We invested in Trenkwalder at a time when temporary staffing was unfashionable. We became convinced of Richard Trenkwalder's story that there were growth opportunities in Eastern Europe. We saw the absence of Adecco and Randstad in Hungary and the Czech Republic, because they still lacked the legal basis for temporary staffing, as a major opportunity. Despite the fact that Trenkwalder was only a small company when we invested in it, with €160 million in revenues, it was able to become market leader in Eastern Europe, growing revenues to nearly €1 billion.

> The Trenkwalder case demonstrates what is important for our investment approach. We invest in industries which don't look sexy at the time, and which may be in the dip of their recession. We had our first talks with Herr Trenkwalder in 2002 when hardly anyone would invest in temporary staffing. At this time, multiples in the sector were low, and the opportunities for realising a buy-and-build concept were high. Two years later, everyone wanted to invest in the sector. The values of the companies took off, which made it an ideal time for capiton to sell its shares.[47]

In the same year, even closer to home for the Berlin team, Borsig came up for sale out of the Babcock insolvency. Given the low point in the recession, very few investors were interested in the business, and the auction quickly narrowed down to a Mexican investor and capiton. Management was crucial as Kogler later recalled:

> It was clear to us from the start that Borsig's problem had been with its parent (Babcock) not with its own business and management. We found a very strong and homogeneous management team, which was key for us to invest.[48]

The same trend-bucking approach was adopted a year later when capiton looked at EHR, a former Mannesmann company, focussed on the piping of large plants, which Technip was looking to sell. Kogler explains how his team got comfortable with the company:

> At the outset we looked at EHR because we thought it might be an add-on acquisition for Borsig. The management looked good, and the business had never made a loss. We brought in L.E.K. to do the commercial due diligence, and their interviews with customers opened our eyes to what a pearl the business was. L.E.K. interviewed all the power stations, and investigated the investments they were planning, and suddenly it was clear that within a year there was going to be a boom in the industry, and none of the strategics had seen this yet, and were not interested in buying. So we made the investment, and within a few months the company began growing.[49]

By the time the boom had reached its peak, capiton had acquired a string of companies, adding GMC (from insolvency) and Misslbeck in 2004, SHW Castings, KOKI (with L-EA Private Equity), and Steco in 2005, Ensys and Gimborn in 2006, and Lahmeyer International and Nora (again with L-EA Private Equity) in 2007.

Montagu

Within one year of von Drechsel's departure, HSBC Private Equity was spun-out of its parent bank and given back its original name, Montagu Private Equity, henceforth majority owned by its senior directors, including Helling and Kroha in Düsseldorf. Over the following few years, the German office closed two transactions, the first being the €470m MBO of Stabilus acquired from Demag in August 2004. Stabilus was the market leader for gas springs used in automotive and various industrial applications. Just a few weeks later, after the Stabilus closing, Montagu acquired Kalle, the world's leading sausage casing business in a further €170m MBO. Both businesses were held by Montagu for around four years and proved successful investments generating healthy returns for the Montagu II fund.

Helling and Kroha recruited several younger colleagues to increase the man power on the ground in Düsseldorf. Using Kroha's relationships from having worked with HSBC Private Equity in the London office during the late 1990s as well as Helling's German experience

Table 15.2 Private Equity Transactions in 2005

2005

Company	Buyer	Seller	Exit year	Sold to
Abellio	Star Capital	City of Essen	2008	NedRailways
Addison Software & Service	HgCapital	Family	2008	Wolters Kluwer Legal
AG KK&K	ECM	BorgWarner	2006	Siemens
Aleo Solar/S.M.D	Hannover Finanz	Family	2007	IPO
Arquana International Print & Media	Arques	Family	2005	IPO
ARWE Group	Afinum	Family	2006	Avida
Babcock Borsig Service GmbH	Bilfinger Berger AG	DBAG/Harvest	Not yet divested	Not yet divested
B.U.S. Group	Star Capital	AGOR AG	2006	Befesa Group
Beissbarth Automotive Group	SG Capital Europe	Facom Tools/Fimalac	Not yet divested	Not yet divested
Benninger	Capvis	Family	Not yet divested	Not yet divested
Berkenhoff GmbH (Bedra)	3i, Granville Baird	ThyssenKrupp	Not yet divested	Not yet divested
Bettmer GmbH	Afinum	Nord Holding	2006	Avida
BHS Getriebe	Halder	EquiVest	2007	Voith Turbo
BST Safety Textiles	PPM	Family	2006	WL Ross & Co. LLC
CABB	Gilde	Clariant	2006	Axa Private Equity
Carl Zeis Vision	EQT	Carl Zeis	Not yet divested	Not yet divested
Casa Reha	Advent	ECM/JPMorgan	2007	HgCapital
Cetelon	Steadfast Capital	Family	Not yet divested	Not yet divested
Clariant Acetyl Building Blocks	Gilde	Clariant	Not yet divested	Not yet divested
Czewo Full Filling Service	Argantis	Family	2008	ColepCCL
Dahlewitzer Landbäckeriei GmbH	Steadfast Capital	Private investors	Not yet divested	Not yet divested
Derby Holding	Finatem	Raleigh Cycle Ltd	Not yet divested	Not yet divested
Dragenopharm	Bridgepoint	Family	Not yet divested	Not yet divested
Duales System Deutschland AG	KKR	Diverse investors	Not yet divested	Not yet divested
Dywidag-Systems International	Industri Kapital	Walter Bau AG	2007	CVC
Elbion AG	3i	Degussa	Not yet divested	Not yet divested
ersol AG	Ventizz Capital	Private investors	2008	Bosch

Table 15.2 Private Equity Transactions in 2005 – *continued*

2005

Company	Buyer	Seller	Exit year	Sold to
Flex Elektrowerkzeuge GmbH	GSO Capital Partners	Black & Decker	2007	Axa Private Equity
Francotyp-Postalia	Quadriga	Röchling Group	2006	IPO
FTE	PAI Partners	HgCapital	Not yet divested	Not yet divested
Garant	Halder	Doorwin B.V.	2007	Looser Holding AG
GMC	capiton	Insolvency administrator	Not yet divested	Not yet divested
Golf House Direktversand	Arques	Karstadt	2010	JAB Josef Anstötz KG
Grammer	Deutsche Bank	Permira	2005	New institutional investors
GSES	Star Capital	Private investors	Not yet divested	Not yet divested
Gutehoffnungshütte Radsatz	SG Capital Europe	Faiveley Transport	Not yet divested	Not yet divested
HAITEC AG	Bridgepoint	Equity swap	Not yet divested	Not yet divested
Herlitz	Advent	Banks	2010	Pelikan
Hofmann Menu	HgCapital	Pricoa Capital	2007	Gilde
HT Troplast	Carlyle/Advent	RAG	2007	Arcapita
J&S Werkzeugbau	Finatem	Private investors	Not yet divested	Not yet divested
Jack Wolfskin	Quadriga/Barclays	Bain Capital	Not yet divested	Not yet divested
Jahnel-Kestermann Getriebewerk	Arques	Private investors	2008	PSM Inc.
Jet Aviation	Permira	Family	2008	General Dynamics
Jost Werke	PPM	Alpha	2008	Cinven
Kaffee Partner	Odewald	Bridgepoint	2010	Capvis/Partners Group
Katz Group	Equivest	3i	Not yet divested	Not yet divested
Klöckner & Co	Lindsay Goldberg & Bessemer	WestLB AG/HSH Nordbank	2006	IPO
KOKI Technik	capiton/L-EA Private Equity	Family	Not yet divested	Not yet divested
KTM Kühler GmbH	Andlinger & Company	CSL-Gruppe	Not yet divested	Not yet divested
Leica Microsystems – SED	Golden Gate Capital	Danaher Corp	Not yet divested	Not yet divested
LEMO Maschinenbau GmbH	Auctus	Tequity	Not yet divested	Not yet divested
Lewa	DBAG/Quadriga	Family	2009	Nikkiso
Machalke	Capvis	Afinum	Not yet divested	Not yet divested

Table 15.2 Private Equity Transactions in 2005 – *continued*

2005

Company	Buyer	Seller	Exit year	Sold to
MAN Heiztechnik	Haspa Beteiligungsberatung	MAN B&W Diesel AG	Not yet divested	Not yet divested
Maredo	ECM/Parcom/Fortis PE	Whitbread	Not yet divested	Not yet divested
MIGUA Fugensysteme GmbH & Co. KG	Indus Holding AG	BPE Private Equity	Not yet divested	Not yet divested
Mikron AG	Swiss investors	CVC	Not yet divested	Not yet divested
Moeller Holding	Doughty Hanson	Advent	2007	Eaton Corporation
MT Misslbeck Technologies GmbH	capiton	Family	Not yet divested	Not yet divested
Neumayer Tekfor Gruppe	Barclays	Equita/Family	Not yet divested	Not yet divested
Nordsee	Kamps/Nomura	Apax	Not yet divested	Not yet divested
ORS Service	Argos Soditic	Family	Not yet divested	Not yet divested
Paper & Design Tabletop	Nord Holding	Family	Not yet divested	Not yet divested
Peguform	Cerberus	Insolvency	2008	Polytec Holding
Pfleiderer Poles & Towers	VTC Partners	Pfleiderer	Not yet divested	Not yet divested
Rado Gummi GmbH	Hannover Finanz	Hella AG	Not yet divested	Not yet divested
Rhodius	Nord Holding	Bürger AG	Not yet divested	Not yet divested
Richter Chemie	Riverside	ITT	2008	IDEX Corporation
Ruhrgas Industries (Elster)	CVC	Ruhrgas	Not yet divested	Not yet divested
Ruhrgas Industries (Ipsen)	CVC	Ruhrgas	2007	Quadriga
Ruhrgas Industries (VTN)	CVC	Ruhrgas	2007	BPE Private Equity
Runners Point	Hannover Finanz	KarstadtQuelle AG	Not yet divested	Not yet divested
Schaetti Group	Afinum	Family	2006	Avida
Schenk Bohemia Group (SBG)	Argantis	Sarna Kunstoff Holding AG	Not yet divested	Not yet divested
Schenk M&P Technologies	HgCapital	Schenk	2007	Industri Kapital
Schlatter Holding AG	Zurmont Finanz AG	Family	2007	Metall ZUG & HUWA
Schneider Verlag	Barclays	Family	Not yet divested	Not yet divested
Schrack Energietechnik	Hannover Finanz	Rexel Group	Not yet divested	Not yet divested

Table 15.2 Private Equity Transactions in 2005 – *continued*

2005

Company	Buyer	Seller	Exit year	Sold to
Schütz Dental	BLB Private Equity	Family	Not yet divested	Not yet divested
Sellner	Equivest	Family	Not yet divested	Not yet divested
SGL Acotec	Adcuram Industriekapital	SGL Carbon	Not yet divested	Not yet divested
SHW Castings (CT Casting Technology)	capiton	MAN	Not yet divested	Not yet divested
Sirona Dental Systems Group	Madison Dearborn	EQT	Not yet divested	Not yet divested
SKS Stakusit Bautechnik GmbH	Arques	Masco Corporation	2007	GEI-Immo AG
Süd Chemie	One Equity Partners	Public to private	Not yet divested	Not yet divested
Swiss Caps (later Aenova)	Bridgepoint	Family	Not yet divested	Not yet divested
The Lacon Group	BayBG	Family	Not yet divested	Not yet divested
Ticketcorner	Capvis	The Kudelski Group	2010	CTS Evention
Tiscon AG Infosystems	Arques	Public to private	Not yet divested	Not yet divested
Tom Tailor	Alpha	Brand Invest	Not yet divested	Not yet divested
trans-o-flex	Odewald/Alpha	Deutsche Post	2008	Austrian Post
TSK	BPE	Family	Not yet divested	Not yet divested
Unicor GmbH	Nord Holding	Uponor Group	Not yet divested	Not yet divested
VAC – Vacuumschmelze GmbH	One Equity Partners	Morgan Crucible	Not yet divested	Not yet divested
Versatel Deutschland	Apax	Family	2007	IPO
Vogel & Noot	Equivest	Vogel & Noot AG	2009	Insolvent
VTG	IPE/Compagnie Europeenne de	TUI	2007	IPO
Webasto Bus GmbH (Spheros)	Granville Baird, HSH N Kapital	Webasto	Not yet divested	Not yet divested
Wendt	3i	Anglo American PLC	2007	Winterthur Techn.
Werkzeugbau Laichingen	BLB Equity Management	Family	Not yet divested	Not yet divested
Westend Druckereibetriebe (Krupp)	Hannover Finanz	ThyssenKrupp	Not yet divested	Not yet divested
YXLON	Adlinger & Co Inc	Invision Technologies	2007	Comet AG

Source: Authors' compilation

Table 15.3 Private Equity Transactions in 2006, A–L

2006, A–L

Company	Buyer	Seller	Exit year	Sold to
Accovion GmbH	3i/Creator Ventures	sanofi aventis	Not yet divested	Not yet divested
ACP – All Computer Products	Capvis	Family	Not yet divested	Not yet divested
ADA Cosmetics International	Halder	Family	Not yet divested	Not yet divested
AHT Austria Haustechnik	Quadriga	Equita	Not yet divested	Not yet divested
AIS Group/IndustrieHansa	Riverside	MCE AG/VAI Metal Technology	2008	Findos
AIS Group/Steelplanner	Riverside	MCE AG/VAI Metal Technology	Not yet divested	Not yet divested
Amor	Pamplona	Family	Not yet divested	Not yet divested
Armacell	Investcorp	CVC/Gilde	Not yet divested	Not yet divested
Auberna Crushing Technology GmbH	Hannover Finanz	Family	2008	Sandvik
Austria Email AG	Global Equity Partners/ UIAG/Cross Industries	Auricon/Wiener Holding	2010	Buy-out Central Europe
AvJS Group	Arcadia Beteiligungen	Family	Not yet divested	Not yet divested
Barat Ceramics	Equita	Boart Longyear	2007	Element Six
Basler	Triton	Alpha	Not yet divested	Not yet divested
Battenfeld	Adcuram Industries	SMS	2007	Insolvency
Bavaria Digital Technik	AdCapital	Family	Not yet divested	Not yet divested
BEA West	Aurelius Investkapital	Röchling Gruppe	Not yet divested	Not yet divested
Benninger Holding	Capvis	Family/Charles Peter	Not yet divested	Not yet divested
BOA	Odewald	IWKA	Not yet divested	Not yet divested
Boart Longyear HSMR/Boart Ceramics	Equita	Longyear Holdings	Not yet divested	Not yet divested
Boehme Group	DyStar Textilfarben/ Platinum	Family	Not yet divested	Not yet divested
Bopp & Reuther	Tequity	IWKA	Not yet divested	Not yet divested
Breitenfeld	DZ Equity Partners	Private investors	2008	Morgan Stanley

Table 15.3 Private Equity Transactions in 2006, A–L – *continued*

2006, A–L

Company	Buyer	Seller	Exit year	Sold to
Brenntag	BC Partners	Bain Capital	2010	IPO
BSN Medical	Montagu	Beiersdorf AG/Smith & Nephew	Not yet divested	Not yet divested
BST Safety Textiles	W L Ross & Co LLC	PPM	Not yet divested	Not yet divested
Burton-Werke GmbH	Nord Holding	SG Capital	Not yet divested	Not yet divested
Buss AG	Fabrel Lotos	Coperion Group	Not yet divested	Not yet divested
CABB	Axa Private Equity	Gilde	Not yet divested	Not yet divested
Cadooz AG	Palamon	Family	Not yet divested	Not yet divested
Clariant Pharmaceutical Fine Chemicals	Towerbrook	Clariant	Not yet divested	Not yet divested
CoCreate	HBK Private Equity	3i/Triton	Not yet divested	Not yet divested
Coventya International	Natexis Industrie	Quadriga/Natexis	Not yet divested	Not yet divested
DC Druckchemie	SG Capital/Quartus	Family	2008	3i
Dematic	Triton	Siemens	Not yet divested	Not yet divested
Deutsche Post Wohnen GmbH	Aurelius	Deutsche Post AG	Not yet divested	Not yet divested
DFA Transport und Logistik GmbH	Aurelius	Private investors	Not yet divested	Not yet divested
DMS Dynamic Micro Systems	Arcadia	Brockhaus PE	Not yet divested	Not yet divested
DNZ (Deutsche Notruf Zentrale)	Finatem	Family	Not yet divested	Not yet divested
Easy Cash	Warburg Pincus	First Data	Not yet divested	Not yet divested
Ensys	capiton	Private investors	Not yet divested	Not yet divested
Eterna Mode AG	Quadriga/Alpha	Ahlers AG	Not yet divested	Not yet divested
Etimex	Alpha	Barclays Private Equity	Not yet divested	Not yet divested
EurotaxGlasse's Group	Candover	HM Capital (Hicks, Muse, Tate)	Not yet divested	Not yet divested
Farbendruck Weber	Arques Industries	Partenaires-Livres Group	Not yet divested	Not yet divested
FEP Fahrzeugelektrik Pirna	Steadfast Capital	Barclays Private Equity	Not yet divested	Not yet divested
FMW Anlagentechnik	Hannover Finanz	Family	Not yet divested	Not yet divested
Fritz Berger GmbH	Arques Industries	Neckermann Versand AG	2010	MH-Beteiligungs GmbH

Table 15.3 Private Equity Transactions in 2006, A–L – *continued*

2006, A–L

Company	Buyer	Seller	Exit year	Sold to
Georg Fischer Schwab GmbH	Arques Industries	Georg Fischer AG	Not yet divested	Not yet divested
Gimborn	capiton	Süd Chemie	2008	Penta Investments
Heinrich Heiland	Arques Industries	Family	2006	Strategic investor
Heissner AG	Hannover Finanz	PeakTop Group (Hong Kong)	Not yet divested	Not yet divested
Highway Automaten	Waterland Private Equity/ Löwenplay	Family	2008	Axa Private Equity
Hirmer Vertag	Aurelius	Private investors	Not yet divested	Not yet divested
Homag	DBAG	Family	Not yet divested	Not yet divested
Hottinger Maschinenbau	Arques Industries	Family	2008	Turnaround Finance Beratungs
Iglo Birds Eye Frozen Foods	Permira	Unilever	Not yet divested	Not yet divested
isu Zeitarbeit	BLB Private Equity	Vedior Konzern	Not yet divested	Not yet divested
JF Hillebrand	Cobepa	Private investors	Not yet divested	Not yet divested
Jil Sander AG	Change Capital Partners	Prada	2008	Onward Holdings
Kabel Baden Würtemburg	EQT	Blackstone	Not yet divested	Not yet divested
Kabel Deutschland	Providence	Apax/Goldman/Providence	Not yet divested	Not yet divested
Karl Eugen Fischer	Halder	Family	2008	Equita
Kentaro AG	Nord Holding	Capital increase	Not yet divested	Not yet divested
Kiekert AG	Deutsche/Morgan Stanley/ Blue Bay/Silver Point Capital	Permira	Not yet divested	Not yet divested
Kienle + Spiess Gruppe	Bavaria Industriekapital AG	Corus Group plc	Not yet divested	Not yet divested
Kinshofer Greiftechnik GmbH	Paragon Partners	Afinum	2007	Lifco
Kion	KKR/Goldman Sachs	Linde	Not yet divested	Not yet divested
Knuerr AG	Emerson Electric Company	3i	Not yet divested	Not yet divested

Table 15.3 Private Equity Transactions in 2006, A–L – *continued*

2006, A–L

Company	Buyer	Seller	Exit year	Sold to
Köhler Automobiltechnik	Hannover Finanz	DURA Automotive Systems, Inc.	Not yet divested	Not yet divested
Konrad Hornschuch AG	DZ Equity Partner/ L-EA Priv. Equity	Halder	2008	Barclays Private Equity
KTP Kunststoff Palettentechnik GmbH	Axa Private Equity	Family	Not yet divested	Not yet divested
KWE Stahl-u. Industriebau	Aurelius	Bauwens Real Estate Group	2008	Kresta Anlagebau
Lautsprecher Teufel	Riverside	Family	Not yet divested	Not yet divested
LEWA	Quadriga/DBAG	Family	2009	Nikkiso
Lista B+L Holding	Capvis	Family	Not yet divested	Not yet divested
Löwenplay	Waterland Private Equity	DDN Capital Partners	2008	Axa
Luk Fahrzeug-Hydraulik (ixetic)	Cognetas	Ina Holding Schaeffler KG	Not yet divested	Not yet divested
Lüscher AG	Global Equity Partners/ UIAG	Family	Not yet divested	Not yet divested

Source: Authors' compilation

through working with UBS Capital in Munich, the team was able to position itself to source and execute mid-market deals. Helling later commented:

> Finding the right balance between local presence, cultural awareness, and Anglo-Saxon deal experience was the right combination.[50]

In 2006, Montagu completed the €1bn MBO of BSN medical, a 50:50 joint venture owned by Beiersdorf and Smith & Nephew after a hotly contested auction. BSN was a leading global business active in wound care, orthopaedic products as well as phlebology. This led to significant post-acquisition support, as Helling explains:

> Over the years Montagu supported BSN with half a dozen add-on acquisitions as well as significant investment in new product development and the business performed extremely well under our ownership.[51]

Government

Even the government felt that it needed to educate itself on what private equity was doing to the German economy. In 2007, the Finance Ministry put out a tender, inviting bids for a project to analyse the impact of private equity. Three consortiums bid: McKinsey, L.E.K., and the Technical University of Munich. The project was awarded to Professor Ann-Kristin Achleitner's group at the Technical University of Munich. The results of the study[52] were published 12 months later, giving a positive verdict on the industry.

Rise of the secondaries market

Perhaps even more significantly as the new millennium progressed, private equity companies began selling companies to each other on a large scale. During the period 2000–2003, most private equity house professionals in Germany claimed that they weren't interested in doing secondaries, the assumption being that all the value would have been extracted by the first private equity investor. But by 2004, secondaries were already accounting for around a quarter of private equity deals, and within a further three years, this proportion had doubled to 50%, and no private equity house could rule out buying a company from another professional in the community.

The peak

The period 2006–2007 saw a peak in valuations, and the private equity industry made fabulous returns on the crop of companies bought during the 2003–2004 recession. Multiple expansion was the biggest influence on the return. The number of deals continued to increase, reaching a peak of over 200 leveraged buyouts in 2007. The escalating valuations, made possible by rapidly rising levels of leverage, that took senior debt up to six times EBITDA in many cases, the level at which enterprise value was estimated a few years earlier, caused many to fear that a bubble was developing. The fear was that a recession would come around the corner, reduce EBITDAs, and cause EBITDA contraction for valuations: a double blow for investors. Anxiety in the market grew, as prices continued to notch further upward. Many PE professionals were convinced that multiples could not keep rising, and that a correction was inevitable. The key issue was whether the correction would involve a soft landing or a hard one. By contrast with the 2002–2003 period, the debt providers were now too enthusiastic, and the fear was that their lending would only become more cautious once loans began to underperform: indeed it was speculated that it would take a number of high-profile buyouts to default on their interest payments to change debt provider behaviour.

As the industry edged ever upwards, with prices, deal sizes, deal volumes ever increasing, it became clear to members of the industry that the bubble would eventually burst. The most likely cause of that puncture was thought to be a global recession. Views differed within the industry on when this recession would occur, ranging from the most optimistic (not until China and India stopped growing) to the most pessimistic (it was about to happen). Perhaps the most common view was that good times lasted seven years and bad times three, which meant that the next recession would be in 2010.

As the year 2007 progressed, many private equity houses began selling their portfolios, cashing in on the high valuations. For the first time, private equity houses themselves accounted for half of the flow of new deals coming onto the market. By contrast, the number of corporate spin-offs was dropping dramatically. Meanwhile, the vendor due diligence market was going through the roof. Corporates were becoming big buyers in the market, limiting the number of LBO deals that could be closed.

In the run-up to the summer of 2007, private equity players in Germany were basking in the image of "masters of the universe", differing only from their US counterparts in the absolute scale of their wealth (being much smaller). Confidence in the profession was running high, in and outside its ranks. Within universities and business schools across the German-speaking region, private equity was becoming the first choice career for the brightest and smartest graduating students, eclipsing the previous stars of investment banking and strategy consulting, now considered commoditised and unrewarding. While there was a general expectation that a correction was to be expected, and there were discussions of "hard landing" versus "soft landing" scenarios, no-one expected what was in store for them.

Table 15.4 Private Equity Transactions in 2006, M–Z

2006, M–Z

Company	Buyer	Seller	Exit year	Sold to
MAN Roland	Allianz Capital Partners	MAN Group	Not yet divested	Not yet divested
Märklin	Knightsbridge	Family	2009	Insolvency
Mecanindus-Jörg Vogelsang Group	Finatem	Family	Not yet divested	Not yet divested
MEDOS Medizintechnik	Ventizz Capital Partners	S-UBG AG/WGZ	Not yet divested	Not yet divested
Minimax	Industri Kapital	Investcorp	Not yet divested	Not yet divested
Moenus Textilmaschinen GmbH	Lone Star	Family	Not yet divested	Not yet divested
MPM – Demag Plastic Machinery	Madison Capital Partners	KKR	2008	Sumitomo
MPM – Mannesman Plastic Machinery	Madison Capital Partners	KKR	Not yet divested	Not yet divested
MTH – Metall Technologie Holding	European Capital	BLB Private Equity/Hannover Finanz	Not yet divested	Not yet divested
MTP Grillo	Aurelius	Siemens	Not yet divested	Not yet divested
MTU Friedrichshafen	EQT	Daimler	Not yet divested	Not yet divested
Myonic AG	Süd Private Equity/ DZ Equity	Capvis	Not yet divested	Not yet divested
Nero	Alpha	Previous investors	Not yet divested	Not yet divested
Nici	Strategic Value Partners	Creditor banks	Not yet divested	Not yet divested
Noske-Kaeser	Titan Hunter/Hunter Capital Group	ThyssenKrupp AG	Not yet divested	Not yet divested
Nukem (RWE Solutions)	Advent	RWE	Not yet divested	Not yet divested
Nybron Flooring	Vestar Capital Partners	HIAG/Nordic Capital Funds	2008	Creditors
Odlo Sports Group	Towerbrook	Partners Group	2010	Herkules PE
OPS Ingersoll	IKB Private Equity	3i	Not yet divested	Not yet divested
Orior Food-Gruppe	capvis	Orior Holding SA	Not yet divested	Not yet divested
Orizon	PPM	GL Aktiengesellschafft	Not yet divested	Not yet divested
Oxxynova GmbH	Arques Industries	Degussa	Not yet divested	Not yet divested

Table 15.4 Private Equity Transactions in 2006, M–Z – *continued*

2006, M–Z

Company	Buyer	Seller	Exit year	Sold to
Parte	Hannover Finanz	Family	Not yet divested	Not yet divested
PAS – Pretti Appliance Systems	Granville Baird	Prettl Gruppe	Not yet divested	Not yet divested
PDS Entwicklungs'-und Service GmbH	Nord Holding	MUK Kapitalbetelligungs GmbH	Not yet divested	Not yet divested
Peine	Steadfast Capital	Family	2010	Gordon Bros
Pfaff Industrie Maschinen	GCI Bridge Capital	Bianchi Marè/Efibanca	Not yet divested	Not yet divested
Pfaff Silberblau	EQT	Family	2008	Columbus McKinnon
Pfleiderer track systems/Rail.one	Axa Private Equity	Pfleiderer AG	Not yet divested	Not yet divested
Pharmazell	Auctus	Noveon-Pharma	2007	EQT
PMA	Equita	Fränkische Rohrwerke	Not yet divested	Not yet divested
Powerlines	Invest Equity	Family	2008	Gilde
Pretti Appliance Systems	Granville Baird	Family	Not yet divested	Not yet divested
Rado Gummi	Hannover Finanz	Family	Not yet divested	Not yet divested
Rasmussen/Norma	3i/Creator Ventures	Family	Not yet divested	Not yet divested
Ratioform	Barclays Private Equity	Family	Not yet divested	Not yet divested
RCE Industrieofen Engineering GmbH	Polysius AG/ThyssenKrupp	DBAG/Hochtemperatur Engineering GmbH	Not yet divested	Not yet divested
Recop Electronic GmbH	Brockhaus Private Equity	Family	Not yet divested	Not yet divested
Rhodius GmbH	Nord Holding	Bürger AG	Not yet divested	Not yet divested
Richard Scherpe GmbH	Aurelius	Private investors	2009	Swiss GJK GmbH
Richard Schöps AG	PHI Private Holdings of Investments Luxembourg S.A.	Borgetti	2007	Arques Austria
Rodenstock	Bridgepoint	Permira	Not yet divested	Not yet divested
Rohner AG	Arques Industries	Rockwood Holdings	2009	BluO
Roncadin/Schröer Eis GmbH	Oaktree Capital	Family	Not yet divested	Not yet divested
Rudolf Riester	Paragon	Afinum	2007	Halma plc

Table 15.4 Private Equity Transactions in 2006, M–Z – *continued*

2006, M–Z

Company	Buyer	Seller	Exit year	Sold to
SAG (RWE Solutions)	Advent	RWE	2008	EQT
Salto Paper	Arques Industries	Creditors	2007	IBET Industrie-beteiligungen
Scharf	Aurelius	RAG AG/DBT GmbH	Not yet divested	Not yet divested
Schleich	HgCapital	Family	Not yet divested	Not yet divested
sds business service	Waterland Private Equity	Deutschen Bahn Logistics	2008	Affiliated Comp. Services
Securlog GmbH/Heros	Matlin Patterson	Insolvency	Not yet divested	Not yet divested
Soudronic – Automotive Division	VTC	Capvis	Not yet divested	Not yet divested
Sport Group/Polytan	Industri Kapital	ECM	Not yet divested	Not yet divested
Stadler Rail	Capvis	Family	Not yet divested	Not yet divested
Stahlhammer Bommern Gebr. Schneider	Brandis Beteiligungs GmbH	Private investors	Not yet divested	Not yet divested
Stankiewicz	Gilde	Continental AG	2009	Insolvency
Stark-Verlag	SG Capital	Family	Not yet divested	Not yet divested
Steco International	capiton	ABN/DDN	2008	IFCO
Striko Westofen	BPE Private Equity	DBAG/Hochtemperatur Engineering GmbH	Not yet divested	Not yet divested
Takraf GmbH	VTC Industrieholding	MAN Group	2007	Techint
Tarkett	KKR	Sommer-Allibert	Not yet divested	Not yet divested
Teufel	Riverside	Family	2010	HgCapital
Textile Processing Chemicals (TPC)	Egeria	Lanxess	Not yet divested	Not yet divested
Time Partner Gruppe	Investcorp	Auctus	Not yet divested	Not yet divested
TITAL – Titan-Aluminium-Feinguß GmbH	DZ Equity Partner	Heraeus	Not yet divested	Not yet divested
Tractabel Gas Engineering	Glenalta Capital	Suez	Not yet divested	Not yet divested
Tuja	Barclays Private Equity	Odewald	2007	Adecco
Uster	Alpha	Capvis/Quadriga	Not yet divested	Not yet divested

Table 15.4 Private Equity Transactions in 2006, M–Z – *continued*

2006, M–Z

Company	Buyer	Seller	Exit year	Sold to
Varta Microbatteries	Global Equity Partners	Varta AG	2007	Montana Tech Components AG
Vestolit	Strategic Value Partners	Candover	Not yet divested	Not yet divested
Vital Fettrecycling/Petrotec	Warburg Pincus	Previous investors	Not yet divested	Not yet divested
Vits-Gruppe	Granville Baird	WD Beteiligungs GmbH	Not yet divested	Not yet divested
VTN Härterei	BPE Private Equity	CVC/Elster Group	Not yet divested	Not yet divested
Walter Services	Gilde	Beisheim family	2008	Odewald
weka Holzbau	BPE Private Equity	Hans Einhell AG	Not yet divested	Not yet divested
Wessel Werk Gruppe	DZ Equity Partners	Barclays	Not yet divested	Not yet divested
Westfalia	Odewald/WestLB	Granville Baird	Not yet divested	Not yet divested
Wittronic (Vogt Electronic Witten)	Adcuram Industries	Insolvency	Not yet divested	Not yet divested
Wittur AG	CSFB/Goldman/Cerberus	Family	Not yet divested	Not yet divested
WKA	Nord Holding	Family	Not yet divested	Not yet divested
WMF AG	Capvis	Public to private	Not yet divested	Not yet divested
Wohnprofil AG	Paragon	Afinum	Not yet divested	Not yet divested
Z&J Technologies	Equita	DBAG/Hochtemperatur Engineering GmbH	2008	J. Hirsch
Zapf GmbH	Les Nouveaux Constructeurs SA/Goldman Sachs/ Deutsch	DBAG	Not yet divested	Not yet divested
ZPF therm Maschinenbau	Auctus	Family	2008	DZ Equity Partner

Source: Authors' compilation

Table 15.5 Private Equity Transactions in 2007, A–L

2007, A–L

Company	Buyer	Seller	Exit year	Sold to
SaSec	ING Parcom PE	Milestone Capital (E.A.C.)	Not yet divested	Not yet divested
Abieta	Auctus	Clariant/Hercules	Not yet divested	Not yet divested
Acomon	Auctus	Chemtura	Not yet divested	Not yet divested
Actebis Gruppe	Arques	Otto Gruppe	Not yet divested	Not yet divested
Almatis	Dubai International Capital	Rhone Capital	Not yet divested	Not yet divested
Alukon	Halder	Axa Private Equity	Not yet divested	Not yet divested
ALVO	Granville Baird	Family	Not yet divested	Not yet divested
Amoena Medizin-Orthopädie	Granville Baird	Coloplast	Not yet divested	Not yet divested
Apcoa	Eurazeo	Investcorp	Not yet divested	Not yet divested
Arwe	Triginta Capital	Afinum	Not yet divested	Not yet divested
AS Electronics	Auctus	Family	Not yet divested	Not yet divested
B2B Construction	GMT Communications Partners/DOCUgroup	Springer	Not yet divested	Not yet divested
Barat Ceramics	Element Six	Equita	Not yet divested	Not yet divested
Battenfeld Extrusion	Triton	SMS	Not yet divested	Not yet divested
Bavaria Yachtbau	Bain Capital	Family	2009	Insolvency
BEA Electrics Group	Arques	Röchling Group	2009	New Investors
Bettmer GmbH	Triginta Capital (Avida)	Afinum	Not yet divested	Not yet divested
Brinkhof	Findos	Family	Not yet divested	Not yet divested
Casa Reha	HgCapital	Advent	Not yet divested	Not yet divested
CBR	EQT	Cinven/Apax	Not yet divested	Not yet divested
CCR Logistics	Monitor Clipper Partners	Family	Not yet divested	Not yet divested
CleanCar AG	DZ Equity Partner	Family	Not yet divested	Not yet divested
Condat	Millhouse	Family	Not yet divested	Not yet divested
Coperion	DBAG	Lyceum (West PE)	Not yet divested	Not yet divested

Table 15.5 Private Equity Transactions in 2007, A–L – *continued*

2007, A–L

Company	Buyer	Seller	Exit year	Sold to
Corden Pharma GmbH	International Chemical Investors GmbH	Astra Zeneca	Not yet divested	Not yet divested
CS Consulting AG	LPR Capital	Family	Not yet divested	Not yet divested
D&B Audiotechnik	Afinum	Private Investors/Management	Not yet divested	Not yet divested
Datacolor Dialog-Medien GmbH	Nord Holding	Family	Not yet divested	Not yet divested
De Sede	Capvis	Private investors	Not yet divested	Not yet divested
Delmod Intern. Bekleidungsi	CFC Industrie	Family	Not yet divested	Not yet divested
Deutsche Essent	Arclight Capital Partners	Family	Not yet divested	Not yet divested
Deutsche Interhotels	Blackstone	Interhotel-Gruppe	Not yet divested	Not yet divested
Deutz Power Systems (MWM)	3i	Deutz AG	Not yet divested	Not yet divested
DocMorris.com	Celesio	3i/HgCapital/Neuhaus Partners	Not yet divested	Not yet divested
Dragenopharm (later Aenova)	Bridgepoint	Adreas Greither	Not yet divested	Not yet divested
Drescher GmbH	Nord Holding	Family	Not yet divested	Not yet divested
Dress-for-Less	Palamon Capital	Family	Not yet divested	Not yet divested
Dywidag-Systems International	CVC	Industri Kapital	Not yet divested	Not yet divested
Eckes & Stock GmbH	Oaktree	Eckes AG	Not yet divested	Not yet divested
Einhorn Mode Manufaktur	Aurelius	Family	Not yet divested	Not yet divested
eismann	Intermediate Capital	ECM	Not yet divested	Not yet divested
Elcon	CFC Industrie	Family	Not yet divested	Not yet divested
EM Test	Riverside	Family	Not yet divested	Not yet divested
Entitec	Auctus	Family	Not yet divested	Not yet divested
Erichsen	BPE Private Equity	Family	Not yet divested	Not yet divested
Eschenbach Optik	Barclays Private Equity	Hannover Finanz	Not yet divested	Not yet divested
Essmann	Quadriga	Taros Capital/3i	Not yet divested	Not yet divested
Euro-Druckservice	3i	Verlagsgruppe Passau	Not yet divested	Not yet divested
Eurojobs Personaldienstl.	Hypo Equity	Family	Not yet divested	Not yet divested

Table 15.5 Private Equity Transactions in 2007, A–L – *continued*

2007, A–L

Company	Buyer	Seller	Exit year	Sold to
European Oxo	Advent	Celanese	Not yet divested	Not yet divested
Eurostyle	Arques	Insolvency	Not yet divested	Not yet divested
Fläkt Woods Group	Sagard PE/Barclays/ICG	Compass Partners	Not yet divested	Not yet divested
Flex Elektrowerkzeuge GmbH	Axa Private Equity	GSO Capital Partners	Not yet divested	Not yet divested
FutureLab	Family	UIAG	Not yet divested	Not yet divested
GEA-Pharmaceuticals	Auctus/Pharmazell	Novartis	Not yet divested	Not yet divested
Geka Brush	Halder	Equita	Not yet divested	Not yet divested
GHD Gesundheits GmbH	Barclays Private Equity	Family	Not yet divested	Not yet divested
Gienandt-Eisenberg	Cognetas	Fink Holding	Not yet divested	Not yet divested
Greisinger Electronic	BPE Private Equity	Family	Not yet divested	Not yet divested
Guillod Gunther	Providente (Natixis PE)	Léman Capital	Not yet divested	Not yet divested
H.C. Stark	Advent/Carlyle	Bayer	Not yet divested	Not yet divested
Heim und Haus	DBAG	Management/Max von Drechsel	Not yet divested	Not yet divested
Hennecke	Adcuram	Bayer	Not yet divested	Not yet divested
Heywinkel Holding GmbH	Nord Holding	Karmann	Not yet divested	Not yet divested
Hofmann Menü	Gilde	HgCapital	Not yet divested	Not yet divested
Holmer Maschinenbau	Triginta Capital	Afinum	Not yet divested	Not yet divested
Homann Feinkost	IFR	Henderson	Not yet divested	Not yet divested
Hörmannsdorfer Fassaden GmbH	BLB PE	BdW	Not yet divested	Not yet divested
HT Troplast (Profine)	Arcapita	Carlyle/Advent	Not yet divested	Not yet divested
Hugo Boss	Permira	Public to private	Not yet divested	Not yet divested
IN tIME Direkt-Kuriere Transport	ECM	Family	Not yet divested	Not yet divested
Ipsen	Quadriga	CVC/Elster	Not yet divested	Not yet divested
ista (Viterra Energy)	Charterhouse	CVC	Not yet divested	Not yet divested
Jobs.CH	Tiger Global	Family	Not yet divested	Not yet divested
Julius Heywinkel	Nord Holding	Karmann	Not yet divested	Not yet divested

Table 15.5 Private Equity Transactions in 2007, A–L – *continued*

2007, A–L

Company	Buyer	Seller	Exit year	Sold to
Kautex Maschinenbau	Steadfast Capital	Adcuram	Not yet divested	Not yet divested
Klöckner Pentaplast	Blackstone	Cinven	Not yet divested	Not yet divested
KMS-Gruppe	DIH Equity	Hauck & Aufhäuser	Not yet divested	Not yet divested
Lafarge Roofing	PAI	Lafarge	Not yet divested	Not yet divested
Lahmeyer International	capiton	SAG Group	Not yet divested	Not yet divested
LBW Refractories	Rhone Capital	Family	2008	Magnesita Refratarios
Leico Holding (Leifeld)	Gruppe Georg Kofler	Hypovereinsbank	Not yet divested	Not yet divested
Leobensdorfer (LMF)	Equita	Nord Holding/Invest Equity	Not yet divested	Not yet divested
Lonstroff Holding	BV Group	3i	Not yet divested	Not yet divested
LTS Lohmann Therapie-Systeme AG	DH-Capital/OH Beteiligungen	Lohmann GmbH & Co. KG	Not yet divested	Not yet divested

Source: Authors' compilation

Table 15.6 Private Equity Transactions in 2007, M–Z

2007, M–Z

Company	Buyer	Seller	Exit year	Sold to
Mateco	Odewald	Family	Not yet divested	Not yet divested
Mauser	Dubai International Capital	One Equity Partners	Not yet divested	Not yet divested
MCE	DBAG	Andlinger & Company	Not yet divested	Not yet divested
Metallum	Alpha	Industry roll-up	Not yet divested	Not yet divested
Mondo	HgCapital	Swiss conglomerate	Not yet divested	Not yet divested
Murnauer Markenvertrieb	Argandis	Family	Not yet divested	Not yet divested
nora	capiton/L-EA Private Equity	Freudenberg	Not yet divested	Not yet divested
NT plus AG	Arques Industries	United Internet AG/ Neue Median Ulm Hold.	Not yet divested	Not yet divested
Ondeo Industrial Solutions GmbH (OIS GmbH)	L-EA	Ondeo France/Suez-Gruppe	Not yet divested	Not yet divested
Otto Sauer Achsenfabrik	Pamplona	DBAG	2007	IPO
Oxea (Oxo)	Advent	Cellanese/Degussa	Not yet divested	Not yet divested
Oxiris	Arques	Degussa	2008	Rasching Group
Oystar	Odewald	IWKA	Not yet divested	Not yet divested
Pharmazell	EQT	Growth capital	Not yet divested	Not yet divested
Pinova	Afinum	Family	Not yet divested	Not yet divested
Pohland Herrenkleidung	Aurelius	Douglas Holding AG	Not yet divested	Not yet divested
PPC Insulators	Seves Spa (Vestar Capital/ Ergon Capital)	Riverside	Not yet divested	Not yet divested
Premiumcommunications (Cyberline)	Barclays Private Equity	Family	Not yet divested	Not yet divested
Procon Holding	Auctus	Heberger Bau AG	Not yet divested	Not yet divested
ProSiebenSat1	KKK/Permira	Public/Haim Saban	Not yet divested	Not yet divested
Prüm-Garant	Looser Holding	Halder	Not yet divested	Not yet divested
Quelle S.A.S.	Aurelius	Karstadt Quelle	Not yet divested	Not yet divested

Table 15.6 Private Equity Transactions in 2007, M–Z – *continued*

2007, M–Z

Company	Buyer	Seller	Exit year	Sold to
Qvesis/Siemens Building Electronic	HSH N Kapital	Siemens	Not yet divested	Not yet divested
R & M Ship Tec GmbH	Nord Holding	Bilfinger Berger Industrial Services AG	Not yet divested	Not yet divested
Rademacher	Nord Holding	Arcadia	Not yet divested	Not yet divested
Reimelt-Henschel	MBB	Kero Private Equity	2009	Zeppelin
Revotar	Millhouse/bmp/Deutsche Life Science	Management	Not yet divested	Not yet divested
Rhiag Group	Alpha	CVC	Not yet divested	Not yet divested
Richard Schöps AG	Arcques Austria	PHI Private Holdings of Investments Lux.	2008	All Wazzan
Rixius AG	BWK GmbH	Family	Not yet divested	Not yet divested
Röder Zeitsysteme	Zurmont Madison	Public to private/Family	Not yet divested	Not yet divested
Rohé Holding	Arques Austria	Italian group of investors	2009	ValueNet Capital Partners
Roventa-Henex	Argantis	Management	Not yet divested	Not yet divested
Saalfrank Qualitäts-Werbeartikel GmbH	Triginta Capital	KarstadtQuelle Konzem	Not yet divested	Not yet divested
SaarGummi	Odewald	Orlando	Not yet divested	Not yet divested
SAG Austria Group	Arques Austria	SAG Group	Not yet divested	Not yet divested
SAG KT	Aurelius	SAG Group	Not yet divested	Not yet divested
Salto Paper	IBET Industriebeteiligungen	Arques	Not yet divested	Not yet divested
Scandlines	ACP/3i	German/Danish Governments	Not yet divested	Not yet divested
Schabmüller Gruppe	Aurelius	Sauer-Danfoss Holding	Not yet divested	Not yet divested
Schaetti AG	Triginta Capital	Afinum	Not yet divested	Not yet divested
Schenck Process	Industri Kapital	HgCapital	Not yet divested	Not yet divested
Schlatter Holding AG	Metall ZUG/HUWA	Zurmont Finanz AG	Not yet divested	Not yet divested

Table 15.6 Private Equity Transactions in 2007, M–Z – *continued*

2007, M–Z

Company	Buyer	Seller	Exit year	Sold to
Schleicher Electronic GmbH & Co. KG	Aurelius	Wieland Holding	Not yet divested	Not yet divested
Schwinn	Finatem	Insolvency	Not yet divested	Not yet divested
Selecta	Allianz Capital Ptrs.	Compass Group	Not yet divested	Not yet divested
SF-Chem	CABB GmbH/Axa Private Equity	Capvis	Not yet divested	Not yet divested
Siemens Building Technology	HSH N Kapital	Siemens	Not yet divested	Not yet divested
SIR Industrieservice	PPM	ThyssenKrupp Industrieservice	Not yet divested	Not yet divested
Siteco	Barclays Private Equity	CCMP (JP Morgan)	Not yet divested	Not yet divested
SLV	HgCapital	Family	Not yet divested	Not yet divested
SM Electronic	Arques	Thomson	Not yet divested	Not yet divested
Sodawerk Staßfurt	ECM	Ciech SA	2007	Ciech SA
Stromag	Equita	Family	Not yet divested	Not yet divested
Süddekor/2D Holding	Quadriga	Odewald/Bain Capital	Not yet divested	Not yet divested
SycoTec	MBG/BGM	Kaltenbach & Voigt GmbH & Co KG	Not yet divested	Not yet divested
Takko	Advent	Permira	Not yet divested	Not yet divested
Tank & Rast	RREEF Infrastructure	Terra Firma	Not yet divested	Not yet divested
Techem	Macquarie/BC Partners	Public to private	Not yet divested	Not yet divested
Tectum	Quadriga	Family	Not yet divested	Not yet divested
Telerob	Equitrust	Rheinmetall	Not yet divested	Not yet divested
Tempton Group	Odewald	Family	Not yet divested	Not yet divested
time matters	Buchanan	Lufthansa Cargo	Not yet divested	Not yet divested
Tiroler Röhren-und Metallwerke AG	Global Equity Partners/UIAG	BFM-Gruppe	Not yet divested	Not yet divested
titus AG	Investor Group	ECM	Not yet divested	Not yet divested

Table 15.6 Private Equity Transactions in 2007, M–Z – *continued*

2007, M–Z

Company	Buyer	Seller	Exit year	Sold to
Tondeo	Findos	Procter & Gamble	Not yet divested	Not yet divested
Transnorm	Equita	Nord Holding	Not yet divested	Not yet divested
Umfotec	Granville Baird	Family	Not yet divested	Not yet divested
UTT	DZ Equity Partner	BPE Private Equity	Not yet divested	Not yet divested
van Netten	Arques	Zuckerfabrik Jülich AG	Not yet divested	Not yet divested
Vautid Verschleißtechnik	DZ Equity Partner	Family	Not yet divested	Not yet divested
VfW	Monitor Clipper Partners	Deutsche Post World Net	Not yet divested	Not yet divested
VWR	Madison Dearborn Partners	Clayton Dubilier & Rice	Not yet divested	Not yet divested
Wanfried Druck Kalden GmbH	Arques	ARQUANA	Not yet divested	Not yet divested
Westfalia Van Conversion	Aurelius	Daimler	Not yet divested	Not yet divested
Woco Michelin AVS (Anvis Group)	Arques	Woco/Michelin	Not yet divested	Not yet divested
Zarges Tubesca	DZ PE/Ganville Baird	Taros Capital	Not yet divested	Not yet divested
Zeeb & Hornung GmbH & Co/ Einhorn	Aurelius	Family	Not yet divested	Not yet divested

Source: Authors' compilation

16
The Ninth Phase: The Fall

There was a feeling of inevitability around the financial crisis which started in the summer of 2007. The sceptics who felt that the collapse would happen sooner rather than later were proven correct on the timing, but wrong on the cause. It was a US house price bust that started the process, not a global recession. The sudden steep fall in US house prices caused immediate problems for mortgages granted to people who could scarcely afford them. These "sub-prime" mortgages had been securitised in the form of collateralised debt obligations (CDOs) and sold around the world. The fall in value of these CDOs burdened the balance sheets of financial institutions which had acquired them. It quickly became apparent that almost every bank in the world was affected, and as a consequence, the credit crunch which ensued was a global one. The credit crunch quickly spilled over into the syndicated debt market, and wiped away the large-cap market for deals, and carried with it much banking enthusiasm for financing mid-cap deals as well. Many people in banks and PE houses were left with the feeling that there was nothing much left useful to do.

The global mega-deal buyout market collapsed overnight. The spill-over to Germany was instantaneous. September 2007 saw an almost complete standstill in the German market, and first the large-cap, and then the large mid-cap markets to all intents and purposes disappeared. Debt in the large PE deals of 2006 and 2007 began to drop in value. This tempted a number of hedge-funds to begin buying the debt, but then as some of the larger companies began to underperform against plan, as with the case of ATU, Monier (Lafarge Roofing), and Klöckner Pentaplast, the hedge-funds, which had leveraged their investments in the debt, began to face margin-calls, and were forced to off-load their debt, plunging valuations ever deeper. By the start of 2008, debt in large PE transactions was trading at 60 cents in the Euro. Against this backdrop, few banks were prepared to lend fresh money to PE houses for new transactions.

To some degree, however, the period September–December 2007 marked a phony recession for many participants in the M&A market. For most of them, 2007 had been a record year, and their bonuses were already guaranteed at high levels. Some deal-makers even hoped that the troubles of the sub-prime market would disappear quickly. But on return from the Christmas break in January 2008 it became clear that the market was in a much worse state than even the most pessimistic had feared. The syndicated loans market had died, and the amounts available on a non-syndicated basis were rapidly shrinking.

Any hopes that some corners of the private equity world might escape the impact of the credit crunch and its aftermath collapsed in September 2008 with the bankruptcy of Lehman Brothers. The shock to the financial system was palpable, not dissimilar in its immediate aftermath to the terrorist attacks on the Twin Towers in September 2001. The scale of the collapse in the financial world was beyond anything that anyone working within the private equity community had either experienced, or imagined.

Many strategy consultants serving the private equity market turned their attention towards analysing the historical impact on various industries of recessions. There were few surprises that automotive, building materials, and outsourced services were the most cyclical industries. What seemed more surprising in hindsight was that so many deals had been closed, with such high leverage, in these areas by private equity houses. Part of the challenge appeared to be that many people had become convinced that recessions were, over time, becoming shorter and shallower. This meant that cyclical businesses were coming to be regarded as less risky, and therefore more leverageable. Leverage reached high levels also for companies with very high levels of fixed costs (which would be vulnerable to a downturn). The WACCs of these companies dropped lower, and their valuations went through the roof.

Once the recession became visible, private equity professionals redid the maths on the risks impacting recession-sensitive, high fixed cost industries, and it quickly became clear that a number of buyouts were hopelessly overleveraged, and wouldn't survive the recession. The bond market for large, heavily leveraged deals, went into free fall. On paper, the equity in such deals became worthless even before the covenants were breached. Analyses revealed that it was not only the absolute exposure to cyclical businesses which could provoke a covenant breach on a PE portfolio

Table 16.1 Private Equity Transactions in 2008, A–L

2008, A–L

Company	Buyer	Seller	Exit year	Sold to
Alloheim Seniorenresidenz	Star Capital Partners	Family	Not yet divested	Not yet divested
Aqua Vital Quell- und Mineralwasser	Buchanan	Family	Not yet divested	Not yet divested
B. Teupen Maschinenbau	Nord Holding	Private investors	Not yet divested	Not yet divested
Bader	EquiVest	Deutsche Zentral	Not yet divested	Not yet divested
Bally	S-UBG AG/Labelux	Texas Pacific Group	Not yet divested	Not yet divested
Bartec	Capvis	Allianz Capital Partners	Not yet divested	Not yet divested
Berentzen	Aurelius	Family	Not yet divested	Not yet divested
Bernd Steudle	L-EA/S-Kap	Finatem/Invest Equity	Not yet divested	Not yet divested
Bigpoint	GMT Communications Partners	Family	Not yet divested	Not yet divested
Blaupunkt	Aurelius	Bosch	Not yet divested	Not yet divested
Breitenfeld	Morgan Stanley	DZ Equity Partner	Not yet divested	Not yet divested
Carl Froh GmbH	Arques	Ruukki	Not yet divested	Not yet divested
CaseTech	Adcuram	Dow Chemicals	Not yet divested	Not yet divested
Casino Royal	Waterland	Family	Not yet divested	Not yet divested
Chemson Polymer Additive	Buy-Out Central Europe/ Global/UIAG	BVP Europe/Invest Equity/ Leman Cap	Not yet divested	Not yet divested
Cinterion Wireless Modules	Granville Baird/EQT	Siemens	Not yet divested	Not yet divested
Computerlinks	Barclays	Public to private	Not yet divested	Not yet divested
Conectis Communications (SBC)	Aurelius	Sunrise	Not yet divested	Not yet divested
D+S Europe AG Retail	Apax	Public to private	Not yet divested	Not yet divested
DBW Group	Süd Kapital	Family	Not yet divested	Not yet divested
DC Druckchemie	3i	SG Capital/Quartus	Not yet divested	Not yet divested
Demag Plastic Machinery	Sumitomo	Madison Capital Partners	Not yet divested	Not yet divested
Dieter Braun	Auctus	Family	Not yet divested	Not yet divested
Erwin Behr	Equivest/Sellner	Insolvency procedure	Not yet divested	Not yet divested
Evonik Industries	CVC	RAG Foundation	Not yet divested	Not yet divested

Table 16.1 Private Equity Transactions in 2008, A–L – *continued*

2008, A–L

Company	Buyer	Seller	Exit year	Sold to
Flabeg	Industri Kapital	EquiVest	Not yet divested	Not yet divested
Flensburger Schiffsbau	Orlando	Egon Oldendorff	Not yet divested	Not yet divested
Frostkrone Engel-Food Tiefkühlkost	Argantis	Family	Not yet divested	Not yet divested
Fruitwork	capiton	Family	Not yet divested	Not yet divested
GANYMED Pharmaceuticals AG	ATS Group	Ingro Finanz/KfW/LBBW/ Nextech Ven	Not yet divested	Not yet divested
gardeur	HSH	Family	Not yet divested	Not yet divested
Geti Wilba	Hannover Finanz	Nestle	Not yet divested	Not yet divested
Giesserei Industrie Holding Isselburg	Hannover Finanz	Family	Not yet divested	Not yet divested
Gigaset Communications (Siemens)	Arques	Siemens	Not yet divested	Not yet divested
Gimborn GmbH	Penta Investments	capiton	Not yet divested	Not yet divested
GolfRange	Waterland	Family	Not yet divested	Not yet divested
H. Schlieckmann	Hannover Finanz	Family	Not yet divested	Not yet divested
Herberg Group	Tempton/Odewald	Family	Not yet divested	Not yet divested
Hobatex	Auctus	Family	Not yet divested	Not yet divested
Holz-Her Reich Spezialmaschinen	Hannover Finanz	Family	Not yet divested	Not yet divested
Honsberg & Co KG	BPE Private Equity/Greisinger	Family	Not yet divested	Not yet divested
Hottinger Maschinenbau	Turnaround Finance Beratungs	Arques	Not yet divested	Not yet divested
Hubert Schlieckmann	Hannover Finanz	Family	Not yet divested	Not yet divested
Hünert Tanktechnik	Rohé/Arques	Family	Not yet divested	Not yet divested
ICTS Holding	DBAG	Fraport	Not yet divested	Not yet divested
IGEL Technology GmbH	Nord Holding	Family	Not yet divested	Not yet divested
IKB	Lone Start	KfW Bank	Not yet divested	Not yet divested
iloxx	Parcom Deutsche PE	Private investors	Not yet divested	Not yet divested
Industrie Holding Isselburg	Hannover Finanz	Family	Not yet divested	Not yet divested
Industriehansa	Findos	Riverside	Not yet divested	Not yet divested
ISE Group	Nordwind Capital	Polytec Holding	Not yet divested	Not yet divested

Table 16.1 Private Equity Transactions in 2008, A–L – *continued*

2008, A–L

Company	Buyer	Seller	Exit year	Sold to
IsselburgGuß und Bearbeitung GmbH	Hannover Finanz	Founders	Not yet divested	Not yet divested
Jahnel-Kestermann Getriebewerk	PSM Inc.	Arques	Not yet divested	Not yet divested
Jil Sander	Onward Holdings	Change Capital Partners	Not yet divested	Not yet divested
Jost Werke	Cinven	Silverfleet	Not yet divested	Not yet divested
Kadi AG	ECM	Family	Not yet divested	Not yet divested
Kägi Söhne AG	Argos Soditic	Valora	Not yet divested	Not yet divested
Karl Eugen Fischer	Equita	Halder	Not yet divested	Not yet divested
Klingel	Odewald	Family	Not yet divested	Not yet divested
Koenig Verbindungstechnik	Capvis/EQT	Klöckner & Co/Debrunner Koenig Holding	Not yet divested	Not yet divested
Kolbe-Coloco	Equita	Invest Equity	Not yet divested	Not yet divested
Konrad Hornschuch	Barclays Private Equity	DZ Equity Partner/ L-EA Priv. Equity	Not yet divested	Not yet divested
KUNDO SystemTechnik GmbH	QVEDIS GmbH/HSH Private Equity	Family	Not yet divested	Not yet divested
Lejaby	Quadriga/21 Centrale Partners	Warnaco/Calvin Klein	Not yet divested	Not yet divested
Löwenplay	Axa PE	Waterland	Not yet divested	Not yet divested

Source: Authors' compilation

Table 16.2 Private Equity Transactions in 2008, M–Z

2008, M–Z

Company	Buyer	Seller	Exit year	Sold to
Maillefer	Alpha	Argos Soditic	Not yet divested	Not yet divested
Martems Elektronik	BPE Private Equity/Greisinger	Family	Not yet divested	Not yet divested
Maschinenfabrik Spaichingen	GCI Management/ACP	Family	Not yet divested	Not yet divested
Meier Vakuumtechnik	Granville Baird	Meier-Gruppe	Not yet divested	Not yet divested
Metallwarenfabrik Gemmingen	Paragon	Family	Not yet divested	Not yet divested
Mode & Preis Versandhandels GmbH	Aurelius	Arcandor/Primondo GmbH	Not yet divested	Not yet divested
Neckermann.de	Sun Capital Partners	Arcandor	Not yet divested	Not yet divested
Nord Süd Spedition	BIP	Argantis	Not yet divested	Not yet divested
Novem	Barclays Private Equity	NIB Capital (Alpinvest)/3i	Not yet divested	Not yet divested
novero GmbH (Nokia Automotive)	Equity Partners	Nokia	Not yet divested	Not yet divested
OLIGO Lichttechnik	LRP Capital	Family	Not yet divested	Not yet divested
Phoenix Dichtungstechnik	GermanCapital GmbH/ Morgan Stanley	ContiTech AG	Not yet divested	Not yet divested
Powerlines	Gilde	Invest Equity	Not yet divested	Not yet divested
Punker	Quadriga	Family	Not yet divested	Not yet divested
Quip	Luxempart	Family	Not yet divested	Not yet divested
REGE Motorenteile	EquiVest	Schaeffler KG	Not yet divested	Not yet divested
Rieter Automatik	CGS Management	Rieter	Not yet divested	Not yet divested
Robert Brill	Auctus	Family	Not yet divested	Not yet divested
Rosner GmbH	CFC Industrie	Link Theory Holdings Co. Ltd., Tokyo	Not yet divested	Not yet divested
RSA Entgrat- u. Trenn-Systeme	BLB Private Equity	Family	Not yet divested	Not yet divested
RSD	Invision Private Equity	Family	Not yet divested	Not yet divested
RTL Shop	Aurelius	RTL Group	Not yet divested	Not yet divested
SAG GmbH	EQT	Advent	Not yet divested	Not yet divested

Table 16.2 Private Equity Transactions in 2008, M–Z – *continued*

2008, M–Z

Company	Buyer	Seller	Exit year	Sold to
Sangro Medical	GesundHeits GmbH Deutschland	Family	Not yet divested	Not yet divested
Sausalitos Holding	EQT	Family	Not yet divested	Not yet divested
SAV Group	Indaver NV/NIBC Infrastructure	Arcadia/E. ON Kraftwerke GmbH	Not yet divested	Not yet divested
Schabmüller	Aurelius	Sauer Danfoss Group	Not yet divested	Not yet divested
Schild AG	Barclays Private Equity	Schild Holding AG	Not yet divested	Not yet divested
Schoeller Arca Systems	One Equity Partners	Stirling Square Capital Partners	Not yet divested	Not yet divested
Schoeller-Electronics GmbH	Nord Holding	Ruwell-Gruppe	Not yet divested	Not yet divested
Schöttli AG	CGS Management	Family	Not yet divested	Not yet divested
Siemens Enterprise Comm.	The Gores Group	Siemens	Not yet divested	Not yet divested
Spectral Audio Möbel	Hannover Finanz	Family	Not yet divested	Not yet divested
SPX Air Filtration	Riverside	SPX Corporation	Not yet divested	Not yet divested
SSB Group	Parcom Deutsche PE	Granville Baird	Not yet divested	Not yet divested
SSP Technology	Ventizz	Plambeck Neue Energien AG	Not yet divested	Not yet divested
Stabilus	Paine & Partner	Montagu	2010	Triton
Stanniolfabrik Eppstein	Cornerstone/Columbus	JL Goslar Gruppe	Not yet divested	Not yet divested
Starkstrom Gerätebau	BC Partners	HCP Capital Group GmbH	Not yet divested	Not yet divested
Sterntaler Holding	Findos	Family	Not yet divested	Not yet divested
Strauss Innovation	EQT	Geringhoff family and Alldata GmbH	Not yet divested	Not yet divested
svt	capiton/CFH GmbH	Gothaer	Not yet divested	Not yet divested
Tenbrink	Afinum	Family	Not yet divested	Not yet divested
Teupen	Nord Holding	Family	Not yet divested	Not yet divested
TKW GmbH	DZ Equity/addfinity	Family	Not yet divested	Not yet divested
Ultimaco Safeware	Investcorp	Public to private	Not yet divested	Not yet divested
VAG Armaturen	Halder	Equita	Not yet divested	Not yet divested
Veritas SG Investment Trust GmbH	Augur Capital	Boursorama SA (SocGen)	Not yet divested	Not yet divested

Table 16.2 Private Equity Transactions in 2008, M–Z – *continued*

2008, M–Z

Company	Buyer	Seller	Exit year	Sold to
W.I.S.	Argantis	Family	Not yet divested	Not yet divested
Walter Services	Odewald/capiton	Gilde	Not yet divested	Not yet divested
Wemhöner System Techn.	FCP	Insolvency procedure	Not yet divested	Not yet divested
Wichard Groupe	Becap	Halder	Not yet divested	Not yet divested
Windrose Fernreisen Touristik	Waterland	Family	Not yet divested	Not yet divested
Xella	PAI/GS Capital Ptrs.	Haniel Group	Not yet divested	Not yet divested
Z&J Technologies	J. Hirsch	Equita	Not yet divested	Not yet divested
Ziemann Sicherheit	Hannover Finanz	Family	Not yet divested	Not yet divested
ZPF therm Maschinenbau	DZ Equity Partner	Auctus	Not yet divested	Not yet divested
ZytoService	capiton	Family	Not yet divested	Not yet divested

Source: Authors' compilation

company, but also the level of leverage applied to the deal. The most fragile deals were clearly those closed in the heady high-leverage days of 2007 and early 2008, and the larger the deal, almost the larger the leverage. Even businesses with little exposure to the recession could breach covenants if they were recent enough and big enough.

Despite the troubles in the larger deal segments, as the months passed in 2008, many in the smaller-cap segments began to think that the troubles in the financial services market might pass them by. Valuations for these deals remained steady, and far from shrinking, there were signs that the market for small deals might actually be growing. As a consequence, while the number of deals closed during 2009 was similar to that for 2003, the average value of each of those deals was much lower. Essentially, raising senior debt of more than €100 million for an LBO deal had become almost impossible.

The experience of the private equity houses depended heavily upon the extent to which they had acquired companies in cyclical industries with high leverage at the peak of the market.

Lehman Brothers

In November 2007, Wolf Wolfsteiner left 3i to join Lehman Brothers Merchant Banking. His departure had been a difficult one, for having been approached by Lehman to join them, he discovered that one of his main competitors on the auction for U.N Ro-Ro, a Turkish ferry service he was working on, was Lehman. Wolfsteiner had to bow out of it in the week before final bids in order not to create a potential conflict of interest.

Hardly had he joined, than Wolfsteiner began to realise that all was far from well:

> From May 2008, it was getting weird, because Lehman wouldn't get out of the headlines. While it was obvious we were in a financial crisis, it hadn't really sunk in how it affected us. Every external meeting I went to began with a ten minute discussion of Lehman's position. Nobody at the time suggested we would go bankrupt: it was always believed we would be taken over. Meanwhile, life went on, and we invested in Istanbul Doors, a deal in Turkey, and Mediclinic, a deal in South Africa and Switzerland, the latter including a business acquired from BC Partners. I also spent time looking at a transaction in Poland.[1]

As the months progressed and September approached, like many others at Lehman, Wolfsteiner didn't expect the worst:

> It was a most spectacular weekend, starting on Friday, 12th September. We went into the weekend knowing that something was going to happen. There were two options: either we would end up being owned by Bank of America; or we'd be bought by Barclays. These outcomes didn't concern us too much within the private equity group, because asset management, of which we were a part, sat in a separate set of negotiations at the time. We were concerned, but not worried.

> Nothing happened at all on the Saturday. On Sunday morning, I received an email which told me that my carry points vested immediately. This was odd. Normally carry points vest over a certain period, and now I was being told that they had vested. It's yours; and can't be taken away from you. I will admit, this email set the alarm bells ringing. But at the same time, we hadn't got any news. Normally, as managing directors, we were part of a closer communication circle. Certainly you would be kept informed, and we were hearing nothing. Then on Sunday afternoon, which was the morning in New York, it was said that if a solution wasn't found by midnight, the company would file for insolvency. Even then I thought that this was just the Fed playing hardball. Why would anyone be so insane as to send a bank like Lehman into insolvency? Clearly they would have to save the bank. So I still didn't pay too much attention to the news.

> I went to bed in the evening. Then during the night, at three o'clock in the morning, one of my children made a noise. So I thought I would check my emails. There was a news line coming through under the title "The final hours of Lehman", so I put on the television, got my computer out. By this time, I was fully awake. Midnight in New York would be five o'clock in the morning in London. When the appointed hour arrived, the news said that Lehman had filed for insolvency.

> It was like someone had died, it was just surreal. It just couldn't happen. I thought I must be sleeping: it can't be. Then, very quickly, we got a barrage of internal emails, along the lines of "sorry to inform you". Our European head said that we should come to the office as usual, and that they were in negotiations with Vodafone to keep the Blackberrys on line at least one day. Amex immediately cancelled all

the corporate cards. All those who were away on business trips were stuck: their flight tickets were cancelled. I knew people who were sitting for days in a hotel in New York, not knowing whether their expenses would be refunded.

On Monday, at 8 o'clock, I went into the office. As I went up the escalator at Canary Wharf, I saw people I recognised carrying boxes coming my way out of the Lehman building. There were so many journalists, and so many camera teams. Police were keeping people to the other side of the road. As I walked towards the building, I had a microphone pushed into my face: "do you work for Lehman's?" Inside it was eerily calm, because nobody knew what was happening or why. We were instructed to do nothing until further notice. By midday the telephones started ringing. On the line were investors, advisors, and friends. That was it, and then we were in limbo for 3–4 weeks.

Merchant Banking, with $4.5 billion assets under management, was not that immediately important to the administrator. It was fairly stable, like a fly in the ointment. So to find someone in PwC who would be willing to listen, and had the competence and authority to decide something in our matter was quite a challenge. The problem was that we had capital calls coming in for several deals that we had signed. Istanbul Doors was one of them, and the single largest Limited Partner for the fund was Lehman, so if they defaulted, the deals, and potentially the entire fund, would crumble.[2]

Luckily for the Lehman Brother private equity team, help was found near at hand. South African entrepreneur, Johan Rupert, stepped in to replace the Lehman equity stake and funds, enabling the group to be relaunched as Trilantic Capital Partners in April 2009.

Quadriga

Even the team at Quadriga including many experienced veterans of the industry was surprised by the severity of the melt-down, and found itself confronted with the need to make some changes in approach, as Burkhard Bonsels explains:

Everyone had to be more involved, and dive deeper into the portfolio companies. We had to become a better counterpart to management, and the industrial approach was even more in demand. The quality demanded from private equity houses had very much increased, in terms of mode of cooperation and collaboration.[3]

The changes however, were not restricted to the private equity community. Hardest hit of all were the members of the banking community, as Bonsels comments:

> Suddenly there was over-capacity in the market, particularly in the banking community. During the days of 2006–2007, there were 40–50 players in the structured finance market, and by the end of 2009 this had fallen to 7–8 players. There was no secondary market anymore, and no syndication. Everything had to come out of prime engagements. Many of the financial players had been sold off or had given up the business.

> Those banks which remained were looking very carefully at the teams they served. Given the lack of syndication, on new deals we had a winner-take-all outcome, but the banks needed to be absolutely sure that the equity player they backed was the right one, and knew how to govern the company, and had solid processes which could deal both with good and bad times. The banks were now very much sticking to your reputation and references. In a recent project in late 2009, we stepped out of a process after initial due diligence, and the banks who were with us decided to step out too, rather than look for an alternative equity sponsor. That is a big change in behaviour. Banks and private equity houses have suddenly become a lot closer.[4]

Figure 16.1   Sources of Private Equity Transactions, 2001–2009

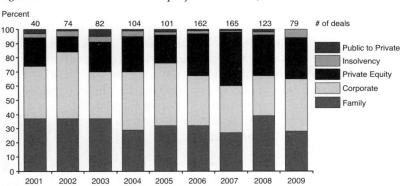

Source: Authors' compilation

HANNOVER Finanz

The team in Hanover, while not relaxed about the crisis, were never-theless calm and collected compared with some of their peers. During the boom, there was a feeling among the team that the prices were too high, and that some houses were not being sufficiently selective, as Andreas Schober comments:

> A lot of bad teams in the market were doing crummy deals, and we knew that the cheque would have to be paid for these sooner or later. Our big concern was that institutional investors would turn away from our industry.[5]

Given its focus on small- to mid-cap deals, HANNOVER Finanz saw little impact from the sub-prime credit crunch which gained traction from mid-2007. It wasn't until the Lehman Brothers collapse that the impact became tangible. Fortunately, the downsides were limited, as Schober explains:

> We never stopped investing, even during the boom. We couldn't escape the higher prices either, although we lost many deals. But we always tried to be conservative, and we nearly always put in 50% equity. The only big instance of us not doing that was with an Austrian company, where it was just too easy to get leverage, and we ended up putting in very little equity. It was operating in a cyclical business, and once the crisis came, revenues dropped by 55%, forcing it into bankruptcy. On the positive side, we didn't lose much because the equity proportion was so low.

Like all other firms, HANNOVER Finanz had to wrestle with the prob-lems of its portfolio companies, but fortunately for the team, only a minority of the deals were new investments through a combination of its long history in the market and its strategy of long-term invest-ments. In many cases much of the leverage had been provided by HANNOVER Finanz's own in-house mezzanine capital.

More of a surprise to the team was the extent to which deal flow dropped, as Schober later commented:

> After the Lehman Brothers collapse, deal flow fell away. That didn't really hurt us. But the big issue was that prices didn't come down during 2009–2010 like they did in 2002–2003. In 2002, the companies

had been very arrogant, and had overestimated their own value, so that when the crisis came, it hit their valuations. But this time round, external factors were at play. The fault lay with bad banks, and the whole world breaking down. So the vendors didn't want to sell their companies until the economy picked up, even if this did not happen until 2012 or 2013.[6]

Silverfleet Capital

In many respects, Silverfleet Capital was one of the luckier private equity houses in Germany during the fall of 2008–2009. The spin-off from the Prudential had occurred at a propitious moment. While many other private equity houses were wrestling with problems in their port-folios, Silverfleet in Germany had relatively little to look after (Orizon, a temporary staffing company, acquired in 2007, and M&W acquired in 2004). Guido May recalls the process of realising that all was not well in the marketplace:

> Back in the summer of 2007, no-one really realised that the sub-prime crisis would have a huge impact, and even in early 2008, while people thought something would come, they were thinking that it would be not so bad. We thought maybe we might have a GDP growth of only half a percent in Germany. But then in August, the Orizon management team called me at around the time they were preparing their budget, and the CEO told me that something serious was coming and they had to prepare for the downturn.[7]

Haing sold most of the rest of their portfolio,[8] and raised a new fund, the German team had time and money on their hands. In 2009, while the rest of the private equity industry in Germany was plunged into near paralysis, Silverfleet pursued the acquisition of Kalle from Montagu in a secondary transaction, as Guido May explains:

> Montagu started doing some market sounding on Kalle in September 2008, and we picked up on the opportunity mainly from market rumours and some calls. We also had an introduction to the man-agement, and we convinced them of our buy-and-build approach. We saw huge potential for them in the US and Asia. But the valu-ation was difficult, and the gap between Montagu and ourselves was substantial. Putting together the banking was difficult given the environment. Two of the banks who had supported the original

transaction rolled-over, but we had to do the full banking process before signing. The whole syndication process that you would normally do after closing was done before signing.[9]

In the event, rather than being viewed as the transaction which paved the way to an improvement in the market, many at the time came to see it as an example of how difficult it was to do even the simplest deal. Rumours in the market suggested that the deal had died a thousand deaths before finally closing, although in reality these were much exaggerated. The key difference was that a large chunk of the work which would typically have been performed after signing had to be completed before signing.

HgCapital

HgCapital also entered the recession in better shape than most. Having made a series of good exits with FTE, Hirschmann, Schenck Process, and Hofmann Menü, HgCapital was left with W.E.T., which was fairly illiquid, being a majority stake in a public company, and SLV, the lighting company, which turned out to be reasonably recession proof. In addition, Schleich and Mondo proved fairly recession resistant as well. The only investment with greater recession exposure was König Verbindungstechnik (KVT) which was made in September 2008. Martin Block explains:

> KVT was a very hot auction. Almost everyone was in there. It boiled down to Capvis and us. We had just lost the Bartec transaction to them, and when they came out on top with KVT as well, they asked us if we would be prepared to join them on the deal.[10]

The KVT deal was affected rapidly by macro economics, and the Capvis and HgCapital teams had to do some heavy-lifting to secure its financing.

Despite all of the challenges, HgCapital completed its move from Frankfurt to Munich during the period and continued to close deals, even during the crisis.

DBAG

DBAG was left with a significant portfolio of companies on its books by the time the crisis hit. Having acquired Preh in 2004, Lewa in 2005, Heim und Haus and Homag in 2006, Coperion in 2007, and ICTS in

2008, its portfolio was both large, and quite recession exposed. Nevertheless, DBAG had been relatively conservative in its leverage of these transactions, as André Mangin explains:

> It was when the crisis came that we drew substantial comfort from the fact that we had focussed on companies in industries we knew. It was also clear that we had been conservative with regard to leverage: this provided some stability in the downturn. Nevertheless, we had to take serious action in our portfolio, and to convince management teams to be much more pessimistic. If you look at Preh, for example, it is tough when you realise that your well-positioned quality car OEM customers are the most exposed, while producers of small cars are better placed. Machinery manufacturers like Coperion and Homag were impacted as well. While we knew these were in cyclical sectors, the sort of downsizing we've had to engage in during this crisis hadn't happened before. Some of the managers of these companies didn't dare to foresee something like this happening. If you asked for a worst case scenario, they would say a 20% drop in revenues. In this case, you needed to prepare for drop in revenues up to twice that big.[11]

Like many private equity houses with cyclical businesses in their portfolio, DBAG worked hard to keep control of some of its companies:

> We've also had covenant breaches in our portfolio during the crisis, and in certain cases we injected fresh capital. Banks appreciated our pragmatic approach, and they could see that Preh, for example, was a good company, performing well relatively to its peers. On Coveright we had very tough times. We did put in extra money, and we told the banks they wouldn't be able to manage it any better.[12]

Thus while by no means unchallenged, by virtue of a relatively conservative approach to leverage, quite typical of most of the transactions in the mid-cap space, DBAG succeeded in riding the storm.

capiton

The capiton team was neither surprised nor alarmed by the recession that struck after the Lehman Brothers bankruptcy, as Stefan Theis explains:

> That the boom which began in 2003 would come to an end was no surprise. Indeed, from 2005 we stopped investing in cyclical

companies and started to sell those companies out of the portfolio, because we were sure there would be a downturn around the corner, and focussed instead on stable industries. In our communication to investors for the fund capiton IV in 2009, we were able to prove that from 2005 onwards we hadn't acquired any cyclicals.

A further important factor was that from the beginning of capiton, we hadn't been doing highly leveraged buyouts. We've always tried to keep the equity level between 30%–50%, and would never drop to 20%. As a consequence, we entered the recession with a robust portfolio of medium sized companies. If you pay close attention to the macroeconomic environment, and maintain a conservative approach to leverage, you can cope with a recession successfully.[13]

The impact of the capiton team's strategy was revealed in the low recession exposure of their portfolio. The capiton III fund portfolio was firmly in the segment of low recession-impacted and short recession-duration-exposed portfolios.

The capiton team considered cyclical businesses to exhibit pros and cons, as Andreas Kogler explains:

From the perspective of making new investments, the position a company holds in its cycle can represent an opportunity. When we look back at our own experience, it is clear that the biggest success driver for an investment is its vintage year. During the period 2001–2003, companies were experiencing low profitability, the scope for leveraging buyouts fell, and so did the valuation multiples. But from 2004 onwards, the M&A market recovered, and enterprise values increased. We think that in the immediate years following the 2009 recession, the prospects for further good investments are positive.[14]

The 2008–2009 period was a wake-up call for all those who had entered private equity thinking that it was an easy profession. Very few members of the industry with experience dating back to the 1980s and early 1990s suffered such delusion, but the collective experience of the private equity houses in Germany had been diluted by the expansion of the industry around the turn of the millennium. Those with fifteen-to-twenty years experience had learnt the hard way that this was not a desk-job, dealing in theoretical values. Private equity involved ownership, and ownership brought responsibility. In times of downturn, such responsibility presented a heavy weight to bear.

Table 16.3 Private Equity Transactions in 2009

2009

Company	Buyer	Seller	Exit year	Sold to
A. Rohe Holding GmbH	ValueNet Capital Partners	Insolvency	Not yet divested	Not yet divested
Adler Modemärkte	BluO	BluO	Not yet divested	Not yet divested
Alex & Gross	Quadriga/Tectum	EKK	Not yet divested	Not yet divested
AlzChem Trostberg GmbH	BluO	Evonik Industries	Not yet divested	Not yet divested
Angell-Demmel Group	CBR/Equivest	Family (Richard Angelin)	Not yet divested	Not yet divested
Angiokard Medizintechnik	equitrust	Masterflex AG	Not yet divested	Not yet divested
A-Rosa Flussschiff GmbH	Waterland	Deutsche Seereederei Rostock	Not yet divested	Not yet divested
Bäckerei W. Middelberg GmbH	DPE Deutsche Private Equity	Family	Not yet divested	Not yet divested
Baumot AG	Perseus Partners	Owners	Not yet divested	Not yet divested
Bauwerk Parkett	Zurmont Madison	Nybron Flooring International	Not yet divested	Not yet divested
Bavaria Yachtbau	Oaktree Capital	Bain Capital	Not yet divested	Not yet divested
Biopharm GmbH	Brockhaus PE	Family/Owner	Not yet divested	Not yet divested
BMG Rights Management	KKR	Bertelsmann AG	Not yet divested	Not yet divested
C&R Stahlhandel GmbH	BayBG	Family	Not yet divested	Not yet divested
CLS Communication AG	Zurmont Madison	MBO	Not yet divested	Not yet divested
Competence Call Center	Axa Private Equity	Thomas Kloiberhofer	Not yet divested	Not yet divested
Constantia Packaging	Sulipo/One Equity Partners	Constantia Packaging B.V.	Not yet divested	Not yet divested
ddp Deutscher Depeschendienst GmbH	BluO	Arques	Not yet divested	Not yet divested
De Maekelboerger Backwaren GmbH	Nord Holding	Hannover Finanz	Not yet divested	Not yet divested
Diehl Elastomertechnik GmbH	mutares AG	Diehl Stiftung & Co. KG	Not yet divested	Not yet divested
Dunkermotoren	Triton Private Equity	Alcatel-Lucent	Not yet divested	Not yet divested
easycash	Ingenico SA	Warburg Pincus	2009	Ingenico
Ebert Hera Group	Odewald	Family	Not yet divested	Not yet divested
Erpo International Vertriebs GmbH	Afinum	Owners	Not yet divested	Not yet divested
Falk & Ross Gruppe	Steadfast	MBO	Not yet divested	Not yet divested
Fastbox Denzel Group	RECAP Restructuring Capital	Denzel AG	2010	Private Investors
Flad & Flad Communication GmbH	Equita	GAB	Not yet divested	Not yet divested
Forstinger	Alcar	Insolvency	Not yet divested	Not yet divested

Table 16.3 Private Equity Transactions in 2009 – *continued*

2009

Company	Buyer	Seller	Exit year	Sold to
FutureLAB Holding GmbH	BC Partners	Vienna Insurance Group/Duff	Not yet divested	Not yet divested
FW Woolworth Co GesmbH (Austria)	BluO	DWW Group Holdings Limited	Not yet divested	Not yet divested
Gebr. Reinfurt GmbH	NICB Capital Ptrs.	Family	Not yet divested	Not yet divested
Gehring	Stargate Capital	Insolvency	Not yet divested	Not yet divested
Ges. für Mikroelektronik Chemnitz mbH	Alster Equity/Wachstumsonds Mittelstand Sachsen	Family/Owner	Not yet divested	Not yet divested
GFKL Financial Services AG	Advent	ABN Amro/RBS/GS/Ergo	Not yet divested	Not yet divested
GRV LUTHE Kampfmittelbeseitigung	Perusa	Turn Around Investments	Not yet divested	Not yet divested
Guss Komponenten GmbH	mutares AG	Perusa	Not yet divested	Not yet divested
Hallhuber	Change Capital	Stefanel GmbH	Not yet divested	Not yet divested
Herlitz	Pelikan	Advent International	2009	Pelikan
Home Shopping Europe	Axa Private Equity	Arcancor AG	Not yet divested	Not yet divested
Integrata GmbH	Cornerstone Capita	Logica	Not yet divested	Not yet divested
Intertrust Group	Waterland	Fortis Bank Netherlands/BLC	Not yet divested	Not yet divested
Ixxat Automation GmbH	BWK GmbH	Family/Owner	Not yet divested	Not yet divested
Jouhsen-bündgens	S-UBG	Family	Not yet divested	Not yet divested
Kalle	Silverfleet Capital	Montagu	Not yet divested	Not yet divested
Karl Kemper Convenience	BPE Private Equity	Royal Wessanen NV	Not yet divested	Not yet divested
Karlie Heimtierbedarf GmbH	Perusa	Family/Owner	Not yet divested	Not yet divested
Kaul	Riverside	Family/Owner	Not yet divested	Not yet divested
Kentaro	DZ Private Equity	Private investors	Not yet divested	Not yet divested
LD Didactic Group	Aurelius	Insolvency	Not yet divested	Not yet divested
MAN Ferrostaal	IPIC	MAN	Not yet divested	Not yet divested
Mdexx Magnetronic Devices GmbH	CGS/CRG	Siemens	Not yet divested	Not yet divested
Median Kliniken GmbH	Advent/Marcol	Private investors	Not yet divested	Not yet divested

Table 16.3 Private Equity Transactions in 2009 – *continued*
2009

Company	Buyer	Seller	Exit year	Sold to
Metalor Technologies	Astrog Ptrs.	Family/Owner	Not yet divested	Not yet divested
Misapor AG	Argos Soditic	Family/Owner	Not yet divested	Not yet divested
OKIN	New Investors	Equita	Not yet divested	Not yet divested
ORS Service AG/OSP AG	Invision AG	Argos Soditic	Not yet divested	Not yet divested
Perrin GmbH	Kitz Corp.	Nord Holding	Not yet divested	Not yet divested
Pit Stop Auto Service	Blu-O	Kwik-Fit/PAI	2010	PV Automotive
Pohland Herrenkleidung GmbH	Men's fashion & lifestyle GmbH	Aurelius	Not yet divested	Not yet divested
Primera GmbH	Endurance Capital AG	Escada AG	Not yet divested	Not yet divested
Reimelt Henschel MischSysteme GmbH	Zeppelin	MBB Industries	Not yet divested	Not yet divested
Remy & Geiser	Aheim Capital GmbH	Family/Owner	Not yet divested	Not yet divested
Rohe Holding	ValueNet Capital Partners	Arques Austria	Not yet divested	Not yet divested
Rohner AG	BluO	Arques	Not yet divested	Not yet divested
RSG Media Holding	GIK GmbH	Aurelius	Not yet divested	Not yet divested
RTS Group	capiton	Family	Not yet divested	Not yet divested
Schülerhilfe GmbH	Paragon Partners	Laureate Education Inc.	Not yet divested	Not yet divested
Schwab Verkehrstechnik AG	Cross Equity Partners	Schwab Holding	Not yet divested	Not yet divested
SCL Chemie	DZ Private Equity	BASF	Not yet divested	Not yet divested
Sitag AG	Nimbus	Samas NV	Not yet divested	Not yet divested
Springer Science+Business Media Deutschland GmbH	EQT	Cinven/Candover	Not yet divested	Not yet divested
SUSPA Holding	Tyrol Equity	Silverfleet Capital	Not yet divested	Not yet divested
Thales Information Systems GmbH	Aurelius	Thales	Not yet divested	Not yet divested
The BEA Group	BluO	Arques	Not yet divested	Not yet divested
TMD Friction GbmH	Pamplona	Insolvency	Not yet divested	Not yet divested
Verivox	Oakley Capital Partners	Family/Owner	Not yet divested	Not yet divested
Weber Benteli AG	ValueNet Capital Partners	Arques	Not yet divested	Not yet divested
Witex	HIG Capital	JP Morgan Chase/Bear Stearn	Not yet divested	Not yet divested

Source: Authors' compilation

By and large, private equity professionals reacted rapidly and astutely to the crisis when it hit. Private equity owned companies probably acted more quickly to cut costs and adjust to falling volumes, than subsidiaries of publicly quoted corporations, or companies in family hands. The threat of covenant breach brought discipline ahead of the threat of insolvency, keeping leveraged companies one step ahead of their non-leveraged rivals. Inevitably, some over-leveraged cases breached covenants, and even became insolvent, but this was very much the exception rather than the rule.

A clear advantage for private equity in the 2008–2009 period was that its capital was overwhelmingly deployed in majority stakes. In previous recessions the level of private equity control over management had been, on average, lower, and the reaction time to outside events slower. While private equity may have appeared "hands-off" during the 2004–2007 boom, once the recession came, it became "hands-on" overnight.

Two categories of private equity house suffered disproportionately during the recession: those that had over-leveraged their acquisitions (generally the large-cap players); and those who had over-invested in cyclical industries (generally those in mid-cap). To be over-leveraged and cyclical was deadly. Fortunately, the fact that private equity houses seldom invest more than 10% of each fund in a single investment meant that they were typically protected against severe cyclical over-exposure.

The experienced professionals, who had seen companies fail, through fraud, poor management, run-away raw material prices, and falling demand, took the recession in their stride. Another rule of thumb they observed was that a fund will have one real winner, one outright loss, and eight players with modest returns. Lost investments were part and parcel of doing business.

The maturity of German private equity by 2008–2009 was also witnessed by the leading positions many of its members had reached. Many Germans and Austrians had become European or Global heads of their funds, including Martin Halusa at Apax, Ralf Huep at Advent, Jens Reidel at BC Partners, and Johannes Huth at KKR. In the case of Apax, the performance of the German-speaking team was such that many of its partners held leading positions in Asia and the US. A generation of private equity professionals had reached the pinnacles of their careers. They had learnt the lessons of experience.

17
What Did Private Equity Ever Do For Germany?

In the Monty Python film, The Life of Brian, a disgruntled and militant Judean asks "What have the Romans ever done for us?" His colleagues begin to give answers: the aqueduct, sanitation, roads, irrigation, education, medicine, education, wine, public baths, civic order and peace. But although the Judean freedom fighters' list is long, the implication is clear: the Romans have never done anything for the Judeans.

From the moment the issue of private equity became politicised during the "locust" debate, it was clear that the default position among public and press was that private equity had never done anything for Germany. On the contrary, it was a harmful foreign influence best banished, or thrown into a deep cell. The private equity industry was poorly organised to respond to such criticism. Private equity professionals are not like occupying Roman generals supported by their centurions. But bit by bit, the debate triggered some soul searching among many quarters of society. Had these purveyors of funny money, these merchants of debt, these worshipers of greed, perhaps been doing something useful after all?

Attitudes towards private equity were already changing among many Mittelstand managers prior to the locust debate. By the middle of the first decade of the new millennium, German managers had a much better idea of what private equity had to offer, and where the money was coming from. Management had witnessed enough examples of what their role would be in a buyout. An old adage of market research is that familiarity and favourability are closely correlated. This was certainly true of Mittelstand manager views on private equity. Countless articles were written about financially sponsored buyouts in every conceivable newspaper and magazine. Nobody in business could remain in a state of ignorance. Many private equity professionals were pleased with the outcome of the locust debate: it had served as a successful PR event. Brian Veitch commented, "I know now what to tell my kids I'm doing".

Part of Thomas Matzen's kudos at the end of the 1980s was that he had made managers into millionaires. At the time of the Ex-Cell-O IPO, the opportunities for a typical German manager to participate in such an enrichment process were about as great as winning the Lotto. But two decades later, with the number of management buyouts reaching 200 a year, the possibilities of participating in an MBO were quite tangible. With every buyout, additional missionaries were found for the private equity industry.

Politicians and economists struggled to establish the impact private equity was having on the German economy. An assessment commissioned by the economics ministry, conducted by Christof Kaserer and Ann-Kristin Achleitner (et al.) of the Technical University of Munich in 2007, produced a favourable result in their attempt:

> Private equity might be an important institution to overcome control and incentive problems in corporate finance. Hence, it should be regarded as a valuable alternative to public equity. As a consequence, private and public equity should be treated equally. Moreover, in private equity financing geographic proximity between the private equity investor and the corporation seems to be important. This is why the legal system should not only be neutral with respect to the choice of private versus public equity; it should also be attractive on an international basis. Evidently, these two goals might be conflicting.

> Benchmarking the legal and tax environment with other European countries, like France, Spain, Switzerland or Luxembourg, leads to the conclusion that there is ample room for improvement in Germany.[1]

But a degree of scepticism surrounded this and other studies, provoked in part by the suspicion that anyone qualified to analyse the impact of private equity would likely be positively disposed towards it, a suspicion not entirely without foundation.

The BVK has attempted to play its role in promoting external assessments of private equity, by developing a database on all private equity owned portfolio companies, prepared and updated by PwC. Inevitably however, it is hard to make an objective statistical assessment of the

Figure 17.1   Sources of Private Equity Transactions, 1984–2009

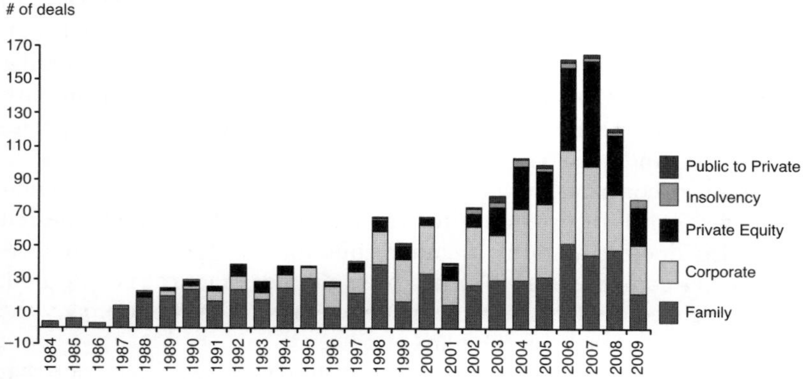

# of deals

Public to Private
Insolvency
Private Equity
Corporate
Family

Source: Authors' compilation

impact of private equity because it is impossible to have a true "control" group with which it can be benchmarked.

Ironically, the most obvious contribution private equity has made in Germany is to take over unhealthy companies. At the outset, no-one thought healthy companies should be sold, and in most cases during the 1980s, private equity was the last resort for companies to turn to. The service that private equity professionals offered during those early days was patchy and unpredictable: not many members of the industry really knew what they were doing. But over time, by a process of trial and error, they became better at identifying ways in which acquired companies could be made fitter, and prepared to better challenge the marketplace.

One of the most obvious ways in which private equity helped improve the strength of companies was to grow them, largely by a buy-and-build strategy. Schroder Ventures and IMM both pioneered the consolidation of smaller companies with significant success. Such consolidation has not been limited to Germany: German companies are increasingly pushed to globalise: stitching together companies from different countries into a single organisation.

Another way in which health in companies has been restored is by improving management control procedures. All too often accounting fulfilled only statutory requirements, and played little role in ensuring that companies were efficiently run. Private equity stimulated a veritable revolution in corporate cash-management, almost entirely with positive effects. These efforts have been of great importance during recessions, particularly in the crisis after the fall of Lehman Brothers. Private equity companies encouraged and empowered managers to make decisions quickly, making sure that they had access to timely and commercially relevant information. Private equity owned companies weathered the 2008–2009 recession well, quickly focussing on cash preservation, and introducing capacity and cost cutting measures to limit losses and preserve balance sheets.

The next contribution private equity made was to provide owner-managers with an exit-route for their investments. It might be felt that this doesn't amount to much, but for many owner managers of smaller companies an IPO has been neither practical nor desired, and private equity has given the trusted lieutenant in the company the opportunity to take over the reins of power.

On the other hand, the critics of private equity will point out that during the early days, the tax loop-holes were ruthlessly exploited, placing a strain on the public purse. This critique has merit. Some of the early tax refunds were large enough to finance the entire equity element of the acquisition. But these practices lasted for only a short time, and were largely eliminated by the beginning of the 1990s.

Critics have also accused private equity houses of asset stripping, buying companies only to reduce employment, close factories, increase indebtedness, and sell them on at a massively inflated valuation. But such criticism betrays a fundamental misunderstanding of how private equity houses make their money. Valuations are based upon future cash flows: stripping a company of its assets, firing employees, and closing factories are not measures which guarantee improved future cash flows. The easiest way to grow EBIT is to grow revenues, not cut costs.

Critics also allege that private equity has increased the indebtedness of companies. Clearly in some cases this is correct. Private equity companies in the early years re-engineered balance sheets to align capital structures to risk profiles. But in many cases, the debt introduced onto balance sheets was temporary, and paid off quite quickly. There has been suspicion of the foreign origins of this money, but private equity has been an effective mechanism of foreign direct investment. During the peak of the market in 2006–2007, the rising levels of leverage, even for highly cyclical businesses, was becoming a cause for concern. Kaserer and Achleitner in their report published in February 2007 warned:

> It should nevertheless be mentioned that there is clear evidence supporting the view that leverage in private equity transactions has significantly increased in 2006. By using an econometric model we

show that the increase in debt-multiples observed over the last quarters cannot simply be explained by fundamental economic factors. It is the financial supervision authority that has to tackle this issue.[2]

If a Monty Python film were to be made of the life of a downtrodden factory worker, slaving under the chains of a private equity owned firm, the hero might well ask angrily "What did private equity ever do for Germany?" His work colleagues might, like their Judean counterparts, begin to provide the answers: a safe harbour for sick companies, funds for buy-and-build consolidation, an exit route for retiring owner-managers, a source of inward investment, transparent management controlling, and a mode of upward mobility for middle management. Indeed the list might be a long one. But the downtrodden factory hero will no doubt continue to believe that private equity has never done anything for Germany.

A Note on Sources

Transactional data

It took considerable research to put together the tables for this book. The volume of information to be captured has of course exploded in recent years, with 2007 taking the record for the most private equity related transactions. But the most difficult tables to research were those in earlier years. During the period 1984–1995 the biggest challenge was that many of today's current M&A news services were not active, including *merger market* and initiative Europe's *Deutsche Unquote*. For more recent years, reliance on these two sources would provide approximately 80% coverage of the transactions. The next challenge is that a number of the early players in the 1984–1995 period are no longer in operation, and consequently have no internet pages or latter-day coverage. Consequently, for the early years we have had to give greater reliance on information from interviews which may not be as complete as for later years. Confirmation of information gained in interviews has been mainly achieved (where possible) through consulting the "history" sections of the internet pages of the companies involved.

For the more recent years we were greatly assisted by having access to Bain & Company's collection of the buyout data for the period 1996–2003, and L.E.K. Consulting's data for period 2002–2009. An additional useful source for the period 1998–2003 were the tables from Nico Reimers' "Private Equity für Familienunternehmen".

We have included in our tables transactions closed in Germany, Austria, and Switzerland. Various terms are used to define this region, most notably "German-speaking region" or "DACH" (based upon car licence plate abbreviations for the three countries). As our book is ostensibly focussed on Germany, some may feel that the inclusion of Austria and Switzerland in our coverage is inappropriate, or that that title of our book is misleading. In this respect, we have chosen to be pragmatic rather than pedantic. Most players in the German-speaking region are active in deal making within all three countries. Only the vagaries of 20th century political history have prevented us from referring to "Greater Germany" in the same way that many now use the term "Greater China".

We have restricted ourselves to the bare minimum of information for the tables, given the difficulties in researching them. For each transaction we identified the target, the buyer, the seller, and determined whether the company was later resold, in which case we give the exit year and the identity of the buyer. The most difficult of these pieces of information to obtain is typically the original seller. The most valuable additional piece of information would clearly be the value of the transaction, which would have allowed us to provide many more statistical insights into the development of the industry. The sad fact however is that the bulk of small and mid-cap transaction values are not disclosed, and we would have been forced to provide either extremely incomplete data, or to develop our own estimates of the values which could have been seriously wide of the mark.

The interviews

From the outset we knew that our book would be an exercise in oral history. Without extensive primary interviews with the key figures in the industry, it would have been nearly impossible to assemble a comprehensive review of the process by which private equity was introduced to Germany. The interviews were conducted in all cases on an "off-the-record" basis in order that they could take place in a relaxed and confidential manner. Each interview was taped, and later transcribed. We then selected those elements of the interviews which were most important for the book, and integrated them into the text. Inevitably, some reworking of the material was necessary in this process, in particular converting free-speech into grammatical prose. Once the content and context of the information was clear, we then passed the relevant material to our interview partners for correction and approval. Everything contained in this book is therefore "on-the-record" in the sense that it has been checked and approved for publication by out interview partners.

Other sources

We relied on comparatively few secondary sources for our book. For the early days of minority participations, Günter Leopold's *40 Jahre Investitionen im Deutschen Mittelstand* was particularly helpful. This also provided substantial coverage of Deutsche Beteiligungs AG and its predecessors.

Ralf Becker and Thomas Hellmann's paper *The Genesis of Venture Capital – Lessons from the German Experience* was critical for our coverage of the Deutsche Wagnisfinanzierungsgesellschaft. The Harvard Business School cases studies on Singulus, Infox, and Sirona (Professor Walter Kuemmerle and Charles Ellis) were important sources. For our coverage of HANN-OVER Finanz, Albrecht Hertz-Eichenrode and Andreas Schober's *Zwischen*

Rendite und Verantwortung was also helpful. In the overall assessment of private equity's contribution to Germany, we referred to *Erwerb und Übernahme von Firmen durch Finanzinvestoren (insbesondere Private-Equity-Gesellschaften)* – Bericht zum Forschungsprojekt 3/06 für das Bundesministerium der Finanzen Berlin, by Christof Kaserer, Ann-Kristin Achleitner, Christoph von Einem, Dirk Schiereck, 2007. For the perspectives of US-based private equity professionals, our principal source quickly became *Done Deals: Venture Capitalists tell their Stories* edited by Udayan Gupta, which was extremely helpful, being a compilation of short essays by the principal actors in the US venture capital industry. These essays were highly complementary to the interviews we conducted in Germany.

One of the best German language literature reviews can be found in Johannes Blome-Drees and Reiner Rang's *Private Equity-Investitionen in deutsche Unternehmen und ihre Wirkungen auf die Mitarbeiter* (Hans Böckler Stiftung October 2006). Blome-Drees and Rang also provide a useful review of the experience with the Edscha transactions of 1997 and 2003.

A number of Diploma theses have been published which are helpful in examining the value private equity has contributed to companies in Germany. These include Volker Kraft's *Private Equity für Turnaround-Investitionen. Erfolgsfaktoren in der Managementpraxis,* and Thorsten Gröne's *Private Equity in Germany: Evaluation of the Value Creation Potential for German Mid-Cap Companies.*

The most important journals of assistance to our book were *Wirtschaftswoche, manager magazin, Der Spiegel,* and *The Economist.*

With thanks to the following for additional support

Ann-Kristin Achleitner
Paul Achleitner
Wolfgang Alvano
John Arney
Charles Barter
Ralf Becker
Stefan Blum
Peter Brooke
Christian Fehling
Rolf Gardey
Horst-Otto Gerberding
Paul Goodson
Nico Helling

Thomas Hellmann
Ivan Heywood
Heinrich Hoyos
Georges Huber
Peter Kroha
Fritz Wilhelm Krüger
Neil MacDougall
Andrew Marchant
Stefan Messer
Klaus Nathusius
Hans Peter Peters
Bertram Plettenberg
David Rubenstein
Franz Scherer
Stefan Theis
Steve Tibble
Christopher Ullman
Otto van der Wyck
Rolf-Magnus Weddigen
Siegfried Weiss
Jochen Weyrich
Stefan Winterling
Philip Yea
Walter Zinsser

Reproduction Permissions

Bild am Sonntag
Central European News
Der Spiegel
Economist Newspapers
Guardian News & Media
Harvard Business School Publishing
International Herald Tribune
manager magazine
MIT Press
Times Newspapers
Wirtschaftswoche

Notes

Chapter 1   Introduction

1   Ralf Becker and Thomas Hellmann: *The Genesis of Venture Capital – The Lessons from the German Experience*.
2   Henry Kravis' views were popularised in the book and film of the same name *Barbarians at the Gate*.
3   For an account of Bruce Henderson's thinking see Pankaj Ghemawat *Competition and Business Strategy in Historical Perspective* HBS Comp. & Strategy Working Paper No. 798010 April 2000.

Chapter 2   Minority Participations: 1965–1975

1   From *40 Jahre Investitionene im Deutschen Mittelstand 1965–2005*, by Günther Leopold, p. 7.
2   Quoted from *40 Jahre Investitionene im Deutschen Mittelstand 1965–2005*, by Günther Leopold, p. 7.
3   Ibid., p. 8.
4   Ibid., p. 8.
5   Ibid., p. 12.
6   Ibid., p. 16.
7   Ibid., p. 17.
8   Ibid., p. 17.
9   Ibid., p. 25.
10 Ibid., p. 36.
11 Ibid., p. 48.

Chapter 3   The Failed Venture Capital Experiment: 1976–1991

1   Ralf Becker and Thomas Hellmann *The Genesis of Venture Capital – Lessons from the German Experience*.
2   Ibid.
3   Ibid.
4   "Peter Brooke: Advent International" in *Done Deals: Venture Capitalists tell their Stories*, edited by Udayan Gupta, p. 249.
5   Ralf Becker and Thomas Hellmann *The Genesis of Venture Capital – Lessons from the German Experience*.
6   Interview with Hellmut Kirchner, 29th October 2009.
7   Ralf Becker and Thomas Hellmann *The Genesis of Venture Capital – Lessons from the German Experience*.
8   Quoted in Ralf Becker and Thomas Hellmann *The Genesis of Venture Capital – Lessons from the German Experience*.

9   Interview with Hellmut Kirchner, 29th October 2009.
10 Quoted in Ralf Becker and Thomas Hellmann *The Genesis of Venture Capital – Lessons from the German Experience.*
11 Ibid.
12 Ibid.
13 Ibid.
14 Ibid.
15 Quoted in Ralf Becker and Thomas Hellmann *The Genesis of Venture Capital – Lessons from the German Experience.*
16 Interview with Hellmut Kirchner, 29th October 2009.
17 Ralf Becker and Thomas Hellmann *The Genesis of Venture Capital – Lessons from the German Experience.*
18 Ibid.
19 Ibid.
20 Ibid.
21 Ibid.
22 "Peter Brooke: Advent International" in *Done Deals: Venture Capitalists tell their Stories*, edited by Udayan Gupta, p. 246.
23 "Kevin Landry: TA Associates" in *Done Deals: Venture Capitalists tell their Stories*, edited by Udayan Gupta, p. 264.

Chapter 4   The Early Shoots: Genes Ventures, Matuschka/TVM, & HANNOVER Finanz

1   Interview with Andreas Fendel, 14th August 2007.
2   Inteview with Hellmut Kirchner, 29th October 2009.
3   Interview with Albrecht Matuschka, 23rd March 2007.
4   Ibid.
5   Interview with Rolf Dienst, 11th January 2008.
6   Interview with Albrecht Matuschka, 23rd March 2007.
7   Interview with Rolf Dienst, 11th January 2008.
8   Ibid.
9   Interview with Albrecht Matuschka, 23rd March 2007.
10 Interview with Reinhard Pöllath, 17th August 2007.
11 Interview with Rolf Dienst, 11th January 2008.
12 Vermögensverwaltung.
13 Interview with Albrecht Matuschka, 23rd March 2007.
14 "Peter Brooke: Advent International" in *Done Deals: Venture Capitalists tell their Stories*, edited by Udayan Gupta, p. 246.
15 Ibid., p. 247.
16 Ibid., p. 250.
17 "Kevin Landry: TA Associates" in *Done Deals: Venture Capitalists tell their Stories*, edited by Udayan Gupta, p. 263.
18 Peter A. Brooke (with Daniel Penrice): *A Vision for Venture Capital*, p. 61.
19 Ibid., p. 62.
20 Interview with Rolf Dienst, 11th January 2008.
21 Peter A. Brooke (with Daniel Penrice): *A Vision for Venture Capital*, p. 62.
22 Interview with Albrecht Matuschka, 23 March 2007.

23 Interview with Hellmut Kirchner, 29th October 2009.
24 Society formed under German civil law for the administration of US stocks.
25 Interview with Hellmut Kirchner, 29th October 2009.
26 Ibid.
27 Ibid.
28 Interview with Reinhard Pöllath, 17th August 2007.
29 Interview with Rolf Dienst, 11th January 2008.
30 Interview with Reinhard Pöllath, 17th August 2007.
31 Ibid.
32 "Peter Brooke: Advent International" in *Done Deals: Venture Capitalists tell their Stories*, edited by Udayan Gupta, p. 250.
33 Peter A. Brooke (with Daniel Penrice): *A Vision for Venture Capital*, pp. 62–3.
34 Interview with Albrecht Matuschka, 13th April 2010.
35 Interview with Hellmut Kirchner, 29th October 2009.
36 Interview with Rolf Dienst, 11th January 2008.
37 Interview with Reinhard Pöllath, 17th August 2007.
38 Peter A. Brooke (with Daniel Penrice): *A Vision for Venture Capital*, p. 63.
39 Interview with Reinhard Pöllath, 17th August 2007.
40 Ibid.
41 Peter A. Brooke (with Daniel Penrice): *A Vision for Venture Capital*, pp. 63–4.
42 Interview with Albrecht Matuschka, 15th January 2010.
43 Interview with Hellmut Kirchner, 29th October 2009.
44 Ibid.
45 Interview with Hellmut Kirchner, 29th October 2009.
46 Peter A. Brooke (with Daniel Penrice): *A Vision for Venture Capital*, p. 66.
47 Interview with Hellmut Kirchner, 29th October 2009.
48 Peter A. Brooke (with Daniel Penrice): *A Vision for Venture Capital*, p. 65.
49 Ibid., p. 66.
50 Haftpflichtverbands der deutschen Industrie (HDI).
51 Interview with Albrecht Hertz-Eichenrode, 17th October 2007.
52 Ibid.
53 Ibid.
54 Ibid.
55 Ibid.
56 Ibid.
57 Ibid.

Chapter 5   The First Phase: From Venture Capital to LBOs

1 Interview with Robert Osterrieth, 20th March 2007.
2 Ibid.
3 Ibid.
4 Ibid.
5 Ibid.
6 Ibid.
7 As estimated by Erik Lindner in: *Die Reemtsmas, Geschichte einer deutschen Unternehmerfamilie*, p. 513. *Der Spiegel* (38/1980) estimated the shares to have been worth DM 370 million.
8 Ibid.

9 Interview with Reinhard Pöllath, 17th August 2007.
10 Ibid.
11 Interview with Robert Osterrieth, 20th March 2007.
12 Ibid.
13 Interview with Brian Fenwick-Smith, 2nd April 2009.
14 Ibid.
15 Interview with Robert Osterrieth, 20th March 2007.
16 Interview with Reinhard Pöllath, 17th August 2007.
17 Interview with Robert Osterrieth, 20th March 2007.
18 Ibid.
19 Email commentary to the authors from Peter Tornquist, 11th April 2010.
20 Metzler Bank did not take long to fully understand and appreciate the attractions of private equity, and a few years later invested in Equimark.
21 T. Boone Pickens was a corporate raider operating in the US during the 1980s, whose takeovers put many independent oil producers out of business.
22 Ibid.
23 Interview with Stephan Krümmer, 17th July 2007.
24 Email commentary to the authors from Peter Tornquist, 11th April 2010.
25 Interview with Peter Tornquist, 9th June 2007.
26 Interview with Nick Ferguson, 8th October 2007.
27 Ibid.
28 Schroder German Buyouts was structured into a Bermuda management company, advised by a UK advisory company, which in turn received advice from a Hamburg-based firm.
29 Interview with Nick Ferguson, 8th October 2007.
30 Interview with Thomas Matzen, 8th June 2007.
31 Interview with Robert Osterrieth, 20th March 2007.
32 Ibid.
33 This approach became standard, confirmed by tax rulings derived from Rodin and Pöllath's work with tax offices and ministries. Later the Government provided "phase-out" (grandfathering) rules when legislation changed.
34 Interview with Nick Ferguson, 8th October 2007.
35 Interview with Robert Osterrieth, 20th March 2007.
36 Interview with Thomas Matzen, 8th June 2007.
37 Interview with Jon Moulton, 4th June 2007.
38 Interview with Brian Fenwick-Smith, 2nd April 2009.
39 Interview with Hans Gottwald, 13th September 2007.
40 Ibid.
41 Interview with Albrecht Hertz-Eichenrode, 17th October 2007.
42 Interview with Andreas Schober, 24th February 2010.
43 Ibid.

Chapter 6   The Second Phase: 3i, CVC, Bain, and Matuschka

1 Interview with Andrew Richards, 26th October 2007.
2 Interview with Friedrich von der Groeben, 30th August 2007.
3 Participation management.

4   Interview with Friedrich von der Groeben, 30th August 2007.
5   Ibid.
6   Ibid.
7   Interview with Friedrich von der Groeben, 30th August 2007.
8   Ibid.
9   Interview with Thomas Schlytter-Henrichsen, 19th April 2007.
10   Ibid.
11   Interview with Andrew Richards, 26th October 2007.
12   Interview with Thomas Schlytter-Henrichsen, 19th April 2007.
13   Interview with Andrew Richards, 26th October 2007.
14   Interview with Thomas Schlytter-Henrichsen, 19th April 2007.
15   Ibid.
16   Ibid.
17   Interview with Andrew Richards, 26th October 2007.
18   Interview with Thomas Schlytter-Henrichsen, 19th April 2007.
19   Interview with Jens Tonn, 19th March 2007.
20   Ibid.
21   Ibid.
22   Interview with Mark Elborn, 17th July 2007.
23   Email commentary to the authors from Peter Tornquist, 11th April 2010.
24   Interview with Fritz Seikowsky, 18th June 2008.
25   Ibid.
26   Interview with Peter Tornquist, 9th June 2007.
27   Interview with Markus Conrad, 18th December 2009.
28   Interview with Fritz Seikowsky, 18th June 2008.
29   Interview with Markus Conrad, 18th December 2009.
30   Interview with Peter Tornquist, 9th June 2007.
31   Interview with Markus Conrad, 18th December 2009.
32   Interview with Peter Tornquist, 9th June 2007.
33   Interview with Fritz Seikowsky, 18th June 2008.
34   Email commentary to the authors from Peter Tornquist, 11th April 2010.
35   Interview with Markus Conrad, 18th December 2009.
36   Ibid.
37   Ibid. Conrad later led the sale of Libri to the Herz family in 1993, where he remained as a buy-in manager.
38   Indeed the Libri deal earned its purchase price back several times, and Marcus Conrad led Libri to a market leadership position in Germany and expanded its position abroad, Libri later became the fulfilment parter of Amazon, who built their German hub next to Libri's main warehouse. Conrad later became the CEO of Tchibo, the Herz family's core business. Reinhard Pöllath was at the time, and remained to the date of this book's publication, the Herz family's advisor and Board Chairman.
39   Interview with Peter Tornquist, 9th June 2007.
40   Interview with Manfred Ferber, 13th June 2007.
41   A major international logistics company with its head office in Switzerland.
42   Interview with Manfred Ferber, 13th June 2007.
43   Interview with Albrecht Matuschka, 15th January 2010.
44   Interview with Albrecht Matuschka, 23rd March 2007.
45   Interview with Rolf Dienst, 11th January 2008.

46 Interview with Albrecht Matuschka, 15th January 2009.
47 Interview with Hellmut Kirchner, 29th October 2009.
48 Interview with Norbert Stelzer, 12th March 2007.
49 Interview with Hellmut Kirchner, 29th October 2009.
50 Interview with Albrecht Matuschka, 15th January 2010.
51 Interview with Norbert Stelzer, 12th March 2007.
52 Interview with Norbert Stelzer, 12th March 2007.
53 Interview with Hans Moock, 9th December 2009.
54 Interview with Vincent Hubner, 29th March 2007.
55 Interview with Norbert Stelzer, 12th March 2007.
56 Interview with Vincent Hubner, 29th March 2007.
57 Ibid.
58 Interview with Jon Moulton, 4th June 2007.
59 Interview with Andreas Fendel, 14th August 2007.
60 Interview with Max Römer, 30th March 2007.
61 Ibid.
62 Ibid.
63 Interview with Andreas Fendel, 14th August 2007.
64 Hauck & Aufhäuser is a German private bank.
65 Interview with Max Römer, 30th March 2007.
66 Ibid.
67 Interview with Chris Neizert, 19th April 2007.
68 Ibid.
69 Interview with Max Römer, 30th March 2007.
70 Interview with Jon Moulton, 4th June 2007.
71 Interview with Andreas Schober, 24th February 2010.
72 Interview with Albrecht Hertz-Eichenrode, 17th October 2007.
73 Ibid.
74 Interview with Andreas Schober, 24th February 2010.
75 Interview with Albrecht Hertz-Eichenrode, 17th October 2007.

Chapter 7   The Third Phase: Trial and Error with LBOs

1   A company formed by Raimund König after he left Bain & Company.
2   Interview with Stephan Krümmer, 17th July 2007.
3   Interview with Fritz Seikowsky, 18th June 2008.
4   Interview with Raimund König, 25th January 2010.
5   Ibid.
6   Ibid.
7   Ibid.
8   Interview with Chris Neizert, 19th April 2007.
9   Ibid.
10 Interview with Hans Albrecht, 1st June 2007.
11 Interview with Hans Albrecht, 8th December 2009.
12 Ibid.
13 Ibid.
14 Interview with Thomas Bühler, 2nd March 2010.
15 Interview with Hans Gottwald, 13th September 2007.

16 Interview with Raimund König, 25th January 2010.
17 Interview with Andreas Odefey, 8th June 2007.
18 Interview with Manfred Ferber, 13th June 2007.
19 Ibid.
20 Interview with Paul de Ridder, 18th April 2007.
21 Interview with Martin Stringfellow, 15th June 2007.
22 Interview with David Martin, 19th November 2008.
23 Ibid.
24 Interview with Christophe Hemmerle, 19th April 2007.
25 Interview with Andrew Richards, 26th October 2007.
26 Ibid.
27 Interview with Thomas Schlytter-Henrichsen, 19th April 2007.
28 Interview with Brian Veitch, 14th June 2007.
29 Ibid.
30 Ibid.
31 Ibid.
32 Correspondence with Peter Cullom, 3rd March 2010.
33 Quoted from an interview with Hans-Dieter von Meibom, 30th March 2007.
34 Interview with Hans-Dieter von Meibom, 30th March 2007.
35 Interview with Wolfgang Bensel, 26th March 2007.
36 Interview with Hans-Dieter von Meibom, 30th March 2007.
37 Interview with Wolfgang Bensel, 26th March 2007.
38 Interview with Eberhard Crain, 24th November 2009.
39 Email commentary to the authors by Christiane Brock, 14th October 2009.
40 Ibid.
41 Interview with Stefan Zuschke, 17th September 2007.
42 Interview with Hans Moock, 9th December 2009.
43 Interview with Stefan Zuschke, 17th September 2007.
44 Inteview with Hans-Dieter von Meibom, 30th March 2007.
45 Interview with Stefan Zuschke, 17th September 2007.
46 Interview with Friedrich von der Groeben, 30th August 2007.
47 Interview with Thomas Schlytter-Henrichsen, 19th April 2007.
48 Interview with Friedrich von der Groeben, 30th August 2007.
49 Interview with Eberhard Crain, 24th November 2009.
50 Ibid.
51 Letter to the authors from Friedrich von der Groeben, 11th March 2010.
52 Interview with Eberhard Crain, 24th November 2009.
53 Interview with Max Römer, 30th March 2007.
54 Ibid.
55 Interview with Max Römer, 30th March 2007.
56 Interview with Norbert Stelzer, 12th March 2007.
57 Interview with Hellmut Kirchner, 29th October 2009.
58 Interview with Reinhard Pöllath, 17th August 2007.
59 Interview with Albrecht Matuschka, 15th January 2010.
60 Interview with Hellmut Kirchner on 29th October 2009.
61 Interview with Albrecht Matuschka, 13th April 2010.
62 Interview with Thomas Pütter, 23rd April 2007.
63 The UK's most complex motorway interchange in Birmingham.
64 Interview with Thomas Pütter, 23rd April 2007.

65 Interview with Albrecht Matuschka, 23rd March 2007.
66 Interview with Vincent Hübner, 29th March 2007.
67 Interview with Norbert Stelzer, 12th March 2007.
68 Interview with Albrecht Matuschka, 15th January 2010.
69 Article in *Wirtschaftswoche*, 18th May 1990.
70 Ibid.
71 Ibid.
72 Ibid.
73 Interview with Hellmut Kirchner, 29th October 2009.
74 Article in *Wirtschaftswoche*, 22nd June 1990.
75 Interview with Albrecht Matuschka, 23rd March 2007.
76 Interview with Vincent Hübner, 29th March 2007.
77 Article in *Der Spiegel*, edition 28/90, 9th July 1990.
78 Interview with Thomas Pütter, 23rd April 2007.
79 Interview with Vincent Hübner, 29th March 2007.
80 Article in *The Economist*, 25th August 1990.
81 Interview with Albrecht Matuschka, 13th April 2010.
82 Interview with Norbert Stelzer, 12th March 2007.
83 Interview with Albrecht Matuschka, 15th January 2009.
84 Interview with Vincent Hübner, 29th March 2007.
85 Article in *The Economist*, 25th August 1990.
86 Article in *The Economist*, 18th January 1992.
87 Interview with Norbert Stelzer, 12th March 2007.
88 Interview with Vincent Hübner, 29th March 2007.
89 Interview with Paul de Ridder, 18th April 2007.
90 Interview with Norbert Stelzer, 12th March 2007.
91 Interview with Albrecht Matuschka, 15th January 2010.
92 Interview with Thomas Pütter, 23rd April 2007.
93 Article in *The Economist*, 18th January 1992.
94 Interview with Albrecht Matuschka, 15th January 2010.

Chapter 8   The Schroders' Story of the 1980s

1 Interview with Reinhard Pöllath, 17th August 2007. He and Andreas Rodin have assisted Schroders in establishing and accompanying the fund since inception to date, and many others.
2 Interview with Thomas Matzen, 8th June 2007.
3 Ibid.
4 Ibid.
5 Ibid.
6 Interview with Thomas Krenz, 30th March 2007.
7 Ibid.
8 Ibid.
9 Ibid.
10 Ibid.
11 Ibid.
12 Comments emailed to the authors by Jon Moulton, 7th April 2010.
13 Interview with Thomas Krenz, 30th March 2007.

14   Ibid.
15   Ibid.
16   Article in *manager magazin*, 1st September 1989.
17   Interview with Thomas Krenz, 30th March 2007.
18   Interview with Wolfgang Biedermann, 7th July 2008.
19   Interview with Thomas Matzen, 30th November 2009.
20   Interview with Robert Osterreith, 20th March 2007.
21   Memo from Nick Ferguson to Thomas Matzen, June 1990.
22   Interview with Thomas Krenz, 30th March 2007.
23   Interview with Robert Osterrieth, 20th March 2007.
24   E-mail to the authors from Robert Osterrieth, 2nd December 2009.
25   Interview with Thomas Matzen, 30th November 2009.
26   Interview with Thomas Krenz, 30th March 2007.
27   Interview with Thomas Matzen, 30th November 2009.
28   Ibid.
29   Interview with Thomas Krenz, 30th March 2007.
30   Interview with Wolfang Biedermann, 7th July 2008.
31   Interview with Thomas Krenz, 30th March 2007.
32   Ibid.
33   Email to the authors from Jon Moulton, 7th April 2010.
34   Interview with Friedrich von der Groeben, 30th August 2007.
35   Interview with Nick Ferguson, 8th October 2007.
36   Interview with Thomas Krenz, 30th March 2007.
37   Quoted from letter to the authors from Friedrich von der Groeben, 11th March 2010.
38   Interview with Thomas Krenz, 30th March 2007.

Chapter 9   The 1984–1991 Experience in Retrospect

1   Interview with Friedrich von der Groeben, 30th August 2007.
2   Interview with Thomas Krenz, 30th March 2007.
3   Interview with Jon Moulton, 4th June 2007.
4   Interview with Hans Albrecht, 1st June 2007.
5   Interview with Jon Moulton, 4th June 2007.
6   Interview with Chris Peisch, 30th March 2007.
7   Interview with Jon Moulton, 4th June 2007.
8   Ibid.

Chapter 10   The Fourth Phase: Frustrating Times 1992–1994

1   Interview with Michael Boltz, 30th August 2007.
2   Ibid.
3   Ibid.
4   Interview with Paul de Ridder, 18th April 2007.
5   Ibid.
6   Ibid.
7   Interview with Christophe Hemmerle, 19th April 2007.

8   Interview with Paul de Ridder, 18th April 2007.
9   Ibid.
10 Interview with Christophe Hemmerle, 19th April 2007.
11 Ibid.
12 Interview with Hans Albrecht, 8th December 2009.
13 Interview with Kai Köppen, 1st December 2009.
14 Interview with Walter Moldan, 16th December 2009.
15 Interview with Hans Albrecht, 8th December 2009.
16 Interview with Thomas Bühler, 2nd March 2010.
17 Interview with Raimund König, 25th January 2010.
18 Interview with Walter Moldan, 16th December 2009.
19 Interview with Raimund König, 25th January 2010.
20 Interview with Hans Albrecht, 8th December 2009.
21 Interview with Kai Köppen, 1st December 2009.
22 Interview with Raimund König, 25th January 2010.
23 Interview with Albrecht Hertz-Eichenrode, 17th October 2007.
24 Ibid.
25 Ibid.
26 Interview with Andreas Schober, 24th February 2010.
27 Ibid.
28 Ibid.
29 Interview with Max Römer, 30th March 2007.
30 Ibid.
31 Ibid.
32 Ibid.
33 Interview with Richard Burton, 28th June 2007.
34 Interview with Thomas Pütter, 23rd April 2007.
35 Interview with Thomas Krenz, 30th March 2007.
36 Interview with Friedrich von der Groeben, 30th August 2007.
37 Interview with Nick Ferguson, 8th October 2007.
38 Interview with Thomas Krenz, 30th March 2007.
39 The Singulus story was written up as a Harvard Business School case study by Professor Walter Kuemmerle and Charles Ellis, published 15th December 1998.
40 Interview with Michael Hinderer, 21st May 2007.
41 Ibid.
42 Ibid.
43 Ibid.
44 Ibid.
45 Ibid.
46 Interview with Martin Halusa, 11th December 2009.
47 Ibid.
48 Interview with Michael Phillips, 11th May 2007.
49 Interview with Martin Halusa, 11th December 2009.
50 Interview with Michael Phillips, 11th May 2007.
51 Interview with Michael Boltz, 30th August 2007.
52 Interview with Michael Phillips, 11th May 2007.
53 Interview with Max Burger-Calderon, 30th October 2009.
54 Interview with Michael Phillips, 11th May 2007.

55   Ibid.
56   The Infox story was written up as a Harvard Business School case study by Professor Walter Kuemmerle and Charles Ellis, published 20th January 1999.
57   Interview with Aman Miran Khan, 27th August 2007.
58   Interview with Michael Phillips, 11th May 2007.
59   Ibid.
60   Interview with Thomas Schlytter-Henrichsen, 19th April 2007.
61   Ibid.
62   Ibid.
63   Interview with Nick Money-Kyrle, 9th October 2008.
64   Interview with Thomas Schlytter-Henrichsen, 19th April 2007.
65   Interview with Nick Money-Kyrle, 9th October 2008.
66   Interview with Aman Miran Khan, 27th August 2007.
67   Ibid.
68   Ibid.
69   Ibid.
70   Interview with Steve Koltes, 16th April 2008.
71   Ibid.
72   Ibid.
73   Ibid.
74   Interview with Jens Reidel, 8th June 2007.
75   Ibid.
76   Ibid.
77   Ibid.
78   Ibid.
79   Ibid.
80   Interview with Chris Peisch, 30th March 2007.
81   Ibid.
82   Ibid.
83   Interview with Eberhard Crain, 24th November 2009.
84   Ibid.
85   Ibid.
86   Ibid.
87   Ibid.
88   Ibid.
89   See Steven Kaplan & Aaron Peck, *Cinven and Tiller Foodservices*, Chicago Business School Case Study.
90   Inteview with Thomas Matzen, 30th November 2009.
91   Ibid.
92   Ibid.
93   Email commentary to the authors from Steve Tibble, 15th November 2010.
94   Interview with Thomas Matzen, 30th November 2009.
95   Interview with André Mangin, 9th December 2009.
96   Ibid.
97   Interview with Jens Tonn, 19th March 2007.
98   See: *Der Fall Balsam. Oder: Über die Unverzichtbarkeit von engagierten Recher-cheuren*, by Johannes Ludwig www. Recherchieren.org.
99   Interview with Raimund König, 29th March 2007.
100 Inteview with Jens Tonn, 19th March 2007.
101 Interview with Fritz Seikowsky, 18th June 2008.

102 Interview with Detlef Dinsel, 12th March 2010.
103 Interview with Fritz Seikowsky, 18th June 2008.
104 Email commentary to the authors from Peter Tornquist, 12th April 2010.
105 Ibid.
106 Interview with Thomas Krenz, 30th March 2007.
107 Interview with Fritz Seikowsky, 18th June 2008.
108 Interview with Clemens Beickler, 25th April 2008.
109 Interview with Fritz Seikowsky, 18th June 2008.
110 Interview with Detlef Dinsel, 12th March 2010.
111 Interview with Clemens Beickler, 25th April 2008.
112 Ibid.
113 Interview with Fritz Seikowsky, 18th June 2008.
114 Interview with Detlef Dinsel, 12th March 2010.
115 Email commentary to the authors from Peter Tornquist, 12th April 2010.
116 Email commentary to the authors from Fritz Seikowsky, 13th April 2010.

Chapter 11   East German Adventures

1 Interview with Albrecht Matuschka, 15th January 2010.
2 Ibid.
3 Interview with Daniel Schmitz, 9th October 2008.
4 Interview with Hans-Dieter von Meibom, 30th March 2007.
5 Interview with Norbert Stelzer, 12th March 2007.
6 "Peter Brooke: Advent International" in *Done Deals: Venture Capitalists tell their Stories*, edited by Udayan Gupta, p. 251.
7 "Kevin Landry: TA Associates" in *Done Deals: Venture Capitalists tell their Stories*, edited by Udayan Gupta, p. 264.
8 "Peter Brooke: Advent International" in *Done Deals: Venture Capitalists tell their Stories*, edited by Udayan Gupta, p. 252.
9 Interview with Chris Neizert, 19th April 2007.
10 Ibid.
11 Ibid.
12 Ibid.
13 Peter A. Brooke (with Daniel Penrice): *A Vision for Venture Capital*, p. 159.
14 Interview with Chris Neizert, 19th April 2007.
15 Peter A. Brooke (with Daniel Penrice): *A Vision for Venture Capital*, p. 159.
16 Interview with Chris Neizert, 19th April 2007.
17 Peter A. Brooke (with Daniel Penrice): *A Vision for Venture Capital*, p. 160.
18 "Peter Brooke: Advent International" in *Done Deals: Venture Capitalists tell their Stories*, edited by Udayan Gupta, p. 253.
19 Ibid., p. 255.
20 Interview with Andreas Odefey, 8th June 2007.
21 Ibid.
22 Interview with Max von Drechsel, 13th May 2009.
23 Interview with Andreas Odefey, 8th June 2007.
24 Interview with Wolfgang Bensel, 26th March 2007.
25 Ibid.
26 Interview with Andreas Odefey, 8th June 2007.

27   Ibid.
28   Interview with Philipp Amereller, 17th July 2007.
29   Interview with Andreas Odefey, 8th June 2007.
30   Interview with Wolfgang Bensel, 26th March 2007.
31   Interview with Philipp Amereller, 17th July 2007.
32   Legal & General Ventures.
33   Interview with Mark Elborn, 17th July 2007.
34   Interview with Philipp Amereller, 17th July 2007.
35   Interview with Wolgang Bensel, 26th March 2007.
36   Interview with Olav Ermgassen, 25th September 2007.
37   Ibid.
38   Article in *Der Spiegel*, edition 17/93, 26th April 1993.
39   Ibid.
40   Interview with Olav Ermgassen, 25th September 2007.
41   Ibid.
42   "Die Rettung des Backkombinats", by Michael Hedtstück, in *Zwischen Rendite und Verantwortung*, edited by Albrecht Hertz-Eichenrode and Andreas Schober.
43   Ibid.
44   Interview with Peter Hammermann, 16th January 2008.
45   Interview with Ekkehard Franzke, 23rd April 2007.
46   Interview with Norbert Stelzer, 12th March 2007.
47   Interview with Ekkehard Franzke, 23rd April 2007.
48   Interview with Chris Peisch, 30th March 2007.
49   Interview with Peter Hammermann, 16th January 2008.
50   Ibid.
51   Interview with Ekkehard Franzke, 23rd April 2007.

Chapter 12   The Fifth Phase: Retrenchment & Spin-offs: 1995–1996

1   Interview with Max Römer, 30th March 2007.
2   Interview with Steve Koltes, 16th April 2008.
3   Ibid.
4   Ibid.
5   Interview with Chris Peisch, 30th March 2007.
6   Ibid.
7   Ibid.
8   Ibid.
9   Ibid.
10   Interview with Georg Stratenwerth, 18th April 2007.
11   Interview with Nick Money-Kyrle, 9th October 2008.
12   Interview with Anthony Bunker, 19th March 2007.
13   Kirk and Maeder left due to the shift in focus from venture capital to private equity. Interview with Anthony Bunker, 19th March 2007.
14   Interview with Anthony Bunker, 19th March 2007.
15   Interview with Hans-Dieter von Meibom, 30th March 2007.
16   Ibid.
17   Interview with Jens Tonn, 19th March 2007.
18   Interview with Mark Elborn, 17th July 2007.

19 Interview with Ivan Heywood, 17th November 2010.
20 Interview with Jens Tonn, 19th March 2007.
21 Interview with Mark Elborn, 17th July 2007.
22 Ibid.
23 Ibid.
24 Interview with Mathias Kuess, 17th October 2007.
25 Email to the authors by Reinhard Blei, 8th April 2010.
26 Interview with Andreas Kogler, 26th February 2010.
27 Interview with Jens Reidel, 8th June 2007.
28 Interview with Dieter Münch, 8th August 2008.
29 Interview with Jens Reidel, 8th June 2007.
30 Interview with Norbert Stelzer, 12th March 2007.
31 Interview with Peter Hammermann, 16th January 2008.
32 Interview with Norbert Stelzer, 12th March 2007.
33 Interview with Hans Albrecht, 8th December 2009.
34 Interview with Raimund König, 25th January 2010.
35 Letter to the authors from Reinhard Pöllath, 14th May 2010.
36 Interview with Walter Moldan, 16th December 2009.
37 Interview with Raimund König, 25th January 2010.
38 Ibid.
39 Ibid.
40 Interview with Hans Albrecht, 8th December 2009.

Chapter 13   The Sixth Phase: The Tsunami Begins

1   Interview with André Mangin, 9th December 2009.
2   Interview with Ron Ayles, 9th December 2009.
3   Interview with Ekkehard Franzke, 23rd April 2007.
4   The Sirona story was written up as a Harvard Business School case study by Professor Walter Kuemmerle and Charles Ellis, published 14th June 1999.
5   Interview with Wolfgang Pietzsch, 25th July 2007.
6   Interview with Wolf Wolfsteiner, 20th November 2009.
7   Interview with Wolfgang Pietzsch, 25th July 2007.
8   Interview with Christof Namenyi, 27th October 2009.
9   Interview with Max von Drechsel, 13th May 2009.
10 Ibid.
11 Schoeller Metternich Beteiligung.
12 Interview with Dieter Münch, 8th August 2008.
13 Interview with Herman Wendelstadt, 17th September 2007.
14 Interview with Tobias Gondorf, 19th November 2009.
15 Ibid.
16 Ibid.
17 Ibid.
18 Ibid.
19 Ibid.
20 Ibid.
21 Ibid.
22 Ibid.
23 Ibid.

24   Ibid.
25   Ibid.
26   Interview with Jens Odewald, 1st October 2008.
27   Ibid.
28   Ibid.
29   Ibid.
30   Comment supplied by Norbert Stelzer, 25th March 2010.
31   Interview with Norman Stelzer, 12th March 2007.
32   Interview with August von Joest, 1st October 2008.
33   Interview with Peter Hammermann, 16th January 2008.
34   Ibid.
35   Ibid.
36   Interview with Michael Bork, 16th November 2007.
37   Interview with Peter Hammermann, 16th January 2008.
38   Ibid.
39   Interview with Klaus Hofmann, 7th April 2008.
40   Ibid.
41   Ibid.
42   Ibid.
43   Interview with Peter Hammermann, 16th January 2008.
44   Interview with Walter Moldan, 16th December 2009.
45   Ibid.
46   Interview with Klaus Hofmann, 7th April 2008.
47   Ibid.
48   Interview with Peter Hammermann, 16th January 2008.
49   Interview with Marco Brockhaus, 14th June 2007.
50   Interview with Ron Ayles, 9th December 2009.
51   Interview with Guido May, 13th January 2010.
52   Interview with David Martin, 19th November 2008.
53   Ibid.
54   Ibid.
55   Interview with Edward Capel-Cure, 17th September 2007.
56   Interview with David Martin, 19th November 2008.
57   Interview with Axel Herberg, 19th March 2007.
58   Interview with Thilo Sautter, 4th June 2007.
59   Interview with Axel Holtrup, 19th November 2009.
60   Ibid.
61   Interview with Thilo Sautter, 4th June 2007.
62   Ibid.
63   Interview with Axel Herberg, 19th March 2007.
64   Interview with Georg Stratenwerth, 18th April 2007.
65   Interview with Axel Herberg, 19th March 2007.
66   Interview with Detlef Dinsel, 12th March 2010.
67   Ibid.
68   Ibid.
69   *Hoechst is to sell coatings manufacturer Herberts*, Business Wire, 19th August 1998.
70   David Rubenstein later confirmed that at this meeting Hans Albrecht said he had no interest in joining Carlyle. Email commentary to the authors from David Rubenstein, 25th October 2010.

71 Interview with Hans Albrecht, 8th December 2009.
72 Email commentary to the authors from Hans Albrecht, 11th April 2010.
73 Interview with Hans Moock, 9th December 2009.
74 Interview with Hans Albrecht, 8th December 2009.
75 "Police called in over Steiner", *Daily Telegraph*, 29th May 2001
76 "So you're looking at funding. Answer these 146 questions", *The Times*, 13th September 2003.
77 Interview with Ervin Schellenberg, 28th October 2009.
78 Ibid.
79 Ibid.
80 Ibid.
81 Ibid.
82 Interview with Peter Gangsted, 24th September 2007.
83 Interview with Reiner Löslein, 18th November 2009.
84 Interview with Peter Gangsted, 24th September 2007.
85 Ibid.
86 Inteview with Steve Koltes, 16th April 2008.
87 Interview with Thomas Rubahn, 2nd July 2009.
88 Interview with Martin Halusa, 11th December 2009.
89 Email commentary to the authors by Michael Phillips, 11th April 2010.
90 Interview with Marc Strobel, 17th July 2007.
91 Interview with Claus Felder, 1st October 2009.
92 Ibid.
93 Interview with Raimund König, 25th January 2010.
94 Ibid.
95 For a brief history of Idéal Loisirs/Majorette/Solido, see: http://solijouet.free.fr/english/365z.htm.
96 Interview with Jochen Martin, 12th November 2009.
97 Bragard joined clinic + job dress, and Walter Schuh in the Mercatura Holding.
98 Interview with Jochen Martin, 12th November 2009.
99 Interview with Kai Köppen, 1st December 2009.
100 Interview with Raimund König, 25th January 2010.
101 Ibid.
102 Interview with Walter Moldan, 16th December 2009.
103 Interview with Thomas Bühler, 2nd March 2010.
104 Interview with Marcus Brennecke, 20th July 2007.
105 Interview with Raimund König, 25th January 2010.
106 Ibid.
107 Ibid.
108 Ibid.
109 Ibid.
110 Interview with Thomas Bühler, 2nd March 2010.
111 Ibid.
112 Ibid.
113 Interview with Andreas Kogler, 26th February 2010.
114 Interview with Eberhard Crain, 24th November 2009.
115 Ibid.
116 Ibid.
117 Ibid.
118 Ibid.

119   Ibid.
120   Ibid.
121   Email commentary to the authors by Neil MacDougall, 1st November 2010.
122   Interview with Jens Tonn, 19th March 2007.
123   Ibid.
124   Ibid.
125   Interview with Ekkehard Franzke, 23rd April 2007.
126   Letter to the authors from Reinhard Pöllath, 14th May 2010.
127   Reflected in a seminar involving academia, Government officials, and practitioners at Münster University, see Birk, Pöllath, and Rodin: *Münsteraner Symposium zu Private Equity, 2002.*
128   See commentary in Pöllath + Partners/Deutsches Venture Capital Institutes, *Private Equity Funds, 2005,* 249 pages. For an English translation of the decree, see www.pplaw.com.
129   Including private equity education for funds and investors such as the popular *Munich Private Equity Training (MUPET)* organised annually, established in 2000.
130   Most funds that hadn't already done so, or which were new to the market, joined the BVK after 2000, and private equity veterans such as Thomas Pütter, Rolf Dienst, and Hanns Ostmeier served terms as BVK presidents.
131   Letter to the authors from Reinhard Pöllath, 14th May 2010.
132   Ibid.
133   The famous § 8 b of the Corporate Income Tax Act.
134   Letter to the authors from Reinhard Pöllath, 14th May 2010.
135   Similar in effect to, but technically more complicated than the statutory US post-acquisition asset-basis step-up election under former versions of the Internal Revenue Code.
136   Earnings-stripping restrictions (Zinsschranke) were introduced by legislation only much later following US and other foreign models.
137   In the first edition of the *M&A Manual,* by Holzapfel, Pöllath, and Drygalski in 1984, this tax treatment was cautiously and generally described on just two pages (pp. 71 and 72).
138   In the fourth (1989) or sixth (1992) edition of the *M&A Manual,* this tax treatment was more fully discussed in a separate chapter (Chapter IV) on LBOs (see pp. 125–97 for the 1989 edition, or pp. 144–220 for the 1992 edition) and given similar coverage in the ninth edition (2000).
139   By the tenth edition (2008) of the *M&A Manual* the respective coverage was once more down to a few pages included in Chapter IV on Private Equity.
140   Letter to the authors from Reinhard Pöllath, 14th May 2010.

Chapter 14   The Seventh Phase: 2001: The Collapse and Its Aftermath

1   Interview with Michael Phillips, 11th May 2007.
2   Interview with Christophe Hemmerle, 19th April 2007.
3   Interview with Max Burger-Calderon, 30th October 2009.

4 Interview with Michael Phillips, 11th May 2007.
5 Interview with Martin Halusa, 11th December 2009.
6 Interview with Michael Phillips, 11th May 2007.
7 Interview with Marc Strobel, 17th July 2007.
8 Ibid.
9 Interview with Reiner Löslein, 18th November 2009.
10 Interview with Axel Holtrup, 19th November 2009.
11 Ibid.
12 Ibid.
13 Email commentary to the authors from Stefan Messer, 29th October 2010.
14 Letter to the authors from Reinhard Pöllath, 14th May 2010.
15 Interview with Axel Holtrup, 19th November 2009.
16 Interview with Dirk Tetzlaff, 30th November 2009.
17 Ibid.
18 Ibid.
19 Ibid.
20 Interview with Detlef Dinsel, 12th March 2010.
21 Interview with Caspar von Meibom, 10th March 2010.
22 Interview with Brian Veitch, 14th June 2007.
23 Ibid.
24 Ibid.
25 Interview with Philipp Amereller, 17th July 2007.
26 Interview with Michael Boltz, 30th August 2007.
27 Ibid.
28 Ibid.
29 Ibid.
30 Ibid.
31 Interview with Christof Namenyi, 27th October 2009.
32 Inteview with Wolfgang Pietzsch, 25th July 2007.
33 Interview with Christof Namenyi, 27th October 2009.
34 Ibid.
35 Ibid.
36 Interview with Nick Money-Kyrle, 9th October 2008.
37 Ibid.
38 Ibid.
39 Ibid.
40 Ibid.
41 Interview with Hans Moock, 9th December 2009.
42 Ibid.
43 Ibid.
44 Ibid.
45 Ibid.
46 Ibid.
47 Ibid.
48 Interview with Jan Janshen, 28th October 2009.
49 Interview with Ron Ayles, 9th December 2009.
50 Interview with Jan Janshen, 28th October 2009.
51 Interview with Hans Albrecht, 10th June 2007.
52 Interview with Jan Janshen, 28th October 2009.

53 Interview with Jens Reidel, 8th June 2007.
54 Interview with Erol Ali Dervis, 17th September 2007.
55 Interview with Peter Gangsted, 24th September 2007.
56 Interview with Georg Stratenwerth, 18th April 2007.
57 Interview with Peter Gangsted, 24th September 2007.
58 Interview with Jens Tonn, 19th March 2007.
59 Ibid.
60 Interview with Peter Gangsted, 24th September 2007.
61 Interview with Peter Hammermann, 16th January 2008.
62 Interview with Georg Stratenwerth, 18th April 2007.
63 Ibid.
64 Interview with Heinz Holsten, 11th December 2009.
65 Ibid.
66 Interview with Thilo Sautter, 4th June 2007.
67 Interview with Klaus Hofmann, 7th April 2008.
68 Interview with Thilo Sautter, 4th June 2007.
69 Interview with Axel Holtrup, 19th November 2009.
70 Interview with Thilo Sautter, 4th June 2007.
71 Interview with Klaus Hofmann, 7th April 2008.
72 Interview with Max Römer, 30th March 2007.
73 Interview with Peter Cullom, 16th April 2008.
74 Interview with Jane Crawford, 18th March 2010.
75 Ibid.
76 Interview with Sebastian Kern, 18th November 2009.
77 Ibid.
78 Ibid.
79 Interview with André Mangin, 9th December 2009.
80 Ibid.
81 Interview with Martin Block, 23rd December 2009.
82 Ibid.
83 Ibid.
84 Ibid.
85 Ibid.

Chapter 15   The Eighth Phase: The Booming Market: 2004–2007

1 Charterhouse Capital Partners began as Charterhouse Development Capital in 1934. It was subsequently acquired by and became a separate subsidiary of Charterhouse Bank. The investment activities of Charterhouse Bank in Germany in the late 1980s described earlier in this book were completely separate from Charterhouse Capital Partners.
2 Interview with Detlef Dinsel, 12th March 2010.
3 Interview with Caspar von Meibom, 10th March 2010.
4 Interview with Klaus Hofmann, 7th April 2008.
5 Interview with Jane Crawford, 18th March 2010.
6 Ibid.

7   Ibid.
8   Ibid.
9   Ibid.
10 Interview with Stephan Krümmer, 17th July 2007.
11 Interview with Wolf Wolfsteiner, 20th November 2009.
12 Ibid.
13 Commentary in e-mail to the authors from Stephan Krümmer, 1st April 2010.
14 Interview with Guido May, 13th January 2010.
15 Interview with Sebastian Kern, 18th November 2009.
16 Ibid.
17 Interview with Martin Block, 23rd December 2009.
18 Ibid.
19 Ibid.
20 Ibid.
21 Ibid.
22 Interview with Reiner Löslein, 18th November 2009.
23 Ibid.
24 Interview with Marcus Brennecke, 20th July 2007.
25 Ibid.
26 "Blitzer comes out all guns blazing", Sarah Ryle article in *The Observer*, 13th March 2005.
27 Quoted in: Sarah Ryle article in *The Observer*, 13th March 2005.
28 Interview with Thorsten Langheim, 24th September 2007.
29 Quoted in: "Blackstone wird Großaktionär der Telekom" in *Handelsblatt*, 24th April 2006.
30 Interview with Thorsten Langheim, 24th September 2007.
31 Interview with Axel Herberg, 19th March 2007.
32 Interview with Thorsten Langheim, 24th September 2007.
33 Interview with Matthias Calice, 15th April 2010.
34 Ibid.
35 Ibid.
36 Ibid.
37 Ibid.
38 Ibid.
39 Ibid.
40 "Was macht eigentlich Ludolf von Wartenberg?", by Christian Rickens, in *manager magazin*, 27th January 2009.
41 Ibid.
42 Interview with Franz Münterfering, published in *Bild am Sonntag*, 17th April 2005.
43 Translation by Wikipedia from SPD: *Programmheft I. Tradition und Fortschritt.* January 2005.
44 Article published in *Stern* magazine, "The names of the 'locusts'", published 28th April 2005.
45 "The buzz on German private equity" by Carter Dougherty, in *International Herald Tribune*, 20th October 2006.
46 Email commentary to the authors from Stefan Theis, 8th April 2010.
47 Interview with Andreas Kogler, 26th February 2010.
48 Ibid.

49   Ibid.
50   Email commentary to the authors from Nico Helling, 15th November 2010.
51   Ibid.
52   *Erwerb und Übernahme von Firmen durch Finanzinvestoren (insbesondere Private-Equity-Gesellschaften)* – Bericht zum Forschungsprojekt 3/06 für das Bundesministerium der Finanzen Berlin. Christof Kaserer, Ann-Kristin Achleitner, Christoph von Einem, Dirk Schiereck. 2007.

Chapter 16   The Ninth Phase: The Fall

1   Interview with Wolf Wolfsteiner, 20th November 2009.
2   Ibid.
3   Interview with Burkhard Bonsels, 27th November 2009.
4   Ibid.
5   Interview with Andreas Schober, 24th February 2010.
6   Ibid.
7   Interview with Guido May, 13th January 2010.
8   Silverfleet sold Jost to Cinven in 2008, and Suspa to Tyrol Equity in 2009.
9   Ibid.
10   Interview with Martin Block, 23rd December 2009.
11   Interview with André Mangin, 9th December 2009.
12   Ibid.
13   Email commentary to the authors from Stefan Theis, 8th April 2010.
14   Interview with Andreas Kogler, 26th February 2010.

Chapter 17   What Did Private Equity Ever Do For Germany?

1   *Erwerb und Übernahme von Firmen durch Finanzinvestoren (insbesondere Private-Equity-Gesellschaften)* – Bericht zum Forschungsprojekt 3/06 für das Bundesministerium der Finanzen Berlin. Christof Kaserer, Ann-Kristin Achleitner, Christoph von Einem, Dirk Schiereck, 2007.
2   Ibid.

Index